FORGING ENVIRONMENTALISM

Justice, Livelihood, and Contested Environments

Joanne Bauer
Editor

An East Gate Book

M.E.Sharpe

Armonk, New York
London, England

An East Gate Book

Library of Congress Cataloging-in-Publication Data

Forging environmentalism : justice, livelihood, and contested environments / edited by
Joanne Bauer.
  p. cm.
  Includes bibliographical references and index.
  ISBN 0-7656-1535-5 (alk. paper) — ISBN 0-7656-1536-3 (pbk.: alk. paper)
  1. Environmentalism—United States—Case Studies. 2. Environmentalism—Asia—Case
studies. 3. Environmental ethics—United States—Case studies. 4. Environmental ethics—
Asia—Case studies. 5. Environmental justice—United States—Case studies. 6. Environmental
justice—Asia—Case studies. I. Bauer, Joanne R., 1962–

GE197.F67 2005 *2006*
333.72—dc22

                                                  2005019733

Contents

PART II. UNDERSTANDING VALUES CROSS-NATIONALLY

PART III. REFLECTIONS ON THE STUDY
OF ENVIRONMENTAL VALUES

Contributors
(in order of appearance)

— Editor —

Joanne Bauer, director of studies at the Carnegie Council on Ethics and International Affairs in New York until 2005, is the founding editor of *Human Rights Dialogue* (published by the Carnegie Council), and coeditor (with Daniel A. Bell) of *The East Asian Challenge for Human Rights* (1999). She currently consults to non-profits and foundations.

— China —

Foreword:
Judith Shapiro is distinguished scholar in residence, American University, and author of *Mao's War Against Nature: Politics and the Environment in Revolutionary China* (2001).

Chapter:
Pan Wei (research, Sanjiang study) is an associate professor of political science at the School of International Studies, Peking University. He is a specialist in comparative politics and the author of *The Politics of Marketization in Rural China* (2002).

Shen Mingming (research team leader) is a professor of political science at the School of Government and the director of the Research Center for Contemporary China at Peking University.

Song Guojun (research, Benxi study) is a professor of environmental economics in the School of Environment and Natural Resources, Renmin University.

The China research reports were adapted and developed for this chapter by Judith Shapiro and Liu Yu, PhD candidate in political science at Columbia University, specializing in the politics of transition in China; Vivian Bertrand, program associate at the Carnegie Council (until 2003), and environmental policy researcher and analyst for the Canadian government; and Mary Child, a writer, editor, and publishing consultant in New York.

— Japan —

Foreword:
Jeffrey Broadbent teaches sociology at the University of Minnesota and is the author of *Environmental Politics in Japan: Networks of Power and Protest* (1998).

Chapter:
Aoyagi-Usui Midori (research) is a senior researcher in the Social and Environmental Systems Division of the National Institute for Environmental Studies, Japan and co-editor of *Culture and Sustainability: A Cross-National Study of Cultural Diversity and Environmental Priorities Among Mass Publics and Decision Makers* (2003).

Arakaki Tazusa (research, Kumamoto-Minamata study) is a researcher at the Environmental Health Science Division of the National Institute for Environmental Studies. Previously (until March 2001) she was employed at the National Institute for Minamata Disease.

Steven Hoffman (research) is an independent consultant on environmental issues and U.S.-Japan relations.

Kada Yukiko (research team leader, Lake Biwa study) is a professor of sociology at Kyoto Seika University, whose research focuses on the Lake Biwa region, as well as Malawi and the Great Lakes of the United States. She was a chief architect in the design of the Lake Biwa Museum, where she is a senior researcher.

Tanaka Shigeru (research, Nagara River study) teaches sociology at Ryukoku University.

Watanabe Shinichi (research, Niigata Minamata study) is an associate professor at Nara University of Education.

The Japan research report was adapted for this book with the help of Mary Child and Jilan Kamal.

— India —

Foreword:
Paul Greenough teaches history at the University of Iowa, where he is also chair of the Global Health Studies Program. He is the coeditor (with Anna L. Tsing) of *Nature in the Global South: Environmental Projects in South and Southeast Asia* (2003).

Chapter:
Amita Baviskar (Delhi study) does research on the cultural politics of environment and development. She has taught at the University of Delhi, Cornell University, and Stanford University. She is currently a visiting fellow at the University of California, Berkeley.

Kavita Philip (Kerala study) is an associate professor of women's studies at the University of California, Irvine. Her current research areas are environmental history, postcolonial and feminist science studies, globalization, and new media technologies.

Subir Sinha (Kerala study) is a lecturer in institutions and development in the Department of Development Studies at the School of Oriental and African Studies, University of London. His current research focus is decentralized development in India, early postcolonial planning, and the global fishworkers' movement.

— United States —

Foreword:
Keith Kloor is senior editor of *Audubon* magazine and author of a number of articles published in *Audubon* and elsewhere, including "Restoration Ecology: Returning America's Forests to Their 'Natural' Roots" (*Science,* 2000).

Chapter:
Diane Austin (research) is an assistant professor at the Department of Anthropology, University of Arizona, and an assistant research anthropologist at the Bureau of Applied Research in Anthropology (BARA), University of Arizona.

Thomas McGuire (research) is an associate professor in Anthropology and an associate research anthropologist at BARA, University of Arizona.

Erin Dean, Trenna Valado, Allison Davis, Candice Clifford, Jane Moody, and Colin Seay, all then University of Arizona graduate students affiliated with BARA, participated in the research of the Sonoran Desert case.

The BARA research report (available at www.carnegiecouncil.org/forgingenvironmentalism) was adapted and developed for this book by Joanne Bauer, David Jenkins, the executive director of the Roundhouse Institute for Field Studies, and Scott Bruton, PhD candidate in history at Rutgers University, specializing in American Indian history. Vivian Bertrand and Anna Ray Davies also contributed to writing of this chapter.

— Commentators —

Sheila Jasanoff is the Pforzheimer Professor of Science and Technology Studies at the John F. Kennedy School of Government at Harvard University. She is the author most recently of *Designs on Nature: Science and Democracy in Europe and the United States* (2005) and coeditor (with Marybeth Long Martello) of *Earthly Politics: Local and Global in Environmental Governance* (2004).

Arun Agrawal is an associate professor at the School of Natural Resources and Environment, University of Michigan, author of *Environmentality: Technologies of Government and the Making of Subjects* (2005), and coeditor (with K. Sivaramakrishnan) of *Regional Modernities: The Cultural Politics of Development* (2003).

Robert Melchior Figueroa is an assistant professor of university studies and program coordinator for environmental studies at Colgate University. He is the author of the forthcoming *Whose Environment? Which Justice? Social Philosophy and Environmental Justice* and coeditor (with Sandra Harding) of *Science and Other Cultures: Issues in Philosophies of Science and Technology* (2003).

Clark Miller is an assistant professor of public affairs, environmental studies, and science and technology studies at the University of Wisconsin, Madison. He is coeditor (with Paul N. Edwards) of *Changing the Atmosphere: Expert Knowledge and Environmental Governance* (2001).

Anna Ray Davies is a lecturer in geography at Trinity College (Dublin), and author of "What Silence Knows: Planning, Public Participation, and Environmental Values" (2001). In 2000–2001 she was a Carnegie Council Environmental Values Fellow.

Acknowledgments

This study could not have been completed without the help of many hundreds of people—in Minamata City, Niigata City, at the mouth of the Nagara River, in the towns along the shores of Lake Biwa, in Benxi City and the Sanjiang Plain, in Delhi and throughout the fishing villages of southern Kerala, of the community of Civano (Tucson) and Grand Bois and its surrounding communities—for so generously agreeing to share their time, their homes, and their insights with researchers throughout the study. This research was possible only because of their willingness to include us in the events marking their communities and their lives. We are also grateful to the many scientists, doctors, journalists, religious leaders, and current and former local, provincial, tribal, state, and national government officials who were involved in the events related in these studies and were willing to share with us their experiences and perspectives. They helped us understand the complex histories of these places and the challenges and choices facing the communities described in this book.

The study and this book would also not have been possible without the generous financial and moral support of the United States-Japan Foundation, former program officers Allan Song and James Schoff, and current program officer David Janes; the Ethics and Values Studies and Political Science Programs of the National Science Foundation and Rochelle Hollander, directorate for social, behavioral, and economic sciences; and The Henry Luce Foundation and Helena Kolenda, program officer for Asia. Very special thanks is due to the Carnegie Council and its president and vice president, Joel Rosenthal and Eva Becker, for demonstrating their belief in this project and in me by so generously and patiently supporting me through the long process of completing it.

Thanks to all the people who participated in the planning and research workshops for the enthusiasm that kept the project moving forward and the insightful comments that informed the project and these chapters: Kenneth Acks, Sanjeev Ahluwalia, Aoyagi-Usui Midori, Arakaki Tazusa, Diane Austin, Tariq Banuri, Vivian Bertrand, Jeffrey Broadbent, Edith Brown Weiss, Robin Cantor, Bruce Chadwick, William Clark, Ken Conca, Anna Ray Davies, Timothy Finan, James Greenberg, Dipak Gyawali, Hao Bing, Hu Dayuan, Peter Haas, Steven Hoffman, Honzawa Kenji, Dale Jamieson, Sheila Jasanoff, David Jenkins, Kada Yukiko, Liu Shuqin, Roger Kasperson, Willett Kempton, Ma Zhong, Thomas McGuire, Clark Miller, Nalini Narayan, Indira Nair, R.K. Pachauri, Talbot Page, Pan Wei, Chandrika Parmar, Kavita Philip, Steve Rayner, Gene Rochlin,

Mark Sagoff, Savyasachi, Seiki Katsuo, Judith Shapiro, Shen Mingming, Robert Socolow, Leena Srivastava, Richard Suttmeier, Tanaka Shigeru, Sarah Trainor, Robert Weller, Brian Wynne, Shyama Venkateswar, Shiv Visvanathan, Song Guojun, Zhang Haibin, Zhang Jianyu, Zhang Lubiao, and Zhao Jimin. I would like especially to acknowledge Sheila Jasanoff for her intellectual leadership in the early phases of the project. Dale Jamieson, Roger Kasperson, Steve Rayner, Kavita Philip, and Judith Shapiro provided essential guidance as advisers to the project at and between project meetings.

I am grateful to all those who took the time to read and comment on select chapters, including Robert Albro, Elizabeth Cole, Mary Lea Cox, Anna Ray Davies, Elizabeth Economy, Richard Franke, William Hurst, Dale Jamieson, Keith Kloor, John Kurien, John Laswick, Madeleine Lynn, Emma Mawdsley, Clark Miller, Andrew Nathan, Hari Osofsky, Steve Rayner, Timmons Roberts, Joel Rosenthal, David Schlosberg, Ajantha Subramanian, Joe Tharamgalam, Lydia Tomitova, and Charles Zerner. In addition, the project was featured at panels of the International Human Dimensions Open Meeting in Rio de Janeiro (2001), at the International Studies Association meeting (2002), and at three Carnegie Council-sponsored faculty development workshops at Columbia University (2001), the College of the Holy Cross (2003), and New York University (2004). Thanks to the individuals who attended those sessions for their interest and feedback.

I am indebted to Katie Mastriani, Rachel Locke, and Vivian Bertrand and interns Deborah Matzner, Karen McGuire, and Josh Seidenfeld, who worked with me at the Carnegie Council, ably handling the myriad details that arise in managing a multiyear project of this scope, and who have all since moved on to important new challenges. When faced with the daunting task of consolidating the country research reports into a single book manuscript, I was fortunate to have close by Kavita Philip, Vivian Bertrand, Jilan Kamal, Mary Child, and (by e-mail) Anna Davies, whose enthusiasm and sharp insights kept the project alive. Mary and Jilan, along with Lauren Osborne and John Tessitore, lent their keen editorial skills in assisting with the chapters, while Rebecca Kraley, Anahita Marker, Zornitsa Stoyanova, and Yesim Yemni provided valuable help in checking facts and preparing the manuscript for publication. Special thanks also to Alice and Will Theide of DBA/Carto-Graphics for their skillful work in creating the country maps, and to Shefali Verma, Nancy Joyce, Yumiko Shimabukuro, and Yin Zhijing for their able transcribing and translating of Malayalam, Japanese, and Chinese interviews and data. I am deeply grateful to Patricia Loo, executive editor for Asian studies at M.E. Sharpe, for her belief in the project from early on. Both she and Angela Piliouras at Sharpe gave the manuscript the benefit of their expert attention and guidance.

This book is the product of more than seven years of collaboration—a far greater time commitment than the participants made when they signed on to the project. I am grateful to all the project researchers and advisors who stuck with me for the duration despite the competing demands and pressures of their lives.

Finally, I wish to acknowledge my wonderfully supportive family. I am grateful to Oliver and Isabel for putting up with my absence as I disappeared on evenings and weekends for "Mommy's project." The peace of mind indispensable to a project of this complexity was provided by Lucie Bittnerova, my peerless babysitter. Most of all, I thank my amazing husband, Andrew Nathan, for his unflagging support, invaluable editorial help, steadfast willingness to make sacrifices, and endless patience. For you, Andy, no expression of gratitude is strong enough.

In the final phase of writing this book, three of the communities who opened their doors to us and agreed to be interviewed for this study—the fishers of Kerala, the Houma of Grand Bois, and the people of the Sanjiang Plain—suffered terrible losses when each was struck by a major disaster (the natural disasters of the Asian tsunami in 2004 and the Hurricane Katrina in 2005 and the manmade disaster of the Songhua River toxic spill in 2005). We extend our deepest sympathy and support to them and to all in the surrounding areas who were affected. In the hope that this book may in some small way help us to better understand their loss and how to prevent and mitigate it, this book is dedicated to them.

Editor's Note

All Chinese and Japanese names in this volume appear with family name preceding given name. The conventional system of transliteration for Japanese is used. Terms from mainland China are rendered using the Pinyin system of romanization.

Currency conversions for the Japan, China, and India chapters are based on historic exchange rates between the dollar and the foreign currency in the particular year in question. In cases where rates have fluctuated greatly, even within a single year, as in Japan, we have taken the year average as a basis for calculation. Numbers in dollars have been rounded off.

An on-line companion to this volume containing supplementary information, further reading, related links, annotated bibliographies, discussion questions, and an on-line-only commentary, "On the Distinction Between Resource Use and Industrial Pollution," by Steven Yearley (York University, Department of Sociology), is available at www.carnegiecouncil.org/forgingenvironmentalism.

FORGING ENVIRONMENTALISM

Introduction

Joanne Bauer

In a talk at the Carnegie Council about his book *Red Sky at Morning: America and the Crisis of the Global Environment,*[1] James Gustave Speth, a world-renowned expert on and leader in combating environmental problems, recited the grave threats facing the planet and lamented the failure of the international community to make progress against them in the past twenty-five years. He concluded that the solution rests largely with ordinary citizens "because the politicians have let us down." Speth warned that "if citizens don't take the helm, we will lose this fight." In order to achieve Speth's vision of "a new movement of consumers and households committed to sustainable living," we need to understand what motivates people to act. We need to understand the social and cultural values that people bring to bear on environmental problems and how they mobilize those values to forge environmentalism—to create and sustain programs and movements of environmental action in their communities and their countries.

The aim of this book is to enhance our understanding about environmental values and their expression in different social and cultural contexts around the globe. Although much of the environmental literature focuses on institutional capacities and available environmental technologies, little of it examines the experiences of communities trying to define environmental values in the context of struggles over livelihoods and lives. This book presents new case material that links the scientific analysis to policy analysis and then goes one step beyond to do what few studies do: to exam the values of all the stakeholders and their processes of interaction. This holistic approach provides a basis for understanding how people in different parts of the world define environmental goals and objectives, how their values related to the environment are shaped by lived realities, cultural contexts, and political struggles in which they forge their ideas about nature and the environment, and whose values matter and whose don't in setting environmental priorities.

This volume draws upon fieldwork conducted at ten sites in four economically, politically, and environmentally important, yet highly disparate, countries—the United States, China, India, and Japan—to analyze community responses to environmental degradation and to government policies that address the degradation. Our studies of growing competition over scarce resources, shifting government policies, and communities grappling with environmental crisis reveal some of the ways in which people make sense of their physical world and act upon it. In these stories we encounter the lived experiences, perceptions, and values that underlie competing claims regarding human interaction with the natural environment, and how those claims get articulated and negotiated within different political, economic, and social contexts. We also gain a clearer picture of how government policy contributes to the creation of environmental values: how it influences people to take steps to value and protect the environment.

Part 1 of this book develops a rich empirical base that brings to light the cultural assumptions, standards, and analytic techniques implicit in environmental values, actions, and policies. We build this base for the four countries both as a foundation for action and a model for future studies that might fill in the tableau of the rest of the world. Because values are complex, we did not try to separate them out as a sole focus of inquiry. Our goal is to report thoroughly on the cases, not to draw any specific conclusions about the relationship between values and policy. Part 2 provides a comparative perspective on the ways in which, in different societies, values come to be publicly "environmental" in the first place. Taken together, the empirical base and the comparative perspective help us to identify what policymakers can do to secure public support for and trust in environmental policies. In addition, the comparative perspective enables us to identify a wide range of factors that contribute to changes in environmental values and behaviors, and to explore the possibilities for a convergence of environmental norms across diverse cultures.

In documenting how the communities we studied make sense of the environmental problems they face and what environmental discourses prevail within them, we draw out the relationships between individual values and collective action and how values are interwoven with power and politics. Our studies demonstrate the fact that not all environmental values are accorded equal weight within the public domain, just as not all expressions of environmental value are seen as legitimately or properly "environmental." Some values enter into environmental debates, policies, and legal decisions, while others are screened out or remain silenced.

Rather than treating environmental values only as a distinct identifiable set of green values, therefore, the studies in this volume treat them as dynamic, and contingent on specific social, legal, political, and economic conditions. Seen this way, environmental values are, in the words of commentary author Clark Miller, "dynamic elements of community relationships and dialogues, shaped by the ways people attribute meaning and importance to scientific facts, weave them into broader social narratives, and to embed them in the tacit assumptions and day-to-day practices of institutions and the broader social order" (p. 380). Context is important because it shapes the ways in which people apprehend and value the environment, and how their environmental values are expressed. Our efforts to contextualize environmental values are aided by cross-national comparison, which helps to avoid essentializing difference, while clarifying particularities and commonalities across different societies and cultures.

The Origins of the Book

This book dates back to early 1992, when under the auspices of the Carnegie Council on Ethics and International Affairs and with the support of the then newly formed Japan Foundation Center for Global Partnership, I organized a series of meetings with Japanese and American environmental policy makers and their close advisers involved with the Earth Summit that was taking place that year in Rio de Janeiro, Brazil. The purpose of what we called the U.S.-Japan Task Force on the Environment was to enhance the efforts of government officials, scientists, and civil society to assemble an action program on the environment by exploring the moral assumptions and ethical principles underlying environmental policy decisions in both countries. The dialogue resulted in two 1993 reports that focused on this theme: *Whose Environmental Standards? Clarifying the Issues of Our Common Future* and *The Politics and Ethics of Global Environmental Leadership*. It engaged with policy debates about American and Japanese leadership roles and responsibilities for global environmental protection, about the U.S.-Japan relationship itself, and about opportunities for both countries to work together to solve shared environmental problems in a rapidly changing context for the conduct of international relations.

The choice of the two countries was significant: whereas Japanese officials had recently and very publicly pledged Japan to be a global environmental leader, among U.S. officials there was much less consensus about what priority to place on environmental issues or whether the problems were even serious enough to warrant that kind of priority. By the time of the summit it had become increasingly clear that a cautious American approach to the environmental negotiations would win out. As a result, Japanese officials were faced with a dilemma: whether to maintain their traditional position of deference to the United States in international diplomacy or break with their American partners. Within the Japanese delegation—and within the very robust contingent of Japanese civil society present at the summit—there was a good deal of frustration with the American position, and our hope was that the task force could help to clarify the points of difference and agreement, and diffuse the tension.

Among the many observations made by task force members, three stood out. First, a hypothesis was put forth that American individualism and Japan's community and consensus orientation had significant implications for the way each country approached environmental issues. For example, in the case of ozone layer depletion, one participant observed that Japan tends to accept general scientific consensus and act on it without insisting on absolute certainty. U.S. policymakers, on the other hand, tend to pay more attention to the dissenter if there is no strong consensus. The practical effect, in terms of the ozone issue according to participants, was that the Japanese favored a strong ozone protection treaty, with stronger controls on the chemical industry, while the Americans did not. Second, we observed that U.S.-Japan dissonance at the Earth Summit was attributable in part to the way each delegation regarded the other. Just as the Japanese delegation members felt that the Americans showed little respect for other cultures, the American delegates felt that the Japanese

placed too much emphasis on the "extractable value" of natural resources—the pecu-
niary benefits realizable from their exploitation—rather than value the eco-systems
themselves. Finally, our task force pinpointed the problem of international dissatisfaction with the American failure of leadership, which, according to several Japanese
participants included a lack of willingness to listen to the ideas of others.

The task force was a valuable opportunity to candidly discuss tensions between
American and Japanese negotiators in a private setting. But a seminar by its nature
allows for the presentation of only a limited range of views—those of the seminar
participants; missing was a clear sense of the range of views and debates going on
within these societies at large, among citizens, activists, educators, scientists, and
local policymakers. Once the hard work of fighting out the language of treaties and
conventions is done and diplomats return home, the next task is to convince their
publics of the need to make good on their commitments. Similarly, after the Carnegie
Council task force reports had been written and sent to the press, questions remained:
To what extent do the cultural, social, and economic priorities that the task force
identified for each nation's team of environmental negotiators accurately represent
the priorities of U.S. or Japanese citizens? Do they reflect the values of ordinary
Japanese and Americans whose lifestyle choices affect the environment and who are
affected by and must respond to local, national, and increasingly international environmental policies and regulations? What kinds of policies should be adopted at home
that can convince publics to embrace the Earth Summit agenda?

These questions led us to want to better understand the dynamics of environmental
politics in each country and the ways in which values towards the environment could
be expressed and acted upon within a policy context. Considering the conclusions of
an important study of environmental negotiations that had just been released,[2] we
reasoned that to improve the quality of communication between parties involved in
international environmental negotiations, researchers and policy makers need better
information on the differences and similarities of environmental values of the constituents of various countries and the political landscapes that shape the expression of
those values in coping with similar environmental problems.

Two years after the release of the task force reports, I initiated the Carnegie Council project upon which this book is based to explore these questions. We expected that
the project would find a gap between citizens' values and public policy, and we decided to explore the gap in each cultural context, why it developed, and how to bridge
it. We were particularly interested in how increasing international economic, cultural,
and political integration—a phenomenon commonly known as "globalization"—was
affecting the ability of local actors to manage the environmental consequences of
growth. In addition, we wanted to understand better the impact upon environmental
values of both globalization and the internationalization of environmental standards.
Along with the United States and Japan, we believed it would be valuable to bring
into the study India and China—two environmentally, economically, and politically
significant developing countries that were coming to be viewed as success stories of
globalization.

The participants in the planning phase were motivated by the possibility that such a study could prompt new thinking about approaches to environmental protection in their own country. The Americans emphasized the importance of providing insight for the domestic environmental policy community working both at home and abroad about the kind of technological and analytical assumptions embedded in American policies. Similarly, the Japanese researchers wanted to promote a new way of thinking in Japan through comparative study. The Chinese researchers wanted to demonstrate to an international audience the particular environmental challenges they face and thereby improve international trust and cooperation with China. Observing that the average citizen and policy maker in India is alienated from national policy, the Indian participants sought in the project a means to incorporate local people and their values into policy making. They also wanted to understand better what prompts people to adopt change either more or less eco-friendly lifestyles and they sought to do this through an exploration of the processes of technology transfer, technology absorption, and the values attached to them. As a group, we also wanted to scrutinize the school of thought promoted in both environmental policy and academic circles that says that people—poor people in particular—are chiefly concerned about their economic well-being, as distinct from their environmental well-being.[3] And considering the tensions at Rio, we hoped that a comparative study of environmental values could point to ways of better promoting international cooperation.

The Study

This project can be seen as an experiment in collaboration. A Millian comparative "method of difference" or "method of agreement" did not fit our purpose, which was not to test explicit theories or hypotheses. Rather we aimed to get a fuller picture of local values, the transactions among stakeholders at different levels, and the interaction of community values and public policy.

Like our research foci, our research method privileged the local: We decided to rely on country-based teams of researchers to select the cases, choose suitable methods, and conduct and analyze the fieldwork. We reasoned that research teams using the qualitative methods appropriate to the sites and the research traditions of each country could most effectively carry out this research. Yet while the research teams in each country were closer to the local scene than a foreign researcher would be, the gap between the foreign researchers and the researchers on the country teams was replicated by a gap between the researchers and their local informants, which had to be mediated in the field and in the chapters that appear here.

To make the project comparative, we used a two-pronged strategy of approximate standardization and continuous interaction. Standardizing the methodology provided the structure needed to keep all the country studies moving in the same direction, while continuous interaction among the research teams enabled us to successively draw the project together by identifying common themes. At eight project meetings that took place at intervals throughout the research and writing phases,[4] we shared ideas, methods, and insights from our fieldwork, worked towards a common vocabulary, and made necessary adjustments to the research design. By bringing into relief the distinctiveness or commonness of what we were encountering in the field, this process informed each team about the findings of the others and influenced the way each team approached the fieldwork and the writing up of findings. In the intimate settings of these meetings, broad cultural and disciplinary differences were magnified, confronted, and usually understood through attention to the cultural context in which they were observed. The similarities and differences that we discovered in our methods and approaches helped shape the analyses of the research findings.[5]

Like the project, the book itself is a product of collaboration, with multiple analysts bringing their distinctive disciplinary and cultural perspectives to bear on the material. Part 1 is the product of researchers who selected the cases and carried out the studies; the chapter authors, who in certain cases are the same as the researchers and in other cases are writers who drew upon and expanded the original field reports; and the experts in environmental politics of each country who introduce the chapters. In Part 2, specialists in environmental justice, law and science policy, environmental politics, and global environmental governance analyze issues across the case material. Drawing upon their own theoretical concerns, they provide insights that might not be apparent to the researchers, and with which indeed the researchers might not always agree.[6] This book, then, is intended to be a sourcebook and an invitation to others to use the material in a similar way.

The country chapters in Part 1 have a common structure. Each begins with an introductory explanation of the significance of the selected cases, a statement of the research biases, and a description of the methods and line of inquiry pursued in the chapter. The case studies follow, first an industrial pollution case and then a resource use case. Each case study section contains a historical narrative of the case and an analysis based upon field interviews of stakeholders—people and groups interested in and affected by the environmental problem detailed in the narrative. The chapter authors frame the studies with a comparative analysis of the stakeholder responses to the two (or, in the Japan chapter, four) cases, developing insights into values and value change and relating these insights to broader trends of environmental policy and political action in the country in question. Immediately preceding each country chapter is an introductory essay by an expert on the environmental politics of the country, who situates the cases within the broader national context.

The Four Countries

Readers will recognize the four countries we cover in this book as four of the countries most responsible for industrial pollution and global resource management and whose cooperation is most required if real progress toward environmental sustainability is to be achieved.[7] Together these four countries account for half the world's population and economic output. They are also responsible for half the world's emissions of carbon dioxide. In 2000, the four countries were among the top five in terms of total carbon emissions, and with GDP real growth rates in China and India continuing to soar, at 9.1 percent and 8.3 percent, respectively, their carbon emissions are expected to rise. Beyond this quintessentially global challenge, which Speth calls "the most serious issue of them all," these countries face serious local resource and pollution concerns that often have cumulative regional and global effects.[8]

For the purpose of comparing and understanding how values are created in different contexts, however, the significance of these four countries lies not in what they have in common but in what makes each distinctive. As Clark Miller notes in his chapter, the four countries were not chosen at random:

> Economically, the four span a diversity of approaches to bridging markets and government planning and the three largest economies in the world. They include the widely regarded icon of Western, laissez-faire, liberal, free trade economics and the intellectual leader of the nonaligned movement. Politically, they are four of the world's current great powers, including the last remaining communist great power, the world's oldest democracy, and two countries whose current forms of governance have been adapted from legacies of occupation by Western countries with noticeably different notions about how to construct a democratic polity. Their inhabitants include some of the world's richest and poorest peoples, not to mention large, influential populations of many of the world's major religions, including Buddhism, Protestant and Catholic Christianity, Islam, Judaism, Hinduism, and Shintoism. Last, but certainly not least, each possesses a highly regarded, well-funded environmental science community. (p. 392)

Thus, these countries present both interesting parallels and important social, cultural, political, and economic differences that affect the relationship humans have with nature, the character of environmental action, patterns of political mobilization, and responses to post-industrial change.

In selecting the case studies within each country, project researchers sought to capture a wide range of variation within their country by including different socioeconomic classes, climates, and ethnic groups. We decided that each team would pick at least one case that involved the environmental impacts of industrial development and at least one case of natural resource protection; yet, while adhering to this rule, the study allowed the research teams to select cases that are particularly salient in the society they were studying, rather than insisting upon strict comparability across the cases. (The full criteria for case selection are described in the final chapter, "How Shall We Study Environmental Values?")

Our decision to distinguish two case types—resource use and industrial pollution —had its basis in the environmental studies literature, where this distinction is widely encountered.[9] Because of their contrasts—in the most basic sense, between nature protection ("backward thinking") discourses and development ("forward thinking") discourses—the two case types would enable us to capture different human-nature interactions as well as the experiences of both rural and urban areas. Furthermore, we expected that the ways in which conflicts develop and are resolved would differ significantly in the two case types. In resource use cases, the resource is always seen to be a public good; the conflict involves a competition of values over how the resource should be used. Pollution, on the other hand, except in its commodification through tradable permit or recycling schemes, is always a public bad, but one that is sometimes ignored. When part of a community ignores pollution and part tries to eliminate it, value differences emerge, and conflict erupts. Thus, whereas solutions to the resource use cases involve resolving a competition over values, we hypothesized that environmentalist solutions to industrial pollution would require facilitating a convergence of values over time by raising awareness of the pollution and its consequences. Still, we recognized that the distinction between the two kinds of cases, which is widely encountered in environmental policy literature, may not in fact be the most analytically important distinction, and thus we endeavored to examine its usefulness in the study.[10]

The China chapter describes two instances of ostensibly progressive policy initiatives to protect the environment undertaken or backed by China's central government. Recent studies of Chinese environmental politics document the rise of public concern for the environment in the form of government-sanctioned environmental civic associations.[11] In our two cases the government's green initiatives provoked a quiet backlash—quiet because of the persistent limits on freedom of speech and organization in China. The pollution study is set in Benxi, a city known for its steel production, in Liaoning Province in China's industrial belt. The air in the city became so polluted that by the 1980s Benxi had earned a reputation as "the city that cannot be seen by a satellite." Reactions from the Benxi public to the effort to turn Benxi into a model environmental city underscore the class stratification taking place in China as a result of the transition to a market economy begun also in the 1980s: whereas the new white-collar class was happy to see blue skies return, the growing number of residents struggling to cope with a transitional market economy betrayed cynicism and contempt for the environmental measures.

Our Chinese resource use case is the Sanjiang Plain wetlands, in the extreme northeastern corner of China, where economic development has been at odds with recent wetlands conservation efforts. Here, public resentment of the environmental campaign has been even greater than in Benxi. For nearly five decades, out of concern about food scarcity, the central government promoted the Sanjiang Plain as a frontier for agricultural production and lured many migrants to the wilderness region to reclaim and cultivate the land. In the late 1990s a sudden about-face of government priorities led to a moratorium on land reclamation for agricultural development and other restrictions on land use. With the designation of a nature reserve in the Sanjiang Plain, initially by provincial authorities, there was growing awareness among both Chinese officials in Beijing and slowly also local officials of the importance of wetland preservation as a way of protecting wildlife and plant species and bringing other benefits—including the national security the sustained forest cover would provide from neighboring Russia. Nonetheless, local officials and residents alike felt betrayed by the more severe restrictions that came when the wetland was upgraded to a national level wetland and designated a "wetland of international importance." While nature reserve officials were optimistic about the possibilities for ecotourism and other forms of economic activity the wetland might bring, the failure to fund the reserve adequately, along with corruption among local officials, fueled anger among most interviewees, who had experienced the damage to their livelihoods and their futures resulting from the upgrading of the wetland.

Still, a contingent of stakeholders at each site were convinced that something needed to be done to clean up Benxi's pollution and preserve China's wetlands, and that doing so would bring other benefits (such as attracting foreign funding) to both locales. The influential political scientist Robert Putnam has coined the term "two-level game" to describe a situation in which international pressure enables government leaders to shift the balance of power in their domestic game in favor of a policy that they privately support but previously felt powerless to undertake.[12] One might expect that, with the Chinese authoritarian system, China's leaders would not need to play the two-level game, but our cases demonstrate that international pressure did provide needed legitimacy to the government's policies.

The Japan chapter presents two industrial pollution case studies and two resource use case studies—in each pair a primary case and a secondary case for comparison. For the pollution cases, the sites are Minamata, a city in Kumamoto Prefecture, where factory effluent caused severe mercury poisoning, leading to intense social and political conflict; and along the Agano River in Niigata Prefecture in northern Japan, where there was a second incident of mercury poisoning, which came to be known as Niigata-Minamata. In contrast to Minamata, where victim suffering slowly gave rise to a powerful citizen's movement, in Niigata, because of a greater social and physical distance between polluter and victim, value and policy changes were not as pronounced, despite the severe human harm and social conflict that also occurred there. The resource use case sites are Lake Biwa, Japan's largest lake, where the national objective of increasing water resources to serve rapidly industrializing cities downstream, led to massive public works projects (including dam construction), which over three decades radically changed the landscape and lifestyles of the lakeshore; and the Nagara River, where a diversified social movement of leisure fishers and nature enthusiasts with conflicting motives mobilized to fight the construction of a dam on Japan's last remaining natural river.

As the Japan chapter shows, a shift in the terminology used to describe environmental problems from *kogai* (literally, "public nuisance") to *kankyo mondai* (environmental issues) tracks a change in Japanese conceptions of human-nature relationships. When the Minamata City and Lake Biwa studies begin, in postwar Japan around the 1960s, Japanese society is at what the Japan team refers to as the "embedded whole" phase—"where environmental values do not translate into a valuing of specific elements of nature or into a discrete concept of nature" (p. 171); rather, in this phase humans are viewed as being at one with nature. The authors trace how, with large-scale and rapid industrial development, marked environmentally by the outbreak of Minamata-like *kogai* crises, most Japanese saw themselves as apart or "abstracted" from nature. Over time, however, each community began to reconnect with nature, thereby approaching what the authors call the "balanced whole" phase, in which the physical environment becomes valued again ("re-embedded") as a fundamental part of human existence. This stage of environmental consciousness is marked by civic environmental movements—in our cases, the anti-detergent movement, or soap movement, taken up by the lakeshore residents of Lake Biwa in the late 1970s, an anti-dam movement at the Nagara River in the late 1980s, and the Moyainaoshi Campaign, the government-led initiative to heal Minamata begun in the 1990s. While the Minamata victims' movement of the 1960s brought Japan's *kogai* problems into the public eye for the first time, these later movements were all carried out in the name of *kankyo mondai*. What became lost in the terminology shift from *kogai* to *kankyo mondai*, however, was the claim of victimhood, which is implicit in *kogai* problems. The new terminology thus represents the influence of elites—in fact, the soap movement was engineered by the prefectural government and the anti-dam movement by a group of leisure fishers—and the obscuring of social injustice in environmental policy decisions and outcomes.

Our India pollution case centers on Delhi, which in 2000 was rated as the world's fourth-most-polluted city,[13] and where, as in Benxi, environmental politics is dominated by a new, politically powerful middle class. Unlike Benxi, where the conflict between environmental policy and livelihood may be more perceived than real, in Delhi the policy solution to industrial pollution—namely, the closure of thousands of factories around the city—directly affected the livelihoods of residents, from industrialists to casual workers, while bringing little if any reduction in air pollution. Even before the legal action that led to the factory closings, poor working conditions rendered factory workers more vulnerable to the toxic burden of the city's polluting factories, and they are also the ones who had to bear the cost of the new green agenda. The study points to the politics of labeling—the politics surrounding what set of values gets labeled as "environmental" and therefore receives national and international recognition and support. In this case the judge who ruled in favor of the factory closings was hailed as the "green judge," and the lawyer who sued to relocate the factories received a prestigious international award. Meanwhile, the middle-class elite regarded the plight of the displaced workers, who mobilized to fight for their rights to earn a living wage, as the unavoidable cost that must be borne for the sake of lessening the city's pollution. The study demonstrates the interrelationship between the two forms of environmentalism, with the green agenda of the rich leading to greater social and economic marginalization of the poor and their concerns over fair distribution of resources and safe working conditions.

The Indian resource use case concerns fisheries in Kerala, the Indian state with the highest rate of literacy, where international aid helped to modernize the fisheries almost six decades ago, presenting fishers with a fundamental choice with which they are still grappling today: whether to maintain their traditional fishing practices, which are more sustainable, or to adopt mechanized technology at the risk of depleting marine resources. The Kerala study brings to light the local effects of technology transfer (in this case, outboard motors and large fishing trawlers) in particular, the ways in which

Kerala fishers made sense of their lives in light of the new choices. Contrary to romanticized images of traditional communities defining their identity in terms of indigenous practices, the authors point out, the artisanal fishers (the local moniker for those who use traditional crafts) shared many of the same interests in access to markets, capital, and technology as their "capitalist" rivals. As a result, the authors argue that the case demands a more complicated account of the material and symbolic relationships between people and resources than is represented by the familiar narrative of "a superior group . . . usurp[ing] the business terrain of a disempowered tradition" (p. 192).

As the title of the chapter on the United States, "Two Faces of American Environmentalism," indicates, the two U.S. cases represent the principal cleavage within U.S. environmentalism: the environment justice movement and its concern with fair distribution of resources and toxic burdens, and the mainstream environmentalist agenda of resource preservation. The cases are thematically linked by the country's addiction to cheap energy supplies. The tiny town of Grand Bois in southern Louisiana, which was sickened by oilfield waste deposited in a nearby pit, is the site of the U.S. pollution study. In the aftermath of the health crisis that results, Grand Bois's Houma Indian and Cajun communities must make sense of their allegiance to their fellow community members, their generations-long commitment to the land, and their ties to the oil industry that has come to sustain them. This incident of a major oil conglomerate, Exxon Corporation, poisoning the community—an act which was entirely acceptable by national and state laws—is representative of many instances of environmental injustice in rural areas in the United States that depend on natural resource extraction for their economic livelihoods.

The residents of Grand Bois contrast with the affluent and mobile families who moved in search of community to the focal point of the U.S. resource use case, Civano, on the outskirts of Tucson, in the desert region of southern Arizona. Civano was a high-profile state- and city-financed housing experiment designed to be a national model of sustainable development. A growth area of the United States, the region had long contended with the multiple threats that population growth and urban sprawl brought to this dry and ecologically sensitive region. While most of Civano residents were originally drawn to the development from both inside and outside Arizona by its promise of community and energy efficiency (which translated for many as lower utility bills), they soon became aware of and committed to the project's conservation goals, seeing themselves as pioneers of sustainable living. The case reveals the values —community, economic, social, and cultural—underlying competing visions of sustainability, the difficulty of shifting from efficiency politics to sustainability politics, the compromises that had to be made in order to maintain an economically sound venture, and how people defined themselves in the process. The case shows that when policy makers create models of sustainable living, they can raise environmental consciousness and promote environment-friendly behavior. Yet the failure of the project to meet many of its original environmental goals and to consider the impacts of continued sprawl produced a limited notion of environmentalism that in the end had limited impact and support.[14]

Understanding Values Cross-Nationally

In Part 2, commentators weave thematic threads through the country chapters into commentary chapters that provide cross-national analysis across these very rich cases. They identify similarities across the cases, that while unsurprising, are nonetheless important: that environmental degradation and environmental policy have similar impacts on the poor and disenfranchised; that rich and poor people respond differently to environmental problems; and that environmental crises trigger social mobilization and social and value change. Yet they also identify significant differences from country to country in social relations and political culture, which affect the ways in which values are articulated and conflicts resolved or not resolved.

Sheila Jasanoff examines the use of the law in the case studies, both as a culturally specific expression of a society's political and moral values and as a reflection of a universal commitment to lawfulness. She focuses on the formal and informal uses of the law by citizens and government bodies "in their attempts to navigate the contrary currents of environmental protection and resource appropriation" (p. 330). Jasanoff compares the cases across five areas of the law: resource allocation and planning; victim compensation; environmental standard-setting; the mobilization of science in service to the law, or "knowledge-making"; and resistance to unjust environmental actions and policy. Jasanoff does not address the problem of non-adherence to the law (as Robert Melchior Figueroa does in a later chapter on environmental justice); yet her commentary is shaped by the understanding that adherence to the law is itself a value that "structures the expression of environmental values everywhere" (p. 330).

Jasanoff sees convergence across the cases in the ways in which the authority of institutions is undermined by interest-driven science (i.e., the manipulation of science by government and industry), the demand of courts and policymakers for indisputable scientific proof of harm, and the inadmissibility of "nonscientific" forms of knowledge, even when people's lives are being ravaged by pollution. But she is even more interested in how the strikingly different and sometimes conflicting values influence both the content of the law in each society and the way it is used, including methods of dispute resolution, the emphasis placed on particular types of legal standards, community building strategies, and social contracts. All of these differences in legal cultural have direct implications for the disparate ways in which environmental values are expressed and negotiated across the cases.

The aspiration to be modern—to attain technology-driven development and to establish democratic societies—motivated many of the people in the studies to accept or reject environmental policies and sometimes to seek to change them. Indeed, probing the communities' aspirations to be modern, and the various meanings they ascribe to the notion of modernity, is one way project researchers assessed environmental values in the field. The authors of the Japan study, who most directly address the modernity drive, observe modernization as manifested in the processes of separating, or "abstracting," humans from nature, and in Japan's democratization, and attribute these processes to the strong aspiration among postwar Japanese to be modern. Notably, they cite one informant who takes issue with the critics of the proposed dam on the Nagara River. "It's just emotional sentimentalism to want a river to remain just as it is," the informant says. "Such thinking has no place in modern society."

In "Environmental Transformations and the Values of Modernity," Arun Agrawal identifies three values of modernity that influence approaches to the environment in all the case studies: the pursuit of progress; reason, based on scientific knowledge; and the belief in equality. All of the cases evolve under the rubric of progress: we see little questioning of modern forms of development except from a key actor in the Minamata case, Ogata Masato. While Jasanoff identifies a conscious effort by some people in the conservation cases to define themselves apart from this trend—what she calls an "antimodern" (as opposed to "premodern") position—Agrawal stresses that these cases are nonetheless driven on both sides by the pursuit of material goods (e.g., economic benefit, flood prevention, and diplomatic leverage). Further, Agrawal observes that all the studies document people on both sides of the disputes engaging in the act of classifying the environment as a distinct policy domain that can be studied in isolation from other social processes. This manifestation of modernity does more than explain environmental problems; such classifications, says Agrawal, can also be seen "to constitute our views about [our relationship to] the environment." Finally, Agrawal notes that in each case an environmental crisis prompted a social movement that revealed modern democratic values. Often, however, this democratic impulse is challenged and even "trumped" by political economic realities—that is, by a competing claim about modernity, as the above-cited quotation by the critic of the Nagara Dam protesters illustrates.

Justice constitutes a central theme in this volume. By examining environmental values in the context of specific policy actions, the studies reveal the varying degree to which people and groups have the power to order their lives—in other words, the degree to which their values matter. Robert Melchior Figueroa proposes an "environmental justice paradigm" that includes distributive justice and recognition justice, and he uses the cases in the book to illustrate the various modes of injustice that often characterize environmental controversies. In the case of Benxi, for example, he asserts that in implementing their green campaign, city officials did not adequately take into account the needs of the many people who have suffered the skyrocketing unemployment that has resulted from the changeover to a market economy. Similarly, he argues that the Civano development project failed to account fully for the interests of those harmed by Tucson's further expansion (the Hopi and Navajo Indian tribes to the northern and inner-city Mexican Americans). This is environmental injustice even if these communities were unaware of the Civano project or had never considered its impact on their lives.

Figueroa traces the theme of justice through the cases to show that in every one of them a community is forced to shoulder a disproportionate share of the burden of a harmful industrial practice or an environmental policy, or is unjustly deprived of a resource. Compounding these inequities is a keen awareness within the victim community that their voices are not heard and that their values, interests, and identities are not respected. Those communities that are repeatedly denied a fair hearing within the policy process are often left feeling despair or anger, which they sometimes convert into social action in the form of an environmental justice movement.

Figueroa also stresses the importance of public recognition of the damage to environmental identity—cultural identity as it relates to one's environmental surroundings—by both environmental assaults and insensitive policies, which is typically overlooked in remedies to environmental injustice. Damage to environmental identity can be devastating and irreversible, and justice measures that do not account for it are only partial. Among our cases, such damage is most severe in Grand Bois, Minamata, and Kerala, although Figueroa suspects that the environmental identity of traditional herders and hunters who live in the Sanjiang Plain and the residents of Benxi may also have been harmed in ways that are not fully explored in the cases.

Clark Miller concludes Part 2 by examining the implications of the case studies for global environmental governance. Miller advises that our project be understood as an instance of "comparative globalism," probing the ways in which people in local settings are jointly "confronting and interpreting key elements of a global environmental agenda." Miller proposes three lenses—framing, styles of reasoning, and trust—through which to view environmental values related to governance while taking into account the culturally grounded ways in which people come to hold environmental values. Framing, Miller writes, is the process by which "people are taught to interpret and value what they see happening around them in new ways." Styles of reasoning are the ways in which people connect their observations about the world to these broader frameworks. And trust in institutions is the crucial element in establishing standards, or "shared styles of reasoning," that can achieve public legitimacy.

Starting with framing, Miller uses two pairs of contrasting examples—first, China and Japan and, then, India and the United States—to show how differently people confront similar environmental challenges. In discussing the first pair, he underscores the distinction between top-down and bottom-up initiatives for environmental improvement. Meanwhile, in the case of the United States, the principal antagonists are corporate interests and activists, whereas in India the sharpest conflicts are drawn in class terms. Furthermore, the United States study frames the problems in terms of consumer choice, whereas the authors of the India case studies are "staunchly critical of consumerism" (p. 385). It is noteworthy that the particular frames Clark identifies are in fact those of the national research team, which in turn reflect local framings. Miller goes on to discuss the lenses of styles of reasoning and trust, explaining that "only as specific frames begin to get taken up and made use of in individual and collective decisions do they begin to have real bite in terms of social and environmental outcomes" (p. 386). He concludes with a lesson for global governance: we need to build institutions of global environmental governance that are able to acknowledge and legitimize the expression of plurality in the world system.

Forging Environmentalism across Cultures

Within the human rights field, there is substantial scholarly debate over whether rights belong to the group or the individual person and how to reconcile the two sets of rights bearers in the implementation of human rights principles. By contrast, in the case of environmental issues, as these studies demonstrate, the line between individual environmental values and community values is blurred. While many social scientists maintain that values do not matter, that individuals may talk about values but act on the basis of interests, these studies show that values are an integral part of a process of identity formation and social mobilization.[15] In all the places we studied —among the Kerala fishworkers, the Minamata disease victims, the Houma and Cajun of Grand Bois, the housewives of Lake Biwa, the Delhi factory workers and owners, the fishers of the Nagara River area, and the residents of Civano—it is by forming attachments to communities that people find ways to confer legitimacy on their values, invoke them, and convert them into action. By documenting this process across the cases, these chapters show how values are synthesized to form discourses, social positions, and shared community norms that influence reactions to environmental conditions and policies, and sometimes bring about policy changes.

We find that the environment is a meeting point for a range of policies and actions. How and when people recognize environmental degradation to be a problem, and how they respond to the problem and to government efforts to address it reflect not only values concerning the natural world, but also values concerning work, health, religion, family, and community. As David Jenkins observed during his work on the United States study:

> Environmental values are deeply embedded in other values, and to separate them does not reflect the lives and concerns of people. . . . Follow the thread of any environmental value—from wilderness preservation to sustainable development—and what one finds is a tangle of politics, science, economics, nature, technology, and individual agency, all informed by local culture.[16]

In other words, we see no distinct sphere of environmental values that stands apart from other values.

This does not mean, however, that talk about sustainable development is merely a smoke screen for self-interested politics. To the contrary, it is evident that people hold deep feelings about the physical world they inhabit. One of the most poignant examples in the book is the reluctance of the Minamata fishers to accept the fact that the fish in Minamata Bay were contaminated, which would mean abandoning their traditional way of life and sustenance. Their belief in the beneficence of nature brought a devastating consequence: some went on eating the fish and suffered the crippling and often deadly disease as a consequence. As a Minamata poet fisherman movingly wrote:

> No one can understand
> why I love the sea so much.
> The sea
> has never abandoned me.
> The sea
> is the blood of my veins.[17]

Similar feelings underlay the ambivalence of many fishers in Kerala about adopting new fishing technology because they fear its impact on Kadalamma, Mother Sea. They reasoned that they have been blessed in the past because they have never disturbed her.

Nobel laureate in economics Amartya Sen lent his weight to the global debate over sustainable development when he argued that the concept should be broadened beyond the narrow "needs" focus given to it back in 1987, when it was first conceived and popularized by the Bruntland Report (also known as *Our Common Future*).[18] Referring to the oft-cited line in the report that defined sustainable development as "meeting the needs of the present without compromising the ability of future generations to meet their needs," Sen wrote:

> Certainly, people have "needs," but they also have values, and, in particular, they cherish their ability to reason, appraise, act and participate. . . . We are not only patients, whose needs demand attention, but also agents, whose freedom to decide what to value and how to pursue it can extend far beyond the fulfillment of our needs. . . . Should we not be concerned with preserving—and when possible expanding—the substantive freedoms of people today "without compromising the ability of future generations" to have similar, or more, freedoms? Focusing on "sustainable freedoms" may not only be conceptually important. . . . It can also have tangible implications of immediate relevance.[19]

Our cases describe both realized and unrealized attempts by people to exercise their freedom to choose how to value the environment. They each give rise to the question of *who* has the freedom to express their values, and produce remarkably similar conversations regarding fairness, justice and privilege that bring into relief class divisions. India, for example, has seen the evolution of two distinct forms of environmentalism: a green agenda for the new middle class and a resource scarcity agenda for the nation's chronically poor, with the former winning out over the latter. While these two forms of environmentalism are very different, they are hardly isolated from each other: the green demands of the rich increase the marginalization of the poor, forcing them to defend their livelihoods. In this political environment resistance to the middle-class-supported environmental campaign is regarded by elites to be an immoral, as well as illegal, act. Similarly in our China cases, we see widespread support for the government's resolve to act upon new scientific evidence of environmental degradation among the new middle class, and cynicism toward the government-led environmental agenda among the widening ranks of the unemployed and the peasant class. The phenomenon of divergent environmentalisms cuts across developing and developed countries. In the United States in the 1980s social justice advocates gave birth to an environmental justice movement to challenge mainstream environmentalism's preoccupation with resource preservation at the expense of the serious toxic pollution concerns facing poor, disenfranchised communities.[20] Our two U.S. cases are emblematic of this divide. And, in Japan, in all the cases lower-class fishers and residents repeatedly lose out to powerful corporate interests.

Across the cases the international environmental movement is a powerful force in conferring legitimacy on a particular set of environmental values—in deciding which of these voices will enjoy the favor of environmentalists. When local groups forge alliances and build networks internationally, they bring about an intentional convergence of values and approaches that can fuel political mobilization and strengthen their movements, as in the cases of the Kerala fishworkers and the Nagara anti-dam movement. We also see the positive impact of international standards on political mobilization, as in the case of Lake Biwa, where the lawyers who filed suit to halt public works projects used human rights language, which they claimed as "Japanese" because it was enshrined in their constitution during the U.S. Occupation. Yet often times, international involvement has the unintentional effect of silencing or radically altering local movements.

In the Nagara case, for example, the recreational fishers succeeded in bringing international attention to their cause through the international networks they forged at the 1992 Earth Summit and later through the World Commission on Dams. However, as they succeeded in popularizing their own movement, they drowned out the local commercial fishers who had first protested the planned dam. As a result, the opportunity was lost for a robust public debate on environmental justice that could have taken the fishers' voices into account. Similarly, international environmentalists ignored the plight of the Delhi workers while praising the Delhi authorities' efforts to clean up their city. The media took notice only when many thousands of protesters took to the streets, bringing traffic to a halt for several days in November 2000.[21] Yet even then, the media framed the problem in terms of worker protests *against* environmental measures rather than as a different expression of environmental values, one that promoted a healthy working environment and better living conditions for all. In the Sanjiang Plain case, local farmers and recent migrants to the region hardly stand a chance of having their voices heard in the face of intense international pressure for China to preserve her wetlands.

In reaction, some communities intentionally avoid terminology associated with the international environmental movement. In Grand Bois, Delhi, and Kerala members of the affected community showed reluctance even to define their problems in terms of "the environment." Indeed, victims and movement leaders saw "the environment" as carrying an agenda that stood in opposition to their own environmental values. In Grand Bois and Delhi the reaction against the term is visceral. In Kerala, a mark of the advancement of the movement was the movement leaders' ability to articulate clearly their problem with the term, which they associate with resource conservation as an externally imposed environmental ethic. The term entered their radar when international environmentalists developed ecolabeling schemes and promoted a proscription on turtle exclusion devices, which the fishworker leaders regarded primarily as means for foreign powers to safeguard market access. Instead of such an "imposed and restrictive form of international environmentalism" (p. 243), they characterized their movement as defending sustainable livelihoods, with a priority on the well-being of vulnerable humans, which they maintain is not the same as resource conservation.

Thus, we find that in many instances local vocabularies do not reflect the international discourse, and vice versa. Such a schism also occurs between local and national levels, creating a roadblock to pubic recognition of certain environmental problems. The national and international attention the Kerala fish workers and Nagara dam protesters gained through NGO networking was absent in the oilfield waste contamination case in Grand Bois, Louisiana, for example, where there was initially no national movement to champion the cause of the affected residents. In fact, because oilfield waste is "nonhazardous" by law, even the American environmental justice movement did not at first notice the problem.

Much has been written about globalization's homogenizing effects and the damage it does to local cultures. With the loss of control for many individuals and communities at the local level has come, paradoxically, a greater attachment to place, a quest for cultural belonging, and a rise in the desire for cultural identity.[22] In Kerala, following the national and international expansion of the fishworkers movement, the fishworkers returned to an appreciation of local roots, leading to revisionist thinking about the value of anything foreign. Calls for local autonomy and a say in the policies that affect one's community also accompany growing environmental awareness in Delhi, Minamata, Nagara, Lake Biwa, Civano, and Grand Bois. As time passes, we may well also hear them in Benxi and in the Sanjiang Plain.

The environmental advocate William Shutkin underscored the intimate connection between values, community, and environment and the imperative of sustainable freedoms when he wrote:

> The environment is the sum of all those places in cities, suburbs and rural areas that play an essential part in constituting our sense of ourselves as individuals and members of a community that demand our care and attention if they are to enhance, rather than diminish, that sense. To ensure the production and protection of a healthy environment requires the participation of those whose quality of life ultimately depends on it: ordinary citizens.[23]

One way to call attention to the global environmental crisis and build a movement that can lead to the large-scale citizen environmental activism sought by Speth is to acknowledge the various ways that people make sense of their world by publicly recognizing environmental and cultural identity. A lesson of all these studies is that we cannot adjudicate resource use and pollution conflicts solely on a scientific and technological basis or through "one world" approaches to environmental problems. In our quest for a solution to the crisis we need to resist a single narrative—as the India study underscores. Rather, we need a "fusion of horizons," where "the moral universe of the other becomes less strange," to borrow the words of the philosopher Charles Taylor.[24]

A principal ethical concern of environmental policy should be to devise systems of governance that hear the voices of all affected citizens. The democratic space must include room for communities to forge environmentalism consistent with what they value in their lives. Some political systems more than others allow people to freely express their values, yet even in the most open systems the right of free expression is circumscribed for certain groups. The convergence of environmental discourses across nations and locales and the silencing of local discourses reminds us that too often movements get valorized as local when they are not only. The multiple scales at which even a seemingly local problem occurs in terms of causes and effects complicate existing ethical questions regarding, for example, who sets the environmental agenda, whose voice counts, who bears the risk, who decides, and who pays? There are and will be conflicts of value frames surrounding such questions locally as well as internationally. Our hope is that in its focus on grounded understandings of the interplay between values and knowledge, this book might help guide us toward ways to resolve those conflicts justly, improve global environmental governance, and ultimately protect our cherished earth.

Notes

1. A transcript of the talk is available at www.carnegiecouncil.org/viewMedia.php/prmTemplateID/8/prmID/4469, accessed 15 December 2004. See also James Gustave Speth, *Red Sky at Morning: America and the Crisis of the Global Environment* (New Haven: Yale University Press, 2004), ch. 9.

2. Edith Brown Weiss and Harold K. Jacobson, eds., *Engaging Countries: Strengthening Compliance with International Environmental Accords* (Cambridge, MA: MIT Press, 2000).

3. See Ragnar E. Lofstedt, "Why Are Public Perception Studies on the Environment Ignored," *Global Environmental Change* 5, no. 2 (1995): 83–85; Raymond M. Duch and Michael A. Taylor, "Postmaterialism and the Economic Condition," *American Journal of Political Science* 37, no. 3 (August 1993): 747–79; and Ronald Inglehart and Paul R. Abramson, "Economic Security and Value Change," *American Political Science Review* 88, no. 2 (June 1994): 336–54.

4. The meetings took place in New York City (in April 1998), where the protocol was agreed upon and the project launched; Kusatsu, Japan (July 1999); New York City again (October 1999); Wuxi, China (January 2000); Beijing, China (July 2000); Udaipur, India (January 2001); and Tarrytown, New York (September 2001). Before or after the formal meetings in Kusatsu, New York (October 1999), Beijing, and Udaipur, researchers also visited one of the sites of the host research team (Lake Biwa, Grand Bois, Benxi, and Delhi/Agra).

5. The research meetings included the principal researchers from the four country teams. In the case of India, however, the researchers who selected the case studies and participated in the process of collaboration across research teams did not submit a chapter for this volume. Thus, after the final project meeting in September 2001, I commissioned the authors—Amita Baviskar, Kavita Philip, and Subir Sinha—to write the chapter that appears here using the research protocol developed by the project. They drew upon fieldwork they had previously conducted in Kerala and Delhi and supplemented it with fieldwork conducted specifically for this study. Despite the change in authorship, the case studies and the approach to the case

studies remain generally consistent with those of the Indian researchers who attended the project meetings and submitted fieldwork reports for group discussion.

6. Project participants considered the idea of allowing chapter authors to respond to the commentary authors within this text, but space did not permit it. As editor, I facilitated dialogue between the commentary authors and the country chapter authors and queried authors when I suspected possible disagreement or misreading of the case material.

7. Steven Gardiner argues that it is wrong to think that climate change can ever be successfully addressed without the full cooperation of China, India, and the United States. See Steven Gardiner, "The Global Warming Tragedy and the Dangerous Illusion of the Kyoto Protocol," *Ethics & International Affairs* 18, no. 1 (2004): 28.

8. For example, according to the United Nations Environment Program, the air in Asia's cities, including Beijing, Shanghai, and Delhi, is among the worst in the world. In China, contaminated drinking water is arguably the country's most serious environmental problem, with as much as 25 percent of the population lacking access to an "improved water source." India is doing only a little better than China, with 16 percent of the population lacking such access. In the United States, the Environmental Protection Agency found that "forty percent of surveyed rivers, lakes and estuaries are not clean enough to meet basic uses such as fishing or swimming because of non-point specific pollution." And in Japan the quality of lake water in a number of areas is deteriorating. For documentation on carbon emissions and all of these statistics, see www.carnegiecouncil.org/forgingenvironmentalism.

9. For a discussion of the distinction in the literature, see Steven Yearley, *Sociology, Environmentalism, Globalization* (London: Sage, 1996), 43–51.

10. Steven Yearley does precisely this in a paper written for this project, available at www.carnegiecouncil.org/forgingenvironmentalism. Unfortunately, space limitations prevented its publication in this volume.

11. The China Environment Forum at the Woodrow Wilson Center for Scholars has done extensive documentation of the development and work of environmental civic organizations in China. See especially, Elizabeth Knup, "Environmental NGOs in China: An Overview," *China Environment Series* (Washington, DC: Woodrow Wilson Center, 1997), 9–15; Jennifer Turner and Wu Fengshi, eds., *Green NGO and Environmental Journalist Forum* (Washington, DC: Woodrow Wilson Center, 2002), available at www.wilsoncenter.org/cef. See also Elizabeth Economy, *The River Runs Black: The Environmental Challenge to China's Future* (Ithaca: Cornell University Press, 2004), ch. 5; and Nick Young, "Searching for Civil Society," *Civil Society in the Making: 250 Chinese NGOs* (Beijing: China Development Brief, 2001), 9–19.

12. Robert Putnam, "Diplomacy and Domestic Politics: The Logic of Two-Level Games," *International Organization* 42, no. 3 (Summer 1998): 427–60.

13. This statistic has been cited widely and attributed variously to the World Health Organization and the World Bank.

14. Advocates of Civano are quick to point out that the Civano experience did pave the way for future, more successful sustainable development projects in Tucson. For example, Wayne Moody, the city planning director during the development of Civano, built on the experience to develop Milagro, a similar, albeit much smaller, demonstration project in inner-city Tucson. Not only does this project directly serve the less well off, but also it was more successful at incorporating environment-friendly features than was Civano (Moody, e-mail communication, 14 July 2004).

15. Of course many social scientists agree with this. See, for example, Sidney Tarrow, *Power in Movement: Social Movements and Contentious Politics* (New York: Cambridge University Press, 1998); and Charles Tilly, Marco Giugni, and Doug McAdam, *How Social Movements Matter* (Minneapolis: University of Minnesota Press, 1999).

16. David Jenkins, *United States Research Report to the Carnegie Council Understanding Values Project*, Carnegie Council, May 2001, 3–4.

17. Cited in Douglas Allchin, University of Minnesota, Resource Center for Science Teach-

ers Using Sociology History and Philosophy of Science, available at www1.umn.edu/ships/ethics/minamata.htm, accessed 2 September 2004.

18. The Bruntland Report, published as *Our Common Future* (New York: Oxford University Press, 1987), is the report of the World Commission on Environment and Development, led by Gro Harlem Bruntland, then prime minister of Norway. Barbara Rose Johnston, *Life and Death Matters: Human Rights and the Environment at the End of the Millennium* (Walnut Creek, CA: Altimira Press, 1997), 9–12, 330–39.

19. Amartya Sen, "Why We Should Preserve the Spotted Owl," *London Review of Books* 26, no. 3 (February 2004).

20. Environmental justice advocates and scholars disagree on the role of race and class in the victimization. See for example, United Church of Christ Commission for Racial Justice, *Toxic Wastes and Race in the United States: A National Report on the Racial and Socio-Economic Characteristics of Communities with Hazardous Waste Sites,* 1987; *Environmental Justice: Hearings before the Subcommittee on Civil and Constitutional Rights of the Committee on the Judiciary, House of Representatives, 103rd Congress* (Washington, D.C.: Government Printing Office, 1994); Bunyan Bryant and Paul Mohai, "Environmental Injustice: Weighing Race and Class as Factors in the Distribution of Environmental Hazards," *University of Colorado Law Review* 63, no. 4 (1992): 921; as well as Bryant and Mohai's edited volume *Race and the Incidence of Environmental Hazards: A Time for Discourse* (Boulder: Westview Press, 1992); Robert D. Bullard, "A New 'Chicken-or-Egg' Debate: Which Came First—The Neighborhood, or the Toxic Dump?" *The Workbook* 19, no. 2 (Summer 1994): 60.

21. For example, see "Delhi Pollution Protest Spreads," BBC News, 21 November 2000, available at http://news.bbc.co.uk/1/hi/world/south_asia/1032513.stm, accessed 3 January 2005.

22. See John Tomlinson, "Globalization and Cultural Identity," in *Global Transformations Reader: An Introduction to the Globalization Debate,* ed. David Held and Andrew G. McGrew (Cambridge, UK: Polity Press, 2003), 269–77.

23. William A. Shutkin, *The Land That Could Be: Environmentalism and Democracy in the Twenty-First Century* (Cambridge, MA: MIT Press, 2001), xv.

24. Charles Taylor, "Conditions of an Unforced Consensus on Human Rights," in *The East Asian Challenge for Human Rights,* ed. Joanne R. Bauer and Daniel A. Bell (New York: Cambridge University Press, 1999), 136. The phrase "fusion of horizons" is originally that of the philosopher, Hans-Georg Gadamer, whom Taylor credits.

PART I

Environmental Values in Four Countries

China: A Foreword

Judith Shapiro

Since the death of Mao in 1976, China's relaxation of Maoist dogmatism, its explosive economic growth, and its integration into the world community have fostered significant and obvious changes in values at all levels of society, including the state. The Communist Party's increased ideological flexibility has permitted the reemergence of some traditional values, such as filial piety, respect for scholarship, and appreciation of traditional Chinese cultural symbols. At the same time, however, the market, the state, and the international community are introducing powerful new values, some of which are in conflict with traditional values, Maoist values, and one another.

China is still recovering from thirty years of intensive government control over thought and behavior. During the Mao years, it was dangerous to hold or express any value or opinion that deviated from official slogans touting the primacy of class struggle, the "eat bitterness" spirit (or, willingness to suffer in the name of state goals), and "serving the people" (which all too often meant serving local officials). A misspoken word or careless deed could lead to criticism, ostracism, or exile; placing a cushion on a hard chair could be construed as counterrevolutionary; and listening to foreign broadcasts like Voice of America or the BBC could mean death. The state determined values, communicated them through propaganda and meetings in which everyone had to "express an attitude" (*biaotai*), and rewarded those who acted in most strident accordance with these exhortations. Because public values sometimes shifted without warning (as after the 1971 Lin Biao incident, when Mao's chosen successor, Lin Biao, a military man, was suddenly labeled a traitor, and the fashion for all things military ended overnight), people became adept at sensing the political winds and adjusting their statements and behavior to match. They grew mute about their values as a matter of survival. Indeed, there was such a profound split between people's internal experience and their public statements that some now say they no longer knew their own thoughts and feelings or how to speak the truth.

While those years are now more than a quarter of a century past, China is still experiencing the "crisis of values" that they left in their wake. Remarkably, the traditional Confucian emphasis on family ties and advancement through educational achievement quickly reappeared after Mao died, as people rekindled ties with relatives sent into exile or political disgrace, and the young vied for precious spots in universities. But the convulsions of the Cultural Revolution produced such profound disillusionment with public goals and exhortations that China's older intellectuals sometimes complain that the country has lost its ethical compass. Individualism, materialism, ambition, and faddish superstitions dominate the national ethos. Meanwhile, government efforts to use the old propaganda apparatus of media, billboards, and institutional meetings to influence people's values and behavior, even for the best of purposes, tend to be met with skepticism. In this context, China's environmental leaders have a singularly difficult task.

China's leaders, like those of many other countries, have experienced a major awakening to the importance of environmental issues during recent decades, beginning even before Mao's death with the country's participation in the 1972 UN Conference on the Human Environment in Stockholm. Their awareness of environmental issues intensified with the 1992 UN Conference on Environment and Development in Rio, when China signed several major international treaties and adopted Agenda 21's blueprint for action on environmental issues. During these and other international meetings, Chinese officials were exposed to world scientific knowledge and concern about growing environmental problems, and they engaged actively in writing the protocols and treaties that the conferences produced. At the same time, they began linking with international environmental organizations and donor institutions that were seeking permission to conduct projects in China, which gave them a hint of the intensity of the world's interest in China's ongoing loss of biodiversity, its carbon emissions, and its use of ozone-depleting substances. Meanwhile, they were learning from their mistakes, as great floods, intense pollution, blinding sandstorms, and other environmental problems forced China to reevaluate its development path. National pride, a sense of global responsibility, and the wish to leverage environmental issues to achieve other foreign policy goals have all contributed to the central government's strong commitment to environmental protection.

During the 1980s and 1990s China developed a large body of environmental laws, and in 1998, the central government elevated the National Environmental Protection Agency to a ministry-level state administration, renaming it the State Environmental Protection Administration (SEPA). However, the post-Mao decentralization of power to the provinces and the emphasis on economic growth at the local level create enormous challenges for those charged with implementing national environmental policies. Moreover, SEPA's ability to oversee implementation is limited by its tiny national-level staff of 270 (compared with 6,000 staff at the U.S. EPA headquarters in Washington).

China's opening toward environmentalism has also been complicated by its turn away from ideological Maoism toward "Market Leninism" and its integration into the global economy, which have brought economic growth beyond the coping capacities of China's environmental protection apparatus. China's adoption of market principles has allowed it to break its "iron rice bowl" commitments to provide lifetime employment and social welfare, while promoting a get-rich-quick mentality that hinders enforcement of environmental regulations. State-run enterprises, with their promises of lifetime safety nets, are shutting and collapsing, leaving millions of unskilled older workers without a livelihood and creating tension between the public goods of social stability and environmental protection. Uncertainty over the stability of land leasing policies, especially in the years immediately following the 1978–1979 "responsibility system" reforms, whereby households contracted with the state to farm assigned lands, led households quickly to exploit their natural resources out of fear they would soon be taken away.

Other recent developments, however, have supported China's nascent environmentalism. Self-reliance in grain has been a goal for China during much of its history, and grain supply has been a perennial source of anxiety owing to the country's large population, its vulnerability to floods and drought, and its long periods of international isolation. But China's integration into the global economy has permitted the country to feel secure about its food supply for the first time in memory. This in turn has allowed policy makers to rethink their emphasis on aggressive land reclamation for agricultural development, while advances in science and technology have allowed farmers to use less land for similar output. Moreover, devastating floods in 1998 and 1999 sparked much Chinese scientific analysis of the role of logging, erosion, dikes, and wetlands in-filling in promoting floods, leading the government toward a new appreciation of the environmental services provided by forests and wetlands. China's culture of pragmatism helps promote the understanding that conservation and restoration are means of hedging against similar future risks. Thus, "wastelands" have been redefined as wetlands, to be respected as "the kidneys of the planet," and logging has been banned in the upper reaches of China's great rivers. In some regions, land reclamation for agriculture has been replaced by wilderness restoration. Moreover, China's popularity as a tourist destination has shown some local people the possibilities of ecotourism as a new source of revenue, and hence allowed them to see their way toward supporting nature preservation.

Meanwhile, China's opening to the outside world has brought intellectual ferment and exposure to environmental writings. The openness is remarkable, considering that a mere quarter century ago contact with outside ideas was still politically risky, and it was considered dangerously bourgeois to read any but a handful of approved writers. Since then, China has published the environmental classics *Silent Spring, Our Common Future, A Sand County Almanac, Only One Earth,* and many other writings on environmental challenges, the global interconnections among environmental issues, and the urgency of rethinking development paradigms. Another source of energy for contemporary environmentalism lies in Chinese philosophical traditions, which emphasize principles of sustainability and reverence for nature.

These ideas and the wish, particularly among educated young people, to reach out to the world community, coupled with revulsion and sadness at China's heavy pollution, deforestation, biodiversity loss, and other environmental harms, have fueled a small but significant environmental movement. Participants include mature intellectuals, college students, independent activists, government think-tank scholars, and foreign donors and partners. Chinese universities are introducing environmental studies into the general curriculum, and basic environmental education is being brought even into elementary schools.

Despite the intense environmental commitment of certain sectors of the Chinese population, institutionalized avenues for activism remain limited. Chinese nongovernmental organizations remain tightly controlled, and they tend to restrict their activities to those that do not threaten the government, such as afforestation, volunteer trash pickup, endangered species protection, and environmental education. Student environmental clubs are administered under the aegis of the Communist Youth League, limiting their potential for independent action. And the level of activism varies greatly by region, with some areas of the country, such as the Southwest, teeming with environmental groups and others, such as those described in this chapter, remaining relatively quiescent at the grassroots level, perhaps because of their remoteness from institutions of higher education. Despite these limitations, the great passion for environmental issues in certain sectors of educated Chinese society provides an important counterpoint to the dominant ethos of consumption and wealth-acquisition, and could be an important source of support for the Chinese government's goals were the Party to relax its fear of the institutions of civil society.

A key mechanism that remains available to the government to communicate values related to environmental protection is China's centralized propaganda apparatus. Media broadcasts of foreign and domestic nature shows have become everyday fare throughout China. News stories about environmental problems and successes are common, and environmental accidents are covered more frequently than in the past. While billboards sending messages about picking up trash may have little effectiveness, news coverage of international Earth Day and other such events, as well as opportunities for public participation in their Chinese versions, provide occasions for the transmission of environmental values in a social context. Finally, public protests about environmental harms such as high local cancer rates or highly polluting factories, and legal actions and protests calling for the redress of such harms, are on the rise, contributing to increased public awareness of the importance of environmental issues not only on a global scale but also on a personal one.

Meanwhile, however, other values that tend to contribute to China's environmental problems resound more loudly still: globalization and economic development, and their coverage in the media, send messages about material success, status symbols, short-term pleasure, automobile ownership, and the Western model of development, energy use, and consumption. In contemporary China, after decades of ideologically enforced abnegation, materialistic calculations often dominate people's thinking to the exclusion of other social values and goals. Naturally, at a time when the developed world has taken few steps to reduce its own overconsumption, most Chinese are skeptical about arguments that the developed world's model should be off-limits to them because the planet's environmental health depends on their taking another path. Moreover, much of China remains poor. In some regions and strata, people are even worse off than they were during the Mao years because of the withdrawal of social safety nets like guaranteed jobs, pensions, and government-provided health care. For broad swaths of the population, survival is the only value that matters.

Under the economic reforms, power has devolved from the center, with the result that local conditions vary greatly, and individual bureaucrats can make an enormous difference in determining whether environmental goals are emphasized in their region. It is thus extremely difficult to generalize about the status of environmental values in China. Even where there are no indigenous environmental movements, environmental concerns may come to the forefront; moreover, China's long-standing penchant for developing models for emulation, whether at the level of the individual person, the town, or the entire region, has meant that some parts of the country have been publicized as ideals for the rest of China to copy.

China's central government now understands that environmental sustainability should be integrated into the country's economic development. There are numerous motivations for environmental policy action, for environmentalism is linked to flood protection, restoration of falling water tables, national energy security, public health, diplomatic leverage, and national prestige. Chinese leaders' pragmatism has even led them to consider the economic costs of China's environmental behavior, and to begin to implement a "green GDP" that would give the country a better picture of the real costs of development. Beijing's challenge is to persuade local officials that these priorities are important, and success in this area varies.

The cases described in the coming pages show that the promise of grassroots organizations and public support for the protection of China's environment has yet to be fully realized. In the case studies of the polluted city of Benxi and the Sanjiang Nature Reserve, local officials have made an effort to clean up and to protect, and in this sense the case studies are partial success stories. However, resources and staff for significant central support remain limited, and endemic corruption contributes to a general feeling among the local populations that they are being asked unfairly to make sacrifices from which elites are exempt. Moreover, weakening safety nets and increasing economic insecurity make it difficult to persuade ordinary people of the merits of environmental action, and local young people have yet to organize themselves into a force for the promulgation of environmental values. The question remains, then, whether China's central government can succeed in transmitting environmental values to the myriad sectors and parties whose activities affect the environmental health of China, especially in the face of so many other conflicting social messages.

Benxi City and Sanjiang Nature Reserve, China

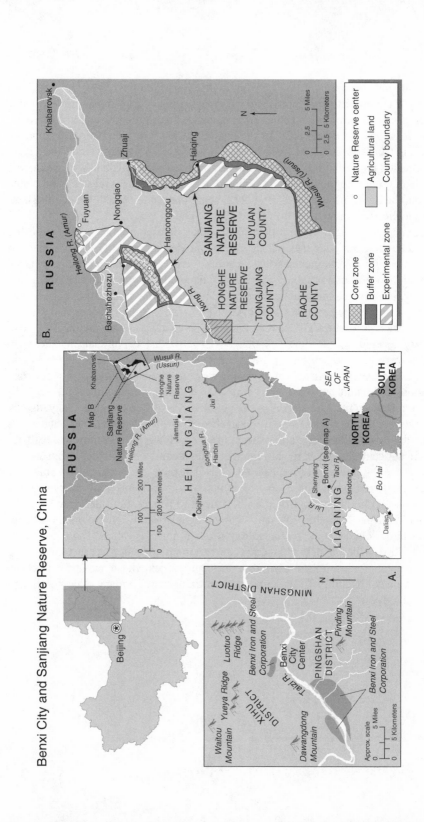

1

The Politics and Ethics of Going Green in China

Air Pollution Control in Benxi City and Wetland Preservation in the Sanjiang Plain

*Liu Yu, Pan Wei, Shen Mingming, Song Guojun, Vivian Bertrand, Mary Child, and Judith Shapiro**

When faced with the choice of developing the local economy or putting resources behind environmental protection, most Chinese local officials choose the former. This is the case despite the devastating extent of Chinese environmental destruction. Sixteen of the twenty most polluted cities in the world are in China. Air pollution alone is responsible for three hundred thousand premature deaths per year. More than 70 percent of the water in five of seven major river systems is unsuitable for human contact. More than 25 percent of China's land is now desert, with the desertification rates twice those of the 1970s. Eight to 12 percent of China's GDP is being lost due to environmental degradation.[1]

In this chapter, however, we examine two instances where local officials chose to pursue progressive environmental policies: in Benxi City in Liaoning Province (historically known as Manchuria) and in Fuyuan County on the Sanjiang Plain, in Heilongjiang, China's northeastern most province. Benxi is a midsized industrial town, which was fabled as a place whose smog was so thick that the city had disappeared from satellite images. The Sanjiang Plain case involves the issues and conflicts surrounding the creation of the Sanjiang Nature Reserve, a wetlands preservation site. Both cases represent environmental campaigns that began in response to the central government's growing commitment to environmental responsibility; both were executed by willing officials on the ground. Both are routinely touted as success stories: Benxi has become an environmental model, while the Sanjiang Nature Reserve's designation as a wetlands site of global environmental importance has brought international attention and approval to China's new wetlands protection initiatives.

Probing how officials came to take action at the two sites and the local reactions to these efforts reveals the complexities of environmentalism in China. What distinguishes Benxi from other highly polluted Chinese cities is that local officials there took advantage of a negative label, transforming the stigma as "the most polluted city" into a source of local identity and cachet. The decision of Benxi officials to step up investment in environmental policies at a time when the city faced economic decline and large-scale unemployment has not been sufficiently explored and explained. Here we qualify the city's success story, as touted by government officials and reported in the Chinese media, by adding in the views of residents, some of whom both resent and question the priority of environmental concerns at a time when economic reform has already jeopardized their livelihood.

The Sanjiang Nature Reserve case also began as a local initiative, but it was heavily influenced by Beijing and its new international obligation to wetlands preservation as a signatory to the Ramsar Convention on Wetlands, an international treaty providing the framework for national action and international cooperation on the wise use of wetlands and their resources. Ultimately, the Sanjiang Reserve case evolved into an instance of central government oversight of a nature reserve and related environmental policies. The central government's sudden interest in the ecological value of the Sanjiang Plain wetlands in the 1990s, fueled in part by international pressure, ran counter to the region's strong agricultural reclamation mandate, which dated back to the Cultural Revolution. In the area surrounding the reserve—and indeed within the reserve itself—90 percent of Sanjiang residents are farmers who migrated to the region in order to farm, and who have seen their livelihoods threatened by the creation of the reserve.

In Sanjiang, we see evidence of the important role that external parties can play in introducing a new awareness among local people. We explore the dynamics of top-down policies (those that flow from political elites to ordinary citizens) and their impact on local engagement with environmental issues. On-site awareness of the material benefits of the wetlands has grown since the establishment of the nature reserve, which has brought new professional opportunities and the promise of foreign funding for nature preservation. The reserve also has brought new responsibilities to various local actors—even the People's Liberation Army. At the same time, we see resistance, even antipathy, toward the environmental campaign on the part of many residents, especially those who, like people in Benxi, feel insecure about their economic future.

Both of these cases are famous in China, as Chinese officials are quick to point out. We knew about the cases when we selected them, and through previous research and cooperative projects, we had already built relationships with the local authorities involved in them. We chose to reexamine them because we wanted to emphasize a dimension relevant to Chinese policy-making as a whole: how various stakeholders interpret government-mandated environmentalism, and whether and how the differing values of these stakeholders are articulated within the policy process. We had three aims: to understand the nature and causes of the environmental conflicts and find potential solutions; to help make decision makers more aware of, as well as informed and concerned about, conflicts over resource use so they are better equipped to resolve them; and to increase international awareness of the particular problems that China faces and its efforts to resolve them.

In Benxi, interviews were conducted during two site visits in December 1999 and November 2000 with local service personnel, factory workers, engineers, administrative staff of the local government, local researchers, government leaders, provincial government officials, and national and international researchers and aid agency personnel. Our interviews also included revealing conversations with ordinary residents.

In the Sanjiang case, we conducted in-depth interviews with people who worked in nearly all trades and professions in the Sanjiang area during a two-week site visit in October 2000. While we were influenced by the work of Ma Zhong, a Renmin University professor working to save the wetlands, whose views are discussed in this chapter, we balanced his viewpoint by reporting sympathetically on the local people who perceive environmental protection measures as unfair and unwelcome interference with established land-use practices and their livelihood. In addition to our visits to local government departments, our fieldwork team went to farmers' houses and ate and boarded with the farmers. They told us their stories of daily life, their feelings and concerns about the nature reserve, and their views on the ways in which it was managed. In this way we learned about the local people's attitudes toward the reserve and the values that are bound up in environmental discourse.

These two cases present some useful contrasts—in terms of their dynamics (the Benxi process was locally driven; the Sanjiang case was externally managed), economic impact (with Benxi a brighter picture), and local attitudes (local residents across the board express resentment toward the nature reserve, while Benxi residents reveal mixed feelings about the clean air campaign). At the same time, both cases partake of a common trend, one that other observers have noted: the Chinese population has been experiencing a rise of environmental awareness since the early 1990s.[2] Government (both local and central) has been the engine of environmental initiatives in China, ensuring an efficient but not always democratic environmental campaign. At the same time, political decentralization has introduced energetic bureaucratic bargaining into the new environmental politics.

Since the early 1980s, when political decentralization began in China, government interests have become differentiated and fragmented at different levels and among departments, impeding the smooth transmission of environmental and other policy priorities from Beijing to the provinces and beyond. Decentralization has created bureaucratic conflict, rivalry, and ultimately the need for negotiation and compromise. By distributing power and interests vertically, political decentralization transformed local governments from puppets of the central government into independent actors maximizing their interests. Rather than relying directly on the central coffers, local governments now had both the right to levy their own taxes and a new need to *lobby* the central government for additional funds. This bureaucratic lobbying, absent the sort of citizen lobbying conducted in Western democracies, is the major driver of the environmental campaigns we examine in Benxi and Sanjiang. Different economic actors in these two cases—not only officials and industrial leaders but also everyday citizens—show different levels of commitment to environmental protection based upon what they could gain from the political bargaining that surrounds Chinese environmentalism.

These environmental campaigns are but two local initiatives spurred by the central government's policy shift toward a new emphasis on the environment. Since the late 1970s, the central government of China has demonstrated an increasing commitment to environmental protection. As represented by the budget alone, the central government's investment in environmental protection increased from RMB200 billion (US$34.68 billion) for the 1991–95 period to RMB360 billion (US$43.2 billion) for 1996 to 2000—an 80 percent increase. The total environmental investment for 2001 to 2005 will reach RMB700 billion (US$84 billion).[3] This rate of increase nearly matches the rate of increase of China's GDP, demonstrating that the Chinese government believes that the growth of the economy and the protection of the environment are mutually dependent. In 1998, Li Peng, then chairman of the Standing Committee of the National People's Congress (NPC) reportedly told an audience that the current environmental situation is "very grim" and that China will pay more attention to environmental protection as a fundamental national policy.[4] It is against the background of this national trend that our two cases emerged.

Benxi: "A City That Cannot Be Seen by Satellite"

China adopted its first national air pollution control law, the Air Pollution Prevention and Control Law, in 1987 in response to public pressure, growing awareness of the health effects of air pollution, international attention to acid rain and climate change, embarrassment that China's cities were being labeled among the world's most polluted, and increasing official recognition that environmental considerations should be integrated into economic planning. This legislation established the responsibilities of emitters ("polluter pays") and government agencies in dealing with air pollution and ambient air quality. It stipulated that local governments are responsible for integrating air pollution and quality management into economic development plans.

Amid China's campaign to reduce air pollution emerged the case of Benxi, a self-proclaimed environmental success story. In 1979, officials of the United Nations Environment Program (UNEP) discovered that Benxi, a city in eastern Liaoning Province, in northeast China, could not be seen on an American satellite image of the region because of heavy smog. With the help of local and national media, government officials carefully tended the story until it became famous throughout China. Local leaders and the central government collaborated to make Benxi, a relatively small Chinese city of 1.5 million people, a test site for new pollution prevention policies.[5] Soon, a number of international organizations, governmental and nongovernmental, recognized Benxi's commitment to pollution control and chose to aid its pollution reduction projects.

Benxi is widely known as one of China's most polluted cities[6]—a significant title, considering China's reputation for having some of the world's worst air pollution. Until the 1990s, however, few cities in China regularly monitored air pollution or kept data on it. By the time a 1998 World Health Organization study revealed that seven of the world's ten most polluted cities were in China, Benxi's air pollution had already improved, and it had escaped the list.[7]

Benxi's industrial pollution problems are typical for Chinese cities. Much of Benxi's pollution is caused by the burning of coal, China's main source of energy. In the late 1970s and early 1980s, when Benxi's air pollution was at its worst, the coal was low grade, with high sulfur and ash content, and it often burned inefficiently. Local officials in Benxi, like their counterparts in other Chinese cities, faced the need to control pollution during a period of transition to a market economy. A city in China's rust belt that had grown up around steel production, Benxi has seen a number of its state-owned enterprises (SOEs) shut down, resulting in vast numbers of unemployed workers in the city, a source of social unrest in recent years.

Yet Benxi is distinct among polluted cities in China for the media attention and financial assistance for environmental remediation it attracted. The central government made an unprecedented move not since repeated for any other city when, between 1988 and 1995, it invested RMB74 million (US$12.8 million) in Benxi's pollution cleanup. This case reveals how a midsized Chinese city came to place priority on the environment despite economic constraints and how it was able to attract significant attention and funds for pollution remediation. It provides insight into how support for environmental protection can be mobilized in China.

Benxi's Air Pollution: The Science Story

The beginnings of Benxi's air pollution story are typical for urban China. Benxi is one of China's oldest industrial cities. As home to the Benxi Iron and Steel Company, Ltd. (known among locals as "Bengang"), one of China's ten largest steel plants, the city produces more steel per capita than any other Chinese city.[8] It is also a center for heavily polluting industries. The largest contributors to air pollution in Benxi are ferrous metallurgy, steel processing, the cement industry, and coal production. The major polluting industries are concentrated in the urban area, which is surrounded by mountains, creating a thermal inversion, whereby air pollution becomes trapped in the river valley.[9]

Benxi's industrial base was a key part of China's economic development before 1979. In turn, economic growth had a significant impact on Benxi. With increased industrial activity, air pollution in Benxi escalated during the 1970s.[10] The main air pollutants included suspended particulates, sulfur dioxide, falling dust, carbon monoxide, and nitrogen oxides.[11] In the 1980s the Benxi economy was booming, a result of the central government's massive investment in Benxi's local enterprises during the period 1975–78. It was then, according to Zhao Zhenyu, chief of Benxi's Environmental Protection Bureau (EPB) at that time, that the city's residents and its political elites, who felt economically secure during Benxi's "golden years" in the 1980s, turned their concern to the pollution and its impacts.

Respiratory illness in Benxi had increased with rising air pollution levels, according to data collected by the city's public health bureau from local hospitals, particularly from the clinics affiliated with large industrial enterprises like Benxi Iron and Steel Company. Under Zhao Zhenyu, the Benxi EPB publicized this data, which showed a significant increase of air pollution–related respiratory diseases from the mid-1970s to the mid-1980s. According to a Benxi EPB study conducted in the mid-1990s, the average death rate from respiratory diseases was as high as 9.3 per 100,000 population in 1975–85, and from 1971 to 1982 mortality from lung cancer in Benxi increased 2.3 times.[12]

In Beijing, concern about Benxi's negative international reputation was growing, and senior leaders like Song Jian became determined to help solve Benxi's problem. Song Jian, then minister of the State Science and Technology Commission, ordered that Benxi be made part of a commission study on the health effects of air pollution during the period 1985–92. This study, carried out by the Center for Environmental Studies at Peking University and the Institute of Labor and Health at Benxi Iron and Steel Corporation,[13] became the first systematic investigation of the linkage between air pollution and health ever conducted in China. The results showed that lung cancer mortality had increased in industrial areas since 1986, but remained lower in areas with less pollution, even though both industrial and nonindustrial areas had similar rates of smoking and similar occupational exposures. These findings were incorporated into a 1995 report that was made available to Benxi city officials, who frequently cited it.

After the Benxi government embarked upon pollution remediation in the late 1980s, Benxi's air began to improve by most measures. Days when the visibility was 10 kilometers or more increased from an annual average of two to three in 1985 to twenty-seven or twenty-eight in 1995.[14] From 1994 to 1998, sulfur dioxide emissions decreased by 28.4 percent, and falling dust decreased 22.4 percent. By 2001 Benxi was no longer ranked as the city in the province with the highest air pollution; instead, it was the third most polluted, after Anshan and Fushun.[15] However, the air quality in Benxi still did not meet the minimum standard for urban areas.

Meanwhile, the central government continued to carry out public health studies. One recent study, undertaken by the Ministry of Health in 2000 and released on June 15, 2001, concluded that lung cancer and other respiratory disease in Benxi result not only from smoking but also from high air pollution levels.[16] To eliminate the statistical disturbance of smoking and occupational exposures, the study looked at Benxi children ages eleven to fourteen. The results showed a statistically significant relationship between the degree of air pollution exposure and incidence of respiratory illnesses. With such scientific evidence in hand, Benxi officials could continue to justify their spending on environmental improvements. Together with officials from the Liaoning Province department of health and NEPA, they would present the reports on pollution and residents' health as classified material to the Central Committee of the Communist Party and to China's cabinet, the State Council.

Benxi Captures the Attention of Beijing and the World

Like many other Chinese cities, Benxi set up its first environmental protection office in 1973, following the 1972 UN Conference on the Human Environment in Stockholm, in order to implement state regulations passed at the first National Conference on Environmental Protection, in August 1973.[17] The Benxi city leadership further demonstrated its commitment to environmental issues in 1979, when it upgraded the office to bureau, an independent agency of the city government. In 1983 Benxi's Environmental Protection Bureau (EPB) was again upgraded, to a department under the municipal government.[18] It was then that the role of the EPB became significant, reflecting the top city leadership's decision to assign environmental issues priority on the city's agenda.

The upgrade took place under Lian Chengzhi, the mayor of Benxi from 1981 to 1983, a key actor in the Benxi story. Mayor Lian first heard the satellite story in 1982, when he received a letter inviting him to make a presentation on Benxi's air pollution problem at the World Cities Conference in Rome. He ultimately declined for fear of losing face in an international setting. But the satellite story prompted him to act: in 1983 he said in his speech to Benxi's first Conference on Environmental Work that as mayor of Benxi he had a duty to take action on pollution control. He also set out to reorganize the EPB. All ranking officials and managers of state-owned enterprises attended the convention, and by the end of his term as mayor, among other achievements, Lian had institutionalized the convention as an annual meeting for all city- and bureau-level government leaders in the city. Lian's successors have since repeated Lian's public pledge, and several have also played pivotal roles in addressing Benxi's air pollution.

Another important figure in Benxi was Zhao Zhenyu, director of the city's EPB from 1983 to 1988. During Zhao's tenure, the Benxi EPB became the most visible bureau in the city, and through his vigorous public campaign, which showcased data from the Benxi Public Health Bureau, he brought the health effects of Benxi's pollution to the attention of city officials and the public. He organized citywide environmental education campaigns, invited members of the Benxi People's Congress to inspect the state of pollution in Benxi, rewarded enterprises that met environmental standards, and promoted a "green schools" program. The green schools initiative led to the opening of the Lixin Primary School in Benxi in 1991, China's first experimental environmental school.[19] From April 1987 to July 1988, Zhao, in cooperation with the central government, held seven news conferences in Benxi and Beijing, inviting journalists from major newspapers and television and radio networks to publicize the satellite story. By 1987, when the municipal government began to take environmental matters seriously, Director Zhao's EPB had assumed an influential role as technical adviser to Benxi decision makers on matters relating to institutional arrangements, personnel, resource allocation, operational plans, and educational campaigns.

Zhao, with his relatively high profile, contrasted sharply with past EPB officials in Benxi, who had held little power. Zhao and his bureau also had a higher status than most other EPB officials in China, where the EPB typically did not have its own listing in government directories, but rather appeared as a subdivision of the bureau of construction. Likewise, at the level of the State Council, the function of environmental protection was weak (as it remains today), and bureaucrats with environmental mandates wielded little power.

The change in priorities within the Benxi municipal government was an important start for Benxi's cleanup, but city leaders could not remedy the problem on their own. City governments in China generally function as implementing agencies of the central government. Thus they have little authority over the large-scale, state-owned enterprises that produce much of the air pollution, which are controlled by the ministries in Beijing that are in charge of raw materials production, steel, cement, and coal. Therefore, it is critical that local leaders gain the attention and support of Beijing when addressing major pollution problems.

In addition to concern over the city's international reputation, Benxi leaders also developed a scientific argument for central government financial support. In 1987, EPB head Zhao Zhenyu had ordered research on the exact sources of pollution, possible solutions, and plans for pollution control. According to the report, the city's total investment in pollution control from 1979 to 1986 amounted to RMB140 million (approximately US$37.7 million). At this rate of investment, it would take another twenty to thirty years to bring fifty-six major sources of pollution into compliance with state air quality standards. Using these figures, Zhao argued that Benxi could not control its pollution without help from the central government. City officials argued that they were entitled to central government funds on the grounds that Benxi was suffering the negative effects of centrally mandated economic reforms, a view that was shared by Benxi's public and industry officials. A sense of abandonment by Beijing had started brewing in Benxi as early as the late 1970s, as in many other Chinese cities with heavy industries. The people of Benxi had made a great contribution to China's development under state planning, but they were not getting the help they needed to control industrial air pollution, and the city was left bearing the cost, both in terms of health and environmental deterioration. A popular local saying at that time was, "Benxi gave its natural resources to the state but kept the pollution for itself."[20] According to Yu Chuanjia, an assistant manager of Benxi Iron and Steel: "The Benxi Steel factory was like a cow in the planned economy era; what we ate was grass, but what we produced was milk. The milk was taken away by the state, and we were left with the excrement."

In July 1988 an elite group of journalists from major national media,[21] including the official Xinhua (New China) News Agency, visited Liaoning Province to report on environmental issues in Benxi and elsewhere. Their visit inspired many media accounts of Benxi's pollution problems, bringing national attention to them. The director of the Liaoning Province EPB, Yu Yuefeng, also persuaded a Xinhua News Agency reporter to write a confidential report on Benxi's pollution for the top leaders in Beijing. In keeping with Xinhua's common practice, the report, marked "confidential," was written specifically for the Central Committee of the Party. In addition, many accounts appeared in the press and on the air with headlines like "A City That Cannot Be Seen from a Satellite." Thanks to this coverage, the city became a national symbol of China's pollution problems.

One month after the journalists visited Benxi, Chen Yun, who along with Deng Xiaoping, was one of the party's most influential elders, was drawn to the Benxi case after reading Xinhua's confidential report. Zhao's EPB had also tried to influence Chen Yun by producing for him a video on Benxi's environmental challenges. On July 23, 1988, Chen penned a note to Premier Li Peng at the top of the report that read, "Improving the environment in Benxi should not be delayed. The State Council should take measures to solve the problem." Chen Yun thereby instructed the State Council to take action, which led to the approval of a major pollution reduction program for Benxi, the Seven-Year Environmental Pollution Control Program. Song Jian, who by then had become the high-profile state councilor of the State Council Environmental Protection Commission (SCEPC), the top environmental oversight body at the time,[22] subsequently made personal inspection visits to Benxi and worked with state and provincial leaders to formulate a pollution control program for Benxi.

Benxi's success in capturing Chen Yun's attention can also be credited to a concerted campaign by then mayor and deputy mayor Yu Guopan and Shen Yucheng. In 1987 and 1988, with other leaders from the Liaoning Province and Benxi governments, they traveled to Beijing twelve times to report on Benxi's air pollution. Yu Yuefeng, then director of the Liaoning EPB, arranged for the director of the National Environmental Protection Agency (NEPA), Qu Geping, to visit Benxi in April 1987. Qu's comment, made during his visit, that he had visited many cities in China and in the world but had never seen a city with such serious air pollution, was made public in Benxi and later made the nationwide news. His visit put Benxi's pollution problem on NEPA's agenda, allowing the Benxi EPB to report directly to NEPA. (It was unusual for the central government to get directly involved in municipal level issues; more typically, this kind of problem would be managed by the provincial government.)

The visits to Beijing for meetings with the central government environment and industry ministries and the resulting inspection visit of SCEPC officials to Benxi helped pave the way for funding for pollution control in the city.[23] With these exchanges, the Liaoning Province EPB director, Yu Yuefeng, was able to convince the provincial government to invest in pollution control in Benxi. In March 1988, the Liaoning government appropriated RMB5 million per year over eight years for pollution remediation in Benxi.

At the end of 1988, the SCEPC issued a document titled "Decision on Pollution Control in Benxi," which called on the Benxi government to bring local air quality up to national air quality standards by 1995, or within seven years. The municipal government then endorsed the seven-year anti-pollution program for Benxi. With this program in place, Beijing considered Benxi a demonstration city for pollution prevention and control in China. The program announcement, while stopping short of stating that economic development had caused the pollution, admitted that the problem stemmed from the city's having ignored pollution for so long:

Benxi is an important raw material production base that has made a great contribution to China's economic development. But because environmental protection has been ignored in the course of economic development, the city's air is seriously polluted, and Benxi has been called "a city that cannot be seen by satellite." Waste materials from coal mines and steel plants are piled mountain-high. The Taizi River is black and brown, with almost no fish or shrimp. Pollution has damaged residents' quality of life, and it also restricts economic development.

With a total budget of RMB388.9 million (US$46.9 million), Benxi launched fifty-six pollution control projects under its seven-year program, with the aim of reducing sulfur dioxide emissions by nine thousand tons per year.[24] Of these projects—all of which used pollution control technologies such as dust-removing devices, electric precipitators, and sulfur-removing engineering—twenty-three focused on Benxi's air pollution, with a total budget of RMB311.57 million (US$37.5 million).[25] Benxi's investment in the project was significant: about RMB150 million (US$18 million), or roughly 39 percent of the total cost. Such high-level investment from a local government was a prerequisite to financial support from the central and provincial governments. Various government sources at the national level provided a total of RMB153 million[26] and according to Yu Yuefang and EPB official Yang Huijan, the Liaoning provincial government contributed RMB40 million. In addition, "special policies"—exemptions Beijing granted only to some favored cities—allowed enterprises such as the Benxi Iron and Steel Corporation and the Benxi Coal Company to sell a certain amount of their products at higher, market prices. (At that time, the prices of iron and steel were still controlled by the government, which intentionally set prices below the market to facilitate and subsidize the development of heavy industry in China.) The companies were then allowed to use the excess profits to cover the costs of pollution control projects.[27] By the end of the seven-year pollution control program, Benxi had spent a total of RMB488.3 million (US$58.5 million), 26 percent more than had been budgeted.

Once the central government got behind the seven-year program, it became a "national special industry program." This designation meant that it was no longer a local initiative, but a piece of the central government's overall environmental strategy. As such, the program was carried out under the direct supervision of the Ministry of Finance and the National Audit Office via expert groups, thus ensuring that Benxi would use the money for the intended purpose of environmental protection. With the program's new status, the central government acquired a greater stake in its success and launched a major publicity campaign. In 1989 the Benxi Daily, Benxi Radio, and Benxi TV sponsored a citywide campaign to expose the city's ten worst polluters—a list that came to include Benxi Iron and Steel and other big industrial firms. The central government also helped Benxi to launch Environment News, the only local newspaper in China that focuses on the environment.

The requirement under China's Environmental Protection Law that state-owned enterprises (SOEs) invest in pollution control was key to the seven-year program's success. In fact, much of the Benxi government's funding for pollution control came from the SOEs themselves. The law assesses pollution levies, fees paid by industries whose discharge of pollutants exceeds the limit set by the state. The size of a given company's levy is based on the quantities and concentration of the pollutants that the company releases. This system is used in most of China to channel funds from polluting industries to government for pollution source control, comprehensive cleanup projects, pollution monitoring equipment, environmental education, and institutional development. Any money that SOEs paid to the Benxi government in pollution levies was thus tantamount to money from the central government in the view of the Ministry of Finance, since SOEs were under the control of the national government.[28] As a sign of Benxi officials' determination to control pollution, the seven-year program doubled the levy for polluting industries in Benxi and enforced this decision strictly. This had symbolic as well as financial benefits: the higher levies helped raise local enterprises' consciousness about the environmental problem, and in the end, pollution levies paid for roughly a quarter of the seven-year program.

The plan's success was also owing to the decision that the ministries in charge of raw materials production, steel, cement, and coal—the Ministry of Metallurgy, the Ministry of Coal, and the State Bureau of Construction and Materials—would have a part in the plan's drafting and implementation, a decision that ensured their support for the plan. The seven-year program set a precedent and became a prototype for programs in other regions with special pollution problems.[29]

In addition to the seven-year program, in early 1989 the State Council approved Mayor Yu and Deputy Mayor Shen's proposal to designate Benxi as a "national heavily polluted recovery city" and to promote the enforcement of pollution fees.[30] The State Council's decision to supervise pollution control in Benxi directly allowed the Benxi municipal government to apply the pollution levy policy more strictly than any other city and to use its leverage in this regard to seek other economic supports from polluting industries in Benxi.

As the seven-year program neared its end, city officials worried about where they would find funds to continue pollution control efforts. They knew they could not rely solely on the central government, since its direct investment in the program had been an exception to its usual practice. Much of the funding would have to come from the enterprises themselves, through such measures as upgrading equipment. Still, there would be a gap, and the city turned to international aid agencies to fill it. Officials from the Benxi Science and Technology Committee, aided by their contacts with scientists in Beijing, persuaded China's Agenda 21 office, the national office created to implement China's international commitments under the Agenda 21 program agreed upon at the Earth Summit in Rio de Janeiro in 1992, to provide funds for research. In 1994, the city proceeded to establish its own Agenda 21 office, the Benxi Agenda 21 Administrative Center, to promote sustainable development. Benxi was one of only a handful of Chinese cities to create such an office. In 1997 the central government chose it, along with fifteen other provinces or cities, to pilot China's Agenda 21.

With Agenda 21 on the table, Benxi officials decided to promote clean production[31] —an innovative alternative to end-of-pipe treatment whereby production inputs and processes are altered to reduce pollution at the source. This process, developed in the 1990s, has been used throughout the world. Yet Benxi industries lacked the technical capacity, including a computer-based decision support system, needed to use clean production. With the cooperation of the central government, including the State Planning Commission,[32] the Ministry of International Economy and Trade, the Ministry of Foreign Affairs, the Ministry of Finance, and SEPA, Benxi sought help from international organizations.

The first international organization to work with Benxi was the United Nations Development Programme (UNDP), which in 1996 agreed to help create and fund a clean production project. The project cost roughly US$1 million, with half provided by the municipal government and half provided by the UNDP. Its main objective was to reduce air pollution by introducing production modifications, restructuring industry, and strengthening the municipal capacity for clean technology promotion.[33] In addition to the UNDP, in the mid-1990s the World Bank, the U.S.-based nongovernmental organization Environmental Defense, and the government of Japan contributed to Benxi's pollution control initiatives. Between 1995 and 1999, the World Bank lent US$12 million to pollution control projects in China, which included Benxi.[34] From 1994 to 2002, Japan's Overseas Economic Cooperation Fund (OECF) provided loans totaling US$81.5 million to support eighteen air pollution reduction projects. Starting in 1997, Environmental Defense began working in partnership with Benxi, along with Nantong, a coastal city in Jiangsu Province, to develop new cap-and-trade legislation for controlling sulfur dioxide, making Benxi a pilot city for emissions trading in China.[35] In addition, Liaoning officials purchased clean production technology from Japan and Europe, where the provincial governments in northeast China had established relationships with manufacturers of pollution control equipment.[36]

Benxi officials even began to turn down some investment opportunities because the proposed investments did not meet pollution control standards, Wang Zhen, deputy director of the Benxi Planning Commission,[37] explained to interviewers. In 2000 an armaments military factory wanted to move to Benxi, but, according to Wang, the city turned it down because of fear of pollution. As he told interviewers later that year:

> Everyone (in the city government) now agrees that environmental protection must be an important component of the city's development plan. In the draft of the next five-year plan, for example, there are more than twenty items about environmental protection and improvement. Any new investment must go through the environmental review process. We turned down several projects because of environmental concerns. This shows we are in the stage of environmental management rather than simple end-of-pipe treatment.

Meanwhile, efforts to reduce Benxi's air pollution continued. In January 2002, Beijing announced a new five-year plan for environmental protection and committed nearly double the funds it had spent on pollution control projects nationwide in the previous five years—a record US$84 billion (RMB700 billion), or US$16.8 billion per year over five years (approximately US$13 per capita).[38] However, the central government provided only RMB65 billion for five years (US$7.9 billion over five years or US$1.6 billion per year), with local administrations and taxes on polluting enterprises expected to finance the bulk of the plan. For Benxi's part, the municipality continued its investment in environmental protection. In its tenth five-year plan (2001–

5), Benxi committed RMB800 million (US$96.65 million) to environmental protection, under a program called the Environmental Protection Project for the New Century —twice the amount spent in the seven-year program. This is a significant investment, constituting about 5 percent of Benxi's 2000 local revenues, which is notably higher than the corresponding figure for many other Chinese cities.[39]

The Project for a New Century included a Blue Sky Program for the reduction of key industrial air pollutants. As part of this program within two years, ambient dust removal programs were to begin at ten of the city's biggest polluters, and energy controls applied, while other heavy polluters were to be closed or moved.[40] Other controls and timelines were established for other sources of pollution, including vehicular emissions. Other components of the Project for a New Century included a clean water project designed to reduce water pollution at the source and treat pollution in the Taizi River, as well as a "green plan" and a "quietness plan" to improve the environmental quality of Benxi's commercial and residential life.[41] The project was supported in part by a UNDP grant of $600,000.

In addition to government appropriations, the plan relied upon municipal government borrowing and revenues from pollution levies. SEPA estimated that Benxi enterprises would contribute about RMB200 million (US$24.18 million) or one-quarter of the RMB800 million total. As of this writing it is too soon to tell whether the plan's goals were met, although typically the government will set very high goals that it fails to meet.[42]

Balancing Economic Growth and Environmental Cleanup

As noted above, it seems strange that Benxi officials decided to step up investment in environmental policies just when the city was coping with economic reforms and rising unemployment. In this section we further explore the financial and social pressures facing Benxi officials and industries. These pressures—and the financial relationships between the central and Benxi government, on the one hand, and the central government and SOEs, on the other—help to explain the multiple motives for Benxi's pollution reduction campaign.

In the early stages of the market reforms launched by Deng Xiaoping, Beijing lifted state price controls on light industry products.[43] This policy harmed raw material-producing cities like Benxi, which had been selling their products at lower prices to support national industrial development; Benxi's economy began to lose strength relative to the economies of cities with light industries that could now sell their products at higher, market prices. Faced with this predicament, Liaoning officials saw poor environmental conditions as a perfect reason to ask for state compensation, using the argument with the Central Committee of the Party, the State Council, and the National People's Congress at almost every national conference they attended.

At the same time, state-owned enterprises (SOEs), which had their own channels to Beijing leaders, also used environmental arguments to ask the central government for funds. Technically, these companies are responsible for treating their own pollution. The standard mechanism is for the EPB to charge them pollution fees, of which the government then refunds 70 to 80 percent with the stipulation that the refund be used for environmental improvements. Yet because of their patronage relationship with the central government, SOEs were able to demand additional funds for pollution control, citing economic hardship under the dual-pricing system of the 1980s.

When, in 1996, the State Council set emissions standards for the country, it stipulated that industrial enterprises in any city that could not meet the standards by the end of 2000 would be shut down,[44] a remarkable departure from the Communist Party's policy of prioritizing development, seemingly at any cost. It is all the more remarkable that such a strict environmental policy would be put in place at a time that coincided with skyrocketing unemployment in many parts of China. Although the officially reported estimate of unemployment in Benxi during 1996 was 5 percent, many scholars believe it was in fact much higher, around 50 percent.[45] Under the State Council's new policy smaller plants were closed more often than large SOEs because they did not have the money to purchase pollution control technology. In an effort to contain the unemployment rate and to maintain social stability, the state seemed to accept the argument that SOEs as major employers deserved preferential treatment. As a result, the pollution control funds that the central government gave Benxi were allocated mainly to the large state-owned manufacturers of steel, namely Benxi Iron and Steel Corporation—the city's largest employer, and one of its largest polluters—and cement. Beijing also favored such enterprises over smaller enterprises through preferential loans and even through the handpicking of SOE heads to be municipal leaders. Of the fifty-six engineering improvement projects designed to reduce pollution under the seven-year program, nearly all were located within Benxi Iron and Steel Corporation, the Benxi Cement Plant, the Gongyuan Cement Plant, and the Benxi Coal Company—all SOEs managed by ministries of the State Council at that time.

In 1999, it looked as though Benxi Iron and Steel Corporation, the city's largest employer, which accounted for approximately 70 percent of the municipal government's tax base, would not meet the State Council's environmental standards; but the company managed to save itself through a combination of measures. At the end of 2000, it purchased a new blast furnace and pollution control equipment[46] and secured a loan from the Deutsche Bank to buy American-made equipment to modernize the steel plant.[47] The government also invested RMB30 million (US$3.6 million) in a high-pressure dust-flushing system, and the company obtained RMB115 million mainly through subsidies and tax breaks, to construct a dust-storing dam that reduces effluent to the nearby Taizi River by 2.9 million tons every year.

By enabling modernization, the support Benxi Iron and Steel and other large enterprises received from Beijing not only gave them the means to meet tougher environmental standards, but also allowed them to increase their production efficiency. In 2000 the State Economy and Trade Commission arranged for Benxi Iron and Steel to be outfitted for continuous casting.[48] By the company's own calculation, the energy they saved in one year as a result of the new technology was equal to 1.25 million tons of standard coal. The added income in 2001 from their more energy efficient products surpassed RMB4.8 billion (US$542 million).

Although some SOEs benefited from close relationships with the central government, most were not immune to economic hardships. In 1997, the central government began a campaign to make its debt-ridden SOEs profitable within three years.[49] Liaoning Province had more SOEs than any other province in China, and in 1997 most of them were in debt. As a result of the three-year campaign, approximately 15 percent of China's SOEs went bankrupt or were shut down.[50] Benxi Mining Bureau, with approximately fifty-four thousand staff and workers, was one of them.[51] Although Benxi Iron and Steel was not shut down, it laid off 1,100 workers during the three-year campaign, and twenty-two of its branches separated to become subsidiary corporations.[52] As a result, the company's per employee steel production doubled in 2001, to more than 100 tons.

Small enterprises have been particularly vulnerable to the squeeze of reform and environmental regulation, since closing one of them does not significantly contribute to unemployment and poses a low political risk for authorities. The story of small coal mines is a prime example of small enterprises falling victim to the environmental campaign. Beginning in 1998, under the orders of the State Council, the Liaoning provincial government criticized the "three smalls" of Benxi—small coal mines, small plaster pits, and small stone pits—and set deadlines for improvements.[53] Those enterprises that did not meet the deadlines, would be closed. The primary criticism involved these enterprises' harmful environmental impacts, although the State Council also took them to task for inefficiency, negligible revenue, and faulty safety mechanisms. The State Council's demands on Benxi's small enterprises were part of a nationwide campaign, in the case of small coal mines reversing a 1980s policy of opening privately managed coal mines under license.

Despite the State Council's deadlines, some coal mines in Benxi were repeatedly closed and reopened: when inspectors came, they stopped running, but after the inspectors left, production resumed. It was rumored that in June 2000, the Liaoning party secretary was offended by the sight of the mines operating on the road to Benxi within sight of visiting officials and international visitors and ordered their immediate closure, resulting in the Benxi government's bombing or closure of eighty-six mines. In August 2001, another sixty-two illegal coal mines in Benxi were bombed. Official reports indicate that a total of fifty enterprises, including small coal mines, were shut explicitly for environmental reasons, affecting approximately 1,200 workers—a small number in comparison to those laid off due to economic reforms. Still, the closure of coal mines intensified the economic strain on Benxi. In 2003, of Benxi's remaining five hundred coal mines—none of which are state-owned "key" mines—more than a hundred were running illegally.

One method local governments have used to balance the demands of environmental protection and economic development is to guarantee loans to enterprises for pollution treatment. Again, these loans come more easily to large state-owned enterprises than to small enterprises—which are already more cash-strapped. According to Wang Zhen, the deputy director of Benxi's planning commission, "The EPB and the planning commission would prefer to give loans to large, stable enterprises, such as Benxi Iron and Steel and the two cement factories, rather than give them to small enterprises."

Enterprises both large and small have sought and received loans for environmental improvements from international agencies and private lenders. Yet these loans put the municipal government at considerable risk. As Mr. Gong, a deputy director of the municipal fiscal bureau, explains, it is the city government that is usually most affected by companies' failure to repay their loans. In fact, since the early 1990s the State Council has prohibited any local government from sponsoring a loan. As Mr. Gong told interviewers:

> Benxi pays much attention to environmental protection, making efforts to get a "green passport" to the 21st Century; these are efforts we should support. But environmental protection must match the level of economic development. Getting loans means you have to pay back at some point. The central government deducts money from the provincial government, and the provincial government does the same to the municipal government, which puts a lot of pressure on us. Environmental projects mostly have only social benefits. If the enterprises cannot pay back the loans, the financial burden will be all on us. This is a huge pressure on our fiscal bureau.

"Benxi's case is common," according to Dan Dudek of Environmental Defense, the U.S.-based NGO that worked with Benxi officials on controlling sulfur dioxide in the early 2000s. "Five to seven years from now, there will be a climax of debt pressure all around China."[54]

Benxi officials saw a means of integrating economic development and environmental protection in the environmental management approach of the International Standards Organization (ISO) in ISO 14000, a program that supports sustainable development by unifying and coordinating the environmental management standards among states, thereby reducing nontariff trade barriers.[55] China has taken these standards seriously, regarding ISO 14000 designation as the means of securing the "green passport" that will allow enterprises to trade on the global market. Benxi submitted an application to SEPA to become the first demonstration city for ISO 14000, and in 1997 the request was granted.

To observers both inside and outside China, this was an innovative request, since ISO 14000 was new and usually applied to an enterprise rather than to a city. But in 1999, Benxi became the first city in China to become ISO 14000-certified. Citing changing "values" Mr. Tong Jun, the director of the Municipal Clean Production Center, a unit of the Benxi EPB, explained the positive impact of ISO 14000:

> Through ISO 14000, our values have changed a lot. We try to integrate environmental protection into economic policy-making. First, we improved government capacity in policy-making. Second, the working style of the EPB changed a lot, too. We used to work all alone, having troubles with all other departments and enterprises; sometimes we had to resort to the courts to ask for enforcement. Now we cooperate. Third, our work is more standardized. Fourth, financial resources have also increased. Prior to ISO 14000, funds for pollution reduction came from pollution levies and appropriations from the govern-

ments, but now we can ask for money from thirty-nine departments. . . . If all departments work in the ISO 14000 framework, the final solution to Benxi's environmental problems is within sight.

Not all agencies cooperated smoothly to promote environmental protection, however, and there was a growing rift between the public and the promoters of environmental values within the Benxi government. In the next section we examine the reason for the rift and the outcomes of these conflicts.

Environmental Values: Reactions of the Stakeholders

Up to this point, we have described how the environmental campaign in Benxi was begun and carried out. Now, we explore views of the campaign held by stakeholders from their varying political and economic positions.

There was no shortage of pro-environmental rhetoric surrounding Benxi's rise to the status of model environmental city. Media reports repeatedly suggested that Benxi citizens and officials alike demonstrated their awareness of environmental damage in the 1980s when they reportedly asserted that "whoever can solve Benxi's environmental problems deserves to be mayor of Benxi."[56]

Interviews suggest, however, that different actors prioritize environmental quality differently and according to their political and economic positions. Furthermore, all the stakeholders use the rhetoric of environmentalism in the service of (and often as a stand-in for) different interests and commitments. Generally speaking, the pro-environmental values expressed by government officials derive from their need to survive in office and to draw public funds, and thus environmentalism contains an element of bureaucratic opportunism. Industry leaders were split; fully state-owned and subsidized industries promoted the environment insofar as they could position themselves to attract investment for technological improvements. On the other hand, small industry officials and their municipal government representatives cast the government's environmental reform mandates as an obstacle to economic development. Finally, while many Benxi residents acknowledge that environmental action is needed, we encountered many, particularly the swelling population of laid-off workers, who also feel that government spending on environmental protection has received attention at the expense of the economy.

In this section we examine the ways in which stakeholders—Benxi officials, EPB officials, SOE industry, small-scale industry, and finally the residents of Benxi—both endorse and reject the new environmental policies. We pay close attention to what their reactions reveal about what environmentalism means to them, and the ways in which they value the environment.

Benxi Municipal Government Officials

Like their counterparts around the world, Benxi municipal officials endorse environmentalism mostly because they can use it as a mechanism for channeling much-needed financial support to the city from central and provincial governments and even international organizations.[57] For individual officials, there is a careerist motivation for aligning oneself with the new environmental policies. Bureaucrats are also sensitive to environmentalism as an international norm, bound up with other norms of modernity and scientific progress; their environmentalist accomplishments thus garner prestige.

Environmentalism also opened up new career opportunities for officials who were able to showcase their environmental achievements before the highest levels of government. This was aided by Benxi's ability to attract attention from officials from other parts of China as well as international visitors: from 1997 to 2002, about twice monthly, Benxi officials made presentations on the city's environmental protection experience to visitors from other cities and sponsored seventeen major exhibitions of environmental technologies. Promotions and other benefits awaited officials within Benxi's environmental bureaucracy. When the environment office was upgraded to a bureau, its officials were promoted, too. The increased size and power of the EPB meant that environmental officials had greater leverage in economic decision-making, and increased city attention to environmental protection translated not just into more money for the bureau but also into new benefits for its employees, such as bonuses and improvements in housing and office conditions.

Nevertheless, some EPB officials betrayed a deep personal and professional commitment to environmental protection in their willingness to risk political capital in supporting environmental projects resisted by other offices within the municipal government. When Environmental Defense worked with city officials to develop sulfur dioxide legislation based on the U.S. acid rain model, the head of the Benxi EPB at that time, Song Kecheng, pushed for the legislation.[58] The local people's congress passed the proposed legislation, but it was subsequently rejected by the mayor's office. After having invested much time and effort into the legislation, the Benxi EPB issued only a "management decree" (*guan li tiao li*), which is less powerful than a law.

In casting about for Chinese cities to work with, a top priority for Environmental Defense was to find policy makers who were genuinely concerned about air pollution. They chose Benxi because the local officials demonstrated an interest in working with a foreign organization to deal with this challenge. In addition, according to Dan Dudek of Environmental Defense, Benxi "officials understood the severity of the task." On a professional level, EPB officials were motivated by Benxi's obligations to the central government under the ninth five-year plan not only to reduce sulfur dioxide emissions but to meet total emission controls standards[59]—standards made even more stringent during the tenth five-year plan.

In field interviews with us, EPB officials routinely and proudly recited the success of their work in pollution reduction. In doing so, they did not mention economic considerations. Here, for example, is how the deputy director of the municipal EPB, Mr. Zhao, described the success of some of the policies enacted during 1996–2000:

> During the ninth five-year plan period, we tried to control pollution within the standard. The sources of pollution in the whole city are 838 enterprises. All except twenty or so have reached the standards under our supervision. . . . In addition, we promote clean production, which contributes a lot to the environment. . . . On one hand, we try to implement the policies of the party and the state; on the other hand, we make our own policies.

Yet, despite some EPB officials' dedication to the bureau's mission, debates continued among jurisdictions about how to balance environmental protection and economic goals. Several agencies outside the EPB were trying to maintain a balance between environmental protection and supporting the state-owned enterprises struggling in a transitional market economy. Mr. Gao, director of the Benxi Coal Bureau, which represents the area's independent mining operations, emphatically condemned the closure of coal mines in Benxi as an example of environmental priorities having upstaged economic and social considerations. Mr. Bi, deputy director of the city's Economy and Commerce Commission took a more nuanced view, however:

> It's not reasonable to say there is no relationship between environmental pursuits and unemployment whatsoever. But the effects are not strong because most employees in Benxi are in big enterprises. The enterprises that closed because of environmental concerns are mostly small enterprises that have a relatively small number of employees.

In closing the coal mines, Benxi was following an order from the central government. In general, the municipal government's enthusiasm for protecting the environment rarely translated into according first priority to the environment when such measures were perceived to be in conflict with economic development. Mr. Wang, deputy chief of the municipal planning commission, explained the struggle of balancing environment and development in these words:

> We feel that between environment and development, development should come first. They shouldn't be reversed. Replacing development with environment in the first place is not feasible. The environmental problems brought by development should be gradually explored and solved in the development.

Naturally, many EPB officials were frustrated by this attitude. Because each district EPB office is under the control of the district government, the latter's views tend to hold sway, and execution of EPB intentions can be thwarted at the district level. As Mrs. Gao, the director of the EPB of Xihu District, explained:

> It's really hard to work at the grass-roots level. It's an institutional problem. We are a part of Xihu District government, governed by the district government, instead of the municipal EPB. . . . Therefore, when we have problems, we have to make concessions to the district government, especially if our job conflicts with the economic interests of this district. If we were governed by the municipal EPB, things would be much easier for us. Environmental concerns would be emphasized.

Industry Officials

Industry officials in Benxi differed in their attitudes toward environmental protection according to the cleanup campaign's economic impact on their enterprise, the size of the enterprise, and the amount of pressure or support an enterprise received from the government. Officials at state-owned enterprises, for example, tended to support environmentalism when it led to subsidies for new equipment and resisted it when environmental policies—derived from new "polluter pays" economic models—placed new burdens on industry. Like the municipal bureaucrats who use environmental values as the basis for their demands for greater funding, SOEs endorsed environmentalism and its policies opportunistically.

If environmental investments can help increase efficiency and profits, they are usually welcome in factories. Engineer Wang of the Gongyuan Cement Plant described the dual benefits of environmental initiatives:

> Because of the nature of dust pollution in the cement industry—that is, recycled dust can be put into the production line again—our enterprises want to do a better job in environmental protection. On the one hand, the profit of enterprises can be increased, and on the other hand, it's good for the health of workers, too. Now every year, recycled dust accounts for one-third of our output value, or RMB10 million (US$1.2 million).

The Benxi No.2 Textile Factory shared a similar experience of success, according to the director of its environmental protection department:

> If the interests of enterprises are hurt, they won't be willing to [make environmental investments]. As a matter of fact, it's beneficial for us to conduct clean production. For example, since we began using low sulfur and high quality coal, our factory has saved tens of thousands of tons of coal. . . . Clean production also reduces the waste of production materials. It saves production costs and increases our profits.

Yet few industries found themselves in such a win-win situation. Even Benxi Iron and Steel felt the economic pinch of implementing pollution control. As Mr. Ren, director of the company's environmental department, explained:

> Now the state has begun to stress the environment. In old times it was a problem if your factory didn't smoke, and now it is a problem if it smokes. . . . The enterprise is pushed to the front line. You have to live on your own,[60] pay salaries, keep running, and take money out to treat your own environmental problems. This creates a lot of troubles for the enterprises.

The enterprises never passively accept government policies; instead, they try to delay the payment of pollution fees, or negotiate with or threaten the government. Sometimes the government has to plea for enterprises to cooperate with environmental regulations and policies. Mr. Lu, the director of the municipal environmental supervision department (a part of the EPB), talked about the recalcitrance of some enterprises:

> According to the national policy, we should charge the pollution fee in proportion to emissions . . . but it's impossible to get the money all at once. Our policy is to allow delays but not to grant exemptions. This year, the fee is RMB1 million (US$120,000), and you can turn in half of it at first, and owe us another half. . . . To get the money, we have to go to the enterprises more than ten times. It is useless to call them, and it is only worthwhile

to talk to the director of the factory. Deputy directors are of no help to us. In old times, we only needed to talk to the directors of environmental departments, and things got solved. . . . Not now. . . . Sometimes the boss hides from you because the economic situation of the factory is not good.

Speaking of the potential conflict between development and environmental protection, an environmental engineer at the Gongyuan Cement Plant said, "The production equipment of our enterprise is backward, and our scale is not big, either; buying a lot of new environmental equipment will increase our financial burden, driving us into a hopeless situation."

Although as SOEs the cement companies are protected by the state and would not be closed, environmental cleanup requirements can put a strain on the enterprise, which affects workers' bonuses and fringe benefits as well as job security.

At smaller industries, managers resisted the environmental campaign almost wholesale, viewing it less as a means to modernization than as an obstacle to development and prosperity. They felt unfairly treated when it comes to the distribution of government subsidies for environmental remediation. Small industries saw little of the "green money" for which the EPB and other municipal agencies lobby. Because they employ fewer people, their closure is less politically destabilizing for China than the closure of an SOE. This gave rise to a justice claim on the part of smaller industries; they felt they shoulder a greater part of the burden of environmental policies on the basis of the inappropriate criterion that it is politically efficacious.

For the small factories, the cleanup of Benxi caused economic hardship including closure or production restrictions. The Xihu District EPB director, Mrs. Gao, talked about their predicament:

The enterprises face their difficulties. It's not easy for them to squeeze out more money. For example, there is an electricity plant in our area; its name is Xihu Electricity Plant. This year, we got complaints from some people about noise and dust pollution [from the plant]. . . . After measuring and investigating, we found it did exceed the environmental standards, so we ordered the enterprise to stop running. . . . This is difficult for the enterprise. They have no money, but still they have to guarantee environmental quality. What are those unemployed going to do?

Mr. Gao of the Benxi Coal Bureau described similar unemployment problems caused by the coal mine closures. The coal bureau represents the independent mining operations encouraged by the government to go into business only a decade or two ago. Now that they do not conform to the new environmental standards issued from Beijing, and because they are not under the direct auspices of the state, they are left to fend for themselves—and the state is not held directly responsible for their failure. As Mr. Gao pointed out that the government's compensation for loss of livelihood is routinely inadequate:

When we protect the upstream forest, requiring the residents there to revert the agricultural field back to forest, we cut off the livelihood of the people there. Basic livelihood is threatened, and the government doesn't give reasonable compensation. Thirty-four coal mines have assets of RMB3 million (US$360,000) but the compensation given by the government is only RMB30,000 to 40,000. . . . Closing the mines causes a lot of unemployment problems.

Not only do smaller industries not receive subsidies to install new green technologies that would help them remain economically and environmentally sound, but they are also saddled with the same pollution fees as the SOEs. And smaller industries do not have the clout to evade these fees as easily as the SOEs do. In 2000, an assistant manager at the Hangang Benxi Beer Factory described the factory's difficulty in securing government support:

> A lack of funding is still a big problem. For example, our new [pollution control] equipment, cost more than RMB8 million; we have still not paid the construction team. We need support from the environmental department. We transferred some money from technical reform funds of our factory to do this. We were originally told we could get loans from the EU [European Union], but it seems unpredictable now. The refinancing from the pollution fee only amounts to RMB600,000 or so; it's far from what we need.

Residents

Before we conducted our interviews, one member of our research team, a longtime resident of Benxi and a former EPB official, had believed that the campaign had widespread support not only among the city's professional class, but among all residents. After all, unlike lavish projects such as skyscrapers, he and his friends and colleagues reasoned, the benefits of Benxi's pollution cleanup are enjoyed by everyone. The interviews the team conducted, however, revealed that Benxi residents hold multiple and conflicting opinions about the new environmental policies. On the one hand, no one we interviewed challenged the idea that Benxi's air was bad. On the other hand, respondents—particularly factory workers and laid-off workers—did not accord much priority to the environment and even spoke disdainfully about the campaign. They routinely shifted the topic of conversation from the environment to job losses and their immediate economic hardship. As an unemployed female worker stated:

> Now the environment is much better than before. It was once a city invisible from a satellite, but now we can see blue sky. . . . Our governments put so much money toward protecting the environment, but why does nobody take care of our lives? People matter the most. If people are starving, it's meaningless to have a good environment.

Although the Benxi municipal government, particularly under EPB director Zhao Zhenyu, made considerable effort to enlist public support for Benxi's environmental campaign, our interviews suggest that many residents are unenthusiastic participants. In a fragile economy where unemployment has soared, basic livelihood needs, health care, and pensions are overriding concerns for many, with environmental degradation often a secondary priority. Similarly, although residents granted that Benxi's air had improved, many of those we interviewed said they believed it was owing to the factory closures—no production, no pollution—and not to new technology in factories or to regulation of factory emissions. While the government characterized improvements in air quality using scientific quantifiers and chemical measurements that signal progress to the international community, Benxi residents gave the improvements mixed reviews on the basis of how (and whether) the improved environment had improved their day-to-day life.

This public distrust of the campaign was fueled, in part, by corruption in the SOEs. In a widely publicized case, Bai Shangxian, the former party secretary and member of the board of directors of Benxi Iron and Steel, was arrested in July 2000 for "arbitrarily extending the period of a promotional price" for some clients and providing fake evidence for counterfeit contracts, and sentenced to five years in jail. Around the same time two other members of the board, Zhang Wenda and Li Zhida, were also found guilty of corruption for personal gain. Corruption charges reached beyond the upper ranks, as twenty-one lower officials of the company were charged with involvement in similar cases of economic crimes. In the early 2000s the company fell from China's fifth-largest steel enterprise to its tenth-largest. It is widely believed that this was due to the corruption cases, which harmed the interests of the company and damaged worker-management relations. More to the point, these cases gained notoriety for a company that has been favored by the environmental campaign; this in turn fostered public cynicism toward the campaign itself.

Those who lost their jobs or businesses in the national campaign to close the coal mines were particularly cynical about the campaign. The owners of those mines were poor local peasants who were ordered to close their mines without any compensation—for the sake of the environment. To many coal mine owners, the Benxi EPB was heartlessly preoccupied with executing the orders of the central and provincial governments. As Mr. Gao, director of the Benxi Coal Bureau, explains:

> After shutting down the small coal mines, our revenue shrank by RMB10 million. Many people lost their jobs because of this. With the revenue decreasing, salaries of government employees are reduced, too. Protecting natural resources should be combined with the protection of social resources. So much unemployment and so much salary arrears are causing social disorder. This is a loss, too.

An unemployed worker who was looking for a job in the local labor market when interviewed also expressed discontent regarding public spending on the greening of Benxi:

> We have nothing to eat. Who cares about the environment? At the Benxi Steel and Iron Company, so many people are laid off, and given no living expenses. We don't know where the money has gone. It's not easy to find a job, but you still have to try; otherwise nobody cares about you even when you starve to death. About the look of the city, have you seen the lawns along the streets by the train station? They reconstructed it three times this year, demolishing and then reconstructing, and then demolishing, and then reconstructing. What the hell are they doing!

When asked if he knew the story of "the city that is invisible from a satellite," one old man who used to work at a factory of Benxi Iron and Steel said, "I know. Everyone knows. Benxi's environment is not good—our factory was very big before, and then it [was closed and] became grassland. The land is green now, but we also lost our jobs. We have nothing to live on now. I'm so old, but still have to go out to look for odd jobs."

When asked if money should be put into cleanup or development, a Benxi Iron and Steel employee responded: "If people can stand the current [environmental] situation, I think the money should be put into economic development. After all, the benefit of economic development is quick and obvious, whereas environmental protection is a long-term and less productive effort."

Nonetheless, some residents see an economic rationale for a clean environment. As an unemployed woman pointed out, "When a company comes here to invest, they look at the city's environment, and that will be one of the factors in their decision. Who will invest in a place with a disgusting environment? Every time there is a trade show or other big event, the city is cleaned up, and Benxi looks beautiful."

Residents have also made a link between their health problems and Benxi's environment, and it is through this link that residents'—particularly workers'—environmental concerns are expressed. Liu Ningrong's novel *Angry Earth* contains the following passage, now well known to many in Benxi: "The white-dressed surgeons . . . don't need you to tell them; they know from looking at your lungs: 'You must be from Benxi.'"[61] William Hurst, an American who has researched unemployment in Benxi and elsewhere in China, recalled his interviews with unemployed workers who attribute their health problems to pollution:

> Among all the unemployed workers that I have interviewed in Benxi and elsewhere, many have mentioned that it is a shame that the environment is so degraded or have talked wistfully about fishing or bathing in what now are filthy or dried-up rivers. . . . Several have even spoken about serious illnesses (most often cancer) they have contracted, they say, because of pollution-related problems.[62]

There have even been instances of workers taking a stand within their companies: some employees of Benxi Steel and Iron, for instance, told us they refused to work in the heavily polluted workshops, such as the benzene and coke furnace workshops, regardless of how much they were paid. Mr. Kang, head of the company's coke factory, explained that workers in the factory did not live beyond age sixty-five due to past pollution exposure, and some of the workers even died at age forty-five. The director of the company's environmental department, Mr. Ren, also expressed concerns regarding the health impacts of environmental problems:

> Those who came to Benxi only a decade ago, 70 to 80 percent of them have pharyngitis, and it's getting worse now, developing into brain tumors and lung cancer. . . . In our fireproof material factories, most of our old workers died of lung disease. If you don't treat environmental problems, what troubles will we bring to our children?

Yet ordinary residents play only a minor role in environmental policy. This is in part a matter of priorities: environmental values are still a luxury for many residents who feel vulnerable to rampant unemployment; people are simply not motivated to fight for the environment, as they are for other concerns, such as their right to their pensions.[63] The low level of citizen environmental activism can also be explained by the Chinese political system, which restricts public participation. As a young, unemployed woman we interviewed put it:

> The major responsibility for environmental protection lies with the government. No one else can do this. There is a dedicated phone line for the mayor. If you can inform the mayor, the problem can get solved pretty quickly. But sometimes the executive level does not act efficiently. The channels for normal people to report their concerns and problems do exist, but they do not work very smoothly.

The residents do complain, however, and do use available channels to make their complaints heard by local officials. One channel is the local people's congress; residents can contact their deputies directly in the hopes that their complaints will be presented at the annual meeting of the municipal people's congress. From 1981 to 1989, for example, the deputies of Benxi's people's congress made forty-three motions and draft resolutions requesting that the government take actions to reduce pollution. During this same period there were fifty-three environmental suggestions or complaints, a substantial number for one issue area, filed by residents at the sessions of the city's political consultative conference.[64] It is, therefore, clear that local environmental concerns over pollution existed, were growing, and had been expressed well before government officials imposed air quality improvement policies via the seven-year program and other programs. This suggests a climate of support for environmental policies among the people's congress representatives and their constituents, the residents.

A second channel for public input, which the young woman above referred to, is the environmental hotline that was set up during the first year of the Seven-Year Pollution Control Program. EPB officials report that through the hotline, they received a flood of complaints about bad air quality and power plants that emit black smoke—an indicator that the plants are out of compliance with pollution standards. Although it took some time for the hotline to catch on, by 2000, the Benxi EPB chief Song Kecheng boasted that as many as three hundred calls were being logged per month. In addition to using the hotline, citizens can write letters or visit government departments to complain about pollution. In 2001 alone, 2,445 complaints (compared with 1,667 the year before) were lodged, primarily through the hotline but also by mail and in-person visits.

Our analysis of the number and content of the public's complaints over the period 1982 to 2001 suggests three things: (1) the residents are much more concerned about their local environmental problems than they were in the 1980s (or at least more likely to express their concern through the available channels); (2) the targets of environmental complaints are often smaller-scale commercial ventures such as hotels, restaurants, and public bathrooms; and (3) air pollution and noise pollution were the top two categories of complaints (outranking water pollution).

The increased level of public participation via the hotline indicates that the environmental campaign in Benxi has heightened awareness of environmental problems among ordinary people. It also suggests some level of confidence that the government will actually respond. Furthermore, it is evident from a review of the proposals for environmental clean up made by the representatives of the Benxi people's political consultative conference, who are charged with representing public concerns, that citizens' consciousness of environmental protection grew during the period from 1990 to 2000, a period that included the years of the seven-year program. While the number of proposals increased, particularly in the years 1990–93, the content had shifted: the number of suggestions targeting individual polluting factories had decreased relative to the number of proposals for dealing with citywide environmental problems. These proposals suggest that Benxi residents want to see broader and longer-term approaches to resolving the city's environmental problems.

Stakeholder Evaluations of the Government's Pollution Reduction Efforts

Benxi residents and officials agree that air quality was formerly very poor and has improved. Elites and nonelites, however, measure the improvement differently. Whereas the public tends to rely on personal experience, government officials use scientific measurements. The deputy director of the municipal EPB, Mr. Zhao Liancheng, for example, said:

> We have basically treated this problem. After the seven-year plan, we continued to emphasize environmental protection to consolidate the results. Now, for the first time, the air quality of Benxi has reached Grade III national ambient air standards.[65] Falling dust is 35.8 tons/square kilometer every month. We have reached all the standards, some even ahead of plan.

A young unemployed woman, on the other hand, offered the street-level perception when she said, "The current environment is much better than before. There was a time when every time you walked in the street, your shoes would be covered with a layer of dust, or if you hung your laundry, it would be dirty in a few hours. The environment has become much better."

Along with this acknowledgment, however, comes a sense that the government's priorities may change with the political winds, and that the job of improving the environmental quality in Benxi remains incomplete. The young woman continued, "But this problem depends on the specific leader. If the leader changes, no one can predict how much attention the government will pay to the environment."

A salesman at a pharmacy agreed: "I've been here for five years. The environment here has been much improved, but it's still dirty here."

Government officials see the improvement as a result of a years-long fight against pollution through policies, investments, and campaigns. The deputy director of the municipal economy and commerce commission, Mr. Bi, stated:

> Now Benxi is quite different from what it was like at the end of the Seventh Five-Year Plan: after so many years of treatment, the problem of dust blowing in one's face has changed. Our municipal party council and municipal government and all government departments took all kinds of measures to achieve this.

Many ordinary residents disagreed with this analysis, however, attributing the improved air quality to economic recession. A fruit vendor, Mr. Gen, expressed disdain for what he perceived to be an excessive emphasis on pollution cleanup amidst rising economic insecurity: "The factories have stopped running; where is the [supposed] pollution coming from? What do we treat now?" A doctor, Mr. Ren, echoed this sentiment: "The factories were running normally before, and the chimneys gave out dust and smoke constantly. The environment was of course bad . . . but now the factories are going bankrupt. [With] no emission of smoke and dust, the environment gets better automatically." To such residents, who remain cynical about government policy, the equation is simple: no more belching smokestacks—a sign of prosperity—no more pollution.

Both elite and nonelite perceptions of why the Benxi environment has improved may have some validity. Later in this chapter we provide further analysis of the tension between perceptions and values as expressed in both this case and that of the Sanjiang Nature Reserve.

The Sanjiang Nature Reserve

The story of the Sanjiang Nature Reserve offers a particularly instructive window on the complex dynamics of Chinese environmental politics. In Sanjiang, the tension between the competing values of environmental protection and economic development is even more powerful than in Benxi. Where the Benxi case offers an example of an urban area plagued simultaneously by choking pollution and state-sector unemployment, the case of Sanjiang illustrates the challenge of protecting nature in a remote and poor yet growing district of China where many local farmers and immigrants strive to make a living off the land. Where Benxi shows how local officials lobbied the central government for funds and other help to combat their pollution problem, in Sanjiang a different scenario unfolded. There, local officials undertook an environmental project—the establishment of a nature reserve—in the hopes that the central government would support and fund their efforts. Instead, the central government assumed the management of the reserve, and the funding did not match its own policy pronouncements about the importance of wetlands to China's environmental preservation. International pressure played a strong role in the central government's decision to become directly involved in, and to co-opt in a sense, the management of the reserve.

The case study below examines the changes in values and other factors that led to the creation of the reserve; the individual people and government entities that have played major roles; and the ways competing interests and values obstruct and facilitate the management of the reserve and the pursuit of environmental protection. The core of this case study is an examination of the bureaucratic conflicts and local resistance facing the Sanjiang Nature Reserve as it tries to carry out its work of protecting biodiversity. From a broader perspective, this account of the reserve shows how changing values at the national level are translated into local policies and actions.

Ecological Significance and Environmental Degradation

The Sanjiang Nature Reserve is located on the Sanjiang Plain in Heilongjiang Province, in the extreme northeastern corner of China. This region was historically known as the Great Northern Wilderness (*beidahuang*). Until the mid-twentieth century, it was a remote, heavily forested wetland area, full of birds, fish, foxes, tigers, wild pigs, and black bears. In the early 1950s the Sanjiang wetlands comprised 5.36 million hectares, about 80 percent of the Sanjiang Plain. Today the wetland areas total less than 1.9 million hectares—less than 30 percent of the plain. The swamp forests have declined dramatically[66] and many species, such as the Siberian tiger, that were once plentiful are endangered, if not extinct.

The Sanjiang Plain is a low-lying floodplain at the confluence of three rivers—the Songhua, Heilong (Amur), and Wusuli (Ussuri) Rivers[67]—hence the name Sanjiang, or "three rivers." It is a triangular area of land that points into Russia, with the Heilong and Wusuli Rivers forming the natural boundaries between China and Russia. The Sanjiang Nature Reserve preserves a small section—about 5 percent—of the total plain, in the far northeast corner, along the Russian border. Today there are several national nature reserves in the Sanjiang Plain, and two—the Sanjiang and the Honghe—are listed under the international Ramsar Convention on Wetlands as "wetlands of international importance."[68] The convention seeks to preserve biological diversity by protecting wetlands, which contain more than 40 percent of the world's species.[69]

As a party to the international Ramsar Convention, China is required to designate one or more wetland sites as wetlands of international importance and take special actions to maintain the ecological character of these sites. A wetland is deemed internationally important if it meets certain criteria outlined in the Ramsar Convention relating to ecology, botany, zoology, limnology, and hydrology. The Sanjiang Nature Reserve is significant because it meets seven of these criteria, more than any other Ramsar Wetland in China.[70] It also contains the largest freshwater wetland in China.

The wetlands of the Sanjiang Plain are northeastern Asia's most important breeding ground and migration route for migratory waterfowl. They provide habitat for numerous species of wildlife, including 232 species of birds, thirty-eight species of mammals, seventy-seven kinds of fish, and five hundred rare plants.[71] Many of these are listed as endangered species in national and international conservation law documents.[72] The Sanjiang Plain is the main breeding area of the red-crowned crane (*grus japonensis*) so beloved of Japanese birdwatchers. It also hosts other rare migratory birds such as the hooded crane, Eastern white stork, black stork, white-tailed eagle, and Steller's eagle.[73]

The Sanjiang Plain wetlands, concentrated in the Sanjiang Nature Reserve and the neighboring Honghe Nature Reserve, the plain's second national-level nature reserve, also perform other important environmental functions, such as water purification, climate moderation, and flood mitigation for the region. However, drainage, overuse of water resources, deforestation, conversion to agriculture, illegal hunting, over-harvesting, siltation, and pollution, including pollution caused by agricultural runoff, have severely degraded the wetlands. A 1983 Chinese scientific study of environmental deterioration in the Sanjiang Plain[74] indicates "a serious decline in environmental quality and resource productivity," including decreased rainfall and increased drought severity, decreased groundwater levels and river discharge, and increased wind and soil erosion, salinization, and sedimentation.[75] While wind erosion was not a factor in the region before land reclamation drained the wetlands, now more than 60 percent of cultivated areas are affected by it.

Changes in vegetation cover have been similarly dramatic. In 1962, 3.16 million hectares of Sanjiang, accounting for almost 30 percent of the region, were forested. By 1976, forests covered only 2.25 million hectares, or about 21 percent—a loss of 916,000 hectares of forest in just fourteen years.[76] By the year 2000, more than 60 percent of Sanjiang wetlands had been turned into farmland, at a rate that would see the wetlands disappear entirely within a little more than a decade.

The loss of swamp forests had a major effect on species diversity, abundance, and distribution. Siberian tigers once inhabited the region. Lu Bingxin, the director of the Heilongjiang Province Wildlife Institute, in Harbin, estimates that there were eighty-one Siberian tigers in Heilongjiang Province and neighboring Jilin Province in 1976 and that only approximately ten to twelve remained in Heilongjiang in 1991 (and none in Jilin).[77] Before the dramatic decline in swamp forests and wetlands on the plain in the latter half of the twentieth century, one could easily catch musk deer and fish there. Fish catches dropped from 22,000 tons in 1960 to 3,200 tons as early as 1970.[78]

National and international attention and funding have helped to prevent the final destruction of the wetlands, however. By 2003, twenty reserves, including the Sanjiang Nature Reserve, covered about 30 percent of the wetlands in the Sanjiang Plain.[79]

Land Reclamation

The Sanjiang region is a Chinese frontier. Before the 1949 Communist revolution, only 3 percent of the province's land had been converted to agricultural use.[80] Its harsh climate and poor soil quality—the wetland is covered with a very thin layer of black soil, which sits atop a layer of saline soil—made it unfit for farming. There were few families living in the region, and most residents relied on fishing for survival.

Since 1949, the region has experienced four major waves of "land reclamation."

The army pioneered the opening of the Sanjiang Plain in the 1950s, starting the cycle of wetland destruction. From 1956 to 1958, a hundred thousand demobilized soldiers were relocated to the area to "settle the border regions" (*zhibian*), establish control over territories that had been contested during the anti-Japanese and civil wars, and increase China's grain supply. These soldiers founded the state farms that still exist in the region today.

The second land reclamation wave occurred during the Cultural Revolution of the late 1960s. From 1969 to 1973, 450,000 "educated youths" from cities all over the country joined the Heilongjiang Production-Construction Corps to reclaim the Great Northern Wilderness; this quasi military force was charged with opening the wastelands (*kai huang*) while defending the motherland. During this time agriculture became more important than fishing in the Sanjiang Plain. Security concerns about a possible Soviet invasion were high, as were the "war preparation movement" and the drive for food security.[81] Guided by the Maoist dicta "take grain as the key link" and "man must conquer nature," security-driven nature-conquest campaigns dominated the domestic agenda. From 1969 to 1979, the educated youths "reclaimed" 310,000 hectares of wetlands in the region, destroying local forests for housing and fuel and building drainage ditches to convert wetlands to farmlands.[82]

Ma Zhong, the director of the Beijing Environment and Development Institute of Renmin University and a former educated youth recalls his experience in Fuyuan County in the Sanjiang Plain:

> From the first, we cut many trees, mostly poplar. We formed woodcutting teams to look for the biggest trees, going by tractor as far as twenty kilometers away. We formed a logging camp during the second winter for about three months. . . . I spent a lot of time alone in nature then. I saw lots of animals—foxes, rabbits, a snow hare, wild pigs, some black bears, roe deer. Nature seemed vast, the snow deep, the trees straight and tall. . . . My feelings for nature date from that time. . . .
>
> During my five years in the county, beginning in 1969 when I arrived, the old forest was almost completely cut down and some animals were wiped out. . . . It was only when I went back in 1988 [and even more environmental destruction had occurred] that I understood what we had done. Before, there were so many trees that you couldn't see the river from the road. But in 1988, the whole forest was gone. There was nothing to eat but farmed fish—the wild fish were gone. Today, there is a tiny bit of forest left in the Great Northern Wilderness, there's a little wetland in the northeastern-most counties. I'm working to protect it, but some people still talk about "opening the wasteland."[83]

This formative experience influenced Ma Zhong to become one of the Sanjiang wetlands' most influential environmental advocates, helping to bring the wetlands to national and international attention.

The third great wave of land conversion took place in the late 1970s, when the state made the Sanjiang Plain a test site for agricultural mechanization, and large state farms were consolidated, with permanent workers who came from all over China. Fuyuan County, which, along with Tongjiang City and Raohe County, has jurisdiction over Sanjiang Plain, became one of only two counties in China that were totally "socialized," with farmers and fishermen earning fixed wages as state employees. To this day, some older farmers there are still enjoying state pensions.

The Heilongjiang provincial government launched the fourth land reclamation effort from the late 1980s until late 1990s when, due to advances in farm machinery, Sanjiang became a major food grain supply base for China. Again the government encouraged migrants to move to the region from other parts of China to farm. In Fuyuan County, this phase led to dramatic increases in population. In 1985, the county registered only twenty-seven thousand residents. By the end of 2000, that number had grown to just shy of fifty thousand, not including people employed by state farms, who accounted for an additional seventy thousand residents, or 60 percent of the county's population.[84]

As Fuyuan County welcomed new farmers, its agricultural output grew impressively. In 1999, the area achieved a record yield, contributing 9 million tons of food grain to China's total production of 500 million tons. It was during the high tide of this fourth phase, from the late 1980s to the late 1990s, that the Sanjiang Nature Reserve was created and developed into a national priority.

In the late 1990s the government had a change of heart about its aggressive agricultural development of the region, shifting policy in a way that has radically affected the disposition of lands there. The Heilongjiang provincial government decided in 1998 to stop the development of wetlands for agriculture, and in 2000, the Heilongjiang Land Reclamation Bureau announced that no more farmland would be opened in Sanjiang and that in three years 180,000 hectares of the farmland would be restored to wetland. The reasons for this shift, and its consequences, are examined below.

The Wetlands and China's Shifting Priorities

Like many other countries, China until recently viewed its wetlands as "wastelands" (*huang*) that should be drained and converted to arable land. A number of domestic and international factors encouraged a shift in attitude and government policy toward wetlands. Song Li, a Chinese environmental protection official at that time, attributed the change to six factors: China's opening to the outside world, government officials' willingness to assume leadership in this area, government officials' willingness to learn from China's environmental failures and mistakes, the role of donor agencies in providing incentives for wetlands preservation, the role of international nongovernmental organizations in promoting preservation, and twenty years of development and rising living standards.

The shift in government priorities toward preserving wetlands was bolstered not only by China's late participation in two major international treaties—the Ramsar treaty (coinciding with the Rio Earth Summit, 1992), which emphasized migratory bird habitat and environmental services, and the Convention on Biological Diversity (which China joined in 1993)—but also by a new understanding of the importance of wetlands in flood control. Changes in international funding priorities, which we discuss below, also played a significant role in changing China's attitude toward wetlands and development programs in the Sanjiang region.

The Ramsar Convention on Wetlands of International Importance was adopted in Iran on February 2, 1971, and took effect at the end of 1975. It held that coordinated international action is necessary in order to preserve wetlands and the seasonal migratory waterfowl that rely on them.[85] China has the largest area of wetlands in Asia and the fourth largest in the world, and it is the world's eighth most biologically diverse country.[86] Naturally, then, the treaty countries pressed China to join.

Pressure to join Ramsar also came from NGOs interested in wetland preservation. Western NGOs had been active on biodiversity issues in China since 1979, when the World-Wide Fund for Nature began its panda conservation activities. Since then, the Nature Conservancy, zoos, and other groups have become involved. Several NGOs took a particular interest in the Sanjiang wetland: Wetlands International, the International Crane Foundation, and the Wild Bird Society of Japan.

China had created its first wetland reserve in the 1970s,[87] but it did not join the Ramsar Convention until 1992. For years, the Chinese government ignored international calls to join Ramsar because of its preoccupation with feeding its huge population. With the threat of famine, the country's vulnerability to flood and drought, and long periods of international isolation, the grain supply issue was a great source of both anxiety and national pride. By the early 1990s, China had achieved grain oversupply, and this was a key factor in changing China's position on the Ramsar Convention.

The other key factor was the need to overcome the diplomatic isolation China faced following the Tiananmen Square tragedy in 1989, when the Chinese army brutally suppressed a massive pro-democracy demonstration in the center of Beijing before the eyes of the world's media. By the time of the Rio Summit, in 1992, China was actively seeking diplomatic interactions and recognition from the world community. The Chinese premier, Li Peng, widely considered responsible for ordering the Tiananmen crackdown, had a personal stake in repairing his reputation and chose to lead the Chinese delegation to the summit. He and Song Jian, the state councilor in charge of environmental affairs, had come to place a high priority on international environmental cooperation as a way to improve the country's diplomatic standing— another motive for joining the Ramsar Convention. China increasingly recognized that its rich natural heritage and its conduct on other environmental issues, such as carbon output, were of great global concern and that its clout on these matters could be a source of leverage on other issues.

Thus, on July 30, 1992, seventeen years after the treaty took force, China ratified it and designated six existing nature reserves as Ramsar sites.[88] By ratifying the Ramsar Convention and the Convention on Biological Diversity, China publicly committed itself to including wetlands in national planning, establishing reserves, and participating in international environmental cooperation. Compliance with convention requirements is monitored by international consensus, and countries that fail to meet them are put on a blacklist. Ni Hongwei of Heilongjiang Province's Natural Resource

Research Institute stated in 2002 that, by participating in Ramsar, China had put enormous pressure on itself to conserve wetlands.[89]

Serious concerns about flooding also encouraged the growing emphasis on wetlands protection. Flooding, a perennial problem for China, reached disaster proportions in several locales in 1998, among them the Songhua River, which runs through the Sanjiang Plain. After the 1998 floods, the State Council developed a framework for ecological conservation for the Yangtze area that included wetland restoration and protection.[90] For example, in the basin of Dongting, a large freshwater lake in the middle of the Yangtze River basin, officials initiated a "grain for water" program meant to increase the lake's water storage capacity in an effort to mitigate future floods.[91] The central government, through policy measures such as this one, showed that it realized that the 1998 flooding had been intensified by unsustainable agricultural development, deforestation, and the uncontrolled development of wetlands.[92] Official newspaper reports carried frequent stories that mentioned the role of wetlands in controlling floods, an alternative to the costly processes of excessive lake-drainage, diking along riverbanks, and moving people out of the floodplains of major rivers—a measure that is nearly impossible to enforce. When water levels in the surrounding rivers rise or when the rivers flood, most of the water is caught by the wetland in the reserve, thereby preventing damage.

Greater awareness of the importance of wetlands for flood prevention helped lead to increased funding for wetland protection in the Sanjiang Plain. In addition, at the end of 1998, following the flood disasters, the Heilongjiang provincial government, under the newly appointed party secretary of the province, Xu Youfang, decided to stop all cultivation within the wetlands province-wide, decreeing that the Sanjiang wetlands should be protected and acknowledging the importance of wetlands as natural reservoirs that prevent flooding.[93] Then, in 1999, the Heilongjiang Land Reclamation Bureau announced that 180,000 hectares of farmland in the region would be reconverted to forest, pasture, and wetlands.[94] The director of the Nature Conservation Department of the State Environmental Protection Administration (SEPA), Zhang Guotai, gave a scientific explanation for the policy change, which alluded to the significance of the 1998 flood incident:

> Wetlands are vitally important in the ecological sense in that they can act as enormous sponges to absorb, hold, and slowly release water that would otherwise cause flooding. . . . They also purify the water and influence local climate. . . . With wetlands greatly reduced, parts of the reclaimed land have become arid. This contributed to the severity of the 1998 floods along the Songhua River basin in Heilongjiang province.[95]

In 2000, the State Forestry Administration put into effect a plan for protecting China's wetlands, and the Ministry of Agriculture declared that all natural wetland previously listed as reserved arable land resources would no longer be considered for agricultural use—actions that the *China Daily* attributed to the government's having "woken up to the disastrous consequences" of ecological damage.[96] On June 20, 2003, the provincial government gave its support for the reserve when the provincial congress passed the

Heilongjiang Wetland Protection Regulation. This law does three main things: (1) it defines the wetlands protection responsibilities of different administrative departments; (2) it defines legal and illegal activities in the wetlands and sets penalties for illegal activities; and (3) it outlines the procedure of establishing a wetland reserve.

International Influences and Shifting Priorities

International funding has influenced China's activities in the Sanjiang Plains for decades. Bilateral and multilateral investors such as the World Bank and Japanese transnational corporations have invested more than US$200 million in agricultural development in the Sanjiang Plain since the 1950s.[97] Beginning in the 1980s, international lending and development agencies began to change their focus in Sanjiang from agricultural development to wetland conservation. By the mid-to-late 1990s, international organizations had become active in conserving the wetland biodiversity in Sanjiang Plain.

In the 1990s, international funding priorities came to reflect changing values. After having contributed to the loss of the Sanjiang wetland, international agencies reversed their priorities and began assisting China with its commitments under the Ramsar and Biological Diversity Conventions. In 1990, the Heilongjiang State Farm Bureau applied for a grant to the World Bank for a $400 million loan, but this time the World Bank refused.[98] Instead, in 1994, the China Biodiversity Conservation Action Plan, which had international funding from the Global Environmental Facility (GEF) of the World Bank through the UNDP, singled out the Sanjiang Plain as a place where wetland conservation could be integrated with agricultural and other development activities,[99] and in December 1999 the GEF awarded China US$11.5 million to support its initiatives in the Sanjiang Plain and three other representative sites.

In the mid-1990s there were other signs that the balance of international support was beginning to tip in favor of wetlands preservation over agricultural development. From 1995 to 1996, with the support of China's State Planning Commission and the Heilongjiang Provincial Planning Commission, two U.S.-based organizations —Ecologically Sustainable Development, Inc., and the National Committee on U.S.-China Relations—and two Russian organizations—the FEB-RAS Institute of Aquatic and Ecological Problems and the FEB-RAS Pacific Geographical Institute—conducted a study of sustainable land use in the Sanjiang Plain. In its final report, the study team recommended "only highly selective conversion of remaining Sanjiang Plain wetlands to farmland," and urged investment in productivity improvements in existing farmland. Because of its international importance to waterfowl, it further recommended Ramsar status for the wetlands, and their preservation as the core of a 914,500-hectare Three Rivers Plain International Peace Park and Wildlife Refuge."[100] The first provincial decree to protect the Sanjiang wetlands, mentioned above, followed in 1998.

In 1996, at the same time that this international collaborative was studying the

Sanjiang wetlands, the Overseas Economic Cooperation Fund (OECF) of Japan funded an environmental impact assessment (EIA) for an agricultural project in Sanjiang Plain sponsored by NEPA. The Japanese agency helped to modify the project to include a wetland conversion component. This was the first EIA of a natural resource exploitation project in China. The Japan Wild Bird Society and the International Crane Foundation provided expertise in making the assessment. Apparently in reaction to the ongoing shift in priorities, that same year in a report to the State Council, the Ministry of Agriculture stressed the importance of coordinating wetland conservation and agricultural development in the Sanjiang Plain.[101]

The Creation of the Sanjiang Nature Reserve: From County-Level to National-Level Management

In its earliest phase, the Sanjiang Nature Reserve was planned, built, and managed at the county level. At the time, Fuyuan County was in its fourth phase of land reclamation and at the high point of the agricultural push, but the agricultural yield of the farmland that is now a part of the reserve was never very high. The soil quality was, after all, poor for farming, and the land's flatness made it difficult to drain. Local officials, therefore, initially saw the creation of a reserve as an alternative means of attracting central government and international funds for local development. Members of the local department of forestry, for their part, also saw a career opportunity in establishing a wetland reserve.

In mid-1993, the Fuyuan County government submitted its proposal to the provincial government to build a nature reserve in the Sanjiang Plain. The EPB team that reviewed the proposal for the provincial government argued in its report that it was an ideal piece of unexploited land to be preserved. The provincial government readily approved the proposal and charged the director of the county forestry bureau, Zhang Xixiang, with setting up an office and establishing and managing the reserve, tasks he began in 1994.

By the time Zhang Xixiang was first assigned to establish the reserve, he had already read an article entitled "Saving the Last Wetlands in the Sanjiang Plain" by the economist and environmentalist Professor Ma Zhong. By his own account, Zhang was deeply impressed with Ma Zhong's call for attention to the wetlands and was enthusiastic about taking on his new duties. Director Zhang was key at the local level to raising awareness of the reserve among area residents and gaining the support of the county and the province for its creation. His enthusiasm for his duties and the energy with which he carried them out were readily apparent in our field interviews. Having worked in forestry for over thirty years, he showed deep commitment to saving forests and expressed delight at having attained a position that allowed him to bring about real changes. He was very proud that the Sanjiang Reserve has received widespread attention and was likewise proud of his staff. "My team," he told us, "is very well-managed. They are highly self-motivated and self-confident. From them, one can see the great strength of good spirit."

While Director Zhang was laying the local groundwork for the administration of the reserve, in Beijing the momentum was building for more serious attention to wetland preservation from the central government. In 1994, Ma Zhong submitted a report to NEPA detailing the risk of wetland damage and argued, using economic analysis, that farms in the eastern part of Sanjiang were not economically viable. He also outlined the benefits of wetlands—flood prevention, biodiversity, and water storage—and argued on economic grounds that preserving the wetland was a better decision than developing the area as farmland. A push for central government support for the reserve also came from the nonprofit group Wetlands International, which met with NEPA officials and urged them to support the reserve. NEPA passed Ma Zhong's report on to the Environmental Protection and Natural Resources Committee (EPNRC) of the National People's Congress, China's legislative body. The committee instructed NEPA to investigate the Sanjiang wetlands matter.

In 1995, in response to this request, Wang Yuqing, vice minister of NEPA, led a team of experts from NEPA and the Ministry of Finance to Sanjiang. Before the mid-1990s NEPA, already burdened with the overwhelming task of reducing China's industrial pollution, had paid little attention to preservation. As a result of the investigatory trip to Sanjiang and the trip report that resulted, however, NEPA officials became enthusiastic about wetland protection. In an unusual sign of bureaucratic cooperation, the Ministry of Agriculture sent a memorandum to China's cabinet, the State Council, recognizing the ecological damage to the wetlands and stating their official agreement with the NEPA report that laid out the risks of wetland degradation and the economic and ecological benefits of protection. In 1995, the State Council ordered the central and local governments to take further measures to protect the Sanjiang wetlands. The EPNRC sent official requests to the central government ministers of agriculture, forestry, and NEPA, the Heilongjiang provincial government, and Director Zhang requiring them to study the NEPA report, reassess development projects, and devise a plan for strengthening the conservation of the Sanjiang wetlands.

In the same year as the State Council order, the central government also established a National Wetland Coordinating Committee involving seventeen ministries and other government agencies. This committee prepared a National Wetland Conservation Action Plan (NWCAP), which laid out the government's goals regarding wetlands: the sustainable use and better protection of important wetland sites, an increase in the number of designated Ramsar sites, and the reform of policies for wetland protection.[102] That same year, the municipality of Jiamusi, the largest city in the region, formally approved the creation of the Sanjiang Nature Reserve Management Bureau, though with an annual budget of only RMB200,000 (US$24,000), barely enough to pay the meager salaries of its thirty-five employees.

Five years later, in April 2000, with the strong support of the Heilongjiang provincial government, the State Council named Sanjiang a national-level nature reserve, one of 140 reserves in China with this status.[103] With this change in status, the reserve management bureau came to report directly to the central government, rising to the same level of authority as the county government. It also acquired some modest financial benefits: that year, the bureau received RMB1.5 million (US$180,000)[104] for the construction of a headquarters and other administrative buildings in Fuyuan. The following year, the provincial and national governments provided another RMB3 million (US$360,000) to finance additional construction and equipment purchases.[105]

With the change of status for the reserve, the county government found itself in the position of taking orders from the reserve management bureau on all matters relating to wetland protection within the reserve; and by cutting out several layers of bureaucracy, the new status empowered the reserve to consider county wishes even less than before. Three parallel administrative institutions, the county government, the reserve, and the state farms thus came to coexist uneasily within the same general geographic area. This has been the source of some of the conflicts that have, as we see below, challenged the management of the reserve.

Funding is another source of discontent within the reserve management bureau. While, as mentioned above, the national government paid for the construction of buildings and the purchase of equipment, it has not contributed any money to the reserve's annual operating budget. Funds for the reserve's operating costs (US$109,000 in 2001) must be covered by the local government, in this case the Jiamusi government, and through other mechanisms. In 2001, local government funds covered only 22 percent of the reserve's operating budget; the reserve made up another 56 percent of its budget through agricultural activities such as rice production. In other words, in 2001, the reserve was operating in the red.[106]

Thus, central government bureaucratic oversight has not translated into money for the staffing and day-to-day operations of the reserve. Some central government officials apparently have noted the dissatisfaction among reserve staff with this arrangement, the economic tensions it causes for local governments, and the obstacles it presents to implementing preservation policies. Several of the relevant ministries are circulating a draft Nature Reserve Law, which proposes that the government should set aside funds for reserves at the national level. As of this writing, in mid-2004, the draft law is still under consideration.

Today, the Sanjiang Nature Reserve comprises approximately 198,100 hectares and, in accordance with the State Council decree that covers national-level reserves, it is divided into three zones: a core zone of 30,000 hectares where hunting, fishing and farming have been completely banned; a buffer zone of 150,000 hectares where there is still some scattered farmland; and an experimental zone of 20,000 hectares where economic activity is allowed. There are still villages within the experimental and buffer zones. Commercial farming (except in the core and buffer zones, where it is prohibited) is the predominant economic activity—51 percent of the reserve's population in 2001 was involved in producing crops such as rice, wheat, corn, and soybeans.[107]

The State Council decree of 2000 lacked the force of law, and despite the subsequent Heilongjiang Wetland Protection Regulation of 2003, enforcement of wetlands protection policies remained a big problem, as we will see below. Thus, while there have been no large, official development projects launched in Sanjiang since 1998, it is widely known among locals, officials, and researchers that there continue to be unofficial, small-scale stealth projects.

Cooperation and Conflict: Managing the Sanjiang Nature Reserve

China's wish to engage with the world, pride in its rich natural heritage, and concern about floods compete with other priorities, such as food production, and with attitudes toward nature as a resource to be conquered and bent to human wishes. This competition among values has played out at the local level in the Sanjiang Plain as the reserve management bureau tries to carry out environmental protection policies, and it intensified when the administration of the nature reserve was elevated to the national level. When the reserve was under local jurisdiction as a branch of the Fuyuan County government, competing interests among stakeholders could be reconciled and coordinated more easily. After the reserve was made a national reserve and became independent from the county government and answerable to the central government, there was rising antagonism between, on the one hand, supporters of the reserve and its preservation policies and, on the other, county officials, who had lost control of the reserve (and thus the tax revenue from it), and local people whose economic activities were restricted by the reserve law.

This section first describes the reserve bureaucracy, its version of environmental values and its methods for managing the reserve, thus providing the necessary background for understanding the reserve's encounters with other agencies and individuals that challenge or aid its policies and agendas. Next, we discuss the role of the People's Liberation Army as a facilitator of the reserve's work. Finally, we explore the reserve bureaucracy's conflicts with its four main challengers: the Fuyuan County government, state farm employees, local residents, and new migrants. As we present the claims and positions of the stakeholders, we will pay special attention to the values to which they are committed.

Bureaucratic Cooperation

The Reserve Bureaucracy

The work of reserve officers is hard. They patrol the reserve, record animal activities, burn fishing nets, destroy fishing boats, and catch hunters and loggers. They have serious conflicts with local villagers and unregistered migrants, and are sometimes threatened at gunpoint. In interviews in November 2000, they spoke of the special hardships of patrolling the reserve in winter. The bureau had access only to one car for a two-year period, and Zhuaji Station, one of the reserve's five patrol units at which we spent the most time, owned just one motorcycle. For the most part reserve officers patrolled the wetlands on foot, walking each day in the icy water. Officers who worked in the local observation stations, such as Zhuaji, lived in nearby farmers' houses, seeing their own families only twice a week. They performed all their work under the stress of inadequate staffing: the reserve had only thirty-five employees, far short of the fifty employees that were deemed necessary according to the March 2001 management plan.[108] Finally, their meager salaries often arrived late.

Sanjiang Nature Reserve officers nonetheless professed to be committed to their jobs. Their view of Beijing's environmental push is bound up with their job: to enforce the new environmental values that led to the creation of the reserve. They defended their work and commitment to the bureau by citing modernity and international norms, career ambitions in a burgeoning new field, and socialist values that emphasize restraint and self-sacrifice. Kinship values also play a role both in the politics surrounding the administration of the reserve and in the desire to protect the values and interests of family members who were among the first migrants to settle the area during the Cultural Revolution and have witnessed the devastating effects of the Maoist value of conquering nature on the place they call home.

The high morale among the Sanjiang Nature Reserve officers rested on Director Zhang's administrative style, which called for iron discipline, but also his promise of a bright and modern future as wetland preservation workers. "Environmental protection is a sun-rising sector in our country," Director Zhang reported he would tell his employees. "The state will give us millions for our important job; tens of millions of U.S. dollars will be available from the Asian Development Bank [ADB] if negotiations in November 2000 are successful, and each local reserve station will get a new building in a few years. All of you will become senior officers when we expand." He managed to build the most beautiful office building in town, a project to which he likes to say his employees even loaned their own money. This building is a symbol of their rising authority and hope for the future.

Director Zhang's own commitment to the reserve has been strengthened by the prestige that his international ties have brought him. One of his favorite topics of conversation was his exchanges with Russian colleagues. He told interviewers that the Chinese consul general in Khabarovsk had written a letter to the Heilongjiang provincial government proposing that he cooperate with Russian officials in charge of the three nature reserves on the Russian side of the Amur and Ussuri Rivers. Following our field site visit, on July 30, 2001, the Sino-Russian Joint Reserve was announced, making big news in the Chinese official media.[109]

Reserve staff appeared to share Director Zhang's view that their environmental commitment would pay off. Twenty-nine-year-old Chen, head of Zhuaji Station acknowledged that he was underpaid. In spite of this, he insisted that he was committed to his work. He tactfully told interviewees: "My work to preserve wetland is significant for future generations. The reserve has a bright future, and my own future in the job is good." In addition to the promise of a bright career, officers' acceptance of poor working conditions was a function of self-sacrifice and austerity, values that Director Zhang had inculcated in his staff by managing the reserve like an old-fashioned Communist-style institution. Director Zhang, we were told, even patrolled with young colleagues in the icy and muddy wetland, sometimes for a week at a time.

The bureau's interest in seeking new forms of revenue for the area—as reflected in the ecotour component of the agreement with Russia and the local support for the anticipated ADB grant[110] that would help fund new buildings—is a sign that the reserve officials were motivated, at least in part, by economic considerations. The reserve administration's deputy director, Feng Wenyi, claimed that the reserve attaches great importance to encouraging local economic development and improving the living standards of the local people in order to improve relations with the county, townships, and villages. For instance, he explained, the bureau helps farmers on existing cultivated lands with technical advice.

Kinship values of loyalty and mutual favors among relatives by blood and marriage often play a role in nature protection work. The two officers posted at the Zhuaji Station maintain good relationships with the local villagers because one of the officers is the son-in-law of the village party secretary and the other is his nephew. The party secretary uses his authority to guarantee their safety and effectiveness, something he would be unlikely to do without the blood relationship.

As with other Chinese institutions, corruption affected the reserve. Though the corruption may well have been an adaptive strategy to obtain resources for the task with which reserve staff were charged, certain of their corrupt behaviors damaged popular perceptions of the bureau. For example, the head of the reserve management bureau's police department owned a used car obviously smuggled into China. When two of our researchers were traveling on foot from Dongsheng to Donghe— two villages in the Zhuaji District of the Reserve—the officer accompanying them hailed a Jeep Cherokee emerging from the core zone. When the researchers got in, they found a hunting rifle on the back seat with blood on it and overheard the driver say to his colleague, "These days, [we] have not seen ducks, and today [we] haven't shot even a single duck." The researchers inferred that the two men may have recently been hunting wild ducks, which is illegal, and later they learned that the Jeep owner was a local official. Such examples reveal that despite the new preservationist rhetoric among officers, old values of personal privilege still persist.

While reserve officials acknowledged the long-term importance of preserving the Sanjiang wetland, the constellation of values that guides them also includes ambitions for a modern life and international engagement, career aspirations, socialist values of discipline and dedication to a cause, and kinship values resting on networks of loyalties and mutual favors. Yet their enthusiasm for their work suggests that there is more than opportunism involved in their support for the reserve, and that the reserve itself has come to have value for them even as it is embedded in their hopes of advancement. Zheng Zhigang, the head of the administration office of the reserve management bureau, spoke favorably of the progress, albeit slow, that the reserve, together with local and county officials, has made since 1997 in educating the peasants in environmental protection. This modest achievement in itself holds value for the reserve staff.

Foot Soldiers for the Environment: Cooperation from the People's Liberation Army

There is today a major military presence in the Sanjiang Plain region because the reserve extends 169 kilometers along the Russian border at Khabarovsk, just across the river from the Fuyuan County seat. Because of this, the People's Liberation Army (PLA) has played an unusual role in the reserve, not only as an enforcer of government nature protection policies but also as a champion of the new environmental values, by pursuing environmental activities such as planting trees and making nests for birds in their leisure time, rescuing animals, and participating in environmental education projects. Their endorsement of environmental policies is nuanced, however, and it has several different motivations. First, for the military, the new environmental values are related to larger issues of national security. Similarly, as we will see, environmental values are linked to patriotism—to the land itself as part of Chinese identity. Finally, the hierarchical military structure promotes the value of top-down dissemination of ideas and actions, which ingrains and reinforces norms handed down from the top of the command structure.

During the Cultural Revolution, when soldiers began opening up the Sanjiang Plain, the military played a key role in the exploitation of the Sanjiang wetlands. Today, on the other hand, environmental protection has become a surprisingly large part of the military's responsibilities. The local PLA contingent emphasizes cooperation with the Sanjiang Nature Reserve Management Bureau, and officers are recognized and promoted for strong performance in environmental protection.

The military instructs soldiers that land use is connected to border defense. One example involves local civilians' practices of using riverbank sand for construction work and riverside bushes for fuel. Now, because of the reserve, these practices are prohibited. Soldiers reported that they have been instructed to explain that "when the riverbank on the China side becomes eroded, the river's central line moves toward China. Digging sand means selling our homeland for private gain." A similar security rationale justifies the local military's role in afforestation within the reserve: According to the head of one outpost, "The Russian side is full of forests, and their observation stations are hidden in the big trees. Our side has few trees, and our observation stations and military moves are exposed." He went on to tell the story of how in the winter of 1998, a nearby state farm sent a truck full of workers to cut trees in the reserve. The reserve station had only six officers then, and they could not stop the workers from cutting trees, but the station head called for military help, and twelve armed soldiers brought the situation under control.

The link between environmental protection and protection of the country is further strengthened by the sharing of resources between the reserve management bureau and the PLA. Military boats, telescopes, manpower, offices, and observation stations are often made available to the cash-strapped bureau, and the army joins bureau officers in periodic visits to local villages to teach about environmental protection and the importance of the reserve. Mr. Wang, commander of Haiqing township's first battalion, second company, explains that the army coordinates its work with the reserve at every level:

> Every year, we work together on propaganda and education. Actually, the reserve uses army resources to reach their goals, and those resources are a great asset to the work of the reserve and create helpful working conditions. . . . The army uses its patrol duty system to assist the reserve in checking fishing activities. At the same time, they can protect the shoreline of the river. And, every year, army members volunteer to do tree planting and reforestation work.

The PLA border patrol is also responsible for animal rescue and monitoring and deterring illegal activities, such as fishing and cutting trees, in the reserve. It cooperates closely with the reserve management bureau and has an impressive record of carrying out these duties. Environmental duties have become more important to the border patrol as the security situation has relaxed. Every soldier is given a notebook in which he is required to write a diary of environmental observations. The army also requires officers and soldiers to take turns receiving training at the reserve management bureau, as a result of which nearly all soldiers can identify the animals, birds, and plants of the region.

The military's centralized hierarchical structure provides a critical example of how new values are transmitted down from the government to the people through propaganda. In the case of the Sanjiang PLA contingent, the norms of environmental protection motivate commands and assignments. As a result, the soldiers become environmentalists "on command." These values, however, extend beyond merely following orders, as evidenced by the volunteer work the soldiers do in addition to mandated environmental protection duties. Indeed, the local military in Sanjiang has become a model for the Chinese armed forces as a whole. Their environmental protection work was publicized in the July 18, 2000, issue of *People's Liberation Army Daily,* in an article that boasted, "Every soldier is a soldier for environment protection." It is also noteworthy that Chinese soldiers serve in the military for only three years, after which they return to their hometowns. This gives them the chance to spread the environmental awareness that they gain during their service in the border area.

Bureaucratic Conflict

The case of the Sanjiang Nature Reserve shows how complex a job it can be to implement environmental policy in a biodiversity-rich region as multiple administrative units carry out their competing missions and mandates. As noted earlier, the central Ministry of Agriculture continues to operate huge state farms in the area near the reserve, some of which were converted from wetlands to farms, or "reclaimed," with World Bank and other foreign donor support. The presence of these farms limits the area of wetlands available for restoration. Similarly, the provincial-level Heilongjiang Land Reclamation Bureau operates according to an outmoded mandate dating from the "grain first" campaigns of the Mao period. In the wetland this approach has been suspended since the provincial government's December 1998 decision to stop the expansion of any existing agricultural areas in the wetland—a policy created under pressure from the central-level Ministry of Water Resources to restore more wetlands to help control flooding after the devastating floods of 1998. Meanwhile the State Forestry Administration, through its oversight of the Sanjiang Nature Reserve Bureau, tries to implement wetland preservation as best it can with limited funding. At the local level, the reserve management bureau has had conflicts with the Fuyuan County government, one of five municipal jurisdictions in the plain.

The Fuyuan County Government

The Sanjiang Nature Reserve, as mentioned earlier, actually lies across three different counties. However, we have concentrated on Fuyuan County, because the reserve headquarters is located there, and because it is the only county with shared jurisdiction over the reserve that touches the Russian border. Moreover, because the reserve constitutes a third of the land of Fuyuan County, the conflict between environmental and economic agendas is especially pronounced here.

All local government officials interviewed for this case study—four officials of Fuyuan County and four officials of Dongsheng village—acknowledged the necessity of preserving the wetlands, demonstrating that environmental protection values had gained official legitimacy. Gao Fazhang, a former director of the Fuyuan County State Farm Bureau, who had helped to open up the wetland for farms, expressed his values vis-à-vis the preservation of what is left of the wetlands:

> When I arrived, Fuyuan was very desolate—forest, swamp, grassland, and lakes everywhere. There were only ten villages in Fuyuan, and Fuyuan town was one of them. The local residents were living on fishing, since natural resources were very rich. . . . We absolutely cannot cut down what little is left. Not only do we have to protect the forests, but also the wild animals living in them.

Despite this general recognition of the problem of endangered wetlands, the Fuyuan County government often comes into conflict with the reserve. In one case, the central government had allocated funds to the county to restore waterlogged farmland, a project that involved digging drainage ditches that needed to pass through the reserve. When the county government and the bureau failed to agree on a plan for digging the ditches, a deputy director of the reserve management bureau ordered police to detain the ditch-digging contractor and confiscate his vehicles. The county government then threatened to obstruct preservation work, even hinting that it would stir up the local people. The crisis was resolved, and the contractor released, only when Director Zhang returned from a conference in Germany to talk things over with the top county leader, a close relative.

The EPB, the water bureau, the forestry bureau, and the land reclamation and cultivation bureau have overlapping areas of responsibility at the local level in Sanjiang, and at times these bureaus work at cross-purposes with the reserve.[111] The Fuyuan

County EPB director, Yu Xichen, contrasted the thorny situation of the Sanjiang Reserve with that of a second reserve that neighboring Tongjiang City also has jurisdiction over:

> In Tongjiang City there is also a reserve, but they didn't form a special reserve administration. The EPB grabbed the job early, before the area was cultivated and opened up, and established a reserve area in order to prevent outsiders from cultivating that land. Later, they opened some parts to cultivation, and the contract fees were used for reserve construction. So the duties in Tongjiang were organized well among departments, and their job is easier. But now, our reserve is a national reserve; thus there are duty conflicts between the reserve and the county.

He went on to acknowledge the inherent value of the Sanjiang wetlands.

> In the entire Sanjiang Plain, this is one of the few areas of natural ecology left, so protecting it is very important. But it cannot be at the cost of economic development. Environmental protection is not only protection, but should also fit with the development of opening-up lands, forestry, the fishing industry, and township enterprises.

Yu Xichen's comment points to the most frequent source of conflict between the county government and the reserve: the perceived tension between preservation and economic development. Although officials we interviewed were aware of the scientific importance of the wetland and expressed bitterness about the exhaustion of fish, wild animal, and forest resources, their positive feelings about the reserve were tempered by their perception that it is a barrier to local economic development.

Another official, Mr. Sun, deputy director of the Fuyuan County government demonstrated the conflict in priorities:

> This summer, we were in the western part of Nongqiao[112] when we got in trouble. Actually, we were only cutting down trees, and . . . only twenty here and thirty there. But the reserve arrested my men and fined me. That section isn't in the core zone. For the local government, whose primary job is to develop the economy and develop agriculture, the central government gives us funds to help increase farmers' income and increase production. So whose job is more important: mine or the reserve's? . . . If there was no reserve, we could reclaim more land, expand fields for growing crops, and we could have greater income from farming, but the reserve leaves something for our grandchildren.

Since the early 1980s, the official central task of the party-state has been economic development, and economic performance indices have decided promotions. Moreover, because of the bloated government there is great pressure to keep salaries low. In September 2000, retired government officials had not received their monthly pension in half a year. Without administrative reform, economic development is the only way to decrease the pressure.

With aspirations for their county to become a growth region—in interviews local officials referred to Shenzhen, in south China, which had grown from a village to a city of 4 million in only fifteen years—Fuyuan County officials want to encourage, rather than restrict, migration. To this end, the government is seeking a change of administrative status from county to city, a move that would require Fuyuan County to increase its locally registered population by a factor of ten, increase its water supply capacity, and build more schools, roads, sewage pipelines, and electric facilities. Officials also talked about constructing an airport for small tourist planes and turning the town into a major port city for trade with Russia and Japan. The reserve management bureau and its goals represent an alien agenda that stands in the way of the county's growth. In the words of the deputy mayor, "What is the sense of preservation if it leads to worse lives for the local people?"

Farming is essential to Fuyuan County's economy, and because of the poor quality of the local soil, land area counts for everything. Thus, farmers use all possible means to open farmland within the reserve. The reserve bureau, in turn, looks to the county for help with law enforcement; yet the county has no interest in helping the reserve enforce the law. Rather, it is interested in collecting more taxes by increasing the acreage of farmland under its jurisdiction. The farmers' economic gain means more tax revenue for local government and more promotions for local officials.

One county official did at least suggest alternatives to existing agricultural development models. Duan Hongguang, director of the Fuyuan County State Farm Bureau, believes the reserve should provide some economic benefits for the county and its farmers, and proposes new economic activities that are more sustainable than current agricultural practices, including tourism and growing rice:

> We need to see policies that give something back to the farmers. Fuyuan wants economic development, so we need to look at what bonuses come out of your reserve. For example, the policy of expanding tourism, how can it work if you don't allow people to enter? The wetlands are protected in the national interest; our county wanted to develop our economy, but both are for the same purpose. . . . We should have some projects in the wetlands . . . Farmers getting out of poverty is a good thing, right? And we are simultaneously protecting the wetlands. For example, assist a few villages on the perimeter to dig wells, and we contribute a few rice paddies; this is also wetlands, right?

Despite the priority placed on development, there have been recent attempts to reconcile the values of economic development and those of preservation. The local government, for example, has supported the efforts of the reserve management bureau to obtain funds that will be spent in the county. Because of the national importance of the Sanjiang Nature Reserve, Fuyuan County gained national attention; in fact, county officials argue that the reserve should have been named the Fuyuan Nature Reserve.[113] Whenever reserve management bureau leaders are willing to help the local economy, the two parties cooperate better. As Duan Hongguang mentioned in our interview with him, Fuyuan County is trying to build a new agricultural base of rice, instead of beans and wheat. Transforming dry land into paddy field is expensive, so the wetland is seen as a better test ground, an idea that is agreeable to both the bureau and the county. As Director Zhang pointed out, "My job is to restore and preserve the wetland, so I have no problem allowing paddy fields into my buffer zone, for it is a kind of artificial wetland."

Resident Resistance

Although environmental protection has, since 1992, been a core element of China's official development rhetoric, the shift to a market economy has unleashed forces that challenge this commitment. Environmental protection continues to be overshadowed by economic development at the national and local levels. The national government, for example, has thus far allocated no budget for the daily operations of the Sanjiang Nature Reserve; what money has flowed in has come from the province.[114] Most Fuyuan County residents, moreover, perceive wetlands preservation to be incompatible with economic development. In Sanjiang the challenge is to create sustainable livelihoods that will not conflict with preserving the wetland, but outside of studies being funded by international agencies, such new initiatives have received little serious attention in China.

Although there are no state farms within the reserve, activities such as fishing and water drainage on farms surrounding the reserve harm the reserve's ecosystem, causing conflicts between the reserve and the state farms. At the provincial level these conflicts pit the reserve against the provincial state farm bureau, which sponsors the state farms. Local residents, particularly long-term migrants and state farm employees, also come into conflict with reserve officials. Even the small population of Hezhe minority people, who are native to the Sanjiang Plain and once supported themselves by fishing, must struggle to adapt to the new agricultural lifestyle and seek a better way of life.

The Sanjiang Plain is an important source of livelihood for local people. "Mr. Z." is a typical example. A new migrant from Huanan County (also in Heilongjiang Province), he survives by doing odd jobs or fishing. Before the reserve was established, he frequently fished in areas that are now in the reserve. Despite the prohibition on fishing within the reserve and the fact that reserve officers have burned or otherwise destroyed his boat and nets, he continues to fish there, sneaking back into the reserve, but he only makes around RMB10, or US$1.25, a day from fishing.

In this section, we examine the attitudes and interests of the residents of Fuyuan County—people who arrived and settled in the area during all four of the phases of land reclamation—and the ways in which their activities and outlooks conflict with the management of the Sanjiang Nature Reserve.

Long-Term Migrants and State Farm Employees

Long-term migrants and state farm employees constituted the first wave of agricultural settlers in the Sanjiang Plain. Their attitudes toward the new preservationist emphasis and policies emanating from the central government cover a broad range. Some, raised on the Maoist drive for agricultural development in that region, recognize that their past activities have led to the loss of the forests and streams that once supported a prosperous life. Despite the economic hardship that the preservation policy has caused them, these residents recognize the nonmaterial value of what remains of the Sanjiang Plain habitat, and they endorse its protection. However, others who settled the area under the aegis of the same drive for agricultural development do not believe environmental preservation should be a policy priority, particularly given the new burdens resulting from the transition to a market economy. Among these state farm workers, a view of reserve land as a resource to be exploited predominates. Others view the executors of new environmental protection policies as opportunists using the new vogue for environmentalism to enrich their own government agencies.

Long-term migrants came to Fuyuan between the early 1960s and the late 1980s, when the county government stopped distributing land to newcomers. They included the state farm workers, who arrived throughout the Mao period. As children, these workers had been taught pre-Communist traditional values, which emphasized family ties and patron-client loyalties, but in the new spirit of Communist selflessness, they answered the call of the party-state and moved to Fuyuan to "construct social-ism," "serve the people," and "eat bitterness"—that is, suffer hardship. Then they experienced yet another change when, after the turbulent years of the Cultural Revo-lution, the new government under Deng Xiaoping told them their Maoist fervor had been a terrible mistake: they were told, as the early 1980s slogan put it, that "to get rich is glorious."

Farmer Sun Jiefang, fifty-six, a typical long-term migrant, is a retired worker from the Donghe village state farm. Sun told our interviewers that his best years were in 1969, when he became a farmer in the local people's commune; at the time Fuyuan was one of just a few counties in China where all farmers were treated as state em-ployees. "We farmed and fished, and our income was handsome," he recalled. "Thirty yuan a month, higher than urban workers. We were told to join the great transforma-tion—there would be guaranteed pension, free medical care, labor protection, hous-ing, and child care." Although many of these promises were not realized, Sun became a party activist and a production team leader. Among a few rare individuals like Sun, the "socialist values" of self-sacrifice and contribution to the state (in exchange for social welfare guarantees) remain strong, and they contrast sharply with new values such as individualism and materialism.

Despite his career as a farm worker, Sun Jiefang supports the reserve. "The reserve is a good thing," he said. "There needed to be administration. Before, there were lots of swans and wild geese . . . many people even killed swans for food. Then, for a long time there were none, but now they are back. Now you can go see them; it's really interesting to watch them!"

Many workers who still farm disagree with this view of the reserve. With the eco-nomic reforms, some of the state farm land was contracted to individual farm work-ers, many of whom live by herding, and the reserve offers the area's best pastureland. On a typical day, hundreds of cows illegally graze within the reserve, destroying the grasses. There are only three officers in the region of the reserve that borders the Qianshao State Farm and their law enforcement capabilities are useless in the face of that many cows and the strong workers who oversee them. Moreover, they have no way to prosecute farmers, for state farms have their own court system. Eventually, through their personal ties, Director Zhang and the state farm party secretary arrived at a compromise, in which Director Zhang agreed to set aside several hundred hectares of wetlands for cattle grazing.

State farm workers have few connections with the local political life in Fuyuan or with the reserve management bureau, since they are sponsored by the provincial state farm bureau and do not fall under the jurisdiction of Fuyuan County. Conflicts over grazing and hunting in the reserve are the main form of interaction. Interviews with state farm workers revealed cynicism regarding the reserve and perceptions of government mismanagement. In particular, they cited the government hypocrisy about publicly stated goals such as reforestation, and its lack of flexibility in allowing local people to engage in practices that would provide even modest economic benefits as reasons why they could not support the reserve.

In one case, an official from the Qianshao farm complained that the forestry management bureau, which is part of the state farm bureau, required workers to grow trees, with annual quotas for each family, usually four hundred bureau-provided saplings. The work is "voluntary," but the trees belong to the state instead of the growers. "We agree that trees should be preserved and forests restored through our efforts," the official said. "However, even if the trees are not for sale, cutting a few to build our own houses should be allowed; after all, we are the growers." Another worker complained:

> Last year, we had to grow trees in front of our residential center, but the trees were neither well planted nor well cared for afterwards. The leaders are only interested in fulfilling the quota; they don't really care about the trees. The year before, we planted trees, and many survived. This year, the leaders decided we needed a livestock farm and cut down all the trees we had planted. We have been planting trees for quite a number of years, but not a single forest has emerged. Why should we care about protecting trees?

In fact, it is not uncommon for state farm workers to steal trees from the reserve. Another state farm worker, who was harvesting beans when we interviewed him, also complained about corruption:

> What is the purpose of wetland preservation? Protecting animals? There are few animals left anyway. There are rules that we cannot fish in the ponds and rivers in the reserve, but if you have money to pay the reserve bureau, they allow you to fish there. Why does the reserve bureau prohibit grazing inside the reserve? They exaggerate the number and kinds of wild animals in it to get state funding. Why do they prohibit fishing? They want the fines. Why do they prohibit cutting trees? They want the fines. But what do they do with the fines? Every year, the grassland has major fires, but what do they do about that?

As he was talking, as if to illustrate his point, a tractor emerged from the reserve carrying a load of logs belonging to someone who had connections with the reserve management bureau. Having done their best to believe in socialist ideals of integrity and selflessness, long-term migrants are deeply offended at what they see as the corruption of reserve officials.

Up to now, it has been too expensive and politically unpopular to move local residents out of the reserve. The long-term goal for the reserve has been to create new sources of income—including work with the reserve itself—so that people living there no longer need to depend on livelihoods that degrade the reserve. Ma Zhong, the Beijing economist who first drew the attention of Beijing officials to the Sanjiang wetlands, worked with the provincial government to draft the Heilongjiang Wetland Protection Regulation, which since its enactment in 2003 has banned economic activities such as agricultural conversion. The provincial government also plans to create a program to reduce human impact on the reserve by controlling the size of villages, preventing the expansion of farmland within the reserve, and encouraging ecologically friendly activities.[115] More recent master plans for the management of the reserve take this agenda a step further, calling for the resettlement of people living in the core and buffer zones. Recognizing the political difficulty of resettlement, the government plans to link it to the creation of sustainable livelihoods and new employment in the area both inside and outside the reserve.[116]

Local officials with whom we spoke before this plan was announced described why such a transition would be problematic. The party secretary of Yanan Township explained to interviewers that when the buffer zone around the reserve was established, farmers had a total of 530 hectares of land under cultivation within it. The reserve allowed the farmers to continue to farm their land, but they no longer paid land tax to the township government; instead, they paid rent to the reserve. As a result, he explained, the government lost about RMB200,000 (roughly US$24,000) of income annually. In his opinion, the reserve would not restore these farms to wetland in the near future, because to do so would mean a double loss: the reserve would have to pay the farmers to leave their land while also losing the rent paid by the farmers. By decree, farmers did not have to compensate the local government, but they violated the decree by farming within the buffer zone of the reserve. Another top cadre leveled more serious charges: "Reserve officers open up virgin land inside the reserve to rent to local peasants."

The attitudes of long-term migrants and state farm employees emerge out of the historical context of Maoist economic development; more important, they respond to how the new environmental policies are being manipulated by corrupt officials, a subject discussed in more detail below. As agricultural laborers lured to Sanjiang to pursue a particular livelihood, they resent forces that threaten their livelihood. Few of them, other than the elderly retiree Sun Jiefang, acknowledged or cited the disappearance of the natural habitat as a problem. Most expressed cynicism towards the new environmentalism because of the way it is being exploited for personal gain by those who enforce environmental policies.

New Migrants

Recent settlers in Fuyuan share their government's hope that one day Fuyuan might become an economic miracle. In the immediate post-Mao liberalization of the 1980s,

Sanjiang represented a land of hope, fortune-seeking, risk-taking, entrepreneurship, and self-reliance, with a view of nature as a supplier of raw materials for a better life. The nature reserve challenges the view of the frontier as cornucopia by putting a third of the land of Fuyuan County off-limits. Many recent migrants are poor, having left their hometowns in search of a better life. Until the late 1990s they were encouraged to come to Sanjiang to farm; and their priority is to farm the Sanjiang wetland. Zhang Hongjin, a new migrant who lives on the edge of the reserve, commented: "The best thing would be to open [the reserve] up and cultivate it so that we could grow more crops."

Their need to survive lead them to exploit the Reserve's resources in any way they can. As a local reserve officer stated,

> We don't worry much about the old migrants, but the new migrants, especially those without land and registration,[117] are the most threatening group. Older migrants identify with this place, and they know how Fuyuan once had rich resources, vast land, plentiful fish, and dense forests. But the new migrants are desperate. They make money from all kinds of risky things, and we might suffer from their crazy retaliation if we strictly enforced the laws.

This officer, an old migrant himself, states the problem in terms of the ability of the new migrants to be good stewards of the land, but the comment also reveals an underlying sense of threat from these new occupiers as economic competitors who bring with them alien values.

The Wang family migrated to Fuyuan County in 1990, settling beside what is now the reserve's core zone. Before leaving home, they sold their single hectare of farmland so they could buy a house in Fuyuan County. They live as hired laborers, earning RMB20 (US$2.40) per day to harvest beans. They also fish illegally in the reserve, and, like many families, they sell fish to survive the seven-month-long winter, when there is no farm work. "Reserve officers burn our nets, but if we didn't fish, how could we live?" they told interviewers. When asked why they did not return to their hometowns, Mrs. Wang replied, "We came here to make money. How could we face people if we came back with empty hands, unable even to buy back our house?" Many families survive on fish during the winter, and they depend on firewood to warm their houses because they cannot afford coal, which has to be transported from afar. Sometimes they cut reserve trees in winter and leave them to be picked up in the spring, since harvesting dead trees is subject to lighter punishment than felling live ones.

Another couple moved to Fuyuan County in 1989 with three children. They rented land to grow rice, but their crop failed. Then they raised three cows, but two of them soon died, and anyway the reserve prohibited grazing inside the wetland. Now they, too, labor for others, illegally fishing and cutting trees to survive. Reserve management bureau officers have twice burned their fish net, and each time the couple has made another. They told interviewers that they hate reserve management bureau officers.

New migrants not directly involved in farming also express disapproval of the reserve. A tavern owner told interviewers:

The nature reserve has no benefits. Besides, establishing an office [the Sanjiang Nature Reserve Management Bureau] to manage it is a waste of human and material resources. . . . It [the bureau] should grow more trees [instead]. It is unnecessary to build a reserve. When peasants are still having trouble surviving, building a reserve is a waste.

Even those residents not yet in the labor force share a deep cynicism about the reserve. As a high school student in the town of Haiqing put it, "The reserve is unnecessary because it only manages common people. The people who have power and money can cut the trees and capture the birds whenever they want."

Pan Jun, thirty-one, a former textile worker, migrated to Yanan Township in 1996, when his state-owned factory collapsed. He borrowed RMB300,000 (US$35,970) to invest in Fuyuan farmland, hoping to make a fortune. Of his eighty hectares, he has dredged twenty hectares of ponds in which to raise fish. The reserve management bureau asked him to pay a RMB50,000 (US$5,995) fine for illegal operations. After negotiations, they reduced it to RMB15,000 (US$1,798.50), still an enormous sum in China. "I don't know where the border [of the zone] is," he complained. Nevertheless, he admitted that he often fishes in the reserve and traps wild animals for food. Interviewers found that Pan had a good basic knowledge of environmental issues (which he said he acquired from watching television), but with fifteen hectares of farmland within the reserve, he cared much more about using his farmland.

The Zheng family migrated from Shandong Province to a nearby state farm in 1977. When, in 1994, Fuyuan encouraged people with livestock-raising skills to settle in the region, Zheng moved to a local village, expecting to earn more money than at the state farm. He purchased a house three kilometers from the village and raised twenty cows. When the reserve was established, however, he could no longer raise the cows since his land was on the reserve, and had to sell them at a loss. "I used to be a state employee, and I understand the importance of the nature reserve," he said. "But I quit my safe job for a better life, not to lose money." Now he has raised two hundred ducks, hoping to sell eggs. He has some income, but the future is not bright. His duck farm is in the core zone, and there is no electricity. By candlelight, his wife spoke of their hopes to return to Shandong once their son had started his own family. But she also had hopes for life near the reserve. "Maybe someday we will open a little inn here for tourists," she said. When the choice is between basic livelihood and nature preservation, there is little contest, but there is also a sense that the reserve may eventually be a source of revenue from ecotourism.

Not all recent migrants suffer, however, and a few acknowledge the legitimacy of preservation even in the face of the need for economic development. Their solution is to adapt by switching to more sustainable forms of agriculture. Zhu Wanchang, fifty-two, migrated to Fuyuan in the early 1980s. He owns 120 hectares of paddy field outside the reserve and sells organic rice, marketing it as chemical-free "green food." He has received national publicity as a "model farmer." When asked about wetland preservation, he expressed support: "I don't want to live in a big city; the pollution is unbearable. Here I will turn my own 'wetland' of rice into a garden of pines and flowers." The government has supported him with loans and agreed that the trees he has planted can be cut and sold as long as he surrenders 10 percent of the revenue to the local government.

Zhu Wanchang's support for the reserve, to the extent that it is genuine and not simply a case of spouting the official line to interviewers, suggests that aesthetic values may emerge when basic survival needs are no longer so pressing, and that even new migrants may become supporters if it will serve their interests. One group banking on this hope in various parts of China is the Trickle Up Foundation, a small American foundation that has made small grants to poor people, often women, near Chinese nature reserves to encourage them to find sustainable livelihoods that won't harm the local environment. So far they have had their greatest successes in the Caohai Nature Reserve, in Guizhou, also a crane habitat. The Global Environmental Fund/UNDP project is also working to encourage alternative livelihood schemes for local communities around wetland areas.

The Expression of Environmental Values in China

Environmentalism amid Political Transition

The environmental campaigns in Benxi and Sanjiang reflect the traditional modus operandi of the Chinese Communist Party: achieve a goal by deploying political, economic, and human resources toward it over a short period of time; and create policy models, such as Benxi, the model city for pollution control. The campaigns also reflect a more modern policy approach, however. At the same time that the central government sought to make a model of Benxi, as it has famously done with many other cities (as well as communes, factories, and towns) in the past, and to position the Sanjiang wetland as a national wetland, it was making broader efforts to institutionalize environmental protection by, for example, legislating environmental laws, establishing environmental bureaucracies, and stabilizing environmental funding. Thus, our two case studies reflect an interesting transition point, or blending, between the old and new approaches, neither of which is likely to supplant the other any time soon.

As we noted at the beginning of this chapter, the environmental cases of Benxi and Sanjiang also have played out against the backdrop of another political transition: decentralization. To the extent that they have been implemented, the central government's environmental policies have been filtered through the local governments' capacity, resources, vision, and interests, as well as their political power and limitations.

The different attitudes of the Benxi and Fuyuan County governments towards the new environmentalism emanating from Beijing can be largely explained by what each was able to gain from political bargaining. The Benxi government won two things in return for its support of the environmental campaign: central government and international funding that enabled it to modernize equipment in its factories; and designation as a national model city in treating pollution, a source of political capital for local politicians, who use the environment field as a new stage to demonstrate their achievements and gain promotion. Thus, despite the escalating unemployment of the 1990s, which raised the political and economic costs of environmental action, Benxi leaders persisted in their support of the pollution cleanup campaign, partly because they still had something to gain from it and partly because they had become "path dependent," having set themselves on a course that was institutionally and politically difficult to reverse.

In contrast, once the Sanjiang Nature Reserve attained national status, in 2000, the Fuyuan County government perceived that it had little to gain from echoing the central government's commitment to wetlands: it had lost its tax base to the independent reserve, and the region's agriculture, forestry, and fishing—the major sources of its revenue—became strictly controlled and restricted. Moreover, even though Sanjiang has become famous for wetland preservation,[118] the political capital resulting from that achievement belongs to the reserve, not the county government. Fuyuan officials' main hopes rest on seeing the county upgraded to a city, meaning a brighter career path for local leaders, but these hopes will be dashed if the reserve maintains its prohibitions on development.

Economic actors have responded to decentralization in much the same way as government officials: by taking more individualized and self-interested actions.[119] Generally, enterprises with greater financial security and more government patronage support the environmental campaigns, while smaller private and town-and-village enterprises tend to resist environmental protection measures. In Benxi, larger industrial interests benefited from the pollution cleanup in the form of an inflow of resources to modernize equipment, whereas in Sanjiang, wetlands preservation has mostly impeded economic development. While some economic actors in Benxi supported the campaign, very few Fuyuan County residents and farmers do. The cases reveal, that apart from those who can gain politically from the environmental campaign—the Sanjiang Nature Reserve Management Bureau officials and Benxi politicians and EPB bureaucrats—environmental commitment among local government officials is highly contingent on the financial flows the campaign can bring to them.

Environmentalism as a Means to an End

A primary objective of this study has been to reveal the motivations behind progressive environmental policy in China. Our emphasis on the official sector is owing to the undeniable fact that the government, as well as government-affiliated scientists and researchers, has been central to the development of China's environmental policy and values. At the same time, however, it is clear that understanding the values of the local people is essential to ensuring the success of any policy, even in China. In this section, we discuss our findings about the motivations of the central government, local governments and officials, industry managers, and local residents in their engagement with environmental policies at both study sites.

International Influence and Diplomatic Motivations

Analysts have attributed the central government's interest in the environment to at least two factors. First, there is the country's environmental crisis, as revealed by a succession of environmental disasters that had direct economic effects. These disasters include the floods of 1998, frequent sandstorms in northern China, and the shrinking of arable land at an alarmingly rapid pace.[120] From such experiences, Chinese leaders learned that China's development had reached the point where it could not be sustained if the country did not incorporate environmental concerns into its economic blueprint.

The second motivation for environmental action is the central government's desire to become a full and respected player on the world stage. China's leaders have seen progressive action on the environment as a means of avoiding diplomatic isolation, particularly following the Tiananmen Square incident. International pressure, particularly organized international pressure, has had a key role in jump-starting China's efforts to protect its environment, and consequently some stakeholders, particularly central government officials, associate a commitment to the new environmentalism with full international citizenship for China. A critical force in the central government's environmental push in the 1990s was Premier Li Peng, the senior leader internationally regarded as responsible for ordering the crackdown on pro-democracy demonstrations at Tiananmen Square in 1989. Li Peng subsequently led the Chinese delegation to the 1992 Earth Summit in Rio de Janeiro and made implementing Agenda 21 a priority of Chinese policy.

In Benxi, the UNDP was the first agency to draw attention to the city's air pollution, and Benxi's subsequent designation as an environmental policy "model city" has made it one of China's environmental showpieces for visiting foreign delegations. In fact, locals believe that the central government order to close China's small mining operations may not have been executed in Benxi had it not been for the fact that they lined the major road leading into the city and thus were declared offensive to visiting foreign and Beijing delegations. Similarly, in the Sanjiang case, the wetlands' ecological significance was impressed upon Beijing by international NGOs and nonprofit organizations such as Wetlands International.

Foreign organizations, including multilateral development agencies, international aid organizations, and conservation groups and their members often provide funding, launch programs, and offer advice that affects policy and behavior on the ground in China. Many of the foreign organizations and individual donors who have an interest in China are not physically present in the country, and some will never set foot anywhere near the regions they seek to protect. But by responding to the prodding from the international NGO community, Beijing has effectively signaled the legitimacy—and ultimately, desirability—of its greater integration into the international community. It is with this in mind that we should recall Director Zhang's pride in his collaboration with his Russian counterparts, and the international network of scholars, researchers, and policy makers with whom he is now in contact.

Local Interests and Environmentalism

On-site stakeholders in our two cases embraced and promoted environmental policies to varying degrees, sometimes at the cost of economic priorities but most often as a means of pursuing economic, political, and/or career motives. Likewise, the local residents in our case studies embraced and supported environmental policies to varying degrees, usually depending upon their level of economic security. Our interviews in Benxi and Fuyuan County elicited a surprising degree of disaffection for environmental policies and projects—what might be termed an "environmental backlash"—from people with more immediate concerns about economic survival. At the same time, however, and over the longer term, environmental awareness and concern have been growing among local people. This is evident in attitudes expressed by Sanjiang Nature Reserve officers, PLA officers, and those in Benxi concerned about health, and from the level of support among the Benxi middle class for the progressive environmental policies, as evident, for example, in the growing use of the environmental hotline.

Our interviews with industry and government officials in Sanjiang and Benxi reveal varying and sometimes idiosyncratic motives and rationales for their response to environmental policies. In Sanjiang, for example, the People's Liberation Army's conception of environmental protection as an instrument of national security (e.g., preserving the forest cover along the border to obstruct surveillance from the other side) was not a concern of other stakeholder groups. In Benxi, since the green money was not uniformly distributed and favored the large SOEs, smaller enterprises cast environmentalism as an impediment to modernization because it checked the enterprises' ability to generate revenues that could *then* be put towards modernization. Thus, we can see that individual actors and institutional actors (i.e., industry and government officials) can often have diametrically opposed views of environmentalism as it relates to one particular good (modernization, for instance).

At the same time, certain motives transcend interest groups, pushing all groups either to embrace or reject the environmental campaign. Perhaps the most widespread motivation for endorsing the new environmentalism stems from an agency or individual's ability to manipulate environmental policies for political advantage. In Benxi, apart from the Environmental Protection Bureau's mandate to carry out environmental policies, maintaining the priority of environmental concerns also meant entrenching the relevance and power of the EPB itself as a force in municipal politics. Although some of Benxi's EPB bureaucrats have acknowledged the clash between the new green regulations and the need to increase industrial output, this has not stopped them from calling for *greater* environmental emphasis in Benxi municipal planning and resource allocation. Those Benxi municipal officials who found their political prestige increased by environmental achievements also touted the new environmentalism. Owing to Benxi's designation as an environmental model, these officials have enjoyed direct contact and political leverage with the central government —unusual for a city of Benxi's size and administrative status. As a result, they have continued to pursue and expand the environmental campaign, despite economic difficulties and widespread unemployment in Benxi.

Similarly, the Sanjiang Nature Reserve's bureaucrats and officers saw their political prestige grow owing to Beijing's 1990s' reversal of course from a development agenda to a preservationist agenda in the Sanjiang Plain. Many cited prestige as a reason for taking a job with the reserve. Career ambition, coupled with assurances from reserve director Zhang that environmental protection was the wave of the future, made the new environmentalism seem like a sound profession for young bureaucrats. This idea could not help but be reinforced in October 2002, when Director Zhang himself received a public commendation from SEPA for his effort to protect the wetlands, an event publicized in the *Xinhua News* under the headline "Loyal Wetland Guard—Zhang Xixiang."[121] And nature reserve officers are not the only ones in Sanjiang who have viewed the new environmentalism as a smart career choice. With promotions awarded in part on the basis of environmental volunteer work and service, the PLA was making environmentalists of soldiers hoping to advance their careers.

The ambitions of nature reserve officials conflicted with those of other local officials, however, most of whom resisted environmentalism. In Fuyuan County, where the economy is based almost exclusively on agriculture, county officials rely on agricultural tax revenues. It would be economic suicide for county officials to endorse preservationist policies when such policies threaten the county's tax base. Thus, the county officials had a careerist motivation to tout the development value of the land in the reserve over its ecological importance. Career motives and economic values were thus intertwined for these local officials.

At times, however, environmental protection, rather than working at cross-purposes with economic development, dovetailed with economic goals. In many cases, good environmental policy was good economic policy in the eyes of local planners. Benxi's enforcement of pollution fees, for instance, and the resulting adoption of new, cleaner technologies promised to, and did, bring modernization, industrial efficiencies, and higher productivity at a time when state-owned enterprises were under pressure to streamline their operations. Similarly, Fuyuan officials' proposal to create the Sanjiang Nature Reserve by converting a portion of the county that was otherwise difficult to farm into a nature reserve was expected to bring an inflow of domestic and foreign investment their way.

Residents, Values, and the Environment

China specialists may be surprised that the oft-cited claim that China's problems result from "too many people" (*ren tai duo*) does not surface in these studies. This suggests that China's population problem, which is publicized by the government to justify its one-child policy, may be a minor concern to people directly affected by pollution, resource degradation, and the policies that address them than the conventional wisdom would have it.

Benxi residents' concerns about the environment were asserted in connection with their concerns about health. The local saying that surgeons could identify Benxi residents by the blackness of their lungs (even though the same thing has been said of some of China's other most polluted cities) resonated with the residents' personal experience of choking pollution and their encounters with pollution-related illnesses such as cancer and respiratory diseases. Their deep concern over health has fostered both support and criticism of the government's cleanup efforts. While many of our interviewees noted improvements in the air quality, suggesting a degree of approval for the campaign, others expressed skepticism that enough was being done. Measures to clean the air (a form of preventative health care, in a sense) are more important than ever at a time when medical care and health insurance are unavailable to many.

Health values compete, however, with the more immediate concerns of many Benxi residents about economic survival, concerns that stem from massive layoffs, loss of pensions, and the disappearance of the social safety net. Thus, despite residents' personal experience of the ill health effects of breathing polluted air and scientific evidence of a link between pollution levels and the incidence of cancer and respiratory disease—evidence that was used by Benxi leaders to build provincial and central governmental support for its anti-pollution campaign—discontent with the campaign runs deep among certain sectors of the population.

The environmental concerns of the residents in both our cases have been similarly overtaken by livelihood concerns. While official media reports lamented the destruction of the biodiversity of the wetland and the landscape of "our beloved Benxi,"[122] few residents we interviewed voiced such sentiments. Instead, we heard practical anxieties about livelihood and complaints that environmentalism is a poor substitute for job security. In Benxi, more stringent emission laws and fees, along with insufficient government funding to meet these standards, have hurt industries (and thus the labor force) already struggling under the economic reforms. Furthermore, the perception that green funds (*huanjing qian*) are being spent to improve the landscaping along roads—rather than being invested in job creation or training—creates cynicism among residents about the environmental campaign. While in 2000 other cities in China were attracting foreign direct investment to shore up their economic base, leaders in Benxi, where employment was estimated to be as high as 50 percent, were attracting investment in the environmental cleanup.

Similarly, in the Sanjiang Nature Reserve case, the preservationist mandates of the provincial and national government put off-limits the resource at the heart of Fuyuan County's economy: land for agricultural development. On the whole, the recent migrants' attitudes toward the reserve lends credence to the Kuznetian notion that until livelihood and survival needs are met, environmentalist agendas that promote the intrinsic (or scientific, or ecological) value of nature have a hard time taking root.

In the eyes of local residents at both study sites, their government officials were adopting a strategy of attracting foreign investment for environmental protection, while in most other parts of China local governments were attracting foreign investment for production and economic expansion. Benxi officials have assumed large risks by taking out international loans to support the environmental cleanup at the same time that many in Benxi are worried about jobs and social programs. In Fuyuan County, local farmers witnessed the erection of a beautiful new office building paid for with provincial and central government funds—just when officials were cracking down on agricultural and fishing practices in the reserve. In both cases, local critics denounced environmental projects as out of step with local needs.

There are few avenues in China for converting this sort of discontent into political action, however, which leaves the public with little power over decisions about their local environments and little direct accountability to the public on the part of the government. And without accountability, policy-making becomes arbitrary and law enforcement un-equal; the people in Benxi and Sanjiang, for example, were left to bargain over how policy directives—over which they had had little or no say in the first place—would be implemented. Stories of big corporations delaying or averting polluter levies in Benxi and people paying bribes for the right to fish or open land in the Sanjiang reserve reveal the abnormal way in which people express their values when democratic channels are unavailable. While new migrants to the Sanjiang Plain have other tactics of subversion—they fish and cut trees in the reserve despite the law—not all stakeholders can interfere in the process in this way. As for the political influence wielded through corruption, it is only an option for the economically and politically privileged, and in both the Sanjiang and Benxi cases we have seen how this practice creates growing resentment among residents, which can in turn undermine public support for environmental policies.

Weak support at the local level puts greater pressure on the government to enforce environmental laws, but funding for environmental administration and law enforce-ment has been inadequate throughout China. In October 2000, the official *People's Daily* reported that 44 percent of China's one thousand–plus nature reserves had no administrative organ and 35 percent had no management staff. Furthermore, only 22 percent of reserve supervisors had received technical training in environmental pro-tection.[123] Poor enforcement has encouraged unlawful practices such as hunting, log-ging, and agricultural development in China's nature reserves. As a sign of its concern over weak law enforcement, in October 2000 SEPA announced that its approach to the management of nature reserves would change "from a quantity-over-quality men-tality" to one favoring ecological benefits over speed of reclamation.

The Future of Environmental Values in China

The Value of Sustainable Development

The idea of sustainable development, despite the central government's rhetorical com-mitment to it, has been conspicuously absent on the ground in this debate. In Benxi, the emphasis on remediation, which poured funds into new clean technologies, over-shadowed the need to diversify the city's economic base. In 2003 Benxi's govern-ment did have plans to retrain workers formerly employed by polluting industries and shift them into new sectors, but these had not yet been broadly tested and imple-mented. Meanwhile, in Sanjiang, with Fuyuan County's economic base in agriculture and its plans to expand to become a major port city, the conflicting mandates of environmental preservation and economic development form a zero-sum game. Unfortunately, the rhetoric of environmentalism-as-nature preservation creates a dichotomy, with environmentalism on one side and development on the other. But this may well be changing, with the aid of international grants for sustainable development initiatives.

In 2002, Chen Yangkai, the party secretary of Fuyuan County, was quoted in the *Heilongjiang Daily* as saying, "Wetland protection and economic development complement each other. Now that we have seen the opening of two customs passages to Russia, more domestic and foreign tourists will come and inspect whether we have a sound ecological situation; if not, they will not come back."[124] Similarly, during our field interviews in 2000 we encountered one resident—a recent migrant—who had changed his agricultural practices, owning a paddy field outside the reserve, using only green technologies, and orienting his crops to the organic market. Although he has been rewarded by the government with loans and publicity, his singular success gives rise to the question of why other residents were not being given the money to start such ventures.

It appears that those residents who arrived in waves during the Mao years, for whom devotion to the old-style farming practices runs deep, have neither the opportunity nor the mind-set to undertake a new venture. The discourse of environmentalism as a threat to development overwhelms the notion that environmentalism may lead the local economy in a different, even prosperous, direction. The central government does not see the need to fund development in the Fuyuan economy in ways that would not clash with the reserve's preservationist mission; instead, it views the antagonism between the reserve and local livelihoods as a given and considers it resolvable through education.

Though the Chinese government may not see the need for them, sustainable development initiatives are being supported by ADB and GEF initiatives throughout China. A five-year GEF wetland project begun in July 2000 covers eleven reserves, including the Sanjiang Nature Reserve, and has a distinctive new vision for development that includes the development and encouragement of alternative, sustainable livelihoods in and around wetland areas as part of a program of poverty eradication.[125] Likewise, an ADB initiative begun in 2003 has the explicit goal of promoting "conservation of wetlands and terrestrial biodiversity in Sanjiang Plains employing integrated approaches to conservation and development to ensure ecologically sustainable production activities, reverse degradation, and reduce poverty."[126] Commercial forestry is one area the ADB has been studying as a potential sector for investment in sustainable development.[127] In supporting such initiatives, international lending institutions have attempted to introduce a new vision that encourages development with "green" characteristics—economically successful commercial activities that at worst will not harm and at best will help preserve and restore the environment. This vision, however, has not yet become a local priority in Sanjiang as well as other parts of China.

Yet, as Secretary Chen suggests above, county and reserve officials have expressed interest in marketing the reserve for ecotourism. Similarly, a recent migrant family that found its hopes of agricultural prosperity shot down by new reserve regulations, nonetheless spoke about possibly opening an inn if and when their duck farm (located in the core zone) was ordered to be closed. The government, however, has been slow to take the lead by supporting sustainable economic endeavors. If it rewards them at all, it is only after they *do* succeed, and most observers admit that, with the weakness of the local economy, the chance that they will take off without outside investment is slim at best.

In China, it is widely believed that basic needs must be fulfilled before it is possible to appreciate nature or value environmental goods like clean air. And many of the residents we interviewed in both Benxi and Sanjiang conveyed the view that this "necessary" level of prosperity has simply not arrived. This priority placed on economic or material concerns by people in Sanjiang and Benxi is representative of attitudes in China as a whole. According to a survey carried out by SEPA and the Ministry of Education in 1998,[128] ordinary Chinese citizens have low environmental awareness. Survey respondents were asked what priority they placed on each of five developmental goals—economic development, progress in science and education, population control, social justice, and environmental protection. Environmental protection came in last, while economic development came in first.

Political Limitations, Public Participation, and the Future of Environmentalism in China

Government-led environmental campaigns in China have been hindered by three conditions: economic hardship; historical values; and ordinary citizens' political impotency and resulting dependency on the government, such that social problems are seen as a matter for the state to deal with, and not a matter of individual concern. In the 1998 survey, when asked to identify the best way to deal with environmental problems, only 10 percent answered "promoting citizens' participation," and only 3.8 percent answered "increasing the role of environmental NGOs," while almost all others provided answers related to education, investment, law-making, and law enforcement, all of which require government action.

The problem of political impotency is compounded by a skepticism, fueled by government corruption, about the government's commitment to resolving environmental problems. Rampant corruption frustrates residents in both Benxi and Sanjiang, and many suspect that corruption has infected the two areas' environmental campaigns. Some residents of Sanjiang talked about how fishing was still allowed in the forbidden zone, but only for those who bribed the officials. In Benxi, we heard from people wondering where the "environmental money" went. Thus, we can infer that residents' passive or even cynical attitude toward environmentalism is not really rooted in their environmental knowledge, but in their general distrust of and frustration with their government.

Economic hardship, as we have pointed out, also contributes to the low priority many residents accord to the two environmental campaigns. In effect, both communities posed the question: "What is the point of a nice environment if people have nothing to eat?" Only 33 percent of respondents to the SEPA survey agreed that "it is acceptable to slow down the growth of economic development in order to protect the environment," while 44 percent disagreed. Thus, the high priority the people of Benxi and Sanjiang assigned to economic development as compared to environmental protection reflects the views of many people across China.

The third factor limiting environmental awareness is the historical value, developed during the socialist era, that "man must conquer the nature." Even today, a majority of Chinese still hold fast to the belief that the conquest of nature made possible the splendid achievements of Chinese socialism—swift industrialization and food security for a country with an enormous population. Thirty-four percent of respondents to the 1998 survey believe that humans must "conquer" nature to achieve happiness, while only 11 percent think people should "conform to" nature, and 28 percent think people should "utilize" nature. Ironically, an environmental notion that helped foster China's economic development for fifty years is now endangering its future development.

Despite the challenges posed by all three of these factors to the future of government-led attempts to protect and preserve the environment across China, our cases reveal signs that some of the attitudes expressed in the 1998 surveys are beginning to change. There is evidence—including the increasing public use of Benxi's environmental hotline and the Sanjiang Nature Reserve and PLA officers' official commitment and volunteer work to maintaining the reserve despite insufficient funding for daily operations—that some local environmental awareness and initiative exists apart from (or in addition to) the central government's proclaimed environmental policy priorities.

This sort of environmental initiative seems promising, but the promise will largely remain unfulfilled as long as channels for public input into policy-making remain limited. Our case studies of Benxi and the Sanjiang Reserve do not reflect the growing emergence and activity of NGOs elsewhere in China over the past decade. Their numbers have increased from nine in 1994 to more than 250 in 2002, most of them student-founded and -led. An increasing proportion, however, are being founded by other concerned advocates for the environment, particularly journalists.[129] These Chinese NGOs differ in some respects from environmental NGOs active in other countries (for instance, if non-student-led, they must register with the government and follow a set of regulations limiting the scope of NGO activities; also, they tend to eschew politically confrontational or provocative tactics), but they engage in the same sort of educational, preservationist, and advocacy activities as environmental NGOs elsewhere. Typically nonprofit volunteer groups, they seek to protect endangered species and natural environments, and to educate and engage citizens in environmental cleanup, restoration, and protection programs. Some have played active roles in raising public awareness of the ecological dangers of major development projects such as the Three Gorges Dam; others have called for immediate attention to endangered wildlife, such as the South China tiger or Tibetan antelope. At least one—the Center for Legal Assistance to Pollution Victims—helps pollution victims take legal action against polluters.[130]

These groups have been allowed to flourish (and many unregistered groups also operate under the radar of regulators) because of Beijing's shift to a new set of environmental priorities and policies. As long as the groups function in the service of these policies (particularly at the local level, where it is often difficult to enforce environmental policies), their continued existence is assured. As political scientist Guobin Yang has pointed out, the spread and success of NGOs have also been promoted by three other factors: the Chinese media, which generally approves of these groups' watchdog roles and educational initiatives; the Internet, which allows them to communicate, educate, and cultivate membership on a large scale; and the influence of international environmental NGOs, many of which have opened China offices, provided funding and expertise, and formed partnerships with local NGOs.[131]

The government-led environmental campaigns in Benxi and Sanjiang could become more successful with the aid of local NGOs, which could, through their work on the ground with neighborhoods and communities, help change people's minds about the importance of protecting the environment at all costs, help give residents a sense of individual responsibility for the future of their environments, and engage them in cooperative projects to protect their local environments. NGOs, in conjunction with the media and international environmental organizations, can also bring the sustained, high-profile attention and resources necessary to resolve an environmental problem. In Benxi and Fuyuan County, these are functions that until now have been the domain of government.

Unfortunately, some of the social and economic factors that foster NGO formation and activities are absent from these two parts of China. NGOs are more likely to emerge in major urban areas with large populations of students and other educated and civic-minded residents. And the digital divide (the byproduct of an economic/educational/employment divide) leaves many of the people who resist environmental policies, such as those who are living hand-to-mouth on the Sanjiang Plain, out of the reach of NGOs' efforts to raise awareness and recruit members via the Internet.

But the largest obstacle to any effort to instill environmental values at the local level in these two cases continues to be the lack of jobs and people's uncertain livelihoods—large-scale unemployment in Benxi and the lack of alternatives to ecologically destructive farming, fishing, and game-hunting on the Sanjiang wetlands. A healthier employment picture may emerge in Benxi—and also in Sanjiang, depending upon the success of incipient sustainable development initiatives for the wetlands, and that would greatly ease the task of inculcating environmental values.

In the meantime, there are signs of the potential for NGO activity in both of our cases. In Fuyuan County we saw the beginnings of individual involvement in environmentally responsible farming in the example of farmer Zhu, who engaged in organic farming on the Sanjiang Plain (albeit with economic support from the local government). In Benxi, we saw precursors to the sort of collective action typically undertaken by NGOs. In the data on the number and content of hotline complaints, we saw that during the period 1999–2001, residents across several neighborhoods banded together to complain about environmental problems: one hundred people collectively complained to the government about a pig yard polluting the drinking water in their area, for instance, and apartment dwellers and block residents joined together to lodge complaints about smog in their neighborhoods created by nearby smokestacks.

But even absent the formidable economic obstacles highlighted by this study, other conditions must exist for the government to succeed in its environmental campaigns. These include a restoration of trust in local governments (in the wake of corruption), an increased sense of civic responsibility on the part of residents, and even a modest measure of political initiative.

Notes

*Research for this chapter was conducted by Song Guojun (Benxi study), Pan Wei (Sanjiang Nature Reserve study), and Shen Mingming (research team leader). Their field reports and analyses were adapted and developed for this chapter by Liu Yu, Mary Child, Vivian Bertrand, Judith Shapiro and Joanne Bauer in consultation with the researchers. Special recognition is due to Ma Zhong, president of the Beijing Environment and Development Institute, who selected the cases, initially led the project, and made himself available to answer questions through the writing process.

1. Elizabeth Economy, *The River Runs Black: The Environmental Challenge to China's Future* (Ithaca: Cornell University Press, 2004).

2. For example, in August 1996, CNN ran a special story on rising environmental awareness. See "Environmental Awareness Takes Root in China," available at www.cnn.com/EARTH/9608/14/china.environment.

3. These figures are from the Eighth Five-Year Plan (1991–1995), the Ninth Five-Year Plan (1996–2000), and the Tenth Five-Year Plan (2001–2005), respectively, and are published by the State Environmental Protection Agency.

4. Available at http://dawning.iist.unu.edu/china/bjreview, accessed 11 September 2003.

5. Benxi is one of 250 prefectural-level cities that report directly to the province. Only four cities (classed as municipalities at the provincial level)—Beijing, Shanghai, Tianjian, and Chongqing—report directly to the central government. The prefectural-level rank is the third of four administrative levels, following the provincial-level rank and the subprovincial-level rank.

6. According to the Asian Development Bank, Benxi is still one of the most polluted cities in the world. Asian Development Bank, "Report and Recommendation of the President to the Board of Directors on a Proposed Loan to the People's Republic of China for the Liaoning Environmental Improvement Project," November 2004, Appendix 2, 25.

7. Energy Information Administration, China Country Analysis Brief: Environmental Issues, 2003, available at www.eia.doe.gov/emeu/cabs/chinaenv.html. Available data show that in 1982 and 1985, Benxi, had a higher level of falling dust than selected major cities in China (National Environmental Protection Agency, China, *China Environmental Yearbook* [Beijing: China Environmental Yearbook Press, 1987, 1992]).

8. "Benxi Cold Rolled Steel Facility, China," Steel Industry Web site, www.steel-technology.com/projects/benxi, accessed 1 October 2002.

9. World Bank, "Reducing Air Pollution in China," available at www.worldbank.org/nipr/china/pix/index.htm, accessed 13 September 2005.

10. In the worst month of 1973 at the most polluted monitoring point in the city, falling dust was approximately 130 tons/month/km^2, and the average yearly dust fall far exceeded the provincial control standard of 8 tons/month/km^2. Falling dust is mainly emitted by industrial production plants and coal boilers. It is defined as particulate matter larger than 100 microns.

11. Benxi Municipal Environmental Protection Bureau, *Environmental Quality Report* (1991–1995), May 1996, 69.

12. *Evaluation Report on Benxi's Seven Year Pollution Control Program* (Benxi: Benxi EPB, 1996).

13. The name changed from Benxi Iron and Steel Company to Benxi Iron and Steel Corporation in the late 1980s, when the entity changed from a state-owned enterprise to a private enterprise.

14. UN Habitat and Together Foundation, "Benxi's Sustainable Development Demonstration Zone," *Best Practices Database*, www.bestpractices.org/cgibin/bp98.cgi?cmd=detail&id=18627&key=rpybfkbfe, accessed 4 March 2002.

15. *Bulletin of Liaoning Environmental Quality in 2002* (2002 nian Liaoning huanjing zhiliang gongbao), Liaoning Environmental Protection Bureau, 2003.

16. Ministry of Health, *Report on the National Project of Scientific Investigation and Research on Asthma*, June 15, 2001.

17. This office, called the Office of Industrial Wastes Management, was located within the city's construction commission. In 1978 the name was changed to Office of Environmental Protection.

18. It was the first environmental protection bureau (EPB) in Liaoning Province to be granted a full-bureau rank. Today every Chinese city has an EPB at full bureau rank, and giving full departmental rank to EPBs has now become a common practice nationwide.

19. The school later became one of the first members of the GLOBE program, an international initiative for promoting environmental education in the classroom.

20. In Chinese, 本溪把原材料贡献给了国家，把污染留给了自己 (*Benxi ba yuancailiao gongxian geile guojia, ba wuran liugei leziji*).

21. The group included *People's Daily*, CCTV, *Economic Daily*, CP Radio, *Science and Technology Daily*, and *China Environmental News*.

22. The State Environmental Protection Commission was the ministerial-level environmental body until 1998, when the National Environmental Protection Agency was promoted to the ministerial level, at which time the commission was dissolved.

23. In June 1987, a team led by Deputy Mayor Shen Yucheng went to Beijing to report to NEPA on Benxi's pollution status. The team included EPB director Zhao Zhenyu and managers with responsibility for environmental concerns from the Benxi Iron and Steel Company and the Benxi Cement Plant. Director Qu Geping, together with chiefs of relevant NEPA departments, after listening to Shen Yucheng's report, agreed that Benxi could not deal with the pollution using its own resources. However, NEPA was short on funds, so he suggested that Benxi appeal to the State Council for special grants to cover the costs. In a subsequent visit to Beijing in January 1988, Deputy Mayor Shen led a team from Benxi to report on pollution to NEPA, the Ministry of Metallurgy, the Ministry of Coal, the State Planning Commission, the State Economic Commission, and the Ministry of Finance. Following this mission, the SEPC sent an inspection team to Benxi, including representatives from NEPA, the Ministry of Metallurgy, the Ministry of Energy, the State Bureau of Construction Materials, and Liaoning Province.

24. In addition to air pollution, the seven-year program also addressed water pollution, industrial waste, and green space. For example, the program created a park around the city.

25. *Review on the Seven-Year Pollution Control Program* (Benxi: Benxi EPB, 1996).

26. The Ministry of Energy and the State Bureau of Construction and Materials also contributed RMB9 million, the State Council contributed RMB74 million, and Premier Li Peng contributed RMB70 million from the Premier's Fund. The Premier's Fund is used primarily for emergencies such as floods, earthquakes, and forest fires but also for some local programs such

as Benxi's environmental program that cannot be listed under the regular national budget.

27. These revenues helped to fill the gap in the RMB388.9 million (US$46.8 million) budget for the seven-year program.

28. SOEs, which were key to China's centrally planned economy and continue to have their own channels to Beijing leaders, were directly administered by central government ministries, including the Ministry of Metallurgy, the Ministry of Coal, the Ministry of Energy, and the State Economy and Trade Committee until March 1998, when this function of ministries was given to industry associations or other government offices, called specialized economic management departments (SEMDs).

29. Following this precedent, from 1998 to 2001, the Baotou of Neimenggu (Inner Mongolian) Autonomous Region received central government financial support of RMB32 million to control its air pollution.

30. The Chinese pollution levy system, a method for charging polluters for emissions, was adopted in 1979 and officially incorporated into law in the early 1980s. A nationwide policy for air pollution levies issued by China's State Council came into effect in 1982. Almost all cities in China now use this economic instrument.

31. Department of International Cooperation, China Economic Information Network, "China to Formulate New Law on Clean Production," available at http://ce.cei.gov.cn/enew/new_gl/pg00g313.htm, accessed 5 November 2002. The UN Environment Program first coined the term "cleaner production" in 1990. European Topic Center on Waste and Material Flows, European Environment Agency, available at http://waste.eionet.eu.int/prevention/2, accessed 19 November 2002.

32. China's State Development Planning Commission, responsible for developing and implementing the national economic strategy, was renamed the State Development and Reform Commission in 2003 when it took over functions from other departments.

33. The UNDP project was called Extensively Promote Clean Production and Enhance the Capacity of the Benxi Municipal Government to Control Air Pollution. United Nations Development Programme project brief, available at www.unchina.org/undp/ee/CPR96307.htm.

34. The World Bank, "Reducing Air Pollution in China," available at www.worldbank.org/nipr/china/pix/index.htm. In Benxi, the project sought to eliminate emissions from four coke ovens and two blast furnaces, establish a district heating company that will deliver heat in the form of hot water, and improve the efficiency of two blast furnaces.

35. By 2003 Environmental Defense had expanded the project to include a number of other cities, including Shanghai.

36. Environmental Technologies Industry, Market Research, China, "Opportunities for Solid Waste Companies in China," available at http://web.ita.doc.gov/ete/eteinfo.nsf/vwQFbyCountry.

37. Municipal planning commissions apply the national five-year and one-year plans locally by setting targets for various government economic units and programs that are consistent with the national plan and ensuring the implementation of these targets. Since the local economy is integrated and interdependent, their work involves forward-looking coordination of different offices and sectors. The official rank of the municipal planning commission is usually a half-level higher than other functional departments of the government. Although some of the local commissions have recently followed the lead of the State Planning Commission by changing their names (in 2003 the State Planning Commission was renamed the Reform and Development Commission) to reflect the new economy, their function remains essentially unchanged.

38. "China Sets Five-Year Plan for Environmental Protection," *People's Daily Online*, 13 January 2002, available at http://English.peopledaily.com.cn/200201/12/print20020112_88510.html, accessed 4 October 2002.

39. Economy, *The River Runs Black*, 117–18.

40. As of 2004 no factories were known to have been closed under this policy.

41. The Green Plan had the goal of creating fifteen green factories, fifteen green residential

communities, fifteen green schools, a thousand green households, and ten green hotels and shopping malls in two years. The Quietness Plan had the goal of creating fifteen model "quiet communities" in Benxi's downtown; this would involve controlling work at construction sites so as not to disturb the communities, and shutting down seventy karaoke rooms.

42. Since 2000, environmental protection investment by Chinese enterprises, in terms of technical improvements, has averaged about RMB100 million (US$12 million) annually, while the pollution levy has been about RMB17 million (US$2 million). See Benxi EPB, "Benxi Environmental Protection Five Year Plans," 2000–2003.

43. This is known as the dual-price system.

44. U.S. embassy, "Curbing Chinese Pollution: A Tale of Two Cities," available at www.usembassy-china.org.cn/sandt/Liaoningweb.htm, accessed 17 October 2003. See also James A. Edmonds, Shi Yingyi, and Kay Storck, "Mid-and Long-Term Strategies for Technological Deployment to Address Climate Change in China," 6–7 May 1999, available at www.pnl.gov/gtsp/conferences/beijing.pdf, accessed 4 October 2002.

45. Zhou Lukuan, a director at the Labor and Personnel Institute at People's University in Beijing, estimated in 1997 that Benxi's unemployment rate was 15 to 20 percent. See Pamela Yatsko, "The Great Job Hunt: Help for China's Jobless Is Patchy at Best," *Far Eastern Economic Review*, 30 October 1997. According to William Hurst, a PhD candidate in political science at the University of California, Berkeley, in a December 9, 2003, e-mail message, "The government uses several figures: one that counts only 'registered unemployed' (5 percent) and other, more inclusive statistics. Probably one can best estimate the true rate of unemployment in Benxi by comparing the number of workers employed in the city around the beginning of the period in which most job losses took place with the number of workers actually 'on post' (*zai gang*) in a recent year. In 1994, there were 612,000 workers in Benxi city. In 2000, only 287,000 workers were 'on post' there. This means that a total of roughly 325,000 jobs have been lost and not replaced. Thus, somewhere around 53 percent of Benxi's workforce is likely unemployed, according to official statistics (*Liaoning tongji nianjian* [Beijing: Tongji chubanshe, 1995 and 2001]). Almost the same figure is reached if one takes the simple ratio of workers listed as 'not on post' (*bu zai gang*)—i.e., workers still associated with their original factories but reported and registered as being out of work through one of a number of mechanisms (this figure probably captures at least half—but certainly not 100 percent of all the workers actually unemployed in Benxi)—to workers listed as 'on post' in 2000. Alternatively, one could say that 35 percent of all Benxi workers not yet retired were listed as 'not on post' in 2000. Complicating any attempt at making such estimates is that officials often do not use consistent indicators to report from one year to the next, and therefore clear or reliable unemployment figures simply do not exist." For more on why calculating any precise rate of unemployment in a Chinese city is difficult, see Dorothy J. Solinger, "Why We Cannot Count the 'Unemployed,'" *China Quarterly*, no. 167 (September 2001): 671–88.

46. "Benxi Iron and Steel Co. (China) No. 5 BF Successfully Restarted after Major Revamping," available at www.paulwurth.com/e/chap5/news/BenxiIronSteel.html.

47. "Benxi Hot Strip Mill Modernization, Liaoning, China," Export-Import Bank, 2 January 2001, available at www.exim.gov/press/jan0201a.html, accessed 27 September 2002.

48. Until that point Benxi Iron and Steel was the only one of China's top ten steel companies that did not have continuous casting. Continuous casting is the process whereby molten steel is solidified into a "semi-finished" billet, bloom, or slab for subsequent rolling in the finishing mills. Prior to the introduction of continuous casting, steel was poured into stationary molds to form "ingots." Continuous casting results in improved yield, quality, productivity, and cost efficiency.

49. This was called *sannian tuokun* ("getting out of difficulties within three years policy").

50. "Official Sure State Firms Can Turn Around," *People's Daily,* 16 August 2000, available at http://fpeng.peopledaily.com.cn/200008/16/eng20000816_48307.html, accessed 9 April 2003.

51. Li Yan, "Nearly 1000 SOEs Drop Out of Market in Past Three Years," *People's Daily,* 22 December 2000, available at http://english.peopledaily.com.cn/200012/22/print20001222_58550.html, accessed 4 October 2002.

52. In that process 5,700 non-production staff were rehired in subsidiary companies, which, like the majority of SOEs, became shareholding companies through joint ventures, listed on the stock market or changing their bank debts into shares. See "Official Sure State Firms Can Turn Around," *People's Daily,* 16 August 2000, available at http://fpeng.peopledaily.com.cn/200008/16/eng20000816_48307.html, accessed 9 April 2003. In 1997, Li Dahong, a company official, claimed that Benxi Iron and Steel Company had laid off, trained, and reemployed sixty thousand workers to meet the new market needs. However, Li later admitted that the company had not retrained the workers. Instead, it had simply reshuffled most of the workers who were now idle. See Yatsko, "The Great Job Hunt," 56.

53. See Wang Qingyi, "Coal Industry in China: Evolvement and Prospects," 1999, available at www.nautilus.org/energy/eaef/C5_final.pdf, accessed 5 December 2005.

54. Phone interview with Daniel Dudek, 3 February 2003.

55. It is a system by which all aspects of the production process—extraction of raw materials, energy use, equipment, production, safety and auditing—are evaluated for their environmental impact.

56. See, for example, Li Song, "Give Me Back Benxi's Beauty," *China Environment News* [Zhongguo huanjing bao], 23 July 1998; and Wang Yadong, "Where Is Benxi? Boundless Smog Covers Benxi—Citizens Say: Whoever Can Clean Up Our Pollution We Chose as Our Mayor," *Economy Daily,* 9 August 1988.

57. While Benxi was one of the first in China, it is not the only city that was successful in channeling funds to their pollution control effort. The China Urban Air Quality Control project launched by the UNDP in 1997 included Benxi, as well as Xi'an, Guangzhou, Guiyang, and Beijing in its first stage, and the second stage now includes thirty experimental cities in China. By the end of 2000 about 113 cities in China accepted financial support for environmental programs from international organizations, NGOs, and funders such as the World Bank and the Asian Development Bank.

58. Dudek interview.

59. The total emission controls (TECs) policy sets national emission standards rather than placing fixed emission limits on individual polluters. This method of pollution control is designed with a view to establishing market-based emissions trading, thereby promoting socioeconomic development and industrialization by allowing some enterprises to emit more pollution than others. After China adopted a TEC policy in 1996, "the central government allocated the total amount of pollutant discharge for each province based on estimates of the provincial-level emission discharges in 1995. Provincial governments in turn began to assign the pollutant quota to various prefectures and cities within their jurisdictions." Dudek et al., "Total Emission Control of Major Pollutants in China," *China Environment Series,* no. 4 (2001): 43.

60. The author is referring to the fact that under the new system factories no longer provide housing.

61. Liu Ningrong, *Fennu de diqiu* [Angry Earth] (Beijing: Zhongguo gongren chubanshe, 1991), 114, 199.

62. William Hurst, e-mail communication, 20 October 2002.

63. See William Hurst and Kevin J. O'Brien, "China's Contentious Pensioners," *China Quarterly,* no. 170 (June 2002): 345–60.

64. The data referred to here and below is unpublished data provided by the Benxi EPB. Today filing complaints before the political consultative conference is the least likely means of political action. Now, the three main ones are sit-ins and other demonstrations, petitions (collective petitions, especially) and class action lawsuits. As of 2005, there have been no suits or sit-ins that we know of to protest pollution in Benxi, although such suits against polluters are proliferating elsewhere in China.

65. "Grade III" refers to the maximum concentration of various pollutants allowed in intensive industry areas under air quality standards issued by SEPA in October 1996.

66. According to national statistics, which go back only to 1952, the forest stock in Heilongjiang Province was 0.92 billion cubic meters in 1952, and 0.57 billion cubic meters in 2000.

67. The Heilong and Wusuli Rivers are better known internationally by their Russian names: Amur and Ussuri.

68. A directory and map of China's wetlands sites, along with a description of characteristics and preservation measures for each, is available at www.wetlands.org/RDB/asia/china_sites.html.

69. The Ramsar Convention on Wetlands, "Reservoirs of Biodiversity," available at www.ramsar.org/info/values_biodiversity_e.htm, accessed 15 January 2003.

70. According to the *Directory of Wetlands of International Importance*, Sanjiang meets criteria 1,2,3,4,5,7,8; available at www.wetlands.org/RDB/Directory.html, accessed 29 May 2003.

71. *SEPA Annual Report*, October 2002.

72. Eight animals found there are listed as top-ranked species in the annex of the China Conservation Law of Wild Animals, and twenty-three are second-ranked. Six species are identified in the Convention on International Trade in Endangered Species (CITES), Appendix I, and thirteen species are identified in Appendix II. Out of 227 migratory bird species protected by the Sino-Japanese Government Agreement on Migratory Birds, sixty-four have been recorded in Sanjiang, of which forty-three breed in the wetlands.

73. Ma Zhong, "Sanjiang Wetland Conservation in the Context of Agricultural Development" (paper prepared for the Carnegie Council on Ethics and International Affairs, November 1999).

74. The study was funded by the United Nations University.

75. Liu Xingtu et al., "The Wetlands of Heilongjiang Province, North-East China," in *Land Resources in the People's Republic of China,* ed. Kenneth Ruddle and Wu Chuanjun (New York: United Nations University Press, 1983), available at www.unu.edu/unupress/unupbooks/80349e/80349E06.htm, accessed 19 September 2005.

76. Ibid.

77. Bruce Marcot, "Report on Tigers and Leopards of the Russian Far East and Northeast China," July 21, 1994, available at www.plexusowls.com/PDFs/report_on_tigers_and_leopards.pdf, accessed 19 September 2005.

78. Liu et al., "The Wetlands of Heilongjiang Province, North-East China."

79. It is difficult to calculate the precise coverage of the wetlands because the boundaries are unclear and changing.

80. Liu et al., "The Wetlands of Heilongjiang Province, Northeast China."

81. Shi Weimin and He Gang, *Educated Youth Memoirs: The Production-Construction Army Corps in the Rustification Movement* [Zhiqing beiwanglu: Shangshan xiaxiang yundong zhong de shengchan jianshe bingtuan] (Beijing: Zhongguo shehue kexue chubanshe, 1996), 12–14.

82. Ma Bo, *A Blood Red Sunset: A Memoir of the Chinese Cultural Revolution* [Xuese Huanghun], trans. Howard Goldblatt (New York: Viking, 1995).

83. Judith Shapiro, *Mao's War Against Nature: Politics and the Environment in Revolutionary China* (New York: Cambridge University Press, 2001), 167–68.

84. It is difficult to count the number of state farm workers, who are seasonal workers. Moreover, there may be as many as five thousand additional unregistered migrants, many of them desperate job-seekers.

85. The Ramsar Convention on Wetlands, available at www.ramsar.org/key_conv_e.htm, accessed 26 March 2003.

86. China is ranked as the eighth most biologically diverse country according to the National Biodiversity Index produced by the Secretariat of the Convention on Biological Diversity and as having the fourth-largest area of wetland in the world by the Ramsar List of Wetlands of International Importance.

87. WWF China, available at www.wwfchina.org/english/sub_loca.php?loca=39&sub=91, accessed 3 January 2002; "Save Our Earth's Kidney," *China Daily,* 1 July 2002, available at www.china.org.cn/English/2002/Jul/35902.htm, accessed 3 January 2002.

88. The six reserves are Hainan's Dongzhai Harbor Nature Reserve, Qinghai's Bird Island Nature Reserve, Heilongjiang's Zalong Nature Reserve, Jilin's Xianghai Nature Reserve, Hunan's Eastern Dongting Lake Nature Reserve, and Jiangxi's Poyang Lake Nature Reserve. In 1992, the Sanjiang Nature Reserve had not yet been established.

89. "China Invites Pressure to Help Curb Shrinking Wetlands," *People's Daily,* 3 February 2002, available at www.china.org.cn/English/DO-e/26353.htm.

90. "College Students Help Restore Ecological Cycle in Wetland," *People's Daily,* 5 July 2001, available at http://english.peopledaily.com.cn/20010705/eng20010705_7433.html, accessed 26 March 2003.

91. "China Restoring, Preserving World's Wetland 'Kidneys,'" *China Daily,* 28 September 2002.

92. GEF, "Project Concept Paper for the Songhua River Flood and Wetland Management Project," available at www.gefweb.org/COUNCIL/GEF_C14/pipeline2/ADB/China%20Songhua .pdf, accessed 29 May 2003.

93. The 1998 decree was entitled Decision of Heilongjiang Communist Party Committee and Heilongjiang Government on Strengthening Wetland Protection. Before his appointment as party secretary of Heilongjiang Province, the most powerful post in the province, by the central party authorities in Beijing in 1997, Xu Youfang was the minister of forestry. In China, the Ministry of Forestry has traditionally held authority over wetlands protection. Thus, it is reasonable to infer that in selecting Xu Youfang, party authorities must have considered his experience and interest in protecting wetlands. His selection demonstrates a shift in priorities for party authorities: Xu's predecessor, Yue Qifeng, had proposed to reclaim 5 million *mu* (roughly .33 million hectares) of land for cultivation in the Sanjiang Plain when he was made the province's top leader in 1994.

94. Zhang Jing, "Wilderness to Reclaim Farmland," *Asia Times,* 16 May 2000, available at www.atimes.com/china/BE16Ad01.html.

95. Ibid.

96. "China Restoring World's Wetland 'Kidneys,'" *China Daily*, 28 September 2002.

97. Ma Zhong, "Sanjiang Wetland Conservation in the Context of Agricultural Development" (paper presented at the Carnegie Council on Ethics and International Affairs, New York, October 1999).

98. We have been unable to confirm whether the sole reason for denying the agricultural loan was because the bank recognized the region's environmental significance, but it is safe to assume that was *a* reason. Just four years earlier, in 1996, the bank had lent state farms $70 million for agricultural development.

99. GEF, Project Concept Paper for the Songhua River Flood and Wetland Management Project, 1994, available at www.gefweb.org/COUNCIL/GEF_C14/pipeline2/ADB/China%20Songhua .pdf, accessed 29 May 2003.

100. "A Sustainable Land Use and Allocation Program for the USSURI/WUSULI River Watershed and Adjacent Territories (Northeastern China and the Russian Far East), A Cooperative Project of: Ecologically Sustainable Development, Inc. (USA), FEB-RAS Institute of Aquatic and Ecological Problem (Russia), FEB-RAS Pacific Geographical Institute (Russia), Heilongjiang Province Territory Society (PRC) National Committee on U.S.-China Relations (USA)," November 1996, 10.

101. GEF, Project Concept Paper Songhua River Flood and Wetland Management Project available at www.gefweb.org/COUNCIL/GEF_C14/pipeline2/ADB/China%20Songhua.pdf, accessed 29 May 2003.

102. Ma Zhong, "Sanjiang Wetland Conservation in the Context of Agricultural Development."; the Ramsar Convention on Wetlands, "National Report of China for COP7, 1999," available at www.ramsar.org/cop7_nr_china.htm, accessed 29 May 2003.

103. General Office of the State Council 2000, no. 30.

104. Of this, RMB1 million (US$120,400) came from the State Forestry Administration (SFA) of the central government, and the rest came from the province and Fuyuan County. Draft final report, field site visit of UNDP-GEF team, 20 September 2001, available at www.wetland-gef-cpr98.org, accessed 29 May 2003.

105. Ibid.

106. Ibid.

107. Ibid.

108. Ibid.

109. A year later, the Sanjiang Nature Reserve and the Khabarovsk Bolshekhekhtsirski State Nature Reserve in Russia held an inaugural conference and signed an agreement to preserve jointly the natural environment in the Wusuli River's lower reaches. In particular, they agreed to work together to carry out scientific research in the area and develop international ecotours. See Zhang Tingting, "China, Russia Agree to Protect Wusuli River," available at www.china.org .cn/English/2002/Aug/39055.htm, 9 August 2002, accessed 18 December 2002.

110. This particular ADB grant, which Director Zhang hoped would be forthcoming after negotiations in November 2000, did not initially come through as expected. A technical assistance grant of US$1.25 million co-funded by the ADB and Global Environmental Facility (GEF) was approved in 1999 to provide assistance to the Songhua River Flood and Wetland Management Project, but the Chinese government later decided to place a hold on funding the Sanjiang component of the grant. According to the ADB's historical records, "In July 2001, a decision was made (with the concurrence of the Global Environmental Facility [which was co-funding these efforts]) to process the wetland protection component as an independent project, focusing on the Sanjiang Plain." In November 2002 the ADB formally awarded a technical assistance grant of $600,000 toward a sustainable initiatives feasibility study for the Sanjiang Plains Wetland Protection Project. E-mail interview with Dr. Kyeong Ae Choe, senior project specialist, Asian Development Bank, June 1, 2004. See Asian Development Bank, TAR: PRC 35289, "Technical Assistance (Financed by the Japan Special Fund) to the People's Republic of China for Preparing the Sanjiang Plains Wetland Protection Project," November 2002 available at www.adb.org/Documents/TARs/PRC/tar_prc_35289.pdf, accessed 21 September 2005.

111. The conflict between the EPB and the reserve, at the local level, mirror in many ways the tensions between the State Forestry Administration (SFA) and SEPA, at the national level. According to the assignments of responsibility made by the State Council, SEPA is responsible for the administration of biodiversity conservation, and SFA is responsible for wetland conservation. SEPA and SFA each has its own reserve program, with SEPA administering its program through the EPB, and SFA administering its program through the forestry bureau. Both SEPA and SFA's programs in Sanjiang are supported by the National Development and Reform Committee and the Ministry of Finance, but through different departments and channels.

112. Nongqiao is a town in Fuyuan County on the border of the reserve. See the map on page 30.

113. This comment does not acknowledge that Tongjiang City also has jurisdiction over the reserve.

114. In June 2004 we learned through the ADB office that the provincial government has committed more than US$26 million over a five-year period to fund not only the reserve but also activities such as land compensation to farmers being forced off the reserve, forestry management, and capacity building within the reserve bureaucracy (K. Choe, ADB, e-mail communication, 5 June 2004). While such sizable funding could well make a difference in local attitudes toward the reserve, at the time of our interviews and several years thereafter no such funding had been provided.

115. Phone interview with Ma Zhong, 24 January 2003.

116. Asian Development Bank, TAR: PRC 35289, "Technical Assistance (Financed by the Japan Special Fund) to the People's Republic of China for Preparing the Sanjiang Plains Wet-

land Protection Project," November 2002, Section II, available at www.adb.org/Documents/ TARs/PRC/tar_prc_35289.pdf.

117. The reference here is to household registration, which is to say legal residence. Every Chinese is, in principle, registered with the police as living someplace, usually at the place of birth. In the past, to shift to another place of registration (i.e., legal residence) was impossible. Thus peasants were born in a place, registered there, and could not legally move to the cities. Today there are many migrant workers in the cities, but they remain legally registered where they came from and do not have full rights where they are living.

118. The lead of a 31 March 1999 *Heilongjiang Daily* article, "Jiansanjiang Land Reclamation Branch Protects Wetland Resource," reads: "The Jiansanjiang Land Reclamation Branch (JLRB) of Heilongjiang Province, the location of the famous Sanjiang Nature Reserve, put 160,000 *mu* (roughly 10,700 hectares) of wetland off limits to its seven farms this year."

119. For a helpful discussion of the impact of economic reform specifically on environmental protection see, Abigail R. Jahiel, "The Contradictory Impact of Reform on Environmental Protection in China," *China Quarterly*, no. 149 (March 1997): 81–103.

120. See Megan Ryan and Christopher Flavin, *Facing China's Limits*, in *State of the World 1995*, ed. Lester Brown et al. (New York: Norton, 1995), 113–131.

121. *Xinhua News*, 4 October 2002.

122. Li Song, "Give Me Back Benxi's Beauty," *China Environment News* (Zhongguo huanjing bao), 23 July 1988.

123. "China to Strengthen Control on Nature Reserves," *People's Daily*, 11 October 2000, available at http://english.peopledaily.com.cn/200010/11/eng20001011_52373.html, accessed 15 January 2003.

124. Li Mingyuan and Fan Yanhui, "The Return of the Beautiful Wetland—A Report on Sanjiang National Wetland Reserve in Huyuan County," *Heilongjiang Daily*, 6 August 2002.

125. UNDP/GEF, "Wetland Biodiversity Conservation and Sustainable Use in China," Grant CPF/98/G32. See the Convention on Biological Diversity's Web site, available at www.biodiv .org/financial/projects.asp?prj=1307.

126. Asian Development Bank, *Country Strategy and Program Update, 2003–2005, People's Republic of China*, Appendix 2, Table A2.2, August 2002, available at www.adb.org, accessed 3 January 2002. As of early June 2004, the scope of the Sanjiang Wetlands Development Project had not yet been finalized.

127. Kyeong Ae Choe, senior project specialist, Asian Development Bank, interview via e-mail, 2 June 2004.

128. The study was conducted by NEPA and the Ministry of Education in 1998 and published by the Chinese Environmental Science Press in 1999 as *Report on the Environmental Awareness of the National Public*.

129. Guobin Yang, "Environmental NGOs and Institutional Dynamics in China," *China Quarterly*, no. 181 (March 2005): 46–66.

130. Ibid.

131. Ibid.

Japan: A Foreword

Jeffrey Broadbent

Traditional Japanese culture—with its ink landscape paintings, its nature poetry, and its cultivation of life-energy (*ki*)—viewed humans as part of an all-encompassing universe. The traditional Japanese words for this unity were "heaven and earth" (*tenchi*) or "all living things" (*ikarumono*). The concepts of *tenchi* and *ikarumono* did not set people apart from other "sentient beings," including animals, plants and often even mountains and trees in that category. The Japanese aesthetic, as in the *bonsai* tree and Zen temple gardens, seamlessly merged the forms of rocks and plants with human artifice. The Shinto gods, too, existed around and within the mountains and trees.

Matsushima, the array of tiny "pine islands" off the north-eastern coast, is one of Japan's "three famous views." The islands were so beautiful, wrote the seventeenth century wandering poet Basho, that he could not compose a haiku worthy of them. In 1980, when I first took the little tour boat out among the Matsushima islands, I, too, was entranced by their beauty. Barely clinging to jagged granite rocks, the islands' crooked pines stretched out over the sparkling sea. "What could better express the Japanese aesthetic?" I thought. Then, looking southward, I saw about a mile away, amid the woods on the bay's far shore, a giant power plant belching smoke. Why, I wondered, would Japanese authorities not better protect the setting of their precious analog to Yosemite?

I eventually realized that Japan's spiritual values and nature aesthetics are personal, not public or political—that is, they rarely become the rallying cry of popular movements that criticize government and corporate policy, nor do they have much effect on public policy. Public policy and public space have always been controlled by a small elite of officials in the government ministries, an elite that has generally favored economic growth over the preservation of nature. Accordingly, the strong nature aesthetic so evident in Japanese culture has remained largely expressed in personal space—temples and shrines excepted.

In the West today, personal concerns readily translate into public action, but Japanese culture has until recently discouraged the public expression of personal preferences. The Japanese feudal system ended only in 1868. Before that, to a greater degree than in European feudal systems, the Tokugawa state forced the people to bend before, rather than stand against, the winds of power. Japan's rulers instituted a rigid status system and demanded unquestioning loyalty, justifying this hierarchy as part of a Confucian ethic. Nor, with some notable exceptions, did Japan's other spiritual traditions, Buddhism and Shinto, offer consistent criticism of the secular order.

Nevertheless, over the past two centuries, popular movements have occasionally arisen in Japan. In the feudal era, peasant villagers and townspeople had a healthy disrespect for their samurai masters, often seeking to evade their control, tax collections, and status regulations. In times of famine, when rice merchants hoarded grain and the government did not stock the emergency granaries, nascent peasant resistance sometimes erupted into fierce revolts (*hyakusho ikki*).

Following the arrival of Commodore Perry's famous black ships (in 1853), the Meiji Restoration of 1868 overturned the *ancien régime*. Faced with the Western threat of colonization, the new government imposed a "social revolution" from above, destroying feudalism and introducing Western-style institutions, but centralizing control over the population and land. Over the ensuing 140 years, in its race to catch up with the West in terms of military, economic and technical power, the state kept a tight grip on public space in Japan. Its narrow focus on economic growth pushed the aesthetic moment so treasured in Japanese spirituality into ever-smaller private spaces. Though the government established national parks, urban and village public land steadily diminished. Today, Tokyo offers the smallest per capita area of public parks of any major city in the world.

The lack of space for nature in Japan's public infrastructure arises from its lack of another kind of public space—the political space devoted to civil society. The western term *civil society* represents the arena of free association and democratic opinion formation—the public sphere. In the feudal era, Japanese cities were allowed to develop an independent artistic culture that sometimes obliquely criticized the elite (a common phenomenon among authoritarian regimes), but this freedom did not extend to the political realm, to a sense of citizenship, with its civic rights and responsibilities. From the start of Meiji, the modernizing elites permitted only limited democracy, keeping the political reins firmly in their own hands. Popular movements in the Taisho Era (1912–1926) pushed open the door of democracy a bit wider, but rising militarism slammed it shut again. In practice, if not in their hearts, ordinary people remained largely conditioned to "leave it up to the ones above" (*okami*).

The U.S. Occupation (1945–1951) refashioned many of Japan's institutions in a democratic direction, but power relations and culture changed more slowly. After World War II, most Japanese people strongly supported rapid economic growth, seeing it as the only path to industrial jobs, prosperity, a "cultured life" (*bunka seikatsu*), and national pride. Many people believed that, in their resource-poor country, disciplined work and cooperation under state and corporate leadership was the way to attain these goals. This conviction only strengthened the long-standing Japanese reluctance to criticize government policy. When labor unions, students, and leftist parties protested too much, the authorities weakened or suppressed them.

In the decades after World War II, the paternalistic government distributed some of the benefits of economic growth to all classes, but it did little to control the environmental costs. The government's policy priorities were power plants and booming factories, not clean air and water. When polluting industries entered communities, they not only destroyed the old ways of life, they made people sicken and die. Such hardships left people disillusioned about the virtues of unregulated growth.

In the 1960s and 1970s, popular frustration peaked. Throughout the nation, quiescent villages and neighborhoods erupted into environmental protest. Minamata was the site of one of the first and most potent of these movements. Photographs of its victims, crippled by mercury poisoning brought on by decades of negligent industrial practice, became symbols of the nation's pollution problem. Disease victims and their supporters challenged the power of business and the state, and went on to win their cases in court. Starting in the mid-1960s and peaking in the early 1970s, a tidal wave of such locally based movements swept Japan, eventually forcing the government to pass effective environmental laws. This wave of environmental protest actualized the democratic potential of the new constitution introduced by the Americans in 1946, giving ordinary people a sense of political empowerment.

Still, when people dared to protest publicly, political elites and even fellow citizens condemned them for failing to observe the traditional Japanese virtue of loyalty to the elites. Indeed, as we see in the chapter that follows, even while suffering the horror of mercury poisoning, the Minamata victims were criticized by society for daring to blame the polluter, a local factory of the powerful Chisso Company. In many pollution cases in other parts of Japan, local residents just grumbled around their dinner tables. Only after someone of high local status decided to take a leadership role would ordinary people band together in public resistance.

Organizing a movement was not easy. Environmental movements usually had to contend with local conservative political "machines," similar to those of old Chicago's Daley machine or New York's Tammany Hall. Local "bosses" (*bosuteki sonzai*), as the Japanese called them, doled out patronage from above: local construction projects, wedding and funeral attendance, and bribes placed on the family altar, all in return for votes and loyalty. If you joined a protest movement, the local boss leaned on your aunt to pressure you to quit. In short, as these examples show, Japanese society and culture posed many informal as well as formal obstacles to the emergence of local citizen advocacy groups.

By the mid-1960s, however, concerns surrounding pollution's effects intensified and overcame customary restraints on political protest. The number of protest movements grew rapidly, peaking in the early 1970s and resulting in a raft of new environmental legislation. With surprising efficiency and much more rapidly than in the United States, Germany, France, or England, these laws and subsequent regulatory action quickly reduced the most visible air and water pollution.

This wave of protest movements permanently altered Japanese political culture; yet few young people adopted the environmental movement as a lifestyle or career. In the 1970s and 1980s, the Japanese economy gained increasing momentum and most young male high school and college graduates were eager to join the ranks of the newly affluent "salarymen" and enjoy the new possibilities of self-indulgent consumerism. Only in the 1990s, after the vast bubble of prosperity collapsed, did the majority of Japanese people begin to entertain "post-materialist" values. Although support for such values was still not high in Japan compared to some other countries,[1] the public became increasingly willing to sacrifice economic gain for the sake of preserving the environment. Moreover, more people recognized a public right to a healthy and beautiful natural environment.

Public policy, however, often ignored this nascent environmentalism. Japan's fiscal problems of the early 1990s led the country into the economic doldrums. The central government tried to revive the economy by spending vast sums on public works, but conservative politicians and general contractors, not the people, defined the character of these projects. As they had done since the 1950s, Japan's huge general contractors used public funds to construct dams, seawalls, roads, tunnels, and buildings throughout Japan, many of dubious necessity and great ecological destructiveness. Moreover, according to one authority, "bid-rigging and political payoffs inflate[d] the cost of public construction in Japan by thirty to fifty percent."[2] Some of the added costs found their way into the pockets of industry-friendly politicians as an incentive to dole out additional dubious government contracts. This led to a vicious cycle that produced what many Japanese call Japan's "construction state" (doken kokka), driving up the public works budget (in 2003, over ¥9 trillion, or US$75 billion) and leaving Japan with a government debt totaling 140 percent of its GDP, a world record. Construction projects on Lake Biwa and the Nagara River, described in this chapter, exemplify the results of this process—the radical transformation of Japan's natural landscape. Pushed by such profit-minded elites, these projects went ahead despite reasonable criticism and popular opposition.

During the 1990s, the government's inability or unwillingness to protect the public interest became increasingly obvious. In one telling example, the government fumbled its response to the 1995 Great Hanshin earthquake, leaving much of the emergency aid work to volunteers. In this time of economic doldrums, the government protected big banks and corporations while small business bankruptcies skyrocketed. The Ministry of Health and Welfare allowed HIV-tainted blood into the national blood supply. Concurrently, new environmental problems emerged: the ubiquitous huge trash incinerators built by the government to eliminate consumer waste spewed forth dioxin-laden smoke, polluting the soil. Toxic waste seeped into the water supply, raising fears of human hormone disruption. Increasingly, the public blamed the ruling Liberal Democratic Party (LDP), with its strong ties to business, for these failures.

All these problems, along with the end of the Cold War, weakened the rationale for further extending the long rule of a single political party. In 1993, for the first time since its founding in 1955, the LDP lost control of both the upper and lower houses of the Diet, the Japanese parliament. After a year out of government, the LDP returned to power, but only at the cost of forming a coalition with its old nemesis, the Japan Socialist Party. The resulting political turbulence opened the way for important new policies. In 1993, the government revised the basic environmental laws to include the new ideas of national and global sustainability, while the 1998 Nonprofit Law gave civil associations the right to incorporate. As a result of these changes, civil society took on a new shape. Japan's educated, middle-class urban society gave birth to environmental groups more like their Western counterparts, concerned not just with the quality of their own neighborhoods but with citywide, prefectural, national, and even global environmental causes. Inspired by the 1992 UN Conference on Environment and Development in Rio de Janeiro and supported by environmental activists nationally and internationally, the Nagara River protest movement, discussed in the chapter that follows, exemplified this new type of citizen activism.

The complex political and institutional changes of the 1990s further weakened the Confucian tradition of obedience and added legitimacy to citizen activism as a way to participate in politics. A new sense of civic capacity and responsibility empowered citizens to act not only on behalf of global environmental ideals but also to express in political form their own deeply held spiritual aesthetics of nature. That such personal values should enter the realm of politics represents something new in Japanese culture. Turning away from wholesale acquiescence to a paternalistic state, people are increasingly getting used to thinking of themselves as citizens empowered by democratic principles, an ethic that can now legitimately support even the public defense of natural beauty.

Notes

1. R. Dunlap, A. Gallup, and G.J. Gallup, *The Health of the Planet Survey* (Princeton: George H. Gallup International Institute, 1992). In this survey of citizens of twenty-two developed and developing countries, the portion that valued environmental protection over economic growth ranged from 72 percent in top-ranked Denmark to 43 percent in bottom-ranked Turkey. The figure for Japan was 58 percent, and for the United States it was 59 percent—eighth and ninth from the bottom, respectively.

2. B. Woodall, *Japan Under Construction* (Berkeley: University of California, 1996), 48.

Minamata City, Lake Biwa, Niigata City, and the Nagara River, Japan

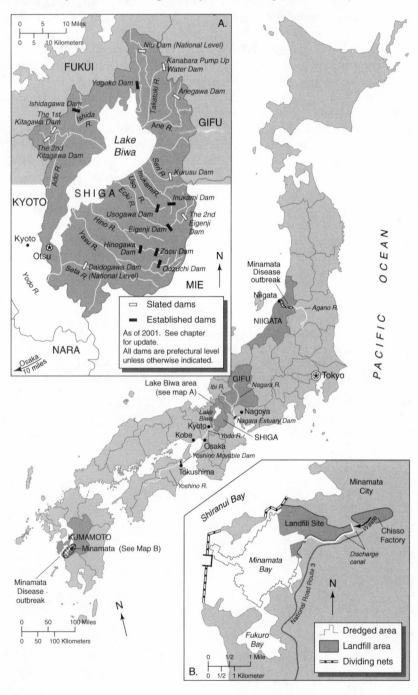

A.

0   5   10 Miles
0   5   10 Kilometers

FUKUI

Niu Dam (National Level)

Kanabara Pump Up Water Dam

Yogoko Dam

Takatoki R.

Anegawa Dam

Ishidagawa Dam

The 1st Kitagawa Dam

Ishida R.

GIFU

Ane R.

The 2nd Kitagawa Dam

Lake Biwa

Ado R.

Seri R.

Kurusu Dam

SHIGA

Uso R.

Ecki R.

Inukami R.

Inukami Dam

Usogawa Dam

The 2nd Eigenji Dam

Hino R.

Eigenji Dam

KYOTO

Yasu R.

Hinogawa Dam

Zaou Dam

Kyoto

Otsu

Daidogawa Dam (National Level)

Oozuchi Dam

Seta R.

MIE

Yodo R.

N

☐ Slated dams

■ Established dams

As of 2001. See chapter for update.
All dams are prefectural level unless otherwise indicated.

NARA

Osaka
10 miles

Minamata Disease outbreak

Niigata

Agano R.

NIIGATA

PACIFIC OCEAN

Lake Biwa area (see map A)

GIFU

Ibi R.

Nagara R.

⊛ Tokyo

Lake Biwa

● Nagoya

Kyoto ●

Nagara Estuary Dam

Kobe

Yodo R.

SHIGA

● Osaka

Yoshino Movable Dam

● Tokushima

Yoshino R.

KUMAMOTO

● Minamata (See Map B)

Minamata Disease outbreak

0   50   100 Miles
0   50   100 Kilometers

N

B.

Shiranui Bay

Minamata City

Landfill Site

Waste

Chisso Factory

Discharge canal

Minamata Bay

National Road Route 3

N

Fukuro Bay

⊔ Dredged area

■ Landfill area

⊏⊐ Dividing nets

0   1/2   1 Mile
0   1/2   1 Kilometer

2

From *Kogai* to *Kankyo Mondai*

Nature, Development, and Social Conflict in Japan

*Kada Yukiko, Tanaka Shigeru, Aoyagi-Usui Midori,
Arakaki Tazusa, Watanabe Shinichi, and Steven Hoffman**

Japan is a nation shaped by water. Its cultural practices, economy, and worldview have been fundamentally influenced by the close proximity of bodies of water and—in the twentieth century—by the use and allocation of water.[1] Over the centuries, floods have been the most frequent natural threat to livelihoods and property. Water is also central to the Japanese diet, in which fish and rice (which requires vast amounts of water to cultivate) predominate. Small rivers and lakes carve up Japan's countryside, and the natural boundaries between watersheds have historically provided administrative boundaries for government.

It is fitting, therefore, that the environmental cases we have selected for this chapter all center upon water. Focusing on the struggle of communities as they cope with transformations to their environments, and the resulting degradation, these cases exemplify the water-related issues faced by many Japanese communities in the postwar era of rapid development.

During its race to industrial development in the latter half of the twentieth century, Japan experienced severe industrial pollution that cost many lives. Our first case—the outbreak of mercury poisoning ("Minamata disease") in Minamata Bay in the 1950s (and, later, in Niigata Prefecture)—is probably the most extreme example of a pollution-related health crisis in Japan. In our case study we examine not only the devastating effect of mercury pollution on the people of Minamata but also the ways in which the community has sought to heal itself and its environment in the aftermath.

Another outgrowth of the postwar development push was an emphasis on "efficient resource allocation." Japan's water policies were increasingly tailored to electricity generation, industrial production, and urban growth. Massive dam and water delivery system projects were planned, and many were built during this period. In our second case study we examine the evolution of Japan's water policies and how they fundamentally altered the Japanese environment and raised awareness of the role of the environment in Japanese society and culture. This case study—of conflicts over government efforts to manage and control water supply at Lake Biwa, the Nagara River, and the Yoshino River—is typical of the water issues many Japanese communities faced in the era of rapid economic development.

In short, the chapter examines the ways in which the communities in and around Minamata and Lake Biwa have been transformed by environmental struggles. We analyze the changes in how people define the environment and the values reflected in the evolving definitions, and how competing notions of the environment are invoked during conflicts among differently situated individuals and social groups.

Japanese environmentalism, as the term is commonly understood in the West, is a very recent phenomenon. Before the 1980s the Japanese referred to problems associated with the destruction of nature as *kogai* (literally, "public nuisance" or "public harm"). This usage implies a clear distinction between polluter and victim, where a demonstrable harm affects specific individuals or groups. However, the term was soon found inadequate for many environmental problems. As we shall see in the cases of the Lake Biwa and Nagara River development projects, beginning in the 1980s there emerged "lifestyle-related" pollution, where household effluent was identified as a cause of environmental degradation but where claims of "victimhood" were absent. This new class of pollution problems came to be referred to as *kankyo mondai* (environmental issues).

After 1990 the term *kankyo mondai* came into common use, and today *kogai* is seldom heard in the public domain despite the persistence of *kogai* issues and effects. As this study will suggest, such shifts in terminology are meaningful, particularly given that before the emergence of the cases presented here, the notion of "the environment" did not exist in the Japanese language.

The cases we have chosen represent these two ways of viewing environmental problems—*kogai* and *kankyo mondai*—in the emerging discourse of Japanese environmentalism and environmental awareness. The *kogai* case, that of the city of Minamata (and Niigata-Minamata), involves mercury poisoning caused by the discharge of untreated industrial effluent. Characterized by government inaction, corporate denials, stigmatization, litigation, and ultimately the introduction of an elaborate bureaucracy for victim certification and compensation, it has played a pivotal role in the rise of environmental protection policies in Japan.

In the water resource cases that exemplify *kankyo mondai*, we see how the effects of invasive natural-resource development policies—characterized by huge construction projects and increased agricultural and industrial activity in the lake region— galvanized local awareness of the importance of the natural environment. At Lake Biwa there emerged calls for "environmental rights" (specifically, the right to clean water) alongside a more spiritual discourse articulating the need for a "living, natural" lake. A related though not identical situation arose during the resistance to the Nagara River Dam project, which evolved from the livelihood-based protests of local fisherman to a conservationist claim taken up not just by local residents but also by nature writers, visitors to the area, and eventually national media.

Of course, these brief characterizations of each case are themselves inadequate representations of the wide range of values and perspectives that shaped environmental politics of these places. Our study tries to attend to the multiplicity of voices, claims, and discourses that have shaped environmental policies and legitimized human interaction with the physical environment. These attitudes and claims as they relate to the *kogai* cases are presented in a "Community Reactions" section; in the *kankyo mondai* cases, which treat Lake Biwa, Nagara Dam, and Yoshino Dam, these "voices" appear in the form of quotations that are interspersed throughout the text.

Our attempt to track the development and articulation of environmental values—the attitudes and intuitions that inform lifestyle choices, cultural habits, and environmental policy-making—is reflected in our methodology. Several aspects are worth noting.

First, our methodology reflects our response to the norms that govern social research in Japan, and the challenge of conducting inductive, values-oriented research in Japanese society. To secure both the trust of interviewees and the acceptance of research results in a society that emphasizes community and group membership, researchers must have prior research accomplishments in their field and research topic. A researcher will have great difficulty eliciting meaningful responses from a Japanese interview subject who perceives the researcher as *ichigen-san* (a one-time visitor). Thus, each researcher associated with this project had already studied extensively various aspects of each of these cases, and the researchers conducted interviews themselves (not via graduate students) at the sites.

We conducted more than a hundred interviews with representatives from all stakeholder groups: the central government, the prefectural government, victims' advocacy groups, and local residents. Highly abstract questions about social problems tended to elicit programmed responses from the interviewees, echoing viewpoints that had been widely disseminated in society through the mass media and government propaganda. Such behavior reflects a cultural feature of Japanese society: the desire to offer socially acceptable answers. Yet the repetition of such language *is* a form of self-expression, and we took it into consideration. However, we found that asking more concrete questions, situated in a particular context or in response to a particular stimulus such as an old photograph of the neighborhood, led us to a more precise understanding of people's environmental attitudes.

In addition to the environmental stories that unfold in this chapter, there is also a political story: the story of a national government increasingly centralizing control over local environments in the name of economic development, and the trouble this presents when people are denied a voice in decisions about local land and water. This theme of loss of control over local environments comes up repeatedly as a cause of disharmony in the case of Minamata Bay (where fishing grounds are transgressed by a major, government-backed industry) and in the Lake Biwa and Nagara River cases (where major public water works projects overrule local wishes to keep water clean and free-flowing).

The water resource cases illustrate how central control of water resource planning and management transformed Japanese people's relationship with water from a "nearby" relationship to a "distant" one, in which local people are divorced (in terms of access and a sense of responsibility) from their traditional water sources. This story comes full circle by the end of our chapter, as Japanese people concerned with these cases begin to voice their opposition to the government's water resource development policies and eventually to regain a voice in decisions about their "nearby water."

Our political and environmental stories go hand-in-hand, and both are driven by the complex and sometimes conflicting values of clean water, health, nature-based livelihoods such as fishing and farming, social harmony, interpersonal obligation, and loyalty, among others. The chapter ends with a discussion of Japanese values and an analysis of how they have come into play in Japan's environmental story.

Industrial Pollution in Minamata Bay

Introduction

The case of industrial water pollution in Minamata, a small city on Japan's southernmost island, Kyushu, is the largest and most emblematic instance of *kogai* in Japanese history. Hundreds of people living along the inland Shiranui Sea died and thousands were debilitated by a devastating neurological disease caused by eating fish tainted by methyl mercury, which had been flushed into Minamata Bay with industrial wastewater from the local chemical plant, Chisso Minamata. The methyl mercury was a by-product of its production of acetaldehyde, which had begun in 1941 and was finally discontinued in 1968. Even before World War II, there were signs of a growing problem of water pollution in Minamata Bay, including periodic fish kills and declining fish catches. For decades the Chisso company had periodically paid "gift money" (*mimaikin*) to the fishing industry in compensation for losses that resulted from pollution in the area near the plant. But it was not until the contamination moved its way from fish up the food chain—first, to cats and, then, to humans —that it began to arouse concern.

Although not understood for decades, the mercury had become incorporated into methyl mercury chloride (mercury combined with carbon), an organic form that could enter the food chain. Humans can absorb it by ingesting it, and after it enters the bloodstream, it can cause brain damage. Further, high levels of methyl mercury in mothers can be passed on to their offspring, causing disfiguration and retardation. What came to be known as Minamata disease is characterized by severe convulsions, episodes of dementia, and in the worst cases, permanent coma before the onset of a high fever and death. Those affected came to suffer external disfiguration and internal, neurological malfunctioning.

Although signs of the disease, known initially only as *ki-byo* (the strange disease) appeared as early as 1953, it was not officially recognized until 1956. Its earliest manifestations were in local cats, which resulted in a second name: dancing cat disease. The Minamata pets had begun to exhibit inexplicably strange behavior, writhing and twisting in the streets and in homes. When Hosokawa Hajime, a doctor at the community hospital affiliated with the Chisso plant, first reported the disease in humans and said its causation was unknown, the city government responded by isolating the patients, members of the fishing community, in hospitals. The quarantine marked the disease with a powerful stigma both within the community of fishermen and outside it, among other social classes. Minamata disease was thus, in a sense, a class-based disease. This unfortunate fact presaged an uphill battle on the part of the victims to get community support in their fight for compensation against the powerful industry-government alliance in Minamata. Disease victims also suffered discrimination in employment and other areas.[2]

Even when the pollution was stopped at its source, the after-effects remained with the community: Mercury remained in the sediment of the bay, and the disease victims and their families, mostly fishers, continued to cope with their personal and commercial losses as well as the social stigma attached to the disease. The now-infamous case of mercury poisoning in Minamata Bay, which has played out over almost five decades, continues to haunt, divide, motivate, and inspire the community.

We selected this case in part because the decades-long story of Minamata is, in many respects, the story of Japan's environmental "coming of age" at all levels of society and government over the past century. During the course of this ordeal (which by some accounts began as early as the 1920s, with a series of suspicious fish kills in the region), Japan has undergone several major value shifts along its path from traditional ways of life to modernization, technological and economic development, and beyond. Government and industry have had to come to terms with the excesses of industrial development and the resulting environmental damage, and to adjust their policy priorities accordingly; and Japanese citizens have acquired higher levels of political and environmental awareness and activism. It was the Minamata case, in fact, that served as a catalyst for many nationwide changes in environmental policy, in pollution regulations for industry and developers, and in legal innovations that provided recourse for pollution victims.

This case also illustrates the real contemporary challenges to environmentalism and environmental policies in a community that was once at the epicenter of an ecological and social disaster. As of 2001, there were 2,955 government-certified victims of Minamata disease.[3] Well over 1,700 certified patients had died.[4] In total, however, more than two hundred thousand people were estimated to have suffered health effects from Minamata disease.[5] A victims' advocacy group, Soshisha, attributed the very large number of "latent" victims to intense social pressure not to speak about the disease and to the fact that many people died unaware that they had mercury poisoning.

The story of the poisoning at Minamata is well documented. In contrast to earlier accounts that emphasize the industrial pollution incident, the cover up, and the impact on the victims, this study focuses particularly upon government and community efforts both to heal the community by remembering the past and to make Minamata, the very name of which once brought shame, a point of pride as an environmental showcase and an instrument for environmental education and awareness. There remain in Minamata, now a city of thirty-two thousand inhabitants, a number of obstacles—some the by-products of the poisoning itself—to the government-led campaign to prioritize the environment and promote environmental values there. Many of the principal figures in this case—including disease victims, activists, fishermen, and company employees—still live in the community. While Chisso ceased vinyl chloride production in 1968, the company still operates in Minamata, employing about two thousand people at the main office and in Chisso-related enterprises involved in the production of fertilizers, chemicals, and computer discs.[6]

Below, we look at how the community of Minamata was altered by this well-known case, and how it has shaped the values and attitudes of the people there regarding community, government, and the environment. We also describe the role of key leaders in pursuing environmental justice and cleanup, and we explore the lasting legacy of the incident for the Minamata community and Japan as a whole. Then, in the "Community Reactions" section, we examine the attitudes and actions of the key actors, and evaluate the prospects for the reforging of community ties and for environmentalism in Minamata.

Healing Disease, Distrust, and Environmental Destruction

Moyainaoshi: Retying Community Ties

In the early 1990s the government of Kumamoto Prefecture (prefectures are akin to U.S. states) initiated a campaign to reinvigorate Minamata City. Not only was the community politically and socially divided over the disease that had affected so many of its citizens, it had also suffered economically both from the contamination of its fish and the downsizing of the Chisso plant, which came as a result of its inability to compete effectively within the chemical field. In an effort to resuscitate the community, the local and prefectural governments undertook a pointed campaign of community healing. The campaign was called *Moyainaoshi*, a maritime metaphor that means "retying the moorings," alluding to reforging community bonds. The Moyainaoshi Campaign emphasizes activities that bring the residents face-to-face to discuss environmental and other community issues and to cooperate together on resolving community environmental problems. It is seen by its architects as a way of healing both differences and the environment.

The language of reconciliation surrounding the campaign was accompanied by government pronouncements that "the Minamata disease problem is important to all citizens of Minamata" and "the Minamata community cannot be revitalized until the Minamata disease conflict [that is, the social conflict connected with the disease] is solved."[7] We examine this local campaign and, later, the community reactions to it because it is widely believed within Minamata that its success is a prerequisite to a shift toward embracing environmental values whereby stakeholders perceive their lives as a part of the surrounding ecological system. In this view, harmony between humans and the environment cannot be fully restored unless community harmony is restored because environmental policies succeed only when the community can put differences aside and get solidly behind them.

Moyainaoshi, originally a grassroots call for the community to come together to support the victims of Minamata disease, became the official, government-adopted name for a range of measures and campaigns to end prejudice and heal rifts, and to promote environmental thinking and values in Minamata and the larger community.

Much of this campaign has played out on a 58-hectare landfill area in the inner bay that has been turned into a green park with the help of local citizens as part of the government's pollution remediation efforts. The area took on symbolic importance as the site of many *moyainaoshi* events, including ceremonies and concerts, and community activists installed stone statues there in an attempt to turn it into a spiritual place where Minamata victims can be remembered.

In addition to the memorial park, the government launched a program to "empower Minamata," increasing the number of outlets for community discussion and victim-outreach initiatives.[8] There have also been memorial services for those who died from the disease, the opening of the Municipal Minamata Disease Museum and two community centers, public education projects, neighborhood cleanups, exhibitions showcasing Minamata's safe and healthful fish products, and international conferences that emphasize the environmental lessons of Minamata. The government even established May 1 as an official day for remembering the victims of Minamata disease.[9]

In the mid-1990s the Kumamoto prefectural government declared Minamata a model environmental city and a lesson (both a cautionary tale and a model of recovery) for the nations of the world. In keeping with the declaration, the city has engaged in a number of projects including a local government program, under the guidance of the Japan International Cooperation Agency (JICA), to teach selected fellows from across Asia about Minamata's methods of environmental cleanup and preservation.[10] In addition, an environmental prize of 1 million yen (about US$8,500) was established for people or groups engaged in outstanding environmental conservation projects in Asia. In 2001, Minamata sponsored the Sixth International Conference on Mercury as a Global Pollutant, attended by five hundred scientists from forty countries.

The local government moved further toward the goal of becoming a model city when Minamata achieved ISO 14001 status in February 1999.[11] The city has adopted recycling as a collective environmental activity, and the municipal government proudly points to that project as one of the community's environmental success stories. The municipal government went to great lengths to run educational programs about the program, which involves a rather extensive garbage separation practice. People are asked to separate twenty-one types of recyclables, which they can then deposit at one of about three hundred waste stations operated by local citizens' groups. The city also has at least four recycling factories.[12] In operation since 1993, the waste collection sites have not only become local gathering places, they have become a showcase of local environmental policy for visitors from Japan and abroad.

If one of the goals of Moyainaoshi was to foster citizen involvement in environmental policy, then the recycling program stands out as an enduring accomplishment. The community healing campaign has also inspired some local citizens to come up with their own ideas about how to promote environment-friendly practices. In 1997, a consortium of sixteen women's groups came up with a proposal for environmental safety and health guidelines for consumers and shops (e.g., avoiding overwrapped foods and products that pose environmental hazards, reusing shopping bags).[13] While these developments are not tantamount to a wholesale absorption of environmental values on the part of local residents, they are signs at least of the beginning of a shift away from a focus on *kogai* toward a concept of the environment as a resource to be protected in its own right and not solely for economic or public health reasons.

As far as community healing is concerned, the campaign has produced mixed results, as we will see from some local residents' comments in the "Community Reactions" section, which follows. Although the campaign has been a top-down initiative, those charged with leading it involved themselves at the grassroots level. In their work on the campaign, Kamakura Takayuki, an official of the prefectural government, and Yoshimoto Tetsuro, a Minamata City official, went far beyond the administrative, bureaucratic tasks to which they were accustomed in their efforts to get people from various social groups to begin talking to one another. Kamakura went to various neighborhoods around the city, listened to diverse groups, and interposed himself—as a representative of the prefecture—as the mediator in their conflicts. He also sought to *identify* with the victims. As he explained in an interview, "Like the Minamata disease victims, I grew up eating the natural fruits of the sea, farm, and mountains." By stressing the commonalities between the disease victims and the larger population, Kamakura has sought to reincorporate the disease victims into Minamata society.

The victims and their families have experienced community ostracism since the outbreak of the disease five decades ago; today, many are still feeling the pain of too little compensation, offered too late. In 1995 the Kumamoto prefectural government set aside about $255 million in state subsidies and bonds to enable Chisso to compensate the worst-affected victims, while refusing to compensate any others. It was not until April 2001—twenty years after the victims filed suit in an Osaka Court—that a ruling was issued ordering the Chisso Corporationto pay $2.18 million in additional damages to the plaintiffs. It was not until the 1990s that the local government finally acknowledged the victims' need for an official apology. On May 1, 1994, the mayor of Minamata, in a memorial ceremony speech, apologized for the local government's part in the history of the disease, and called it a day to recreate *moyai*.[14]

Minamata: A "Company Castle" Town[15]

The extent of the social disruption caused by the pollution and disease in Minamata can only be understood when one considers the prominent role of the Chisso company in the life of the community. When Chisso opened the *Nippon Chisso Hiryo* (Japan Nitrogen Fertilizer) factory in Minamata in 1908 bringing outsiders to work for the company, fishing families from the region also moved to Minamata in the hopes that the new factory would bring an increased demand for fish. As a result, a social gap was created between people who had farmed the region for centuries or engaged in commerce (the longest-term residents were known as *jigoro*) and these migrant fishers (*nagare*), who occupied the lowest rung on the social ladder.

The factory, which produced chemical fertilizers, acetic acid, vinyl chloride, and plasticizers, grew and as it grew, Minamata grew, from a village to a town, and from a town to a city. Over the decades Chisso became the major employer and taxpayer in the region; at one point in the 1950s it provided 60 percent of all city tax revenues and dominated social and economic life.[16] This was not unusual in Japan, where large companies engaged their workers in practically feudal relationships when it came to things like loyalty and benefits.

Chisso's prosperity became the city's, as its economic and political clout in the region was paralleled by its social standing. Chisso employees came to be called *Chisso-sama* (*sama* is an honorific title for a social superior). The factory was commonly referred to simply as *Kaisha*, meaning "The Company." Many believed that Chisso had brought a *yoi kurashi* (a rich, modern life) to the small seaside town of Minamata. The people of Minamata thus began to understand themselves as sharing, on the community level, the destiny of the Chisso chemical plant.[17]

The plant's future was assured as long as it enjoyed pride of place in the government's postwar industrial development and modernization plans. The Minamata Chisso chemical complex was the only one in Japan that could produce a chemical used in a popular product and that otherwise had to be imported—polyvinyl chloride plastic. The production of acetaldehyde, which involved the mercury-based compound that was spilled into the bay, was a step in the manufacture of polyvinyl chloride.[18]

Between 1956, when Minamata disease was identified, and the early 1970s, Chisso Minamata employed almost 20 percent of the local workforce, occupied 68 percent of the city's land area, and consumed 93 percent of its water supply.[19] Employees from Minamata mostly worked in menial positions, while managerial jobs were largely filled by recruits from the main office in Tokyo. Even when the Chisso company began to downsize its Minamata plant in the early 1960s, the plant still had an overwhelming influence on the local economy and government, accounting for almost half of the city's tax revenues.[20] To understand the company's grip on local politics, it helps to know that beginning in 1950 and for almost twenty years, the Chisso plant manager also served as the city's mayor. According to the Kumamoto University sociologist Maruyama Sadami, "By identifying [the company] as 'Chisso of Minamata,' corporate leaders . . . encouraged the belief that the firm and the community shared a mutual destiny."[21]

That the national government impeded efforts to determine more specific causes of the Minamata disease, as described below, is unsurprising given its emphasis on national development goals. In 1956, Japan was just entering a period of rapid economic growth. The economy was growing by more than 10 percent per year, and as a chemical factory, Chisso stood to benefit from the boom. As Japan's top chemical company, Chisso's government protection, prestige, and political influence in the region were guaranteed throughout the 1950s and well into the 1960s.

Investigation, Denial, and Cover-Up

Understanding the community's need for *moyainaoshi* requires a look back at the history of Chisso and the government's response to the disease. Through the 1950s, while the crippling new disease struck local fishing families, the medical research community and their government (at all levels) were failing them.

In 1956 the local and national governments separately commissioned studies to investigate the disease. The Kumamoto University medical researchers initially tapped by the government of Kumamoto Prefecture to investigate *ki-byo* (strange-disease) determined in 1959 that organic mercury was the likely cause. The national government, however, had begun its own study, funded by the powerful Ministry of International Trade and Industry (MITI) and using professors from Tokyo-based universities, who put forward alternative claims about the cause that were widely publicized.[22] Largely because of the Tokyo universities' reputations as Japan's premier academic institutions, it took many years for the Kumamoto University findings to be accepted, a fact that confused the policy process and delayed moves toward a solution. MITI's minister at that time, Ikeda Hayato, who later became prime minister, even blamed the Kumamoto research group for causing social conflict by publishing their findings.

Even granting the Kumamoto group's theory that the disease was linked to heavy metal–contaminated fish, the absence of a scientifically proven link between the disease and its manufacturing processes allowed Chisso to deny responsibility, citing the support of the national government's MITI-funded study. The company even issued its own report, countering the Kumamoto group's finding.[23] The company was also involved in an outright cover-up. Hosokawa Hajime, the doctor at the community hospital affiliated with the Chisso plant who had first reported the disease, secretly continued to pursue the Kumamoto findings, despite orders from the company to come up with evidence to the contrary. When, in 1962, Hosokawa confirmed the Kumamoto theory, the Chisso company ordered that his finding be kept secret.

In 1963, Kumamoto University's researchers publicly released a report linking the disease, methyl mercury in fish, and pollutants from the Chisso plant that had settled into the sludge of the bay. It was only in 1968, after five more years and a great deal of community rancor and activism, that the company stopped its production of acetaldehyde, as it had come to rely on the production of other chemicals as its main source of revenue. And it was not until that same year, that the government finally publicly acknowledged Chisso's industrial waste as the cause of the disease.

The Fight for Compensation

> While the modern chemical industry was secretly depositing poisons, some of my own people died a sudden and anguishing death, and through ten and twenty-year periods, parents, children and then grandchildren were more slowly murdered. However, these people, caught in an unprecedented disaster, saw through those who sought to destroy them with the penetrating sight of unseeing eyes at death.

This is how Ishimure Michiko, a novelist and housewife who became an important witness and advocate for the victims, described the injustice of Minamata disease.[24] When the cause of the disease was still uncertain, victims were feared to be contagious (or genetically defective) and accused of harming the fishing trade; after the disease was confirmed to be linked to the Chisso chemical complex, it was feared that any threat to Chisso could destabilize the local economy, and thus the victims were shunned. Once the victims' compensation claims and payments were under way, a cloud of suspicion was cast over them; some were accused of posing as victims (labeled "fake patients") in order to collect money. These accusations and general community anger against the victims who chose to take the company to court for compensation grew in the 1960s, a decade when, for market reasons, the Chisso plant's fortunes were waning.[25]

In the early years, Minamata disease victims and their families quickly fell into poverty. If the family breadwinner contracted the disease, a source of income was lost while family medical expenses skyrocketed. As a result of this dual hardship, many victims simply went untreated and died. Victims' groups today bitterly recall not only those years but also the years after the Chisso Corporation was found to be at fault. The diagnosis and disease certification processes devised by the government to mete out compensation money were flawed from the start. The onus fell upon the victims and their families to prove (using narrow definitions of the disease, which manifests itself to varying degrees and with a wide array of possible symptoms) that their illnesses had resulted from mercury pollution in the bay. As a result, many victims over the years were left out of a succession of compensation arrangements despite multiple applications to be certified. This led to a series of bitter lawsuits brought by the victims against the company (and more recently, against the government), which have played out from the 1970s to the present.

Local fishing families played an early role in the activism by demanding compensation from the Chisso company in 1959. The disease was killing their business as well as them and their neighbors, as fears of eating fish spread. After a violent demonstration against the plant by four thousand fishermen and their families, the Kumamoto government stepped in to broker a deal. The company, while still denying responsibility, agreed to make a one-time payment of *mimaikin* (gift money) both to the fishermen and to disease victims. This payment came with the condition that there would be no more inquiry into the cause of the disease. The payment process proved inadequate, as the amounts were small, and in the case of the disease victims, the clinical requirements for qualifying excluded all but the most extreme cases.

Nine years after Minamata disease was named, the fight for compensation took a new turn. In 1965 a mysterious neurological disease appeared in another part of Japan —along the banks of the Agano River in Niigata Prefecture, in communities downstream from another chemical processing plant. The Showa Denko factory, which used the same acetaldehyde-based procedures as Chisso, was dumping untreated effluent into the river. The contaminated wastewater carried methyl mercury downstream to settlements along the river. The symptoms of the disease in Niigata bore a suspicious resemblance to Minamata disease.

As in Kumamoto, those affected were predominantly fishers. Showa Denko, however, did not have the paternalistic, economic, or political reach of the Chisso Corporation. The economic life along the river was varied, and not overwhelmingly defined and influenced by the chemical plant. This fact, as well as the time lag between these two cases, would result in a speedier course of action on the part of the Niigata disease victims.

As in Minamata, the industry and government attempted to obscure local research findings through manipulation and cover-up, but this time, they did not succeed as well. In Minamata, the Kumamoto University Medical Department, under pressure from supporters of the chemical industry, had kept to conservative, classic definitions of the disease, but in Niigata, careful epidemiological studies showed that methyl mercury poisoning could be manifested in a variety of neurological effects and symptoms.[26] By scientifically demonstrating the causal link between industrial practices and the disease, these findings aided the movement in Minamata to assign responsibility for the disease to Chisso. In 1968 the national government officially accepted that the Kumamoto and Niigata diseases were pollution-based diseases caused by the same substance, organic mercury.

Despite the differences in the two cases, the Niigata disease victims, like those in Minamata, felt enormous pressure to stay silent, not to "bring shame" on their families, neighbors, or towns, and not to hurt fish sales in the area. Victims who spoke out were subjected to slander and social discrimination, even threats and vandalism. Some lost their jobs. But the Niigata victims wasted little time in pressing their claims. In 1967, after Showa Denko was found to be the culprit, seventy-seven Niigata patients took their case to court. Early support from medical and legal professionals was critical in moving the quest for justice forward more quickly than in Minamata.[27] Yet thereafter Minamata activism began to build momentum. From the time the Niigata victims began their lawsuit, in 1967, the story of Minamata disease activists played out largely on two fronts: on the streets (as demonstrators took their calls for justice all the way to Chisso headquarters in Tokyo) and in courts of law.

After the government's declaration in 1968 that Chisso's manufacturing processes were to blame for the contamination, most victims signed an agreement to abide by the settlements to be reached by a government mediation committee, but a minority, distrustful of such processes because of the government's past behavior, chose to pursue their own legal action. In June 1969 twenty-nine families (112 people) sued the Chisso Corporation for damages in the Kumamoto District Court, the first lawsuit in the Minamata case.

Those who chose to sue Chisso faced huge pressures from the community to drop their legal claims. One fisherwoman, Sugimoto Eiko, said the lawsuit against Chisso worsened prejudice against disease victims and resulted in bullying by the company, Minamata residents, and even their own relatives. According to Sugimoto, Chisso used relatives of Minamata victims to pressure them to end the lawsuit. Her own relatives sided with Chisso despite strong evidence that the company was to blame.[28]

The plaintiffs in the Minamata lawsuit, with the aid of socially conscious lawyers (opposition political party members and supporters), pressed their case in the courts, however, and eventually prevailed. In 1973 Chisso was found professionally negligent in polluting Minamata Bay. This outcome opened the door for victims to pursue their claims based upon a legal judgment, rather than mediation with the company. The 1974 Pollution Health Damage Compensation Law entitled victims of pollution to compensation from the industrial polluter. That same year, the central government set up the Minamata Disease Certification Applicants' Council to deal with these claims. However, many applicants were stymied by the red tape and medical reports required to become certified by the council.[29]

The same 1974 law relieved the polluting industry of having to bear the burden of remediation and victim compensation on its own: The damage sustained by the polluter was to be relieved in part socially, through tax money. In this context, victims' claims for compensation were seen as a drain on and a possible threat to the rest of the community, increasing resentment against victims.

Because of Chisso's status as the single most important employer in Minamata, the citizens of Minamata shared with the government a concern over the company's financial stability. These concerns were not entirely unwarranted. Large payouts and remediation efforts (wastewater treatment and dredging polluted sediment from the bay) threatened the Chisso plant's operations. By 1978 the company was reportedly having trouble making payments to the victims, so the prefectural government stepped in, subsidizing the plant through bond issues, with the understanding that the money raised would be a partial loan. Under this government arrangement, Chisso received 18 billion yen ($86 million) in relief funds.[30]

The Minamata case has pushed Japan's pollution policies, albeit slowly, toward protecting people and punishing polluters. Today victims of pollution are certified based on the Pollution- Health Damage Compensation Law, which bases certification criteria on medical science. In the case of Minamata disease, medical science has a much broader definition for the disease than in the days immediately after its discovery.

Moreover, since 1992, the government has been conducting medical examinations of citizens in areas with high incidence of the disease, and has provided financial assistance for medical care to people exhibiting neurological signs of the disease.[31] It has also established the National Institute for Minamata Disease for the continuation of research into chemical and clinical aspects of the disease. Cases, though far fewer now, are still being reported, and people are still being certified as suffering from the effects of methyl mercury poisoning dating back to the 1950s and 1960s.

Collective Action and the Fight for Justice on the Streets

Despite pressures on victims to keep their problems to themselves, from about 1968 onward, more and more people were beginning to see that the victims' claims were about more than money. Local volunteer groups, Chisso labor union members, and researchers—inspired by Niigata victims—began to join together to support Minamata victims. Lawyers, doctors, leftists, university students, and journalists were drawn to the cause. The new Niigata cases brought media attention to the disease as something that endangered people beyond Minamata; they also widened the scope of activism, leading eventually (in 1971) to the largest sit-down strike in Japan's history of social activism. Minamata disease became the poster-case for *kogai* pollution issues. At that time, an American photographer, Eugene Smith, who supported the Minamata disease victim advocacy groups, captured world attention by publishing a photo essay documenting the horrors of the disease with images of children who had been deformed in their mothers' wombs.[32]

While the court cases moved slowly and the certification process frustrated victims and their families, some took their case to the streets. Sit-ins and imaginative demonstrations, some of which turned violent, also brought national and even world attention to the cause. In 1970, Minamata victims, dressed as Buddhist pilgrims, and a thousand supporters disrupted the Chisso annual shareholders meeting in Osaka. The following year a fisherman/activist named Kawamoto Teruo led other uncertified victims and their Tokyo supporters in a high-profile sit-in in front of Chisso headquarters in Tokyo. The sit-in, in support of the victims' demands for direct negotiations with the company president, lasted eighteen months and brought international attention to the struggle of the victims. Their efforts paid off. Although Kawamoto's group was unable to achieve direct negotiations, through negotiations mediated by the director of the Environment Agency, they were able to extract an agreement from Chisso to pay designated victims more than was provided by the court decision in March of 1973. Moreover, Chisso accepted responsibility and expressed regret for the first time. Frustrated that the Japanese government was not addressing the victims' plight, activists appealed directly to the world: Minamata disease victims attended an international meeting of nongovernmental organizations (NGOs) in Stockholm in 1972 in connection with the United Nations Conference on the Human Environment.[33]

Labor unions also played an active role in this social justice issue, but they were by no means united in their position on the Minamata victims. The Chisso conglomerate was large, and its unions, like the conglomerate itself, were geographically dispersed and diverse. While for historical reasons related to a wage freeze controversy one union, the first Chisso plant union, came out in support of the victims, other unions saw the victims as a threat to the company and opposed them, in a few cases with violence.[34] The relationship between the labor unions and the Minamata disease victims, who were supported by leftist students and other antigovernment activists, played out against the backdrop of the general political struggle in Japan between the Communist and Socialist Parties and more conservative supporters of the ruling Liberal Democratic Party.

The history of the movement was also shaped by a number of key individual actors. Harada Masazumi, a doctor on the faculty of medicine at Kumamoto University, began to treat the first patients with Minamata disease–related birth defects in the early 1960s. Disturbed by these defects, which often included cerebral infantile paralysis,[35] he began speaking out publicly, an unusual step for a medical professional at that time. Similarly moved by a sense of professional duty to address social injustice, Togashi Sadao of the Kumamoto University law faculty began to offer victims free legal advice. Journalists such as Takamine Takeshi brought the stories of the victims to a larger public, emphasizing the perspective of fishers, the victims whose liveli-hoods were most closely tied to the natural world.

Ui Jun, a young scientist in the 1960s, inspired by the early findings of the Kumamoto researchers, went to Minamata to help compile chemical evidence of the connection between Minamata disease, mercury poisoning in the bay, and effluent from the Chisso plant.[36] Most accounts, including this brief one, of Chisso's misdeeds in Minamata owe a debt to Ui Jun's chronicling of the scientific and political aspects of the story.

Some leading activists, a few of whom we hear from them directly below, got drawn into the case through their personal involvement with the disease. That was the case of Ogata Masato, who became a leading spokesman. Ogata, the son of a prosper-ous fisherman who had died of Minamata disease in 1959, became involved in activ-ism through his efforts to gain certification in 1974, and he soon began to help uncertified victims gain certified status as chairman of the Minamata Disease Victims Certification Association. He is credited with first applying the boating phrase *moyau* (which refers to two boats that link up with one another at sea) to the Minamata reconciliation effort.

Like Ogata, Kawamoto Teruo, whose father had also died of the disease, was drawn into activism by the injustice of the certification process. He devoted himself to mak-ing the company accountable to victims. His dramatic staging of large public victims' demonstrations in Tokyo brought the movement headlines.

Ishimure Michiko, a poet who had worked on behalf of the victims, published in 1969 a book entitled *Paradise of the Bitter Sea* [Kugai Jyodo],[37] which raised aware-ness of Minamata disease throughout Japan. Though not herself a victim, as a native of Minamata, Ishimure knew well the life and philosophy of the fishing community. She organized the first victim support organization in 1968 and helped to found a second organization in 1975, the nonprofit advocacy group Soshisha, whose goal was to end the victims' isolation.[38]

Other advocates settled in Minamata and joined Soshisha, which helped mobilize victims during lawsuits and foster community awareness of the disease. Its members were derided as "newcomers," and some locals warned that they were "violent stu-dents," but some members stayed in Minamata for ten or twenty years, eventually gaining the trust of the local residents.[39] Soshisha still actively supports disease vic-tims and is committed to "clarifying the truth and meaning of the disease" by collect-ing and publicizing oral histories, operating the original Minamata Disease Museum, with exhibits that document the history of Minamata fishers lives, the Chisso Corpo-ration, and Minamata disease, and educating visitors (especially school children from all over Japan) about Minamata disease.

Healing the Bay: The Environmental Story

The story of Minamata disease and its impact on people, public health, and the poli-tics of activism has long overshadowed the underlying story of ecological damage to the sea and its impact on the fishing industry and fishing community life. In this section we look at efforts to clean the bay and to restore it for fishing.

As we have noted, the fishing community was doubly hard hit by the water contamination. Disease victims were preponderantly from fishing families, which also faced devastating commercial losses due to the pollution. Today the fishing industry and families remain, but their numbers are reduced from the days before the disease emerged, when roughly two hundred thousand people along the coast made their living from the Shiranui Sea.[40]

Although the Kumamoto prefectural government did not take any effective steps to regenerate the fishing industry, the national government enacted industrial pollution controls designed to prevent such massive mercury contamination of sea life from happening again. According to the Ministry of the Environment Web site,

> the case of Minamata disease in Japan makes it clear that activities which give priority to economic goals but lack proper attention to the environment cause irreparable damage and bring undesirable results even from an economic point of view . . . since so many measures, huge costs, and a long time period are required to repair these damages.[41]

One of the first tasks of the Japan Environmental Agency, formed in 1971 and later upgraded to the Ministry of the Environment,[42] was to clean up Minamata Bay. The agency set a temporary safety standard to guide remediation efforts whereby any sediment exceeding 25 parts per million (ppm) of contaminant had to be dredged. Nets dividing the bay and sea were put in place in 1974 to contain contaminated fish and keep other fish out of the bay while contaminated sludge was being removed, and fishing cooperatives were recruited to help catch and isolate the contaminated fish. Local residents knew that fish were getting through anyway, either through the nets themselves or through areas in the bay that remained open for the movement of ships.

The sediment-dredging project was controversial among residents. On the one hand, it would help to regenerate the economy (in addition to the promised, long-term impact of the cleanup, the project itself could provide jobs and income at a time when the Chisso Corporation was increasingly cash-strapped); on the other, it could worsen fish contamination by stirring up mercury from the sea floor. With this opposition in mind, Kumamoto prefecture, in cooperation with the university, formed a committee to determine the safety of the dredging project. An opposition group of Minamata disease victims and local citizens sought a legal injunction against the plan, but they lost in court, and from 1977 to 1989 the government dredged and reclaimed 1.5 cubic meters of the bay floor at a cost of 48.5 billion yen ($346 million in 1989 dollars) to the national and prefectural governments and to the Chisso Corporation.

It was only in 1997, more than forty years after the disease first appeared, that the fish and shellfish in Minamata Bay were declared officially safe for eating.[43] This was a necessary step in the economic recovery of the region, for the area's reputation for tainted fish not only paralyzed commercial fishing, it also thwarted the development of many shore-related businesses, including tourism. Soon after the bay's fish were deemed safe for eating, fishing reopened in the bay for the first time in twenty-four years.

Many residents and fishers remained skeptical, however, about the safety of eating fish from the bay; at the time of this writing they had yet to resume fishing—especially for large fish—aware of the possibility of the bioaccumulation of mercury. The official government position, however, remained that the dredging project had been an unqualified success. In a speech at the 2002 Johannesburg Summit for Sustainable Development in which he explained Japan's experience with industrial pollution at Minamata, former Prime Minister Hashimoto Ryutaro claimed that the *average* concentration of mercury in the bottom sediment was 4.65 ppm, well below the minimum standard adopted by the government.[44] However, a healthy skepticism of government claims continued to exist in Minamata, as evidenced by the comments from people in the community featured below.

Community Reactions

In this section we look at how people's views about the community, government, and the environment have been shaped by the mercury poisoning incident and by the policy effort to heal the social and environmental wounds. We draw upon our own interviews as well as published sources. The diversity of views expressed in this section suggests that while the government has made admirable efforts at environmental cleanup and healing, there remain political and social issues that must be resolved before the community can embrace its environmental goals.

Views on the Role of the Chisso Corporation

Minamata residents today remain conflicted about the role of the Chisso Corporation in the environmental disaster. Some hold bitterly to the sense of injustice they and their community suffered at the hands of the powerful company. Others, while they agree that the company's actions were disastrous, take a more nuanced view about the company's guilt, reasoning that Chisso's misconduct dates back to a time when most Japanese people were preoccupied with economic development and were largely ignorant of the effects of mercury pollution. Little of the conversation about Chisso relates to its treatment of the environment and the ethical implications thereof; true to the Japanese casting of the Minimata incident as one of *kogai*, the discourse is mainly about Chisso's relationship to individuals and to the community. Here, former employees, disease victims, and activists reflect back upon the Chisso company's role in Minamata disease, its behavior during the years that followed, and the company's place today in the community.

Ogata, the prominent fisher and activist, described to us the warlike atmosphere between the company and the fishing community. He recalled first hearing about Chisso at age six, upon his father's death from the disease:

> The whole of Chisso—the president, the factory managers, and the regular workers—became the enemy, because there wasn't any way to specify blame. Of course the opposite was also true: From Chisso's perspective all fishermen—the fishing community—were victims, and from the company's profit-making point of view, all victims are their enemy. . . . If this happened in the *yakuza* [gangster] world, taking revenge would have been easier since the two parties would only need to kill off a few, but with Chisso, you're up against a whole organization, "the Chisso *gumi*" [gang], so it's nearly impossible to identify an enemy.[45]

Those working for the chemical complex at the time were able to see both good and bad sides of the company. As Yamashita Kikuko, a former Chisso employee and activist, commented:

> I think some of my bosses were pretty good people, and they did do some good things. But these types of people were not rewarded in their careers. Only those that were good at getting on in the world advanced in their careers. Many managers left Chisso. Chisso used to have a strong group of Tokyo University graduates, but they left . . . because [Chisso] lacked human compassion.

Yamashita saw a connection between the way Chisso treated its employees inside the company and how it treated the local community. The Fuji Film factory decided in 1934 to build a water treatment facility at its plant near the famous Mount Fuji on the principle that the company should return to society water of the same quality as that which it used. When asked whether Chisso would do something similar, she replied:

> Chisso doesn't think like that. . . . If they had a conscience, they wouldn't have caused Minamata disease. . . . Even when they expanded to Korea, it is said that they went in telling managers to not think about the laborers as human beings, but as cows. That way of thinking continues to this day. . . . The founder of Chisso, Noguchi, used to emphasize the importance of "having a human heart," but this seems to have been lost.[46]

Despite this jaundiced view of Chisso's corporate culture, which is now fairly prevalent, many people do not want the next generation to suffer from the same, bitter divide between community and company. Kamakura Takayuki, the prefectural official spearheading the government's Moyainaoishi Campaign, remarked that Chisso employees continue to face recriminations from society. "It is sad and unfair for those young employees in Chisso who are still treated as if they were to blame for what the company did in the past," he said.

There is an ironic sense, too, that, although the company long ago lost its position as a Japanese industrial powerhouse, its continued presence in Minamata is in the best interest of the victims and serves an important function for the community. As Kamakura put it:

> Chisso hasn't filed for bankruptcy because, although it doesn't have money, Kumamoto prefecture borrowed money from a bank to lend it to Chisso so that it can pay for compensation and damages. If we destroy Chisso, thousands of certified Minamata patients and others would suffer more.

Yet many citizens feel that the company, because it is now so embedded in the community and vital to the local economy and because it has received financial protection from the government, has managed to escape the full consequences of its actions. Ogata explained how the company came to be in such a unique position:

> Around fifteen years ago, Chisso's domestic market share in liquid crystal [screens for TVs] was around 60 to 70 percent. It was impossible to say to anyone that "I don't have any memory of being helped by Chisso," especially when so much of what we consume, including camera film, cassette tapes, televisions, and videotapes come from Chisso. Really, their market share is impressive, and their technical skills are remarkable, even to this day. That's one of the reasons why [the government] makes sure Chisso doesn't go bankrupt.
>
> Now we have all become Chisso. . . . For over twenty years now, Chisso has not been able to unilaterally manage its strategic planning, facility investment decisions, and act in other ways that normal independent companies do. It has to get approval from the Kumamoto prefectural government, the Japan Environment Agency, the Ministry of Finance, and so on. Without this approval, Chisso's hands are tied. This is because they owe money to the government, which they are not able to repay. Meanwhile debts are ballooning, while they keep borrowing. . . . It's now getting clearer that they will take all the money from the government's general expense account. . . . Just like "Japan, Inc.," the idea of "All Chisso" is outrageous because just like the national debt, no one is taking responsibility.

The journalist Takamine Takeshi[47] expressed concern about what he called Chisso's doctrine of innocence (*seizensetsu*).

> I heard [the view] from Chisso's general manager that even to this day Chisso has not done anything wrong. By this he means that Chisso expressed sympathy through monetary contracts [*mimaikin*] even when the causes of the disease were unknown. After they found what was causing the disease, they compensated the victims. It could not have been prevented because Chisso didn't know. Chisso was always innocent. This view of Chisso's innocence is prevalent in the company and may end up leading the company to repeat its actions.

Despite the history of antipathy between the company and the victims, and the persistence of anti-Chisso sentiments, particularly among the older generation, efforts to heal have sometimes included representatives from the Chisso Corporation. According to Kamakura:

> There was a memorial ceremony . . . under the administration of Mayor Okada. . . . Because the event was held for everybody who suffered from the Minamata disease, Chisso also got involved. Chisso wanted to be recognized as a wonderful company, despite its problematic past.[48]

Chisso's community involvement may be another sign that Minamata's bipolar dynamic of the powerless, injured fisher-victims pitted against the powerful polluter, Chisso, over financial compensation has begun to shift. Restoring the city's social harmony is a long-term project, and viewing all the parties as victims as well as agents in this incident—in terms of the excesses of industry, the discrimination against those who dared to speak out, the failure to value the environment for its own sake—may be a necessary step in the healing process. Some victims of the disease, having suffered enough already, don't choose to put more energy toward blaming Chisso. Ogata Masato's niece Hitomi, who has congenital Minamata disease, "is getting by," said Ogata, "although her limbs are unsteady. 'Don't you hate Chisso?' I asked, 'No,' she answered. 'Because I'd rather focus on how I'm going to live in the future than on what happened in the past.'"[49]

Many Minamatans share this wish to move on. Ogata himself, once one of the most fervent anti-Chisso activists, eventually came to feel that the substitution of monetary compensation for responsibility had become a greedy game, no more morally supportable than the company's behavior. Ultimately, despite his role as a pioneer in the advocacy efforts on behalf of the victims, he withdrew from the victims' lawsuit. As he explained:

> I could no longer bear to be a part of it. . . . The idea of assuming responsibility is an illusion. Our legal proceedings are premised on this illusion. . . . It is not the responsibility of a particular person in a particular time and place but a deeper, more abstract responsibility, borne by the human race.[50]

Views on Discrimination Against Victims

For victims of Minamata disease memories of discrimination evoke perhaps even more bitterness than the Chisso company's misconduct. Sugimoto Eiko, a disease victim and activist whose mother succumbed to the disease in 1958, recalled how her family was shunned by neighbors. Her father had been a local fishery boss; after her mother fell ill, his employees left, and people in the village cut the family's nets and used their boats without permission. "My most painful memory," she said, "is the way we were treated by others in the hamlet."[51] As we have pointed out, the diversion of tax money to Chisso to help it make its compensation payments only increased the stigma Minamata society placed on the afflicted. To this day, Minamata victims are referred to in Japanese as "patients" (kanja), reflecting a persistent cultural predilection to avoid attributing the cause to a particular perpetrator.

The casting of fisher-victims as "other" was promoted by the cultural gulf between the traditional fishing people and villages, on one hand, and the middle class residents of the newly urbanizing town of Minamata, the educated employees of Chisso, and the medical and legal communities, on the other. This cultural and educational gulf was poignantly on display at the compensation trials. Kumamoto University professor Togashi provided legal support to the victims during the first Minamata trial (1969–73) and in successive lawsuits. He said of their behavior at the trial, "the disease victims laughed in a loud voice, jeered and heckled others, and so forth; it often seemed utterly like a theater to them. . . . It seems that, at times, the trial took on a kind of [religious] festival atmosphere to the victims."[52]

As Mr. Kanasashi Junpei, the leader of one of the citizens' movements, explained, "During the Minamata trial, I had the feeling that the people were not living in a democratic modern society. They didn't seem to grasp the idea and framework behind legal proceedings. . . . Even after the preliminary hearing, Minamata people couldn't really comprehend this."[53]

From the victims' perspective, the coldly formal courtroom context underscored the bias against them. A journalist-turned-activist, Mishima Akio, described how Ishimure Michiko, a prominent victims' advocate, remembers one important trial in Kumamoto City in 1973:

> To Michiko, the trial had the brittle artificiality of a second-rate drama: the absurdity of ordering a woman out of the courtroom when the child she was holding, a congenital victim of Minamata disease, uttered involuntary cries; the courtroom histrionics, such as the anachronistic custom of prohibiting note taking; the pompous posturing of the defendants and their lawyers. There was something about the trial that got on the patients' nerves.[54]

Tsuchimoto Noriaki, a well-known filmmaker who filmed Minamata in the 1970s, described the fears underlying the early phase of discrimination against the victims:

> What the people in the fishing villages without information were most worried about was whether or not . . . the disease was contagious or hereditary. It was a big problem back then when people would say, "Don't marry into a family with Minamata disease, and don't have them marry into your family." Moreover, those with fetal Minamata were considered to have a malignant hereditary disease, and they were discriminated against strongly.[55]

Discrimination associated with the disease remains an issue with which the victims must contend even today. Kamakura, the prefectural official who has led the Moyainaoshi Campaign, said he sees persistent discrimination as the fundamental challenge that Minamata faces and the stumbling block to the success of *moyainaoshi*:

> Rich locals [gossip] among themselves that the Minamata disease victims who received compensation are [doing well] because now they can just spend all their time playing pachinko. . . . I asked these people what they mean when they say such things. . . . [The victims] are permanently disabled. They play pachinko because there is no joy in living; they cannot experience happiness through work, love, mobility, etc. . . . In my view it's because of such vulgar comments and meanness that the Minamata community remains divided and unhealed.

Kamakura's comments point to several aspects of the discrimination. In large part, it has been and continues to be class-based. The fishing community was already considered to be part of a lower social class by townspeople engaged in other occupations, particularly employees of Chisso. The disease outbreak widened this class divide. Kamakura's remarks also suggest that there is lingering suspicion about the victims, particularly the suspicion that many of them are really "fake victims." Finally, the remarks suggest some degree of envy of those surviving victims who are compensated and do not work—their moderate or severe disabilities notwithstanding. These residual feelings continue to impede the Moyainaoshi Campaign, which is designed in part to heal rifts between the victims and others in the community.

Views on the Role of the Academic, Medical, and Professional Communities

The actions of the local medical and academic communities—during the early phase of the poisoning epidemic, when they were pressured by the Chisso Corporation to support its position; and later, when some hindered the disease victims' attempts to obtain diagnoses and certification—appear to many in the city to be more self-protective than professionally responsible. The ethical implications of this behavior are still felt and discussed.

Harada Masazumi, the doctor who spoke out on behalf of victims in the 1960s and who has become a renowned expert and writer on Minamata disease, told us in 2000:

> The medical community is in disarray. It is still running away from the issue, and for this it should be blamed. . . . Although the disease was a social issue, the medical community would only speak about it in medical terms . . . It was stupidly confined to a study of symptoms. It was disastrous. People from the medical community molded the Minamata issue like a dumpling, but the victims' movement broke this. From a professional perspective, it seems almost insolent and improper for nonexperts to venture into a specialist's territory. But if they hadn't, the Minamata issue would not have been able to emerge.

By contrast, according to Togashi, the Kumamoto law school professor, the law school encourages and nurtures discussion of the Minamata disease. He reports that he is free to do research on the topic, and he explains that his own involvement in Minamata disease cases was born of the great sorrow he felt when he saw child victims of the disease. The law profession's history of involvement on behalf of the victims during the lawsuit meant that lawyers were closely exposed to the social justice issues created by the disease.

Kamakura, the prefectural official leading the Moyainaoshi Campaign, noted that the government (like the medical community) was guilty of narrow-minded and socially neglectful behavior. For him, a Moyainaoshi Campaign that engaged directly with the Minamata victims was the only solution. He argued that

> the problem with the way Minamata was handled is that the local government was operating only from medical and legal perspectives. . . . But the problems are social, psychological, and macroeconomic, and their solutions need to be grounded in these understandings. . . . It was irresponsible for the government to ignore the pain of the Minamata people. . . . In the beginning [those involved in developing the Moyainaoshi Campaign] were in conflict with the pollution division that dealt with the certification and registration of disease victims. . . . But I told them that they had been working for forty years and had failed to solve this problem and so now it was time for them to be quiet and watch us do our work.

When Yoshimoto Tetsuro, a Minamata city official, learned that a number of medical, legal, and sociological investigations had been conducted by outside researchers who had never shared their results with Minamata, he was also struck by the distant and disengaged attitude of the research community. In response, in the early 1990s he began a movement, which came to be called *Jimotogaku*, or "Community Self-Study," whereby Minamata residents conduct their own research on their natural surroundings as well as their local history. As he explained:

> We have started to make study about our mountain, rivers, and local plants and wildlife by ourselves. . . . We have learned that the name "Minamata" means "water network," that our land of Minamata had once been rich with the charm of mountains, rivers, and seas, with the vitality of many living creatures, and that our life has been historically and ecologically maintained by the profound and beautiful whole of our environment.[56]

At the same time, Yoshimoto also came to see that Japanese tend to place high value on that which is from "outside," and to import ideas about development, particularly from entities with a wide reach, like the national government and major Japanese companies. In its call to people to look within their own locales for value and meaning, his Jimotogaku movement, which has now spread throughout Japan, is a counterweight to that tendency.[57]

Views of the Moyainaoshi Campaign and Environmental Cleanup

The planners of the Moyainaoshi Campaign came to believe that in Minamata social healing and progressive environmental policies must go hand in hand. The policy rested on the idea that a society still divided cannot cooperate on the project of restoring and protecting the environment and revitalizing the economy. As we have seen, it is difficult to forget, even decades later, the deaths and the wrongs committed by industry and facilitated by the government. At the same time, most people wished to move beyond this case of *kogai* and Minamata's infamy. Local views about the campaign were mixed. Many people supported the ostensible purpose and general goals, and applauded the government. The fishing cooperatives in particular took up the rhetoric of community restoration, supporting all efforts to neutralize the social stigma against fishing since the mercury contamination. Others resented the campaign's top-down nature or thought it was belated and somewhat superficial.

Despite its top-down origins, Kamakura, the Kumamoto government official who helped to initiate and coordinate the campaign, made great efforts to take this campaign to the people. To work successfully in the campaign, he said:

> You have to dress and eat like [ordinary citizens]. . . . You cannot just talk in pretty academic words and pretend you know everything because this is a real human problem that the residents are facing. When people recognize [that you feel a] moral obligation [to them], residents/victims will open up and talk honestly. An eighty-year-old man may say, for example, that he knew about Minamata, but he didn't feel able to come forth and say what he felt about it when he knew his grandchildren were working at Chisso; honesty comes out in the end when you're acting morally.

Kamakura was proud of his accomplishments with the Moyainaoshi Campaign and feels that it is working. "People are coming to value the protection of the environment as part of city-building," he explained. "It is still a work-in-progress, but it seems that people are shifting from being ashamed of the Minamata disease to building a supportive neighborhood."

A typical view of the campaign was expressed by a young woman working at a volunteer *moyainaoshi* center, who said, "Somehow or other, the government is doing its utmost, and what we are doing now has gradually become second nature."[58]

Few local residents expressed doubts about the campaign. As the sociologist Maruyama explained, "Feelings run deep for most residents, and in many cases the feelings remained buried. So on the surface, people endorse Minamata's effort to revitalize the environment. Given how strong the rhetoric of the value of the environment is, it is impossible to voice opposition."

Our research team had difficulty interviewing people who opposed the Moyainaoshi Campaign; those citizens seemed to fear having their views publicized and facing possible further ostracism. Yet some did forthrightly express their misgivings about the campaign. One source of bad feelings that surfaced surrounds the government's decision to go ahead with its plan to build a landfill over the most contaminated part of the floor of the bay despite local opposition. In 1977, Mishima Akio, argued that the landfill in the bay added a permanent element to the injury to the bay environment, which had once been a "treasure-trove of fish":

> The sea will probably never revert to its former pristine condition. In fact, the national government, the prefectural government, and Chisso have already spent 20 billion yen [$74 million in 1977 dollars] to dredge the bay and fill it in. The voices of happy children that once echoed along its shores have long since fallen silent. An evil spirit now resides in what was once a kind and gentle sea. A national policy of prosperity at any cost has allowed a single corporation to damage the environment irreversibly. The beautiful Shiranui Sea has been sacrificed to the pursuit of profit.[59]

Ogata Masato described why he felt the government's having filled in the bay should be considered a continuation, rather than a reparation, of the environmental damage in Minamata:

> The reclaimed land in Minamata Bay illustrates the laws of karma. It demonstrates more clearly than any other place I've seen the relationship between cause and effect. Looking at the original topography of this region, we see first the ocean, then the tidelands. Hills lead into the mountains. Mountain forests are the source of our fresh water, which flows back down to the seas. Land and ocean are intimately connected. Here at the reclaimed land these natural links have been severed by concrete barriers and terraces. The reclaimed land is highly symbolic. It reminds us that Minamata disease represents the destruction of natural cycles.

Others argued that the government had no choice but to fill the bay. As Professor Maruyama said, they did it "to put closure on the problem and move forward. If they still had a polluted Minamata Bay to deal with, that would not have been possible; by cleaning and making landfills, they were able to do their job better."

Yet some still recalled with skepticism the government's approach to measuring the safety of the bay that underlay the dredging plans. Takamine Takeshi, the journalist who followed the case beginning in the 1970s, remembered:

> The 25 ppm [safety level] was arrived at based on the amount of money Chisso Corporation had available to pay for remediation measures. After the monitoring of the bottom mercury level and deciding which areas needed remediation, the Kumamoto prefecture government decided [on the] 25 ppm level, and the bottom mercury of these areas was dredged, and the sludge was dumped in the inner, most-polluted area of the bay. Finally, 58 hectares of reclaimed land was created in 1990. This 25 ppm was not scientifically decided.[60]

It is not surprising, perhaps, in light of widespread misgivings about past government policies regarding the environment that some people were reluctant to embrace enthusiastically a government-led campaign to get people to commune with their neighbors, reach out to disease victims, and get involved in environmental cleanup and protection. Others resisted the campaign simply because it forced people to confront a traumatic past they would like to wish away.

When we surveyed Minamata citizens in 1999 to gauge their attitudes toward the Moyainaoshi Campaign,[61] 70 percent evaluated it as "a step in the right direction" (toward healing the city), yet almost 40 percent still felt ashamed of the city's association with Minamata disease. In interviews they made such comments as, "I'm tired of the disease problem" and "It's [draining] to participate in events connected with Minamata disease." This kind of fatigue was evident even at the start of the campaign. Upon first hearing about the campaign, citizens said they would prefer to spend the government money on a "theme park" or "something enjoyable."

Takamine Takeshi confirmed the ongoing public lassitude toward the disease when he explained that although his newspaper, *Kumamoto Nichinichi*, continued to report on Minamata disease "widely" and "independently from the government," "the public is not interested and it's not a major political issue."

For advocates of the surviving victims, the government's role was more at issue than the actual goals and activities of the campaign. Kanasashi Junpei, the citizens' movement leader, is resentful that the government usurped control over the Moyainaoshi Campaign, pointing out that the idea, which originated with the fisher-victim activist Ogata, was co-opted by Yoshimoto Tetsuro, a Minamata city official and campaign planner. Kanasashi told us:

> Moyainaoshi should not have been an initiative of the top; it should have come from below. . . . Now the government is proudly projecting the image that they are building an "environmental city." But the wind that is blowing at the top is different from that of the bottom. It's completely different!

We encountered this view again with respect to the government's recycling initiative. Although Minamata citizens widely participated in recycling, as do people in many other parts of Japan, some felt their participation is not a genuine reflection of the citizens' newfound environmental values. Yamashita Yoshihiro, husband of Kikuko, whom we heard from above, and also a former Chisso employee and labor leader, said, "I think the idea is wonderful, but it seems residents are just doing it because the government says so. It's not a self-sustaining movement backed by residents, and it doesn't reflect what they want."[62]

He admitted that the campaign had good intentions but added that the government's top-down approach and the lack of a grassroots mandate posed a problem for a town torn by years of anti-industry and antigovernment activism. He went on to complain about the discriminatory nature of the Moyainaoshi Campaign in practice:

> Prior to the establishment of the [*moyainaoshi* community center], the administration listened to the residents; however, once it was set up, they acted completely differently. We [victims group members and advocates] held a meeting of those who were born of mothers with Minamata disease. They [the municipal government officials] built a coffee shop, and I proposed that they make it into a place where disabled people could work. Unilaterally and without justification, they prevented the disabled people from working there. Instead, they brought in regular, healthy people to work and just made it look like disabled people were working there. Later, at a meeting, I told the officials that we had been deceived. While I think these initiatives are needed, if it's going to be a superficial *moyainaoshi*, it may be better not to have one.

This last observation may be another example of how the victims and the government continue to approach the history and issues surrounding Minamata disease from different perspectives and with different values, almost as if they were speaking a different language.

Hatano Hideto, an active citizen supporter and a self-employed carpenter who for more than twenty years fought on behalf of uncertified disease victims in the Niigata-Minamata case, likened the underlying value differences between the disease victims and industry and government officials to "the difference between the *shakkan* system and the metric system." *Shakkan* is the centuries old Japanese system of weights and measures, based upon the size of various parts of the human body. (For example, one *shaku* is the distance between the elbow and end of the hand; one *hiro* is the length of both hands when fully spread out.) Certain values and ideas are lost with the adoption of new, modern systems; the language of economic and technological development does not have the terms to convey traditional ideas and perceptions, nor, for that matter, do the imported languages of environmentalism and law.[63] Indeed, one of the differences between the government's and the residents' approaches, Kanasashi explained, is that Minamata residents are trying to cope with the emotional scars of the disease, so the topic of the environment seems to them beside the point:

> Right now, the emotional problems people are facing have been erased from the debate, and there seems to be no way to bring them in. . . . Because they believe that Minamata disease is a problem of the heart . . . if you shift to the subject of the environment, these people will not immediately get it.

Kanasashi went on, however, to frame the "problem of the heart" in terms of financial worries:

> The reason why the wind that is blowing at the top is different from that at the bottom is that the most serious issues that the citizens are facing are economic concerns. Minamatans are very anxious about the economy. The garbage separation-collection effort has been driven under the guise of protecting the environment, but in reality the initiative is built around the notion that you can create monetary value from garbage. . . . The city is telling people to "build an environmental city," but when they mobilize residents, they are doing so by giving monetary incentives. There's an economic logic driving this. And this will leave residents without any sense of environmental awareness.

Kanasashi added that the process needs to be driven by the people, saying, "I told one of the city's planning officers that I don't think it is right for the city to ask the people to make reparations for Minamata disease. It should be a new era . . . a time in which those who wish to do something can do something. If people are not given the opportunity to decide for themselves what they want [rather than being told what to do], the town will never change!"

Kanasashi said he believed that meaningful change would come only when residents begin to get past the injury to humans and recognize the Minamata incident as relating more broadly to the environmental order:

> Minamata disease should not be treated as a "pollution problem" *(kogai)* but as an environmental problem *(kankyo mondai)* because environmental problems are built on a relationship between nature and humans, whereas *kogai* are principally about the relationships between people—about the betrayal of people by other people.

The Minamata official, Yoshimoto Tetsuro, commented to us on the tendency for the word "environment" to be used principally by government officers and scientists "who are detached from actual contact with land and water," and much less so by average Minamatans. Yet while they may not have often used the term "environment," as people who live and work closely with the land and the sea, Minamatans always had an intuitive respect for nature's power and gifts. The Minamata incident appeared to have enlarged their appreciation for the delicate balance of nature, and for man's critical role in protecting it. At the time of our field study there were signs that farmers and others who work with the land in the area were beginning to develop environmentally conscious ways of cultivation. Similarly, the victims' movement leader Sugimoto Eiko, who after the nets were lifted from the bay in 1997, began to catch sardines again and to sell them, was very careful not to use any chemical additives to process them. As she explained, "Since I was poisoned by the Chisso, I do not want to poison people with my products."[64] In this context one can see that while activities such as the garbage-recycling project have an economic impetus, by engaging citizens in environmental protection activities, such policies can also serve to build environmental awareness.

The Name Minamata Disease and Minamata's World Reputation

As with Benxi, the smoggy Chinese city discussed in Chapter 1 of this book, the light of world attention shone upon Minamata for negative reasons. As our survey indicates, Minamata residents are tired of being known for their tragedy and its ugly aftermath. The municipal government, as well as the local tourist industry, wants to escape the stigma of the disease and has pushed, so far unsuccessfully, to change the name of the disease that so many locals suffered from "Minamata disease" to "organic mercury disease."

Surprisingly, Kamakura, the government Moyainaoshi Campaign leader, sees in the notoriety brought to Minamata by having a disease named after it both an economic and public relations benefit to the campaign. In response to those in the tourist industry and other businesses who criticize the naming of the disease and the resource center after the city, he remarked:

> We can't change the name of Minamata disease, but we can make the city more appealing by showing how we supported each other and [made a lot of progress]. This will improve the reputation of the city because others will look at us and be impressed by how much [Minamata] has changed. . . . The economic pie is only so big. . . . I want to convince Minamata residents that they should cooperate rather than fight, and reap gains from tourism that helps increase the size of the pie.

Mayor Yoshii Masazumi, Minamata's mayor from 1994 to 2002, also saw some value in Minamata's experience:

> The name Minamata is known worldwide. However, its image is a dark one. . . . We must value the fact that our name is well known and change the image of Minamata. I believe that it is important for Minamata's citizens to change—change minuses to pluses. This means that because we are a city that suffered from environmental experiences, we must turn this picture around and become a city that takes the best care of the environment in all of the world.[65]

Minamata residents still seem to disagree over whether to embrace the negative experience or simply to bury it (like the mercury-contaminated sediment in the bay). Kojima Toshiro, who was formerly in charge of Minamata disease control at the Ministry of Environment, takes the former view. "Some people say 'let bygones be bygones,'" he observed, "but Minamata disease must not be a bygone; it must not be forgotten. Minamata's negative legacy (Minamata disease) and positive legacy (the sea, mountains, rivers, people) are both part of Minamata's self worth."[66]

These ideas were repeated in the form of an apology to the victims by the Environment Minister Koike Yuriko on October 15, 2004, following a Supreme Court ruling ordering the Japanese government to pay the victims $703,000 in damages. "We assure you that this horrific incident won't ever be repeated," Koike said. "The government will teach the lessons learned here for generations to come."[67]

Minamata victims and victims' advocates have also expressed the desire to tell their story so that a similar catastrophe will never happen again anywhere not only in Japan but also in the world. In this way, they may be able to redeem their tragic experience and make it valuable to the world. The Minamata Disease Municipal Museum, which educates visitors about the disease and its cause, is one indication of their dedication to the task. Becoming a model environmental city is another. Public apathy and the scars of the social rift that accompanied the disease are but two of the obstacles that remain in the path of a united effort to promote environmentalism by government officials, industry leaders, and other residents from all walks of life.[68]

Water Wars: Power and Preservation at Lake Biwa and the Nagara River

Introduction

While our case study of Minamata *kogai* describes the impact of industrial pollution and the public policy response to it on the way people think about their environment and their community in one locale of Japan, the case studies of Lake Biwa and the Nagara River Dam describe conflicts over water resources and their protection in a changing society. By the time these conflicts were aired in public forums and tried in courts of law, the infamous case of Minamata disease had influenced, to an appreciable extent, Japanese methods of framing and advancing environmental concerns. Minamata had, in a sense, laid the groundwork for grassroots environmental activities in Japan, having set a precedent for collective lawsuits against polluters and raised awareness about the importance of greater public participation in policy affecting local environments. The two water cases presented here exemplify an ongoing, gradual shift in Japan from considering environmental concerns only when they constituted *kogai*—pollution incidents that harmed people in obvious and dramatic ways—toward an awareness of environmental issues within a larger, ecological framework, as *kankyo mondai*.

The environmental disruptions in all of our cases took place in the context of Japan's vigorous push for industrialization during the post–World War II period. The two water projects described here, the "comprehensive development" of Lake Biwa and the Nagara River Dam, were part of the central government's program to harness water to support industrial and urban development nationwide. The case of Lake Biwa is particularly significant because it involves a multipurpose system of dams designed simultaneously for flood control and to provide water to industry and downstream urban areas. For that reason, initially it had strong local and national support. Though plans for a dam at Nagara had less direct regional and national import, opposing the dam to conserve the water and the river's fish became an environmental *cause célèbre*, attracting activists and sport fishing enthusiasts from around the nation as well as international support. Both cases involved sparring over resources between local and outside interest groups of a kind that can be seen in many other cases in this book.

Both cases were also shaped by a historic transfer of power over water-resource management from local governments to the central government, which led to clashes between national and local interests across Japan. Rural Japanese people have a long tradition of managing their own environments and resources; moreover, local water and fishing rights have long been honored in Japan. The relationship between people and water was traditionally direct and close. However, as the central government sought to modernize and nationalize the country's laws and infrastructure, beginning in the Meiji period and extending throughout the twentieth century, decision-making power over land and water was increasingly transferred from the local level to the prefectural and national levels of government. Rural people's daily relationship with water became increasingly distant, as water was piped in from far away and the central government took on massive water engineering projects to control unpredictable and life-disrupting floods.

While many rural people welcomed the flood control efforts, water development plans met with local opposition where they threatened or adversely affected local fishermen's livelihoods, their water rights, and the areas in which they lived. By the 1970s, when poor water quality became a contentious issue, the mismatch between local needs and the central government's development projects became more pronounced. The need to return to citizens power over water management and preservation in their own locales was a recurring, though often unstated, issue underlying conflicts between the national government and local people. Through the 1970s, opposition political parties, such as the Japan Socialist Party and the Japan Communist Party, often used local citizen positions on environmental and other social justice conflicts (such as that of Minamata disease victims) for political gain against the ruling Liberal Democratic Party. But calls for more local power and input from non-party-affiliated citizens on an array of environmental and social issues grew bolder in the late 1980s and the 1990s. A trend toward "localization" and participatory decision-making with respect to waterways such as the Nagara River and the Yodo River system, which includes Lake Biwa, has recently brought citizen groups more genuinely into environment-related decision-making processes.

Both cases reveal the growth in Japan not only of new, grassroots approaches to environmental decision-making, but also of new understandings of the interdependence between water and land ecosystems as well as between those ecosystems and the quality of human life. By 1974 environmental issues had become enough of a public concern that a candidate for governor of Shiga Prefecture (where Lake Biwa is located) could run—and win—on a platform prioritizing *kankyo mondai*. By 1977 citizens downstream from Lake Biwa had brought a lawsuit against the prefectural government alleging contamination of their drinking water through eutrophication, using arguments reflecting a broad range of *kankyo mondai*. And since 1997 plans for dams and other water projects have required input from local citizen committees, which have integrated *kankyo mondai* and participatory decision-making. While efforts to harmonize water management with local needs and values continue to be challenging (particularly where sewage treatment is concerned, as the Lake Biwa case illustrates), the two cases in our study have advanced both the protection and localization of water resources management across Japan.

Water Power: From Local to Central Control

The story of water resources management in Japan throughout most of the twentieth century is one of progressive consolidation of planning, decision-making, and management under central government control. Until Japan's rapid industrialization in the early to mid-twentieth century increased the country's need for water, the management of local watersheds was left to local communities. Before the 1868 Meiji Restoration, village and town governments built levees to control flooding in their jurisdictions. Although the 1896 River Law technically assigned responsibility for river systems to prefectural and national governments, local governments were still responsible for "resource management," which included jurisdiction over claims of land ownership, fishing rights, and other local activities, such as farming, that relied on water. Nevertheless, Japan's nineteenth century engagement in modern nation-building included efforts to centralize government control over water resource management, among many other important arenas. In terms of flood remediation measures, the central government had broad de facto control over water resources because the prefectural governors who were formally assigned the responsibility under the River Law were appointed by the central government. This gave the central government a broad legal mandate to carry out the nationwide hydropower schemes developed shortly after the law's enactment.

As a result of the U.S. occupation of Japan (1945–52), Japanese political institutions underwent fundamental reform. In the arena of water resource management, concepts and methods used by the Tennessee Valley Authority in the United States strongly influenced Japan's development planning process. In the American model an integrated agency regulated industrial resource use, land allocation, hydropower, and more. Unlike the U.S. government, however, Japan's central government sought to retain de facto authority over water resource development throughout the country.

When, as part of the democratic reforms instituted during the American occupation, the post of governor came to be decided by election, the central government lost its control of the assignment of governors within prefectures, and thus it lost its free hand in river management. Thus, to retain water management control, the central government needed a new legal framework. That framework was provided for beginning in 1950 with the enactment of the National Comprehensive Land Development Act (NCLD).

Then in 1962, the passage of the Water Resources Development Law gave the central government further authority to develop water resources in the service of electricity generation and industrial use as well as flood control. This law, together with the establishment that year of a quasi-governmental company to carry out major public water works—the Water Resources Development Public Corporation (WRDC), led by the Ministry of Construction—set the stage for that ministry's domination of water resource policy and management throughout Japan. Two years later, in 1964, the Japanese government revised the River Law, largely removing river system oversight from the prefectures and placing Japan's water supply at the disposal of the central government. Under the new Unified Management of Entire River Systems Policy, national government approval was required for all local water plans and development. This central control, which facilitated grand-scale water projects, was a key cause of disharmony in the relationship between the residents of Shiga Prefecture and their water. At the same time, while the law gave the central government sole authority to issue water allocation rights for grade one rivers, such as the Yodo River and its source, Lake Biwa, prefectural and municipal governments retained jurisdiction over grade two and lower grade rivers, which were deemed less important water resources. This multi-tiered system of water management set the stage for the ambitious and controversial water engineering projects at Lake Biwa and the Nagara River.

Lake Biwa: Water Development; Water Degradation

Lake Biwa and Its Past

Lake Biwa, Japan's largest natural freshwater lake, is situated in Shiga Prefecture, near the center of the country. The boundaries of the Lake Biwa watershed nearly match the boundaries of the lake's home prefecture. The lake receives water from more than four hundred rivers and tributaries, and it feeds the Yodo River system to its west and south. Today the lake supports the lives of roughly 1,300,000 people in the catchment area, and provides water to approximately 14 million people in the downstream areas.

One of the world's oldest lakes, Lake Biwa has a geological history that dates back four to five million years. Since the lakeshore became inhabited ten to twenty thousand years ago, it has been used for fishing and transportation. Renowned for its beautiful waterfront scenery, it is also a destination for spiritual pilgrimages and tourism. Until the end of the nineteenth century it seemed as if the interaction between the lake and its inhabitants could be sustained indefinitely, dominated as it was by farming and fishing, activities that depended upon renewable natural resources and manual labor. Although historical documentation is limited, the major environmental issue involving the lake during the Edo period (seventeenth through nineteenth centuries) appears to have been the flooding that occurred because of the limited drainage capacity of the Seta River, the lake's only natural outlet.

Industrialization in the latter half of the nineteenth century brought drastic changes to this picture. During Japan's Meiji period (1868–1912) the national government opened the door to trade with Western countries and began to import technology and science. Japan's modernization forced Shiga residents to reevaluate Lake Biwa's traditional role and meaning; concerns for livelihood and economic expansion were at the forefront of this reevaluation. The lake was also regarded in several other ways: as a source of floods, which could be managed and controlled using Western technology; as the scene of "traditional living," which revolved around fishing; and as a resource for many other industrial processes.

Floods, considered a major threat to livelihoods in the region, have been a constant throughout Japan's history. Although flood control on the lake and its many rivers has been the main goal of water policy since the early Edo period, following the Meiji Restoration and under the 1896 River Law, flood control came for the first time to rely on Western technology. In 1905, the national government constructed the Nango Araizeki weir across the lower end of the lake to control the lake's water level. While the weir did not entirely eradicate flooding, it harmed the living creatures in the lake. Since the weir, a series of adjustable water gates, cut the lake off from Osaka Bay, it stopped the upstream and downstream migration of the commercially important sweetfish (*ayu*) and eel (*unagi*) between Lake Biwa and Osaka Bay. With the advent of modern technology and engineering in the construction industry, particularly the creation of new building materials, the construction of the weir to regulate inland water flow augured the wave of the future.

In 1937 the national government changed its approach to inland water problems entirely. Instead of focusing on small, localized floods, it began to take a broader view, setting up the Water Control Research Commission to investigate how best to neutralize the flooding threat posed by seasonal changes in water volume in Japan's watersheds. Lake Biwa's position as the largest lake in Japan, and its location near two rapidly urbanizing industrial areas—Osaka and Kobe—made it a prime candidate for the government's plans for water management, which would be realized with devastating effect on the lakeshore ecosystem in the decades to come.

From the perspective of the local inhabitants, however, the lake was not only the source of a threat to livelihood; it was also the very source of livelihood and a centuries-old way of life. From the Middle Ages until the present, approximately two hundred rural (and now urban) communities have dotted the perimeter of the lake.[69] If these communities were growing, it was owing to the diverse livelihoods supported by the lake, with its inland rice paddies, lakeshore wetland plants (reeds), aquatic plants, and fish. Relatively few villages and hamlets, those with no agricultural land, made their livings entirely from fishing. Most localities in the region survived on a combination of agriculture and fishing.

It is clear from the region's history and from several sociological studies of its lakeshore communities that were carried out in the 1980s that the lake has always accommodated small-scale human economic activity, including potentially nature transforming activities such as farming and fishing.[70] Even until the late 1960s with the industrialization and urbanization of the lake area, and in spite of dense lakeshore populations, traditional production systems and lifestyles kept Lake Biwa oligotrophic, a scientific designation for a deep, low-nutrient, or "clean," lake. Cattle manure and human night soil—potential sources of nutrient contamination of the lake—were recycled for agricultural production as precious fertilizer, and thus they caused minimal pollution.[71]

At the beginning of the twentieth century an estimated ten thousand people relied directly on the lake fisheries for their livelihood. The local government attempted to increase fishing production by introducing artificial spawning techniques. After World

War II the national government responded to severe nationwide food shortages by declaring a need for more agricultural land, and ordering the reclamation of 2,600 hectares of lakeshore lagoons for rice production. Some of the newly developed farmland was allocated to fishing villages. Years later fishing families and environmentalists would criticize this land reclamation program, citing loss of spawning grounds and, in the case of environmentalists, the degradation of the ecosystem, especially the loss of reed beds around the lagoons and the lakeshore macrophyte zone. Post-1970 rice surpluses intensified the criticism.

The lake region first became a host to industry (and pollution) in the 1920s, when a major production center for rayon, the Toyo Rayon factory,[72] was built near Otsu in southern Shiga Prefecture. Without any pollution laws, untreated wastewater effluent was released into the southern part of the lake and began to kill off a small species of cobiculid clam native to the lake that had been a mainstay of the fisheries. The fishers complained, and like the Minamata fishers, the company paid them "sympathy money." It would not be until much later, following the enactment of the 1958 Industrial Effluent Control Law (*Kogyo Haisui Kiseiho*), however, that the company introduced any wastewater treatment mechanism.[73]

In the 1960s, Japan's industry-fueled economy grew explosively, resulting in larger and larger urban centers. The government forecast that if water resources were not reshaped and harnessed for production, there would be massive shortages of water, which was needed for continued economic expansion and urbanization. In retrospect, the Japanese government's 1960s estimate of future water needs seems highly inflated,[74] a theme that returns in the Nagara River Dam project discussed below. Nonetheless, in the early 1960s the Japanese government began to cast around for development projects and policies that could provide an ever-increasing water supply to satisfy an ever-increasing demand.

Harnessing Lake Biwa: The Lake Biwa Comprehensive Development Plan

Local attempts to prevent flooding on Lake Biwa had been ongoing for centuries and had included, at various times, dredging the Seta River, the lake's only natural outlet, and as mentioned above, building a weir across the lake's southern end. There were long-running tensions between the lakeshore people, who wanted to dredge the Seta River as deep as possible to prevent lakeshore flooding, and downstream people who believed that dredging the Seta River would cause flooding downstream. The downstream people had always been stronger politically because the downstream area included Osaka, the center of Japanese commerce throughout the Edo and Meiji periods. In building the weir in 1905, the national government was exerting third-party control over the conflict. The weir proved moderately effective but environmentally disruptive.

The need to increase the supply of water from Lake Biwa for urban and industrial uses came later, in the late 1950s, with the start of Japan's rapid economic development which was concentrated in the downstream areas. It took more than fifteen years before agreement to send more water from Lake Biwa to the industrializing downstream areas was reached among the downstream and upstream communities and the national government. In 1972 the parties agreed to the Lake Biwa Comprehensive Development Plan. Though it helped Japan move toward the national goal of increasing the industrial and urban residential water supply, the plan would alter Lake Biwa's water levels and ecosystem in unprecedented ways. The plan included a comprehensive water engineering project for the entire Lake Biwa watershed. The resulting system of dams on the rivers feeding the lake, water gates, and water diversion channels, and the deepening of the existing weir across the southern lake—all of which lowered the lake's water level—would transform the entire natural lake, in a sense, into a multipurpose dam.

Three powerful national ministries bid to lead the new government corporation that would oversee the development and management of Lake Biwa: the Ministry of Construction (MOC), the Ministry of International Trade and Industry (MITI), and the Ministry of Agriculture, Forestry, and Fisheries (MAFF). MOC's plan was by far the most extensive, and invasive. Its grand water resource development scheme, which was touted for the many jobs it would create, included lowering the volume of Lake Biwa by over a meter in order to increase water supply downstream. It also included many large-scale dams around Japan, including a Nagara River Estuary dam. Yet, at the time, Shiga prefecture officials thought it would be the least damaging plan for the lake, and the MOC's plan won the day.

The MOC's goal for Lake Biwa was to increase the water supply for urban areas and industries downstream from the immediate Lake Biwa area. The cities of Osaka and Kobe stood to benefit, as did neighboring industries that needed water for manufacturing processes. However, because those cities' needs were not *purely* industrial, the MOC had to be careful; they needed a plan that would not only increase the volume of water but also provide water suitable for drinking.

Despite the presence of industry along the lake region and creeping pollution, the natural waters of Lake Biwa were noticeably fresher than the water downstream. As Yamaoka Kansuke, then a Shiga Prefecture official and a leader of the Lake Biwa Comprehensive Development Plan's compliance unit, recalled in an interview with our research team:

> We frequently visited Osaka from [1968 to 1969] in order to negotiate [various matters]. When we went there, we always drank tap water, and I thought: "How can these people drink such smelly water?" Then, I thought how great it would be for them to use natural water from Lake Biwa and its surroundings.[75]

The idea of turning the lake into a reservoir of sorts for the downstream communities, however, had not seemed possible to prefectural officials until the Lake Biwa Comprehensive Development Plan (LBCDP) offered the blueprint and the technology. According to Yamaoka:

> The thought of using Lake Biwa as a *mizugame* [water jug] didn't occur to us. We thought, well, it was not usable as a *mizugame*. The MOC's plan for comprehensive infrastructure development showed that controlling the [Seta] river weir made it possible. I think that's when people started talking about using [Lake Biwa] as a *mizugame*.

Those who stood to lose from the plan to use the lake as a reservoir for downstream populations were the people who lived around Lake Biwa itself. Some journalists called the ensuing negotiations over this plan "the Water War," where upstream and downstream parties vied for control over the water supply, which had become a precious resource. The negotiations were carried out between the national government, downstream officials and Shiga prefectural officials. The Shiga authorities were adamant that water resource development should be pursued alongside regional (Shiga) economic development, which at the time lagged far behind that of Osaka and Kobe downstream.

After lengthy bargaining a new deal was struck. Water resource development would be carried out together with upstream economic development through financial support from the national government and by the downstream areas shouldering a greater portion of the costs than upstream areas. In 1972 the LBCDP was launched; it was not officially completed until March 1997.[76] Its aim was to modify the lake in a variety of ways and for a variety of ends: the construction of levees for flood control; the construction of multipurpose dams to provide flood control, water supply, and electricity; and the lowering of the lake's water level by as much as 1.4 meters to provide additional water—a 40-ton-per-second increase—to downstream areas. After the LBCDP was finished, Lake Biwa was commonly referred to (as noted above) as the "Water Jug of the Kinki Area" (*Kinki no Mizugame*), signaling a shift in the lake's role from source of livelihood for local residents to resource for a growing national population. The "water jug" concept became the primary value that downstream residents projected onto the lake, while those living around the lake continued to value it for its multiple roles as a source of livelihood, leisure activities, and symbolic meanings—values that they became conscious of only in the 1990s after the severe damage the LBCDP had caused to the lake ecosystem became apparent. Then, and as part of a new campaign to promote environmental consciousness in the region, the lake came to be referred to as "Mother Lake Biwa."

Environmental conservation—specifically, the maintenance of potable water for the downstream residents of Kobe and Osaka—was also a stated goal of the final LBCDP, a hard-won victory for the Socialist party. Yet despite the rhetoric, water quality was not a strong component, as the plan's only budget items within this category were sewer construction, lakeside park construction, and even road construction. The inclusion of environmental conservation as a goal may have placated affluent downstream residents and others who cared about Lake Biwa's water quality; it may also have been in harmony with the central government's economic development plan, because its real aim was to provide potable drinking water to a growing population and industrial water to a growing economy. However, given the wide variety of environmentally destructive activities that the LBCDP involved (for example, road and dam construction) this goal was ultimately no more than *tatemae* ("for show").

Local Support, Local Opposition

The people living along the shores of Lake Biwa by and large believed that the comprehensive development plan would bring good things to the community, not least among them the means to control the frequent flooding of their region. In addition plans for pumping the lake water for farm irrigation and drinking water were welcomed especially by residents in the area where water shortage was a historical concern. Many shared the view of Shiga official Yamaoka Kansuke that using modern technology to control floods and increase the water supply could only improve their livelihoods. During an interview Yamaoka explained how his childhood experience with floods had affected his view of the comprehensive development of Lake Biwa:

> I was scared of floods. I used to fall into the river, and I got stuck in there once, when a rainstorm flooded the village bridge. I was swept away by the current. . . . There were poles in the river for mooring boats, and the current drove me into them. I have scars [to prove it]. . . . I have heard from other people that they were also injured [this way]. . . . After being involved with the Lake Biwa Development Project, I really think that the public wishes to control Lake Biwa. This is . . . tied to my childhood memory, and I can fully understand the utility of river works [that control the flow and the level of the water].

Yamaoka opined that the prefectural government kept the public informed about its policies and strategies for infrastructure and water development, and that the LBCDP seemed to reflect the will of the people. In the late 1960s and early 1970s, he argued, the promise of modernization outweighed public opinion (or knowledge) about any harmful effects on aquatic life that might result from the water engineering plans. This was true among Shiga officials as well as ordinary residents. As Yamaoka remembers:

> By December [1971], the fundamental attitude of the prefecture became clear. . . . The main [objective] was to develop the water resources [and help] Shiga prefecture to develop as the downstream regions have done. In [1971], Shiga prefecture's level of [socioeconomic] development was quite low. In a national statistical survey, Shiga's economic performance was that of a backward prefecture, ranked always at the very bottom or second from the bottom. . . . For Shiga Prefecture, it was not just about managing the water. [The LBCDP] coincided with the public's desire to get rid of the strong image of Shiga as a backward prefecture, and so they viewed [a better water system] as a chance to attain higher socioeconomic status.

Among those who opposed the comprehensive development plan (at least those components of the plan that would affect their own interests) were fishermen, whose time-honored fishing rights were threatened by the plan. Fishing rights, protected by the Japanese national fishery law, were a category of water use rights that had remained with local people despite the government's moves to bring water resources under central control. The plans for construction and other development would result in the decrease of the fishery catch, especially by the artificial fluctuations in the water levels and these were bound to affect the fish ecology upon which their livelihoods depended. The fishermen, via their fishing cooperatives and under the umbrella of the Federation of Shiga Fishing Cooperatives, negotiated with the Ministry of Construction for compensation for their losses.

Far from a spontaneous grassroots opposition movement, the fishermen were part of an official negotiating process, a relatively standard procedure when the government planned major public works that would affect fishing. Academics and other specialists could be called in to help the parties decide on appropriate compensation amounts. As in Minamata, the payment of "sympathy money" was not new to the fishermen in the Lake Biwa area, where pollution from industrialization had already affected the shellfish population.

So although there was, at times, vocal opposition to the Lake Biwa Comprehensive Development Plan from within Shiga prefecture, it was mostly confined to a few intellectuals.[77] There was not much precedent in rural Japan at the time for spontaneous civic activism. What little opposition did arise during the early phase of the LBCDP was largely stirred up by opposition political parties, such as the Socialist and Communist Parties—in other words, by experienced organizers whose aim was to spawn a large political movement.

One such group, the Return Lake Biwa to Citizens Life Association, was formed in early 1972 to support the effort of the prefectural-level Socialist Party to get conservation measures included in the final LBCDP. The group was launched with the help of Hosoya Takuji, a Socialist Party leader and Chisso employee at the plant in Moriyama in Shiga prefecture, who had long been deeply concerned about the poisoning at Minamata. Yet despite its leafleting and other public education efforts, the group failed to spark mass concern about the LBCDP.

Holding steadfast to the issue of water quality, opposition parties and their supporters targeted planned sewage treatment plants. Significantly, these small opposition groups were composed mainly of new residents, not people who had lived along the lakeshore for generations.[78] Typically, new residents were interested in environmental conservation, and old residents cared more about concrete needs like flood control and practical uses of water. The new residents tended to be bolder and more aggressive, in the view of long-time residents. According to a regional wastewater plan created for Lake Biwa, between 1966 and 1976 four sewage treatment plants were to be built at different locations along the lake using funds from the "environmental conservation" budget line. The wastewater was to be dumped into Lake Biwa after treatment. In 1974 activists coordinated by the opposition parties opposed the construction, in particular of the Yabase sewage treatment plant, as a tactic in their general opposition to the infilling of the lake that it would require. Among the concerns was whether setting in large-scale sewer pipes and wastewater treatment facilities was worth the cost, particularly given the inevitable damage to the lakeshore environment. There were also fears that chemicals in industrial wastewater would be difficult to treat and would end up in the lake, causing health and ecological problems. Those who opposed sewer construction were in the minority, however, as most Shiga residents welcomed the flush toilet and other modern conveniences that sewers and waste treatment would bring. In addition, the prefectural government's public campaign claiming that sewerage construction would improve the lake water quality and prevent water pollution undercut any effort by opponents to convince people otherwise.

The story of Shiga Prefecture and the LBCDP is the story of a prefecture in Japan that voiced its needs. Its officials, who generally approved of plans that promised to bring money to their district, played the role of intermediary for their constituents, representing the economic and environmental concerns of Lake Biwa residents in negotiations with the central government, and presenting the MOC's plan to the people of Shiga. In the face of a central government plan to "take" more of the prefecture's main resource, Shiga prefectural officials were able to negotiate a reasonable deal— that it should receive, in essence, a local economic development plan as part of the LBCDP. Their leverage came from the fact that they were agreeing to supply lake water to downstream users. They pointed to the loss of fish and the economic impacts of lowering the lake level, and they demanded compensation—primarily in the form of public works projects, such as sewer, road, and dam construction, farmland consolidation, that would provide jobs, improve infrastructure, and increase the overall economic well-being of Shiga prefecture. Thus, even though at this stage there was not much public participation in Shiga decision-making (indeed the public knew very little since at this point there was little scientific information on water quality circulated), Shiga prefectural officials were able to exert a measure of local control, even at the height of centralized power over water resources.

The prefecture's efforts in negotiating the LBCDP deal were aimed at mitigating losses as well as modernizing Lake Biwa's water infrastructure. In the end, the plan provided some compensation for the lake's declining water levels. Specifically, the MOC subsidized the construction of spawning canals for fish, the dredging of the lake bottom for ship navigation, the expansion of water irrigation inlets into the deeper parts of the lake to offset the lowering of the lake water level, and monetary compensation for fish catch losses. The prefecture also received non-lake-related social benefits, including farmland consolidation permits, expanded tap water systems, sewer construction, the construction of bank and drainage facilities, as well as lakeshore roads, and other projects aimed at modernizing the infrastructure that provided water for domestic use.

What the LBCDP did *not* include was adequate protection for Lake Biwa's water quality and its ecology. The people of Shiga had to take other routes to achieve that end. One of these came to be called the "soap movement."

Fighting the Red Tide with Soap: The Local Struggle for a Clean Lake

Even before the comprehensive development plan was hammered out and under way, poor water quality had become an issue of deepening concern for the residents of the lake region. Increased use of tap water by residents, agriculture, and industry had brought degradation in the form of increased wastewater, laying the ground for a shift in public debate from water management to clean water. Thus, when the LBCDP was introduced, its pollution consequences, both anticipated and actual, began to play a role in public debates and environmental politics in Shiga.

In the late 1960s lakeshore residents reported reduced fish catches and foul-smelling water. A prefectural government investigation blamed agricultural pesticide and fertilizer runoff. This finding cast doubt on LBCDP arguments that Shiga Prefecture would benefit from the increase in agricultural land resulting from the draining of marshlands surrounding the lake. Because of the loss of these marshlands—whose reeds served to filter and purify water naturally—and the increased agricultural activity, however, agricultural runoff further contaminated the lake, resulting in fish kills and more bad odors.

In 1969 lakeshore residents launched yet another in a long series of complaints about the lake's foul-smelling water. Partly in response, the national Diet enacted the 1970 Water Pollution Law, which established water quality standards—specific "acceptable" levels of water contamination. The responsibility for making sure Lake Biwa met these standards rested with the Shiga prefectural government. The law included two kinds of water quality standard: first, a "health" (*kenko*) code, which set out acceptable levels of toxic pollutants such as mercury and other heavy metals; second, a "living environment" (*seikatsu kankyo*) code, which listed acceptable levels of nutrient-related indicators, such as COD (chemical oxygen demand) and BOD (biological oxygen demand), phosphorus, and nitrogen. Both kinds of standards were concerned largely with the chemical content of the water and its effects on human health, and much less with its impact on the health of the Lake Biwa ecosystem, including the fish population.

In any case, the creation of water quality standards was not accompanied by effective measures and therefore did not alleviate the pollution problem. Water quality worsened, and residents continued to complain. In 1974, Takemura Masayoshi successfully challenged the incumbent Shiga governor on a platform that centered on *kankyo mondai*. Thirty-nine years old at the time he was elected, he was the youngest governor of any prefecture. Takemura had been heavily influenced by German environmental policy, which he learned about while living and studying in Germany in the 1960s as a young Interior Ministry bureaucrat. His candidacy drew support from the two parties that formed the national opposition at the time—the Japan Socialist Party (JSP) and the Japan Communist Party (JCP), which liked to claim attentiveness to local problems, and was actively supported by Mr. Hosoya, the labor union leader. Mr. Takemura was also supported by Shiga Prefecture's labor union movement, which was heavily JSP-influenced. The JSP and JCP saw as their purpose attentiveness to local peoples' problems, and Takemura, as the "environmental candidate," represented the concerns of the local people.

In 1977 a new phase of water degradation occurred in a changed political atmosphere. With the election of Takemura Masayoshi as governor in 1974, environmental complaints found a more sympathetic ear, as urban and upstream lakeshore residents continued to report foul-smelling and -tasting water. The first freshwater red tide (noxious algae) outbreaks in 1977 further awoke the public to the issue of Lake Biwa's water quality. Thereafter the outbreaks became increasingly frequent and extensive, having spread as far as the northern central part of the lake. This was particularly alarming because the northern part of the lake was considered the cleanest part owing to its relatively low population density and industrial activity as compared to the southern part of the lake. Because of the red tide, drinking water purification plants had to take additional measures, using charcoal to clean the water.[79]

Red tides, like any kind of disproportionate algal bloom, are indicators of eutrophication, the process whereby a body of water becomes overloaded with nutrients, thereby enabling algae to grow rapidly. Unchecked algae growth uses up the oxygen in the water, which is needed by other organisms. It can also form an opaque cover over the lake, blocking out the sunlight that other aquatic plants need. There are naturally eutrophic lakes that may simply be shallower and more nutrient rich than other lakes, and therefore prone to algae blooms. But Lake Biwa was not one of these, and its eutrophication presented problems for the human population as well as for the natural flora and fauna. Because it does not necessarily signal pollution, the red tide was seen as a qualitatively different environmental problem from the straightforward industrial contamination that had characterized *kogai* problems. As we shall see below, although eutrophication at Lake Biwa resulted from human activity, its appearance as a "natural" phenomenon in other contexts would play a role in the courts' adjudication of the issue.

What differentiates diminished poor water quality resulting from eutrophication from the effects of straightforward pollution is the *kind* of agent that contaminates the water and its relationship to human health. Eutrophication is not the result of a poison such as mercury or polychlorinated biphenyls (PCBs)—highly lethal compounds associated with increased incidence of cancer.[80] Ironically, such poisonous contamination—an instance of which occurred as a result of a 1972 industrial accident in the southern part of the lake—did not arouse as intense a public debate as did eutrophication.

In response to the public outcry over perceptions of deteriorating water quality, Governor Takemura ordered the environmental division of the prefectural government to study the causes of the change. That study determined that the domestic use of synthetic detergents containing phosphorus was a major cause of the algal blooms. Prior to the red tide, a small but vocal group of housewives in the region had been concerned that the still relatively new laundry detergents were causing health problems, such as skin irritation. Now that eutrophication was being attributed to detergent use, housewives organized to promote the use of soap in place of detergent. This new "soap movement," as it came to be called, was essentially engineered by the Takemura government. Thus, a government-supported "social movement" was born that capitalized upon the increasing trend toward health-related campaigns by housewives.

The soap movement, which quickly attracted national media attention, provided tips on how to use soap in washing machines. The movement also urged the Shiga prefectural government to undertake a product comparison and concluded that soap was better for the environment than detergent in terms of chemical contents. In response, the prefectural government changed the water treatment processes at all the sewerage plants it managed.

The movement was not without its critics, however. The detergent industry pounced on the government, claiming that detergent had become the scapegoat for government inaction in not providing adequate water treatment and sewers. The industry also disputed the movement's claim that synthetic detergent products contributed 18 percent of the total phosphorus inputs into the lake; it claimed that the true figure was closer to 12 percent. The industry mounted a fierce campaign against the Shiga government after the government announced its intention to ban the use and sale of detergents, declaring the action unconstitutional.

While local governments in Japan rarely defied industry, the Takemura government continued to champion the soap movement. Largely due to the movement's effectiveness, in 1979 the prefectural assembly unanimously enacted the Shiga Prefecture Eutrophication Prevention Ordinance, the first in Japan to prohibit the use of phosphorus-containing detergent. An opinion poll conducted at the time showed that two-thirds of the population approved of the ban.[81] In addition to the detergent ban, the government ordinance included: controls on industries that used phosphorus, subsidized coupons that citizens could use to exchange their detergent for soap, and a system of penalties and fines for violators. According to the prefectural government, the law resulted in an increase in the use of powdered soap from 26 percent in 1979 to at least 70 percent in 1980.[82]

Significantly, while household use of phosphorus was prohibited, its industrial use was controlled but not banned outright. By focusing on domestic use, the ordinance left the responsibility for reducing phosphorus input to the citizens, even though domestic use was estimated to be responsible for, at most, 18 percent of the total phosphorus released into the lake. Thus, the malodorous red tide continued to be nearly an annual occurrence in certain parts of the lake, particularly between April and June.[83]

The soap movement did not directly criticize the many construction projects of the LBCDP, which were probable contributors to eutrophication. And yet it did succeed in placing water quality squarely on the agenda of the prefectural government. In addition, after Governor Takemura took office, in 1974, the prefectural government put much energy into the measuring and monitoring of water quality. It created a water quality advisory council, composed of scientists, biologists, industry professionals, and prefectural assembly members, which reported to the governor. In its attempts to understand eutrophication process as well as the role of synthetic detergent, the Takemura government also brought in researchers from the American Great Lakes and other parts of the world and even organized an international symposium on water issues, the first of its kind in Japan, which drew researchers from the United

States and Europe. In addition, in 1982 again under Takemura's leadership, the prefectural government created the Lake Biwa Research Institute, the first basic research institute in Japan financed entirely by the local government. Its purpose was to study water quality as well as the social impacts of environmental degradation; but it also enabled the prefecture to develop its own scientific data on the lake, thereby decreasing its dependence on the national government.

Until the late 1970s opposition to the LBCDP was limited mainly to fishermen, biologists, ecologists, and some residents of the smaller villages where dam construction was planned. The soap movement served as a kind of wake-up call. According to Hosoya, the movement's leader, red tide outbreaks were probably the event that "turned the tide" for the movement to protect Lake Biwa:

> With a single stroke, the red tide outbreak [in 1977] alerted residents that Lake Biwa's water quality was at a critical [level], and this called the residents to be more aware of the lake's situation. . . . Of course, it happened at a time when we were thinking about how we could popularize the Lake Biwa issue. [Before the red tide incident,] movements such as the 1972 Association to Return Lake Biwa to Citizens' Life did not spread. [People] cried out: "[we're] against the movement to develop Lake Biwa!" They opposed and took action, but it was not built on popular support. It seemed like the soap movement [changed this] by providing a cause that the masses could support.

Kunimatsu Yoshitsugu, a prefectural official in 1970s and the governor of Shiga at the time we interviewed him in 1999, also pointed to the red tide as the occasion for the "coming of age" of environmental awareness for the people of Shiga:

> It was said that "developing is good." But suddenly, people realized that "it was wrong" and noticed that they were destroying the natural environment. . . . For Shiga Prefecture it was definitely the red tide [in 1977] that showed how [development can be environmentally destructive]. Nothing would have happened if it weren't for those who actively worked on this issue in Shiga.[84]

Governor Takemura's early warnings about Lake Biwa's problems earned him credibility once the red tide broke out, and this helped to popularize other movements concerned with lake quality and social dislocation. For example, concern over the red tide appears to have aided smaller groups opposing the construction of dams on rivers emptying into Lake Biwa. In fact, the lakeshore residents' involvement and large-scale response to the visible problem of red tide, compared to their earlier lack of concern about the impact of the LBCDP, can be explained in large part by the fact that Takemura's prefectural government engineered and endorsed the soap movement. This official endorsement gave a measure of legitimacy to Shiga residents' concerns about water quality.

It is important to point out that the housewives who had supported the banning of synthetic detergent did so because they saw it as a threat to their own health—that is, as a potential carcinogen. They were angered that the government had "co-opted" the movement, changing its agenda from human health to eutrophication—that is, the health of the lake itself. In one of several interviews for this study, Hosoya in fact admitted that the campaign's focus "was secretly switched to an environmental issue" since at that time government officials did not accept that the problems with Lake Biwa were health-related.[85] Governor Takemura had been reluctant to see Lake Biwa as a health issue, since it seemed very much unlike the Minamata disease crisis, which was raging at the time. In the mid-1970s as a newly elected governor he visited Minamata at the urging of Mr. Hosoya, a close confidant. As Hosoya told us: "I brought the governor to Minamata to ask him to really think about the environment through the Minamata [experience]. Minamata is the apex of saltwater problems, and Lake Biwa as a freshwater lake is the apex of freshwater problems in Japan."[86] But to Takemura, Minimata was a very different kind of problem from that of Lake Biwa— a health problem as opposed to an environmental problem. It was not until much later that he recognized the commonality of Minamata and Lake Biwa's problems in terms of the ill regard for human life.[87]

The housewives were in a minority of residents concerned about Lake Biwa as a health issue. Others—especially new residents—actively embraced the Shiga government's new-found concern with Lake Biwa as an environmental issue by speaking out or engaging in protest. As mentioned above, in Japan an important distinction is made between "old residents" and "new residents" of Shiga prefecture (and other parts of Japan). "New residents," who have generally moved to an area during the past two or three decades, tend to be better educated, more affluent, more urbane, and more mobile than "old resident" families, which have generally lived in a place for many generations. Old residents have often tended to view environmental activism as "egoistic" or "immature," though that is changing. Governor Kunimatsu told us:

> I think the newcomers have always had these values and high expectations. There is a saying in Shiga that "if you are born in Shiga, you can only succeed by going outside [of Shiga]." . . . These [newcomers] came into the picture when we were reflecting upon what we should do about Lake Biwa, which was quite an issue. . . . People believed that Lake Biwa had rich natural surroundings, but then newcomers started describing the lake using strong words like "death" and "dying."[88]

The media helped to bring new attention to the problem for all residents. But as Kunimatsu pointed out, old residents were not inured to the degradation and had taken notice on their own. "Even those who frequently used the lake—fishermen and residents who drank water and washed their bowls and utensils in the lake—noticed that there was something wrong," he said. The poor quality of the water, in fact, concerned all residents. According to Kunimatsu:

> There were those [old residents] who had witnessed the transformation [of the lake] over a long time . . . and there were those [new residents] with a certain wishful image of the lake in mind. Both sides were shocked when they found that the lake was hurting. This gave impetus to a unified residents' movement.

Despite this claim, Hosoya felt that the difference in attitudes between old and new residents was profound and ultimately threatened to weaken the movement to improve water quality. He told us:

> I was quite amazed by how new residents were [the most concerned] when Lake Biwa was in trouble. This makes sense because these new residents moved here primarily because they appreciated the lake's beauty. [Old residents] just assumed that Lake Biwa would change naturally, and so they were insensitive to these transformations of the [environment].

Hosoya speculated that the reason the movement did not "take off" was that the "old residents" did not feel that the pollution of Lake Biwa was "destroying their lives."[89] In fact, at times it took complete outsiders—downstream water users—to call the government to account for the lake's water quality, as we will see in the next section.

Despite the significant social investments in water quality management made after Takemura's election and in the wake of the 1979 Eutrophication Prevention Ordinance, the regional development and modernization projects of the LBCDP continued apace, bringing more dramatic changes to the Lake Biwa landscape. Artificial levees continued to be built, riverbeds were lined with concrete, and farmland consolidation proceeded.

Because the LBCDP's environmental conservation policies took the form of large-scale public works projects, the financial investment involved was enormous. For example, the main environmental policy carried out during and after the introduction of the eutrophication standards in 1979 was the construction of sewers to address the problem of wastewater effluent. As the effluent that was once poured into rivers and ditches was routed into the lake, the river and ditch water quality naturally improved. But even though the sewer project—essentially a system of long, underground pipelines—used the most sophisticated engineering methods, at a very high cost, it could not treat the wastewater in such a way as to maintain the lake's water quality. Nonetheless, in accordance with the LBCDP, in the early 2000s a vast system of pipelines for sewerage was under construction all across the lakeshore region.

Only recently have policy officials and residents come to realize the huge financial burden that this construction brings. It is estimated that the cost per family of four for sewer construction in the less-populated areas is 7 million yen ($50,000). This realization caused the planner of the Lake Biwa sewerage pipelines, Naito Masaaki, the engineer behind the original Lake Biwa sewerage plan, to admit in 2001 that his plan had been a bad idea, both economically and ecologically.[90]

The Struggle for a Clean Lake Redirected: Launching
a Landmark Lawsuit

Lake Biwa residents complaining about Lake Biwa's water quality were joined in their activism by downstream water users, who since 1976 had been against the LBCDP.

That year, they filed a lawsuit against the Shiga prefectural government, citing the LBCDP as a threat to their safe water supply. The suit sought to stop LBCDP-related projects, particularly sewer construction, and argued that changes in the lake level, as well as construction of embankments around the lake, were damaging the lake's ecosystem. This was the first time that a Japanese environmental campaign had taken to the courts for the broad reason of environmental protection.

Spearheaded by two key leaders, Tsujita Keishi and Orita Yasuhiro, the lawsuit named 1,186 plaintiffs, who asserted the importance of the "conservation of the ecosystem." In addition to conservation arguments, which one movement leader later explained had been borrowed from the American nature preservation movement,[91] the plaintiffs' lawyers drew upon Article 25 of the Japanese constitution, claiming the right to clean water as a basic human right.[92] This was the first time in Japan that human rights were made the basis for an environmental claim. The Shiga prefectural government countered that the LBCDP was not degrading the Lake Biwa water quality, even though Takemura's government had demonstrated its awareness of the problems of eutrophication.

Of the plaintiffs, only eight were Shiga residents, and these were either intellectuals or political activists (members of the Socialist or Communist Party). In forming an opposition movement and taking their grievances to court, the plaintiffs, almost all of them urban, downstream residents, had flouted an unwritten norm of Shiga's conservative political culture. Even the staunchest of the plaintiffs, however, began to withdraw from the suit as the case dragged on. By the time the case was decided in 1988, thirteen years after the suit was filed, fewer than a dozen plaintiffs were left. The court ruled for the defendants, denying the plaintiffs the right to clean water on the grounds that it lacked legal precedent to do so. Despite this legal setback, the Lake Biwa lawsuit is another example of a pioneering citizen action that attempted to take back a measure of citizen control over water resources, and raised awareness of potentially serious environmental problems.

* * *

Having overcome the hurdle of the lawsuit, Shiga officials proceeded with the implementation of the Lake Biwa Comprehensive Development Plan unhindered.[93] In all, the LBCDP took twenty-five years to complete and cost 2.2 trillion yen (about $20 billion), roughly 600 billion yen ($6 billion) of which was spent on sewer construction that did not protect water quality as expected. By the time the project was formally completed, in 1997, the ecosystem and scenery of the lake had changed dramatically. Flood control and water supply targets had largely been achieved, but at a steep environmental cost. The artificial lowering of the lake's water level during the rainy season from mid June to mid October deprived fish and other aquatic life of access to spawning grounds in rivers, lagoons, and rice paddies since indigenous fish naturally spawn in these areas during the high water rainy season. As a result, the artificial levees had also prevented families living along the lake from engaging in the age-old fishing method called *okazu-tori* (side-dish catching), from which they supplemented their diets.[94] Nonnative species of fish like largemouth bass and blue-gills, introduced by humans into the lake from North America, had proliferated, while native species had declined. (This sometimes required strong countermeasures, such as Shiga Prefecture's prohibition in 2002 of the catch-and-release of large-mouth bass and bluegill sunfish.) Reed beds along the lakeshore, important for filtering toxins and absorbing water flows, had in many cases been uprooted and replaced by concrete banks and other shoreline development. And the water quality—while worse in some measurements like COD (chemical oxygen demand)—was no better than in 1977.

The river dam construction projects, which continued even after the official end of the LBCDP in 1997, were also socially disruptive. For example, the Daidogawa Dam project displaced one village and fifty-four families, and roughly forty families moved in anticipation of the proposed Niu Dam.

Still, the efforts of local citizens were a significant catalyst for change. The soap movement resulted in a ban on the use of phosphorus-containing detergents. The lawsuit forced the prefecture and courts to take stock of what was happening to the waters of Shiga. It also aired these issues before the public, helping to set the stage for later expressions of discontent regarding other public works projects, such as proposed dams or sewer lines that are costly and may not serve local interests. Years of environmental controversy in Shiga Prefecture ultimately compelled both industry and government to play closer attention to the environmental concerns of local residents.

From Comprehensive Development to Comprehensive Conservation

The "Lake Biwa lawsuit," as it is often called, also helped change policy at the local level. After the official end of the LBCDP in 1997, the prefectural government decided to study the adoption of a "comprehensive conservation" policy. The decision reflected an increasingly widespread concern with *kankyo mondai*; it was also a strategic maneuver of Shiga officials who endeavored to take advantage of this new concern to gain new funding from the national government. The effort led to the formulation (with input from six national ministries and agencies)[95] of the Mother Lake 21 Plan, a nationally approved and nationally supported project to transform Lake Biwa into a model of lake conservation in the twenty-first century.

The policy, finalized in 2000, included plans to review and adjust land use in the catchment area around the lake; recycle water used in agriculture and create rainwater storage facilities; and improve the filtering capacity of the nutrients into the lake. To this day, these nature conservation goals for Lake Biwa have continued to be a policy priority for the new Ministry of Land, Infrastructure, and Transport (the ministry that replaced the Ministry of Construction in 2001). In order to sell its policies to the public, the ministry used appealing but sometimes misleading project names. For example, the *Shizen Saisei* (Nature Rebirth) plan was, according to the promotional literature, a public project to construct a natural lakeshore along Lake Biwa and natural river beds along the flowing rivers. In fact, the project used reeds to cover a concrete lakeshore project.

The government's promotional literature for Mother Lake 21 invoked values relating to *kankyo mondai*. "The ultimate solution to these problems lies in the revival of an environmental culture," the literature said. "We must make the transition from the modern way of life based on mass production and consumption to one that is in harmony with the environment and is based on symbiosis of humans and nature." It also called upon residents to participate, arguing that "the government cannot be the only or even the main actor in this enterprise. The solutions must begin with changes in the behavior of citizens of the prefecture and the business sector."[96]

The overall environmental plan asked citizens to do their part by recycling, using soap, and adopting environmentally safer behaviors. Industries were called upon to review and amend their production processes, to recycle water, and manage waste safely. For decades, Japanese citizens who were concerned about *kogai* (pollution) focused their efforts on compelling local industrial firms to stop polluting, but that generally would occur years after the firms had begun polluting, and only well after local residents had started suffering the health and environmental effects of the pollution. Since then fines and regulations have, to a significant extent, prevented the most egregious forms of industrial pollution. But the conservation plan took a more proactive approach, asking businesses to think ecologically (and preemptively) across the full range of their activities. Thus, the plan went beyond the *kogai* issues involving conspicuous toxic pollution to the question of conservationist behavior. As Governor Kunimatsu explained to us in 1999:

> Our current lifestyle contains elements that are environmentally destructive. So we need to think about a lifestyle that minimizes the negative effects. Instead of treating it as an individual problem, we need to frame the issue at the production stage and make changes to the production of various goods that are commonly used in our daily lives so that they become environmentally friendlier and have a positive impact on the environment. This way of thinking is new and different.

Kunimatsu went on to explain that this new thinking was not only about the conservation of a lake but about working out a new form of coexistence between people and the water, in which each nurtures the other. The potential benefits of adopting the new lifestyle Kunimatsu talked about went far beyond improvements to the lake itself. According to Kunimatsu:

> I don't know if the word "strategy" is appropriate here . . . but . . . I think the strategy is to have a big experiment to [examine] the relationship between human beings and water, or between the environment and mankind and move beyond thinking that Lake Biwa is just an "ancient lake." . . . This is a big experiment that can contribute to the human race. . . . If this succeeds, others around the world can use the know-how that we gained. . . . Plus, this can also benefit the more than 14 million people who use the lake.

The Shiga government's efforts to develop a broader environmental vision, through the creation of a more comprehensive plan to preserve the lake, contrasted sharply with the LBCDP. The new efforts revealed an evolution of thought, from the central government's (for example, the MOC's) former one-size-fits-all approach to water resource development to a vision that integrated local businesses' and local residents' daily activities and concerns. Arguably, the Shiga governor's words were designed, in no small part, to enhance his (and Shiga Prefecture's) image. At the same time, however, they did integrate, to a greater extent than ever before, the concerns of local people who, by speaking out and acting to take back control of local water resources and environments, seriously challenged water management from a distance.

Cultivating Environmental Values from the Top-Down

For decades, Japanese activists sought to change the government mindset so that it incorporated *kankyo mondai* into policy decisions. At the start of the twenty-first century, as in Minamata, government officials began to speak of changing the citizens' mindset—in other words, of inculcating environmental values in citizens. This has been an uphill struggle for officials in Shiga Prefecture, where efforts at enlarging public participation have not always gone smoothly, in large part due to the divide between old and new residents. Kotani Hiroya, a Shiga prefectural official with responsibility for setting policy on Lake Biwa, saw the divide as a hindrance to the government's program to get local people to adopt environmental values and live by them:

> Initially we organized around a group of respectable leaders, including those residents who have been living here for a long time. But the problematic gap emerged and hampered progress. New residents voice their opinions more than old residents, and the presence of new residents at town meetings overwhelms that of the old residents. This is the biggest reason why things become confrontational. The old residents are very frustrated because even when they have opinions, they cannot voice them; the [new residents'] louder majority voice tends to get heard. And so we need to formulate a system in which the old residents' opinions are articulated and embraced. The way to solve this problem must come from within.[97]

Despite these challenges, Kotani felt that the government had an important leadership role to play in pushing for progress on environmental issues, particularly in shifting emphasis from the *kogai* mind-set to *kankyo mondai* mind-set. As Kotani told us, Japan's narrow focus on pollution control, *kogai*, lent itself to a centralized approach to decision-making that relied exclusively on science. Science alone, as he pointed out, cannot address the environmental concerns of people, which cannot be captured only by statistics that measure human health. Having recognized this, the Shiga prefectural government, like other local governments around Japan, began to seek out ways to better integrate local people's concerns into policy. The prefectural government continued to function as a middleman between the local people, whose needs and values had become more complex and varied, and those of the national government, which has stepped back from its role as the patron of industrial development. As Kotani implied, in this context citizens needed to find ways to work more effectively with government officials.

To some, a top-down environmental initiative was by its very nature a stumbling block to progress. Though Hosoya, who spearheaded the soap movement of the late 1970s, lamented a lack of grassroots organizing and environmental values among the ordinary residents, he said government efforts to mobilize people resulted in what he calls YGOs—"Yes Government Organizations," which are neither effective nor self-sustaining. NGOs, on the other hand, are more credible in the eyes of the public and thus in a better position to organize campaigns and to work with citizens to influence changes in values and practices that will protect the environment. For this reason Hosoya believed that, in the top-down nature of the project to protect Lake Biwa, the government had it wrong. He told us, "It seems like the government is trying too hard to think about ways to get residents to ride along."

Hosoya also believed the government placed too much emphasis on its own "report card" of progress enacting environmental policies and not enough on results in terms of the health of the lake itself. Providing independent information on the status of the lake and calling attention to unresolved problems is one function that an independent citizens' organization could perform. Most importantly, perhaps, despite divisions between new and old residents, and other, traditional schisms within Japanese society, Hosoya wanted to see more independent citizen participation in policy decisions. We argue in this chapter that a wide range of citizen efforts—including the soap movement, the Lake Biwa lawsuit, and the anti-dam movements, all of which had their critics and unique flaws—have nevertheless demonstrated the benefits of such participation. Each of these movements has taken Shiga (and Japan as a whole) closer to a political culture and situation in which the values and concerns of local residents are more fully integrated into environmental policy decisions. Increased local control of local environments and resources is a notion whose time has come. As Hosoya stated, Japan's environmental problems remain considerable, but progress has been and is being made.

In retrospect, Lake Biwa's comprehensive conservation program was hard-earned. How it will be implemented remains an open question. To what extent will development be reined in? To what extent will industry and other entrenched interests be forced to sacrifice? At the same time, it is clear that the efforts of Shiga residents, documented in this chapter, helped to fuel change and helped focus attention on local needs.

The high-profile struggles at Lake Biwa inspired a new vein of environmental activism in Japan. Environmentalists and local residents in other areas began to see the need to block outdated, grandiose water development schemes based on inflated projections of water demand, prevention of "hundred-year floods," and questionable political dealings that hand lucrative construction projects to politically influential construction companies—with inadequate regard for aquatic ecosystems. The Nagara anti-dam movement, the story of which follows, advanced awareness of problems with water projects all across Japan. It is yet another manifestation of the growing dissatisfaction with the old-style water planning process.

The Nagara River Estuary Dam and the Yoshino River Moving Dam

The Nagara River Estuary Dam Movement

Although Lake Biwa residents mobilized around the problem of eutrophication, a locally conceived and locally led movement against the Lake Biwa Comprehensive Development Plan failed to coalesce. In the case of the Nagara River Dam, by contrast, a public works project became the center of a major opposition movement that gained national and international attention and support. We offer this case as an example of the development of a Japanese citizen movement that adopted *kankyo mondai*, in this case a resource conservation problem, as its central cause and rallying call. This opposition movement, which gained momentum in the late 1980s, represents a further departure from the narrower agendas and arguments of earlier environmental activism in Japan, and from the focus on *kogai*. While the movement ultimately failed to stop the dam construction, it had a critical impact on public participation and government decision-making over major water works projects across Japan.

The Yoshino River Moving Dam project, another controversial case that began to unfold in the mid-1990s, offers yet a more recent example of activism. This project, in which a popular referendum was held on whether a dam should be constructed, played out in a changed political environment in which Japanese citizens, in the wake of the Nagara Dam controversy, have increasingly demanded a voice in the planning and decision-making affecting dam construction in their locales, and have endeavored to extend that participation beyond water works to major public works of all kinds. By 2004, Japanese citizens were increasingly calling upon the government to stop unnecessary public works projects that would harm the environment.

Dam Construction vs. Fishing Rights: Nagara Fishermen Bring Their Case to the Courts

The Nagara Dam opposition movement became known both within and outside of Japan for its high-profile protest actions. Most accounts of the controversy over the dam make little mention, however, of the early phases of opposition in which fishermen (as with Lake Biwa) were the primary opponents. Yet in our view the early history is an important part of the story. Unlike their counterparts at Lake Biwa, fishermen opposing the Nagara Dam stepped beyond their traditional mode of asking for compensation via their fishing cooperatives and took their plight (and the government) to court. More important, their arguments and early resistance to the project laid the groundwork for a more confrontational form of grassroots activism.

The controversy began in 1960, when the central government formally announced a plan to construct a dam at the mouth of the Nagara River in Gifu Prefecture (in the Chubu region of central Japan). The original purpose of the estuary dam was to supply water for industrial use. Japan had entered a period of rapid economic development and the development of water resources for industry had become a top priority for the Ikeda cabinet. Then in September 1959 the Isewan Typhoon caused the Chubu area to experience the worst flood damage in its history: more than 5,000 people died. This experience led to the idea of a dam at the mouth of the river that could both control floods and provide water to industry. At the time, controlling floods by damming at the river mouth was a new idea, one that would prove controversial in the decades to come.

From the start, local fishers vigorously opposed this plan, which would entail construction in, and the damming of, their fishing waters. As with Lake Biwa and the comprehensive development plan, however, local rights over water resources were overridden by economic and political priorities. Following the legal path created by the National Comprehensive Development Plan (NCDP) of 1950, the Electric Power Law of 1953, and the establishment of the Water Resources Development Corporation (WRDC) in 1961, the central government assumed the sole authority to decide on natural resource allocations and their economic uses, *without* parliamentary debate or approval.

Thus, in 1968, the central government decided to construct the dam, and in 1973 the Ministry of Construction gave its approval. To local government officials like Koreto Hisatake in the town of Yogo, the water resource development laws enacted in the 1960s and the institutions formed to carry them out rendered the Ministry of Construction "emperor-like" (*tenno no yo*)—that is, all-powerful. The resistance of local residents and sport fishers, who registered opposition, however sporadic and small-scale, through their fishing cooperatives, could do little to change MOC policies; but the objections and claims of the fishers, whose fishing rights in local waters were protected by law, could and did *delay* the construction. Just as the commercial fishers of Lake Biwa could demand compensation for damage to their "property" (under Japanese law, fishing rights are a form of property), Nagara fishermen technically were within their rights to block any construction that would harm the fish in local waters.

With the Ministry of Construction's official approval of dam construction, the fishermen, after years of resistance, decided to adopt more confrontational tactics. In 1973, over twenty-six thousand local fishermen from seven fishing cooperatives along the upper and middle regions of the river and other people living near the site sued the national government to halt the project. This number of plaintiffs is much larger than the number who filed in the downstream lawsuit in the Lake Biwa case; indeed, the list of plaintiffs was one of the longest ever for a preventative environmental lawsuit in Japan. (The Minamata disease suits, by contrast, were damage claims.) The Nagara plaintiffs had a case: an estuary dam would affect their fish catches, their major source of livelihood.

Within the next few years, the underlying rationale for the dam—a projected increase in demand for water, based on projected economic growth—had begun to weaken. Regional economic growth slowed, with the oil shocks of the 1970s, and the demand for water began to drop significantly. Nevertheless, the government continued to forecast large increases in water demand, but this only intensified opposition to the dam; critics claimed that the predictions had no basis in reality, and were merely a "bureaucratic exercise." According to at least one independent analyst, the new realities made not only the Nagara River Dam unnecessary, but also the Tokuyama Dam on the neighboring Ibi River, which was already in the planning stages.[98]

The lawsuit lost some of its steam after 1976, when severe flood damage occurred in the town of Anpachi, which lies along the Nagara River. Following the floods, the public rallied behind the dam's function of flood control, just as it had after the floods of 1959. In 1978, the governor of Gifu Prefecture, where most of the flood damage had occurred, consented to the building of the dam, the bill for which would eventually be 150 billion yen ($1.7 billion in 1995 dollars).[99]The fisher plaintiffs had originally claimed that the dam would actually cause more flooding, but the Anpachi flood swayed public opinion in support of the dam. "Fish or human life, which do you conserve?" was a common argument against the fishers, who had been silenced in their arguments about loss of fish.

In 1981 the fishing cooperatives dropped their 1973 legal action because of procedural problems stemming from the huge number of plaintiffs, the settlement of fishing compensation payments, and political pressure from the prefectural and municipal governments. It was replaced by a second lawsuit filed only by the Akasuka Fishing Cooperatives of the lower Nagara River, which made the same claims to loss of fish and livelihood. Eager to move the project forward, in February 1988 the government offered the protesting fishers of the Akasuka Fishing Cooperatives compensation in exchange for their consent to the dam project, and the fishers accepted. One month later, the Water Resources Development Corporation signed a contract with three major construction companies, and the construction work began in 1989. The prefectural government planned to finance the construction with profits they made from the sale of water, which they expected to be larger than they turned out to be. According to a 1998 editorial in the left-leaning national daily *Asahi Shimbun*, "The prefectural governments of Aichi and Mie [both would be users of Nagara River dam water]were counting on revenues from selling that water to pay back their debts on dam construction. But now that this has become impossible, they have to dip into taxpayers' money."

The compensation to fishermen was calculated on the basis of forecast decreases in the fish catch. Although the total amount dispensed in the Nagara case was not made public, the Akasuka Fishing Cooperative's newsletter reported 30 million yen for each of 200 members, or about US$250,000 per fisher, which roughly amounts to several years' income. The sufficiency of this settlement remains controversial, however, because the decline in the catch persists today. Even in 2004 activists were locked in fierce debate with the Ministry of Land, Infrastructure, and Transport about the inadequacy of a few years of income to compensate for a lifetime of projected losses, to say nothing of the loss of a way of life.

Environmentalism Comes to Nagara: Amano Reiko Incites New Opposition to the Dam

> Our leaders sacrificed all our rivers for economic development. . . . The Nagara River was the last that remained.[100]
>
> Amano Reiko

Until 1988, despite the large numbers of people involved in the lawsuit and the official settlement, protest against the dam received little public attention in Japan. With the fishermen's resistance swept aside, other local residents who had opposed the dam lost an important ally. But as with Lake Biwa, the entry of outsiders into the fray had an important effect on the environmental debate. In the Nagara case, however, outsiders brought about much more dramatic change.

In 1988, Amano Reiko, an Osaka resident, journalist, and sport fisher, began a movement that attracted recreational fishers, nature writers, and other concerned people from *outside* the Nagara River area. The movement grew into a coalition—the Society Against the Nagara River Estuary Dam Construction (SANREDC)—made up of sixty-three opposition groups. SANREDC quickly grew to sixteen thousand members, with branch offices in towns along the Nagara River and in Tokyo and other cities.[101] In addition to sport fishers and canoeists, the movement included academics, environmental scientists and activists, photographers, politicians, and celebrities.[102] At its height, the movement used celebrities more effectively than any Japanese opposition movement ever had done to gain favorable media attention and broad support.

While some local residents joined the coalition, the activists were primarily repeat-visitors to the area who saw the Nagara River as an important site for leisure activities. In their arguments against the dam, they stressed their opposition to the destruction of nature, especially the destruction of habitat for the sweet fish (*ayu*) and trout. In framing the issue, the activists treated aquatic life symbolically stressing the traditional importance of *ayu* as reflected in Japanese art and literature, and the movement became tinted with romanticism. Amano explained that her leadership of the movement was based on her determination to "save the last natural river in Japan," as nearly all other large rivers in Japan were by that time already dammed.[103]

Those who supported the dam felt that the claims of the environmentalists were nostalgic and impractical. Mizuno Mitsuaki, an official of a water resource agency affiliated with the Ministry of Construction, said at the time, "It's just emotional sentimentalism to want a river to remain just as it is. Such thinking has no place in modern society."[104] A spokesperson for the Ministry of Construction offered a similar line of thinking when he declared:

> A river is there for humans to develop and make appropriate use of. That should be obvious to any sane person. . . . We are concerned with the total environment for humans. And if the natural fish happen to die in the process, we possess the technology to supply new fish raised in captivity. So, you see, there is really no problem.[105]

Yet the language and spirit of the movement had an impact on the way that people, young and old, speak of the Nagara environment. Yasufuku Koji, an eighty-five-year-old fisherman we interviewed in 2000,[106] said he had joined the fight against the dam in the early days because he supported "the conservation of fishing resources like *ayu* fish and *sijimi* crab." His use of the terms *conservation* and *resource* was a sign that he had been influenced by the movement, because traditionally the environment was not perceived or referred to as a resource. Other statements of this long-time resident reflected a more traditional conception of, and personal relationship with, nature. "I know what environment fish like to live in," Yasufuku commented. "I can tell what fish want because I have engaged in *ayu* fishing for more than seventy years."

The sport fisher outsiders brought new arguments as well as new energy and determination to the opposition. They were not willing to sacrifice the qualitative contributions the river made to their lives, particularly when the increased water supply the dam project would yield was unnecessary. The movement denounced the government—especially the Ministry of Construction and the ruling Liberal Democratic Party—for using taxpayers' money for such an unnecessary project, particularly when the public had been offered little opportunity to participate either in developing the policy or in its implementation. After all, the economic projections were faulty: water demand had not grown as the government had predicted.

Despite the strength and energy of this environmental movement, the powerful combination of government and engineering contractors prevailed. The dam was built and began operations in 1995. The opposition movement, however, continued to criticize the dam, broadened its agenda by questioning the government's entire program of long-planned and outdated "public works" projects, which had absorbed massive tax revenue.

Also, unlike the earlier resistance by local commercial fishers and residents, the SANREDC movement directed considerable media attention to the questions surrounding public works projects. By criticizing the projects as *muda na kokyo jigyou* (useless public works) and condemning the policies that promoted them, the movement popularized its message beyond the stratum of intellectuals and activists who usually agitated for environmental causes. The movement attracted broader support from all over Japan, and from abroad as well. Internationally known environmental luminaries such as David Brower, founder of the Sierra Club in the United States, attended anti–Nagara Dam demonstrations. The movement's strategy of making its events socially enjoyable as well as political—including live music concerts and canoe races—raised awareness and drew many into environmental activism. The image of hundreds of canoeists at the site of the dam, raising their paddles while chanting protest slogans, is famous in Japan. In large part, the political achievements of the movement before 1995 were due to the efforts of Amano, who had lobbied members of the Japanese parliament twice a week for seven years[107] and on two such visits to parliament staged hunger strikes to demonstrate the urgency of the cause.

While Amano's movement popularized environmentalism as "conservation" and drew considerable support among people outside of Nagara, it was not embraced by many of the local fishermen, who had started their resistance decades earlier. Promoted by the media, led by intellectuals from outside the community, and energized by celebrity participation, the anti-dam movement of the late 1980s and 1990s remained a thing apart for the Nagara fishermen. Amano was charismatic and well able to enlist outside support, but the qualities that recommended her to a broader, urbane public did not endear her to the local fishing community. Though they were reluctant to criticize her in their interviews with us, the local fishermen would reiterate their concerns for the conservation of fish as the source of their livelihood, in distinction to Amano's group, which they described as more concerned with ecosystems and criticism of public works.

Even where older residents agreed with the outsiders' movement on the issues, they were divided from the outsiders by culture. "The dam puts us in more danger, not less danger," said Ito Yoshinobu, a local farmer and sometime fisherman. "Many of my neighbors are frightened as I am. But they feel it is un-Japanese to protest or even to question the decisions of government."[108]

Still, the movement inspired other, particularly younger and more urban, residents of Gifu Prefecture to speak out. Adachi Takashi, a sportsman and graphic designer from the city of Gifu, inspired by his involvement in Amano's movement, formed his own protest group called Save the Satsukimasu (a trout that is threatened by the dam). He explained that he also found inspiration abroad, in the experience of Americans who had opposed the Tellico Dam on the Little Tennessee River on the grounds that it endangered the snail darter, a native fish. Takashi said he opposed the dam not only for the sake of the fish themselves but because their reduced numbers would harm commercial fishermen and because citizens had been cut off from the policy-making that paved the way for the dam. "My fight is as much a struggle for democracy in Japan as anything else," he said, wistfully.[109]

The Society Against the Nagara River Estuary Dam Construction was influenced and supported by international NGOs and environmentalists active in and outside Japan. When NGOs operating in Japan, such as the international group Friends of the Earth, swayed Japan's bilateral foreign aid agency, the OECF, to withdraw financing for the controversial Narmada Dam in India because of environmental concerns, members of the Nagara movement could point to the inconsistency between the policy at home and abroad. Furthermore, Amano Reiko's personal networking at the 1992 Earth Summit in Rio and beyond brought international attention to the Nagara issue. It also brought many world-renowned environmental experts and officials to Nagara to speak about the hazards of dam construction.[110] Their warnings linked the Nagara movement to a broad international movement to limit environmentally damaging dam construction around the world.

One of the outcomes of this international exchange was the formation by the Japanese Diet of a nonpartisan organization—the Diet Members' Association for a Mechanism of Public Works Review (DAMPWR)—that called for independent reviews of major public works projects. This group spearheaded information-gathering about and assessments of public works and helped to convince legislators of the need to cancel, or at least cut budgets for, the longest delayed, costliest, and most controversial of them.[111]

This development, of course, did not come in time to stop the Nagara River Dam. Construction of the dam, completed in 1995, cost 150 billion yen ($1.7 billion in 1995 dollars). Eight years later, in 2003, water consumption in the Nagara Dam region was about 6.3 million tons per day, but local officials predicted the figure would drop because of Japan's low birth rate. Even if consumption remained stable at 6.3 million tons per day, though, it was significantly below the 9.1 million tons per day of water consumption that the Ministry of Construction often cited in its defense of the dam.

Despite the failure to stop the Nagara Dam construction, Amano believes that her movement was instrumental in bringing about key changes to the River Law. The Ministry of Construction has denied her claim; in fact, the head of the river section of the ministry, Hirose Shunichi, in response to court testimony by scientists about the risk of damage to the *ayu* ecology that the the dam posed, had led his team in the early 1980s to study the river ecosystem. This, the ministry argues laid the groundwork for policy change. Still, when Japan's national River Law was amended in 1997, clauses were added calling for careful consideration for living creatures and for citizen participation before dam or river construction could go forward, ideas that the movement had vigorously promoted. In addition, the phrase "in order to improve and protect the river environment" (*kasen kankyo no seibi to hosen ga nasareru yo*) was included within a clause in the first section. While the new language did not refer to living creatures, the term *environment* was understood to include living creatures and their habitats. On citizen participation, the following clause was added: "When developing plans for river management, managers need to provide mechanisms for public input of affected parties, such as public hearings."[112] This was a significant change from the previous, long-standing policy-making process, in which "river managers"—meaning the MOC or prefectural government, for larger rivers—were able to make decisions without public input.

In accordance with the amended law, in 2001 the Ministry of Land, Infrastructure and Transport formed a new kind of citizen committee, the Yodo River Basin Committee (*Yodogawa Suikei Ryuuiki Iinnkai*), comprising fifty-three people, including more than ten local residents to review the plans for the Yodo River system. In addition to including citizen representatives as full members, this committee differed from those that came before it because it actually authored the recommendations, compared to the past when bureaucrats would author them and the citizen involvement would be nominal.[113] By the spring of 2004, the committee had convened more than three hundred times to deliberate on issues related to the river environment, how to involve society in flood prevention and water conservation, rethinking dam construction, and resident participation in decision-making. The committee aimed to establish a basic framework for community involvement that could be adopted throughout Japan. That year it publicized a recommendation that dams should only be constructed when all other measures of flood control have been examined and only after assessing the full social impact. The impact of the committee was profound. In July 2005, the Ministry of Land, Infrastructure and Transport decided to stop the construction of two dams in the Yodo River system, the Daidogawa Dam and the Yonogawa Dam. This was the first time in Japan that a decision was made to stop dam construction when construction was already under way. In addition, the ministry decided to reduce the size of two planned dams, the Niu Dam and the Kawakami Dam.

Those who sought to mobilize local resistance to other dam projects, such as the proposed "moving dam" for the Yoshino River, learned from the experience at Nagara. The local government wanted the dam, which would cost more than 100 billion yen ($900 million in 1999 dollars), for the funds it would inject into the local economy; because it was solely a flood control project, the national government would be responsible for bearing the full cost. Himeno Masayoshi, a court reporter and a resident of Tokushima City, where the Yoshino River flows, led a movement to hold a citizens' referendum on the need for the dam. The MOC had refused to make public the details of the construction plan, and thus Himeno saw a referendum as the citizens' only option.

Himeno was aware of the limited role that Amano Reiko, as an outsider, had been able to play in mobilizing local public opposition to the Nagara Dam. By adopting a strategy that brought insiders, local residents, to the center of his movement, Himeno forced the government to hold the referendum on damming the Yoshino. The referendum —the country's first on a public works project[114]—took place on January 23, 2000, and more than half of those who voted opposed dam construction. The minister of construction called the vote a "mistaken exercise in democracy."[115]

Despite the referendum, the Ministry of Construction did not change its plans for dam construction; over the following two years the Yoshino Dam issue moved to the epicenter of local politics. In 2002, Himeno and his group successfully supported the candidacy of Ota Tadashi, who campaigned on an anti-dam platform, as governor of Tokushima Prefecture. Just one year later, however, in April 2003 a no-confidence bill was passed by members of the Tokushima Prefecture Assembly (made up largely of Liberal Democratic Party members), and Ota was forced to resign. On May 18, 2003, another gubernatorial election was held, and Ota lost to Iizumi Kamon, a young LDP bureaucrat from the national government. During his campaign Iizumi publicly pledged to oppose dam construction, and as of 2004 the Ministry of Land, Infrastructure, and Transportation was putting pressure on him to change his position.[116]

The Legacy of Lake Biwa and the Nagara River

The long process of recovering local control over local environments—which began with the tragedy of Minamata disease, found limited expression in the Lake Biwa soap movement and trial, and advanced more dramatically during the anti–Nagara Dam movement—increased the popularity of citizen referenda in Japan. These referenda are now being called on a broad range of public projects, including roads, land reclamation, and waste disposal plants as well as dams. Thus, concern over public works, particularly their effect on Japan's changing landscape, is continuing to shape and change the nature of citizen participation, environmental policy-making, and Japanese democracy as a whole. Citizen demands for greater accountability and more sensible planning are converging with economic demands—specifically, Japan's need to remain competitive in an increasingly globalized economy and to reduce its sizable national debt. The result is widespread recognition that the Japanese government must maximize the social and environmental efficiency of its investments in infrastructure and water resource management.

The process of rethinking major public works construction projects was given an international boost during the anti–Nagara Dam movement. At the beginning of this section, we noted that in seeking a model for modernizing its water resource management, Japan had adopted concepts and methods used by the American Tennessee Valley Authority (TVA) when it developed dams to produce hydroelectric power that could fuel industrial growth. But by the early 1990s the TVA itself had come to view some of its projects and practices as environmentally destructive. Robert Herbst, a TVA representative, visited Japan in 1992 at the invitation of Nagara's environmental activists. At an annual anti-dam event, he explained the shift in the TVA's thinking about dams and spoke persuasively against the Nagara project. In meetings with Ministry of Construction officials, he stressed the same points. His personal presence helped demonstrate to Japanese policymakers that other industrialized countries were well into the process of scaling back major dam works because they had become too costly (environmentally and socially as well as financially), and that a reevaluation was also in order for Japan.[117]

The globalization of the Japanese economy has also helped change the way in which public works projects are considered and run. Japan's huge debt level has made public works boondoggles economically unfeasible as well as politically dangerous, placing in jeopardy international trust in the Japanese government and the yen. Thus, since fiscal year 1996 the government has abandoned more than ninety-two dam construction plans.[118]

Safety issues have also played a role. Severe floods in 2002, which hit particularly hard Nagoya City, and in 2004 Niigata, Fukui, northern Kyoto and Hyogo, reminded citizens and government alike about the vulnerability of urbanized areas, and how ill-equipped a central administrative system is to cope with these emergencies at the local level.[119] Kada Yukiko, this chapter's lead researcher, has been engaged in a movement to encourage every Japanese community to take "small" flood prevention measures, such as creating community planning committees, which would add up to a significant national prevention effort and would also empower local communities and conserve the ecology of the country's rivers.

A major earthquake that racked the city of Kobe in 1995 had already spurred a trend away from nationally planned and managed infrastructure projects. The government's slow response to the earthquake helped convince people that national-level bureaucrats could not take care of all local problems. The shortcomings in the government's response to the earthquake highlighted the need for more local control and thus more local capacity to deal with public infrastructure issues, among them water resources.

The political fallout from citizen environmental movements such as the Nagara Dam movement and the Yoshino Dam referendum has moved the review of major public works higher on the agenda of politicians and policy-makers. Amano Reiko, speaking at the Third World Water Forum Participation Session, in Kyoto on March 21, 2003, described the developments made possible by the changed political atmosphere:

> The members of an assembly called "the construction group" of the Liberal Democratic Party held a study meeting to restore meandering rivers in December 2001. Then, they concluded a nature-restoring promotion bill in December 2002. A woman governor in Kumamoto prefecture made a decision to remove a dam for the first time in December 2003. She could do so because the construction group of the local Liberal Democratic Party considered removing dams to be "new public works."[120]

Opposition parties have promised to go much further, pressuring the ruling Liberal Democratic Party to demonstrate its intentions to correct its past mistakes. In the run-up to the general election in November 2003, the Democratic Party of Japan, the largest opposition party,[121] declared as one of its "five pledges" its commitment to "immediately terminating wasteful public-works projects, such as the Kawabe river dam . . . and Yoshino River sluice-gate dam."[122]

If the political process for effecting change in national public works policies has been slow and partisan, consensus-building at the local level, which is often divided along insider versus outsider and new resident versus old resident lines, has also been difficult. Since the 1997 River Law, citizen referenda on river dams have granted local citizens a means of taking back a measure of control over plans for dams in their locales. But this recovery of local power has not come easily or always gone smoothly. Some local city or township assembly members, often those tied to powerful local construction companies and other business interests, dislike resident participation and it is common for the local assembly to use the legal process to deny public referenda since to accept the referenda means a diminished role and status for the local assembly. Furthermore, increased local participation does not always translate into votes in favor of local environmental protection over the development of local resources.

The planned Niu Dam on the Takatoki River offers one example of the sometimes confusing effects of increased local participation. Local residents in villages along this river, which feeds Lake Biwa, had opposed the dam for years on the grounds that the risk was far too high: If the dam broke, their village would be destroyed. After thirty years of opposition to the construction, in the 1990s the residents finally accepted it in the expectation that with the dam would come the economic development of the area, including leisure facilities that could lure the younger generation back to the region, as part of a compensation package promised by the Ministry of Construction. The residents whose homes would be flooded by the dam were relocated in the late 1990s, and for a time it looked as if the issue was settled, and the opposition to the dam quelled.

However, only a few years later the Yodo River Basin Committee, described above, recommended that the dam be stopped both because of its harm to the environment and on the grounds that the slowdown of the economy in 2002 meant that the need for water was not as great as had been anticipated. The committee found that their recommendations against constructing the dam were being opposed by those same local residents, many of whom had come to favor the dam for its advertised advantages. Furthermore, the forty or so families who in the 1990s relocated from the villages that the dam was to have flooded were now bitter that the construction had been delayed—and could possibly be cancelled altogether. These pro-dam residents would rather allow the prefectural level of government the authority to proceed with the dam (in 2005 the prefectural governor, Kunimatsu, favored the dam) and overrule local input to the contrary.

The Kawabe Dam controversy, another struggle where consensus-building has been difficult, provides evidence that the central-local struggle for control over water resources continues to be hard fought. The Kumagawa Fishermen's Union (which represents about two thousand members) has held out against the project the strongest and longest, arguing that the dam would threaten fishing in their territory. The national government and the fishermen were unable to agree on compensation, and without the fishermen's consent, the government could not proceed with construction. Thus, for the first time in Japanese history the national government attempted "compulsory confiscation" of fishing rights. This controversy has also pitted the central and prefectural governments against one another, with the prefectural governor backing the fishermen.

While dams and river administration issues have been high-profile targets for local citizens' groups and activists, local residents have been slow to recognize or criticize poorly planned and potentially harmful sewer and wastewater treatment projects. These have long been considered quality of life improvements, understood to bring cleaner water (as well as the convenience of flush toilets) to residents. Sewer and wastewater projects account for the largest component—30 percent—of public works budgets in Japan today.[123] But the link between sewage treatment and harm to local waterways has not been widely understood, a particular problem in the Lake Biwa region, where sewage treatment is now the most costly in Japan.

While it remains uncontroversial for the moment, sewer construction may well be the next front in the struggle for local participation in decisions about public works. Many small towns have become financially saddled (and some bankrupted) by huge sewer systems that they were compelled to install by decisions of the national government (Ministry of Construction) and prefectural government. Central government subsidies for running these systems have long since dried up, and local communities have had to foot the bill. In addition to financial considerations, there is a strong environmental argument for cutting back vast, centrally planned sewage disposal and treatment systems and returning to smaller-scale, more independent, and locally managed wastewater treatment systems.

Japan has come far from the days in which citizens accepted without question major transformations to their environments in the name of development. These days, there appears to be a genuine dialogue between government officials and local citizens over the management of local water resources.[124] The story of Lake Biwa and the Nagara River (and other regions recovering from environmental damage) in the twenty-first century is the story of an effort to forge a new, more appropriate relationship between local people and local waters in vastly transformed environments.

Environmental Values in Transition

The cases we describe above reflect an evolution in Japanese society and its values over the last half century. Each case contributes to our understanding of Japan's progression from societal concern for the environment stemming from *kogai* (a reactive concern about pollution) to societal concern for *kankyo mondai* (a proactive and preemptive concern about ecology and environmental conditions of people's lives). This evolution involves three phases: the traditional, or "embedded whole," phase, during which humans are seen as one with nature; a second, "disembedded" phase, marked by a clash of values and by social division; and a third, "balanced whole" phase, in which competing values are balanced out so that none receives sole or disproportionate emphasis. Japan is well into a transition from the second phase to this third phase, in which *kankyo mondai* is weighted equally with values of economic development, human livelihoods, and safety.

As we saw in the case studies, this transition was accompanied by a shift in the nature of Japanese citizens' relationship with local waters. In the resource-use cases in particular, lakes and rivers that once were valued as "nearby" water supplies, were transformed over the decades by modern water delivery systems into "faraway" water. By the end of our case studies, we see the beginning of a shift in perceptions and environmental values concerning water toward a form of awareness of the coexistence of humans and nature.

By *environmental value* we mean a cultural and social standard for attitudes and behavior related to the interaction between nature and people. Through our research we have identified three types of values—instrumental values, intrinsic values, and compassion values. *Instrumental values* are those connected with people's motivation to secure their material needs; people operating from instrumental values see the worth of an entity in terms of its practical use or the material benefits it affords. This category includes the value placed upon production, scientific and technological progress, and material security (safety issues, avoiding hazardous damage). *Intrinsic values* are those that place primacy on human and other life, seeing life itself as intrinsically valuable. *Compassion values* are those that motivate and foster communion with both nature and people as a means of seeking mental or spiritual satisfaction.

These three value types are active during all three societal phases described above; however, when one type predominates, social friction results. Instrumental values were evident in water policy, for example, during the flood control efforts (which focused on human safety) that immediately followed the Meiji Restoration and in the postwar emphasis on water resource utilization for economic development. *Intrinsic values* were evident in the Nagara Dam controversy, where the anti-dam movement emphasized the importance of the survival of *ayu* fish. They are also evident, though tempered by other values, in recent Lake Biwa policy attempts to "coexist with water" as part of the Comprehensive Conservation Plan.

In each case there were "framers," activists, intellectuals, or politicians who cast developments and arguments about the environment in a light that influenced and rallied people to support or oppose environmental causes.[125] These people are responsible in no small part for helping to bring environmental values—in other words, values that emphasize *kankyo mondai*—to the forefront of public policy debate, nudging Japanese society from the second to the third phase of environmental consciousness. International influences have also helped promote a shift in values toward concern for *kankyo mondai* and "peaceful coexistence" with the environment.

Phase One: "Embedded Whole" Society and the Role of Nature

In the past, people at the four key sites we examined—Minamata, Niigata, Lake Biwa, and the Nagara River watershed—depended on a sea, lake, or river for their livelihood. At each site a distinct set of social arrangements, a so-called environmental culture, emerged out of long-standing human and human-nature interactions. Each of these traditional environmental cultures governed the use of resources and the ways in which environmental conflicts were managed within the community. Usually, these arrangements produced environmentally sustainable outcomes for the next generation.[126] For example, the people of Lake Biwa understood that floods promoted the spawning of fish in the lake, a rich resource for the local people. According to Nakagawa Taiyu, a farmer living near Lake Biwa, "The flood is not always bad. It brings fish to our village."[127]

We call traditional Japanese communities coexisting with their environment "embedded whole" societies. For embedded whole societies, environmental values do not translate into valuing specific elements of the environment, or even into a discrete concept of nature. Rather, in these societies people see themselves as central to and indistinguishable from the "lifeworld" in which humans and the environment are parts of the same whole. Ogata Masato, the Minamata fisherman/activist, described the traditional mind-set about nature this way:

> In the past we had no use for the word *shizen*, nature. It's only in the last twenty years or so that we've started to hear this word. Our lives were so immersed in nature there was no

need to distinguish it [from ourselves]. If people fell into the river or the sea, we would say they had been sucked up by *garappa*, a water goblin. . . . This is how our people described the powers of nature; on the one hand, they warned us against its vagaries, and on the other, they expressed feelings of closeness and affection.[128]

In Japan's traditional societies, terms such as *environment* or *nature* that refer generally to the physical environment are unknown. Animal and plant species are considered individually, and referred to familiarly by name (such as *garappa*, above). This type of interaction with nature (which has animistic elements that are enshrined in the Shinto religion) prevents total extraction of humans from nature or the idea of the environment as a thing apart. Rather, people in this phase feel a connection to nature and understand its multiple meanings, as in the case of Mr. Nakagawa's complex understanding of floods. Ogata bespeaks the sense of interconnectedness with nature that governed the life of traditional fishermen in the areas of Japan where we conducted our case studies when he said:

When I catch a lot of fish, I love the sea. But if I catch too many, I begin to get scared. To take fish is to take lives. If I take too many, I fear that I will pay with my own life.[129]

Phase Two: The "Disembedded" Phase, in Which People Are Distanced from Nature

The deep connection between people and nature was the cultural context of rural Japan in the 1950s and 1960s into which "innovators" brought modern industry and bureaucracy. The innovators in Minamata and Niigata were the modern chemical manufacturers, Chisso Corporation and Showa Denko. In the Nagara River and Lake Biwa regions, the innovators were government officials who dammed a natural lake and rivers to satisfy a burgeoning demand for water. Modernization was accompanied by two important, interrelated transformations: a specialization of social roles, which created divides between rural and urban communities and between technocrats and lay people; and the abstraction of nature through science, which resulted in a new emphasis on the material value of natural resources.

In Japanese, the abstraction of nature from its traditional role in people's social and cultural lives is called *datsu-bunmyaku-ka* (disembedding). After disembedding, people came to believe that a man drowns in the sea because of bad weather rather than the *garappa*'s power. After nature became valued as an economic resource, people welcomed enormous fish catches for the higher economic return they would yield them instead of worrying about overfishing or taking more than their due from nature.

The concept of "the environment" gained currency in Japan during this phase, as a byproduct of the pollution that accompanied modernization and industrialization. The pollution, along with resource-use problems, caused friction among organizations and people holding different values. It is during this second societal phase that environmental problems came to be perceived as serious.

The clash of traditional and disembedded values regarding nature led to tragic consequences in Minamata on many different levels. The instrumental valuing of nature allowed industry to run roughshod over the environment. At the same time, traditional views of nature as a familiar friend encouraged fishermen to continue their old dietary habits, which proved deadly to some of them. Even when the local people realized that fish taken from Minamata Bay were poisonous, they continued to eat them. They continued to trust the natural world, against all evidence. Many disease victims saw their parents, siblings, and relatives killed—but none of the managerial class of Chisso employees who had been sent to Minamata from the head office in Tokyo, whose livelihoods did not depend on the water, and for whom nature was decidedly abstract, died of Minamata disease.

Even after the cause of Minamata disease became known, local fishing families continued to have children, despite fears that the children would be born with birth defects. As Ogata explains, "We were granted this life, and we would not turn away from it." Pregnant women and their families did not choose abortion but instead accepted the life they were given, a fact that demonstrates their traditional values regarding life and also their compassion for living things. Eventually, however, the disease eroded the Kumamoto fishermen's deep trust of fish that lived in nearby seas and rivers. They came to see the fish as "dangerous," and thus their relationship with nature was fundamentally transformed.[130]

Changes in human relations and values are also reflected in the conflicts over water resource use. Traditionally, people regarded rivers and lakes as the home of living creatures, a source of sustenance as well as beauty, and places that offered recreational opportunities. Once the Lake Biwa Comprehensive Development Plan, with its objective of increasing water output, was announced in the early 1970s, the primary meaning of the lake shifted, however. The government no longer talked of Lake Biwa as a habitat for living creatures but in instrumental terms, as a key resource supporting Japan's industrialization and urbanization.[131] Lake Biwa's exclusive new role as a reservoir for the region was captured in the phrase "the *mizugame* (water jug) of Kansai."

Value Clashes, Social Conflict

In the cases we studied, social conflicts occurred between Minamata disease victims and Minamata residents, the Chisso Corporation, and its patron, the government; between residents downstream of Lake Biwa and the Lake Biwa lakeshore residents; between Nagara River fishermen and the dam planners in Tokyo, and, later, between the conservationist opponents of the Nagara and Yoshino River Dams and the government-industry development complex; and between old and new residents and between local residents and outsiders in all of these cases. All these conflicts were rooted in fundamental clashes about the environment—its meaning, its value, and its purpose.

The introduction of Chisso and its cadre of professionals to Minamata led to a clash between traditional and more modern (disembedded) lifestyles and means of production. While both long-term residents and new residents emphasized in their defense of their actions and beliefs the economic value of nature as a source of livelihood (fishermen during the period of the conflict increasingly came to view the sea as their economic resource), the different way in which each community responded to Minamata disease demonstrates a value gap between them. The "production first" attitude of Chisso management was manifest in rural Minamata in their discrimination against the disease victims. By contrast, the victims were reluctant at first to see their symptoms as stemming from an industrial offense against their resource. When the government supported the Chisso Corporation in its insistence that it had not caused the disease, it appears that modern, rationalist economic concerns (instrumental values) in the policy response prevailed over the intrinsic value of human life.

The social conflicts at Lake Biwa resulted from the same fundamental value conflicts, with fishermen seeking to preserve the lake and their traditional way of life from the water engineering projects (i.e., water level controls, dredging, sewers) that were driven by material, economic development values. The material compensation they eventually won came at the cost of their traditional livelihoods.

The LBCDP was founded on the instrumental values of human safety and economic development. The government's priorities for the lake were evident in its policy response to community complaints about the quality of lake water in the 1970s. Though the Shiga and national governments added an environmental preservation component to the Lake Biwa Comprehensive Development Plan at the final hour, this component, to the very limited extent the implementing agencies took it seriously, dealt with water quality in narrow, scientific terms (with a focus on reducing concentrations of specified substances in the water) that failed to account for quality-of-life improvements, either for humans or other species. In other words, the government policies improved the lake water according to selective measurements that did not take into account threats to the broader lake ecosystem (such as the destruction of reed beds and fish populations).

These government priorities conflicted with those of residents in the surrounding areas who relied on the lake. When downstream water users took the LBCDP to court, they asserted the importance of two types of values: the conservation of the ecosystem, an intrinsic value, as well as the right to drink clean water, an instrumental value, and pressed its claims through the modern system of legal action.

The disembedding process by which people became distanced from nature is clearly part of the story of water in Japan. From the late nineteenth century through the 1980s, Japanese people's connection with water changed from a close relationship with the nearby water resources upon which their daily lives depended, to a more disengaged sense of "water as far away," a consequence of development of major public water works. This was true both physically (their new water supply may have depended on a dam that was farther from their homes than their old water source), but also socially (the central government was now managing a resource that used to be locally managed). As a result, water also became farther away spiritually and emotionally; people lost interest in their local rivers and streams.

In the last two decades of the twentieth century, environmentalists—those people who emphasize compassion values—sought to encourage local people to "take back" their water and in doing so to revive an emotional connection with it on the premise that the people who live near and off the water, those with the greatest interest in its preservation, will be its best custodians (by embracing intrinsic values). This premise still has not been fully tested because that process of localized governance in Japan—evident in such cases as the Yoshino Dam, where citizen referenda have been used effectively to express the local will, and in the formation of the Yodo River Committee—is still developing. When it is fully realized, communities around the waterways can be said to have reached the third societal stage, in which water resources will be treated in a way that finds an appropriate balance between intrinsic values and instrumental values.

Toward a "Balanced Whole" Phase

The same disembedding process that allowed people to consider nature for its instrumental value to humans also has allowed them to consider it for its intrinsic value, a prerequisite for a form of "peaceful coexistence" between people and water. Japanese society, as our most recent water cases illustrate, is still in transition toward the last societal stage—the "balanced whole" stage.

If the early part of the second (disembedded) societal phase was marked by a preponderance of material values, which challenged traditional values, the late second phase can be said to be one in which compassion values predominate. These values, which involve communication among people in a way that promotes identification with other people and healing relationships with nature, are consistent with traditional values in Japan, although they do not replace them.

The leaders of the Moyainaoshi Campaign, Kamakura and Yoshimoto, provide a good example of the pursuit of compassion values. Both men worked within a context where "the revitalization of Minamata," a phrase used both within and outside policy circles, was valued as an undisputed public good. In their work on the campaign, they went beyond their role as public officials, linking to that role values that related to their identity as a resident of the community, or as someone who had grown up in rural Japan, where traditional values prevailed. Their activities even came to be accepted by their superiors, including the governor of Kumamoto prefecture and the mayor of Minamata.

The Lake Biwa case offers another example of how first citizens and then policy makers, successfully advanced compassion values.[132] Around the same time that scientists and local residents began to notice that species native to Lake Biwa were on the verge of extinction, they began to raise doubts about the materialist rationale for government policies. As community members, they began engaging in water-related conservation activities that emphasized the interaction between living creatures and human beings. In 1996 the Lake Biwa Museum opened, with exhibits emphasizing the strong cultural and spiritual ties between the people and the lake.[133] In 2000 the Shiga government departed from its policy emphasis on "comprehensive development" and began its program of "comprehensive environmental conservation" of Lake Biwa.

It is important to consider the impact of globalization on values in the transition between the second and third societal phases we have described. The environmental movements in all our cases have been influenced by the imported concept of the global environment, which implies that damage to a local ecosystem (a bay, a river) is damage to the earth, of which people of all nations should be responsible custodians. And our water resource cases offer many examples of the influence and support of foreign individuals and groups on local ideas about environmental degradation, the overdevelopment of water, and especially dams. Environmental movements across the globe are interconnected and mutually supportive as never before, aided by the efficiency and "megaphone" capabilities of the Internet; Japanese environmentalists have welcomed the support of international groups. In recent years, these groups, and sometimes local Japanese governments, have sponsored international environmental conferences in Japan—on mercury poisoning in water, on dam construction, and on other environmental issues. It is notable that the involvement of international groups has increased over time. Among our cases the environmental movements (to oppose the Nagara and Yoshino River Dams) have benefited from stronger international influence and support, helping to reframe the terms of the Japanese environmental debate.

With government and industry at its center, for more than half a century economic and material values have reigned supreme in Japanese society. Yet the 1990s saw the enactment of a Basic Environmental Law and the strengthening of the River Law, both expressions of life values. Transformative experiences such as the Kobe earthquake of 1995—also known as the Great Hanshin Earthquake—further increased the awareness of the interdependence of humans and nature. This awareness is anchored in the first, traditional phase of society that we described at the beginning of this section. It involves a sense of life that encompasses animistic experience, and the physical senses.

While Japanese society has identified the "environment" as an object of value (as understood in the term *kankyo mondai*), the third societal phase of balanced values is a goal that seems almost unattainable in the sense that instrumental values still dominate. How far Japanese society moves toward that goal will depend upon the next generation. Their custodianship of water, in turn, will depend upon the proven strength of compassion values, including institutional efforts of intergenerational communication about the value of water and all living things.

Notes

*The authors wish to thank Mary Child, who played a major role in adapting their work for this chapter, and Yumiko Shimabukuro for her assistance in translating the interviews.

1. This essential element of Japanese society has been well documented by Japanese sociologists. See, for example, S. Tamaki, *Mizu Shakai no Kouzou* [The Structure of Water Society] (Tokyo: Ronsousha, 1983).

2. See "Approaches to Water Pollution Control (Case Study-2) Minamata City, Kumamoto Prefecture," sec. 4, "The Social and Economic Impact of Minamata Disease," available at the International Center for Environmental Technology Transfer Web site, www.icett.or.jp/contents.nsf/Main?OpenFrameset, accessed 7 September 2005.

3. Japan Ministry of Environment, "Minamata Disease: The History and Measures (2002)," available at www.env.go.jp/en/topic/minamata.html, accessed 7 June 2004.

4. Mizoguchi Kozo, "Court Orders Japan to Pay in Mercury Case," Associated Press, 15 October 2004.

5. Soshisha Minamata Disease Center, ed., *E de miru Minamata byou* [Minamata Disease in Illustration] (Yokohama: Seori Shobo, 1993, rev. 2004). Soshisha's estimate of the number of latent patients is based upon heavy fish eating in the 1950s and 1960s in the Shiranui Bay area, where the mercury-containing fish migrated and were caught.

6. Douglas Allchin, "The Poisoning of Minamata," 1999, available at http://www1.umn.edu/ships/ethics/minamata.htm, part 1, para. 6.

7. In an interview with our research team on 7 December 1998, the incumbent mayor, Yoshii Masazumi, repeated these phrases.

8. Mayor Yoshii Masazumi, interview, 9 December 1998.

9. "Mercury and Solid Waste Countermeasures in Minamata," available at www.iges.or.jp/kitakyushu/Meetings/KIN1/Presentations/Session%20I/25%20Minamata.doc, accessed 13 November 2003.

10. This educational program, entitled Administration Management for Environmental Restoration and Conservation by Minamata City Government, was supported by JICA for five years, beginning in 2000. Trainees stay in Minamata for approximately thirty days. More information is available at www.jica.go.jp/branch/kic_e/minamata_e.html, accessed 29 March 2004.

11. ISO 14001 certification indicates that Minamata has used the International Standards Organizations environmental management system criteria to increase the efficiency of its delivery of day-to-day services, encourage citizens to assume more environmental responsibility, and move toward sustainable development. See www.denix.osd.mil/denix/denix.html, accessed 29 March 2004.

12. Ibid.

13. Ibid.

14. Minamata residents have adopted the verb *moyai*, a fishing term meaning to moor the boats together, to refer to residents engaging cooperatively in their daily lives. "Mercury and Solid Waste Countermeasures in Minamata," available at www.iges.or.jp/kitakyushu/Meetings/KIN1/Presentations/Session%20I/25%20Minamata.doc, accessed 13 November 2003.

15. The Japanese term is *kigyou jyokamachi.*

16. See Ui Jun, ed., *Industrial Pollution in Japan* (Tokyo: United Nations University, 1992), available at www.unu.edu/unupress/unupbooks/uu35ie/uu35ie00.htm.

17. Ibid.

18. Ibid.

19. Maruyama Sadami, "Responses to Minamata Disease," in *The Long Road to Recovery: Community Responses to Industrial Disaster*, ed. James K. Mitchell (Tokyo: United Nations University Press, 1996), chapter 2, section 4, available at www.unu.edu/unupress/unupbooks/uu21le/uu21le00.htm#Contents.

20. Masatomi Funaba, "Chisso and the Community and Municipality," *Research into Industrial Pollution* 2, no. 4 (1973), cited in ibid.

21. Maruyama Sadami, "Responses to Minamata Disease," section 4, para. 4.

22. Kiyora Raisaku of the Tokyo Institute of Technology claimed that the disease was caused by toxic animes, a consequence of bacterial spoilage, which can build up in dead fish. Tokita Kikuji of Toho University endorsed this theory and also claimed that poor people were more susceptible to the disease because they ate leftover fish. Another widely publicized theory, put forth by Oshima Takeji, managing director of the Japan Chemical Industry Association, was that the cause was corroded explosives dumped in Fukuro Bay south of Minamata during World War II. Mishima Akio, *Bitter Sea: The Human Cost of Minamata Disease* (Tokyo: Kosei, 1992), 50–51. Mishima was a staff writer for the national newspaper, *Asahi Shimbun.*

23. Ironically, the company's denial of responsibility was based, in part, upon selected portions of the research of Hosokawa Hajime, the Chisso company doctor and city hospital director who had first identified the disease. His own research into the mercury-disease connection, using cats, confirmed the role of pollution from the factory.

24. From Ishimure Michiko's speech accepting the 1973 Ramon Magsaysay Award for Journalism, Literature, and Creative Communication Arts, available at www.rmaf.org.ph/ RMAFWeb/Documents/Awardee/Response/mi_01res.htm, accessed 13 November 2003.

25. In response to changing market conditions, in the 1960s the company oriented its production toward petrochemicals.

26. These studies were planned and undertaken by Niigata University together with the Niigata prefectural government. Such proactive action by a local university and the prefectural government had not been seen in Kumamoto case. Two Niigata individuals can be credited: Mr. Kitano Hirokazu of the Niigata prefectural government and Dr. Tsubaki Tadao of Niigata University.

27. One of the reasons for the greater activism in Niigata is the geographical and social significance of Niigata City, where most of the victims were concentrated. This was the capital city of the prefecture and the prefectural hub for media, lawyers, union leaders, and other sources of antigovernment political power.

28. Kurihara Akira, *Testimonies: Minamata Disease* [Minamata Byo] (Tokyo: Iwanami Shoten, 2000).

29. Since the first lawsuit by Minamata victims in 1969, there have been more than twenty-two lawsuits in Minamata, most of which were decided only in 1995–96, as well as three suits in Niigata. In 1996, the national government and uncertified victims agreed upon a final settlement: a one-time payment of 2.6 million yen (about $24,000) each would be available to more than 10,000 uncertified victims, and 4.94 billion yen ($46 million) awarded to five victims associations. (Takamine Takeshi, "Kecchaku ni Itarumadeno Prosesu" [The Process Toward Political Settlement], *Minamata Byo Kenkyu,* no. 1 [1999]: 16–36.) The final case to be resolved, the Kansai suit, was concluded after twenty-two years on October 15, 2004, when the Supreme Court upheld an Osaka Court's ruling from April 2001 holding the national government responsible for mishandling the disease. Mizoguchi Kuzo, "Court Orders Japan to Pay in Mercury Case," Associated Press, 15 October 2004.

30. Oiwa Keibo and Ogata Masato, *Rowing the Eternal Sea: The Story of a Minamata Fisherman* (New York: Rowman and Littlefield, 2001), 144.

31. Ibid.

32. Eugene W. Smith, *Minamata,* trans. Nakao Hajime (New York: Holt, Rinehart and Winston, 1975); published in Japanese as *Shasinshuu Minamata* (Tokyo: San'ichi Shobo, 1980).

33. Ui Jun, "History of Activism," in *Industrial Pollution in Japan*.

34. When a group of victims went to try to meet with union representatives of the Chisso plant in Chiba Prefecture in 1971, they were beaten by employees there. Mishima, *Bitter Sea,* 176–78.

35. This condition has become known as fetal Minamata disease.

36. His findings, originally published under a pseudonym in a series of articles, were eventually published as *Kogai no Seijigaku: Minamata-byo o Otte* [The Politics of Pollution: Tracking Down Minamata Disease] (Tokyo: Sanseido, 1968).

37. The book was selected in 1970 for the first Oya Prize for Nonfiction, but the author declined the award. See Mishima, *Bitter Sea,* 229.

38. Ishimure has published more than twenty books related to Minamata disease and Minamata environmental culture. Most recently, she wrote a Noh drama, *Shiranui,* which was performed in August 2004 at the infill area known as the Minamata Bay Victims Area. The play's stated purpose is the remediation of the souls of the human victims and the fish and other creatures that have been killed in the bay.

39. Today the government encourages NGO's and other "private bodies" to participate in environmental activities such as street and water cleanup and tree planting. There is even a section of the Basic Environmental Law that states that all government bodies must support and encourage such activities.

40. Harada Makiko untitled essay for Think the Earth Project (a nonprofit project that encourages environmentally responsible business practices), available at www.thinktheearth.net/thinkdaily/report/rpt_03.html, accessed 7 June 2004. The number of fishers today is not clear, in part because the boundaries of the Minamata disease–affected area are vague.

41. Ministry of the Environment of Japan Web site, available at www.env.go.jp/en/topic/minamata.html, accessed 13 November 2003.

42. The Environmental Agency was upgraded to the Ministry of Environment in 2001.

43. This occurred after the fish showed below minimum mercury safety standard—the provisional regulatory standard for fish was set at 0.4 ppm for total mercury and 0.3 ppm for methyl mercury—for three years in a row.

44. Hashimoto's address to the Johannesburg Summit on Sustainable Development, 2002, is available at www.iadb.org/intl/jpn/seminars/mexico/downloads/takemoto-eng.pdf.

45. Interview, 18 February 2000.

46. Interview, 17 February 2000.

47. Interview, 16 February 2000. Takeshi is editor of the *Kumamoto Nichinichi* newspaper.

48. Interview, 17 February 2000.

49. Oiwa and Ogata, *Rowing the Eternal Sea*, 59.

50. Ibid., 145–46.

51. Ibid., 21.

52. Interview, 21 February 2000.

53. Interview, 17 February 2000.

54. Mishima, *Bitter Sea*, 193–94.

55. Available at www.city.yamagata.yamagata.jp/yidff/docbox/8/box8-2-e.html, accessed 8 December 2003.

56. Interview, 7 December 1998.

57. His movement focuses on the three parts of Minamata life that were most involved in the crisis: water, locally produced food, and waste. In fact, it was Yoshimoto who devised Minamata's recycling program.

58. Harada Makiko for Think the Earth Project.

59. Mishima, *Bitter Sea*, 216.

60. Interview, 28 June 2003.

61. The survey was in the form of a mail questionnaire to male and female adults (over twenty years old) living in Minamata City. The number of survey respondents was 1,182, out of 2,513 who were selected randomly from a list of 25,130 Minamata residents as of December 1998. The response rate was 47 percent. The survey was conducted by the National Institute of Minamata Disease; Arakaki Tazusa, a co-author of this chapter, was one of the members of the survey team.

62. Interview, 17 February 2000.

63. Interview, 28 April 2000.

64. Reporting on a July 2001 ecotour of Minamata for the Think the Earth Project, Harada Mariko noted a number of people engaged in environmentally safe agricultural projects, including a family that grows pesticide-free tea and the use of ducks to eat weeds in place of herbicides.

65. Case Study Vol. 5, Minamata City, 20 Percent Club for Sustainable Cities, Global Environmental Forum, Tokyo, March 2000, available at www.shonan.ne.jp/~gef20, accessed 8 December 2003.

66. Think the Earth Project Web site, available at www.thinktheearth.net/thinkdaily/report/rpt_r03.html, accessed 16 August 2004.

67. Mizoguchi Kozo, "Court Orders Japan to Pay in Mercury Case," Associated Press, 15 October 2004.

68. Ibid.

69. Torigoe Hiroyuki and Kada Yukiko, ed., *Mizu to Hito no Kankyoushi-Biwako Houkokusho* [Environmental History of Man and Water-Lake Biwa Report] (Tokyo: Ochanomizu Shobou, 1984), 29.

70. Kada Yukiko, *Seikatsu Sekai'no Kankyougaku* [Environmental Studies of our Everyday Life World] (Tokyo: Nousan Gyoson Bunka Kyoukai, 1995).

71. Ibid., 217–44.

72. In the 1940s, this was the largest rayon company not only in Japan but in all of Asia.

73. The impetus for the law was pollution of the Arakawa River in Tokyo. Although this law existed at the time of Minamata, it was not enforced there because of Chisso's political influence, its importance to the national economy, and the geographical remoteness of Minamata from any urban center.

74. Kada Yukiko writes: "Recent research has found that, although Kyoto city authorities planned this second canal project [for the lake] as a drinking water project, this was actually a manipulation of public opinion. The amount of water that would be drawn from the lake was ten times more than would be needed for Kyoto's population (about five hundred thousand)." The hidden purpose of the canal construction was additional hydropower/electricity. Kada Yukiko, "Biwako/Yodogawa no Mizuseisaku no Hyakunen to 21 Seiki no Kadai" [A Hundred-Year History of Lake Biwa Yodo River Basin and the Issues for the Twenty-first Century], in *Mizu wo Meguru Hito to Shizen* [Man and Nature around the Water], ed. Kada Yukiko (Tokyo: Yuhikaku, 2003), 111–52.

75. Interview, 23 April 1999.

76. Shiga Prefecture Report, available at www.pref.shiga.jp/biwako/koai/mother21-e/0.pdf, accessed 7 June 2004.

77. One academic, Suzuki Norio of Shiga University, was particularly outspoken. He was thought by many to have close ties to opposition political parties, but his public statements and writings were primarily about the ecology of Lake Biwa. As early as the 1970s he was writing about the ecological impact of the comprehensive development plan, and he described the lowering of the lake levels as "extremely serious" even in early 1970s.

78. Yet there were some long-term residents, such as the people who lived in Yogo, where the construction of a dam was planned in 1972 for the Takatoki River, who knew the probable effects on the LBCDP and resisted it: the dam would have flooded five villages and forced the people of Yogo to uproot themselves and move elsewhere.

79. Development Forum archives, World Bank, available at www2.worldbank.org/hm/pollmgt/0020.html.

80. Hiroshi Tsuno, "Water Pollution and Preservation in Lake Biwa," Research Center for Environmental Quality Control, Kyoto University, available at http://greenkorea21.kist.re.kr/teams/gk21/act/file/oral/tsuno.rtf, accessed 21 April 2003.

81. Development Forum archives, World Bank, available at www2.worldbank.org/hm/pollmgt/0020.html.

82. Lake Biwa Comprehensive Preservation Promotion Council, "Lake Biwa Comprehensive Preservation Initiatives," 15, available at www.mlit.go.jp/crd/daisei/biwako/pamphlet/pamphlet_en.pdf, accessed 2 March 2004.

83. Ibid., 12.

84. Interview, 27 June 1999.

85. Interview, 24 January 2000.

86. Ibid.

87. Governor Takemura, personal communication with Yukiko Kada, 10 October 2005.

88. Interview, 17 June 1999.

89. Interview, 24 January 2000.

90. He made this admission at a public symposium that was part of the International Lake Conference held in Shiga, 13 November 2001.

91. Tsujita Keishi, *Uo no Saiban* [Lawsuit by Fish] (Tokyo: Nihon Hyoronsha, 1984).

92. This article is part of the basic human rights chapter, inserted by the U.S. occupation authorities, which helped to draft the postwar Japanese constitution. It does not refer to human environmental rights, such as the right to clean water.

93. It is worth noting that there were some modifications of the plan. For example, initially the route of the levee along the southern shore was planned to run far offshore of the lake. Governer Takemura changed the route in the 1980s to minimize destruction to the water area. He did so at the recommendation of Kira Tatsuo, then the director of the newly built Lake Biwa Research Institute.

94. Kada Yukiko, "Socio-Ecological Changes Around Lake Biwa: How Have the Local People Experienced Rapid Modernization?" in *Ancient Lakes: Their Cultural and Biological Diversity,* ed. Kawanabe Hiroya, George W. Coulter, and Anna C. Roosevelt (Ghent: Kenobi Productions, 1999), 245.

95. The six ministries and agencies are the Environment Agency (now the Ministry of the Environment); the National Land Agency (now the Ministry of Land, Infrastructure, and Transport); the Ministry of Health and Welfare (now the Ministry of Health, Labor, and Welfare); the Ministry of Agriculture, Forestry, and Fisheries; the Forestry Agency; and the Ministry of Construction (now the Ministry of Land, Infrastructure, and Transport).

96. Shiga Prefecture, "Mother Lake 21 Plan: Lake Biwa Comprehensive Preservation and Improvement Project," March 2000, available at www.pref.shiga.jp/biwako/koai/mother21-e, accessed 5 September 2005.

97. Interview, 15 December 1998.

98. Shiro Kasuya, "Destructive Effects of the Estuary Dam on Nagara River's Environment and the Program for Its Regeneration," available at http://gumail.cc.gifu-u.ac.jp/~kasuyas/english/wwf.html, accessed 23 October 2003.

99. Douglas McGill, "Scour Technology's Stain with Technology," *New York Times Magazine,* 4 October 1992, also available under the title "Nature in the Mind of Japan" at www.mcgillreport.org/nature_in_the_mind_of_japan.htm, accessed 31 October 2005.

100. Kate Douglas, "Last Stand on the Nagara," *New Scientist,* 18 November 1995, 43.

101. Niikura Toshiko and Heather Souter, "The Citizens Campaign to Save the Nagara River: Raising Consciousness and Concern Regarding Public Works Projects," Environmental NGOs' International Symposium on Dams, available at http://216.239.39.104/search?q=cache: C2pPujqG_kAJ:english.kfem.or.kr/international/symposium/99dam%2520citizen.doc +Nagara+River+dam&hl=en&ie=UTF-8], accessed 21 March 2004.

102. Owen Kyle Cameron, "The Political Ecology of Environmentalism in Japan: Protest and Participation: 1983–1995" (Ph.D. dissertation, University of Cambridge, Trinity College, 1996), cited in Kim D. Reimann, "Going Global: International Politics, NGOs and the Environmental Movement in Japan" (paper presented at the Grassroots Environmental Movements in Japan and the United States International Conference, University of Kentucky, April 25–26, 2003), available at www.uky.edu/~ppkaran/conference/Going%20Global.pdf.

103. McGill, "Nature in the Mind of Japan."

104. Colin Nickerson, "Japan to Still Its Last Wild Waters," *Boston Globe,* 15 April 1992.

105. Ibid.

106. Arifuku Ichiro, interview, 19 September 2000.

107. Douglas, "Last Stand on the Nagara."

108. Nickerson, "Japan to Still Its Last Wild Waters."

109. Cited in McGill, "Nature in the Mind of Japan."

110. Kim D. Reimann, "Going Global."

111. Ibid.

112. In Japanese this read: "Kasen kanrisha wa kasen seibi keikaku no an o sakusei suru baai

ni wa, kochokai no kaisai nado kankei jyuumin no iken o hanei saseru tame hituyo na sochi o kojinakeraba naranai."

113. One of the committee's members is Kada Yukiko, the lead researcher for this study.

114. There was an earlier referendum, in 1996, on the construction of an atomic energy plant in Maki City, Niigata; however, in this case the plant was proposed by a private company, Tokyo Denryoku.

115. "Kawabegawa Dam Issue Update" February 2000, available at http://kawabe.technologic .co.jp/eng/engtop.html, accessed 15 August 2004.

116. In April 2004 Himeno ran for Tokushima City mayor on the Yoshino River Dam issue, but he lost to the LDP candidate, Hara Hideki, the former head of the prefectural assembly. Hara ran not on the Yoshino River Dam issue but on a pledge to improve city management.

117. Herbst attended the annual 1992 Nagaragawa Day. See Reimann, "Going Global."

118. Takahashi Yutaka and Monma Yoshiko, "Consensus Building with Participation in River Management," *Dams, Rivers and People* 1, no. 2–3 (March–April 2003), available at www .waterresourcesgateway.com/Proceedings/WorldWaterCongress2003/Yutaka%20Takahasi.pdf, accessed 7 June 2004.

119. Shiga Prefecture, for example, has only fifty river managers. Lake Biwa, which is located there, is connected to more than one hundred large rivers and many hundreds more smaller streams and rivers.

120. Available at http://kjc.ktroad.ne.jp/030322eama.html, accessed 29 March 2004.

121. The Democratic Party of Japan (Minshuto) was launched on 28 September 1996, uniting fifty-seven dissenters from other parties into Japan's third-largest political party. Many Minshuto members are liberal renegades from the Social Democratic Party, the name for the Japan Socialist Party since 1991.

122. Foreign Press Center/Japan, "General Election Set for 9 November; Parties Prepare to Do Battle with Manifestoes," 17 October 2003, available at www.fpcj.jp/e/shiryo/jb/0349.html, accessed 26 March 2004.

123. From 1997 to 2003, 23.7 trillion yen ($204 billion in 2003 dollars) were spent on sewers and waste water canal construction in Japan. See Kada, *Seikatu Sekaino'no Kankyougaku*, 40.

124. Indeed, the dialogue is extending beyond water. In spring 2003, Kada Yukiko was invited by the Shiga prefectural government to give a talk titled Citizen Participation in Public Works Projects—something that would have been unthinkable a few decades earlier.

125. For more on the concept of framers, see www.carnegiecouncil.org/forgingenvironmentalism.

126. There were exceptions. For example, in the Edo period, farmers wanted to dredge a shallow section of the Seta River so that the river could flow freely during times of high water instead of spilling over onto their farmland and ruining their crops. But the Tokugawa shogunate would not let them because the shallow water was considered a strategic point for transporting armies and supplies across the river. In addition, there was strong opposition from downstream residents in Osaka and six hundred village communities. Thus it was dredged only five times in two hundred years (not counting the times that farmers dredged it secretly in the night at the risk of severe punishment).

127. Date of interview difficult to specify. Kada had frequent contact with this fisher once every month from 1982 until his death, in 1990.

128. Oiwa and Ogata, *Rowing the Eternal Sea*, 165.

129. Ibid.

130. Ishimure Michiko, *Kugai Jyoudo* [Bitter Water Became Heaven] (Tokyo: Kodansha, 1969), 71.

131. Ikemi Tetsushi, *Mizu Sensou—Biwako Gendaishi* [Water War—Modern Lake Biwa History] (Tokyo: Ryokufuu Shuppann, 1982).

132. In order to understand better how the new ideas filter through society and change social values, we have identified "framers" for each case, those who articulated and promoted environmental values. For more on this concept, see www.carnegiecouncil.org/forgingenvironmentalism/

133. Kada Yukiko played a key role in developing the mission and design of the museum.

India: A Foreword

Paul Greenough

In attempting to explain India's daunting array of environmental problems, most authors point to the enduring effects of colonialism.[1] A standard environmental narrative traces a downward spiral over the past 150 years from an era of ecological harmony, distributive justice, and material abundance to the present era of ecological disruption, massive social inequity, and widespread poverty. According to this narrative, between 1830 and 1850 foreign rulers shattered the traditional rural economic system, forcing market capitalism on self-contained villages, exacting taxes beyond the capacity of cultivators to pay, draining wealth to Europe through fiscal trickery, closing avenues for indigenous entrepreneurship, and wresting away ancient commons by appropriating rivers, wildlife, and forests. The long-term effects have included rural flooding, waterlogging, and desiccation, the cultivation of marginal soils, the ruinous monoculture of cash crops, and the collapse of village self-sufficiency and moral concern for the local environment—in short, the disappearance of the subsistence arrangements upon which India's well-being had depended for centuries.

This narrative describes a wise peasantry whose once-instinctive respect for natural processes resulted from a richly detailed knowledge of crops, animals, and wild plants. Such knowledge was codified in vernacular taxonomies, proverbs, and songs and found its expression in myths and rituals that celebrated natural forces and enjoined the worship of a nature goddess, Prakriti, and her epigones. Material welfare in this precolonial world was in equilibrium with nature, markets were only a marginally significant economic feature, and every caste and tribe was ensured minimal subsistence.

Although historical evidence shows this standard environmental narrative to be accurate in many specifics, it is erroneous in large matters: its vision is too nostalgic (there is little evidence for pervasive precolonial social harmony and self-sufficiency), its hostility to the market system is misplaced (it was India's trade goods and merchant capital that caught Europe's attention in the first place), its chronology is undoubtedly mistaken (the impact of foreign investment was felt in rural India well before the Victorian era), and it fails to acknowledge the powerful spiritual bonds (or at least nostalgic longings) that still connect Indians to animals, water, and woods. The relationships among colonial practices, peasant-level social and economic responses to colonization, and current environmental crises are too complex to allow us to attribute all virtue to one party and all evil to another. Indian environmental history is thus in a state of active revision as researchers continue to dig in the archive.

Reflection on the origins of India's urgent environmental problems needs to be supplemented by thinking about ways in which these problems can be addressed in practice. The burden of human demands weighs heavily over all of India—in the forests, wetlands, deserts, coasts, and hill areas as well as in Bombay (Mumbai), Calcutta (Kolkata), Delhi, and the thirty-two other cities with more than a million inhabitants. In the Americas and Africa, large tracts have been cleared of their inhabitants for national parks that sustain the illusion of wilderness, but in India people and environment are fused into a single complex object of concern. While India has nearly six hundred million square kilometers of forest (and is home to 7 percent of the world's wild animal species and 13 percent of the world's plant species), inside this forest there are thirty-five million tribal hunters, fishers, cultivators, and herders pursuing their livelihoods—and millions more non-tribal people work steadily at the edge of the forest to open new ground to rice, millet, cotton, and sugar cultivation. Similarly, India's substantial desert in Rajasthan is thoroughly peopled and routinely crisscrossed by herders and traders.

Further, 74 percent of India's more than one billion people live in rural and coastal areas, where hybrid seeds, pesticides, chemical fertilizers, fishing trawlers and other motorized boats have enhanced the ancient practices of cereal cultivation and net fishing. Yet while cereal and fish productivity have shot up in the last four decades, and India has become a net exporter of food grains and fish (including shellfish), the prices paid to actual producers are predictably meager, and their engagement with unpredictable world markets both raises and dashes their economic prospects for reasons that are rarely evident. In addition, for small farmers and fishermen economic liberalization means that the subsidies they were once offered to adopt new technologies, such as high-yielding grains or outboard engines, or to enter new markets in East Asia and Europe are disappearing. Meanwhile, the externalities of the new agriculture and fishing methods, such as the contamination of water, soil, and air, along with changes in groundwater salinity and a loss of biodiversity, are noxious new realities to be borne. Water for drinking and irrigation is scarce everywhere, and most workers have only minimal shelter because of the scarcity of timber for fuel and construction—hundreds of workers and their dependents freeze to death each winter during the coldest nights. A sizable portion of the Indian populace is exquisitely sensitive to even slight reversals of weather, food and fuel prices, or their own health, and this group is chronically mired in debt, disease, and underemployment. While outright famine hasn't occurred for four decades, Indian economists agree that at least 30 percent, and probably 35 percent, of the population is chronically undernourished.[2]

The indirect impact of globalization and rapid economic changes causes millions of rural Indians to flee to India's great cities each year, adding to the existing urban hazards. Industries spew out streams of pollutants; drinking water, clean air, and open spaces for leisure activities are conspicuously absent; animal and human wastes are trodden into particulates that foster asthma and other lung diseases. Municipal governments struggle with these problems but never solve them; no large city in India meets global air quality standards or has a comprehensive sewage treatment system.

In sum, the survival needs of huge numbers of people shape and are shaped by India's physical environment, which is the determining context for popular welfare. Poor people's responses to ever-worsening price inflation and a deteriorating natural environment add up to what notably Joan Martinez-Alier and Ramachandra Guha call the "environmentalism of the poor." These responses, some barely noticed such as stripping leaves and bark from trees in public spaces without ever quite cutting down the trees, some very loud and public like blockading contractors' access to groves and ponds that are vital to local survival, have to be distinguished from those of environmental movements based on esthetic preferences or scientific values—by default, the environmentalism of the rich—which all too often force tribals, poor cultivators, and proletarians to defend their livelihoods: for example, *your* biosphere reserve versus *my* lost source of fodder, herbs, and grazing. In these contests, the poor nearly always are the losers.

But the environmental situation in India, while challenging, is hardly hopeless. The country has a surprising array of official, NGO, and popular mechanisms for preserving natural diversity and ensuring that air, food, and water are safe for humans. For example, the Indian constitution calls on the government to "endeavour to protect and improve the environment and to safeguard the forests and wild life of the country" (section 48A), while citizens are obliged by the same document "to protect and improve the natural environment, including forests, lakes, rivers and wildlife and to have compassion for living creatures"(section 51A). A Central Pollution Control Board monitors air, water, and solid-waste contamination and sets the standards that are intended to trigger abatement measures. Since the 1970s dozens of laws have criminalized poaching and trading in rare species, fostered biodiversity, constrained the release of hazardous chemicals and industrial wastes, restricted air and water pollution, and even regulated noise pollution. While these laws and regulations are rarely enforced, from time to time the Supreme Court, acting on its own or in response to public interest litigation, compels bureaucrats to address particularly offensive hazards or to enforce environmental rules that government otherwise cannot bring itself to face, as we see in the Delhi case study that follows. Meanwhile, nearly half the forested area in the country's twenty-eight states is still under public control, and a central Ministry of Forests and Environment oversees 450 national parks, biosphere reserves, and sanctuaries that make up Asia's largest protected area network. The venerable Forestry Research Institute (founded in 1906) and the Wildlife Institute of India (founded in 1982) train highly competent forestry professionals and conservation biologists, and key academic institutions like the Centre for Ecological Sciences (founded in 1982) train ecologists and conduct field research

There are also professionally staffed NGOs—for example, the Bombay Natural History Society (BNHS, founded in 1883), the Centre for Science and Environment (CSE, founded in 1980), and the Ashoka Trust for Research in Ecology and the Environment (ATREE, founded in 1996)—which use the courts to push back against heedless poachers, resource-grabbing contractors and industrialists, and malfeasant officials. These NGOs use the media effectively, and their websites, videos, and journals, models of green conviction, are consulted around the world. Finally, the Indian press is alert to environmental crises and regularly berates the government when public welfare is threatened.

Yet despite all its environmental legislation, technical expertise, and media and citizen commitment, India at the beginning of the twenty-first century shows an unmistakable will to rush headlong into unregulated development and modes of "first world" consumption that will cause ever greater harm to the environment and the public's health and welfare. After enduring for decades what an economist sardonically dubbed the "Hindu rate of growth," the country's middle class and business elite are enjoying explosive GDP growth that has averaged 6 to 7 percent annually since 1993. Accompanying this growth has been a jump in the number of collaborative agreements with foreign governments and corporations, many of them aimed at extracting minerals, timber, and other forest products and at opening the Indian market to foreign firms in accord with WTO agreements. Even in cases where official motives were once welfarist in intent, as in the 1950s agreement between Norwegian donors and the state of Kerala to improve both the productivity of fisheries and the well-being of fishers, which we read about in the chapter to follow, the government has proven incapable of ensuring the sustainability of marine resources or of preventing their looting by entrepreneurs.

Thus, present-day India suffers from repeated crises where the survival needs of the landless and the urban poor, the hopes of small farmers, fishers, and micro-entrepreneurs, the rational calculations of foreign development agencies and the ecological dreams of NGOs and conservation biologists, the relentless ambition of global capital, and the vacillations of judicial and regulatory agencies all jostle together in environmental free-for-alls. These collisions of opposing values and interests are often accompanied by lawsuits, demonstrations, and media campaigns, as well as behind-the-scenes political threats and feints, and it is usually impossible to know who all the players are. The best-organized middle class environmental groups frequently go to court or appeal to public opinion to demand that the government take responsibility for the evident chaos. But they have met with repeated setbacks, in which the state and central governments themselves wheel and deal to seize the best surface water, give away mineral deposits, and open up biomass reserves, and the highest elected officials launch highly dubious public works projects, such as the damming of the Narmada River network in western India and the more recent and highly controversial proposal to link together many of India's major rivers for navigation and irrigation. Private interests, too, move aggressively to claim choice sites for industrial parks, tourist hotels, open pit mines, hydroelectric plants, port facilities, and so on, inducing politicians to put back into play prime lands and waters once thought safely within protected areas.

Neither the government nor the mainstream NGOs can articulate the threats hanging over the environment-survival nexus as forcefully as the numerous peasant- and worker-based movements that have sprung to life in the past fifteen years. Arising from tribal people's, untouchables', landless laborers', women's, and industrial workers' day-to-day struggles and building on the methods and traditions of the anticolonial movements of earlier generations, organized protest groups have stirred India and attracted world attention—not least because their elite supporters have made skillful use of new communication technologies. The most famous of these groups, the gender-based Chipko movement of the 1970s and 1980s, which strove to protect timber resources and forest livelihoods, and the tribal- and peasant-driven Save the Narmada anti-dam movement along the Narmada River in the 1980s and 1990s, paved the way for the current National Alliance of People's Movements, which advocates humane development from below and worker unity and opposes WTO-led globalization. In these movements thousands of activists of both sexes have shown the capacity to endure physical punishment and imprisonment, after which most of them promptly return to the struggle for land, work, and full political rights. Indian officials and corporate interests have become wary of these "people's movements," which in recent years have found external allies through global networking and have sometimes even grasped political power, as in the case of the tribally based movement that since 2000 has controlled the new mineral- and timber-rich state of Jharkhand.

India is too large, too varied, and too populous for one to capture in a few pages the changing relation of its people to their environments. Competing needs and values have resulted in two distinct forms of globalized environmentalism—first, a well-organized movement from above of middle class environmental NGOs with strong links to leading Euro-American conservation groups; and second, a more dispersed array of justice-seeking survival movements that are impelled from below and also have supporters in the global North and among similar movements in the global South. Blowing against both like a strong wind is India's laissez-faire surge, aided and abetted by state and national governments whose many branches and agencies seem all too often divided against themselves in their efforts to protect and punish the poor. Meanwhile, the legal and political frames for effective environmental regulation and meaningful sanitary and subsistence reform are shifting rapidly, so that the outcomes of ongoing environmental struggles are unpredictable and will only emerge piecemeal in the courts, in the streets, and in village enclaves. Case studies like those that follow, by Amita Baviskar, Subir Sinha, Kavita Philip, and their co-workers, are the best sources of insight we have as India does not so much resolve its environmental predicaments but wobbles along its distinctive environmental path.

Notes

1. See Vandana Shiva, *Ecology and the Politics of Survival: Conflicts over Natural Resources in India* (New Delhi: Sage, 1991); and Madhav Gadgil and Ramachandra Guha, *Ecology and Equity: The Use and Abuse of Nature in Contemporary India* (London: Routledge, 1995).

2. See Jaya Mehta and Shanta Venkatraman, "Poverty Statistics, Barmecide's Feast," *Economic and Political Weekly*, July 1, 2000; and J.H. Cassen, "Well-Being in the 1990s, Towards a Balance Sheet," *Economic and Political Weekly*, July 6, 2002.

Kerala Fishing Villages and Delhi, India

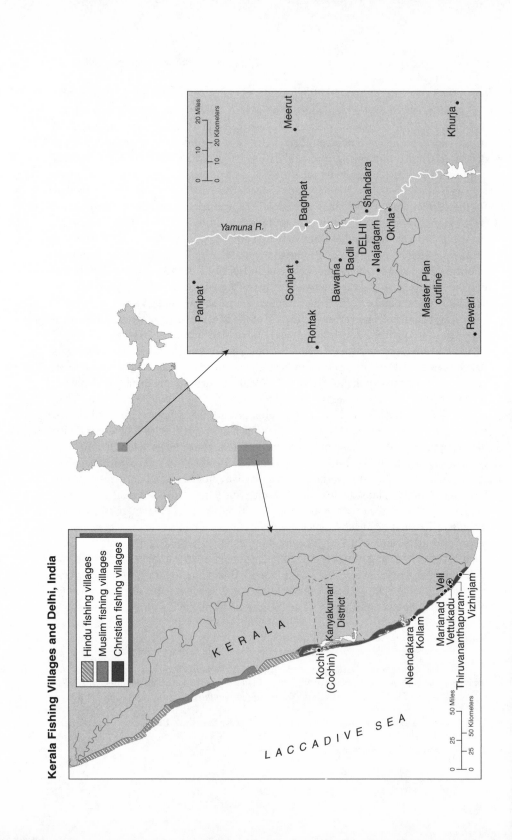

Hindu fishing villages
Muslim fishing villages
Christian fishing villages

KERALA

Kanyakumari
District

Kochi
(Cochin)

Neendakara
Kollam

Marianad Veli
Vettukadu
Thiruvananthapuram
Vizhinjam

LACCADIVE SEA

0   25   50 Miles
0   25   50 Kilometers

Yamuna R.

Panipat

Sonipat

Rohtak

Bawana
Badli

Baghpat

Meerut

Shahdara

DELHI

Najafgarh

Okhla

Master Plan
outline

Rewari

Khurja

0   10   20 Miles
0   10   20 Kilometers

3

Rethinking Indian Environmentalism
Industrial Pollution in Delhi and Fisheries in Kerala

Amita Baviskar, Subir Sinha, and Kavita Philip

The discourse of development has dominated India's debate over diverse environmental questions. Since the country became independent in 1947, its leaders have invoked the "national interest" as a pre-eminent justification for their reorganization of the management, control, and exploitation of resources. The cause of national development has enabled widely divergent environmental policies to be reconciled and pursued, simultaneously and sequentially. Both natural resource extraction and environmental conservation, which appear to be contradictory state policies, in fact emerge from a common logic that assumes a state monopoly on safeguarding the public good. Thus, the state sponsors both deforestation, which boosts national income, and the creation of protected biodiversity habitats, which advances another sort of "national interest," even as both policies impoverish and displace forest-dwellers, already vulnerable citizens of the nation.

Yet in claiming to represent the welfare of all, the discourse of development also offers opportunities for critique and compromise. Social groups divided by class, caste, gender, and region experience national development differently. These differences generate contested meanings, creating new political fractures and alignments through which social groups aim to recover the variously imagined promise of development. Constructing flexible alliances and global networks, concerned citizens seek to halt specific forms of dispossession and ecological degradation by reclaiming resources and asserting their right to a voice in political decision-making. They draw upon a rich repertoire of political action, often turning development's tools against itself by deploying alternative scientific expertise, legal authority, and the language of citizenship and the nation. At the same time, they also invoke preexisting social solidarities and alternative forms of knowledge, challenging the very premises of development. These heterogeneous strategies for recasting development's relationship to its diverse publics are evident in the varied careers of two environmental campaigns in India.

In the 1990s Delhi, India's capital and one of the world's most polluted cities, witnessed a concerted campaign to reduce air and water pollution. Environmentalists, backed by the authority of the Supreme Court of India, succeeded in closing down thousands of industrial units in the city. The petitioners and the court justified their judicial activism as serving the "public interest" by securing the universal benefits of cleaner air and water. Their actions were supported in the media and by a broad spectrum of middle-class urban citizens. Marginalized by this pursuit of "public interest" were many factory owners as well as hundreds of thousands of poor workers who lost their livelihood as a result of the campaign.

How did the pursuit of an environmental good—clean air and water—result in starvation and malnutrition, worsening the living conditions for some of Delhi's most vulnerable citizens? Why were the environmental priorities of workers not considered by the environmentalist activists or the court? How did the antipollution campaign articulate with other processes of urban restructuring related to economic liberalization? How did campaigns for environmental improvement and urban development mobilize competing scientific accounts of the pollution problem to legitimize and oppose widespread displacement? Questions about (a) environmental values, (b) democratic representation, and (c) scientifically informed decision-making and government action must be answered before we can understand the outcome of the Delhi antipollution campaign.

The same questions are crucial to understanding the environmental struggle over offshore fisheries in the southern state of Kerala, although in Kerala they have generated radically different answers. The conflict there began in the 1960s as a clash between small-scale fishers and the owners of large, mechanized trawlers over rights to the region's rich fisheries. State policies that encouraged "fisheries development," or the commodification of marine resources for export to generate national revenues and increase local incomes, provided the context for heightened conflict. Poor, lower-caste artisanal fishers and their supporters in the Catholic Church and various political parties mobilized against trawler owners and multinational fishing companies, demanding justice and asserting that the fishers' right to a livelihood must be the chief concern of state fisheries development policies.[1] Also at issue were questions of scale and the ecological impacts of a range of "improved" technologies and fishing practices, from outboard motors on catamarans to fishing nets and factory ships. Over time, as political alliances shifted in response to new policies of economic liberalization, so did competing claims about scientific knowledge. Arguments about safeguarding livelihoods and the primacy of local knowledge articulated, sometimes uneasily, with national and transnational environmental and labor campaigns. Over the course of four decades, the fishworkers' movement has successfully argued that "fisheries development" as promoted by the state leads to adverse consequences, both ecological and social. In the process, the campaign has also increased understanding of the complex relations between technology and capital ownership, the politics of production and the politics of consumption, economic development and ecological sustainability, locality and nation, and gender and religious belief.

The conflicts over air pollution in Delhi and offshore fisheries in Kerala demand attention because they provide an important corrective to dominant perspectives on Indian environmentalism. The two major frameworks used to analyze Indian environmentalism might be described as "spiritual ecology" and "political ecology," both of which attribute a distinctive ethos to Indian environmental action. "Spiritual ecology," as exemplified in the work of Vandana Shiva,[2] asserts that Indian environmental struggles are anchored in a civilizational critique of Judeo-Christian values, such as the masculinist desire for mastery over nature. According to this analysis, the women of the Himalayan foothills who protest against state forestry projects embody a Hindu ethic of respect for nature that is based on their recognition of shared feminine essence. Shiva's thesis about Hindu environmental values relies upon an ahistorical construction of precolonial Indian society as frozen in time and untainted by inequality and conflict, and it ignores the contradictions generated by the coexistence of multiple religious and ideological beliefs and practices, including the multiplicity of Hindi practices (high/low, scriptural, and folk) as well as other religions on the Indian subcontinent (Islam, Buddhism, Sikhism, Christianity), and non-religious beliefs (Western bioscience, capitalism, and socialism). However, despite thoroughgoing critiques that have demolished its credibility within academic circles,[3] Shiva's account has circulated widely and has been influential in shaping the perceptions of a wide range of readers—from Western New Age acolytes seeking Eastern enlightenment to Hindu nationalists looking for cultural superiority in a glorified past, to many activists seeking solidarity with distant strangers.

The "political ecology" school of thought, exemplified by the scholarship of Ramachandra Guha and Madhav Gadgil,[4] tends to characterize environmental conflict as a confrontation between "vicious states" and "virtuous peasants," in the words of political economist Henry Bernstein.[5] "Political ecology" represents environmental activism as resistance to state-sponsored development, whereby poor farmers, forest produce gatherers, and fishers seek to retrieve their means of subsistence from the jaws of an extractive corrupt state that serves the interests of elites. Such environmental action combines the "red" and "green" values of social equity and ecological sustainability. Although Guha takes care to separate the different ideological strands that coexist and combine within Indian environmentalism, his account builds the case for a distinctive Southern environmentalism that seeks to redress injustices in the distribution of productive resources.[6] Instead of the extractive economy of state-led capitalism, according to Guha's interpretation, Indian environmentalism calls for an alternate moral economy that gives priority to the subsistence needs of the poor.

The struggle over air pollution in Delhi defies both these frames of interpretation. It has elements of the "vicious state" paradigm because it brings together some state actors—Supreme Court judges, Pollution Control Board scientists, and administrators—to throw thousands of laborers out of work. Yet in this case state action does not facilitate the extraction of natural resources for capitalists; in fact, it adversely affects many small factory owners in Delhi. Indeed, in this struggle capitalists and workers are thrown together in an uneasy alliance that includes trade unions, human rights organizations, and politicians across party lines, while state initiatives aimed at protecting the health of the entire urban population are supported by middle-class citizens' groups and NGOs such as the Center for Science and Environment, who feel that the "public interest" has been subverted by sectional interests. But, as we shall see below, more authoritative action to protect the common weal further undermines the position of the most vulnerable members of the public. As for the spiritual ecology framework, far from invoking any inherently Indian environmental value that is rooted in religious belief, the discourse around air pollution in Delhi criticizes bureaucratic inertia, incompetence, and corruption, and approvingly cites the example of Western countries that have more efficient, rational processes of environmental action. The failure of both schools of interpretation to account for what happened in the Delhi case demands a rethinking of Indian environmentalism that recognizes its complexity in terms of its transnational articulations, the heterogeneity of state projects and practices, and the collaboration as well as resistance of citizens.

At first glance, the conflicts in Kerala seem to belong to a broad twentieth-century trend whereby global forces threaten local interests, technological modernization renders obsolete traditional livelihoods and cultures, and big foreign business swamps small local enterprise. The Kerala fisheries story appears to follow the familiar narrative line in which one heavily capitalized, technologically superior group—big commercial fishing vessel owners—usurps the business terrain of a disempowered tradition—local fisheries. Another representation pits local, traditional communities distinguished by their indigenous knowledge and practices and their ethic of ecological stewardship against a dispersed, modernizing, capitalist machine seeking new resources and driven by the need to maximize profits. But the fisheries conflict is only partly about the swift and painful intrusion of neoliberal economics and high-tech resource exploitation into a place where resources had been harvested on a modest scale for small but resilient local markets. On closer study both sides deploy sophisticated scientific knowledge, mobilize global networks and complex institutional structures, and address local needs and interests including access to markets, capital, and technology.

In short, both the Delhi and Kerala campaigns challenge analysts to come up with complex and contingent narratives that do justice to the dynamism and creativity of the social actors they seek to describe and to the complex material and symbolic relationships between people and resources. Both campaigns challenge a North-South binary analysis, and resist the very notion of an "Indian environmentalism." Both the spiritual and political ecology approaches have, explicitly and implicitly, assumed that it is the rural poor who respond to environmentally damaging development and its social effects. The cases here show that environmental action in India is not the exclusive preserve of the rural poor. In Delhi, activists representing middle-class interests are pitted against poor migrant workers who are unable to organize in defense of their livelihood. In Kerala, while the struggle is first taken up by poor fishers in coastal villages, over the past two decades, its supporters have formed a multi-class coalition that now includes urban-based fish merchants, as well as owners and operators of mechanized fishing craft who had initially opposed the small fishers' cause. This indicates that "the environment" is a field of fluid political alliances.

Another challenge to the established interpretive frameworks is thrown up by the modes of environmental activism in Delhi and Kerala. Spiritual ecologists have stressed popular religion and culture as the idioms in which both a critique of development and an alternative to it are articulated. Political ecologists, for their part, have pointed to "subalterneity," or the experience of inhabiting subordinate social positions, as structuring relations between people and resources and fueling resistance to modern development. But our case studies show that activists against pollution and overfishing come from different class positions and that activists in both conflicts use law and the language of science and development, in pursuing their claims with the state. While fishers certainly exploit the currently powerful discourse of "culture," "caste," and "tradition," they imbue these concepts with a dynamism that is usually not attached to them in the conventional explanatory frames. Also, the international networks of which the fishers' movement, in particular, are an important part give it added power and take their activism beyond the authenticity and isolation implied in the "subaltern" concept.

A final challenge concerns the coherence and singularity associated with the notion of "Indian environmentalism." To be sure, the Indian state, national development, and nationalism itself are powerful institutions and ideas. At the same time, regionally, at the level of state politics, they have taken on various forms and dynamics. The Kerala state government is no mere regional reflection of the Indian state; since the 1960s, it has developed in a social welfarist and social democratic direction with an emphasis on benefits to the poor, as compared to states like Bihar and Uttar Pradesh, which are organized primarily on caste, and Punjab and Gujarat, which explicitly favor agrarian and industrial capitalists. Sociologist Patrick Heller has shown that in Kerala a close relationship exists between organized labor unions, political parties, and the state government. Kerala's unusual politics help explain the fact that the fishworkers' movement has taken the union and cooperative as its predominant organizational form.[7] Similarly, the strong middle-class bias in Delhi's definition of the public interest has its basis in the city's demographics and its privileged position as national capital. Rather than being exceptions to the general pattern of Indian environmentalism, these particularities indicate the intrinsic diversity of environmental activism in the country. This suggests that political configurations vary widely across India, and that regional contexts and transnational histories articulate in radically different ways despite overarching national projects. The cases we present here show the problems implicit in the search for a singular narrative of Indian environmentalism as a response to modern development and globalization.

Pollution in Delhi: Environmental Activism, the Public Interest, and Delhi's Working Class

Introduction

"I was waiting this morning for the school bus to pick up my son, and I noticed that three of the four kids at the bus stop carried inhalers in their pockets. Man, that's scary!" said Anand Kapoor, an architect. Kapoor, who lives in Delhi's affluent Defence Colony neighborhood, has a ten-year-old who is asthmatic, a condition that seems more and more common among the city's children. The oft-quoted statistic that 25 percent of Delhi's children suffer from some chronic respiratory ailment provides a numerical gloss to the everyday experience of impairment, visits to the doctor and pharmacist, and the anxiety and expense suffered by parents.

On a drive through Delhi's rush-hour traffic, pollution manifests itself in the black gusts of smoke belched out by trucks and old buses, and the acrid smell of unburned hydrocarbons that cause burning, streaming eyes, coughing bouts, and, later, blinding headaches. Many people on two-wheelers (as motor scooters and motorcycles are called), who have no windows to roll up as they drive at the level of vehicular exhaust pipes, tie ineffectual handkerchiefs across their noses and mouths. When asked whether it works, they shrug.

At some of Delhi's major intersections, the Central Pollution Control Board (CPCB) has installed giant digital readouts of pollution levels. As people wait for the lights to change, they can check exactly what toxic cocktail they are imbibing: how much lead, carbon monoxide, and suspended particulate matter. The metro news broadcast on the Star News and NDTV channels regularly features a "Pollution Watch," which follows the weather report. It surveys the pollution levels recorded every day in India's four biggest cities.

A child's body, a ride through the city, statistics reported on television—these varied sites are connected by a chain of signification that links somatic symptoms to proximate causes, suggesting diagnosis and remedy. The narrative that is created—the problem of air pollution in Delhi—conjures up a cause and a constituency, authorizes action and enables exclusions, and obscures as much as it reveals. Air pollution in the sense of an objectively verifiable series of chemical changes, may have existed in Delhi for some time, but it was only recognized as a *problem,* and especially one that demanded public action, at a particular historical and cultural conjuncture. The everyday experiences and media coverage described above were not "natural" reflections of a preexisting concern but informed a collective cognitive process whereby a "problem" came to be perceived. The narrative about "the problem of air pollution" is produced by multiple historically and spatially located agents, whose practices are informed by complex and sometimes contradictory values that fuse ethics, politics, and aesthetics. This section examines these values as they are manifested in discursive and material practices that shape environmental action in Delhi. In particular, it focuses on the construction of a "public interest" around the environment that brings together different state agencies and an assertive middle class to legitimize authoritarian interventions in the lives of that segment of the city's working classes employed in large and small industrial firms.

In the latter half of the 1990s, in response to litigation filed by an environmental activist-lawyer, the Supreme Court of India issued a series of directives that resulted in the closure of thousands of industrial units in Delhi. The petitions and the court directives addressed the issue of air and water pollution, and were justified as being in the "public interest." The media and middle-class citizens, many affected by the increased incidence of respiratory diseases in the city, widely supported the environmentalist initiative. Affected factory owners' and workers' organizations widely opposed it, but they could not get the court to amend its decision. As a result, not only did many factory owners suffer significant financial losses, but thousands of poor workers lost their only means of livelihood.

The pursuit of the "public interest" deprived a large section of Delhi's working class of their means of subsistence. Environmental benefits—clean air and water— were obtained at the cost of losing *working environments*, resources that sustained some of the most vulnerable citizens of Delhi. How did the middle class succeed in presenting health and hazard, beauty and order as environmental concerns that superseded the welfare of Delhi's working class? Why were the environmental priorities of workers—jobs, food, and shelter—overlooked? Why were workers not represented in the decision-making process that led to the factory closings? Why was action routed through the judiciary when the Indian government has an extensive administrative setup for monitoring and regulating pollution? Was the closure of factories the most effective way of improving air quality?

This case study attempts to answer these questions by tracing the factory closings to the convergence of several processes, including the emergence in recent decades of an assertive middle class, one that has privileged access to the media and courts and is impatient with bureaucratic processes and the politics of compromise and accommodation. Detached from Delhi's industrial economy, the middle class derives its socioeconomic status from professional and financial/commercial occupations, and has the ability to fulfill its aspirations toward a consumerist lifestyle that combines wealth, well-being, and "good taste."[8] Middle-class desires for a clean environment are reflected and taken up by an activist judiciary, willing to step into the breach left by the executive and legislative branches of the state, especially a regulatory structure that is susceptible to political pressure and corruption.

The conjuncture of processes that ultimately enabled judicial action against air pollution was also partly created by the capitalist restructuring of the real estate market under the regime of liberalization and privatization. Meanwhile, economic restructuring has strengthened Delhi's service and commercial sectors and weakened an industrial economy that relies heavily on "informal" labor—ill-paid workers without any job security who live in illegal shanty settlements in the city, are often migrants, and are denied recognition as legitimate urban citizens. The invisibility of workers in the air pollution debate is also related to the dominance of corporate-owned media, which prefer to produce "infotainment"—selling consumer products through the coverage of "news" about health, beauty, and lifestyles rather than exposing the realities of starving workers' families, hazardous industrial working conditions, and a weakened public transportation system. Connecting these processes, practices, and positions enables an understanding of how a "public interest" around the problem of air pollution was created.

It must be recognized at the outset that several environmental initiatives have been under way in Delhi simultaneously, of which the campaign against air pollution is only one. There is also the removal of encroachments and squatter settlements from public lands, ordered by the courts in response to several public interest petitions filed by consumer rights organizations and affluent residents' welfare organizations— all carried out in the name of "cleaning and greening" the city. There is the Yamuna Action Plan, which, among other orders, directs the Delhi government to build several sewage treatment plants. The Delhi government has sought to involve neighborhood bodies and residents' welfare associations in the decentralized management of solid waste. (This new mode of decentralized urban governance is supported by the World Bank through its urban water supply and sanitation projects, which emphasize efficient management and cost recovery, to be achieved by turning state functions over to private corporate bodies.) At the same time, the government has encouraged environmental education in schools and, in partnership with nongovernmental organizations (NGOs) and school administrations, has run two public awareness campaigns: "say no to plastic bags" and "say no to firecrackers." Finally, the state government is improving transportation infrastructure in this congested city of twelve million by building a metro rail network funded by Japanese capital. Each of these initiatives brings together a range of social actors working at and across multiple scales—courts, elected governments (both state and central), administrative departments, residential and business associations, transnational funding agencies, NGOs, media, and even schools. Each initiative merits examination on its own, as do its linkages with other initiatives. For the purposes of this case study, however, they form the larger context within which to understand the air pollution case.

There are certain distinctive characteristics of the Delhi case and of this study that must be noted before we begin to examine its details. The Delhi air pollution initiative is remarkable in its focus on the courts and its lack of focus on reforming legislative and executive functioning. The exercise of power by the Supreme Court exemplifies Foucault's notion of sovereign power—at once peremptory and erratically paternalistic. This sovereign power has been well demonstrated by the Court in recent years; its order that the government evict within one year all people living inside areas designated as National Parks and Wildlife Sanctuaries is one instance.[9] Another is the court's decision to allow the Sardar Sarovar Dam to be built on the Narmada River because "dams are needed in the interest of the nation," a ruling that glossed over the troubling issue of the displacement by the dam of thousands of tribal and Hindu peasant families.[10] Approaching the Court and inviting its sovereign intervention in Delhi's air pollution issue is, therefore, a political strategy that demands closer examination. This mode of action is a departure from the techniques of public protest familiar from other Indian environmental movements, which often employ Gandhian methods of nonviolent *satyagraha*, in which activists use self-denial to increase their moral force and impress their opponents and audiences with the justice of their causes.

This case study analyzes information gathered from several sources, including interviews, newspaper reports, and other published accounts. All these situated sources of knowledge are refracted through the lens of coauthor Amita Baviskar, a long-term resident of Delhi who has been involved with rights-based groups, including Kalpavriksh, the People's Union for Civil Liberties, and Saajha Manch (Joint Forum on Urban Issues). The case study thus relies as much on participant observation and informal conversations as on formal interviews and published sources.

This study also departs from positivist notions of "evidence," where every statement must be attributed to a definite source and verified through cross-checking. As a long-time resident of Delhi, coauthor Baviskar draws upon tacit cultural understandings that, while often unspoken, powerfully shape the practices of different social groups. Such knowledge, part of what Bourdieu calls "habitus," emerges from particular subject positions, at the intersection of class and caste, gender and ethnicity, space and time. Members of a given social group provide themselves with a representation of their social relations and organize reality by performing "symbolic violence," "tacitly laying down the dividing line between the thinkable and the unthinkable, thereby contributing towards the maintenance of the symbolic order from which [they draw their] authority."[11] When people are marked by the stigma of class or gender and treated as lesser beings, these discriminatory practices are usually normalized and naturalized. The middle-class belief that poor migrant workers are lesser beings is not necessarily expressed in so many words, and is unlikely to be encountered in an interview,[12] but the silence on the subject of workers' concerns is eloquent testimony to middle-class indifference. When significant silences mark normalized exclusions, attention to practices other than speech is necessary. We discuss nonverbal communications in later subsections of this essay. Coauthor Baviskar's proximity to rights-based activist groups in Delhi has allowed her to gain important insights into these practices, which would otherwise escape attention. In particular, we aim to make explicit the consequences of constitutive exclusions and unstated assumptions that invisibly yet powerfully shape the construction of "public interest."

Jump-Starting Environmental Action Through the Courts

In 1985, environmental activist and lawyer Mahesh Chander Mehta filed a public interest petition asking the Supreme Court of India to order the closure of stone crushing units in Delhi, which, in Mehta's words, "caused dust pollution, affecting half a million people. More than 2,000 tons of dust was being emitted into the air."[13] Mehta contended that these industries violated the Air Pollution Act of 1981, as well as Delhi's Master Plan. In 1992, the court agreed—but this was not the end of Mehta's petitioning. He also asked the court to move 1,200 polluting industrial units away from Delhi,[14] arguing that, since many of them were located in residential and commercial areas, they violated the Master Plan's zoning provisions. As the following account shows, this category of "nonconforming" factories (those that violated urban zoning regulations) was to become a major bone of contention in struggles against pollution in Delhi. Finally, in yet another petition, Mehta approached the court to act on the issue of the pollution of the Ganga[15] and its tributaries, including the Yamuna, which passes through Delhi.

The issue of air and water pollution in Delhi was therefore on the Supreme Court's agenda starting in the late 1980s, and periodic statements and orders were issued from the bench. But little definitive action was taken until 1994, when the court took *suo motu* notice of a newspaper report[16] about the pollution of the Yamuna. The Central Pollution Control Board (under the central government's Ministry of Environment and Forests) and the Delhi government were made parties in the matter. In 1995, the court asked the Delhi Pollution Control Committee (DPCC), a state-level unit under the Delhi government, to categorize all industrial units in the city according to the pollution hazard they posed, using a classificatory system employed in the Master Plan. It also ordered the Municipal Corporation of Delhi, the agency responsible for licensing commercial activities in the city, not to renew the licenses of polluting industries. In February 1996, the court ordered the Delhi state government to construct common effluent treatment plants (CETPs), which the industries were required to pay for, to reduce water pollution, and it appointed the National Environmental Engineering Research Institute as a consultant to this process. It stipulated that industries that failed to install effluent treatment plants by January 1, 1997, would have to close. In April 1996, the court ordered the relocation of all factories away from residential areas.

These overlapping, even contradictory, orders, which demanded prompt action from several state and private actors with different organizational capacities, had little immediate effect beyond signaling the court's desire to address the pollution issue. Yet this spate of judicial orders precipitated several processes that unfolded over the subsequent decade. Although the various orders and their effects are interrelated, for purposes of clarity, they are presented here in three parts: (1) the 1996–97 closure of hazardous, large, and heavy industries; (2) the closure of industries that discharge effluents into the Yamuna in the year 2000; and (3) the closure and relocation of nonconforming industries, also in 2000. In addition to the judicial orders affecting industries, the Supreme Court in 1998 also ordered a major transformation of Delhi's transportation system, again in response to a public interest petition on air pollution. It is difficult to convey the complexity and ambiguity of these developments in the space of this brief account, and some generalization and simplification cannot be avoided.

The First Closures: Hazardous and Heavy Industries

In July 1996, the Supreme Court targeted 168 factories classified in the Master Plan as "H"—noxious and hazardous. These factories, the court ruled, violated Delhi's 1990 Master Plan and must be relocated or shut down within five months. If factory owners chose to relocate within the National Capital Region—adjoining districts of the states of Rajasthan, Haryana, and Uttar Pradesh—they would have to pay each worker monthly wages during the period of the move, as well as one year's salary as a resettlement bonus. If owners opted to close their factories, workers would be entitled to six years' wages as a retrenchment allowance. Two months after the ruling, in September 1996, the court ordered the relocation or closure of another 513 nonconforming factories by January 1997. In October 1996, it added another forty-six hot mix plants, twenty-one arc/induction furnaces, and 243 brick kilns to the list, all of which were to be closed down or moved by 1997.

The events around the closure of the initial 168 "H" category factories have been documented by the Delhi Janwadi Adhikar Manch (DJAM—Delhi Socialist Rights Forum). The Manch, a federation of trade unions and other human rights organizations[17] that was formed in December 1996 as a response to the Supreme Court's orders, immediately started investigating the impact of the judicial orders on workers, organizing meetings and public hearings, publishing reports,[18] and attempting to represent workers' concerns before the court. Three trade unions affiliated with the Manch approached the bench separately through their lawyers, asking to be heard in the air pollution case. The judges brushed them aside, merely remarking that the court would protect workers' interests and did not need the intercession of the unions. This verbal assurance was not recorded as a part of court proceedings, and thus trade unions were later unable to appeal the judgment, since they had not been recognized as affected parties.

Imminent factory closure had already spurred owners to take preemptive action. The managers of many larger units saw the court's order as an opportunity to profit from the sale of the land on which their factories stood,[19] and they were quite reconciled to the prospect of shutting down their industries and selling off capital assets. Anticipating closure, managers had begun laying off workers well in advance of the Supreme Court deadline. The Birla Textile Mills, for instance, reduced its workforce from 8,000 to 2,500. Bhagsons Paint Industries laid off forty-four workers over a year before the court's deadline, leaving only six workers eligible for compensation,[20] and Sahni Tyres reduced its workforce of 1,800 to 300.[21]

Managers also used other devices to minimize their liability for workers' compensation. Only one factory, Ayodhya Textile Mills, the only government-owned unit ordered to close, declared closure and gave six years' wages in compensation to its workers. Through various subterfuges, the owners of the remaining 167 factories avoided paying the court-ordered compensation. Some factories declared that they were moving out of Delhi. This reduced their liability to one year's wages, and they also found ways to avoid paying workers during the months when the factory was being moved. In all cases, the number of workers employed in the relocated unit was drastically reduced, and in some cases local workers replaced those previously employed by the Delhi factories. For instance, Shriram Foods and Fertilizers[22] announced that it would move to Rajpura, but only 150 of its 1,304 workers were actually transferred there.[23] Birla Textile Mills, for its part, moved to Baddi, in Himachal Pradesh, and the Swatantra Bharat Mills moved to Tonk, in Rajasthan. Since many workers' families were unwilling to move to these sites, which had skeletal infrastructure and were far from the National Capital Region (Delhi and contiguous districts of adjoining states), they forfeited their entitlement to six years' wages. Thus, relocation meant that in effect most workers were laid off without compensation.

Furthermore, factory management limited its liability to the narrowest possible definition of "workmen," those who were on the rolls as permanent employees. This meant that large numbers of workers employed year after year as *badli*—casual workers or those hired through contractors—were denied compensation.[24] According to the Manch's survey, up to 90 percent of workers in some firms were not classified as permanent, even after decades in service. For instance, G. D. Rathi Steel, Ltd., had twenty-nine permanent and three hundred casual workers. Punjab Potteries employed 150 workers, all of whom were casual. In Birla Textile Mills, only 800 of the 2,800 workers were permanent employees. Firms denied that casual or contract laborers were their employees, even though social security benefits were deducted from their wages, indicating the firm's long-term, direct relationship with them. The majority of workers employed in these units were thus laid off with no compensation.

Permanent workers fared little better. According to the Manch,

> Of those entitled to compensation under Section 25 F of the Industrial Disputes Act (read together with Section 25 B which defines "continuous service"), our survey shows that *compensation has not been paid to any worker* although more than one year has passed since the order was issued on 8 July 1996, and seven months since the 168 units ceased production in [sic] November 30, 1996. This is in total disregard of the order of the Supreme Court dated December 4, 1996, which fixed April 30, 1997, as the deadline by which compensation had to be paid.[25]

When the Manch approached the Supreme Court and pointed out that the judges' orders were being violated, the court suggested that they take their complaints to the labor commissioner, an official whose previous inaction had already demonstrated his total lack of interest in protecting workers' rights. Clearly, the attempt to clean up Delhi's air and water had a severe adverse impact on workers' livelihoods.

What was the scale of displacement? Notably, the only source of data on the number of workers rendered jobless by the Supreme Court is a survey conducted by the Manch in 1997.[26] No detailed figures are available from any government agency, and as their heavy use of casual and contract laborers indicates, factory owners systematically underreport the number of people they employ.[27] The Manch's survey of a hundred (out of 168) affected factories shows that 12,668 workers lost their jobs. And if displacement from the other sixty-eight factories, 513 nonconforming firms, forty-six hot mix plants, twenty-one arc/induction furnaces, and 243 brick kilns is taken into account, the number of affected workers is clearly much higher. The Manch estimates that "in this first phase, no less than 50,000 workers have lost their jobs and been dislocated with their families."[28] To this estimate should be added the number of workers in ancillary industries supplying materials and services to the closed or relocated factories. Thus, of Delhi's total population of 12 million, the number directly affected by loss of employment (workers and their families) far exceeds 250,000.

The Closure of Water-Polluting Factories

The second phase of factory closures occurred in 2000. As mentioned above, in February 1996, the Court had stipulated that factories that failed to install effluent treatment plants by January 1, 1997, would have to close. Although the Delhi government agreed to share the costs of the effluent treatment plants, factory owners still refused to install the plants, arguing that they were still too costly and that some of the factories were being unfairly targeted. Thus, over the next three and a half years no effluent treatment plants were built. On September 13, 1999, the Supreme Court judges scolded the Delhi administration:

> As observed in our order dated August 27, 1999, there are enough laws at the command of the state to enable it to take appropriate action against the polluters. . . . No effective action has been taken so far. It is for this reason . . . [that] we . . . hereby direct the National Capital territory of Delhi . . . to take such measures as it may deem proper . . . to ensure that no industrial effluent is discharged into the river Yamuna.

The court set a deadline of November 1, 1999, one and a half months from the date of the order, to reach this goal. On December 17, the judges issued a notice to the chief secretary of the Delhi government, asking why nothing had been done to prevent untreated industrial discharge. And in January 2000, reiterating its previous order of 1996, the court forbade the discharge of any untreated effluents from any factory in Delhi and Haryana into the Yamuna.

In late 1999, the Delhi Pollution Control Committee (DPCC) sent notices of closure to 1,142 industrial units. These firms were chosen by means of a survey conducted by twenty-nine subdivisional magistrates (administrators) of the Delhi government and engineers of the state pollution control committee, and on the basis of information provided by various industrial associations. To ensure effective closure, not only were the factories' gates locked, their water and electricity were also cut off.

The closures did not go unopposed. On February 12, 2000, factory owners in the Seelampur area of the city physically attempted to block the government's "vigilance squads" from closing their factories. Many other industrial units and associations also protested, arguing that they did not discharge effluents and met existing standards, or that they had already installed treatment plants. Of the closed-down factories, 372 were allowed to reopen by January 2000. The process of closing and reopening continued throughout the year: by July 2000, while 3,177 units had been issued closure notices, an unspecified number had actually been shut down and an unspecified number had been allowed to stay open or reopen.[29]

Almost all the firms closed down during this phase were small, most reporting that they employed fewer than ten workers. While the closed firms were scattered across the city in designated industrial areas, nonconforming but de facto industrial areas, and residential and commercial spaces,[30] the closures were concentrated in certain industrial areas.[31] The court issued no directions about compensation for workers laid off during this phase, and since almost all the firms employed unorganized laborers, there is no documentation about the scale and impact of closures on the workers.

The Closure of Nonconforming Factories

The third, related, set of closures focused on "nonconforming" factories (factories that violated the zoning provisions of the master plan). The Supreme Court first ordered the relocation or closure of nonconforming factories in residential areas in April 1996, setting a deadline of January 1, 1997. In 1996, the DPCC contracted schoolteachers to conduct a survey[32] of industrial units. Of the city's 126,218 industrial units in the city, 97,411 (almost 80 percent) were nonconforming. The Delhi administration was galvanized into action by the deadline and by the court's threats to punish government officials who failed to carry out its orders. Owners of nonconforming units were allowed to apply for a license to operate from a high-powered committee, appointed by the chief secretary of the Delhi government. "Household industries"—those that did not pollute, employed fewer than five workers, used no more than one kilowatt of power, and occupied an area smaller than thirty square meters—would be granted the licenses. But most nonconforming units did not meet these stringent criteria, and of the 51,000 industrial units that applied for licenses, only 5 percent qualified. The court directed that alternative sites be found for the ineligible firms.

In October 1996, the Delhi State Industrial Development Corporation (DSIDC) began to acquire land in Bawana, on the outskirts of the city, where small factories from residential areas could relocate. Meanwhile, in June 1996, a manufacturers' association[33] had appealed the closure order, and the high-powered committee established by the court decided in 1997 that those owners who had applied to the DSIDC for alternate plots would be granted temporary licenses to continue operating in their old locations. The DSIDC also began raising money (10 percent of the total projected cost of a developed industrial plot) from the applicants. This process continued for three years. By July 2000, 52,000 applications for alternate plot allotments had been received—and not a single firm had been relocated. Since Bawana had only enough land for 16,000 plots, the flood of applications caused consternation among DSIDC officials. They rejected 27,000 applications on what applicants claimed were "flimsy" technical grounds. DSIDC also raised its demands, insisting that factory owners pay 20 percent of the value of their plots by October 30, 2000,[34] failing which their applications would be rejected. When manufacturers' associations approached the Supreme Court to complain that DSIDC was demanding large sums of money without allotting any land, the corporation capitulated by allotting plots of land on paper to *all* applicants! No land was actually given (indeed, there wasn't enough to resettle all the applicants, nor had the parcel of land in Bawana been developed), yet DSIDC demanded another 20 percent by December 31, 2000, failing which a firm's application would be rejected and the firm's factory closed. At the same time, the corporation told the court that it needed at least five more years to develop the land in Bawana.

At this point, the Supreme Court apparently decided that enough was enough. On September 12, 2000, the judges announced that "all polluting industries of whatever category operating in residential areas must be asked to shut down." Two months later, on November 14, the court issued a show cause notice to the chief secretary of the

Delhi government and the commissioner of the Delhi Municipal Corporation, asking why they should not be punished for contempt of court for not implementing the court's orders. In panic, the Delhi government ordered the immediate closure of *all* nonconforming industrial units (and not just the polluting ones). This order, which affected more than 97,000 factories, was unprecedented in scale. Over the next few days, as government officials, escorted by heavily armed policemen, went around sealing factory premises (locking their doors, disconnecting electricity and water), there were riots in Delhi. Factory owners and workers were out on the streets protesting. There was a citywide *bandh* (shutdown)[35] on November 20. Protesters set fire to government buses and stoned municipal officials. Police retaliated by firing on the protesters. Three workers were shot dead, and hundreds were injured. Even the media, which had reported only desultorily on the progress of the Supreme Court litigation, took note of this outbreak of violence. Yet, restricted as they were to the industrial pockets of the city, even these dramatic events received only a few inches of column space and only for a few days. There were no in-depth accounts of how workers or small factory owners were affected, nothing that indicated that a huge section of the city's population stood to lose its livelihood.

On November 28, 2000, the Supreme Court chided the Delhi government for not distinguishing between polluting nonconforming and nonpolluting nonconforming firms. Soon after, undeterred by the protests, the judges criticized the government for its tardiness and set a deadline of December 15, 2000, for identifying all the nonconforming factories, and a deadline of January 7, 2001, for shutting all polluting factories among them.

On December 15, the Delhi Pradesh Congress Committee, the state-level unit of the political party ruling Delhi, and the Delhi Manufacturers' Association staged a large demonstration near Parliament, trucking in thousands of workers. The target of their protests was the central government's Urban Development Ministry, which controlled the Delhi Development Authority, the body that prepared and implemented the city's Master Plan. The protesters blamed the urban development minister, Jagmohan, for arbitrarily trying to remove all industries from Delhi. It was not clear how the authority was defining polluting industries, they said. Moreover, the livelihood of hundreds of thousands of workers and factory owners was more important than the Master Plan, and the protesters saw no reason why the Plan could not be amended.[36] The protest, in other words, blamed the assault on nonconforming units on the land-use classifications mandated in Delhi's Master Plan. This was also an attempt to deflect criticism from the Congress-led government of Delhi and attribute the closure fiasco to the BJP-led central government. The Delhi government proclaimed a *nyaya yuddha* (battle for justice) against the central government and BJP members of Parliament elected from Delhi.

Between 2001 and 2003, many polluting nonconforming factories appear to have shut down. The Supreme Court extended the deadline for closing all polluting nonconforming industries to December 31, 2002. The Delhi government submitted a revised list of thirty-three categories of polluting factories[37] to the Supreme Court and announced that factories in these categories would be closed down in phases. The government also agreed that industrial units that were nonconforming but did not pollute would be allowed to operate from their present premises for the time being. By November 2002, construction had started in the new Bawana Industrial Area, where 14,500 plots had been allotted by the DSIDC. A common effluent treatment plant, housing for three thousand workers' families, bicycle paths, and other facilities were also planned. In February 2001, the Delhi government announced that it would approach the Ministry of Urban Development to "regularize" (or redesignate as industrial) twenty-four areas classified as residential in the Master Plan.[38] It argued that more than 70 percent of the land in these areas was occupied by industrial units, and thus their de facto industrial status simply needed to be legitimized. Such a step would prevent the closure or displacement of twenty thousand factories.[39] Almost two years later, on December 12, 2002, the Delhi Development Authority reversed its stand and accepted the Delhi government's proposal for in situ regularization in the twenty-four areas of the city.

This change of heart in the DDA, which was controlled by the Ministry of Urban Development, was criticized in the English-language press. *The Hindu* reminded its readers that the ministry had earlier rejected the change of land use from residential to industrial "keeping in view the already deteriorating environmental conditions in Delhi and the ever-growing menace of illegal constructions and unauthorized encroachments."[40] The newspaper darkly hinted that "there are political and other interests involved in the exercise which on the face of it seeks to prevent the closure or displacement of nearly 20,000 industrial units but in reality overlooks not only the interests of residents of these colonies [neighborhoods] but all other citizens of Delhi as well."[41]

Dealing with Vehicular Pollution

Most Delhi residents' most direct experience of air pollution comes from travel through the city that brings them in contact with automobile exhaust. In 1993–94, according to the Central Pollution Control Board (CPCB), 64 percent of Delhi's air pollution came from vehicles, 16 percent from thermal power plants, 12 percent from industrial sources, and 10 percent from domestic sources.[42] Because automobile emissions are the largest source of air pollution, one would expect them to have been the first target for cleanup, but they were not. As we have noted, the Supreme Court's first move against air pollution in Delhi focused on "H" category factories, which were shut down during 1996–97. In a public hearing organized by the Manch in 1998,[43] researchers from the Delhi Science Forum, an independent group investigating the social impacts of science and technology-related policies, deployed CPCB data to point out that Delhi's transportation sector contributed far more hydrocarbons, nitrogen oxide, and carbon monoxide to the air than did industrial sources; only in suspended particulate matter and sulfur dioxide emissions were the proportions reversed.[44] Yet attention had been concentrated almost exclusively on pollution caused by industries. If clean air were truly a priority, the court needed to focus elsewhere.

In 1997, the Centre for Science and Environment (CSE), a nongovernmental research and advocacy organization that had conducted a hard-hitting public campaign against automobile emissions called Slow Murder, filed a public interest petition asking the Supreme Court to issue a series of directives aimed at the government, the petroleum industry, and automobile manufacturers. In 1998, the court appointed an Environmental Pollution (Prevention and Control) Authority, widely known as the Bhurelal Committee after its chairperson, retired bureaucrat Bhurelal. Anil Agarwal, the director of CSE, was one of the committee members. The Bhurelal Committee recommended several steps, the most far-reaching being that (1) vehicles that run on gas switch to unleaded fuel;[45] (2) public transportation (buses, taxis, and auto-rickshaws) switch to compressed natural gas (CNG);[46] (3) public and private vehicles older than ten years be taken off the roads; and (4) all vehicles undergo an emissions check every three months and that vehicles that pass get a "Pollution Under Control" certificate to be displayed on the windshield. Those vehicles that failed to meet these specifications would not be allowed to ply. It must be noted that all these directives were to be implemented in Delhi alone, and not in other parts of the country.

The Supreme Court accepted the Bhurelal Committee's recommendations and gave the government and other involved parties three years to implement them, with March 31, 2001, as the deadline. Yet action happened in fits and starts. The Delhi government, the central petroleum ministry, the automobile manufacturers, and other involved parties often failed to coordinate with each other. The shift to unleaded gas was relatively smooth, despite arguments that the new fuel, though lead-free, emitted significantly more benzene, a known carcinogen. Those who drove their own vehicles —cars, motorcycles, and scooters—were relatively unaffected. But the conversion of gasoline- and diesel-fueled public transportation to CNG was (and continues to be) a long nightmare. Many vehicle owners, most of them lower-middle-class owner-operators,[47] had to sell their vehicles at a loss and go into debt to buy new vehicles. Owners then had to wait in line for hours, often overnight, at the CNG filling stations, because the supply of CNG fell far short of the demand generated by the pace of vehicle conversion. A sign painted on the back of one auto-rickshaw sarcastically summed it up: "Gaadi gas ki, zindagi aish ki. Hotel par khana, petrol pump par sona. Isi ka naam zindagi" (A vehicle on gas, a life of luxury. Eat in a restaurant, sleep at the petrol pump. This is life).

CNG scarcity eased only in late 2002, when new supply stations came into operation. Over the two-year period when CNG was scarce, taxi and auto-rickshaw owners sustained huge losses in their earnings at a time when they were financially overextended, forcing many out of business.[48] Meanwhile, the entire state-owned Delhi Transport Corporation bus fleet had to be drastically downsized because the corporation could not afford enough new CNG buses to replace the old diesel-powered ones, and the shortage of CNG kept many buses off the roads. As a result, commuters who depend on public transport spent more time waiting for buses that were even more crowded, and stress levels rose as people battled every day to get around the city. In short, the improvement in Delhi's air has been achieved on the backs of commuters who use public transportation (mainly working-class and lower-middle-class people) and small owner-operators.

The Supreme Court directive raises several other important issues which this brief account does not adequately address. For instance, critics have complained that the conversion of all public transportation to CNG makes the entire city dependent on one relatively untested technology. There are also concerns about the safety of CNG tanks, especially after wear and tear. The Bhurelal Committee did not consider alternate technologies such as ultra-low sulfur diesel. According to Dinesh Mohan of the Indian Institute of Technology, a transportation policy analyst, the Bhurelal Committee and the Supreme Court should have prescribed a set of standards for vehicle manufacturers, the petroleum industry, and the government to meet, and left it to them to find the best ways to meet them. The committee's reliance on blanket directives instead brings up a larger issue, that of the process by which decisions about transportation policy are made. The absence of a consultative process that can examine issues in a wider context means that alternatives such as encouraging bicycle use were not considered at all.[49] The long-term benefit of converting public vehicles to CNG may also be limited. Public vehicles constitute only 4 percent of the motor vehicles in Delhi. Private vehicles that run on diesel and out-of-state vehicles that used leaded gas continue to pollute. And ironically, by weakening public transportation, the court provided an incentive to those who can afford it to invest in private motor vehicles, increasing the numbers of polluting vehicles on the road. It bears examining whether, in the long term, the absolute increase in the number of vehicles offsets the benefits accruing from the decreased emissions from each vehicle.

Analyzing the Court's Actions

The Supreme Court orders to close factories contain many vexed assumptions and ambiguities. What is a *polluting industry?* The commonsense notion that a manufacturing unit must actually pollute—generate noxious or hazardous wastes (or noise) in excess of permissible levels—in order to be identified as a polluting industry does not hold in this case. The 1990 Master Plan lists twenty-seven polluting industries, an expanded version of a list produced by the Central Pollution Control Board.[50] The designation of a factory as polluting is based not on its actual emissions but on what it produces and whether the manufacture of that product is classified as polluting or not. The classification of products in the 1990 Master Plan also has anomalies. "While corrugated boxes are listed under category A," observes one writer, "paper products are in category F and, in many cases, corrugated box manufacturers have been targeted for closure by the sealing squad under the argument that it is also a paper product."[51] Rather than investigate the specificities of each case and the particular practices of individual factories, the court uses the CPCB's categories as an approximation. Thus, even if a factory has reduced its emissions to permissible levels, it may still be designated as polluting industry. But the issue is moot because the Delhi Pollution Control Committee (DPCC), the state-level counterpart of the CPCB, is woefully understaffed and thus incapable of checking emissions for every factory even if the court were to order such checks. Factory owners and politicians accuse the DPCC, moreover, of fudging its lists for a fee to let individual factories off the hook.

Through their protests, public statements and publications, workers' organizations and the Manch tried to downplay the importance of industries' contribution to air pollution, arguing that the vehicles of more affluent urban residents should be targeted before workers' livelihoods. But other analysts offered a different perspective, arguing that industrial emissions were also a serious hazard. An analyst argued that:

> even though the contribution[s] of industry may seem less significant, their effect is more lethal because of the localized effect and the higher toxicity of the emissions. A component of industrial air pollution in Delhi, particularly in non-conforming areas, is toxic fumes from the electroplating and anodizing industry. Obviously, the workers are the first to be affected by it. Rolling and pickling units too generate toxic gases. Some of the industrial areas like Wazirpur . . . where there are many such units, are close to residential localities. With the expansion of the urban sprawl in Delhi, many residential areas are now dangerously close to industrial areas housing hazardous units.[52]

Yet relocation, which simply transfers the problem elsewhere, out of the Supreme Court's sight, is no answer. And closing down polluting factories to protect workers' health, without providing them with safe alternate livelihoods, merely exchanges one form of vulnerability for another. The Manch had initially adopted a "jobs versus environment" stance on the issue of factory closure, dismissing pollution as the concern of privileged elites who did not care that workers were being deprived of their livelihood. But confronted by the overwhelming concern about air pollution in the media and elsewhere, the Manch eventually conceded that pollution was not a trivial issue and modified its stance, asserting that the primary victims of polluted working conditions were laborers and yet neither the court nor the government had addressed their plight. In the words of a commentator affiliated with the Manch, writing in the progressive journal *Economic and Political Weekly*:

> If the aim is to fight pollution and improve the health of the citizens then it [public policy] should begin by addressing the issue in terms of the disproportionately high impact of pollution on the lives of the underprivileged sections of the population. Let alone this no provision [sic] was made to protect their interests, thereby sending a message to them to fend for themselves. Where are they supposed to go for pleading their case and for enforcement of their rights? What happens if they are denied any hearing by the administration which even otherwise neglects them? What happens if they lose their jobs or employers refuse to give them their rightful dues? What happens if under the pretext of implementing Court orders employees are wrongfully dismissed from service? What of the impact on their families and children's future? Are all these non-issues?[53]

The same commentator justified the protests in the city, asserting, "When the central issue of survival of the workers becomes non-justiciable then they are being compelled to take the law into their own hands." This impassioned plea, however, made little headway in a Supreme Court that had decided that reducing air and water pollution constituted a public interest that overrode the concerns of a large, disadvantaged section of the public.

Another key concept on which the court's orders hinged was that of the nonconforming industry, an industrial unit that violates the land use provisions of Delhi's Master Plan of 1962, which designated functionally segregated zones for residential, commercial, institutional, and industrial purposes. The Master Plan has emerged as a key point of contention in the debate over the closure of factories, and thus it merits some explanation. Delhi's population almost doubled in the months after August 1947, when the Partition of India drove more than 450,000 Hindu and Sikh refugees to the city. In order "to check the haphazard and unplanned growth of Delhi," the Delhi Development Authority (DDA) was created in 1957 by an act of Parliament. The DDA, a unit of the central government's Urban Development Ministry, has primary responsibility for planning, acquiring, and developing land in the city. The DDA prepared the first Master Plan in 1962, with expert help from the Ford Foundation. This plan, intended to cover the period 1961–81, divided the city into functionally segregated zones.[54] In accordance with the plan, and pursuing the goal of rapid industrialization set out in the second and third five-year plans of the Indian government (1956–61, 1961–66), industrial estates were established in Okhla, Badli, Shahdara, and Najafgarh Road on the outskirts of the city as locations for small-scale industries.

However, industrial development in the city did not entirely follow the Master Plan. Industrial growth outpaced the limited space provided in the industrial estates, with thousands of small factories sprouting up around the industrial estates and commercial centers to take advantage of the proximity of labor, materials, and markets. Despite being in violation of the Master Plan, most of these nonconforming factories were recognized by the government in the sense that they were licensed, registered with the sales and excise departments, and received government subsidies and bank loans. Also, since the plan had made virtually no provision for housing workers, squatter settlements had mushroomed all around the factories.

Such violations were not merely tolerated, they were actively encouraged by politicians and corrupt bureaucrats. Government practices regarding encroachments on public lands and nonconforming industrial units have been complex and contradictory; many different, often conflicting, pronouncements and acts have provided a fertile field for enterprising power-brokers. The possibility of eviction, after all, provides the context for bribing government officials to look the other way. The simultaneous possibility of "regularization," or retrospective legalization of nonconforming sites, spurs encroachers and nonconforming factories to stay on and stake a claim. Meanwhile, the most egregious violator of the Master Plan has been the Delhi Development Authority itself, which, in the early 1980s, suddenly constructed several unplanned flyovers and sports complexes for the 1982 Asian Games, and which has generally followed a policy of ad hoc accommodation of construction whenever it has been politically expedient.

After the lapse of the first Master Plan, the DDA prepared its Perspective Master

Plan 2001, which was published in 1990 in the *Gazette of India*. After independent planners publicly criticized the document as "unsatisfactory,"[55] the Delhi Urban Arts Commission, a body formed by a 1974 act of Parliament, was entrusted with the task of reviewing it. The legal status of this plan is ambiguous, yet it is frequently invoked in public interest litigation. This plan designated twenty-eight industrial areas in Delhi and identified at least thirty-seven areas where industries had proliferated even though the area had been earmarked for some other use. The plan also categorized various industries in terms of the pollution they engendered, in order to select those industries that were suitable for an urban environment and identify those that should be shut down, relocated, or prevented from setting up shop in the first place.

At various points, the Supreme Court indicated that a nonconforming industry, even if it did not pollute, should either relocate or close down. Even in cases where a unit had been operating before the formulation of the Master Plan, it was retrospectively deemed to be in violation of it. The 1962 Master Plan (and the later Master Plan of 1990), which the court treated as sacrosanct in this case, is a highly contested document, produced by planners without any process of representative consultation, and the courts have consistently condoned the Delhi government's systematic violation of its provisions over the years. Most of the nonconforming industries were able to establish themselves only by making regular under-the-table payments to municipal authorities, an active collaboration between officials and factory owners. The Master Plan is based on projections about the rate of growth of Delhi's population and the city's anticipated and desired industrial and commercial profile—projections that were more than thirty years old at the time of the court's rulings and that have proved wrong by several orders of magnitude. As the Manch pointed out,

> if the MPD 1962 is indeed, according to the Judges in their order of April 30, 1996, a "charter for deciding land use pattern," then they ought to have considered the premises on which various projections were made in the MPD. Its estimate of population in 1981 was 5.5 million, which became 6.2 million in actuality. The size of the workforce was estimated to be 440,000 in 1981 compared to 460,000 in actual fact. By now even these figures have become irrelevant. By 1996, Delhi's population crossed 10 million, and the number of workers climbed to 910,000.[56]

Another relevant document in this debate is a 1997 white paper by the central government's Ministry of Environment and Forests titled "Pollution in Delhi, with an Action Plan." The paper attempted to address the problem of pollution, "keeping in view pollution trends and prescribed ambient standards."[57] The white paper attributes Delhi's pollution to "the rise in population and growth in economic activity." After examining various sources of pollution, the document emphasizes the need to plan and develop infrastructure in ways that will mitigate pollution. Towards this end, the paper focuses on the need to "contain the pressure of population on Delhi." It envisages the diversion of two million people from Delhi. "Accordingly, the development of priority (satellite) towns and complexes in the National Capital Region outside Delhi has been projected."[58]

Gautam Navlakha, an activist affiliated with the Manch, points out that the white paper merely echoes the wishful thinking of the 1990 Master Plan, which sought to develop the towns of Meerut, Rewari, Khurja, Rohtak, and Panipat in order to decentralize and decongest Delhi. As Delhi has continued to grow and expand, these "satellite" towns have grown at an even faster rate, and are themselves suffering from severe air, water, and noise pollution. Thus, the policy of moving industries out of Delhi into adjoining areas may actually worsen the problem of pollution by displacing it into towns with already stretched infrastructure and which lack even rudimentary regulatory capacity.

The biggest ambiguity in the Supreme Court orders was the fate of the several hundreds of thousand workers who were laid off by one stroke of the judicial writ. Ostensibly, the court had been kind; it had stipulated norms for compensating permanent workers employed in the factories being relocated or shut down. But, as we have noted, the vast majority of workers who were affected by the court order were "casual laborers," not officially registered as employees of their firms. As discussed above, factory owners are increasingly resorting to the strategy of underreporting the number of workers they employ, as industrial production is subcontracted to smaller firms in the "informal" economy. Much of this informal economy—an umbrella category encompassing complex and myriad work arrangements, from family labor to seasonal employment, escapes the state's regulatory apparatus. Unorganized and not even recognized as employees, hundreds of thousands of workers in this sector had no way of representing their point of view before the judges or the media, and thus inevitably lost their livelihoods.

The Supreme Court order that closed down Delhi factories in order to end air pollution choked off a larger debate about alternative policy options. As noted earlier, the overwhelming contribution to air pollution came from automobile emissions, yet the court orders focused on industrial pollution.[59] The Manch marshaled the evidence to make this case in a series of public hearings in the city, arguing that it is the vehicles of affluent citizens that should be the target of public action. As Amit Sengupta of the People's Science Movement,[60] one of the constituents of the Manch, remarked, "The undue emphasis on removing industrial pollution makes one wonder whether the intention is to remove pollution or to remove the poor from Delhi."[61] It was only in the late 1990s, with the CSE petition, that automobile emissions became the subject of court action. This raises some important questions about social justice. Since the closure of factories would cause immense suffering to large numbers of industrial workers, was there a need to threaten nonconforming units that did not pollute but were only in violation of the Master Plan? And was closure the only way of dealing with polluting industries? A few chose to relocate outside Delhi, and presumably continue to pollute in other states, hardly an ideal solution to the problem. Meanwhile, the option of helping firms adopt cleaner technologies or install pollution control equipment was not seriously examined. Admittedly, in 1996, the court directed factories to set up common effluent treatment plants, but it failed to pursue the matter, so even that possibility fell by the wayside. As the failure to consider alternatives underscores, the flurry of unilateral action by the court completely foreclosed a democratic process of representation, discussion, and informed decision-making.

One reason for the court's swift and peremptory decisions has been the participation in the pollution cases of Justice Kuldip Singh, later famous as a "green judge." Kuldip Singh's reputation rested on the speed with which he dispatched complex legal problems and the strong diktats he issued to recalcitrant bureaucrats, among them senior officials, failure to implement which would lead to censure and the threat of jail for contempt of court. Singh drew legitimacy from the radical tradition of public interest litigation begun in the late 1970s by Justices P. N. Bhagwati and V. R. Krishna Iyer that invoked constitutional rights to justify decisive court intervention in instances where government action had caused a miscarriage of justice, even in areas that had earlier been perceived as outside the court's purview. Initially, such public interest litigation was used to release prisoners held without trial for decades or to safeguard the rights of pavement-dwellers in Bombay—cases in which the victims were poor and powerless and unable to seek justice. Since then, however, the concept has been greatly expanded to encompass a variety of concerns, including those that should be addressed to administrative agencies.

Instead of being the last resort, then, the Supreme Court has permitted itself to become the first body to which petitioners appeal, thereby short-circuiting the administrative process and even weakening it in the long term. Yet this new way of doing business is hailed by those who have access to the courts because it cuts through red tape and avoids a painful, drawn-out struggle for administrative responsiveness and accountability. As M. C. Mehta, the lawyer who initiated the pollution litigation, said:

> If there is a law, you respect it, you obey it, you enforce it. . . . You cannot set up hazardous and polluting industries in Delhi. . . . The law was there and all the industries, all the associations knew it very well. . . . They [should] have voluntarily . . . gone out of the city. Instead of doing that, they started lobbying with the government. All these politicians, they are vote-hungry people. They are all the time looking out for their seats and for their elections. . . . So they were doing that [and] all these industries were influencing them. . . . Nobody is complying with [the law]. . . . [There is] negligence on the part of the industries, on the part of the government of India, on the part of the state government and every possible machinery. So when they failed to protect the life and health of the people in this city then the court came into play.[62]

What this account leaves out is that environmentalists like Mehta made no direct attempt to influence or even address politicians, manufacturers, or leaders of regulatory agencies. Yet they cite their frustration with these people as their reason for approaching the Supreme Court. The partnership of environmentalists M. C. Mehta and Kuldip Singh, advocate and judge, which resulted in directives that affected the lives and livelihoods of hundreds of thousands of workers and their families, people who had no representation in court, exemplifies the new efficient dispensation of justice in the "public interest" that middle-class people acclaim.

Yet M. C. Mehta and Kuldip Singh do not act alone. Like most vigilante icons, they command the admiration and support of a broad public (excluding, of course, the displaced workers and their supporters), and their actions are widely and favorably reported in the media. Both have received prestigious awards[63] and frequently figure as invited speakers and celebrity guests at public ceremonies of the kind organized by the Rotary or Lions Clubs. Together, they attract the accolades of the upper classes, partly because they embody effective state action and partly because they are seen to serve "the public interest" by protecting the environment, with clean air and water appearing as transparent, universal goods that supersede questions of political economy. How and for whom did clean air become such a transcendental value, one that could trump issues of livelihood and social justice?

Pollution and the Constitution of a Public

For a subcontinent with a centuries-old obsession with matters of purity and pollution, a matrix that still organizes much of social life, the problem of air pollution seems strangely inassimilable into older frames of understanding. While orientations to people, objects, and spaces, especially in practices regarding food and sexuality, are shaped by ideas about caste and life-cycle event-related pollution,[64] that set of concerns seems to be curiously at odds with the western biomedical discourse around toxicity and risk. How can mourners, for example, who come to cremate corpses at Delhi's Nigambodh ghat, on the bank of river Yamuna, believe that they are cleansed of death's pollution by bathing in water made filthy by sewage and industrial sludge? Extending Thomas Rosin's analysis of the use of dust as a cleansing agent in India, one may trace beliefs about the relative harmlessness of water- and air-borne wastes to Ayurvedic notions of the elements—air, water, fire, earth—as marked by constant traffic and flow of energy. In this conceptual framework, the renewal and recycling of wastes and debris is perceived to be part of "an active . . . alchemy stirring among castaway substances"[65] that dilutes and diffuses the danger that these substances embody. Thus, for example, sulfur dioxide from the Indraprastha thermal power plant is simply borne away by the wind, and cannot be a form of pollution that matters.

Resisting this set of environmental values, with its built-in inertia when it comes to things deemed toxic by western biomedicine, demanded tapping into a different discourse, one already made familiar by colonial and postcolonial health and hygiene projects. Ideas of improvement, of husbanding resources, of controlling lands and peoples for the purpose of conservation, and of better management for more efficient exploitation were an intrinsic part of the colonial enterprise.[66] Empire was justified as an instrument of development that would lead "new races of subjects and allies in the career of improvement."[67] Promoting "the internal Improvement . . . of a Powerful Empire" involved "the improvement of the people in regard to their health, industry, and morals," and not merely agriculture, mining, and fisheries.[68] The pursuit of improved health and morals ranged over such diverse terrain as education, agricultural policy, public health and hygiene, population control, prison reform, and personal law.[69] The government as guardian drew upon expertise in new forms of knowledge,[70] based on techniques of taxonomic classification and inscription that included maps, censuses, and surveys of all kinds. Enumeration was essential to the act of producing order, rendering unruly reality legible,[71] and enabling bureaucratic action. It helped shape (without determining) new collective identities—the modern politics of caste, religion, region, and language—and new modes of action. After independence, the same techniques of government that had been used by India's colonial overseers were inherited by the postcolonial state and employed to achieve planned national development.[72]

It would be misleading, of course, to point only to continuities between colonial and postcolonial forms of government. The postcolonial discourse of sovereign nation-states, anchored though it was in the paradox of aspiring to independence by adopting a development path that required participation in the familiar inequities of global markets, an "aid" regime, and Cold War militarism,[73] created novel political opportunities.[74] The postcolonial era opened new institutional arenas for negotiating the conflicting imperatives of accumulation and legitimation—from electoral representation to socialist planning, liberal democracy created the possibility of new freedoms. Ideas of citizenship, forged in the freedom struggle's "crucible of cultural politics,"[75] informed the sensibilities of assertive social groups, who could make new demands upon the state. The Indian state created a large public sector that included research and educational institutions, capital-intensive infrastructure, and heavy industries, as well as a large bureaucracy to control and regulate this sprawling edifice. The prominent position of the Indian middle class can be traced to the rise of nationalism in the colonial period,[76] but its consolidation as a decisive hegemonic power occurred in the aftermath of independence.[77]

Though middle-class people saw themselves as upholders of the public interest, speaking for nature and the nation, their interests and ideologies had been shaped by their subject positions. Their social location in the urban economy—in the professions and in commerce and finance—kept the middle classes detached from working class lives and concerns. Moreover, the absence of an organized working class in the city meant that working-class points of view could rarely make themselves heard in the public sphere. Instead, middle-class visions of the ideal city came to dominate and drive public action. Images of Singapore inform the model urban lifestyle which middle-class Delhites desire and to which they aspire.[78] The "benevolent authoritarianism" of this city-state appeals to their sense of civic order and security, efficiency and prosperity. A city where spitting on the streets is punished by a hefty fine and where shopping and commercialized recreation are twenty-four hour activities seems like a utopia for urban middle-class Indians, who bemoan Delhi's chaos, dirt, and lack of amenities.

By the 1980s, the promise of development in postcolonial India and the dream of model cities were perceived by the middle class to have been betrayed by a corrupt and inefficient bureaucracy. While it maintained its faith in the optic of enlightened public interest, to be determined by technocrats and judges, the middle class saw the process of governing as having been subverted by the "politics" of vested interests. In their view, governing should ideally be a rational, technically informed process that "takes all factors into account" and then generates enforceable decisions that will be passively accepted by compliant subjects. The state's failure to live up to this ideal led to disillusionment, which was only displaced by the emergence of activist-citizens like M. C. Mehta and activist NGOs like CSE, who cut through red tape, disciplining not only erring bureaucrats but also working-class citizens. A middle-class citizen approvingly commented on the success of these initiatives in getting a moribund state to act:

> In terms of air [pollution] they've done a lot—moved to CNG, restricted entry time for trucks.[79] Air quality has improved. [I know] through newspapers, TV. Now they have it on TV, everything about NO [nitrogen oxide], CO_2 [carbon dioxide] and dust. . . . It is only the judiciary and media which [are] keeping these things under control, otherwise the government machinery has failed. It is all because of the interfering politicians [who] do not support good officials. Two major factors that have led to failure are politicians and corruption. Media and judiciary are the only impartial ones. If they are not there, no one will know the truth.[80]

Hidden Violence, the Workplace, and "Free" Labor

When middle-class citizens of Delhi praise the action against air pollution, they rarely acknowledge the issue of displaced workers. To them, workers remain faceless, an amorphous mass that blurs into the distance. Delhi's layout means that residents of middle-class localities may never have to venture into parts of the city where manufacturing firms are concentrated. This spatial segregation contributes to the invisibility of the city's industrial workers. Middle-class privilege also includes the power to screen out facts that may disrupt the comfortable fictions of everyday life. One of these organizing fictions is the idea of "public interest." When confronted with the issue of workers' loss of livelihood, M. C. Mehta defended his campaign by saying, "Here twelve million people are suffering. . . . What is more important—people's life and health or jobs to a few people?"[81] In this view, protecting the general population from respiratory diseases is a larger cause that overrides the specific suffering of a "few people," even if they may be poorer and more vulnerable to malnutrition and ill health than the rest. Mehta's formulation of the issue—benefit to many versus loss to some—conceals the class-specific effects of the air pollution initiative.

When critics point out the asymmetrical impact of the air pollution campaign, middle-class residents shelter behind self-serving reassurances. "Oh, the government is bound to do something for workers," Mehta asserted. "The court has fully protected the interest of the workers. . . . Where is the injustice?" Mehta takes at face value the court's orders about compensation, without acknowledging that factory owners did not comply with them. When challenged about the efficacy of these orders, he shrugged off responsibility: "It was the role of the politicians; it was the role of the trade unions. . . . When the court order was there, they should have protected [workers'] rights through that order. If they don't do anything, then [what] can you do?" In blaming politicians and trade unions for betraying workers, this account ignores the fact that the court gave them no room to represent workers' interests. That the court saw air pollution as a "technical" problem devoid of social content is clear from the fact that, besides excluding trade unions as affected parties in its deliberations, its advisory committees were made up entirely of technical experts and environmentalists, with no representatives of factory owners or affected workers. The media, for their part, made only token inquiries about the fate of workers, by and large reporting court proceedings without bothering to investigate their impact on the ground. Middle-class hegemony, operating through the court and the media, worked to conceal the violence perpetrated on workers.

That workers' concerns do not matter to the middle class is clearly expressed in this November 2002 interview with S. P. Marwah, an officer of the Indian Administrative Service who, as labor commissioner for Delhi, was the most senior official responsible for safeguarding the rights of workers in the city:

> Marwah: The main issue of concern before the Delhi government is population—unchecked immigration in the city. This is the basic cause of all problems. . . . It also results in environmental problems. There have been two landmark judgments by the Supreme Court banning vehicles with non-clean fuel and the relocation of industries in non-conforming areas.
> Interviewer: Landmark judgment . . . in what way?
> Marwah: The Supreme Court acted on public interest litigation and acted to clean the air. Delhi is the fourth most polluted city in the world.
> Interviewer: Has it improved?
> Marwah: Oh yes. Recently kids were asked if they could see the sky and stars and they responded that they could see the stars now. It was bad [before], you could not see the sky, only black clouds.
> Interviewer: But what about the workers?
> Marwah: They were given compensation.
> Interviewer: But what about the unorganized labor?
> Marwah: Some must have gone back to their villages and others took up [other] jobs in the city. Water finds its own way. In practice no workers were laid off or dislocated. There are large-scale development activities. . . . Overall it seems everyone welcomes the efforts and is happy. Who would want to see dirt and no development?

In terms of improving Delhi's air quality, the Supreme Court's campaign can be regarded as a success. Air pollution levels have been reduced. Children can see the stars. The incidence of asthma and other respiratory ailments will also decline, one hopes. But what of the injuries suffered every day by the children of laid-off workers? They breathe cleaner air, but it doesn't fill their stomachs. They live in worse conditions; many have been pulled out of school because their parents cannot afford the expense.[82] In the quest for cleaner air, why were these children not considered? The effects of the Supreme Court judgment on the vulnerable bodies of poor children, men and women remain invisible in the public eye.

Workers offer a different perspective on the links between pollution and health. They assert the importance of work and livelihood for health, both physical and mental. Prem Kaur, the wife of a laid-off foreman from the Birla Textile Mills, described their situation a year after the factory closed:

> We live in Kamla Nagar New Birla Lines.[83] Since last year, when my husband was dismissed from work, our home is always full of stress and discord. The children's schooling has stopped. My [elder] daughter was studying for a master's degree; she had to leave midway. Now she gives tuitions[84] to keep things going. Our little daughter has a kidney problem that was being treated the past two years. That's all stopped now. We've just been told that she needs surgery. If my husband was still working, we'd have gotten something from his ESI [social security]. Now all his work has stopped. We can't do anything at all.
>
> While my husband worked in the factory, there was no impact on his health. Actually he stayed healthy from working; now that he sits at home, he's tense all day. Can't do anything properly, doesn't eat or drink properly. So many of our neighbors are in such difficulties; it's hard to describe. One family doesn't have enough to eat; they've started vending snacks from a cart, and all they can feed their children is dry rotis.[85]

This account details the travails of a permanent employee, a member of the so-called labor aristocracy. If this is what a relatively well-to-do worker has experienced, the condition of casual and temporary workers is clearly much worse.

In their pursuit of stable employment, workers and their families express their own distinct set of environmental values. These relate to the environment as a site for productive and remunerative work, and as a place to live in dignity and relative comfort. Workers' views about pollution vary. Some deny that their factory caused any pollution or that their health was affected by working there, and they see the entire pollution issue as a smokescreen intended to conceal other motives. Hari Singh, a foreman in the Birla Textile Mills, asserts:

> As far as pollution is concerned, it is just a drama. There was absolutely no pollution from our factory. I've worked for thirty-two years in this factory, and I've never had to go to the doctor even once. We've worked for sixteen hours at a time in the mill; pollution didn't affect us. Actually the owner [closed our factory] after realizing the value of vacated land. This fiasco has been deliberately created. The management has been trying for several years to close the unit. They just needed an excuse. I can't understand why, even though we keep shuttling around the courts, we never get heard for months on end, and Mehta's petition is heard immediately. What law is this? What sort of justice is this?

Another worker asserted that the Birla mill had installed pollution control equipment in the late 1980s,

> when the V. P. Singh government came and ordered it. So the chemical-filled water from the mill was actually cleaned and would then flow out in the drain. That equipment worked. Even after this, they closed factories in the name of pollution. There was no external pollution—just a little bit of smoke and effluent.

By contrast, Hardwar Dube, the president of the Shriram Foods and Fertilizers workers' union, explained that poor workers could not afford to worry about pollution:

Neither the workers nor the trade unions knew anything about the environment. And when workers would raise the issue of pollution inside the factory, the manager would say, "What do you care? If it's dirty work, take two rupees extra, but don't fuss." And it's also true that we think that we're all going to die someday anyway. And if you tell a worker that this environment is bad for your health, he might listen once or twice, but when it threatens his daily bread, he won't listen to you.

Other workers acknowledge that there were pollution-related occupational hazards in their work, but, unlike the court, they offered a nuanced, specific understanding of threats as embodied in particular industrial processes. Another worker from the Birla Textile Mill, Jaiprakash, said:

We produced cotton thread and a synthetic thread—polyester—neither of which caused pollution. Yes, there was a process department which did generate some pollution, but the company had, for the sake of appearances, installed some pollution control device, which wasn't switched on. In the weaving department and the process department people could get respiratory problems because of the steam. They would get TB. Cotton fibers would enter through their lungs and affect them.

Such a nuanced understanding of polluting work processes suggests that the problem could have been tackled by modifying technologies and providing worker safeguards. As another worker remarked, "You don't kill off a person just because they have a disease in some part of their body." But instead of exploring factory-specific solutions, the court simply closed down production.

Which environmental values are implicit in workers' knowledge of industrial activity and the court's refusal to acknowledge them as legitimate. Workers' everyday experience of the workplace and the urban environment is marked by intense, routine exploitation and stress.[86] Many workplaces are unsafe, and accidents abound, but workers chronically exposed to hazardous materials and processes are unable to demand either protection or greater compensation. The polluted workplace remains invisible to the judicial eye until it affects the city's air. Dunu Roy, an environmental planning expert at the NGO Hazards Centre, points out that if the Factories Act and other labor laws had been systematically and routinely enforced to ensure workers' safety, much of the pollution from factories would have been checked at the source. Working and living in and around polluting industries, laborers had been constantly and intimately at risk, yet their predicament was not seen as part of the "public interest." The Manch struggled to represent their interests, but in the absence of support from the court and the media, it remained a voice in the wilderness.

The construction of the "clean air" cause by a middle-class constituency with privileged access to the courts represented "the environment" as a universal good, to be protected in the "public interest," never mind the effects on workers. Workers, if they were considered at all, were dismissed as mobile migrants, who could return to their distant villages or find other employment. Middle-class unconcern about the devastating effect of displacement for the poor is summed up in Labor Commissioner Marwah's remark that "water finds its own way," which naturalizes the poor workers' trauma as the simple ebb and flow of footloose and fancy-free nomads. Officially, then, the poor do not exist; they are absent from official records, and as long as they do not agitate, they are invisible. The desperation of jobless workers and the crushing burden of debt and poverty borne by their families are visible only on rare occasions, as on May Day 1997, when Sarvesh Chand, who had been laid off from a category "H" firm, committed suicide by setting himself on fire at a workers' rally.

Conflicts over Livelihood and Sustainability in Kerala Fisheries

In the Delhi case, middle-class activists convinced the courts to improve environmental quality by curbing polluting industries, with an adverse effect on the livelihoods of poor and largely unorganized workers. The case we explore here—a conflict over ocean resources in Kerala, a southwestern coastal state—involves the introduction of new technologies, which are opposed by a social movement of fishworkers, who unlike the Delhi workers, succeed to some degree in effecting policy changes. Industrial pollution, a very recent concern for environmental activists in India, is treated as a local problem wherever it occurs. By contrast, the struggle over rights to Kerala's rich fisheries began over four decades ago and has fueled a political and social movement that is active nationally and internationally. The story of the fisheries movement reveals competing understandings of relations between people and resources.

Among Indian states Kerala is responsible for the second-largest annual catch of marine fish; in fact, with only 8 percent of India's seaboard, it accounts for more than 20 percent of the country's total fish catch. It has about 190,000 active fishers scattered over 222 fishing villages, the largest population of fishers in India.[87] Until the middle of the twentieth century, these fishers made a living by catching mainly fourteen species of fish, primarily from 40,000 artisanal crafts including catamarans, dugout and plank-built canoes, and plywood boats. The conflict that eventually gave rise to an international movement began in the 1960s, when Kerala's poor fishers began to fight for their rights to marine resources. Their protests, initially about the Kerala fisheries department's unfair distribution of new, mechanized boats, evolved into a broad popular struggle that became known as the Kerala fishworkers' movement.[88] The movement took shape over concerns about social justice, fishworkers' rights, fishing communities' access to marine resources, and the ecological sustainability of rapidly changing patterns of resource-use. It challenged official fishery policy and the power of the capitalists who were its primary beneficiaries. It initially represented poor Catholic fishers, but subsequently expanded to include fishers from *dalit* Hindu castes and Muslims.[89] Over the next three decades, the movement became a key component in national and global fishworker activism and in a national alliance of social movements. It engaged with almost every major political issue of the times, including nationalism and globalization; entitlements and free trade; caste and community; gender and class. By the late 1980s, ironically, the movement had even grown to encompass the very fishery capitalists it had fought against in the 1960s, as fishworkers and

Indian capitalists joined together to oppose the entry of multinational corporations into Indian waters.

The shifts in the scale and scope of the Kerala fisheries conflicts make clear that those conflicts were not the modern/traditional, global/local or North/South binaries they might appear to be at first glance. Producing for export has been a feature of Kerala fisheries as long as records have existed.[90] It was only in the 1970s that local fishers began to complain, about the combination of new technologies, foreign investment, and export-fixated state policy they believed had come to threaten marine ecology and their livelihoods. Their objections were no Luddite responses to new technology. The fishers themselves, in the decades that followed, gained access to sophisticated scientific knowledge, global networks, institutional structures, markets, capital, and technology.

In the early 1960s, Indian planners abandoned the gradualist approach to rural development and decided to increase productivity rapidly by adopting new technologies and export-oriented strategies. Two and a half decades later, with this model exhausted, they adopted neoliberal policies and encouraged foreign investment in the national economy. These two policy shifts created antagonisms throughout India: between modern and traditional technologies, and between national and transnational economic interests and local livelihoods. In Kerala, these policies also created an antagonism between overly efficient, ecologically destructive fishing methods and less productive yet more ecologically sustainable technologies.

The story of the transformation of Kerala's fisheries and the resulting social movements is well known within India, and some of the lessons of the movement have circulated in international policy and academic circles. However, the relevance of this case for debates over the forms of Indian environmentalism[91] and the local benefits of globalization has gone relatively unexplored. It is with these concerns that this study brings to the fore the diverse meanings of environmentalism and of social justice, how they are expressed, and how they shape this case of resource conflict.

The Evolution of the Fishworkers' Movement

The Indo-Norwegian Project: The 1950s and 1960s

The preconditions for the Kerala fisheries conflicts were set in the 1950s, with an experiment in international development that had drastic and unforeseen consequences over the next fifty years. This experiment was made possible by the convergence of two broader trends: a global consensus (supported by UN development funds) about the need to bring newly independent states and war-ravaged economies into the world market; and India's post-independence stress on a policy of "community development."

From the late colonial period forward, development was considered a key function of the state, not only by colonialists but also by Indian nationalists. The state created new administrative departments to manage development, including a department for fisheries, which experimented with cooperatives and new technologies, created new "scientific knowledge" about seas, fish, and fishers, and searched for new markets.[92] Despite these efforts, income from fisheries remained low, and thus fishing remained a low-status activity—that is, until a postwar international discourse that promoted the developmental role of international aid, technology transfer, and production for export brought them to the renewed and intense attention of the state and international agencies.

In the case of Kerala, the development donor was the Norwegian government, which founded an agency designed to put Norway at the forefront of international development work.[93] In January 1953 the Indo-Norwegian Project for Fisheries Community Development in the States of Travancore-Cochin (INP)[94] began as a result of a tripartite agreement signed by the United Nations, India, and Norway. The project was part of the UN's Expanded Program for Technical Assistance, an avenue for channeling development assistance to newly independent countries, and was active until the early 1960s.[95] It was the world's first bilateral development assistance project seeking to place technological progress front and center, a model that would become standard in the decades to follow.[96]

The INP chose the artisanal fisherman living on the coast of Kerala to receive Norway's aid. The project shipped some traditional Indian fishing boats to Norway, fitted them with engines, tested them in fjords, and shipped them back to India, only to find them unsuitable to Indian conditions. The Kerala coastline, which drops sharply in depth relatively close to shore, has wave patterns that make it difficult to beach craft with outboard motors. From 1953 to 1957, the INP continued to try, without much success, to motorize indigenous boats. During this time, some Kerala fishermen accepted Norwegian motorized boats as gifts, but few actively sought them out. The Norwegian experiments with motorizing indigenous boats, however, had laid the groundwork for the motorization that would occur three decades later, in 1980.

It was not INP aid but an individual merchant who set off the explosion in export-oriented fisheries that was to bring far-reaching changes to the lives of fishing communities in Kerala. In 1953, a local shrimp merchant,[97] chartering a Japanese trawler and using the freezing equipment of a large local company, exported thirteen tons of shrimp to the United States. His success brought new entrepreneurs and mechanized fishers to Kerala, and in 1957–58, a total of six private companies exported more than 450 tons of shrimp to America per year.[98] Freezing technologies, trawling nets and boats, and faster communication systems promoted an expansion in scale and reach that was unprecedented in Kerala. Demand expanded as well, as postwar recovery in western Europe and Japan opened up markets other than the United States.

With the emergence of the lucrative niche market in shrimp, the INP directed its efforts toward providing technical and scientific surveys of the Kerala waters to help guide the nascent shrimp industry. Together with the Central Marine Fisheries Research Institute (CMFRI), the scientific agency that had been established in Kochi in the 1950s to modernize the sector, the project identified the waters off Kochi and Kollam as "one of the world's richest shrimp grounds."[99] They introduced bottom-trawling techniques to increase productivity and opened large freezing plants, both developments that further encouraged the boom, which came to be known as the "pink gold rush."

The Kerala government maintained that this boom was necessary to reduce poverty and generate employment among fishers, but its interventions had ambiguous results. The imported nylon nets introduced in the 1950s significantly increased catches, but they also displaced the cotton nets whose manufacture had provided livelihoods to many women in fishing communities. Technological and market innovations also significantly increased fish catches in Kerala, but the related export boom provided the preconditions for the emergence of fishery capitalists, powerful new groups of trawler owners, merchants, and middlemen whose interests would threaten the livelihoods of artisanal fishers.[100]

Neither the INP-created sales organizations that marketed local fishermen's catches nor the numerous government-endorsed fishing cooperatives springing up in Kerala[101] could compete with the fishery capitalists, who either took over these institutions or used their market power to drive small fishers out of business. By 1968, the investments of fishery capitalists in new technologies were close to ten times those of the INP. As John Kurien, the leading scholar of the fishworkers' movement, has said:

> The change in the technology and labor process in the realm of fish harvesting and processing taken together with the entry of this new segment of merchant class interests into the fish economy can be considered as the death knell of the fisheries development policy in Kerala, which viewed fishing as a source of livelihood and fish as a source of food for local consumption. The Norwegians played the role of chief pall bearers.[102]

The Emergence of "Modern" and "Traditional" Fishers: The 1970s

With the development of a market for frozen shrimp in the United States in the 1960s, and in Japan in the 1970s, the mechanization drive became more aggressive. Kerala's fishing economy began to polarize into "modern" and "traditional" sectors. Initially these terms referred to fishing technology. The "modern sector" referred to those who used motors for propulsion and operated trawl nets; the "traditional sector" to those who used oars or sails for propulsion, and a diversity of fishing gear.

This distinction, always ambiguous because "tradition" is never static, was further blurred by waves of technological change that affected all kinds of fishers. Some "traditional" fishers became hybrids, adopting modern technologies such as motorized craft to compete and survive but still using traditional nets and gear. At the same time, they resisted those technologies, such as trawlers, that seemed drastically to diminish fish stocks. In addition to technology, power, which flowed from caste as well as access to capital, also played a role in delineating the boundaries of "tradition" and "modernity." Boat owner-operators, mostly members of fishing castes, controlled production in the traditional sector, whereas merchants, often from outside the traditional fishing castes, controlled marketing. Trawler owners and merchants often were not from the fishing community; in many cases they were urban capitalists.

A further complication arose from the split between those who served the export market, and those who were linked primarily to domestic markets. This distinction, too, is blurry because state support has dramatically strengthened the export market, driving many artisanal fishers to participate directly or indirectly in national and global markets. At the same time, because women from fishing families were deeply involved in the marketing of fish in local and regional markets, they were directly affected by the shifting dynamics of the sector. Women working in fish processing plants associated with the export trade complained of exploitative work conditions, including sexual harassment.

One transformation of the Kerala fisheries was its dramatic increase in output. Trawlers' fish yield steadily increased, rising from about a thousand metric tons in 1960 to more than forty-seven thousand metric tons by 1970.[103] Until the end of the 1960s, despite a looming crisis, the artisanal sector held its own in terms of yields: in 1969, it caught more than eight times the catch of the trawl sector.[104]

It was the shrimp boom that converted these differences into conflict. Trawlers are designed to operate far from shore, but shrimp are concentrated in relatively shallow inshore waters. For that reason, and to save on fuel, the trawlers fished in the inshore waters, also the fishing ground of artisanal fishers. While artisanal fishers' catch tended to come from near the surface, trawlers dragged their nets along the sea bottom, their nets indiscriminately dragging up all species, not just shrimp. This left little for artisanal fishers working the same area.[105] At first, many trawlers threw back less valuable species to save space on their vessels for shrimp. By the end of the 1970s, however, extensive overfishing had reduced shrimp catches, and trawlers began to target the species traditionally caught by artisanal fishers.[106]

The sources of tension were manifold. Because most of the trawler operators were from outside the artisanal fishing communities, they had no direct interest in their welfare. Wary of the growing levels of organization among local fishers, they preferred to hire more vulnerable migrant labor from the neighboring state of Tamil Nadu to work on their vessels. So the anticipated developmental benefits of the INP, such as year-round employment and income stability, never materialized. Similarly, the social development goals promised in the INP model of community were never achieved: fishers remained poor, with low levels of health and education, and high vulnerability to seasonal fluctuations in markets and weather conditions. Facing trawlers' outright grab for species traditionally fished by local fishers' boats, the local fishers also worried about the effects of current overfishing on future marine stocks. They feared that incessant trawling in the inshore waters during the monsoon months would destroy the eggs and larvae of fish such as mackerel and sardines, on which they depended heavily. Trawlers also sometimes destroyed the craft and gear of artisanal fishers, a sign of growing competition for space. Even if the destruction was inadvertent, the trawlers often steamed off without paying compensation for the loss. In a few cases, accidents with trawlers resulted in the death of local fishers, further angering the locals.

With the heightened interest in the fisheries sector of the state, international agencies, NGOs, and researchers, the shifts in sectoral dynamics and their effects on lives and livelihoods were documented thoroughly. This was to play an important role, as we show below, in the formation of the new political collectivity called "fishworkers." By the early 1980s, it was clear that the mechanized sector of the fishing industry had brought economic polarization. Between 1969 and 1980, artisanal fishers' share in Kerala's total marine fish catch fell from 88 percent to 62 percent. Over the same period the output per traditional fisher dropped by about 50 percent.[107] The per capita income per worker in the trawling sector increased over that time—from 1,600 to 8,000 rupees (approximately from $125 to $1,000)—but this did not help local fishing populations because trawler owners preferred to employ migrant workers. At the same time, Kerala state's revenues from marine fisheries rose from Rs. 11.5 crores in 1966 to Rs. 124 crores in 1981(from just below $1 million to almost $14 million).[108] Furthermore, the composition of the catch indicated that the stocks of a number of species were being depleted, and that mechanized vessels had made inroads into the fish stocks in inshore waters. By the late 1970s, the conflict between the mechanized and artisanal sectors erupted into violence. There were numerous reports of the two sides destroying each other's craft and gear, and of collisions at sea that led to violent fights. All the changes in the local economy, ecology, and social relations that took place as a result of mechanized fishing animated a new politics that concerned itself with rights, justice, and sustainability.

The Emergence of the Fishworkers' Movement

By the time the economic and ecological consequences of mechanization were starting to be felt, traditional fishers had organized into the broad-based and popular Kerala fishworkers' movement. This movement, which began in the 1970s, became the platform for a critique of state policy and discussion of alternatives to it. Even before the emergence of a formal movement, however, Kerala fishers had engaged in collective action. In the late 1950s, officials of the Nehruvian state realized that they could not accomplish their goals for community development without help. They therefore invited voluntary organizations to participate in community development efforts. In response, Bishop Peter Pereira of the Archdiocese of Trivandrum authorized the formation of the Trivandrum Social Service Society (TSSS) to work among the poor Catholic fishers of south Kerala. TSSS activists established a model village called Marianad, or Mary's Land. In Marianad, Catholic priests helped local activists set up service organizations, women's and children's groups, and production, credit, and marketing cooperatives, including a fair price shop that sold commodities essential to the fishers' survival.

These new organizations threatened the entrenched power of local fish merchants. Moreover, the traditional money-lenders and middlemen, holders of power in Kerala fisheries, violently opposed new collective savings and credit systems introduced by the Marianad-based activists. Local fishers nevertheless managed to use these new resources to purchase equipment, and the cooperatives succeeded in a hostile environment, becoming the model for similar institutions that grew up in other villages.

Marianad also proved to be a training ground for future leaders in the fisheries move-ment.[109] By the early 1970s, the local, collective organizational forms introduced there had spread to the south and central coastal areas of Kerala, in part due to the efforts of priests influenced by liberation theology.[110] Some cooperatives managed to tap into international development funds for housing, education, and employment programs, as well as to set up transport and freezing facilities.[111] Some early unions, such as the Kerala Fishworkers' Union, were registered under the Charitable Societ-ies Act and remained under the supervision of their dioceses.[112] The main nonde-nominational group to emerge in these early days was the Programme for Community Organisation (PCO-Trivandrum), founded in 1978 by many of the activists affiliated with the Marianad project,[113] whose networks had grown, and in the early 1970s began a widely circulated newsletter.

In 1977, several Catholic and other social service organizations, including the unions mentioned above, came together to form the first unified organization of fishers, the Kerala Latin Catholic Fish Workers' Federation. But the church affiliation limited both union membership (by excluding Muslim and Hindu fishers) and the federation's power, because the church hierarchy was reluctant to get involved in conflicts. A secular and more militant union, the Kerala Independent Fish Workers Federation (Kerala Swatantra Matsya Thozhilali Federation or, more commonly, KSMTF), was formed in 1980. It operated as a federation of district-level unions, allowing its constituent units to retain their emphases on local issues. Its broad base and its independence from church and political party control made it quite different from other Kerala unions. Moreover, it viewed its members not as "fisherfolk," objects of charity, but as "fishworkers," who were bearers of rights. The union demanded fishers' inclusion in state planning bodies, transportation for women to sell fish at markets, and more controversially, exclusive access to inshore waters and a ban on trawling during monsoon months to allow regen-eration of fish stocks. Through the late 1970s, the KMSTF and other fishers' organiza-tions held marches and sit-ins to call attention to their demands.

In 1978, the leaders of the fishers' movements in the states of Kerala, Tamil Nadu, and Goa formed the National Fishermen's Forum (NFF) to press for the rights of tradi-tional fishermen and for the conservation of marine wealth. Father Thomas Kocherry, a Marianad activist who had led the KSMTF, played a leadership role in the NFF, which pressured national legislators and the Indian central government to put controls on trawlers and other mechanized craft and gear. The NFF recast the question of mechanization in terms of social justice and workers' rights, and linked these demands to ecologically friendly fisheries policy, resource management, conservation, and regeneration. Its fa-mous Protect Water, Protect Life campaign of 1989 made clear connections between a range of ecological concerns—including the depletion of fish and reduced water qual-ity due to pollution and pesticide runoff—and the very question of survival.[114] The issue of pesticides had emerged because catches were declining where inshore waters were polluted as a result of industrial and agricultural activities. Further ecological con-cerns, regarding deforestation, arose as a response to the increasing price of some artisanal boats, the result of wood shortages due to overfelling.

The fishworkers' movement politicized fishers and fisheries in new and deep ways. Prior to the struggles of the 1970s, center-right parties had taken fishers' votes for granted, owing to the close relationship between the Congress Party and the Catholic Church.[115] But in the 1980s, as the KSMTF became the strongest fishers' group, other political parties began to court the fishers and formed their own fishers' unions. Meanwhile, the movement's strong women's groups made alliances with progressive women's groups elsewhere in Kerala. Because electoral results in Kerala were often close, and because the center-left and center-right alliances alternated in power, political parties realized that their electoral fortunes partly depended on whether or not the fishers' interests were included in their agenda. The movement thus ended the fishers' political marginality. Fishworkers' rights organizations were visible everywhere, from seaside fishing villages to street protests, addressing fishers' needs while putting pressure on the state for attention to their demands.

Contesting Fishing Rights through Law and Science

Through the 1980s, the fishworkers' movement grew in strength, numbers, and level of sophistication. As it increasingly used the language and rules of development, law, and science, the struggle moved from the seas and the streets to the legislature and the courts. The movement's efforts during this period centered on the regulation of the fishing industry and the passage and enforcement of a law that would ban trawling during monsoon season. The political debate surrounding these proposed measures brought into play the full range of conflicting environmental and social justice values at issue in this case.

The KSMTF's mass mobilizations of the 1970s, including public meetings and large demonstrations in prominent locations calling attention to fishworkers' human and economic rights, enjoyed widespread success among fishworkers, and its slogans, chants, songs, plays, and graffiti reached a wide audience.[116] Faced with an increasingly militant and successful movement, however, fishery capitalists also began to organize, forming lobby groups and issuing reports. This forced the union to move beyond appeals to class interests and use scientific evidence and current development thinking to frame its demands. Its analysis of the fisheries crisis relied equally on the fishers' experiences with loss and injustice, on the one hand, and the findings and recommendations of scholarly reports, on the other. In invoking such concepts as "appropriate technology," "institutional change," "maximum sustainable yield," "common property resources," and "sustainable development," it tapped into ideas influential in bilateral and multilateral development aid programs.

In 1980, after years of militant and legislative politics, the fishworkers' movement forced the Kerala government to pass the Kerala Marine Fisheries Regulation Act (KMFRA), having first gained entry into the commissions of inquiry whose work formed the basis for the act. The legislation, celebrated as "a landmark in the history of the fisherfolk movement in Kerala,"[117] banned trawlers bigger than twenty-five gross registered tonnage (GRT) from waters less than twenty-two kilometers off the coast, and smaller trawlers and all mechanized boats from waters less than ten kilometers out. It also provided for the closure of fisheries during spawning season in the monsoons for the sake of resource conservation. The law entrusted the task of protecting the exclusive fishing zone to the state police and coast guard. Once it was passed, the fishworkers' movement concentrated on getting the new rules enforced. Fishery capitalists remained powerful, however, and one of them, Baby John, was powerful enough to earn places in both center-left and center-right ruling coalitions.[118] Fishery capitalists mounted annual legal challenges to the monsoon trawl ban, arguing that the science was indeterminate, and loss of incomes and employment an unacceptably high public cost. Fishers organized legal challenges and mass mobilizations to enforce each legislative victory—exclusive zone, monsoon ban, and police support for enforcement.

As a result of KSMTF's aggressive lobbying, union activists were invited to participate in further discussions about fisheries legislation. But fishery capitalists challenged the law on two grounds: that the evidence on the impact of trawling on stocks was inadequate and that the monsoon trawl ban and conservation measures would have seriously negative effect on their incomes, local fish supply and the wages of their workers. Twice in the early 1980s, the Kerala government appointed committees to "probe into the need for conservation of the marine resources and allied matters."[119] The first committee looked into the pros and cons of enforcing a ban on trawling during the monsoon season. By 1982, the committee had made several recommendations, but it could not reach a unanimous decision about the trawl ban. The near-term economic losses resulting from such a ban, it felt, trumped the KSMTF's environmental argument that overfishing harmed marine life and interfered with spawning. The committee found the data to support the claim that trawling destroyed eggs and larvae to be insufficient, and even the scientists appointed to the committee were vehemently opposed to the [monsoon] trawl ban. Fisheries activist A. J. Vijayan recalled that scientists on the committee understood the decline in fish numbers as having resulted from pollution caused by emissions and oil leakages from trawlers. Instead of a seasonal trawl ban, the committee's report recommended measures like regulating the size of the mesh to allow juvenile fish through, and suspending fishing for a week to be determined each monsoon season.

Through participation in this committee and the ones that followed, activists gained valuable experience working with members of other, better politically connected unions. Their actions generated public debate and attention in Kerala and nationally. When the government decided not to follow even the mild recommendations made by the first committee,[120] the KSMTF's call for joint action by all unions to press for these and more changes in policy took place in a context of heightened public awareness of the issues, with prominent citizens, writers, and religious leaders supporting the positions of the union.[121] There was wide media coverage of the demonstrations. By the mid-1980s, the "fishworkers' agitation" was being covered in news reports and written about in editorials. These mobilizations kept the issue of trawl-bans alive and kept pressure on the state, and by 1985, the government had come around to the fishers' position that trawling was destructive and needed to be restricted.[122]

For a number of reasons, curbs on fishing were difficult to enact, implement and enforce. Environmentally destructive devices, such as purse seines and mini-trawlers, had become widely popular among local fishers. In addition, fishery capitalist interests were well represented in state government, making enforcement even more difficult. Many politicians involved in the process had private interests in mechanized fishing, and some were themselves boat owners and major fish exporters. One tactic they used to defend their interests while appearing to agree to movement demands was to declare a ban and then exempt the best fishing areas.[123] In the face of such evasions, the movement resorted once again to militant mobilization. In May 1988, Fr. Thomas Kocherry, then the leader of the KSMTF, started a hunger strike in front of the state secretariat. Mass demonstrations and blockades of Neendakara harbor followed, and the news media covered all these protests widely.

Finally, on June 23, 1988, after many years of protests, the left-wing Kerala government announced a ban on monsoon trawling throughout the state, excepting the Neendakara trawler base. While still short of the movement's demands, this partial ban established the movement as a political and economic force that had created a new regulatory framework to define access, rights, and concerns in the sector. The minister of fisheries stated that in agreeing to a ban, the government had accepted the movement's claims that "the trawlers were not only depriving them of their livelihood but also causing damage to the marine ecology." He also claimed that Neendakara had been exempted because it was the only region where a particularly lucrative species of shrimp was found. Detractors pointed out that Neendakara was the biggest center for mechanized fishing in Kerala and that its exclusion benefited Baby John, then the state's irrigation minister, who owned fishing boats in this area.

With continuing dissension over the ban's nature and scope, the Kerala government convened yet another committee. In its 1989 report the Balakrishnan Nair Committee came down decisively in favor of a total ban on trawling by all types of vessels in the waters of Kerala during the monsoon months, including fishing technologies and practices (such as the ring seine and the mini-trawls) that had been adopted by artisanal fishers but were potentially damaging to the ecology. This total monsoon trawl ban that was enacted in Kerala in 1989 has been acclaimed as "the most important fishery management decision made by any government in the country since Independence."[124] The committee proposed the implementation of the ban initially for three years, during which it suggested investigating its impact on the conservation and use of local resources, and on the socioeconomic life of fishermen and the industry over the next three years. The state fisheries department, however, did not follow this recommendation (leading the committee to chastise it in a second report, in 1991), and the government asked the committee to reconsider how long the ban should be enforced, indicating that it would be willing to revisit the issue.[125]

These episodes reveal that government policy regarding the fisheries was in a state of flux that cannot be accounted for by a monolithic view of state interests. Explicit state policy no longer denied ecological and social justice arguments for trawl bans, but paradoxically, as the movement entered the legislative, legal, and public arenas and began to gather and demand scientific evidence, fishery capitalists and state elites adopted weapons of the weak: foot-dragging on enforcement, failure to comply with regulations, and so on. Thus, although the fishworkers' movement in these years dislodged conventional power relations in the sector, it could not sufficiently affect the exercise of state power. Because the bans on monsoon trawling were temporary, fishers had to agitate every year to convince the government to reissue the ban. For their part, trawler owners challenged the ban every year. while the KSMTF demanded its continuation, arguing that the fish catch had increased in the previous three years because of the ban. In 1991, when the government agreed with the fishers, the trawler operators went on strike, after which the government immediately capitulated by reducing the length of the ban. The policy arena became highly volatile and contested.

The mechanization of the fisheries, and the organization of "fisherfolk" into "fishworkers" in response, changed public perception of both the resource and the fishers. The relation between traditional fishers and resources had been mediated through cultural and religious practices, and relied on intimate knowledge of marine conditions. Successive states had revenue interests in fish, but before mechanization these were not decisive in changing production and exchange conditions. International development agencies and the state saw mechanization as a way to increase productivity, and thus to address the needs and interests of poor fishers. Fishers' groups took this notion of needs and transformed it into demands for rights. They made demands on the grounds first of social justice, and then on the grounds of ecological and scientific knowledge, increasingly used state institutions to pursue them, and attempted to change state policy. In short, the value of the fish resource became multiply articulated, a source of wealth in one discourse, a right of citizenship in another, and in regulating interactions between the state, social groups, and resources. In addition, it generated a dense network of activists involved in unions, cooperatives, NGOs, media, academia, the church, and some state and aid agencies.

Over time, new trade unions organized by political parties led to a decline in the activity and influence of the KSMTF (the very body that had inspired the formation of the new unions). Its influence declined further in the late 1980s, when the central government enacted neoliberal reforms that encouraged foreign investment and joint ventures, which made local action less effective. The site of militant politics has therefore moved to the national and international arenas, where the World Forum of Fish Harvesters and Fishworkers (founded by KSMTF activists) plays a key role. The importance of NGOs such as PCO—once a vital source of new ideas, slogans, and cadre training for KSMTF members—has declined in the new context.

Structural Adjustment Policies and the Effects of Globalization

Until the early 1990s, the chief conflict in the fisheries remained framed within state and national politics. In the 1970s, it had occasionally coordinated strategy with state-level unions from Goa and Tamil Nadu on issues that were common to the three states or those that needed national-level action. The Kerala movement pushed for the formation of state-level unions in other maritime states, and its activists were crucial to the creation of the national apex union, the National Fishworkers' Federation (NFF) in 1984. Beginning in the late 1980s, when neoliberal reforms were introduced, the Kerala union began coordinating strategies with unions from other states (those concerned with factory fishing in Andhra Pradesh and Gujarat, for example, or shrimp aquaculture in Orissa) to pursue fisheries issues nationally. In the 1990s, when the Indian government granted licenses for joint ventures between multinational and Indian business firms, along with subsidies for very large factory ships the demands and dynamics of the movement changed significantly.

Just as the 1960s policy of spreading mechanization came in response to India's inability at the time to pay for large food imports, the globalization of the fisheries came about because of the political and economic factors at play in the 1990s. From the mid-1980s onward, the Indian economy was being slowly deregulated, but in 1991 when the Congress Party returned to power, deregulation gathered speed. This was due in part to a realignment among Indian political elites, and in part to structural adjustment and stabilization programs imposed on the Indian government by the IMF and World Bank following India's foreign exchange crisis of the late 1980s. In addition to deregulation, these new economic policies involved liberalization, state withdrawal, privatization—in short, neoliberal globalization. The transfer of capital and technology deemed crucial for Indian growth now took place through foreign direct investment and joint ventures between Indian and international capital, where previously it had taken place on a state-to-state level. Furthermore, the World Trade Organization (WTO) intervened in the Indian economy by mandating programs to rationalize fisheries policies.[126]

In March 1991, the government began granting permits for deep sea fishing to foreign vessels, in keeping with a new deep sea fishing policy that assumed significant fish resources were inaccessible to Indian vessels.[127] The new joint ventures with foreign companies that resulted brought together two formerly antagonistic groups to protest globalization—the artisanal fishers, on the one hand, and the Indian trawler owners and fish merchants, on the other. The latter group now sought (and were granted) membership and even leadership positions within the NFF. The centers of the large-scale fishing against which the artisanal fishers had protested now became centers of fishworker militancy.[128] The former antagonists both feared that multinational companies would over-exploit marine wealth, leading to a drastic reduction in catches. The new alliance, named the National Fisheries Action Committee Against Joint Ventures (NFACAJV), mobilized nationwide for protest, staging nationwide one- and two-day strikes that paralyzed the fishing sector and gained renewed government and media attention.[129] Because the NFF was a key constituent of a larger alliance of more than forty different social movements, its actions had wide support. Ironically, the local Kerala issues that had inspired the movement faded into the background once the movement began acting on the national and international stage.

The government responded to the NFF actions by convening a committee that eventually recommended that all joint-venture fishing licenses be cancelled and that Indian fishers be sold diesel and kerosene at subsidized rates to enable them to fish in mid-sea waters.[130] But the government ignored these recommendations, and most maritime states threw their seas open to joint venture factory fishing.[131] The Kerala government took another route, however.[132] In a 1994 report, it called for "a multi-pronged approach" to fisheries regulation that focused on resource sustainability, the economic viability of the industry, the provision of a decent level of living to workers in the sector, and a good supply of fish for local consumption and export.[133] Further-more, it called for the active participation of fishworkers in fisheries management and promised a restructuring of the state fisheries department. Implementation was, how-ever, imperceptible in the years following the report. Still, the fact that Kerala did not endorse joint ventures demonstrates the continuing power of the movement, the movement's impact on state policy, and the politics of the left-front government with respect to deregulation.

Globalization altered the political terrain on which the fishworkers' movement was waging its struggle. It brought in new players with new interests and technolo-gies, dispersed the fisheries crisis across other states, and produced new coalitions. Neoliberal valuations of resources brought a pure market logic to fishing: New coalitions were developed not only between various classes within the Indian fish-eries but also with national fisher unions from the forty other countries in the World Forum of Fish Harvesters and Fishworkers. The NFF and the Kerala movement were important components of and inspirations for this transnational movement, which in turn helped reshape the original movement. Under the influence of the transnational movement, the Kerala fishers began talking not just about ecological and social justice but also about economic nationalism, which they treated as a form of populism. The fishworkers' movement was thus able to institutionalize, though at the level of state policy more than of state practice, a new set of under-standings about the fisheries and their limits. But even though the movement in-creased the fishers' collective power, among other ways by linking them with national and international networks, enforcement of the new regulations inspired by the movement remained lax. While the movement acquired power in shaping policy, state, and fishery capitalist interests retained power to render new policy weak by thwarting its implementation.

Reflections on the Fisheries Conflict

In this section we explore the environmental values expressed by the principal groups with a stake in the fisheries sector: traditional fishers, trawler operators, the state, those who have managed and assisted the movement, and intellectual-activists. Though we focus upon individual people who represent these groups, we do not mean to suggest that within each of these contending groups there exists a univocal, unani-mous discourse of environmentalism. Rather, we cite the people who most clearly articulated particular lines of argument, with the understanding that their arguments might not be the only ones within their groups. In addition, the people we quote were active at the time of our latest site visit, in November 2002. Several people who played major roles at earlier stages of the movement could not be interviewed or contacted.[134] We present the voices as a sampling of some key positions in the field of fisheries debate.

Traditional Fishers and Trawler Operators

The state of Kerala, even more than most other Indian states, has had a long record of responsiveness to the people's needs. However, the successes of the movement appear to many fishworkers to have been quickly assimilated into a welfarist bureaucracy. For example, in November 2002, women fish vendors in Vizhinjam (a largely Christian fishing village near Kerala's state capital, Thiruvananthapuram), expressed frustration with the state government, which talked the language of rights and uplift but rarely delivered satisfactory results. Fishworker Seetha reported:

> Women come forward [with demands for aid] in large numbers. But they don't get any aid from the government. Panchayat [village council] members use their power to help those who work for their political interests. . . . But they have not given any money to groups who are really doing active work. When we complained at the collectorate, they told us that it was a matter of influence exerted by the Panchayat member. To whom are we supposed to address our complaints? . . . We ask the Panchayat member: "Dear member, haven't we formed the society [a reference to cooperative welfare societies]? Why don't you help us to receive the aid offered by the government?" He asks us to wait. But nothing happens.

The specific welfarist successes of the KSMTF had, by the end of the century, been co-opted by a plethora of new fishworkers' unions, each affiliated with a political party. Many KSMTF activists perceive that their independent federation is increasingly pitted against party-affiliated unions. For example, N. and B., two KSMTF activists in Vizhinjam complained:

> N.: See, our union fights for the benefit of fishworkers irrespective of politics, whether it be Congress in power or the communists in power. But when other political parties come here to form unions, they primarily give importance to their political interests.
> B.: Yes, the fishworkers' union [i.e., KSMTF] stands for the people, whereas unions formed by political parties stand for the parties' political interests.
> N.: Also there are different groups and factors within them. Now politics has become a trade. It is not easy for people like us to receive any aid [from the government]. They give preference to party members. For example, CITU [the Center for Indian Trade Unions][135] helps only their people.

Activist fishers often feel pride about having participated in mobilizations, and their awareness of rights and their expectations of the state reflect their empowerment. Despite changes in policy at the official level, however, union members' inter-actions with the local government indicate that these changes have not translated into universal access to good governance. In Marianad, we met several men sitting on the shore one day in October 2002. The catch had been poor that day, as it had been for months. Many of them had not even taken their boats out to sea that morning. According to one of them,

> trawling boats destroy our artificial reefs.[136] . . . Though [our generation] invests a lot of money and uses many modern tools, we are not able to earn sufficient money to meet even the fuel expenses. That's why these boats remain at the shore. If this is our fate, what will be the condition of the next generation? How will they live? . . . According to the government, the sea is full of fish. There are too many fish in the sea. That's why they are giving license to foreign fishing ships!

Artisanal fishworkers see themselves as increasingly assimilated into the new market economy. They recognize the magnitude and significance of this change for their way of life but feel that they cannot direct or control it. (State officials, on the other hand, see themselves as keeping a finger on the pulse of global economic flows, and as successfully riding the shifting wave of global demand and opportunity.)

Among many KSMTF activists, who work to raise awareness among fishers, anti-trawling, and anti-outsider rhetoric has been important in mobilizing resistance; in fact, by the late 1990s it was the union's most successful argument among its own constituents. KSMTF organizer Maglin[137] recalled:

> Competition started problems, as we were not getting any fish from our sea. It really started in the 1975–80 period [with the spread of outboard motors]. Actually, we did not start this competition; foreigners did when they introduced outboard engines as an experiment. The Indo-Norwegian Project was not an experiment by the Indian government. [The foreigners] gave it [outboard motors] to the fishers here on an experimental basis. Fishers got attracted to it because it reduced their labor.

Fishers experience the introduction of market reforms and the emphasis on ex-ports as a loss—of once strong connections among family and community, of strong local markets, and of generous seas. Now the sea disappoints, and markets seem more distant and impersonal. According to one fisherwoman, Sheela,

> Nobody goes fishing these days. We don't have any income from fishing. . . . We earn something from [the local fish market]. . . There are no fish in our sea . . . If they stopped trawling, the fish would lay eggs. Then there will be more fish. But now trawling boats catch all the fish. How can the poor survive?

K.M. George, a fisherman for more than forty years, reported that he used to be able to see jumping shark, eagle rays, sting rays, and other fish from the shore, and he would run to his boat to fish only after having seen them from the shore. He reasoned that because he and his fellow fishermen never disturbed Kadalamma (the Mother Sea), she always blessed them with adequate fish.[138]

In both Maglin's and George's account, the memory of what has been lost is somewhat idealized. Fishers, after all, were among India's poorest people, the most exploited by markets and intermediaries. But such memories and the sense of loss they generate provide another means for understanding some key dichotomies raised in the fishers' struggle, namely those between "foreign" capitalism and "local" community life, and between hyperefficient technologies and ecologically benign artisanal fishing practices. Maglin's account above gives only a partial view of the role of "foreigners" in the history of the movement, for foreigners have played a variety of roles. In addition to introducing disruptive new technologies, they have also played a large part in the movement itself. Starting with the founding of Marianad, the movement has included activists from Canada, and in the 1970s it developed links with the London-based Intermediate Technology Development Group, and with foreign bilaterals, NGOs, and liberation theology activists. In the context of globalization, however, the idea of "foreignness" stands in opposition to "national" and "local" interests. It is stripped of memories of past instances of solidarity and imbued with a purely negative meaning.

Several fisherwomen we interviewed saw themselves as having been progressively squeezed out of their roles in the fishing economy ever since nylon nets, introduced in the 1950s, replaced the cotton nets they wove. But women also appreciated many aspects of modernization, such as convenient transportation (which saved them long hours of walking with loads on their heads), cooking gas (which replaced firewood), and instant and packaged foods that they perceived as highly nutritious. Most women from fishing families expressed appreciation for "their" bus—a bus run especially for women fish vendors by the state cooperative federation for fisheries development, Matsyafed, an amenity won as a result of protests in the 1970s. They emphasized, nevertheless, that technologies could be of dubious benefit. One woman, Sara, pointed out: "Now we have vehicles, but the sound of engines repels fish." Likewise, trawlers, an apparent technological advance, caused enormous social upheavals by allowing their owners to appropriate a disproportionate share of the fish. Another fisherwoman, Carmel, commented on how technology both helps and hinders her, saying, "Today we don't have to walk. In [past] times, we had to walk. We brought only one basket of fish. The profit was not much. But the cost of living was also less."

Of the problems associated with the new technologies, the most obvious to the fishers was the direct effect on the marine ecosystem of indiscriminate fishing by trawlers. In addition, the storage, processing, and canning industries built to cater to the mechanized sector released effluents that polluted the artisanal fishing zone close to the shore. Fishers who operated trawlers or boats with outboard motors could escape the effects of the pollution by fishing in mid-sea waters, but this meant higher fuel costs. Meanwhile, the small-scale artisanal fishers without motorized boats were the losers in this competition for ocean resources. One such fisher, Baby, sees the effects of the pollution on his livelihood this way:

> Big trawling boats and ships catch all the fish. . . . Also, the acid flushed out from [a Titanium factory near Veli] is another thing. . . . It has largely affected areas like Veli and Vettukadu. . . . When acid mixes with the water, fish move to the mid-sea. Those fish are caught by big ships and boats with outboard engines.

Many fishworker activists point out that fishers suffer not only from economic hardship but from the weakening of their social and cultural beliefs. This is not the result of a straightforward exchange of old ideas for new—in some cases, old practices are given new meanings, and in others new technologies have brought new practices. KMSTF activist Maglin expressed dismay about the general decline of a formerly respectful attitude to the sea.

> "You should not stand near the sea with your hair undone, flowing down," he said. "Mother sea wouldn't like it. . . . Also, the men considered themselves unclean after sexual intercourse. So they did not want to go to the sea unclean."

In the 1980s women activists viewed such beliefs as restrictions on women's sexuality and as cultural barriers separating the sexes. During fieldwork in the same area in the late 1990s, KSMTF activists declared that their analysis of the crisis in marine resources was "scientific" and that belief in Kadalamma was "superstitious." But activists soon revised their opinions, arguing later that "unscientific" traditional beliefs were closely tied to a respect for the environment. Among activists like Maglin, it is now a commonplace claim that traditional fishermen did not even perceive the environment as something separate from themselves. The sea was a mother, a provider; they refused to fish at spawning time even if they faced starvation.[139] Now, according to Maglin, fishers show less concern for the purity and cleanliness of the sea, and of fishers' relationship with it. "All sorts of waste materials are dumped in the sea [by fishers]," she complained. "It has happened after the introduction of outboard engines. You know that they use kerosene and petrol in outboard engines. Waste from these engines gets mixed with seawater."

New technologies have altered traditional attitudes in other ways, too, Maglin claims. "Today [when you use an outboard engine], you just board the boat and sit in the boat as if you are sitting in a hired auto-rickshaw. And that feeling is individualistic," she said. "Then competition started. Now, the women fishworkers [vendors] have to [travel to fishing harbors to] buy fish, which they used to get at their own shore."

Decrying the use of outboard motors as a selfish practice, as Maglin does here, was popular in the early years of the movement. However, artisanal fishers have adopted many of the more modest forms of mechanization, such as mini-trawlers, motorized plywood boats, and modern fishing gear. In other words, fishers have adopted hybrid strategies in order to survive—and not all of their short-term strategies are unselfishly collective or unambiguously eco-friendly.

Memories of earlier collective action inspire today's Marianad residents to seek to preserve the community spirit that used to dictate that fish catches be distributed throughout the community. During our site visit in 2002, more than forty years after the founding of the village, fishers in Marianad commented that, despite the harsh economic climate, "people in this village are very generous, as they are better off compared to other villages." They attributed their relative good fortune to the success of the cooperative movement (which had its heyday from the 1960s to the 1980s but whose spirit lives on in the form of cooperatives that offer low-interest loans to fishers) and to the persistence of a community ethic of responsibility and sharing.

Yet even fishers in Marianad have been affected by the resource crisis. Recalling traditions of sharing their catch with fellow villagers, regardless of their fishing abilities and economic resources, a Marianad fisher said in 2002, "[Now] we cannot give fish to all. If ten [needy] people came to us, we would give fish to at least five of them. That is how we do it even today. If fifty people came, we would at least give fish to twenty-five of them. It has been our tradition."

These practices, which have their roots in the high variability in catch among artisanal fishers, help spread the risk of a bad day at sea across all fishing units. But falling catches made practices of generalized reciprocity difficult to sustain.

KSMTF organizer Elizabeth Anthony commented that the new conditions of the fisheries had compromised the dignity for a people, or caste, that was already marginalized. In the past, said Anthony,

> the sea belonged to those who lived at the coast. Now it belongs to everyone. People from other areas, irrespective of caste or religion, catch fish from our sea as a result of the growing unemployment. This has led the coastal inhabitants into poverty. It has increased the rate of suicide.

Earlier, the organizers attempted to downplay caste identities, emphasizing a more universal solidarity among "workers." Caste-based demands for resource entitlement today, however, seem to many to be an appropriate way to safeguard the ocean's resources from dominant-caste Indians as well as from foreigners. It may also be true that the current upsurge in caste-based demands for rights and entitlements across Indian politics has influenced the way the fishers frame their demands. Indeed, the movement seems to have placed itself squarely inside the new political terrain, both drawing on and expanding idioms of caste politics, while deploying them in a politics opposed to neoliberalism.

In addition to their other harmful effects, the resource crisis and the changes in the market economy exacerbate deep gender differences among fishers. As Maglin pointed out, "Most of the ecological problems have been created by globalization. And its impact had been mostly on women." Faced with men's apparent helplessness to alter the fact of resource depletion, women must work harder and longer, or they must come up with new ways to provide for their families (women traditionally sell fish at market) and keep their households intact. Arguing that most social science and policy research still tends to ignore fisherwomen's double burden, Maglin emphasized the need for additional scientific studies on gender disparities and caste inequalities, a clear sign that she recognized the importance of scholarly recognition in positioning the fishers' struggles for rights.

Maglin, Elizabeth Anthony, and other women from fishing communities raise important questions about who controls research agendas, about what issues research should investigate, and about who benefits from economic liberalization. The fishworkers' movement has succeeded in promoting such discussions. At the same time, it is important to note that the discourses of the movement and its activists have changed substantially over time. Caste, community, and economic nationalism now dominate over liberation theology, class, and gender discourses in the way the movement frames justice and ecological issues. While these new frames were increasingly being used by fishworkers' movement activists, they were also changing the terms of the debate for the fishworkers' original adversary, the trawler operators. The fortunes of these two groups have now merged for the most part—but they still disagree on many key points, especially on the impact of mechanization.

The views of the trawler owners are well represented by M.S. James, the general secretary of the Kollam District Trawler Operators Association, which, with a membership of around 1,300 trawler owners, is the largest subgroup in a four-thousand-member statewide trawler owners' association. Apart from lobbying the government on issues of interest to mechanized fishers, this association runs a group insurance program for trawler owners and workers. James, who in addition to the office he holds with the Kollam District group, serves as vice president of the statewide trawler owners' group, does not concede anything to the small fishers' argument that trawling has negative environmental effects. Instead, he argued in our interview with him that trawler owners are being victimized by artisanal fishers and transnational factory ships:

> The destructive fishing practices employed by the traditional fishermen, such as small mesh ring seines, dynamite fishing [exploding dynamite just above the water and then scooping up the large numbers of dead fish that result], and stake net operation [setting up stationary barriers that divert fish into nets] in the estuaries during high tides, and marine pollution caused by the discards from deep sea fishing vessels lead to resource depletion.

James pointed out that trawler owners are unanimous about the need for a seasonal trawl ban, but he argued that it should take place over the winter, not during the summer monsoon. In his view, this is the more important breeding season, and James believes there is no good scientific evidence to support either position. So convinced is he about his stand that he argued that "those who advocate a trawling ban during the southwest monsoon are the agents of foreign fishing vessels that fish in our sea even during the monsoon."

James thus ties the fishworkers' movement demands for a trawling ban into the globalization debate, placing the fishworkers and the state on the same side of the issue (a position that the fishworkers would be surprised to find themselves in). In fact, the Indian trawler operators and small-scale fishers, despite their disagreements about environmental impacts of mechanized fishing and the timing of the trawling ban, are often on the same side of the globalization debate. James, for example, said he sees globalization as a loss of national sovereignty:

Under the pretext of globalization, the government of India is granting more and more licenses to foreign companies for fishing in the Indian Exclusive Economic Zone. But, on the other hand, it could not equip even a single vessel of ours to get license to fish in another country's EEZ. Moreover, there is no proper monitoring of the operations of the deep sea fishing vessels in our country.

The State

On the opposite side of the globalization debate from both the fishworkers' movement and trawler owners are the representatives of the state. Since the rise of the fisheries movement, the Indian government has appointed a secretary of fisheries to define and implement the state fisheries policy. Through the 1960s, fisheries belonged administratively to the department of agriculture and allied activities, and the fact that they now merit their own ministry is significant, as it indicates fishing communities' rise to a status worthy of state attention. As secretary of fisheries in 2002, K. K. Vijaykumar casts the fisheries as a sector of undertapped production potential, and one whose crisis could easily be managed. He is enthusiastic about the sector's export potential and skeptical of the belief that multinational corporations and foreign trawlers pose a grave threat to local fishers. Indeed, he maintained that

> there are now no multinational companies operating here. Huge trawlers used to come into our waters from international waters, but now we are blocking them with the coast guard, who are very vigilant now. . . . Of course, Vietnam and Japan have their factory ships, which catch fish, do all the processing on board, and go on to other international ports and sell their product.

The secretary further insisted that the operation of factory ships outside state waters does not affect artisanal fishers' catches and that India still catches more than enough fish to supply both domestic and international markets. "Depletion of the resource [in Kerala]," he claimed, "is nominal," thanks to the innovative ways that were being found to restock fish resources in alternative sites, such as in inland lakes and rivers. What little depletion has occurred has been caused, in his view, by climate changes, overfishing, pollution, and defective trawling techniques, not by foreign ships. During our interview, he pulled out a book of official figures and educated us on gains in fish productivity, citing the growth statistics for Kerala's share of Indian fish exports. In his view, then, the conflict between trawler operators like Mr. James and small fishermen is also overblown, and can easily be resolved by confining each group to its own specific zones of operation (inshore for small fishers and deep sea for trawlers).

"There may be occasional fights at sea," he said. "For example, three to four months ago there was a fight between a Tamil Nadu boat and one from Kollam; but this is a law and order problem, it is not an issue specific to fisheries."

This assumes, of course, that what happens beyond 5 kilometers from shore doesn't affect small fishermen (in contrast, ecologists and resource systems managers see the entire coastal ecology as interconnected).

Although he knows of the history of conflict over fisheries resources, Vijaykumar adheres unquestioningly to mainstream doctrines of development, environmental science, and resource management. He is interested in the findings of scientific and technical studies, and enjoys receiving and keeping up with information from all around the world.

Vijaykumar said he also believes that "some of our traditional fishermen are repositories of environmental knowledge. Our traditional fishers had different nets for each species; their techniques were highly developed." He acknowledges the loss of traditional livelihoods, but he believes that development and welfare agencies are taking care of the subsistence needs of the poorest fishers. Vijaykumar's view is fully in line with the official narrative of modernization: things have turned out as planned, problems are minor and manageable, those who oppose modernization lack the right knowledge and statistics, and anyone left behind by its inexorable march will be taken care of by state-led welfare schemes. As he pointed out,

> we support fishermen in the lean period and have twenty-seven types of welfare activities which through our Fishermen's Welfare Board offers[sic] help with things like insurance, educational concessions, assistance for marriages and funerals, housing, sanitation, and so on. And in the most recent budget the government of India has just increased this budget by 15 crores [Rs. 150 million, about $3 million].

As for the cultural effects of the fishing crisis, he implied that it is backward-looking to associate identity with livelihood. As he put it:

> We do have sons of fishermen getting educated and moving out of the occupation, and also people from outside coming into fishing. In Kerala we have three castes primarily in the occupation of fishing—Latin Catholics; Hindu fishermen, who live on the cost from Kollam north up to Kasargode; and the Malabar Muslim fishermen. You cannot insist that a fisherman's son should become a fisherman.

Here again, the secretary is staking out a position against current activist rhetoric, which wants to reserve artisanal fisheries for particular castes and communities. However, his view—which is bound up in the economic value of the fisheries, which trumps other meanings such as fishing as caste-based destiny or identity—finds a parallel in some of the early positions of fishworkers' cooperatives themselves, such as Trivandrum District Fishermen Federation (TDFF), which recognized the impending crisis in fishing in the 1970s and sought to create alternative livelihoods for fishers.

Resource Managers and Providers of Technological Assistance

Despite the views of Vijayakumar, artisanal fishing practices are not inherently anti-technology or antimodern. This becomes evident when one talks to representatives of fisheries support organizations, such as the South Indian Federation of Fishermen's Societies (SIFFS) and the International Collective in Support of Fishworkers (ICSF).

V. Vivekanandan is a management professional trained at one of India's premier rural management schools. As chief executive of SIFFS, his main concern in the mid-1980s was helping local fishers gain access to the new technologies that would make them competitive in an international market. That meant helping them with marketing, bulk purchases, and the dissemination of new technologies. SIFFS was founded in 1980, when, in Vivekanandan's words, "it became very clear that the village society [would] need a regular support system, which means monitoring, supervising, troubleshooting, linking with banks for credit—many things."[140] Although local community groups—such as the Program for Community Organization (PCO) in southern Kerala or the Catholic diocese in Kanyakumari (at the southern tip of the state of Tamil Nadu)—were trying to do these things, they were not trained or equipped for the role. "So," Vivekanandan recalled, the PCO was "very keen that some of these [banking and credit] functions be taken over by a federation. We took over a lot of PCO work, including subsequently organizing new cooperatives."

The creation of movement-oriented, nongovernmental cooperatives was a significant achievement for the fisheries movement. The cooperatives had more success than the state in disseminating new institutional and technological methods to fishers. According to Vivekanandan, in the 1970s the fishers'

> collective response [to a perceived resource shortage] was to fight with the government, fight with the trawlers. Individually [their response] was to look around for technologies which will help them survive, do better, which means to go [into] deeper waters, go in search of fish, be less dependent on the sail and the rowing, [to find] whatever fish is there.

In the 1980s, with the post-Emergency return of Indira Gandhi's government, the basic ideas of national development and international political economy were vigorously debated in Parliament. Fisheries policy changed in accordance with a national shift away from a "structural" approach to poverty alleviation—which emphasized equalizing the distribution of property and wealth—toward an "individualist" approach, which encouraged the accumulation of wealth by individual entrepreneurs. Vivekanandan recalled that during this time the SIFFS was overwhelmed by fishers rushing to upgrade their technology and enhance their productive power:

> Membership grew tremendously. It is not very easy to get a bank loan. They [banks] were under pressure to give loans, but [they believed that] giving individually to fisherman would have been a total flop. . . . So my job, among other things, was to go around head offices of banks and convince managers that our people are very nice guys, give them the loan. And they [fishermen] used to get loans.

This kind of help, however, came with a sustained need for support. In order to help the fishers keep up with loan payments, as Vivekanandan puts it, "we were forced to get into technology-related work."

> We developed boats that were in tune with the new needs and technology. We had this [nonprofit] U.K. connection that provided technical support; they even provided financial assistance. We started boat building, which after a lot of initial problems has become a

> very big activity, very successful. So today, this technology that we developed and disseminated dominates the complete southern part of this region—from Kanyakumari to Kollam, this is the main craft.

In arguing that local innovation, global demand, and nonprofit organizations worked together to assure the best possible outcome for small fishers, Vivekanandan's story of the popular rise of motorization differs from the KSMTF's "movement perspective." This is not to deny the truth of the reflection by many fishers, twenty years later, that motors have not helped them weather the resource crisis, and have put them further in debt. Nevertheless, it offers an account of motorization as more than a simple one-way coercive imposition of external technology. It also suggests some of the ways in which perceptions and needs on the ground are shaped by global markets, as well as by the abilities and networks of service and nonprofit organizations. This view thus complicates the category of fishworkers, and the movement's rather idealized view of fisheries before globalization.

Like SIFFS, the International Collective in Support of Fishworkers (ICSF), headed by Sebastian Mathew, is an important fishers' support group. Mathew describes ICSF's objective as "supporting small-scale fisheries that need guidance." The ICSF hopes to make resource management part of fishers' daily practices. He scoffed at the claim that artisanal fishers are engaged in a battle against multinational companies for their survival, calling foreign fishing sporadic and saying its effects have been "exaggerated beyond proportion. I really don't think it is a main issue, and multinationals are not an issue."

For Mathew the primary problem is with overfishing by locals. "You always try and find an external enemy so it is easier for you to do . . . what you have to do," he said. "But I think we have to confront our own biases, and I don't want to exonerate small-scale fishers. Small-scale fishers . . . need some order in their house."

On the subject of overfishing and depletion of resources, Mathew denied that there is a crisis, if by crisis we mean extinction of species. He argued that the problem is one of managing human activity more rationally so as to create sustainable ecological outcomes:

> If you talk to people, they will say that you don't see the particular size of fish anymore. . . . Now we have to go so far out. These signs of overfishing are there. But there is no kind of extinction of resources, so overfishing, overcapacity, these are problems we have to address. . . . We have to basically . . . put our act together, put our house in order.

Unlike KSMTF activists and others who advocate the movement perspective, Mathew does not regard fishing as an occupational heritage inherently worth preserving. He sees, rather, a dynamic global economic field in which one has to move flexibly in order to survive and grow. Mathew avoids the rhetoric of political mobilization and concentrates on how best to manage a finite resource, and how to educate people to be good managers of their livelihoods as well as their resource base. In our interview with him, he said:

Right now [we're] caught in that language of "movement" and "globalization" . . . and we keep debating that. My position is that we cannot ignore the export context. The export fishing market is subject to environmental standards . . . We need a standard for fishing, quality standards, working labor standards. We should have national standards . . . and then we can see how we can engage the world rather than seeing how we react to the world.

Mathew's overall position, however, is sympathetic both to environmental protection and to the protection of poor and lower-caste populations. He differs from the movement perspective principally on the ways in which both might be optimally protected, advancing a position of institutional change and resource management.

Intellectual Activists

From the beginning, intellectual activists have been an important part of the fishworkers' movement. One of the most influential is Nalini Nayak, who has been active in the fishworkers' movement since its early days, and today argues for "grassroots sustainability" and a "contextual environmentalism," by which she means an expansion of environmental concerns to include cultural and historical as well as economic and management issues A.J. Vijayan, like Nayak, was active in the fisheries movement in the early days of the KSMTF, having served as the union's representative on the first government committee to consider the trawling ban. When the two were interviewed for this study, in November 2002, neither was formally affiliated with the KSMTF any longer, but they continued to argue for social and environmental justice. They were starting a new organization to promote these causes by combining scientific and social insights, scholarship, and activism.

Since 1967 Nayak has worked among and with fishers, specifically women. She was involved in the Marianad experiments, the emergence of the Kerala Independent Fishworkers Federation, and the National Fishworkers Federation. Through her fisheries activism, she emerged as one of the key framers of the gender-environment aspect of the fisheries debate. For Nayak, the Kerala fisheries movement is about sustainable livelihoods, which is not the same as resource conservation. In the interview, she argued that

environmentalists . . . don't understand this whole concept of livelihood because if you look at it from a western point of view, yes, you can transfer [to other resources and occupations], but you can't do that on a global scale unless then you divide the resources of the earth. . . . So if we have to live on our resources as they exist physically, then livelihood issues are a main part of the whole thing. But environmentalists don't make this kind of a link.

Neither Nayak nor Vijayan rejects international environmentalism per se; rather, they object to the international and supposedly universal version of environmentalism that gets imposed in local contexts, often as a result of corporate lobbying. They contrast this kind of international activity to the networks that they have learned to work within. According to Vijayan, the fisheries activists were having great trouble defending their livelihood against trawler owners and government scientists, who insisted on imposing what he calls a model of "fisheries management in temperate waters" that was not applicable in Kerala's tropical setting:

> But then we found there were other examples [of environmental movements in developing countries]. We had . . . contact with [them] because by '84 we had some opportunity for global exchanges. For example . . . in '84, just after an international meeting of the FAO [Food and Agriculture Organization of the United Nations] we had a parallel conference of fishworkers. . . . We were able to visit and also exchange [ideas] with so many other groups. It was then that we found out about the trawl ban in Philippines, trawl ban in Indonesia. Since these are also tropical contexts, we knew we could easily also push for that here.

Other global initiatives, such as "sustainable marketing," were equally suspect to those looking to build a contextual environmentalism. In one such campaign, announced in early 1996 by the international NGO World-Wide Fund for Nature (WWF) and the multinational corporation Unilever, a global eco-labeling initiative was begun to promote sustainable fishing. (Eco-labeling refers to the practice of labeling products as ecologically friendly.) The right to use an eco-label is conferred by an impartial third party rather than by manufacturers, so products with the label must meet independently established criteria. Applying eco-labeling to fishing was designed as both a step toward sustainable resource management and an innovative response to the ongoing crisis in fisheries. Consumers would be able to select sustainably harvested fish products, the environment would be protected, and the worldwide crisis in fisheries resources could be averted.

The initiative, however, met with strong opposition from artisanal fishers and small producers in Canada and India, who drew analogies to the experience of fishers in Senegal, where French and other European fleets took advantage of the Senegalese government's limited enforcement capacities and fished illegally in excess of their legal quotas. In forging this alliance with Senegalese fishworkers, Kerala fisheries activists began what was to emerge as a transnational arc of solidarity that transcended simple dichotomies between East and West, Asia and Africa. The very notion of sustainability was at stake in this conflict, they argued. Sustainability for whom? Which markets should be valued—global (served largely by large trawler owners) or local (served by subsistence and local fisheries)? Are there uncertainties and blind spots in the scientific definitions of sustainability? In Kerala, fishers rejected the eco-labeling plan and began to market their fish instead through an alternative Fair Trade initiative, linking local producers with green consumers in Germany under a banner that prioritized livelihoods and the food security of the poor, over more abstract green values.[141]

In the Indian case, the eco-labeling process required fishers in Orissa state to use "turtle-excluding devices" (TEDs). Nayak commented:

> It had less to do with environmentalism than it had to do with safeguarding access to a particular market. The dolphin-safe tuna issue of the United States was market-based. They were fighting Mexican tuna vessels. And then they exported [eco-labeling] through

the Earth Island Institute. What India is suffering from now is the TEDs . . . which they say have to be used [to win eco-labeling]. Now, that is a market strategy. The company which wants to sell a TED can control you. We are saying: Stop trawling. They're saying: No, you use this device, and trawl. How environmentalist can that be? How ecologically safe is that?

In a separate interview, John Kurien, the preeminent scholar of the fishworkers' movement, described TEDs as an imposed and restrictive form of international environmentalism, an unacceptable loss of sovereignty that may not even have the positive ecological effects that proponents claim for it. According to this view, people are lured into thinking that trawling is environmentally safe as long as TEDs are used, but that is not the case.

On a related point, Vijayan suggested that the fishers' movement, with its network of international contacts, was actually better acquainted with the latest research on fisheries than were the scientists on the Kerala government's expert panels. He recalled that the Indian scientists on the 1981 Babu Paul Committee panel

> were saying . . . that trawling was like plowing a field. [They claimed that] it makes the sea bottom more fertile! . . . They are the authority, so you had to listen to what they were saying. . . . It was funny. Even at the international level trawling was not that popular, and the scientific news had still not reached our Indian scientists.

Today, fishworkers' movement demands continue to be at odds with the resource management approach favored by governments. As Nayak explained:

> Now fishers all over the world are asking for an [inshore artisanal fishing] zone. And no government is willing to give it because . . . the [inshore] zone is the most productive zone. That's where all fish come and go from whether they are in the deep sea or not. Now no government wants to give [artisanal fishers their own] zone, and they're moving faster towards . . . quotas. What the internationals are pushing is a quota system.

While Nayak celebrates the movement's successes and the range of actors it mobilized, she regrets that grassroots sustainability remains peripheral to the movement:

> We've tried to establish links between the community and the resource. The [artisanal] fishing community lives on this resource; but at the same time the community can be sustained only if the resource is. So there is this very dynamic relationship. . . . The initial struggles were really struggles for conservation of the resource—the demand for the ban on trawl fishing, demand for the demarcation of the zones. . . . But what surfaced gradually was . . . that even [artisanal] fishing was becoming unsustainable because of the way it was evolving.

When Nayak articulates the need for more sustainability activism at the base, she is referring to the need for a grass-roots understanding of environmentalism that combines livelihood and justice issues with a technical and scientific understanding of ocean ecosystems. And yet Nayak argued, "We don't have a management model for tropical waters," and the "northern model imposed on us" has proved destructive to the resource and inappropriate for Indian waters, because of the particular relations among monsoon systems, local fish reproductive cycles, and artisanal fishing communities' local knowledge.

To fill this void, Nayak advocates a grassroots environmentalism that combines social history, livelihood and justice issues with a technical and scientific understanding of ocean ecosystems. Although concerned with the loss of some traditional practices, she does not advocate a return to the past. While she recognizes the importance of demanding welfare and support from the state, she also would like the movement to devote more attention to the hard work of shaping new sustainable fishing methods. However, as Nayak noted, it is the welfarist demands that have gained priority over the demand for bans on monsoon trawling and restrictions on unsustainable fishing.

"The major demand of the fishermen in Kerala," she said, "has been the closed season for trawlers during the monsoon. After a decade, the union had only succeeded in getting a forty-five day closure. But there have been numerous other things they have demanded and got" such as social services.[142]

Though the state takes credit for providing social services, Nayak points out that it was in fact the result of fishworkers' movement agitation.[143] She also points out that state social services became necessary only after strong local communities were almost destroyed by the economic impact of the crisis in fishing. When resources were abundant, community practices and structure supported poor and sick community members.

According to Nayak, destructive fishing practices weaken the social fabric and result in dispossession of lower caste coastal populations, particularly women. As she put it in our interview,

> we saw women being marginalized by the increase in technology. . . . Fishing became more centralized. . . . So by the mid-'80s . . . technology was getting aggressive at sea, and there was an aggression on women on shore as well. So we had a saying: "Without women in fisheries, no fish in the sea."[144]

Nayak insisted, however, that we cannot assume that fishing practices will evolve in a sustainable direction. She pointed out that the competition has already caused artisanal fishers to make choices that might be good for them in the short run, but are bad for the ecosystem:

> The inshore [artisanal] fishers themselves have become so high-tech. They are actually searching out every last fish in the water. This is the sad part. You know, when you look from the point of view of the struggle, we've been making demands, but we haven't looked at ourselves. So we haven't been able to translate the demands on the state into an action proposition for ourselves.

In this, Nayak concurs with Sebastian Mathew's judgment that there is an urgent need for ecosystem management among traditional fishers. She sees destructive fishing practices as linked to the changes in social fabric and the processes of modernization and globalization. Nayak's contextual environmentalism, then, does not represent indigenous knowledge as isolated and static. Rather, she sees indigenous knowledge as dynamic, the product of solidarity with fishers in other parts of the world and engagement with global debates and policy initiatives.

The Evolution of New Arguments for Sustainability and Survival in Kerala

Our interviews in Kerala show that individual representatives of the state and the movement espouse diverse and often incompatible environmentalisms, despite significant overlaps. From the state's point of view, Nayak's position may be indistinguishable from Maglin's—just more nostalgic, insider-versus-outsider narrative. From the inside, however, there appears to be a divergence in the views of sustainability embraced by various actors in this debate: the new KSMTF organizers like Elizabeth and Maglin (who often prioritize livelihoods and identity politics over sustainability), the organizational ecologists like Sebastian (who are trying to introduce international management principles), the contextual ecologists like Nayak, and service organization directors like Vivekanandan.

The work of the KSMTF and other activist groups over a long period has given many fishers hope for a better future, but also an awareness of the dynamically politicized nature of Kerala fisheries. In field interviews, we found a divergence in the attitudes and political stances of fishers who had become politicized by the movement and those who were more distant from it. In interviews with nonactivist fishers we heard despair, isolation, and helplessness, while in interviews with activists and organizers we heard empowerment and a determination to fight for their rights and for what they perceived as a just outcome to the fisheries conflict. Activists were also more certain that their actions would bear results, an interesting insight into the formation of ecological citizenship.[145] Yet every fisher we spoke with knew about the trawl ban, and believed in the importance of pressuring the government to protect their livelihoods against larger forces, both national and global.

Kerala's marine fishers, once inert vote banks for the Congress Party, have over four decades been transformed in the depth of their knowledge of and attitudes toward resource depletion, rights to resources, and alternative development. But policy changes and class compromises achieved at the level of national policy or a statewide compact do not automatically become the consensus among the various interests in the fisheries. Partly, the logic and narrative of the movement itself have changed. With the site of movement politics becoming national and international, intellectual-activists are producing new arguments about local sustainability and livelihoods.

At the same time, it is important to recognize that these outspoken and articulate champions of the rights of fishers in developing countries did not emerge from a static local context or an ideologically anti-Northern environmentalism. Rather, they emerged out of a locally grounded yet transnationally linked social movement that benefits from several decades of sophisticated scientific and social analysis of tropical fisheries. Mathew, Nayak, Anthony, and others speak on a global stage not only as individuals deeply embedded in a local context, but as fisheries advocates within a transnational network of solidarity and activism.

The Kerala case study should also be read through the history of global aid and North-South development assistance. The histories of colonial conquest and military domination are, naturally, pertinent to the analysis of states and social movements, but so is the history of "uplift," "improvement," and "cooperation." In the wake of World War II, a complex set of technological changes transformed societies and economies by making possible new forms of mass production and distribution. There was a global consensus about the need to help developing or war-ravaged economies to acquire new technologies so that they could participate in the world market. This paradigm shift in economies and technologies did not leave the world's fisheries untouched. Small-scale fishermen and coastal communities all over the world found themselves caught up in large and permanent changes in the nature of production and markets.

While all these communities expressed anxieties and fears over the loss of local self-determination, the ways in which these fears played out varied, of course, with state institutions and local contexts. For instance, the cultural pluralism and decentralized regulatory structure of the United States created a "fragmented array" of groups in the New England fisheries, each attempting to influence policy through highly specific, locally defined initiatives. In Norway, by contrast, similar coastal anxieties and demands were nationally coordinated, and translated quickly into state-supported measures to protect small-scale fishers against multinational incursions.[146] By the 1950s, while privatization and liberalization had become entrenched in developed countries, several developing countries could still boast of open-access seas, traditional fishers, and cheap fish for the masses. These boasts were, then as now, based on somewhat romanticized narratives—narratives that reappear, however, as wistful memories for the fishers of Kerala.

There is no one true narrative of the movement, nor any one lesson to be learned. The voices of actors from different sides of the conflict, however, show us that the various positions are both overlapping and constantly changing—it makes little sense to be simply for or against traditional fishers, trawling, globalization, and so on. The themes of national economic sovereignty, opposition to globalization, the role of the state, the value of tradition, and the advantages and disadvantages of technology run throughout the fisheries debate today—but they cannot be neatly parceled out among the different actors in the Kerala fisheries narrative. If anything, the positions are becoming increasingly complicated, and it is only by understanding the shifting nature of the debate that we can hope to understand how fisheries politics will play out as the process of globalization continues.

Indian Claims for Ecology and Equity

The events in Delhi and Kerala cannot be understood as a simple trade-off between the environment and livelihoods, or as "ecology versus economics." Nor can they be understood in terms of a conflict between the "universal" interests of the public or nature and the "particular" interests of the working classes. At stake are different modes of appropriating nature, different conceptions of the environment as a place for gaining a livelihood. Both Kerala fishers and Delhi industrial workers make nuanced claims about which environmental values need to be prioritized, and they argue for both ecology *and* social equity.

In the Delhi case, middle-class activists were effectively able to present themselves as protectors of the environment by moving polluting industries out of sight. Cleaner air in Delhi was obtained by shifting the burden of air and water pollution elsewhere, and thus it is dubious that the Delhi campaign achieved a net improvement in air quality. Middle-class environmentalists also have refused to recognize the role of their own consumerist lifestyles in fueling the demand for manufactured products, especially private vehicles, that helped create the pollution in the first place. Most important, they have avoided the difficult task of democratic environmental planning and implementation, preferring to take judicial shortcuts that penalize workers.

Under these circumstances, workers' insistence on jobs before clean air was not an anti-environmental stand. Their perspective had been shaped by the compromises they were forced to make by an economic system and labor conditions not of their choosing. Because their jobs were on the line, workers were not in a position to demand cleaner or safer technologies, but in a world where their concerns mattered, workers would probably have opted for jobs that did not expose them or others to pollution. That choice was never offered to them, however, in the air pollution controversy. Excluding workers' concerns from the court eliminated the possibility of creating ecologically sustainable as well as socially just economic arrangements.

In Kerala, too, the challenge has been to craft sustainable fisheries management techniques that support people's livelihoods while ensuring the survival of marine species. As activists argue, the artisanal fishing community can be sustained only if the resource is sustained. The long-term future of fishers and the fate of offshore fisheries are interlinked. Both the Delhi and Kerala struggles highlight the difficulty of assuming congruence between particular "public interest" environmental campaigns and the pursuit of social justice. Closing the polluting factories in Delhi and requiring that Kerala fishers use turtle-exclusion devices in order that their fish catch be labeled eco-friendly both seem to serve a transcendental public interest—universal health and ecological benefits. Yet the consequences of these actions are visited selectively, exacerbating previously existing social disparities. Like the industrial workers in Delhi who point to the need to devise context-specific pollution-control techniques and regulatory processes instead of blanket bans on industry, Kerala fishers argue for fishery management policies that respect their situated, experiential knowledge of complex ecological processes. Standardized models of marine ecosystems that form the basis for seasonal bans or the regulation of catch need to be replaced with information-based models that draw upon locally monitored fisheries data. In short, environmental decisions are soundest when they incorporate the perspectives and knowledge of those whose labor brings them closest to the resource.

Export-oriented "fisheries development" in Kerala since the 1960s, which led to over-fishing, and industrial restructuring in Delhi in the 1990s, which led to a shift away from manufacturing into a service economy, represent two different moments in the context of postcolonial development and liberalization. This changing context, as much as po-litical alliances on the ground, shaped the different fortunes of the Kerala and Delhi campaigns. The anti-trawler movement drew its environmental and social legitimacy from Kerala's vigorous trade unions, progressive churches, and the People's Science Movement—the movement committed to promoting scientific literacy[147]—at a time when the discourse of development had generated provocative critiques and challenges. Industrial workers in Delhi defended a rearguard position against middle-class environ-mentalists for whom a liberalized economy had created new means of imagining them-selves as urbane citizens living the good life. Nonunionized workers, ill-paid and laboring under insecure conditions, could not withstand the overwhelming power of the courts and a corporate-controlled media to shape the debate on environmental values. The differences between these two campaigns and the imperfect fit—even outright contra-diction—between dominant environmental narratives and the Delhi and Kerala experi-ences suggest that Indian environmentalism cannot be understood via a single narrative. The rich multivocality of these environmental narratives reflects the multiplicity of lived experiences that constitute modern development and its antinomies.

Notes

*Amita Baviskar researched and wrote the Delhi study; Kavita Philip conducted inter-views for the Kerala study in November 2003 and coauthored that study with Subir Sinha. Antonyto Paul conducted supplemental interviews in February 2004 and assisted in writ-ing the Kerala study.

This chapter did not emerge directly from the collaborative research process. While initial work on these cases was conducted by a research team, the authors of this chapter were commissioned separately to write it after the research process had ended but according to the guidelines established by the process. See chapter 9 for further explanation of the evolution of this chapter.—Ed.

1. "Artisanal" is a term used to denote the small scale of the operations, based on skills rather than machines. This term is used even in official documents to describe a subset of the "fisheries sector."
2. Vandana Shiva, *Staying Alive: Women, Ecology and Survival in India* (New Delhi: Kali for Women, 1988).
3. Bina Agarwal, "The Gender and Environment Debate: Lessons from India," *Feminist Studies* 18, no. 1 (1992): 119–58; and Subir Sinha, Shubhra Gururani, and Brian Greenberg, "The New Traditionalist Discourse of Indian Environmentalism," *Journal of Peasant Studies* 24, no. 3 (1997): 65–99.
4. Madhav Gadgil and Ramachandra Guha, *Ecology and Equity: The Use and Abuse of Nature in Contemporary India* (New Delhi: Penguin, 1995); and Guha, Ramachandra and Juan Martinez-Alier, *Varieties of Environmentalism: Essays North and South* (Delhi: Oxford University Press, 1998).
5. Henry Bernstein, "Taking the Part of Peasants?" in *The Question of Food: Profits Versus People?* ed. H. Bernstein, B. Crow, M. Mackintosh, and C. Martin (New York: Monthly Review Press, 1990), 56.

6. Ramachandra Guha, "Ideological Trends in Indian Environmentalism," *Economic and Political Weekly* 23, no. 49 (1988): 2578–81.

7. Patrick Heller, *The Labor of Development: Workers and the Transformation of Capitalism in Kerala, India* (Ithaca: Cornell University Press, 1999).

8. It is hard to assess accurately the size and significance of India's urban middle class. The group is heterogeneous in terms of income, consumption, education, occupation, and property ownership. The characteristics of the middle class are inflected by regional cultural understandings (e.g., *bhadralok*, in Bengal indicates an intelligentsia that partakes of high culture—music, literature, and film). For purposes of this study, we use the term *middle class* to capture what in Hindi are referred to as *padhe-likhe log* (educated folk), a group instantly recognized by its dress, deportment, and language. These are professionals, usually educated in private English-medium schools and holding jobs as civil servants, bank employees, engineers, and university lecturers. They are likely to own their own homes and automobiles over the course of their lives, and are, in short, owners of symbolic and material capital.

9. Amita Baviskar, "Forest Management as Political Practice: Indian Experiences with the Accommodation of Multiple Interests," *International Journal of Agricultural Resources, Governance and Ecology* 1, no. 3/4 (2001): 243–63.

10. Amita Baviskar, "Red in Tooth and Claw? Looking for Class in Struggles over Nature," in *Rethinking Class and Poverty: Social Movements in India in a Transnational Age,* ed. Mary Katzenstein and Raka Ray (Lanham, MD: Rowman and Littlefield, 2005).

11. Pierre Bourdieu, *Outline of a Theory of Practice* (Cambridge: Cambridge University Press, 1977), 21.

12. The statements that respondents make in an interview are often shaped by their desire to present themselves in a favorable light, based on suppositions about what the interviewer wants to hear.

13. Interview with M.C. Mehta, *Frontline,* 22 December 2000, 17.

14. Vinish Kathuria, "Relocating Polluting Units: Parochialism vs. the Right to Live?" *Economic and Political Weekly* 36, no. 3 (2001): 191.

15. The Ganga (Ganges) is India's most important river, originating in the Himalaya Mountains and flowing east through the vast alluvial plains of northern India. The river and its tributaries support both rural and urban material life and have great cultural significance for Hindus.

16. "And Quietly Flows the *Maily* Yamuna," *Hindustan Times,* 18 July 1994.

17. The trade unions include All India Federation of Trade Unions, Progressive National Labor Union, United Trade Union Congress, Rashtriya Kisan Mazdoor Ekta, Sarvahara Mehnatkash Sangharsh Samiti, Delhi General Mazdoor Front, Nirman Mazdoor Panchayat Sangam, Mazdoor Ekta Committee, Indian Federation of Trade Unions, All India Coordination Committee of Trade Unions, and Sangharshsheel Mazdoor Samiti. Rights organizations include People's Union for Democratic Rights, Jhuggi Jhonpri Nivasi Adhikar Samiti, Saheli, Aids Bhedbhav Virodhi Andolan, People's Union for Civil Liberties, and Human Rights Trust. Some students' and teachers' unions were also a part of the Manch. Many of the groups in the Manch are Marxist-Leninist, ideologically on the extreme left of the Indian political spectrum. It is notable that trade unions affiliated with the major political parties—Congress, BJP, CPI, and CPI (M)—were not a part of the DJAM. Thus the Manch represented fairly small, radical groups with limited constituencies.

18. Reports/pamphlets published by the Delhi Janwadi Adhikar Manch (DJAM) in Delhi: *The Order That Felled a City,* February/March 1997; and *The Day After,* July 1997.

19. In many cases, the land had been given to them by the government at subsidized prices. The huge rise in the price of real estate in the heart of the city made closing aging manufacturing units and converting the land to commercial use a very attractive proposition. The Supreme Court had stipulated that a certain portion of vacated factory land would have to be handed over to the government (30 percent for factories below a certain size and 60 percent for factories above that size), but several illegal land transfers happened anyway. A similar process happened in downtown Mumbai, when the closure of "sick" textile mills opened up prime real estate for commercial development, at great profit to mill owners (Darryl

D'Monte, *Ripping the Fabric: The Decline of Mumbai and Its Mills* [Delhi: Oxford University Press, 2001]).

20. DJAM, *The Day After.*

21. DJAM, *Jansunwai* [Public Hearing], 1998, 24.

22. Shriram Foods and Fertilizers was the firm responsible for an oleum leak in the late 1980s. Toxic fumes from this accident affected several hundred people living near the factory. This event prompted Mehta to initiate public interest litigation to prevent another Bhopal-type tragedy.

23. DJAM, *Jansunwai,* 16.

24. The term *"casual" laborer* means that the worker is continuously employed for fewer than ninety days by the same firm. Employers prefer casual laborers because, compared to permanent workers who have job security and are entitled to employment benefits on a higher scale, casual laborers are cheaper and easier to control. It is a common practice in Indian firms, including government establishments, to employ people for several years but avoid the liability of recognizing them as permanent workers by firing them after ninety days and then rehiring them. In some cases, the worker is rehired under a fictitious name to maintain the façade that the firm employs a workforce of changing, casual laborers. Most workers, especially those who work for smaller firms, are not unionized, and are too poor and vulnerable to fight such illegal practices.

25. Emphasis in original. The Manch report goes on to note that Ayodhya Textile Mills, a government-owned factory, was the only exception to this rule. DJAM, *The Day After.*

26. Ibid.

27. Underreporting is a strategy to circumvent the Labor Act and the Industrial Disputes Act, which mandate that firms employing more than ten workers provide them with certain entitlements. Under these laws, firms are required to contribute to workers' pension and provident funds and other social security benefits, and must allow collective bargaining.

28. DJAM, *The Day After.*

29. Ibid.

30. Ibid.

31. Wazirpur and Badli (both dominated by steel pickling and processing firms), Maujpur, Seelampur, and Okhla (dyeing), Anand Parbat, Vishwas Nagar, and Mayapuri (electroplating).

32. Schoolteachers in India are often conscripted to conduct enumeration exercises for the government, such as collecting census data.

33. The Subhash Nagar Residents' Welfare Association.

34. A clause inserted into the DSIDC notice says that if the Master Plan is amended so as to declare that a firm's present location is in an industrial area, the money deposited will be refunded. This indicates that factory owners and the Delhi government were hoping to resolve the problem of nonconforming units in one stroke, by simply redesignating residential zones as industrial.

35. A *bandh* is a common form of collective protest, sometimes spontaneous but more often sponsored by a political party or neighborhood association. A bandh may also be a mark of respect (upon the death of a public figure) or a precaution (in the case of anticipated violence such as riots).

36. *The Hindu,* Delhi edition, 16 December 2000.

37. According to the Delhi government, the list of categories was "worked out by experts after a thorough study." Of the forty-four categories in the original list, nine were deemed nonpolluting, reducing the total number of categories to thirty-three.

38. The Delhi government proposed another sleight-of-hand: changing the definition of a "household [production] unit" from a firm employing up to five workers and using up to one kilowatt of power to a unit employing up to twenty workers and using up to five kilowatts of power. This move would literally domesticate the problem by reclassifying many current industrial units as "household industries," giving them immunity from the court's orders. But even this expansion, complained the Association of Small-Scale Industries, did not go far enough.

39. *The Hindu,* Delhi edition, 13 February 2001.

40. *The Hindu,* Delhi edition, 21 December 2002.

41. It was rumored that Jagmohan, the urban development minister, had been removed from his post because his intransigence regarding factory closures was adversely affecting the popularity of BJP members of Parliament from Delhi. Small manufacturers and merchants form a significant chunk of the BJP's electoral base in Delhi. Jagmohan was replaced by the more "flexible" Ananth Kumar, who was willing to accommodate the concerns of his party members from Delhi.

42. Central Pollution Control Board, *Pollution Statistics: Delhi 1993–4* (Delhi, 1995), quoted in Centre for Science and Environment, "Slow Murder: The Deadly Story of Vehicular Pollution in India" (New Delhi: CSE, 1996).

43. DJAM, *Jansunwai,* 23.

44. Motor vehicles emitted 310 metric tons per day (mt/d) of hydrocarbons, 157 mt/d of nitrogen oxide, and 810 mt/d of carbon monoxide, while industrial sources released only 6 mt/d of hydrocarbons, 20 mt/d of nitrogen oxide, and 128 mt/d of carbon monoxide. As for suspended particulate matter, industry released 60 mt/d compared to transportation's 13 mt/d, while for sulfur dioxide the figures were 35 mt/d for industry to transport's 11 mt/d.

45. This order was limited to vehicles registered in Delhi. It also excluded private vehicles that ran on diesel.

46. The term "public transportation" is a misnomer; apart from a few thousand buses run by the Delhi Transport Corporation (DTC), all other buses, taxis, and auto-rickshaws are privately owned, in most cases by small owner-operators.

47. Delhi had 86,185 registered auto-rickshaws in 2001, of which 65 percent were driven by their owners. A new auto-rickshaw can cost as much as Rs 80,000 (about $1,700). Since net earnings average Rs 3,000 per month ($60), close to the minimum wage, the investment in a new vehicle represents an onerous financial commitment. Dinesh Mohan and Dunu Roy, "Operating on Three Wheels: Auto-Rickshaw Drivers in Delhi," *Economic and Political Weekly* 38, no. 3 (2003): 177–78.

48. Ibid., 177.

49. Dinesh Mohan and Geetam Tiwari, "Sustainable Transport Systems: Linkages between Environmental Issues, Public Transport, Non-Motorized Transport and Safety," *Economic and Political Weekly* 34, no. 25 (1999): 1589–96.

50. Nagraj Adve, "Industrial Water Pollution in Delhi: The Yamuna Maily Case: An Overview."

51. Kathuria, "Relocating Polluting Units: Parochialism vs. the Right to Live?" 191.

52. R. Ramachandran, "The Lethal Zones," *Frontline,* 22 December 2000, 18.

53. Gautam Navlakha, "Urban Pollution: Driving Workers to Desperation," *Economic and Political Weekly* 35, no. 51 (2000): 4471.

54. Some critics of the Master Plan challenge the basic premise of spatial and functional segregation. There has been a long-standing debate among urban planners in India about the appropriateness of functionally segregated urban planning in the Indian context, where urban spaces have tended to move toward mixed land use. Some planners have contended that, in consonance with the spatiality of traditional Indian cities, planning in Delhi should encourage mixed land use, recognizing and adapting to the complexity of a multiethnic, multiclass society with spatially overlapping functions. A school of opinion within urban planning circles, drawing upon the work of Patrick Geddes, who had traveled widely in India and designed plans for several Indian towns, espoused this model of the planned city, thereby questioning the appropriateness of the Master Plan's fundamental categories. Patrick Geddes, *Cities in Evolution: An Introduction to the Town Planning Movement and to the Study of Civics* (London: Williams and Norgate, 1915).

55. Kathuria, "Relocating Polluting Units: Parochialism vs. the Right to Live?" 191.

56. DJAM, *The Day After.*

57. Quoted in Navlakha, "Urban Pollution: Driving Workers to Desperation," 4470.

58. Ibid.

59. Similarly, the bulk of water pollution is caused by untreated domestic sewage. Although the court ordered the Delhi government to set up more sewage treatment plants, it has been far less energetic in pursuing this line of action.

60. The People's Science Movement is a loose federation of activist groups across India that work to popularize science-based reasoning and promote appropriate technology. Their activities include adapting school science curricula to local materials and conditions, and critically appraising the social and environmental effects of introduced technologies. See M. Zacharaiah and R. Sooryamoorthy, *Science for Social Revolution: Achievements and Dilemmas of a Development Movement* (London: Zed Press, 1994).

61. Quoted in Rakesh Kapoor's unpublished essay "The Ugly Face of Green Justice."

62. Interview by Kavita Philip, 25 October 2002.

63. Mehta has won the prestigious Magsaysay Prize, which honors outstanding social service in Asia.

64. Life-cycle events such as births, deaths, menstruation, and menarche are marked by heightened levels of pollution.

65. Thomas R. Rosin, "Wind, Traffic and Dust: The Recycling of Wastes," *Contributions to Indian Sociology* 34, no. 3 (2000): 404.

66. M.P. Cowen and R. W. Shenton, *Doctrines of Development* (London: Routledge, 1996); Uday Singh Mehta, *Liberalism and Empire: A Study in Nineteenth-Century British Liberal Thought* (Chicago: University of Chicago Press, 1999).

67. Stamford Raffles, quoted in Richard Drayton, *Nature's Government: Science, Imperial Britain, and the "Improvement" of the World* (New Haven: Yale University Press, 2000), 94.

68. Ibid., 104.

69. Personal law refers to Indian jurisprudence for individuals belonging to different religious communities.

70. Bernard Cohn, *Colonialism and Its Forms of Knowledge* (Delhi: Oxford University Press, 1997).

71. James C. Scott, *Seeing Like a State* (New Haven: Yale University Press, 1998).

72. David Ludden, "India's Development Regime," in *Colonialism and Culture,* ed. Nicholas B. Dirks (Ann Arbor: University of Michigan Press, 1992).

73. Philip McMichael, *Development and Social Change: A Global Perspective* (Thousand Oaks, California: Pine Forge Press, 1996).

74. Sunil Khilnani, *The Idea of India* (New Delhi: Penguin Books India, 1997).

75. Donald S. Moore, "The Crucible of Cultural Politics: Reworking 'Development' in Zimbabwe's Eastern Highlands," *American Ethnologist* 26, no. 3 (1999): 654–89.

76. Partha Chatterjee, *The Nation and Its Fragments: Colonial and Postcolonial Histories* (Princeton: Princeton University Press, 1993).

77. Satish Deshpande,. "From Development to Adjustment: Economic Ideologies, the Middle Class and 50 Years of Independence," *Review of Development and Change* 2, no. 2 (1997): 294–318.

78. Many upper-middle-class Indians have traveled to Singapore on vacation, and a growing number work there in the banking and IT sectors.

79. The movement of heavy vehicles such as trucks through Delhi has been restricted to avoid congestion during peak-hour traffic.

80. B.M. Gupta, a retired teacher and a member of the B Block, East of Kailash Residents Welfare Association, in a discussion of public action on environmental issues in Delhi.

81. This and all subsequent Mehta quotations, unless otherwise noted, come from an interview conducted by Kavita Philip on 25 October 2002.

82. The lack of systematic survey data on the situation of affected workers is further evidence that they are invisible to official eyes.

83. This is company-owned housing that workers' families will soon have to vacate.

84. Coaching for school and college examinations.

85. DJAM, *Jansunwai,* 34.

86. At the Sahni Tyres factory, for instance, workers were routinely pushed to achieve production targets that exceeded their physical capacity. Several workers reported that injuries, some permanent, such as the loss of hands, occurred regularly.

87. Government of Kerala, *Marine Fisheries in Kerala at a Glance* (Trivandrum: Government of Kerala, 1991).

88. "Fishworker" is a translation of "Matsya Thozhilali" and was coined by the movement to indicate the importance of class-position and the movement away from a purely caste-community affiliation.

89. While the word *dalit* literally means "oppressed," it is now a potent term in Indian politics, connoting demands of identity, justice, and rights as compensation for centuries of oppression by Hindu dominant castes.

90. See Francis Day, *The Fishes of Malabar* (London: Bernard Quaritch, 1865); James Hornell, "Administrative Report of the Department of Fisheries for the Year Ending 30th June, 1922," *Madras Fisheries Bulletin* 17 (1923).

91. Debates over varieties of environmentalism typically refer to "deep" ecology (concern for "nature-in-its-own-right") and "social ecology" (concern for "nature-in-social-relations"). For details, see David Pepper, *Eco-Socialism* (London: Routledge, 1995).

92. Because the nationalist movement also believed in development as a key function of the state, the colonial intervention in the fisheries was continued by the postcolonial state. On the creation of such a development regime as an effect of contestations between the colonial state and nationalists, see David Ludden, "India's Development Regime," in *Colonialism and Culture,* ed. N. Dirks (Ann Arbor: University of Michigan Press, 1993).

93. The Norwegian Foundation for Assistance to Underdeveloped Countries sought out aid projects that would enhance Norway's national image by promoting peace and stability through economic growth in the developing world. The foundation's agenda resonated with India's philosophy of community development—the central rural intervention of the Nehruvian socialist state. This paternalistic philosophy, which aimed to create social transformation with minimal social conflict, had it roots in earlier Gandhian, Christian missionary, and late-colonial initiatives, and was supported by bilateral and international agencies and foundations (including Ford and Rockefeller).

94. Travancore and Cochin are the two former principalities that, along with the Malabar district of the former Madras Presidency, were combined in 1956 to form the state of Kerala.

95. John Kurien, the leading authority on the case, argues that 1963 should be regarded as the end point of Norwegian influence, even though some Norwegian sponsorship continued in the area of "integrated fishery complexes" in Cochin, Karwar, and Mandapam. See John Kurien, "Technical Assistance Projects and Socioeconomic Change: Norwegian Intervention in Kerala's Fisheries Development," *Economic and Political Weekly* 20, no. 25/26 (June 1985): A76.

96. Ibid.

97. He remains unnamed in all the accounts we have read.

98. Kurien, "Technical Assistance Projects and Socioeconomic Change," A74.

99. Ibid.

100. Kurien, "Technical Assistance Projects and Socioeconomic Change," A76.

101. The chief executive of the South Indian Federation of Fisherman's Societies (SIFFS), V. Vikekanandan, commented to us in 2002 on these early cooperative societies: "The '50s–'60s in fact was a period when probably all over India, the government, as part of its development efforts, had promoted cooperatives in fisheries. . . . Kerala in particular had gone very far ahead with more than one thousand cooperatives registered . . . and they were a miserable failure."

102. Kurien, "Technical Assistance Projects and Socioeconomic Change," A76.

103. A.G. Kalawar, M. Devaraj, and A. Parulekar, *Report of the Expert Committee on Marine Fisheries in Kerala* (Bombay: Versova, 1985), 84.

104. Ibid., 203.

105. Trawling involves dragging a conical net along the seabed. The net is fitted with two wooden boards to keep the mouth of the net wide open and an iron chain, called the tickler chain, to rake the seabed.

106. According to a study by the Central Marine Fisheries Research Institute, shrimp resources were under threat in the most important shrimp fishing ground of Kerala. The catch per unit effort in that ground declined from 82.6 kg/hour in 1973 to 7.6 kg/hour in 1980. CMFRI data cited in Kalawar et al., *Report of the Expert Committee on Marine Fisheries,* 12.

107. The per fisher output fell from over 3,000 kg to less than 2,000 kg per annum (Kurien, "Technical Assistance Projects and Socioeconomic Change," A77).

108. Babu Paul Committee Report, report, Government of Kerala, 1982. A crore equals 10 million rupees.

109. Among those trained in Marianad were Tom Kocherry, Nalini Nayak, John Kurien, Eugene Culas, John Fernandes, and A.J. and Eliyamma Vijayan, all important leaders of the fishworkers' movement.

110. Liberation theologians advocate compassion and focus on creating a better life on earth rather than on salvation in the afterlife.

111. The Trivandrum District Fisherfolk Federation was one such cooperative; examples of international agencies to whom the cooperatives commonly applied for grants are NOVIB (Dutch Oxfam) and GORTA (a leading Irish Catholic charity organization).

112. Although these groups were strongest in the Catholic areas of Kollam, Alapuzha, and Thiruvananthapuram (Trivandrum), similar groups were started among Hindu fishers, primarily by the Dheevara Sabha, an umbrella union with members from various caste groups. Muslim fishers in the north of Kerala suffered harsh living conditions similar to those of fishers in other parts of the state, but little has been written about the history of organizing in northern Muslim fishing villages. It may be that traditional fishers took more quickly to trawling in these areas, without the same conflicts between trawlers and catamarans.

113. Gabriele Dietrich and Nalini Nayak, *Transition or Transformation: A Study of Mobilisation, Organisation and Emergence of Consciousness among the Fishworkers of Kerala, India* (Chennai: Sri Venkatesa Printing House, 2002), 82–109.

114. Gabriele Dietrich and Nalini Nayak, *Transition or Transformation,* 4. Kocherry later went on to lead the World Forum of Fish Harvesters and Fish Workers (WFF), which involved unions across thirty-five maritime nations worldwide.

115. Mathew Aerthayil, *Fishworkers' Movement in Kerala (1977–1994): The Role of Non-Party Political Organizations in Social Transformation in India* (New Delhi: Indian Social Institute, 2000), 37. Leftist parties did not even attempt to gain a constituency among fishers. Wicky Meynen, "Fisheries Development, Resources Depletion and Political Mobilisation in Kerala: The Problem of Alternatives," *Development and Change* 20 (1989): 738–39, 742. While the Congress Party was center-right in the 1970s, today it is center-left as the political spectrum has moved to the right.

116. Antony Gregory and G. Placid, "Fishermen's Struggle Against Mechanised Fishing in Kerala," Society for Participatory Research in Asia (PRIA), available at www.ids.ac.uk/ids/civsoc/final/india/ind1.doc, accessed 17 November 2003.

117. Ibid.

118. Kerala politics over the years has involved a conflict between coalitions clustering around the Communist Party of India (Marxist) and the Congress Party. Lately, with the rise of the Hindu nationalist Bharatiya Janata Party, these distinctions have blurred, with the left parties supporting the Congress in the national elections but opposing it in state politics. Baby John, as a prominent fishery capitalist, was given a place in both right and left wing coalitions because of his power over the mechanized sector, on which Kerala depended for foreign exchange.

119. These committees were the Babu Paul Committee, in 1981, and the Kalawar Committee, in 1984. The Babu Paul Committee made several recommendations but could not reach a unanimous decision about a trawl ban. A subsection of the committee, however, submitted a dissenting report that recommended the cessation of trawling during the monsoon season.

When the Kalawar Committee met, it did not agree to a total monsoon ban on trawling, either, but it did call for reducing the number of mechanized boats. See Kalawar Report (Trivandrum: Government of Kerala Press, 1985), 5.

120. These included the establishment of fish sanctuaries at important spawning places and the banning of purse-seining along the coast. Purse-seining is a method of fishing in which a long rectangular net with a buoyant top and weighted bottom is dropped into the water to surround a school of fish, usually at the surface.

121. Aerthayil, *Fishworkers' Movement in Kerala,* 68.

122. Ibid., 76.

123. Because of their need for infrastructure such as transport and storage, a lot of the shrimp- and export-oriented fishing fleets, which employed large numbers of people, were clustered around harbors such as Neendakara, which had such facilities. Fishery capitalists pointed out that they had agreed with the ban in other places, where mechanized and artisanal boats both plied. But near areas like Neendakara, there were fewer artisanal boats, they claimed, and thus fewer chances for conflict between trawlers and artisanal fishers. Legislative success foundered on faulty implementation, and the debate over the ban remained unresolved.

124. John Kurien, "Ruining the Commons and the Responses of the Commoners: Coastal Overfishing and Fishworkers: Actions in Kerala State, India," in *Grass Roots Environmental Action*, ed. D. Ghai and J. Vivian (London: Routledge, 1992), 249.

125. There was also a 1992 Silas Committee, which recommended that artisanal fishers be given an exclusive fishing zone. For more on these committees, see V. Vijayan, L. Edwin, and K. Ravindran, "Conservation and Management of Marine Fishery Resources of Kerala State, India," *Naga: The ICLARM Quarterly* 23, no. 3 (July–September 2000): 6–9, available at www.worldfishcenter.org/Naga/feature2.pdf, accessed 10 January 2006.

126. In the past the Food and Agriculture Organization of the United Nations had been involved in Indian fisheries as a supporter of fishworkers via the Bay of Bengal Program, an intergovernmental program which supports sustainable fisheries development in the Bay of Bengal.

127. The government issued seventeen licenses and signed agreements for three joint ventures with foreign companies (Aerthayil, *Fishworkers' Movement in Kerala,* 105). Under these agreements, the foreign company would own a 49 percent share of an Indian company but would bring in all of the investment. Therefore, while the resulting enterprises may have been joint ventures in theory, in practice they were foreign ventures. The policy also allowed the vessels to transfer their catch on the high seas, thereby avoiding reporting of the catch and Indian laws against overfishing. The latest available data, from 1995, indicate that at that time 180 joint venture vessels, forty chartered vessels, and 180 Indian-owned vessels were operating in India's Exclusive Economic Zone, according to the United Nations Law of the Sea, the coastal state has sovereign right to explore, exploit, conserve and manage the natural resources. See S.K. Das, *Recent Policy Initiatives on Promotion of Deep Sea Fishing Industry* (New Delhi: Government of India, 1995), cited in T.S. D'cruz, *Artisanal Deep-Sea Fisheries: Prospects and Problems* (Trivandrum: Kerala Research Programme on Local Level Development, Centre for Development Studies, 2001), 22.

128. These centers included Vishakhapatnam, in Andhra; Gujarat, where intensive factory fishing had begun; Orissa, where shrimp aquaculture had been encouraged; and Madras, Bombay, and Calcutta, which had large fish markets.

129. The strikes occurred on 4 February 1994, and 23–24 November 1994. For details, see Aerthayil, *Fishworkers' Movement in Kerala,* 107.

130. This committee was the Murari Committee. It was initially composed solely of officials, but after pressure from NFACAJV the government expanded it to include a diverse group of forty-one people, including bureaucrats, experts, politicians, activists, and representatives from the fishing communities. In 1996 the Committee presented twenty-one recommendations— many of which came about not so much because of NFF protests as because the government was incurring huge losses on the subsidies given to joint ventures.

131. Mukul Sharma, "Fishworkers' Struggle: Resources of Hope," *Labour File* 2, nos. 7 and 8 (1996): 6.

132. Up to this point, it had failed to formulate a comprehensive marine and fishing policy, even though the central government left the enactment and enforcement of national policy up to the individual states.

133. Government of Kerala, *Fisheries Development and Management Policy* (Trivandrum: Government of Kerala, 1993).

134. The bulk of the analysis in this section draws on interviews conducted by Kavita Philip in 2002. In addition, in February 2004, Antonyto Paul conducted a follow-up interview with M.S. James, the general secretary of the Kollam District Trawlers Association. These interviews were designed to address the Carnegie Council project's research questions, although they could not be conducted over the course of four years because the first interviews were conducted late in the project. There were fourteen interviews in all, ranging from thirty minutes to three hours long. The Marianad fishers and women members of the fishworkers movement were interviewed in groups of several people each. We did not interview fish processors, fisheries entrepreneurs and corporations, and fish consumers, whose views we have assumed to be reflected in the official perspective that, because of economies of scale, the people of Kerala stand to gain more than they lose from large-scale fishing operations. The results of the interviews were consistent with the findings of field researchers who interviewed Kerala fishers during the early years of the project (1998–99); some of those interviews are also included here and referenced as such in the footnotes. This section thus relies on intensive research visits and activist publications more than on long-term, locally based participant observation.

135. The major national trade unions all have political party affiliations; for example, the CITU, cited here, is affiliated with the Communist Party of India (Marxist).

136. Artificial reefs, which attract fish, are constructed of objects made by humans, such as wood posts or old tires.

137. In southern India it is common to use only their given name; interview respondents generally did not give a surname.

138. Chandrika Parmar and Shiv Visvanathan, "India Team Report 2000" (paper on file with the Carnegie Council on Ethics and International Affairs, New York), 20.

139. Ibid., 19–20.

140. By "village society" Vivekanandan means the village-level cooperatives established in Kerala in the 1960s and 1970s.

141. The debate has continued into the early twenty-first century, involving critiques of the notion of environmental stewardship, the international role of artisanal and small-scale fishers in global fisheries markets, the nature of "sustainability" certification by the independent accreditation certifying firms, and the role of developing countries in multinational resource management.

142. Aliou Sall, Michael Belliveau, and Nalini Nayak, *Conversations: A Trialogue on Power, Intervention and Organization in Fisheries* (Chennai: ICSF, 2002), 114–15.

143. Ibid.

144. Here, Nayak is referring to widespread domestic violence, malnutrition, marginalization from artisanal fishing practices, and other forms of abuse and discrimination that women fishworkers were subjected to.

145. By "ecological citizenship" we mean a bundle of rights and responsibilities to nature that becomes a central feature of the relations of citizens with the state.

146. Frank Alcock, "Scale Conflict and Sectoral Crisis: The Fisheries Development Dilemma," in *Global Environmental Change and the Nation State,* ed. Frank Biermann, Rainer Brohm, and Klaus Dingwerth (Potsdam: Potsdam Institute for Climate Research, 2002), 448.

147. In Kerala, the People's Science Movement has been led by the Kerala Sastra Sahitya Parishad, a grassroots organization that has campaigned effectively against ecologically destructive projects such as the Silent Alley hydropower project.

The United States:
A Foreword

Keith Kloor

The historian Samuel Hayes has written that the "environmental drive in modern society stems from new human values about what people want in their lives."[1] In America, this drive has been discernible since the late 19th century, when technological advances and the industrial economy led to markedly improved living standards, giving birth to a leisure class. As recreational activities like hunting, fishing, and hiking became popular, especially with affluent urbanites in rapidly expanding cities who sought to reconnect with the country's rural heritage, this new leisure class soon became concerned about overexploitation of the country's forests and wildlife, and began advancing a philosophy of "conservation," the sustainable use of natural resources. The federal government, prompted by the growing trend toward outdoor leisure pursuits, started establishing national parks and wildlife refuges in the early decades of the twentieth century. Meanwhile, the conservation ethic was vigorously incorporated into public policies after being strongly embraced by President Theodore Roosevelt (an avid outdoorsman) and other government officials.

By the middle of the twentieth century, as the country grew more prosperous, the environmental drive expanded to include wilderness preservation, a nature-centric movement that advocated setting aside forests and mountains for their aesthetic beauty and ecological properties. This cause, championed by many national environmental groups whose memberships consisted largely of affluent whites, led to the 1964 Wilderness Act, a federal statute that defined wildernesses as areas where "man is a visitor who does not remain" and set aside millions of acres as nature sanctuaries.

The late 1960s saw the creation of another strand of environmentalism, as increasing evidence of pollution caught America's attention and people started linking public health to environmental quality. Decades of steady modernization and unbridled economic growth had brought higher-paying jobs and material comforts to a growing middle class; many now expected clean air and water and a healthy environment for their children. But cities, beaches, and parks had become intolerably foul as a result of industrial waste and car exhaust. In addition, wildlife began dying off because of indiscriminate spraying of pesticides across the land. Several infamous incidents from this era crystallized the view of generalized environmental decay: a river in Cleveland burst into flames after chemicals dumped into its water ignited, for example, and the coast of Santa Barbara, California, was blackened by an oil spill.

New environmental groups that emerged to address these alarming problems mobilized average citizens, who had already become increasingly politicized by societal changes and the controversial Vietnam War. On April 22, 1970, 20 million Americans took to the streets around the nation to demonstrate their concerns about the environment and their health. Many participated in volunteer trash cleanups, planted trees, and protested in front of the offices of major oil companies. This event, now referred to as Earth Day 1, marked the arrival of the contemporary environmental movement, which merged ecological concerns with those of human health—a connection later popularly described as the "web of life."

Politicians quickly got the message. In a burst of activity the U.S. Congress enacted a raft of landmark environmental laws that President Richard Nixon said would "help repair the damage we have done to our air, to our water, and to our land." New federal agencies were created to enforce the new laws and carry out further environmental protections.

Since then, nature appreciation, ecological awareness, and pollution prevention have formed the core tenets of mainstream environmentalism in America. It is a movement whose values have been expressed on both the personal and political levels, influencing individual habits (as in recycling) and public policy (in measures ranging from the safeguarding of endangered species to the regulation of industrial pollution). In recent years, the environmental movement has widened its purview to include everyday quality-of-life issues. Middle-class Americans, for example, have become distressed by the increasing "sprawl" in their communities—poorly planned housing and commercial developments that have congested their highways with traffic and eaten up treasured open space. The disenchantment is so widespread that many have been moving to less crowded states where open space is still abundant and where they can enjoy greater exposure to nature, a deeply embedded "environmental drive."

Still, for all its broad appeal, environmentalism has failed to develop a platform that can unify conservationists and social justice advocates. Instead the movement has become balkanized into competing groups with competing messages: some groups continue to focus their efforts largely on preserving nature, while others emphasize the dangers of environmental contaminants to human communities. To a large degree, this schism reflects the competing groups' constituencies and their differing agendas. The nature groups are mostly national in scope, and their members are still mainly affluent whites who care about issues like biodiversity and sustainable development. The groups most concerned with pollution are localized, and often based in low-income, minority neighborhoods, where the residents live in close proximity to factories or dumps (and sometimes both).

If it is true, as Hayes asserts, that the country's "environmental drive" reflects what Americans "want in their lives," then it would appear that America today has two distinctly separate sets of environmental values—one that is expressed in ecological terms, the other in human health terms. The U.S. environmental movement splits along this divide not because of disagreement over these two environmental values but because they have been treated unequally on the political and policy levels.

The two case studies in this chapter bear this view out. One covers a small town in the Louisiana bayou where over a million barrels of oil field waste were dumped in pits, sickening the residents. The other involves the Arizona desert, where the world's largest "sustainable" housing project was built with energy-saving and water-conserving features.

The common thread between the two cases is energy. One is about the idealistic mission of saving it; the other is about its toxic byproducts and the people who have to live with them. The Tucson study exposes the perverse ironies within one dominant school of environmentalism, in that it shows how some popular environmental values and projects are divorced from the problems they purport to address. Similarly, the Louisiana study exposes serious gaps within the social-justice-oriented environmentalism that has arisen in recent decades, and the fact that these health-related environmental values have not included recognition of a certain class of people and the environmental problems they have faced.

Concerns over oil scarcity and global warming are triggering a new wave of angst over energy-related issues in the United States today. The Arizona and Louisiana case studies presented in the chapter that follows are instructive lessons for the larger debate over energy—that is, how to both conserve it and produce it. The first step is to revisit key policies from 1980 that, coincidentally, set the stage for the unfolding events in both case studies. This was the year the U.S. Congress passed a law protecting a hundred million remote acres in Alaska from development, including 19.6 million acres officially designated as the Arctic National Wildlife Refuge. The law, a reflection of continuing support for wilderness and biological preserves, a hallmark of the American environmental movement, closed the refuge, which contains oil reserves under its coastal plain, to oil and gas exploration. In ensuing years, the refuge would become an iconic symbol for environmentalists, who have periodically battled attempts by oil companies and their supporters to open it to exploration.

In 1980, Congress also approved an amendment exempting oil field waste from being regulated as a hazardous substance under the Resource Conservation and Recovery Act (RCRA), passed in 1976. That act had required that the transportation and disposal of industrial hazardous wastes be tracked and monitored. In addition to petroleum, oil drilling produces a watery soup of toxic chemicals, such as arsenic, lead, mercury, hydrogen sulfide, and benzene, but the petroleum industry argued that the health effects of such waste were unclear and that federal regulations would be too costly to their operations and even slow down the domestic production of oil. Their lobbying won the day, and in some states, like oil- and gas-rich Louisiana, where officials have historically exercised lax oversight of industry, indiscriminate dumping of oil field waste in one community would go on unchecked for years.

Also in 1980 this same Congress created a historic environmental program, known as Superfund, to clean up abandoned toxic waste sites around the country. Sites with oil field wastes, notably, were not included. Nonetheless, the Superfund law gave impetus to a grassroots movement already underway that was known as the "anti-toxics" campaign—community groups fighting the disposal of toxic waste in their neighborhoods. The issue of toxic waste as a health concern had exploded into public view a few years earlier, when a group of outraged mothers in the Love Canal section of Buffalo, learned that their community had been built atop a 20,000-ton chemical waste dump, leading to a spate of strange, unexplained illnesses among residents. One resident in particular, Lois Gibbs, won national fame for leading her fellow residents in the search for accountability; she would go on to establish an effective network of community groups engaged in similar battles around the country, a precursor to the grassroots environmental justice movement that emerged in the 1990s, which has sought to remedy the disproportionate placement of landfills, toxic waste sites, and factories in minority communities.

Meanwhile, in the Arizona desert, 1980 was the year that a group of university researchers, solar power advocates, and eco-friendly developers sketched out their vision for the Tucson Solar Village, an environmentally sustainable community that was to supply all its energy needs through solar power. During the sixteen years that passed before the idea took root, the solar component was deemphasized, and the building design was remodeled in New Urbanist fashion, as a pedestrian-friendly townscape that encouraged social interaction and neighborhood ties, civic virtues that, many Americans were beginning to feel, had been lost with the onset of sprawl. The ecologically conscious residents who would move here came because of their desire to live more harmoniously with nature and be part of a healthy, vibrant community.

In 1980, as all these events started to play out, the two faces of American environmentalism were becoming increasingly distinct from each other: upwardly mobile, white Americans were searching for a higher quality of life that included a deeper connection with nature, while less economically advantaged Americans in blue-collar towns, inner cities, and backwater bayous were coming to grips with the fact that society's waste products were now contaminating their community.

The paired studies in this chapter illustrate those two faces of American environmentalism—how they were expressed on an individual and public policy level, as well as how their differing environmental values shaped the outcomes of the two cases.

Note

1. Samuel P. Hayes, *A History of Environmental Politics Since 1945* (Pittsburgh: University of Pittsburgh Press, 2000), 22.

The Sonoran Desert and Grand Bois, United States

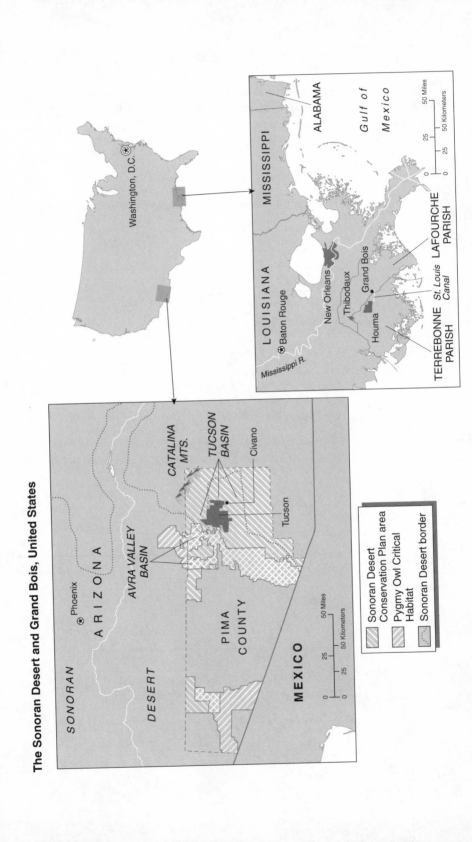

4

Two Faces of American Environmentalism

The Quest for Justice in Southern Louisiana and Sustainability in the Sonoran Desert

David Jenkins, Joanne Bauer, Scott Bruton, Diane Austin, and Thomas McGuire*

In an important sense, the subjects of this chapter's two case studies—toxic oilfield waste in southern Louisiana and diminishing water supplies in the Sonoran Desert of Arizona—are linked. The U.S. economy in the twentieth century was founded on cheap supplies of energy, mostly derived from fossil fuels. Keeping the cheap energy flowing required lax governmental regulation—or so the oil and gas industry argued, and Congress concurred. The cost has been damaged ecosystems and the impaired health of people in places like southern Louisiana. Cheap energy supplies make it possible, among other things, to pump tremendous amounts of water from underground sources and to make rivers flow uphill. Without cheap supplies of energy, the southern Arizona city of Tucson would not have been able to pump millions of acre-feet of groundwater for municipal purposes, nor would the U.S. Bureau of Reclamation have been able to build a system to pump Colorado River water deep into the Sonoran Desert in an attempt to stem the flow of precious groundwater into Tucson's faucets and toilets. Oilfield waste in Louisiana and real estate development in the Sonoran Desert are thus linked through the extraction and use of cheap energy, but the link is not reflected in the environmental values of either place.

The discovery and production of fossil fuels, with myriad environmental effects, and the development of water sources, with a different set of environmental effects, result from government policies that seek to maximize the use of a valued resource. Local environmental values do not always or even frequently inform such policies, especially when they are at odds with the instrumental rationality of the state. In outlining the Bush administration's 2001 energy policy, Vice President Dick Cheney placed personal values in opposition to public policy. "The aim [of the energy policy] is efficiency, not austerity," he said. "Conservation may be a sign of personal virtue, but it is not a sufficient basis for a sound, comprehensive energy policy." Why not? What keeps conservation, as a personal or social virtue, from becoming the basis of energy policy? As many commentators have pointed out, conservation measures such as raising the fuel economy standards for light trucks would save more oil than can be extracted from beneath currently protected areas such as the Arctic National Wildlife Refuge in Alaska—an area the Bush administration would like to see developed as an oil source.[1]

Cheney's statement is emblematic of a disjuncture in American society between environmental values and policies that have environmental effects. As the following case studies show, the disjuncture can be found in diverse social contexts. It is also not unique to the current federal administration. In fact, it may well be characteristic of American culture.

This chapter attempts to uncover some of the relationships between environmental values and policy in the United States and to understand why the disjuncture between them persists. The chapter is divided into three sections. The first examines the policies, practices, and effects of oilfield waste disposal, focusing on Grand Bois, a tiny community of three hundred Houma Indians and Cajuns in southern Louisiana. The second section examines attempts to develop an alternative environmentally sustainable housing complex, known as Civano and based on "traditional" community ideals, in the rapidly growing desert city of Tucson, Arizona, whose population now stands at more than 830,000. The Louisiana case explores problems associated with extreme pollution. The Arizona case explores attempts to sustain economic and population growth despite the constraints of a limited and rapidly diminishing water supply. Both cases indicate that local environmental values are complex and do not always coincide with or inform the government's environmental policies. The concluding section discusses the relationship between values and environmental policy as illuminated by the two case studies.

Each case study begins with a description of the environmental, sociocultural, and political contexts of the case. The focus then turns to the lived experiences of people in southern Louisiana and the Sonoran Desert region of Arizona, with special attention placed on how residents interact with and talk about their environments and how their experiences and perceptions relate to environmental policies. The study methods include interviews, observation, document reviews, a survey, and community mapping.[2] Two research teams consisting of faculty members and graduate students from the Bureau of Applied Research in Anthropology at the University of Arizona conducted most of the research.[3] We reviewed documents appropriate to each study, including planning documents, minutes of meetings, newspaper archives, court documents, legislative histories, publications of the oil and gas industry, and scientific papers. We talked with residents in their homes, on their front porches, in their gardens and orchards, and at their workplaces; we observed them at informal local gatherings; and we shared meals and drinks with them. We attended public hearings, city and advisory council meetings, and other sessions where residents described, and confronted others about, their situations; we also visited schools and community centers and took formal and informal community tours. Residents were not our only source of information, however. We also talked with local and state officials, scientists, doctors, religious leaders, architects, planners, university professors, builders, bureaucrats, and activists, all of whom influenced and were influenced by the residents.

During our onsite research period, from the summer of 1999 through the spring of 2001, changes were occurring in the communities under study—in Civano in particular, residents moved in or out, houses were built or torn down, and research reports were issued and discussed. In both cases, some residents resorted to lawsuits when they were ignored in other venues. The methodology that allowed the researchers to monitor and adapt the study to pay attention to and analyze these changes is called processual ethnography. Following this approach, the case studies are organized chronologically and residents' thoughts and concerns are described at more than one point in time, capturing how they perceived the evolving situations.

It is important to note, therefore, that these cases are not static and that, even taken together, they are not representative of all American communities. In fact, it could be said that both cases represent relatively extreme versions of environmental justice and conservation efforts in the United States. Louisiana is widely regarded as a democratic backwater, where big business has a privileged seat in the halls of government and participation by ordinary citizens in public policy is constrained. In fact, Grand Bois sits in the region that is infamously dubbed "cancer alley." Because of the nature of the contamination at Grand Bois—toxic oilfield waste, which American lawmakers exempted from hazardous waste laws—the problem eluded even the environmental justice movement. Similarly, in the environmentally sensitive desert region of Arizona the urgency of containing sprawl is greater than in many other cities, as is the public resistance to anti-sprawl measures because of the continuing draw of the region's temperate climate and breathtaking scenery for businesses and families.

Despite their differences, the cases involve a set of overlapping concerns that can help us draw a composite picture of how people live within and interact with their environments. These concerns involve energy production and use, population growth and change, the just distribution of risks and benefits, the sway of the market, and a litigious culture (in both cases, residents resorted to the courts when they were ignored in other venues). Both cases also concern the relationships between citizens and their local, state, and federal governments, and the tensions that arise from the way in which those governments allocate responsibility for the environment among themselves. Finally, both cases involve the interactions of individual communities with the markets (national and international) that they depend upon and serve. In this sense the two cases, taken together, provide a window on the concerns and conflicts that underlie the circumstances in which many Americans find themselves at the start of the twenty-first century.

Oilfield Waste Pollution in Southern Louisiana

In southern Louisiana, the oil and gas industry is ubiquitous. The region is full of shipyards, ports, service and supply companies, tugs pushing barges up and down the bayous, and trucks speeding up and down the highways carrying oil and related products. Local residents quote the price of a barrel of oil the way Midwestern farmers talk about corn prices.

The benefits to the local economy of the oil and gas industry are clear to many Louisiana residents; the risks to health and ecosystem are less so. Although the region is rich in environmental "goods" (natural resources), oil exploration has produced considerable environmental "bads" (pollution and waste byproducts). Waste from federally owned offshore oilfields can contain high levels of naturally occurring radioactive material, heavy metals, and volatile liquid hydrocarbons such as benzene and naphthalene. This waste is brought back on land and disposed of in open waste pits or through underground injection. Oil and gas waste regulation has lagged decades behind the scientific evidence of the hazards posed by oilfield waste. Even now, U.S. state and federal laws classify oilfield waste as nonhazardous, and ecosystems and human communities in states such as Louisiana have suffered the consequences.

The regulation of the oil industry in Louisiana takes place within a social context that includes long-standing political, economic, and social inequality. This is acutely evident in the case of Grand Bois, a tiny community of three hundred Houma Indians and Cajuns about sixty miles southwest of New Orleans. The residents of Grand Bois are poor and undereducated, and have long confronted social, economic, and political barriers in the race-conscious American South. The Houmas and Cajuns first moved into the region in the eighteenth century, and they survived well into the twentieth by lumberjacking, trapping, and fishing, including shrimping. In the 1950s the shrimping industry began to decline, and by the 1970s oilfields and related service companies had begun to dominate the local economy. Houmas and Cajuns had little choice but to take the new jobs, thus intertwining their fate with that of the oil industry.

Almost as soon as the Houmas and Cajuns began working in the oil industry, the industry began dumping oilfield waste from all over Louisiana—and even from neighboring states—in Grand Bois. The first waste pit was dug in the mid-1970s. From then until the mid-1990s the number of waste pits grew rapidly. By 1994, the industry was dumping some 1.4 million barrels of oilfield waste annually into the Grand Bois pits.[4] At first, leakage from the pits caused the local community little concern. During the 1980s and 1990s, however, scientific evidence of rising levels of cancer in southern Louisiana communities (those near the petrochemical plants along the Mississippi River) came to light.[5] Gradually some Grand Bois residents began to connect the nearby open oilfield waste pits and the rising incidence of the disease. After one particularly noxious waste shipment in 1994, the citizens of Grand Bois decided to fight for their health and their land. The dramatic story of their efforts to ban oilfield waste from their community attracted national attention and was instrumental in effecting changes in the state's environmental policy. More important for our purposes here, however, the case of Grand Bois offers a clear example of environmental values in the making. In particular it demonstrates the potential for community action and the emergence of individual actors who can bring social change regardless of their socioeconomic status. The case also demonstrates how citizens' attitudes toward the environment, their economic security, and the state changed as they struggled to make sense of the changes around them following an environmental crisis.

In the account that follows, we tease out and analyze the values of different actors:

Cajun and Houma residents, newcomers, newspaper and television reporters, scientists, state courts, and local, state, and national policy makers. We chart the actions of these stakeholders—and how they justify them—as they attempt to change or maintain the status quo in a situation of progressive poisoning of the environment and local residents. We show how powerful business interests wield their power and how, even after minor victories, the community members remain powerless in its face. Before turning to the actions and reactions of the stakeholders, however, we will examine just how Grand Bois got into its predicament, and in particular, why oilfield wastes were considered nonhazardous in the first place. The history of federal and state regulation of the oil industry is a long and frustrating one, but it is crucial for understanding what happened to the people of Grand Bois.

The History of Hazardous Waste Regulation

Federal Laws and the RCRA Exemption

The debate over how to define hazardous waste, what to do with it, and how to measure its effects on the health of both environments and people was one of the most extensive national environmental debates of the last quarter of the twentieth century. At the federal level, this debate produced the1976 Resource Conservation and Recovery Act (RCRA), which amended the 1965 Solid Waste Disposal Act. RCRA required businesses to track and control hazardous waste from its point of origin through transportation, treatment, storage, and eventual disposal. Its main goals were to protect public health and the environment from improper hazardous waste disposal. Yet in 1980 Congress caused a major controversy by exempting from the act "drilling fluids, produced waters, and other wastes associated with the exploration, development, or production of crude oil or natural gas or geothermal energy."[6]

Industry arguments had convinced members of Congress that because it was hard to determine the contents of oilfield waste, the enormous volume of such waste would overwhelm the regulatory process. In fact, produced water—one of the major constituents of oilfield waste by volume—had already been the subject of considerable scientific investigation, especially in the Gulf Coast field.[7] Produced water is salty wastewater that is brought to the surface during oil and natural gas drilling. Although the water is treated before release, it still contains traces of oil, salt, organic compounds, heavy metals, and other toxic materials. Early studies of produced water focused on the effects of high salt content on water supplies and soils, the presence of hydrocarbons in bottom sediments near produced water outfalls, and the level of radioactivity, specifically of radium isotopes, in produced water.[8] With indications of the toxicity of produced water, Congress directed the Environmental Protection Agency (EPA) to conduct further studies on whether produced water and associated wastes should be included under the 1976 Act. In the meantime, Congress deferred regulation of oilfield waste to state authority and its discharge to combined state and federal (EPA) authority under existing laws.

The EPA, which repeatedly delayed reporting on the further studies, was finally goaded into action by a lawsuit in 1987; it issued a draft of its three-volume report in March and the final version in December. The EPA had found organic and inorganic pollutants in produced water at levels one hundred times higher than the EPA health-based standards—a finding that caused the agency some "potential concern." Yet in the final report the EPA concluded that wastes from oil and gas exploration and extraction should not be regulated under RCRA, a conclusion that contradicted the conclusions of the draft report. The agency asserted, "The presence of constituents in concentrations exceeding health- or environment-based standards does not necessarily mean that these wastes pose significant risk to human health and the environment." Not coincidentally, the final report also noted the high cost to industry of regulating the oilfield waste—between one billion and 6.7 billion dollars a year—a cost that would reduce domestic oil production by as much as 12 percent.[9]

In spite of its failure to recommend regulation, the EPA continued to monitor oilfield waste. In 1988, the agency estimated that 10 to 70 percent of large volume oilfield waste (produced water, drilling fluids, and drilling cuttings) oilfield and 40 to 60 percent of the associated waste stream (completion fluids, production storage tank sludge, produced oily sands and solids, production pit sludge, and washout water and sludge from tank cleaning operations) would be classified as hazardous if the special exemption were removed.[10] Such reports encouraged national environmental and citizens' groups to bond together to change the regulatory structure.[11] In October 1990, for example, representatives of seventeen environmental, public interest, and citizens' groups met at the offices of the National Audubon Society in Washington, D.C., and created the National Citizen's Network on Oil and Gas Wastes.[12] The group agreed to "develop, draft, finalize, and promote a citizens' consensus position for regulating oil and gas wastes under federal laws," formed platform and public outreach action groups, and shared information such as the damage case reports gathered during the EPA study. In 1991, this group tried to bring oil and gas wastes under federal law. Members worked with an Ohio member of Congress to draft and support the introduction of the Oil and Natural Gas Exploration and Production Waste Management Improvement Act and lobbied Congress in an effort to persuade lawmakers to abolish RCRA's exemption for oilfield wastes.

Despite their efforts and those of other national groups, the oil and gas exemption emerged unscathed, and regulation of oilfield waste remained in the hands of the individual states. State agencies had—indeed, still have today—the option of imposing their own requirements on oil and gas drilling firms operating within their borders. Alabama law, for example, forbade the disposal of waste with high benzene content; Louisiana regulations did not—a fact that set the stage for the crisis at Grand Bois.

State Control of Oil and Gas Production

The major oil- and gas-producing states are concentrated in the south and the west—regions recognized for their belief in states' rights, especially on natural resource issues. U.S. oil and gas production policies thus evolved under the strong influence of regionalism and states' rights ideologies. The ongoing and deliberate introduction of "just enough" state and interstate controls has helped forestall national regulation of oil production.

In Louisiana the Department of Conservation began to regulate the drilling and production of oil and gas in 1939 through Statewide Order No. 29-B. Common scientific knowledge extending back at least to the early part of that decade indicated that produced water contained much more than salt. Nevertheless, the order referred to the waste as "brine" and "salt waters." The few regulations that were developed subsequently focused on protecting public health and flora and fauna by preventing highly saline discharges into freshwater lakes and streams. Louisiana's coastal waters were largely excluded from the regulations, and issues other than salinity were not mentioned. At first, this emphasis on salinity may have resulted from ignorance, but in later years it was a primary means of silencing the concerns of the public and legislators. Not until the 1980s did the state finally issue a series of comprehensive rules and regulations on oilfield waste, including those related to the design and construction of waste pits, groundwater monitoring, mandated testing and sampling of pit contents, and permits for produced water discharges.[13] In addition, a 1986 regulation required levees to be built around waste pits at drilling sites located within inland tidal waters, lakes bounded by the Gulf of Mexico, or saltwater marshes. Yet neither pit liners nor specific levee heights were mentioned. As one state environmental official noted facetiously, Louisiana's toxic oilfield waste pits would never lack sufficient capacity: As waste pits filled, storms periodically flushed them out [I-241].[14]

In 1988, Buddy Roemer was elected governor of Louisiana, and the environment finally became a priority. A panel he appointed concluded that Louisiana had the poorest environmental program of any "highly industrialized state" and recommended moving the regulation of oilfield waste from the Department of Natural Resources (DNR) to the Department of Environmental Quality (DEQ).[15] The DNR was responsible for both promoting and regulating the oil industry in Louisiana—a situation that Paul Templet, then secretary of the Louisiana DEQ, argues was a conflict of interest.[16] The move never took place, anyway. Roemer tested the waters by talking with legislators about the proposed move, and found it dead on arrival. The oil and gas industry's considerable clout in the Louisiana legislature translated into a strong preference among legislators for regulatory powers to remain with the Department of Natural Resources, where the environment would remain a secondary concern. Consequently, the DEQ was given only a minor role in regulation.[17]

In spite of this failure to change the way oilfield waste was regulated, the governor did move quickly on many environmental issues, including recycling, air pollution, and industrial emissions. Through meetings with grassroots, trade, and environmental organizations, state administrators galvanized public support. The speed with which they did so indicates that many citizens were waiting for a way to express their concerns about environmental protection.[18] One issue that received significant attention was produced water, which was then being discharged into surface waters. Maureen

O'Neill, assistant secretary for Water Resources of the DEQ, noted in an interoffice memo on the topic of produced water: "The more I see the more I am convinced we have a serious problem on our hands."[19]

In addition to older studies on the contents of produced water, there was more recent and increasing evidence that produced water contained naturally occurring radioactive materials (NORM). In 1988, the administrator for the DEQ's nuclear energy division noted a "growing awareness of related problems of the radioactivity content of produced waters and contamination of equipment and facilities in the oil and natural gas production and processing industries."[20] Once oilfield waste was characterized as radioactive, it quickly became a subject of wider public concern. By the end of January 1991, radioactivity had been reported at six thousand oilfield waste sites. By then, Louisiana had enacted laws requiring underground injection of produced water—and "zero discharge" into surface waters.

When it became evident that the Louisiana DEQ was serious about regulating produced water discharges, the U.S. Department of Energy (DOE) became involved in the debate, requesting that the Louisiana DEQ delay action until yet another study could be completed. Louisiana attorney general William Guste objected strongly. Using bold-faced text in all upper-case letters, the attorney general exclaimed:

> It is heresy to suggest that Louisiana should delay action despite the findings of numerous scientific studies—so that one more study can be done. . . . It is an affront to the sensibilities of the people of this state to suggest that we continue to subsidize the oil and gas industry with the ecological integrity of our coastal zone. . . . To rally for no-net-loss of wetlands and at the same time politic for continued unregulation of these toxics laden discharges into our remaining coastal wetlands is Janus-faced.[21]

This rhetoric was a distinct departure from what the federal government was used to hearing from Louisiana officials before the Roemer administration. Despite federal objections, Louisiana's 1990 "zero discharge" rules prevailed.

State support for the rules did not last long, however. After the state had stood up to industry and the U.S. Department of Energy, the zero discharge rule was rescinded a mere two years later by a new Louisiana governor, Edwin W. Edwards, under whose administration those environmental regulations that were not overturned were ignored. Edwards thought that repealing the oil companies' exemption from federal hazardous waste regulations would be "very, very bad and environmentally upside down. Oilfield waste, in almost every instance," he insisted, "is not hazardous."[22] Thus, the window of opportunity for environmental regulation closed as quickly as it had opened.

Even during Roemer's relatively enlightened administration, families in many communities often remained isolated with little help for their concerns coming from the halls of government. It was one thing to participate in public meetings as a way to vent concerns—and quite another to confront pollution in one's immediate environment in the face of powerful industrial forces keen to maintain the status quo. But in Grand Bois, with increasing evidence of poisoning, residents did just that. Grand Bois residents did not rely on scientific studies to convince them that there was a causal relationship between oilfield waste in their community and the dead trees, dead fish, and human health problems that they suddenly were seeing all around them. Without other recourse, they sued the owners of the waste facility. In doing so, however, they entered a system of conflict resolution that demands expert scientific evidence of causality—evidence that, in this case, was nearly impossible to obtain. In order to understand why Grand Bois's residents, sued, we now turn to the subject of who lived in Grand Bois and how oil came into their lives.

The Poisoning of Grand Bois

Houmas, Cajuns, and the Oil Industry

Houma Indians and Acadians, or Cajuns, who were descended from French-Canadians, dominate many of the bayous of southern Louisiana.[23] In years past, the Houma and Cajun people lived off the rich natural resources of the region's swamps, marshes, and coastal waters. Many Cajuns practiced small-scale agriculture. Upon reaching adulthood, children would build their homes on the family land, with each generation moving farther from the bayou and toward the marsh. Most families had their own small cattle herds to provide meat for their families, and the cattle ran free. Those who did not want the cattle on their property had to fence them out.

Arriving as exiles from Mississippi after conflicts between French and British explorers and subsequent eviction by the Tunica from north of Baton Rouge and largely excluded from Louisiana's plantation economy, the Houma Indians settled mainly in several small undeveloped areas along the bayous of south Lafourche and Terrebonne Parishes, where they could trap, fish and hunt undisturbed. The social isolation of the Houmas from mainstream Louisiana society was aggravated by their culture and language. At the same time, as anthropologists have noted, Houmas readily absorbed and became incorporated into other Indian and non-Indian groups. Many Houma settlements were formed by the offspring of Indian and non-Indian unions who retained their Indian identity. Nevertheless, they came to speak French because, like other Louisiana native people, they began incorporating French words into their vocabulary from the time of first contact in the late 1600s. By the turn of the century they had retained little of the Houma language. The local whites' term for the Houmas, "sabines," was derived from the Spanish word for cypress tree or "red-and-white-spotted."[24] Because of their mixed race, they faced further discrimination from white society.

The mixing would also prove a legal liability: in December 1994, the same year as the environmental crisis in Grand Bois, the U.S. Bureau of Indian Affairs (BIA) turned down a United Houma Nations' request for federal recognition as a tribe on the grounds that the seventeen thousand Houmas scattered over seven parishes did not constitute a "community" characterized by close-knit bonds and leaders who address the problems of all members of the tribe. As members of a state-recognized tribe, the Houma residents lacked the legal, political, and social rights available to federally recognized tribes.

The BIA's refusal to grant tribal status to the Houmas reflects the difficulty all Louisiana tribes have had in obtaining legal recognition and access to public services. No Louisiana tribe was federally recognized until 1973. The Houmas began research to obtain recognition in the 1960s. In 1979 they established the United Houma Nation as a nonprofit corporation recognized by the state of Louisiana. The tribe petitioned for federal acknowledgment in 1984. Significantly, because of the tremendous value of the land occupied by members of the United Houma Nation, tribal leaders became concerned that their petition would be denied if they claimed any title to that land and its resources. In 1990, the tribal chairman testified before the U.S. Senate Select Committee on Indian Affairs that the tribe had no land claims against any entity. Nevertheless, eight individual members of the tribe filed a lawsuit against the Louisiana Land and Exploration Company and other landowners, seeking recognition of Indian title to thousands of acres of property in southern Louisiana. That action led attorneys representing the Louisiana Land and Exploration Company to oppose the tribe's petition for acknowledgement and, in letters to Secretary of the Interior Bruce Babbitt, to argue against tribal land claims.[25]

Until recently both Houma and Cajun parents generally saw little value in formal schooling, needed their children to work on their boats and traplines, distrusted outsiders, and maintained languages and cultures distinct from those who came into the area as teachers.[26] Consequently, as in most small towns and rural areas of the South in the first part of the twentieth century, few residents acquired a formal education. Their penchant for practical knowledge and its transmission via mentoring further separated the bayou residents from their northern neighbors. There was also a racial divide: In the black/white world of the American South, there was no official designation for those who considered themselves Indians. The most obvious consequence of Louisiana's failure to acknowledge the native populations was their exclusion from the public schools until the federal government forced desegregation upon an unwilling South in the 1960s.[27]

The bayou residents' lack of education and their geographic, linguistic, and cultural isolation left them vulnerable to those who came to their region in search of natural resources, including oil, timber, and gas. The owners of the timber companies, for example, pressed Grand Bois locals into service to dig the nearby St. Louis Canal as a means of transport for logs. Outside interests controlled local resources such as furs and cypress forests and contributed to ecological damage, but the longest-lasting invasion attended the discovery and exploitation of oil and gas resources. Local custom had long treated marshes and swamps as common property, so when the oil companies came in search of swampland to lease or purchase, the transactions went unnoticed and unchallenged. Language barriers, low literacy, and segregation meant that word of official contracts—such as the 1928 deal that gave the Texas Company exclusive rights to prospect, drill for, and produce oil, gas, and sulfur on properties held by the Louisiana Land and Exploration Company—never reached local residents.[28] Soon stories that land had been taken from residents traveled up and down the bayous by word of mouth. When residents resisted selling their properties and accepted offers to lease them instead, pride coupled with their inability to read made them vulnerable to unscrupulous operators. As a Cajun oil worker recounted:

> One time in Leeville, surveyors came in to open Bayou Blue to the Gulf. They asked around, looking for the landowner, and the people told them to talk to the Indians. There were lots of Indians back there. Louisiana Land and Exploration paid them five cents an acre. They put in lots of oil rigs, and the people got nothing.[29]

Integration of the Houma and Cajun locals into the oil industry began in earnest during the oil boom after the conclusion of World War II. Initially, Houmas and Cajuns were not hired to work on oil-related jobs. Instead, experienced workers were imported from Texas and Oklahoma, and local residents generally avoided interactions with the outsiders. As the growing labor needs of the oil and gas industry brought more workers to southern Louisiana, however, locals, mainly Cajuns, eventually began to work in oil-related jobs, transporting crews and supplies to offshore oil wells. Houma Indians were still excluded from such jobs; the men continued to fish and trap for a living, while Houma women and youth worked in shrimp sheds, until those industries died out.[30]

At first, as Cajun oil workers began to earn money and adopt new lifestyles, the economic disparity between Houmas and Cajuns widened. Yet in the 1970s, when oilfield and related service companies began to dominate the local economy, both Houma and Cajun alike came to depend upon oil for employment. Fabrication yards, drilling mud companies, and pipeline companies were established throughout the area, and Houmas and Cajuns used their boats and trucks to transport people, supplies, and equipment for the offshore industry. Worker shortages led companies on a desperate search for employees. Many youth left school as soon as they could and went straight to the oilfield. Restrictions that had prevented nonwhites from working offshore were lifted.

Around the same time, an open pit appeared in a grove of trees near Grand Bois. Locals didn't know the purpose of the pit, which was on private property, and some remember sneaking onto the property to swim in the pit when they were young. Even after learning that the pit contained oilfield waste, few residents regarded it as dangerous; after all, putting the waste in pits was an improvement over discharging it directly into streams and bayous. One resident of a nearby community stated, "I started [a] protest in Grand Bois—when they dug the first little hole. I told [the Indians] they wouldn't want it, that they were dumping poison in there, but I didn't get any support back then" [I-253]. Before long, however, the surrounding trees began to die, yet residents, who feared retaliation from the non-resident landowner, still did not press city officials to close the pit. Only after a New Orleans reporter exposed the problem in 1980, was the pit shut down. That year, the EPA listed the Grand Bois pit as a potential Superfund site,[31] though in the mid-1990s the site was removed from the list.[32]

By 1980 pits like the one at Grand Bois had caused enough trouble—in the form of wastes flowing out of the pits and contaminating soil and water—that Louisiana revised its gas law to require that oilfield waste be injected back underground, spread on land, or placed in pits with bermed edges. Owners of such pits quickly sold their operations to avoid the expense of compliance with the revised law, and the consolidation of Louisiana's commercial oilfield waste business began. In 1981, near the closed Grand Bois waste pit, Intracoastal Oilfield Fluids began construction of a new facility intended for the underground injection of sludge and residues from oil and gas exploration and production. The firm eventually decided, however, to use open pits, also known as "land treatment cells," instead. Officials at the firm circumvented the new law by claiming that the pits were temporary, designed to hold only mud and salt water from drilling and production operations ("drilling mud") prior to underground injection, and in 1983 the state issued permits to dig three land treatment cells on the site.

The company hired several area residents to help excavate the pits and work at the facility. The facility grew rapidly, and by 1987 contained eighteen pits. The pits were open so that waste could oxygenate, allowing microorganisms to break the hydrocarbons down into water and carbon dioxide. Volatile substances present in the waste, such as benzene and hydrogen sulfide, and gases generated during decomposition simply entered the atmosphere, while heavy metals and radioactive materials sank to the bottom of the pits with the sludge. As the facility expanded, the sludge and other toxic materials that remained in the pits after drying were excavated and used to construct levees around the facility. Once these levees were dry, dust containing heavy metals and radioactive substances began to enter the air.

As the activity at the facility increased, residents began to discuss the facility among themselves. They knew from facility employees eating lunch in Grand Bois when shiploads of toxic materials were coming in. Yet initially they did little to act upon this news. Although many residents believed that the oil and gas industry was causing environmental damage, they also felt there was little they could do about it. As one person remarked, "Sure I'm concerned, but I'm just a little guy who doesn't matter, like a lot of other little guys don't matter" [I-121]. When asked whether the community opposed the facility, one resident replied by describing an earlier battle between the community and parish officials who had sought to open a solid waste landfill in Grand Bois. The community managed to stop the landfill but paid a heavy price—the local government denied public services to Grand Bois for the foreseeable future. This taught the local residents an unforgettable lesson: not to fight with powerful outsiders.

There was also another reason that residents were reluctant to protest. The growth of the facility occurred during the period when the oil and gas downturn of the 1980s was turning into a major bust. Unemployment skyrocketed throughout southern Louisiana. Long-term residents with strong ties to the area were unwilling to leave, returning instead to fishing, hunting, and anything else they could do to make a living. But increased population in the town, new lifestyle expectations, continued shrinkage of fish and shrimp populations, the rapid decline in the fur industry, and eroding wetlands all made a return to a subsistence economy impossible in the long run. There was a mass exodus of residents from southern Louisiana, primarily (but not exclusively) newcomers and the younger members of longtime resident families. One entrepreneur even created bumper stickers that read, "Last one out, please turn out the lights." In this kind of economy, residents saw the waste facility as a needed source of work.

In spite of the drop in drilling in the region, the Grand Bois facility was used more heavily than ever during the 1980s. As the frequency of shipments increased, facility workers began to express their concerns to community residents. By 1989 the pits were filled to capacity, and residents anticipated that the facility would close. But the pits were designed as temporary storage—which meant that the volume of waste was constantly reduced through evaporation, mechanical removal, and seepage. By 1991 the pits were no longer full, and another company, Campbell Wells, Inc., bought the facility. The state office of conservation transferred the operating permits to the new company with no revisions, and the rate of shipments increased again. In 1994, U.S. Liquids bought the operation from Campbell Wells and began to accept particularly noxious Exxon waste.[33] The pits containing this waste were only a few hundred feet from some Grand Bois homes.

During this period, residents occasionally called the state environmental and health departments to report noxious odors and physical symptoms such as headaches and nausea, which they believed were caused by the facility, but state officials gave them little help. The Louisiana DEQ conducted regular inspections and recorded various violations in the operations of the facility, including contamination of nearby bayous, but it told concerned residents that the cells contained only nonhazardous oilfield waste. With little help from officials, residents were left with few sources of information. Even the public Toxic Release Inventory was of no use to them, since exploration and production facilities were not required to report their emissions.[34]

Oilfield Waste and Local Action

The impact of oilfield waste disposal on the Grand Bois community was felt most heavily during ten days of March 1994, when eighty-one trucks driven by men in protective gear arrived to unload Exxon waste from Alabama at the U.S. Liquids facility. Exxon reportedly saved more than $500,000 by disposing of the waste at Grand Bois, oilfield instead of in Alabama where the waste is more tightly regulated.[35] The Alabama shipment affected local people's health in immediate and dramatic ways. Grand Bois resident and community leader Clarice Friloux recalled, "The smell was unreal. . . . It would cut your breath. We watched our kids get off the school bus that day with their T-shirts over their faces."[36] The pollution, she said, "was like a fog," adding that everybody got sick in 1994 when they brought that stuff down from Alabama. We had, well, first we'd feel weak, dizzy, nauseated all the time, stomachache all the time, diarrhea all the time; some would throw up. And I'd get it, it was just as bad, I'd get so nauseated. And when you'd get up in the morning, about an hour later, you'd be ready to hit that bed again. You were sleepy all the time, weak all the time. You'd start washing dishes, you'd have to stop. Your legs were weak, your arms were weak. The burning of the eyes and the nose. You'd start coughing, you couldn't stop coughing. The smell was bad. And when we'd leave from the house to go somewhere—oh man, you needed some fresh air. I didn't know if it would ever be clean. [I-222]

A truck driver who was passing Grand Bois when one shipment was unloaded was sickened by the smell. She felt a burning sensation all over her body, along with chest pains and dizziness. Many local residents reported headaches, burning sensations in their noses, and later, chronic diarrhea, vomiting, fatigue, coughing, and general weakness. These are common symptoms of exposure to hydrogen sulfide, which in extreme cases, can cause severe neurological dysfunction. Yet, while LDEQ inspectors did take air samples at the time of the dumping, they did not look for hydrogen sulfide because the LDEQ had specifically instructed them not to test for the compound.[37]

Eventually, a deluge of citizen phone calls to state offices led the sheriff's department to stop the trucks and examine their shipping records, which indicated that benzene and other highly toxic materials were being transported and released in the open cells. But such wastes, which came from a cleanup of natural gas facilities in Alabama, were defined as nonhazardous under Louisiana law, and no citations were issued. To avoid further public attention, however, Exxon rerouted the remaining trucks to another waste facility in Mermentau, Louisiana (approximately 155 miles northwest of Grand Bois). A Grand Bois resident contacted local media, and the story of the rerouting was published in the *Baton Rouge Advocate* the following day.

Residents began to talk to one another about the situation. The March events and increasing media attention fueled community concern and led members of the community to form the Grand Bois Citizens Committee which began a petition drive to shut down the waste facility. Community members constructed and displayed signs denouncing the facility and warning passing motorists that they were being exposed to toxic fumes. Though these efforts had little immediate effect, they did catch the attention of people outside the community. As a result, residents came into contact with scientists and others experienced in dealing with the problems of oilfield waste. They met, for example, Wilma Subra, a Louisiana environmental chemist who was a leader in the national struggle to regulate oilfield wastes, and who provided the group with information about the chemical composition of oilfield waste in an effort to toughen state environmental regulation of the waste. The director of Catholic Social Services, an office of the Diocese of Houma-Thibodaux that provides social services to the community, also played an important role, first by providing envelopes and stamps so that residents could mail letters to local, state, and federal officials and then by organizing community meetings to compose letters for those who could not read or write, and to translate letters for those who spoke and wrote in French. Working through her networks, the director eventually involved priests, a bishop, the sheriff's department, and some state politicians in the effort to shut down the Grand Bois disposal facility.

When state officials still refused to act, Louisiana lawyers and other advocates with whom Grand Bois residents consulted advised them to file a lawsuit. In April 1994, a young, Mississippi-born attorney, Gladstone Jones III, began what was to become a six-year ordeal. On behalf of nine named individuals and all persons residing in the immediate vicinity of the facility, he filed a class action suit against the waste facility.[38] Several months later, he amended the suit to include the facility owners (U.S. Liquids and Campbell Wells) and Exxon as defendants. The judge broke the class action suit down into thirty separate suits of ten plaintiffs each, a move that residents feared would prolong the litigation and wear them down.[39]

Following the March 1994 events and throughout the trials, Grand Bois residents set out to educate themselves about oilfield waste. They learned more about its chemical composition, and they wrote out associated health effects longhand on cards, which they distributed around the community. They also paid close attention when people exhibited symptoms, and they talked increasingly with scientists, health specialists, medical professionals, and activists, some of whom called Grand Bois to offer assistance. Grand Bois locals became convinced that they were in danger. In 1995 and 1996, residents urged the state environmental quality department to restrict fishing in the bayous and to post warning signs near the facility. Although the state ignored these requests, residents stopped fishing near the facility.

Grand Bois residents also tried to effect change through their elected officials. Parish officials took residents to the state capital to meet with Governor Edwin Edwards and officials from the Department of Environmental Quality. The residents showed the state officials the bill of lading from the 1994 waste shipment, which indicated the presence of benzene, and the governor promised to increase surveillance and shut down the facility if any hazardous materials were found there. He left office in 1996 without having taken any action, however. In 1997, then state Senator Michael Robichaux, whose district included Grand Bois, introduced several bills aimed at getting the facility shut down by increasing the mandatory buffer zone around oilfield waste sites and requiring the relocation of facilities, such as the one at Grand Bois, that were too close to residents' homes. During the public hearings on the bills, Grand Bois residents traveled to the state capital and told their stories again and again. Wilma Subra, other scientists, representatives from the Tulane Environmental Law Clinic, and medical professionals from Louisiana State University's Occupational Toxicology Outreach Program all testified in support of the bills.[40] The oil and gas lobby, however, mounted a fierce opposition, and the bills were defeated.

In 1996 a CBS news correspondent contacted residents for a program about oilfield waste. The show, which focused on Grand Bois, was delayed and postponed several times, reflecting the low priority accorded to waste issues by both the media and the public. Finally, on December 23, 1997, CBS aired the one-hour program, *Investiga-*

tive Reports: Town Under Siege. In it, U.S. Environmental Protection Agency administrator Carol Browner attributed the oilfield waste exemption in federal environmental law to the influence of big oil, and argued that, "Congress should revisit this loophole. You know, big oil got a sweetheart deal."[41] In October 1997, shortly before the broadcast but because of the advance publicity for it, Louisiana's new governor, Mike Foster, held a press conference in which he announced that he had instructed the state Department of Natural Resources to prepare an emergency rule that required testing of oilfield waste prior to shipment into Louisiana for disposal at commercial facilities. Critics greeted it as a publicity move with no substance, and some observers have argued that both the news special and the emergency rule had little effect.[42] Yet both created a public audience for additional data on the actual components of oilfield waste, and videotaped copies of the news program have aired across the country at environmental conferences and youth retreats, and in university classrooms.

In 1998, Gary Holley, one of the workers who had loaded the waste destined for Grand Bois in 1994, made a phone call to the Grand Bois plaintiffs' attorney. Holley subsequently testified that he had become ill as a result of exposure to toxic oilfield waste at the Alabama facility, and his medical records (including information about the contents of the waste) were submitted as evidence at trial. His testimony directly contradicted Exxon's claim that no workers had become ill at the Alabama site. Despite a subpoena to produce all documents involving illnesses of workers at the Alabama facility, Exxon had failed to provide the paperwork on Holley.[43]

Holley's testimony and medical records were compelling enough to encourage Campbell Wells and U.S. Liquids (whose case had been tried separately from Exxon's) to settle out of court. The settlement was sealed, but certain details soon became obvious. The facility owner publicly agreed to build a twenty-foot-high soil berm (levee) to separate the facility from the community and prevent flood and hurricane spillage. The company also agreed to close and clean the four pits closest to town.[44] For their part, the residents agreed to take down the handmade signs they had posted along the highway. After attorney's fees, Grand Bois residents received, on average, less than $14,000 each.[45]

Grand Bois residents continued to pursue their claims against Exxon, which had not been party to the settlement. They were banking on the evidence that Exxon was hiding significant evidence that Holley had brought them and that company officials were indeed aware that the wastes were hazardous before they left Alabama. A civil trial ended in August 1998. The company was ordered to pay $7,500 to two Grand Bois residents and $15,000 to a trucker who had fallen ill after breathing fumes from the waste, but otherwise the jury rejected the plaintiffs' claims. Based on the undisclosed documents concerning Gary Holley's health problems, attorney Jones petitioned the court for a retrial.

The Grand Bois case hinged on the residents' ability to demonstrate scientifically that their health problems were linked to oilfield waste. Yet the small population of the town was unable to produce statistical analyses that would satisfy the courts. The first attempt to establish a profile of the local population relied on individuals to self-report lifestyle, behavior patterns, and medical history.[46] After industry and state officials challenged the scientific adequacy of self-reports of health problems, Senator Robichaux, himself a doctor, enlisted the help of scientists and health professionals, including Wilma Subra and Patricia Williams, director of the Louisiana State University Medical Center's Occupational Toxicology Program, to produce a more rigorously scientific study. The follow-up study included data collected during a one-year medical surveillance program focusing on women and children. The study, published in five volumes in September 1999, reported that the people of Grand Bois had been exposed to heavy metals and to substances such as benzene and hydrogen sulfide, which, although not classified as hazardous, were nevertheless toxic chemicals.

The judge in the court case ruled that the study was inadmissible as evidence because its findings were "correlational" rather than causal.[47] On this basis the judge denied the motion for a new trial but he found sufficient cause to sanction Exxon and ordered the company to pay $325,000 in court costs, litigation expenses, and attorney fees.[48] Jones appealed the judge's decision, but the appeal was rendered moot in September 2000, when Exxon (called ExxonMobil after their 1999 merger) settled out of court. The final settlement excluded many current and former residents of Grand Bois and nonresident property owners, leading to internal conflict and the dissolution of the Grand Bois Citizens Committee.

In the end, the residents of Grand Bois have borne the full cost of the waste facility. In addition to health problems caused by the facility, they live in a polluted neighborhood with devalued properties and thus cannot afford to leave. Property in Grand Bois has been so unattractive that between 1997 and 2002 no new residents moved into the community.[49] According to one resident, prospective buyers come to the area because of the relatively inexpensive land and homes for sale, but when they find out about the waste facility, they go elsewhere.

On the positive side, the Grand Bois case and the negative publicity that attended it did lead to the creation of new rules for the handling and storage of oilfield waste.[50] On November 27, 2001, the Louisiana Office of Conservation presented new rules to the Louisiana House Committee on Natural Resources, which dealt with some of the issues highlighted in the Grand Bois case. For example, the new rules increased minimum buffer zones between waste pits and residences, a provision that Senator Robichaux had included in his unsuccessful bills. They also included testing requirements for benzene in waste prior to shipment, and acceptance criteria for materials containing benzene if they were to be disposed of in cells located less than two thousand feet from residents. The DNR acknowledged that the Grand Bois case was the impetus for these regulatory changes. As stated in a paper written by two DNR officials, Carroll Wascom and Gary Snellgrove: "The basis for regulatory changes began in 1997 and 1998 with implementation of a comprehensive E&P waste sampling and analytical testing program implemented statewide as a result of concerns voiced by residents living near a commercial E&P waste treatment and disposal facility in Grand Bois, Louisiana."[51] Kathy Wascom of the Baton Rouge–based grassroots organization, Citizens for a Clean Environment, publicly commented on the rule change, saying, "It's a shame that the people of Grand Bois had to cause such a hue and cry to get something done."[52]

Since the trial, the Grand Bois facility has received much less waste than it did in the early 1990s. Yet the court cases and the new rules did not achieve what Grand Bois residents wanted most: closure of the waste facility. As of 2003, sixteen of the seventeen original pits were still open. The facility had closed only the cell that received the 1994 waste. Furthermore, the owner had still not built the levee promised in the settlement.

Nevertheless, some residents of Grand Bois, such as Clarice Friloux, who had founded the Grand Bois Citizens Committee, kept on fighting. "Our roots have been here for the last hundred years," she told a reporter. "We belong here. It's not finished for me, no matter what. I still have to shut down the waste site."[53] In addition, the incident at Grand Bois attracted the attention of Louisianans at large, who began to recognize that the events of this tiny bayou community were just one piece of a larger problem of human-induced environmental change. Coastal erosion, a subject of widespread debate in the region, has had dramatic effects on the abundant and diverse terrestrial and aquatic animals and plants of Louisiana's estuary system. The waste from the closed Grand Bois pit migrated to nearby bayous and waterways, contributing to the erosion, but dredging, clearing forested wetlands for development, and natural processes such as subsidence and rising sea levels were as much to blame. Some Louisianans recognize how such events are intertwined, but halting the resulting environmental degradation is a problem that is bigger than Louisiana alone can handle.

Stakeholder Reactions

Government Officials

Even within local and state government there exists no consensus on the issue of oilfield waste in Grand Bois. In interviews, some top state officials denied that the oil and gas companies had caused environmental problems and instead dwelled upon the economic benefits provided by the industry. As one parish council member in an adjoining parish explained, "We are doing better than yesterday. . . . The water is not polluted. . . . I would eat any fish out of it. . . . DEQ and EPA regulate all the dumping sites used by the oil industry. . . . All are being handled correctly. Everything is operating under permits" [I-239].

A businessman who had been involved in local government work was even more extreme in his defense of the oil industry:

> An expert who knows this area says no damage has been done to marsh and water by oil—
> oil is a natural thing—there is more damage with today's chemicals. Oil is no problem for
> the environment—if it seeps out, nature takes care of it. It's not bad for the marsh, shrimp,

or oysters, but it's bad for the fishermen's boats. It makes them dirty. . . . Every experience shows that if you leave it on its own, it will disappear. [I-243]

But other officials, both state and municipal, provided insightful commentary on the effects of oil on the community. For some, the effects were an unavoidable byproduct of modern industrial development and the displacement of the region's subsistence economy by a cash economy. In this view, such changes were not unique to Grand Bois but typical of the processes attending modernization in the wider society. For other officials the exploitation of oil resources had brought modernization in the form of environmental regulation. In premodern times fishing and other extractive industries caused environmental degradation, but they were never regulated; nowadays, by contrast, there was legislation to protect the environment from extractive industries such as oil- and gas-drilling. If the oil industry was operating within the laws, these officials reasoned, then it could not be harming the environment.

Not all officials shared such optimism, however. For example, some state officials countered the optimism of their colleagues on the municipal level, saying that the problem lay with enforcement. According to one,

> Louisiana has *very* good regulations . . . water regulations . . . but they are not enforced. It is the tragedy of the commons. It will only work if people in charge will protect them. There is a difference between who is responsible and who is accountable. Agency heads are accountable, but all people are responsible. [I-241]

These comments reflect the familiar conflict between environmental degradation and economic prosperity achieved through modern exploitation of resources—the dilemma that environmental philosopher Kristin Shrader-Frechette has termed the "bloody-half-loaf," whereby a poor community will accept risky technologies based on the calculation that they are better off with a bloody half-loaf than with no loaf at all.[54] This conflict is not lost on southern Louisiana's local government officials. An official from outside Grand Bois summed up the community's relationship to the oil industry as follows:

> People love the oilfield. It brings jobs and money. We have the best technology in the world. . . . [It] can solve any problem. . . . There is a lot of confidence in the oil industry. . . . [It's the] safest, most technically advanced in the world. . . . The biggest problem with the environment and civilization is that civilization moves in faster than it can recognize its impact on the environment. Some care, some don't. Then it's too late. [I-239]

The problem, as identified by this official, is technical and social. This position recognizes that significant patterns of power and influence will affect which decisions are made and whose voices are heard in policy-making forums. In this case, systematic exclusion of the views of certain sectors of the community has led to an inactive and passive public, one not willing, except under extreme circumstances, to challenge the hegemonic practices of big business and legislative frameworks. This same official later stated that

> people in Louisiana don't want to involve themselves with the government in its day-to-day activities. . . . Lots of people here are non-formally educated. They have lots of common sense, but people were not allowed the education that they needed to become informed about how government works. Their opinions are not sought. People believe government is something else—separate. Little people can't get involved. They don't understand that the vote is the ultimate power. Only 20 percent vote. It is the history and culture. They have not been informed that they can make a difference. [I-241]

Others in power shared this official's perceptions of a defeatist attitude among residents. Even though the citizens of Grand Bois proved the prejudice to be ill-founded, many southern Louisianans do have a weak sense of their own efficacy, and still wonder why they should bother to fight for justice.

The Catholic Church as Advocate

During the unfolding of the events in Grand Bois, most environmental justice groups were unaware of what was happening there. Public awareness of and concern about waste generally arises only when the usually invisible disposal processes for household, business, and industrial wastes are made visible. Because oilfield waste is categorized as nonhazardous, it has been largely excluded from national debates on hazardous waste, and consequently, the communities living near oilfield waste sites have remained outside the focus of the environmental justice movement. This is in stark contrast to the prominent debates over wastes from nuclear power plants and other uses of nuclear energy. Even on the rare occasion when a national newspaper or television station has reported on the topic of oilfield waste, political reticence and lack of public awareness have kept it in the shadows. In 1996, for example, a CBS news correspondent decided to do a national story that highlighted the situation at Grand Bois, the community that is the focus of this case study, but the show was postponed and delayed several times and not aired until Christmas Eve, 1997.

One advocate of environmental justice did get involved in Grand Bois, however: the Catholic Church. The Church saw Grand Bois's crisis as directly related to the community's poverty. It first became involved in the case when the director of Catholic Social Services for the Houma-Thibodaux diocese, Sister Miriam Mitchell, began helping the residents in their struggles against the facility. Her involvement led the bishop to speak out against environmental pollution and against permits for additional facilities, even when those actions resulted in threats by moneyed businessmen to withdraw financial support from the Church.

Although the Grand Bois case marked the beginning of its ongoing involvement in toxics issues, the Church had long played an active role in local environmental issues. In the early 1980s, the Catholic Social Services office provided a grant to the Organization for Louisiana Fishermen, who were concerned about the effects on fishers' livelihoods of wetlands erosion and efforts by private landowners to restrict fishers' access to some marsh areas. And in some of the areas still available for fishing, there was oil on the water from drilling sites. To the Church, the degradation of and loss of access to fishing grounds were social injustices, and local Catholic leaders were soon tackling other social injustices as well. They became involved with larger groups such as the Coalition to Restore Coastal Louisiana—groups that were making the connections between poor environmental conditions and human poverty. According to one Church leader,

> It is always the poor people who live in the most polluted areas, the places that are most quickly eroding. Everyone is affected—health, way of life, and recreation. The environmental concerns could not be separated from the people who live here. Down here, it's not an "oh, those environmentalists" kind of thing. . . . From the church perspective, the dignity of the human individual could not be separated from the environment. . . . You had some very fundamental value issues but [also] practical concerns. [I-279]

In 1987, the Catholic Charities/social concerns committee of the Louisiana Catholic Conference sponsored a resolution that passed unanimously urging "the people of Louisiana, particularly those in coastal parishes, to recognize our moral responsibility to learn about coastal restoration efforts, and to support groups active in protecting our wetlands."[55]

The resolution included a four-step plan for implementation that involved extensive public participation. Several months later, the United Methodist Church passed a similar resolution, and by fall it had been adopted by the Louisiana Interfaith Council.

The church activity on behalf of environmental causes in Louisiana paralleled efforts throughout the United States. In 1984, for example, the United Methodist Church's general conference passed a resolution that called stewardship of natural resources a fundamental responsibility of Christian discipleship. In January 1990, the Pope's world day of peace message, entitled "The Ecological Crisis: A Common Responsibility," supported environmental efforts across the globe. In 1991, the U.S. Catholic bishops followed with a directive on the environment that launched the Catholic Church into a broad stewardship movement. Several years later, "care for God's creation" was added to the Catholic social teaching, the Church's "rich treasure of wisdom about building a just society and living lives of holiness amidst the challenges of modern society." According to the U.S. bishops,

> Care for the earth is not just an Earth Day slogan, it is a requirement of our faith. We are called to protect people and the planet, living our faith in relationship with all of God's creation. This environmental challenge has fundamental moral and ethical dimensions that cannot be ignored. . . . This central Catholic principle requires that we measure every policy, every institution, and every action by whether it protects human life and enhances human dignity, especially for the poor and vulnerable.[56]

Catholic Church officials in the Houma-Thibodaux diocese continued to lead on environmental and social justice issues, speaking at public hearings and urging the closure of the waste facility. The Church's involvement in toxics issues have since expanded to include retreats for priests, youth weekends, and taking formal positions on local facility siting decisions.

Residents

Among Grand Bois residents, the values that emerged in our interviews were many and disparate. The most prevalent were a sensitivity to the land; strong opinions (pro and con) about the oil industry's role in environmental degradation; the connection of environmental protection with community protection; concerns about health; new attitudes toward the power of the community to create change; and opinions (favorable and unfavorable) about legal remedies for environmental problems.

Although there is disagreement about the oil industry's impact on the local environment, the crisis of 1994 made communities more sensitive to their local environment. This sensitivity is not the stereotypical "green" awareness associated with ecocentric philosophies; it is rather an articulated sense of connection with the land and sea, and an awareness of how that connection has been damaged by human activity. Youth and adults alike talked about canals, levees, and coastal erosion; reduced alligator population; and contaminated fish. When asked about changes to the area, two boys described their most recent hunting trip into the marsh, during which they had watched a leaning tree finally topple into the bayou as the soil underneath eroded away. Several residents noted that human sewage leaking from old septic tanks and cesspools was a major source of water pollution, and one argued that he would not eat the fish in the area because of health concerns related to the sewage and not the waste facility.

Some residents harkened back to a golden age of environmental harmony. A Houma man in his late sixties recalled his life as a young boy on the nearby Isle de Jean Charles in the 1930s and 1940s, when people made clothing out of flour sacks, yet no one went hungry:

> [W]e had gardens, we had fish. Most of our people were fishermen. We had whatever the sea had to offer—at least the estuaries. They were selling everything—shrimp, trout, redfish, oysters. We had our gardens and our cattle. We had community type of cattle—a ranch, you might say. . . . Nobody really owned anything that I knew of. If you wanted to slaughter a bull, when he's dead, everybody would divide it. There were only twenty families at most on the island. [I-251]

While infused with nostalgia, this statement is a useful indicator that the local communities did not isolate themselves from their surroundings. Environmental issues were represented by virtually everyone we talked with as inextricably linked to broader social and personal issues. Many spoke of the traditional knowledge of the environment and its cycles that had been passed down through their families. One resident recalled lessons he had learned from his grandfather: "You don't want to harm or deplete [natural resources]. You'd catch in one place and then move, not staying to deplete it. I was taught to respect the land . . . I learned lots from the older generation" [I-247].

During interviews, we heard anecdotes about family life and leisure activities (such as gardening and alligator hunts) that often centered on connections among people, place, and nature, although again, they were not couched in traditional environmental language. Residents described with pride working in the local shipyard, owning and operating boats that serviced the offshore oil and gas industry, shrimping, trapping, traveling up and down the bayou in small motor boats, and walking or riding four-wheelers to their hunting blinds. Members of the older generation expressed concern that, with the decline of fishing, the younger generation would not get to know the local environment. As one said:

> It's a totally different feeling when you're out on the boat. There's no phone. There's nothing above you telling you how much to catch, when to come in. My husband's mama and daddy got into it. That's pretty much how my daddy raised all of us. . . . I don't know what my grandkids are going to do. [Everyone is] talking of a time when shrimping won't be around forever. [I-278]

While the older interviewees noticed most markedly the more modern, instrumental attitudes toward the environment that had taken root within and surrounding the community, concern for environmental preservation was not limited to elders. Several boys talked about the recent changes in the fish and amphibian populations, demonstrating that the changes had been rapid and perceptible even to the young. "We do not have as much fish anymore," one boy told us. "I don't know what's happening to them. The fish I like to catch are all getting chased off from the salt water. . . . We don't have that many frogs anymore. I like to go froggin'. Gradually they just went down" [I-283].

Despite widespread concern about natural resources, our discussions with residents turn up noconsensus on the role of the oil industry and other resource exploitation in changes to the area's natural surroundings. Some residents refused to believe that oilfield waste was the problem, citing instead other poisons, including domestic solvents; some refused to believe than an industry as successful, rich, and technologically sophisticated as the oil industry could be responsible. Still others acknowledged that the oil industry was to blame, yet were reluctant to make the economic trade-offs that would be necessary if the industry changed radically or shut down.

A man in his mid-seventies told interviewers that it was the decline of fishing that had sent him into the oilfields. He attributed the decline to pesticide runoff, yet agreed that oilfield waste had harmed the community in other ways. "You know what ruined the trapping?" he asked. "The oilfield. I had leased a lot of land [to oil drillers]. They started drilling, and it ruined this country. My daddy and uncle said the same thing. . . . The oilfield ruined a lot, and it's going to ruin a lot more. But we got to have it, they say" [I-248].

Alongside divergent views of who caused the current changes to the environment we also heard diverse views of what accounted for the recent upsurge in environmental awareness in the community. One community member noted that environmental awareness extended beyond the oilfield waste crisis: "People are becoming more environmentally aware. . . . [They] are littering less. In the old days we burned our garbage without thinking about it" [I-245]. Another said, "The changes that have affected us are more changes in the awareness about the environment . . . than the actual [environmental] change. . . Now we are more conscious" [I-246].

Such changes were not dramatic, nor were they community-wide. Some residents, for example, continued to hold that oilfield wastes had had few if any long-lasting deleterious effects. Referring to a waste facility under construction in a nearby town, one man commented, "There's more dangerous chemicals under your sink then they will have there." Another resident explained, "There are a lot of threats . . . There are oil spills and chemical spills, but the land recovers easily down here. It takes a lot of punishment, but recovers by next year. Like a hurricane—looked like a bomb hit, but the next year it looked beautiful" [I-247].

Some residents resented the policy steps the government had taken in response to Grand Bois. Some even went so far as to say that there was no pollution. Despite the evidence that oilfield waste deposited in pits can spill over into adjacent waterways during storms, causing surface water contamination and affecting fishing, one resident complained that "the government is trying to ban commercial fishing any way they can. . . . I haven't noticed pollution, but I've fished where [the government claims] they've got pollution . . . I don't see none at all really" [I-232]. Other residents were more forceful, blaming governmental intervention for undermining local communities and their way of life. "It's all between the politicians, the government, and Fish and Wildlife," one maintained. "They are destroying our way of life. If it keeps going like this, we're going to be another Russia. That's how bad it looks. It's not like it used to be" [I-232].

Some people's hesitancy to bite the hand that feeds them—in other words, to attack the oil industry—led to wildly different appraisals of the industry's behavior during the lawsuit, the industry's operating practices, and its benefits and drawbacks for the community. One resident stated:

> The oil industry has been good for Louisiana. They brought millions of dollars into the state. Some aspects have been detrimental to the environment. They dig canals and run up and down in these big boats and wash away land. They contribute to the loss of land in Louisiana, but I don't blame the oil companies; we go fast in our boats, too. . . . I see the oil industry as giving families options, especially those members who may not be successful at fishing. [I-221]

Other residents were more circumspect. Said one:

> Before, you could just drain a swamp and start planting beans or whatever. . . . Now draining is regulated. . . . You have to do environmental impact statements. . . . While oil used to be swabbed into salt water, it is now swabbed into a tank. That still has to go somewhere, but out of sight, out of mind. [I-221]

Another dominant theme among residents is the connection between environmental protection and protection of community traditions and ties. For example, some long-time residents linked environmental changes to the influx of immigrants and new industries, which had also changed the social fabric:

> The biggest changes . . . are changes in society's [treatment of] natural resources. I'm a south Louisiana native. I grew up in a small town fifty miles south of here. When I grew up, it was agriculturally driven. . . . You had in my lifetime a heavy industry along the river. In the heyday we had gas development. All of that, in my mind, has changed society, and when I talk about society, I mean people who grew up in Louisiana. You had people that came in that were not from south Louisiana, and they altered the coast. [I-220]

Environmental protection was also synonymous for many with health. Some residents were very much aware of the health effects of oilfield practices, particularly after the events of March 1994.

Residents had long associated their community with fresh air and peace; now illness had disrupted that peace, and many began to relate their illness to the invisible, and often odorless, materials at the facility. As one resident explained:

> Look at my family. I lost my dad to cancer, my mother to cancer. My wife has cancer; my sister has problems, and they think it's cancer. My brother-in-law has prostate cancer. My sister has heart cancer. I never even heard of heart cancer. It's a tumor of the heart. It's very rare. We've lost so many people. It used to be people died of heart attacks; now we all die of cancer. [I-250]

The issue of health proved a rallying point both for residents suffering from the oilfield waste pollution and outsiders interested in their plight. Had the linkage between the facility and health problems not been found, environmental concerns about the oilfield waste facility would likely not have grown so powerful—not as long as people continued to hold high paying oil industry jobs. Because of health concerns, some residents discouraged their family members from having children. In a community that values large families, such advice was traumatic for young couples. One young couple learned that the wife had high levels of lead in her blood during her pregnancy, a known cause of birth defects; families were reluctant to hold baby showers or otherwise celebrate a pregnancy because of fear that the baby would not live or would be terribly damaged.[57]

Many residents were deeply worried about the health of the next generation, so much so that they will move if they can. "My little girl, she's not getting any better," said one woman. "My other one's getting sick, too. It hurts me that I've got to leave, got to find a home for them so they can breathe better and be happy." Some stay because of strong ties to the area—as one resident said, "This is where my people's at, you know, and—and it's all here. I don't think they have another place like it that— well, that I know of. I mean, you got beautiful places in this world, but not like my place here." Others stay because they have no choice. Anna Matherne, one of the original plaintiffs in the lawsuit, felt herself "going down fast," she said. "Tired all the time, throat hurts, ears ringing just about all the time now." But when a reporter asked why she didn't leave, Matherne retorted, "I can't afford to. I can't sell this place. Who would want to buy it? I'm a thousand feet from a waste facility that—that has hazard-ous material."[58]

Physical symptoms such as those mentioned above, and the knowledge that they couldn't leave the area, galvanized residents into action. As outlined in our narrative of the Grand Bois crisis, they formed a committee, circulated a petition, and wrote letters to politicians. Many soon came to feel that their actions were useless, however. One young Houma woman lamented to interviewers that all of the letter-writing had had no effect because the recipients of the letters, local and state officials, claimed that they had no authority to shut down the Grand Bois facility. These official reac-tions were not the only reason for residents' defeatism, however. There had long been a notion in the community that government would never respond to residents' con-cerns. This notion had been encouraged by an earlier environmental conflict, when Grand Bois residents approached their parish government with a request for a levee to protect the community from coastal erosion. The parish officials agreed, but a local resident and the community's major landowner, a nonresident, refused to give up land for the levee and the government made no effort to seize the land by eminent domain. In another locale, the residents might have sued those two individuals to have their property condemned, but the Grand Bois residents concluded that the po-tential for reprisals was too great and therefore took no action. As a community leader explained:

> To understand the sense of helplessness around the [waste facility] issue, one needs to understand the past. It began with the cyprus industry that demonstrated perfect igno-rance of the environment. . . . This was followed by the seafood industry. . . . The reason it boomed here was because the east coast and Florida had been fished out, so they came here and discovered jumbo shrimp, which might have developed in the east had it not been overfished. . . . Then came the oil/energy industry and [it] came on the same foot . . . armed by the same mind-set as the others when it came to environment. For ex-ample, only in the last two years was saltwater discharge from rigs regulated, which has contributed to erosion and destruction of the estuary. A major problem with the oil industry was that years ago, when oil started, Congress passed legislation that declared that any waste coming out of the oil industry was not hazardous. But any of the same substances, if found in other industries or products, were considered hazardous. [I-240]

What made the oilfield waste case unique, then, was residents' willingness to sue the facility owners. According to one resident: "It felt good when we went to court last year, and we hit [the company] pretty hard" [I-222]. Some community members' willingness to fight a legal battle cannot be construed, however, as community cohesion. Rifts over the waste facility became visible during the legal fight. According to a community leader, the legal battle was "costly in both social and psychological costs. There are very good arguments both for and against [the waste facility]. It split families to the extent that family members don't talk to each other because of it" [I-240]. In fact, from the time the court case began, there was no consensus within the community that a legal battle could resolve anything. By the time the case ended, with a small monetary settlement, people were exhausted, and underlying conflicts surfaced. In particular, the final settlement with the oil company created conflict over who should receive payments. This led to the dissolution of the Grand Bois Citizens Committee and comments from some members that their future efforts would be for the benefit of their own families rather than the entire community. As Clarice Friloux explained:

> We originally thought litigation would make a difference. We thought people would see that it is time to stop allowing these companies to do this. But in Louisiana, oil and gas is our number one industry. We are fighting some big people here. In fact, I think our litigation has hurt the larger struggle against the industry in the long run. We have raised awareness, but it is clear that the people in south Louisiana will keep fighting for their oil and gas, no matter what. It doesn't matter how many communities are being poisoned, as long as their husbands and wives are bringing home those big paychecks. . . . You can't get a jury to sit on a trial in south Louisiana that hasn't been affected by the oil and gas industry.[59]

Conflicts over the impact of the oil industry and the court settlements surfaced in interviews with little prompting. Some residents argued that concern over the waste facility was misplaced. They claimed that earlier environmental problems caused by the oil industry had been addressed, and that the Army Corps of Engineers, with its penchant for dredging and building canals, had wrought the longest-lasting environmental damage.

Families have reacted to the legal settlement in a variety of ways. In 2001, the overall feeling appeared to be relief that the lawsuit was finally over. As one resident remarked, "We just want to go back to the way we were, to a regular life" [I-252]. This "live and let live" attitude was prevalent in Grand Bois, and it sets the residents there apart from those in our next case study. In our study of Civano, we encounter residents who fit more easily into the so-called mainstream of American environmentalism, whose primary focus is not environmental impacts on human health but nature preservation.

Desert Conservation and Development in Southern Arizona: The Case of Civano

Residents of the American urban west have long struggled with how to live in the desert. Conventional post–World War II housing developments are often woefully inadequate for life in an area of water scarcity and rich (but endangered) wildlife. Civano, a mixed-use housing development in the Sonoran Desert but within the city limits of Tucson, Arizona, was designed expressly to help its residents live better in the desert. As the largest sustainable housing project ever attempted in the United States,[60] Civano has brought national and even international attention to Tucson. Civano was designed, financed, and built over a twenty-year period, during which time concerns about the form, pace, and consequences of urban development had coalesced under the banner of "urban sprawl." Civano was planned and initiated before sprawl became a national concern; early proponents envisioned the development as a solar village, and environmentalists, developers, and politicians initially greeted the concept with great enthusiasm. Yet as the project developed, critics maintained that Civano (on the outer fringe of Tucson proper) added to sprawl, and that the ideal of sustainable development was being compromised by competing market and ideological values.

With only one of three planned neighborhoods completed as of 2004, Civano represents an ongoing attempt to actualize a vision of sustainability—an attempt that has required the close involvement of both private and public interests. Unusually, both the city of Tucson and the state of Arizona have been directly involved in financing Civano, facilitating land transactions, legislating energy standards, and even adjudicating ownership at the development, providing in all almost $4 million from city and state coffers. Yet city demands and regulations have cost the developers more than they have received, making it clear that large-scale alternative development can be financially difficult even when backed by powerful interests and community support.

The drive to build Civano grew out of pressing concerns and broad public debate in the region about energy scarcity and rising costs, sprawl and its environmental impacts, and the availability of water. We first describe in brief the political debates about and policy responses to such concerns. We then describe the development of the idea of Civano—its inception as the Tucson Solar Village, the attraction of essential political and financial resources, the controversy over vision, which resulted in significant changes to the project goals, and the building and marketing of the development that resulted.

It is impossible to understand the values Civano represents without knowing something about the people who chose to make it their home: the challenges they face to make it a home and a community; the compromises, conflicts, and disillusionments, but also the commitment, conviction, and solidarity; and how they negotiate and define what it means to be a Civano resident. Basic demographics can offer us a quantitative description of a place, but they do not fully explain who lives in Civano. To get a more inclusive picture, the research team relied on participant observation of residents at Civano and on surveys and in-depth interviews about residents' motivations and reactions. These findings appear in the final section of this study, an analysis of reactions to Civano—both positive and negative, from inside and out.

We might have focused our study on other desert communities, such as those of the Navajo and Hopi, whose native lands are exploited by outside industries to service Tucson with water and coal. But we chose instead the well-off community of

Civano, in order to reveal another face of American environmentalism: namely people and communities who ostensibly have the power to choose the way they want to order their lives. While it is the largest and most prominent, Civano is just one of a growing number of Tucson developments that market their ecological consciousness. The study examines the compromises even well-meaning people often must make to get by, and their degree of awareness of the broader environmental and social consequences of their choices. Overall the case study reveals the political, economic, and social dynamics of siting urban areas in a desert, the devil's bargains that have been made to make such cities possible, and the ironies of creating "sustainable developments" that rely upon a desert infrastructure.

Tucson: Growth of a Desert Metropolis

Tucson, 63 miles north of the Mexican border, is nestled in a valley ringed on all sides by mountains. The city proper covers more than 220 square miles in Pima County, Arizona, and the Tucson metropolitan area covers 495 square miles. Elevations in the Tucson Basin and surrounding area vary from 2,200 feet in the city to 9,100 feet in the Catalina Mountains north of Tucson. This topographical variation creates varied environments, including a desert scrub environment in the city and a deciduous forest environment in the mountains. This variety is one of the features that encouraged settlement in Tucson—prehistoric dwellers could exploit both desert and forest resources, and more recent residents could bear the harsh summers by fleeing into the mountains. Unfortunately, this same variability also puts local ecosystems at greater risk of damage from development. Many plant and animal species are concentrated in small geographic areas, making development of even small parcels of land potentially devastating.

By the 1970s, there was mounting public concern in the region that too many people had come to southern Arizona. Groundwater resources were pushed to their limits, and residents already in Tucson were fleeing a decaying inner city and joining new arrivals on the urban fringe. By the 1980s, there was a growing realization that the urban fringe was expanding too rapidly into the surrounding desert and upward into the foothills. In the 1990s, it was acknowledged that Tucson's growth was encroaching on critical habitats for endangered species and that such growth—sprawl—had to be managed. The great engineering feats and complicated political deals required to supply Tucson's water needs, and the knowledge that much of Tucson's regional character relies on an environment that its growth endangers, together motivated Civano to position itself as a model of "sustainable development."

Bringing Water to the Desert

Although Tucson sits atop huge aquifers containing about 63 million acre-feet of water in the Tucson Basin and the nearby Avra Valley Basin,[61] only a small portion of this water can be pumped out of the ground to meet the projected needs of this rapidly growing desert city.[62] The rate at which water is removed is twice that at which it is naturally replenished—and as the water table drops, it takes more energy to lift water from the depths. As a result, Tucson, along with Phoenix, relies on the Colorado River to help solve its water problems. The Central Arizona Project (CAP), authorized in 1968 as part of the federal Colorado River Basin Project Act, delivers Colorado River water to arid central Arizona. Completed in 1993 at a cost of $4.7 billion, CAP lifts water 2,900 feet from Lake Havasu, a lake in Arizona created by the damming of the Colorado River to the south side of Tucson through fourteen pumping stations and 336 miles of canals and tunnels. Much of the power for such heavy lifting comes from the coal-burning Navajo Generating Station near the northern Arizona town of Page, in which the Bureau of Reclamation, which built the Central Arizona Project, owns nearly a 25 percent interest. Coal for the plant is strip-mined on Black Mesa, 273 miles away.

Complicating matters is the fact that rights to water, which are key to development in the arid Southwest, have been taken from the Navajo and Hopi, on whose reservations Black Mesa sits. The Peabody Western Coal Company leased rights to the coal from the Navajos and Hopis, and also negotiated an arrangement to use Navajo water to transport the coal by pipeline in the form of a slurry. (Because Black Mesa is so remote, lacking rail or other means of shipping, a slurry was the only way to move the coal.) According to a report in the *Los Angeles Times*, Black Mesa is "the only mine in the world to use a water-propelled pipeline for coal delivery," and it does so from one of the most arid regions in the United States.[63] Starting in 1973, the Navajo and the Hopi, who consider water the center of their existence, sued Peabody, claiming that the company's Black Mesa slurry is overdrawing water from the Navajo aquifer—the principal water source of the Navajo and the Hopi. The Navajo and Hopi are frugal in their use of water. Water consumption of the Hopi Nation averages 28 gallons per capita per day (gpcpd). By contrast, the average use of water by neighboring non-Indian communities in Arizona was 160 gpcpd, while residents in other parts of the United States typically average more than 200 gpcpd.[64] The Navajo and Hopi lawsuit against Peabody was still pending in 2004. If they were to win, and regain their water rights, the intricate system providing water to Tucson might have to be reengineered.

Ironically, after billions of dollars, dozens of lawsuits, several decades of political maneuvering at state and federal levels, and twenty years' anticipation, there were few takers when CAP water finally began to flow to Tucson. As predicted by a handful of renegade agricultural economists,[65] farmers—the original beneficiaries of the massive diversion—could not afford to pay for CAP water. And after the initial delivery of CAP water in 1992, urban consumers wanted no part of it—CAP water tasted bad, had a foul smell, and was acidic enough to corrode old pipes. The water damaged dishwashers, water heaters, evaporative coolers, and other water-dependent appliances.[66] The city of Tucson has, in fact, paid out $1.9 million worth of CAP-related claims to some 5,300 claimants, apparently a fraction of the actual damage.[67] In 1995 Tucson voters passed a Water Consumer Protection Act, which restricted the ways in which Tucson could use the CAP water it had already contracted to buy. The city could sell it or exchange it for other water; allow its use for agriculture, mining, parks, golf courses, and schools; use it to prevent land subsidence and, if it was properly treated and deemed "free from disinfection byproducts," inject it into wells. Tucson's water utility, after some consternation, started using its CAP allocation by injecting it into the aquifer and repumping it as "blended groundwater."

Even before the use of CAP water was restricted, Tucson's leaders were looking for other ways to solve the city's water problems. In 1980, the state legislature passed the Groundwater Management Act, which mandated "safe yield" (in which groundwater take does not exceed groundwater recharge) for all exploited aquifers by 2025. The act restricts the expansion of agriculture and calls for incrementally stricter conservation measures for municipal and industrial users. In response, Tucson has been encouraging water conservation measures such as the use of low-water plants for landscaping, rainwater harvesting, and reclaimed water recycling, yet the city, along with Phoenix and Prescott, will probably fail to achieve safe yield by 2025.[68]

Since safe yield is not working, Tucson is sustainable only because of the Colorado River. So far, the river has not failed Tucson, yet severe and lasting droughts do periodically come to the West. And even if the river flows forever, a continuous supply of energy will be needed to pump Colorado River water into the Sonoran Desert. Black Mesa will eventually be strip-mined bare, unless Navajo and Hopi litigation stops the process before that happens, and a new energy source will have to be found. All this water pumping, of course, also requires money. Tucson has been able to grow, partly through tax revenues that have funded the CAP project and partly by allowing federal agencies such as the Bureau of Indian Affairs to approve contracts that benefit the metropolitan West at the expense of Indians who have had a much longer presence in the area. Furthermore, even if drought, energy, and money do not prove to be obstacles to a sustainable supply of water, population will. There is no sign that Tucson's population growth will slow dramatically in the near future—and if it does not, all the region's existing groundwater, and all the water Arizona can squeeze out of the Colorado River, will be insufficient.

Protecting Desert Ecosystems from Development

Overuse of scarce water resources is not the only problem with Tucson's rapid growth. Uncontrolled growth also threatens open space, air quality, and wildlife habitats. In 1992, with these concerns in mind, the Pima County Board of Supervisors adopted a comprehensive land use plan, which specified recommended housing densities and uses for vacant lands and also spelled out a Sonoran Desert conservation plan.[69] This plan covered elements such as ranch conservation, historic and cultural resource preservation, and riparian restoration.

By far the most controversial element of the plan was its proposal to protect fifty-six endangered and vulnerable species.[70] Since only 13 percent of Pima County is open for development, species protection is a highly charged issue for developers and preservationists.[71] Unsurprisingly, builders and growth advocates staunchly opposed the plan, but supporters gained an important ally in 1997, when the U.S. Fish and Wildlife Service declared the cactus ferruginous pygmy owl endangered.[72] The Fish and Wildlife Service made a preliminary designation of 730,000 acres of prime pygmy owl habitat in four Arizona counties, of which some 260,000 acres are in Pima County. Nevertheless, the Pima County Board of Supervisors approved building permits for more than 1,300 single-family detached houses in the pygmy owl habitat between March 1997 and November 1998, which subjected the Fish and Wildlife Service to charges of not acting forcefully and swiftly enough.[73]

In March 1999, the county board of supervisors finally took its first action to implement the Sonoran Desert Conservation Plan, agreeing to a two-year rezoning hold on environmentally sensitive land within the county, authorizing funds to begin comprehensive surveys and studies of the pygmy owl, and establishing guidelines for an eighty-member steering committee to prepare an endangered species protection plan. As with most environmental regulations, builders and developers worried about the impact of such conservation measures on the economy. The Southern Arizona Home Builders Association quickly released a study that priced the protection of pygmy owl habitat at $8.5 billion over fifteen years in lost jobs and tax revenues and declining property values. Because the plan allowed developers to harass, harm, or kill individual owls, even some environmental groups opposed it.[74] Despite the grumbling, the supervisors continued to take steps toward implementation of the plan. In 2001, they unanimously passed interim guidelines to protect a proposed 1.2 million acre biological reserve that includes most of the county's mountain ranges.[75]

Although the presence of pygmy owls delayed some development plans on the northwest side of Tucson,[76] the overall effect on urban sprawl was minimal. The Southern Arizona Home Builders Association and other growth advocates challenged the designation in court and simultaneously channeled growth into other areas of the city where endangered species are not an issue. By 2001, approximately thirty-seven subdivisions with twenty thousand new homes were under construction in southeast Tucson, with another fifteen thousand to eighteen thousand units awaiting approval.[77] According to the Fish and Wildlife Service, the number of adult pygmy owls in Arizona has dropped from forty-one in 1999 to thirty-four in 2000 to thirty-six in 2001, and eighteen during breeding season in 2002.[78] Still, the pygmy owl controversy and the Endangered Species Act have been the most potent force in containing Tucson's sprawl. In November 2002, in an effort to reestablish protection in a way that could withstand future court challenge, the Fish and Wildlife Service proposed designation of the 1.2 million acres that make up the county biological reserve as "critical habitat," an act that enraged the developers.

The county's desert protection plan carried a high price tag—$300 million–$500 million[79]—but it nevertheless has enjoyed widespread support. In addition, the plan attracted significant national attention for addressing issues of municipal growth and eco-regional planning, and it was a first step in establishing a comprehensive land use plan for the city of Tucson, Pima County, and incorporated jurisdictions around Tucson.[80]

The Birth of an Idea: Tucson Solar Village

The desert conservation measures of the 1990s came out of a decades-long quest for new ways to conserve resources. Water conservation, desert ecosystem management, and increased use of solar energy all came into play in the building of Civano. When the development was first conceived, however, it was thought of primarily as a solar energy project.

The solar energy movement dates back to the 1973 Arab oil embargo, which sent shock waves through the United States, which had become highly dependent on petroleum. Conservation measures were quickly introduced, and the modern solar industry was born. In 1975, Arizona governor Raul Castro created the Arizona Solar Energy Commission, an independent state agency charged with funding solar development projects. Because of its unusually sunny weather Tucson emerged as a prime location for the development and testing of solar products.

A second embargo, in 1979, strengthened support for solar research and development. By 1980, there was an active informal dialogue on solar building in Tucson, to which the city contributed by forming, in partnership with Pima County, the Metropolitan Energy Commission (MEC), an appointed, volunteer civic commission. Its activities include public education, technical analysis, review of energy legislation, and sponsorship of community activities and projects. The following year, Governor Bruce Babbitt participated in a Showcase of Solar Homes sponsored by the Southern Arizona Home Builders Association. A conversation there between Babbitt and local solar advocates marked the beginning of a vision of a community powered only by solar energy—the Tucson Solar Village. Before members of Tucson's solar and planning communities could fully develop the solar village idea, however, the U.S. solar industry took a nosedive. In 1984, federal solar energy tax credits expired, and within two years the number of manufacturing firms in the U.S. solar industry declined from 225 to 98.[81] In 1986, world oil prices dropped, and the decline in solar industrial companies intensified, with the number of companies dropping to fifty-nine in 1987 and thirty-six eight years later. In Arizona, the decline was reflected in lost jobs; in 1985, seven hundred solar-related companies employed four thousand people across the state, but by 1992, fewer than 150 people were working full time in the industry.[82]

Despite the downturn in the solar industry, Governor Babbitt wanted the state to provide seed money for the solar village. The federal government had revenues, generated through financial penalties to oil and mining companies,[83] to allocate to states for environmental uses. The Arizona portion amounted to more than $1 million, all of which the state legislature allocated to the Tucson Solar Village vision. The Arizona Energy Office used $500,000 to fund a study and Arizona's state land department committed 820 acres of undeveloped desert, southeast of Tucson, to the "Arizona Solar Village Environmental Showcase." Then, at the urging of MEC, local builders, and environmentalists, the energy office released a request for proposals (RFP) to design the solar village project. P&D Technologies, headed by Wayne Moody (the former planning director for the city of Tucson), assembled a team of experts from across the country to develop a proposal for the site, and in May 1989 P&D was awarded the contract. Moody then spent more than two years engaged in a legally required public input process to plan development of the parcel. This process included over sixty public meetings—both small meetings geared to specific groups such as business groups, the Audubon Society, or home builders, and larger open public meetings that were usually attended by thirty to fifty people.[84]

The development of the Tucson Solar Village required close collaboration among the city, state, and MEC. Public support for the project was also critical, given the many policy decisions required to move the project forward. These included rezoning, the transfer of water allocations from the Central Arizona Project to Tucson Water, and funding for the project from the city of Tucson. Letters of support came from congressmen, developers and builders, and local organizations such as the Neighborhood Coalition of Greater Tucson and the Tucson Urban League. Fortunately, in the early 1990s the solar industry recouped a little of its former strength. New technologies increased the potential for centralizing solar power production, and new government programs required utility companies to generate at least some portion of their energy from renewable resources. Still greater efforts to reinvigorate the solar industry came from the Arizona Corporation Commission (ACC), which has jurisdiction over public utilities along with other state constitutionally mandated responsibilities. The ACC recommended that the state's four regulated public utilities install units to produce a cumulative 19 megawatts from renewable energy resources by 2000.[85] In 2000 ACC replaced these recommendations with a new measure mandating that by 2007 utilities generate 1.1 percent of their electricity from renewable sources with at least 50 percent of that from solar. While not the first state to develop policies requiring utilities to generate power from renewable sources, Arizona was the first to establish a percentage requirement for solar generation. Nationally, President Bill Clinton's 1997 Million Solar Roofs Initiative, a plan to install solar energy systems on the roofs of one million buildings in the United States, also helped to revive interest in solar.[86]

From Vision to Reality

Tucson Solar Village Becomes New Urbanist Civano

As a result of public meetings and debate the vision for the Tucson Solar Village rapidly expanded. The public, the steering committee of the MEC overseeing the planning process, Wayne Moody, and Wilson Orr (the project manager hired by the MEC to supervise Wayne Moody's work) all wanted to expand the community's goals beyond mere energy consumption to include water conservation and other environmental measures. To reflect this change, MEC decided in 1990–91 to solicit ideas for a new name for the proposed development. Finding a name proved more controversial and time-consuming than expected, but when the development plan was unveiled, in 1992, so, too, was the new name: Civano.

Civano is the name of a phase of one of the earliest civilizations in the Tucson area, the Hohokam, characterized by extensive trade networks and irrigation systems and by highly developed pottery production and architecture.[87] The name was thought to capture and promote a Civano "vision" by referring to a time when the Hohokam were able to maintain complex social systems using the local resources of southern Arizona. The city of Tucson's Web site praised "the golden era of native Hohokam civilization, which exhibited balance between human needs and the natural environment," and went on to declare that the new Civano would "demonstrate the marketability of sustainable community development on a large scale at affordable prices."[88]

The 1992 master development plan for Civano called for a community of three neighborhoods—each with its own neighborhood center—2,500 homes, a community school, a visitors' center, a conference center with hotel, a village center with 285,000 square feet of retail and commercial space, and an industrial park geared toward light industry. An additional 400 acres of public open space and recreation areas were to be preserved next to the community. The plan specified goals in five basic performance areas: reduced consumption of fossil fuels; decreased potable water consumption; reduced internal automobile traffic buildup; decreased solid waste production; and the provision of jobs in the community.[89] The mayor and city council unanimously adopted P&D's plan in 1992. Other nearby developments, including high-end developer Don Diamond's Rocking K Ranch, ran into serious controversy when they were proposed because of growing public concern over urban sprawl, but Civano, planned to be two or three times denser than any surrounding development, sailed through.[90]

In 1994, after a period of inactivity, the city council hired John Laswick to oversee the development of Civano, and in 1995 adopted a Civano IMPACT (Integrated Methods of Performance and Cost Tracking) System for Sustainable development. The system set performance targets based upon goals outlined in the 1992 plan, and when compared to Tucson's 1990 average, mandated a reduction of 75 percent in energy demand, 65 percent in water use, 90 percent in solid waste, and 40 percent in automobile traffic. The system also called for increased innovation in energy supply, affordable housing, and one job for every two housing units. Although these standards applied only to Civano, the IMPACT system would come to influence the targets set for future developments, including the neighboring subdivision of Mesquite Ranch and the planned Rio Nuevo in downtown Tucson. Ultimately, Civano developers were held to less ambitious targets, but even the lowered standards were expected to save the city $500,000 annually in water, landfills, and road-building costs.[91]

Shortly after he was hired, John Laswick commented, "People come to live in Tucson because of its beautiful desert environment. Ironically, though, more of the desert must be destroyed in order for more people to live here. Our goal is to attract people and to preserve the desert environment."[92] In pursuit of this goal, Laswick soon contacted David Butterfield, a developer who had worked on the Bamberton project in Canada. The promotional materials for Bamberton mirrored the vision for Civano: "A community that emphasizes human-scale architecture and embodies the traditional values associated with small town life, ecological sustainability, and a positive vision of the future." While Bamberton was never built,[93] Butterfield felt that lessons learned in the process of planning the community could benefit Civano. His vision for Bamberton had drawn on principles of New Urbanism—a theory based on traditional concepts of town planning that advocates high-density, mixed-use building to encourage an active community life. New Urbanist planners prefer small-scale commercial areas and shops that are integrated with residences. New Urbanism is the "lost art of place-making," according to its advocates, who see sustainability as an outgrowth of traditional design, especially in reducing car dependence and creating more local production.[94]

Financing, Marketing, and Building the New Urbanist Community

David Butterfield was keen to develop Civano, but he could not come up with enough base capital on his own to bid for the land. In 1995 his Trust for Sustainable Development partnered with Case Enterprises, which consisted of local developers David Case and Kevin Kelly. In exchange for agreeing to meet the IMPACT standards, the group secured a promise of municipal investment (including an offer to provide physical infrastructure such as roads). The city reasoned that the publicity associated with Civano would bring special grants and other funding.

With this support in place, the developers hired New Urbanist architects Moule and Polyzoides of Los Angeles to work under the direction of Civano's chief planner, Wayne Moody. The city soon issued a municipal improvement district bond, which financed the infrastructure at a very low interest rate of about 5 percent. (Normally, developers pay for such improvements with loans as high as 10 percent.) The bonds would be repaid in the case of Civano not through increased home prices, as would normally be the case, but through separate bills to the homeowner, with payments compounded into the buyer's monthly mortgage payments. The effect would be to reduce the price of a home at Civano but increase the mortgage payment until the bond was paid off. The individual homeowner could choose to pay off his or her portion of the bond at the end of seven years without penalty or further interest payments.

Even with this bond, the project still needed start-up capital. In October 1997 the Federal National Mortgage Corporation, commonly known as Fannie Mae, became a minority equity partner in Civano. From 1997 to 2000 Fannie Mae, chartered by Congress to increase the supply of funds for housing, contributed substantially to Civano through its American Communities Fund. The ACF was designed to reduce urban blight, improve distressed areas, and finance the building of low-income housing. Investing in Civano was a stretch for this fund, for Fannie Mae did not press Civano to provide low-income housing or recruit low-income residents. Nevertheless, Fannie Mae eventually became the major investor in the project, buying out David Case and David Butterfield, and collaborating with now-minority investor Kevin Kelly. Throughout this period of changing financing, Civano was looking for builders. The city of Tucson received a grant from the state, again out of its oil overcharge revenues, to fund the implementation of a Civano Builder Program, known as the "Guide for Sustainable Development in Arid Climates."

As discussions with builders began, the vision of Civano changed even further. Solar energy goals were modified. Although the original purpose of Civano was, according to the Metropolitan Energy Commission, to "demonstrate the beneficial uses of solar energy,"[95] the development's focus changed to a broader goal of conservation, with the role of solar energy much reduced. As a result, Civano's configuration evolved to the point where it did not incorporate even the most basic passive solar technique of proper structural orientation. The issue of orientation reflected the constraints under which the development was operating and the compromises made by builders and developers. Lots were divided by the city and by builders in ways that prohibited passive solar orientation because such orientation did not fit with the New Urbanist designs [I-034]. The structural layout of individual houses and the density and proximity of houses that are key components of New Urbanism exclude large-scale solar exploitation; thus, the most basic solar concept of passive orientation gave way to orientation designed to induce neighborliness and community.

The original Civano planners also lost the battle to introduce innovative hydrological principles in the community. Planners and developers aimed to adapt building plans to local topography so as to preserve the existing runoff patterns, maintain existing vegetation wherever possible, reduce soil erosion, and maximize water infiltration, but the city's flood control and health policies, designed to channel rainwater runoff away from developed areas quickly to prevent flooding and the accumulation of standing water, forced Civano developers to fully grade lots and channel runoff into the city's flood control system. In addition, Civano developers had hoped to collect and recycle water on site. They eventually opted to extend the city's reclaimed water system to each house instead, at an additional cost of approximately $5,000 per home. Recycled (gray) water systems are restricted under city health ordinances because improperly maintained systems can foster the growth of mosquitoes and potentially harmful bacteria, and the city would not grant Civano permits for individual gray water systems for each home.[96]

When discussions with builders were well under way, Civano began to market itself to potential residents. Selling homes in new developments is about selling image —Fannie Mae's company description opens, "For most of us, a home is more than simple shelter, or a good investment. A home of our own is a dream come true, and symbolizes who we are."[97] Civano was created to bring alternative building technology into the mainstream of the American new housing market, and therefore it did not stray far from the currently popular style of suburban residential development: large single family homes with high ceilings and plenty of amenities. The city of Tucson's Web site explained, "Civano addresses the growing desire for a new development pattern that enables people to meet their economic needs, yet maintain social values and ecological harmony."[98]

Civano became awash in public relations materials. *Civano Magazine* identified as sustainable features at Civano "high efficiency," "renewable energy," and "designing for tomorrow." A wall display at the Civano Community Center invoked "the ancient Hohokam legacy." While appealing to environmental values, Civano marketers specifically directed their campaign to a group known as "cultural creatives," in the words of a participant in the marketing process, those who are, "typically pretty well educated and put a high value on concepts of community and being involved in community." This person went on to explain,

> Cultural creatives . . . hate to be marketed to. They want to be informed. . . . So you always want to try to find a way to not try to be selling, but to talk about the authenticity and the reality of the community. . . . You would come to this "welcome center"—not a "sales center"—and you get an education about what's Civano trying to do. [I-033]

Some of that education comes in the form of promises (many as yet unmet) about the community. Civano's Web site proclaims that the "commercial, cultural, and civic activity clustered in the village center will foster a small town ambiance. Half the population and two-thirds of the jobs will be within a five-minute walk of Civano's town center. Businesses in the Community of Civano will provide jobs for many of the residents, reducing the need for automobile travel and its attendant air pollution."[99]

Construction at Civano began in 1998, and the development's grand opening was celebrated in April 1999. In a congratulatory letter to the Civano partners Vice President Al Gore wrote:

> Once in a great while each of us is lucky enough to have an opportunity to clearly see the future. Today, the grand opening of Civano is one of those unique times. Since Henry David Thoreau spent his years at Walden Pond, America has had a vision that, to be truly free, one must live in harmony with nature. Civano demonstrates that through creativity and imagination—and some risk—we as a nation can build stronger communities whose development does not conflict with environment, but actually can support and enhance a sustainable society. I want to congratulate the staff of the Community of Civano partners, Mayor Miller, and the city of Tucson, for showing us that a 19th Century dream can become a 21st Century reality.[100]

When it opened, Civano had a neighborhood center containing Le Buzz Café (a small coffee shop and restaurant) and other retail stores (mostly selling home decorating and home improvement products), a certified public accountant's office, a nursery and garden center, and the builders' offices. GlobalSolar, a solar panel manufacturing plant, was operating in the industrial park located on the fringe of the development. All of the buildings showcased alternative building technologies.

After residents moved in, Civano was transformed from a design template, an interesting building and policy debate, and a marketing campaign into a functioning community. People began occupying the spaces that grew out of the vision, and the fifteen years of planning faced the ultimate test of practice. A new set of stakeholders —the residents—were now on the scene and projecting their values and interests onto Civano's future. Designers, developers, builders, managers, and residents alike were soon to discover the difference between marketing and experience, expectation and reality, a planned community and a lived community. As a headline in the *Arizona Daily Star* read: the " 'Future Community' Is Now."[101]

Stakeholder Reactions

Though the project was off to an auspicious start, political controversy over its compromised environmental goals and the very concept of a large-scale development that
would contribute to rather than contain sprawl had been brewing and continued to
grow. In fact, months after its opening the project seemed as beset by difficulties as
ever. In 2000, Civano Development/Kevin Kelly, one of the original visionaries of
Civano, sold the remainder of its interest in the development to Fannie Mae, which as
a result came to own 100 percent of Civano.[102] This change dampened the enthusiasm
of the new residents, who were dubious about Fannie Mae's commitment to the
project's goals.

From the development phase onward, reactions to Civano have varied enormously.
There has been little consensus about what it means to live sustainably in the environmentally sensitive Sonoran Desert. Critics have questioned the primacy of "community" over solar technology in Civano's ultimate New Urbanist design, suggesting
that the only value of an initiative like Civano was its role as a testing ground for
large-scale technological innovation. Once the project let go of its original solar vision, critics argue, it became just *another* development on the fringes of Tucson—
adding to sprawl and drawing municipal funding away from poorer areas of the city.
Civano advocates, on the other hand, see Civano as a model of sustainability. Its
homes consume less water and electricity than other Tucson homes,[103] and its various
intended benefits from reducing sprawl by reducing car dependence, to conserving
conventional sources of energy, to reducing water consumption and waste, and even
to creating new jobs—have been touted as part of a larger program of sustainable
development for the region.

Residents' reactions have been even more complex than those of nonresident critics. Some residents value the sense of community they feel in the place, and others
have been drawn by the promise of sustainable living. Still others have focused on
purely economic benefits—low electric and water bills. The interplay between environmental concerns and market forces, however, has resulted in an uneasy tension.
The community has met its own environmental standards, yet there are still questions
about whether or not a project that has traditional growth goals—attracting more
people and business, and continuing to expand—can be called "sustainable."

Civano's Critics

Civano received national and international attention during its development phase. It
was touted as a housing development that incorporated the most innovative environmental resource-use technologies, such as solar heating and alternative building materials, while also being a "traditional" community with a "small town" feel.[104] In
1997, the President's Council on Sustainable Development praised Civano, and in
2000 the U.S. Department of Energy sponsored a visit from a delegation of forty-
eight African energy ministers to Civano.

Yet among locals, Civano had become the target of mounting criticism, particularly as a project receiving government funding. One set of criticisms came from Tucson's solar community.[105] By 1998 the project had replaced its plans to incorporate multiple solar technologies in all structures with an overall, not specifically *solar*, focus on energy efficiency. The latter, the developers believed, could be achieved as readily by insulation as by solar energy technologies. Homes in the first phase of the development, neighborhood one, have active solar water heating, and homeowners there can choose to install other solar features, but for neighborhoods two and three, yet to be built at the time, Fannie Mae proposed that solar technology be optional. Those in the solar lobby who criticized this turn saw sustainability not just as a movement to reform existing technologies for efficiency or reduced consumption, but as a means to create completely new ways of satisfying resource demand. A former director of the Arizona Solar Energy Commission expressed the sentiments of others in the solar community when he said, "Many of us are asking what about Civano is worth $1 million to the people of Arizona as a model solar-energy project."[106]

Solar technology advocates were not the only environmentalists who criticized Civano. Others focused on apparent incongruities in the design and planning of the "sustainable" development. One major issue was that the project's location, on Tucson's eastern outskirts, contributed to the city's suburban sprawl and created additional automobile traffic and pollution at a time when the city was trying to manage growth. The *Arizona Daily Star* noted in 1999 that "residents probably will burn more gas commuting twelve to fifteen miles to town than they save heating and cooling their 'energy efficient' homes."[107] Some critics have even argued that Civano's presence, along with the subsidies needed to get infrastructure to the site, has promoted unsustainable development in that part of town. The new roads leading out to Civano have largely been developed for business and retail use, although Civano residents must still drive four miles to reach a grocery store, undercutting the New Urbanist principles.

Even Wayne Moody, the original planner of the Tucson Solar Village, objected to Civano's shift to New Urbanism. From his point of view, a "community" design wasn't necessary; a design that is in harmony with the natural landscape and climate of a region maximizes energy efficiency and creates a community indirectly by tying people closer to each other through their connection to the local environment. In other words, the more people are aware of the environment in which they live, the stronger their allegiance to place and neighborhood. Moody was especially chagrined that principles of permaculture—land use principles that strive for the harmonious integration of dwellings, climate, soils, water, and animal and plant life—had been scuttled in the final Civano plan due to several factors, including city flood control policies and time constraints. The desired spatial arrangement of houses and pedestrian walkways—facing inward for a "community feel"—made it impossible to preserve the neighborhoods' natural hydrology. New Urbanism, Moody argues, can be terrible for the environment.[108]

Critics also challenged—and continue to challenge—the claims of "sustainable" development. The basis of this critique lies in the original aim to make Civano a national example of large-scale alternative development based on innovative technologies. In the 1980s, the planners purposely sought out a large parcel of land, and the only affordable parcel they could find was on the fringes of town. It is true that since the development of Civano, the area between it and downtown Tucson, known as the Houghton corridor, has rapidly developed cookie cutter divisions, but the fault does not lie solely with Civano. Although it was hoped that Civano would establish a new trend, it had long been predicted that this area of Tucson would be the city's growth corridor— so infrastructure would have been extended there even without Civano.

The concerns about Civano became a significant issue in Tucson's 1999 mayoral race. Molly McKasson, a city councilwoman who was running for mayor, had been on the losing side of a city council vote that approved a $3 million city grant to Civano. Echoing widely held concerns, McKasson denounced Civano's location and its weak commitment to solar energy, saying, "It's so far out, everything you save on heating your house is going to be burned in your tank . . . The homes aren't even oriented to take advantage of passive solar uses anymore." She also criticized the project for taking funds that could be used for more pressing needs. "The worst thing about the project is, we needed that money in a lot of other areas around the community," she said.[109]

In fact, Tucson has struggled with inner-city development for decades. In the 1960s, as residents moved to the urban fringes, many Mexican-American barrios were demolished, and no comparable low-cost replacement housing was provided.[110] Property values in revitalized areas tended to rise, effectively barring low-income people from the urban housing market.[111] Advocates for Tucson's homeless are still struggling with this problem. According to Don Chatfield, executive director of a foundation that works with Tucson's low-income and homeless residents, "There are signs that Tucson may go the route of other cities that have wanted to sanitize downtown to pave the way for revitalization."[112]

Predictions that the energy saved by Civano's energy-efficient building technologies would be canceled out by commuting distances have been borne out. The IMPACT system set a goal of one neighborhood job for every two residences, and the city of Tucson boasted that within eight to twelve years of opening, Civano would become home to more than five thousand people and the location of light industry, offices, and retail businesses.[113] It was unclear by 2004 whether Civano had met its goal of jobs for residents[114]—most remained commuters, and only 6 percent of respondents to our 2001 survey cited jobs as their reason for moving to Civano. Further, there is no mass transit linking Civano to the rest of Tucson, and few residents carpool to work. In fact, Civano now has a parking problem. In 2003, the Civano Neighbors Neighborhood Association created a working group to look into parking in the community.[115] Employment opportunities at Civano do appear to be growing. Some residents work at the community school, the nursery, home-based businesses, and at facilities located on Tucson's southeast side. Overall, however, Civano has not been able to transform the commuting patterns that are typical of suburban residents.

The aggregation of these criticisms led the alternative press in Tucson, particularly the editorial pages of the *Tucson Weekly*, to call Civano yet another offspring of the "cancerous" growth lobby—"a fake, pure and simple." The municipal money fronted for Civano was approved specifically for a *solar* village, and in the view of the *Weekly*, merely conserving energy from conventional sources does not justify the construction of a new suburb. Tucson should instead revise the city building code to require the environmental measures taken at Civano. As the *Weekly* put it:

> Any idiot can see that shade, insulation and pedestrian-friendly streets are important. The real task involves imposing these requirements on out-of-town mega-developers used to having their own way when it comes to throwing up the cheapest crap imaginable at the lowest possible cost in order to maximize sales and, hence, profits.
>
> It sure as hell doesn't take some over-hyped, stuccorama-in-the-sticks development to show these bottom-line-oriented bozos the way. No, it takes firm leadership and a local government willing to enforce beefed-up building codes. But, of course, that's precisely what Tucson has always lacked.[116]

Public and Private Supporters: Investors and Marketers

In spite of these critiques, many observers also acknowledged Civano's environmental accomplishments. Every home has solar water heating, and many have additional solar panels for heat and electricity. Reclaimed water is a standard feature of Civano houses, in spite of the expense of the system. The developers attempted to save and replant most of the desert vegetation disturbed by the construction of the community, with a success rate as high as 99 percent for some species, such as mesquite [I-010]. Green building techniques, drawing on ecologically safe materials like RASTRA block to provide advanced insulation, are employed in the construction of most of the houses in the community.

The federal government declared Civano a "success story" even before its opening. Mark Ginsberg of the U.S. Department of Energy pointed out in 1999 that Civano need not have incorporated solar energy to be novel and effective. Civano's use of better insulation, shade, more efficient heating and cooling systems, and better windows still makes it a standout when it comes to energy efficiency. Although other homes may have some of these features, Ginsberg touted Civano as an example of how they can be coordinated on a large scale.[117] John Laswick, the city of Tucson's project manager for Civano from 1994 to 2000, also defended Civano's energy-saving measures, pointing out that solar requirements were not abandoned entirely. "One myth is that the solar part dropped out," he said. "Every house is still required to have some solar feature."[118]

Fannie Mae also stood behind Civano, claiming that the project has reached all its IMPACT goals,[119] even though it had modified some of its strategies for achieving these goals—for example, by using other methods of saving water in neighborhoods two and three in addition to requiring reclaimed water use for individual homes. Fannie Mae also cited the developers' commitment to the "creation of non-vehicle circulation systems"—bike paths and walking trails—and to "developing mixed uses on-site so that residents have employment and commercial opportunities at Civano," though they fail to mention that only the first of these goals has been reached. In reality, there are few other employment opportunities within Civano for residents, and many of the on-site jobs originally proposed (at the coffee shop, community garden, post office, and so on) were not suitable for Civano residents in any case due to the disparity between the wages those jobs pay and the cost of living in Civano. Fannie Mae's PR representatives were also ambiguous about Civano's energy *supply* requirements. They cited "encouragement" of "innovative technologies not dependent on fossil fuels" as one of the project's successes even as they advocated eliminating the solar requirements for the yet-to-be-built neighborhoods two and three.

Some Civano supporters steer clear of energy consumption questions and instead focused on Civano as the embodiment of New Urbanism. According to John Lawsick,

> New Urbanist principles really reinforced the kind of environmental principles that Civano or sustainable developments were trying to promote, which was not just an environmentally better community, but a socially more interesting and dynamic community, which made money and flourished in the marketplace. So you have the three legs of environmental, economic, and social benefits. And what I think New Urbanism brings to development is essentially "curb appeal"—not everyone wants to live in a house that is energy efficient but isn't particularly attractive. You need both.[120]

Lee Rayburn, formerly head of CDC Partners, which managed and designed Civano's development, asserted that the emphasis on community that has replaced some environmental goals is as much a point in Civano's favor as a strike against it. "The way the place is designed," according to Rayburn, "invites social interaction; it doesn't demand it."[121] In other public comments Rayburn has added that the developers were "trying to go further to make sure that we retain the special look and feel of the Sonoran Desert," suggesting that they were banking on Civano's aesthetic appeal to lure potential homeowners.[122]

Of course, Civano's developers (and their patrons, the municipal and federal governments), wanted Civano to represent it all: innovative alternative energy technologies, conventional energy conservation, community planning—all while contributing to economic growth. And some advocates have held fast to this vision. In 1996, an eco-industrial park workshop in Virginia sponsored by the President's Council on Sustainable Development featured Civano as a case study.[123] And in 2003, a senior economist for the EPA commended the *economic* benefits accruing from sustainable development communities such as Civano insofar as they contribute to job creation, technological innovation, and reduced resource consumption.[124] Laswick, for his part, said he believes that "Civano has been successful in showing builders that they can build a much more environmentally appropriate kind of house without significantly affecting the economics of construction."[125] In addition, the Civano developers' successful battles in the city council and planning chambers over things like zoning ordinances and traffic-calming measures have inspired, and smoothed the road for, more recent projects. For example, the planner of Armory Park del Sol, a new development in downtown Tucson that embodies some of the same principles as Civano, found it much easier than Wayne Moody had to attain city approval for his plans. One member of Civano's management team expressed hope for the project's continued market potential:

> I've gotten really tired and really discouraged sometimes thinking, why am I doing this? And then I go to a conference, and I hear a speech, and people come out all aglow and energized by the fact that someone's insane enough to do this crazy whatever, so I feel good about that, because I know this is right. There's a market for it. . . . We're. . . . trying to show that there is a market for it, we're trying to convince Fannie Mae and the insurance companies and the banks who control mortgages that there is a market for this kind of development, but it's all in the context of real hard economic realities, and unless you've dealt with time and interest payments and that clock that just ticks away every second of every day, it's tough to understand the [pressure]. [I-033]

For its promoters, then, Civano is a model for continued economic growth that tries to offset the traditional byproducts of development, namely resource depletion and environmental degradation. Some highlight the project's environmental record, others its New Urbanist pedigree—and most either ignore or play down the fact that commitments to New Urbanism and energy conservation sometimes conflict. John Laswick summed up supporters' feelings when he said, "Civano shows people that there's a different kind of development that can occur." Civano may have modified its vision over the years—but at least it was greener than its neighbors.

Residents

Civano residents, yet another set of stakeholders, became a powerful voice in shaping the development. While promotional literature for Civano implied that environmental concerns were a common core value for residents and the environmental components of the development a central attraction,[126] our 2001 survey, interviews, and discussions suggested a more nuanced and variable assemblage of motivations and values among Civano's new residents. Those most often mentioned were the economic benefits of sustainable living; the importance of building community; the power of a cohesive community to change human interactions with the environment; and the power of individual voices to effect change in the laws and institutions that govern their lives.

Approximately 48 percent of the thirty-six Civano households surveyed (out of a total of sixty households in residence at the time of our survey) moved there from other neighborhoods in Tucson, and an additional 10 percent moved from elsewhere in Arizona. The remaining 42 percent came to Civano from out of state. For residents moving from outside of Arizona, job relocation, family, and climate were common reasons for relocating. Approximately 33 percent of those moving from out of state did so because of a job transfer or military base closure, but many also wanted to live in a particular kind of environment. As one resident put it, "I didn't want to be an anonymous home owner in Rita Ranch," a typical suburban development nearby. Of those who moved to Civano from other neighborhoods in Tucson, about half moved from centrally located neighborhoods, and the remaining half moved from other out-lying parts of the city. Many cited a concern with congestion and lack of safety in their old neighborhoods, as well as an attraction to the Civano concept, as reasons for their move.

Despite Civano's incomplete success in meeting its environmental goals, there were residents for whom the environmental components of Civano were a central attraction. Twelve percent listed environmental concerns as a reason for moving to Civano; an additional 15 percent cited the project's energy and building standards; and almost all residents interviewed talked about the environmental sensitivity of the desert and, in the words of one resident, "the need to live as lightly on this fragile land as possible."

In addition to its New Urbanist and environmentalist features, Civano advocates advertise their wish for community diversity, but demographically the development appears little different from the traditional suburban sprawl that is quickly surround-ing it. Only 11 percent of survey participants identified themselves as ethnic mi-norities. The remaining 88 percent identified themselves as white only, significantly more than the 54.2 percent of Tucson residents who identify as white (not Hispanic or Latino). Though the price of a house at Civano predetermines a certain income level for residents, within that economic stratum there appears to be a wide span of occupations represented. Residents include engineers, teachers, scientists, mechanics, investors, designers, consultants, students, and train conductors. These are clearly not the low-income people that Fannie Mae's American Communities Fund was designed to help.

The residents of Civano took pains to distinguish themselves and their vision of Civano from that of the developers. Following our interviews, they created their own neighborhood association Web site, www.CivanoNeighbors.com, and newsletter, the *Town Crier.* In May 2003, the *Town Crier* covered a recent conflict between Civano residents and the developers: the residents' opposition to Fannie Mae's push to elimi-nate the solar power requirement for future building. Nevertheless, residents' reac-tions to Civano focused more on what Civano is and less on what it could have become. Detractors pointed to Civano's failure to achieve its initial goals, but residents com-mented on its successes in sustainable resource consumption and on the community's other, nonenvironmental attractions.

In most cases, residents attracted to Civano by the community's energy efficiency standards identified the economic benefits of energy efficiency—in the form of lower home heating and cooling costs—more often than the environmental benefits, dem-onstrating that although environmental concerns are not absent from energy discus-sions, economic concerns are prioritized. As one resident explained, "We knew that the costs of heating and cooling could be really high, so we were looking for some-place that would give us the energy savings we were looking for" [I-025].

Home buyers who chose to move to Civano also understood they would have small yards with no grass, share a community swimming pool instead of having their own pool, and pay extra for reclaimed water and alternative building materials. Though such amenities are unaffordable for many residents in Tucson, the middle-income residents in Civano's housing market can afford them if they want them. Once they have moved in, many residents opt to work on neighborhood committees that promote their idea of an appropriately developed environment—for example, the landscape and architecture committee donated hundreds of volunteer hours to the task of preparing a report that listed recommended plants for landscaping and identified water-loving species that should be banned from the neighborhood. (The final document was endorsed by the resident advisory council and adopted by the board of the Home Owners Association [HOA] for Civano.) Not surprisingly, then, some residents described their decision to move to Civano as a personal sacrifice for the sake of the environment:

> I mean, that's the funny thing about Civano. It's not financially smart to be in the conservation business. What's financially smart is to use up your resources while they're cheap and make as much of a bundle on them and move on. The world is getting too small to do that anymore. . . . Right now, I don't think people are planning for the shortage of water, or shortage of electricity, or shortage of fossil fuels, or shortages of land uses, burning it up because it's cheap and plentiful and they can do that. . . . I guess from our point of view, it's worth some personal sacrifice now as part of Tucson, or U.S., or North American continent to start looking for [ways in which] people can start transitioning to different ways of living and using resources, instead of this consume, consume, consume attitude, which works when things are plentiful but doesn't when [they're not]. [I-006]

Residents often talked about the need for a group of people like themselves to make the initial efforts to live "outside the box," despite the hardships it involved. According to one resident:

> I think, some days we just go, "Let's move to Rita Ranch and give it up. It's just too much work." But realistically, you have to believe. . . . I guess in some respects it's about trying to put out a new way of viewing this whole thing of building these giant subdivisions. . . . Someone has to start. [I-007]

Still, the level of environmental commitment varied within the community. Some residents came to Civano for its environmental goals, while others claimed to have become more aware of environmental concerns since moving to the community.[127] For many, care for the environment was just one piece of what it means to live a good life. Environmental values were mediated by and articulated along with values connected to community, safety, and economics. In fact, 55.5 percent of the residents surveyed emphasized community as the main reason they liked living in Civano. As one participant stated, "Everyone out here feels very strongly that they aren't just moving into a house; they're moving into a community" [I-025].

In addition, many residents saw environmental goals as achievable only within a community. As one said:

> People can't really afford to do a lot of environmental things personally. Some people can, but to really do great things . . . like water harvesting. . . . It's different than living out somewhere in some wildcat subdivision[128] where you can do anything, you can just put a big wacky silver giant thing to collect water in and who cares? [I-007]

Community as a value embodied in design was a major selling point for Civano, and residents mentioned it frequently. Overall, Civano residents are highly conversant with the principles of New Urbanism, whether or not they use the label, revealing beliefs in an explicit relationship between a neighborhood's physical-spatial design and increased positive interaction among residents. One resident described the appeal of the original vision as follows:

> Things were self-contained, so you didn't have to drive 5 miles to the supermarket; there would just be a market there. There would be a café, there'd be a place to do postage, there'd be kind of all these things a little town would have, be right there in the center. So you wouldn't have to depend on the outside world for all your needs. [I-006]

During 2001 interviews, residents cited the closing of Le Buzz Café in 2000 as a major disappointment. The resident community was too small to support an internal business, and city ordinances prohibiting advertising along Houghton Road had limited the ability of Civano businesses to draw outside customers. A mixed-use commercial area was one of the key components of the Civano design, and with the café went a central meeting place and a vital part of the neighborhood center. When asked in 2001 how Civano had differed from their expectations of it, fully 25 percent of survey participants complained of promised amenities that were not available, while only 5 percent complained that there was less green building than they had expected. When asked what they would change about Civano, 25 percent wanted more small businesses in the community, and 22.2 percent prioritized a functioning neighborhood center.

Although the vision of merging environmental goals and community life was not yet fully realized as of 2004, many firmly believed that it would be. As Simmons Buntin, a leader of the Civano Neighbors Neighborhood Association wrote in the *Town Crier* in September 2003:

> Is it possible for a New Urbanist community also based on principles of sustainability to become a town that does substantially reduce energy and water use, preserve the environment, enhance pedestrian and social access, and create a variety of long-term jobs onsite? The answer . . . must be yes. . . . In Civano's case, I believe long-term success will be defined in large part on whether the town center comes to fruition. More than simply a grouping of commercial buildings, a town center is the core and focus of the community, commercial and civic.[129]

As they waited for the completion of the town center and the arrival of small businesses, two critical New Urbanist features, Civano residents took their own steps to strengthen the community. Besides informal socializing among neighbors, they created three long-term forums for community interaction: monthly potlucks, committee meetings, and an on-line chat room. In 2001, 61 percent of our survey respondents attended a monthly potluck at least once every few months, while 30 percent claimed to attend committee meetings at least once a month. Clearly, community has in many ways trumped the environment as an attraction for Civano residents. It remains to be seen whether that will hold true for future residents, as well, but by May 2003 the Town Crier was reporting that a new restaurant/social center would open and that the hours of the neighborhood center would be extended.

An outgrowth of the strong commitment to community was many residents' active involvement in decision-making at Civano. This begins with home buyers' control over the designs of their homes, a significant departure from the usual practice in "cookie-cutter" subdivisions. As of the summer of 2001, buyers could choose among five different builders offering a range of prices and a variety of features, and many residents mentioned control over design as an important reason for moving to Civano.

Residents extended this desire for control to the governance of the community as well. The original planners established a three-member board of directors to oversee the Civano Homeowners Association, the entity established to manage common property and make decisions about the covenants, conditions, and restrictions (CC&Rs) of the development.[130] Every property holder in Civano held one vote per lot in the homeowners association.[131] Because most of the lots are still unsold, however, the developer still legally controls decisions. A residents' advisory council to the homeowners association has little autonomy, and some residents consider it to be no more than a mouthpiece for the HOA.[132] This is the reason why in 2002 they formed their own neighborhood association.[133] According to its Web site, the Civano Neighbors Neighborhood Association uses a modified consensus form of decision-making because "we live in a unique community environment and the consensus form of decision-making reflects that uniqueness and lets all of us participate freely and openly."[134]

The RGC and Don Diamond Incidents and the Elucidation of Resident Values

Extensive resident involvement in the Civano community made for an unusual level of interaction, not all of it friendly, between residents and developers. Several incidents — the multiple contract default of one of the original builders, as described below — underscored the tension between these two groups. Many residents expressed the sentiment that the developers "missed that connection between the ideals of planning this community, and what happens if we bring in human beings" [I-027]. Residents were particularly dismayed to see the original vision of the Civano project continue to wane, as when Fannie Mae threatened to lower environmental standards in the Civano neighborhoods two and three.

By far the most damaging incident with builders was the bankruptcy and multiple contract default in 2000 of RGC, one of the original builders. RGC was unable to meet its production demands and pulled out of the development, leaving many potential residents homeless, perplexed, and angry. For RGC contract holders, the failure of the builder to meet the contract obligations was much more significant on a personal level. Many families had contingency contracts with RGC. They sold their homes to pay for the construction of their new homes at Civano and moved into rental houses or apartments to await their completion. When the builder defaulted on the contracts, they could choose to get their money back and build elsewhere, but many contract holders still wanted to live at Civano. Moreover, housing and production prices had risen since they had purchased contracts from RGC, and the homebuyers could not get the same house at the same price in the inflated market.

At the most basic level, the RGC pull-out was a breach of contract that left many people homeless. However, because of the visibility of Civano within the community, this default had much larger implications for the reputation of the project. The fact that the builder could not meet his contracts led some people within Tucson to question whether such a project—large-scale sustainable development—was even feasible. Rumors circulated that Civano itself was bankrupt, and this affected sales of other builders' homes within the community.

After repeated attempts to negotiate with RGC and Fannie Mae, on August 16, 2000, the homebuyers filed a lawsuit against RGC, Civano Development, and Civano Realty in order to recoup the money that they had lost in changing housing markets and extended rental fees. Another suit filed by CDC Partners, then the management entity at Civano, was settled out of court, allowing CDC Partners to regain options on several lots owned by RGC that had not yet been sold to homebuyers.

These lawsuits, the first in Civano's twenty-year history, underscored the complexity of the financial negotiations involved in building the community. Moreover, they represented an undesired form of conflict resolution for many residents, who were fully aware of the harm a lawsuit could inflict on the Civano community. But it is exactly the rhetoric of community from the developers and the perceived betrayal of that concept by the builder and the developers that inspired the lawsuit and gave it significance beyond mere financial motivation. As one couple involved in the suit explained, "It was a last resort." The RGC contract holders were families and individuals drawn to Civano for various reasons, but united by the common values of community and environment. Yet the RGC default made clear that environmental values (energy efficiency, water conservation, aesthetics, etc.) and community values (neighborliness, safety, diversity, etc.) had to be mediated and filtered through the residents' own economic concerns and the builder's need to meet a bottom line. Faced with these external impediments, the homeowners sought to regain control over their lives through litigation, despite the disdain of many of the residents who were not affected by RGC's actions.

Also in 2000, another unsettling moment came when word leaked out that Don Diamond, a Tucson developer with a reputation for building sprawling subdivisions on the fringes of the city, might purchase neighborhoods two and three. Much of the community rallied in opposition. Several residents wrote, and posted on the Internet, a "white paper," endorsed by the resident advisory council, to represent resident interests and beliefs during the period. In it, the authors write:

> While many years of thoughtful planning have gone into shaping The Community of Civano, that legacy has now been passed to its current residents, as we are known, the early adopters. . . . It is our economic, cultural and ideological investment that is at stake in the future development of Civano. Therefore, we have not only the right, but the responsibility, to help safeguard the vision of Civano as written into current public law and the foundation documents.[135]

Our interviews were conducted during this time period, and many residents voiced their concerns: to them, Don Diamond represented exactly the kind of development that Civano had been created to counter. And because Diamond Ventures' nearby developments were among the first to benefit from the city-subsidized infrastructure out to Civano, some began to feel as if they were part of a scam.[136] Some residents began an aggressive letter-writing campaign, demanding assurances from the city that the development standards could not be altered. Individual community members targeted specific city councilors, seeking to speak with them in person about their concerns for the community. Though the energy and conservation standards for Civano are part of the city's constitution, for two of the three neighborhoods they can be changed by a vote of the city council. Don Diamond is a powerful figure in the city, and residents worried that he could persuade the council to make those changes. Management at the welcome center at Civano removed from its promotional material all references to the two neighborhoods, neighborhoods two and three, where changes were still possible, and instructed staff to speak about Civano only in terms of neighborhood one, which could not be changed.[137]

The potential loss of neighborhoods two and three to cookie-cutter development greatly concerned the residents in neighborhood one. The Civano name itself symbolized what alternative development hoped to achieve, and thus the threat to that achievement had symbolic importance. Additionally, residents in neighborhood one would be affected by development decisions regarding features such as roads, drainage, and lighting in the other two neighborhoods. Finally, the residents in the other neighborhoods would outnumber the residents in neighborhood one, and potentially outvote them on decisions that might come before the homeowners association.

The Don Diamond scare exacerbated another anxiety for Civano residents. Fannie Mae could make deals and contracts without any input from residents, but residents would have to follow through on those contracts when they transitioned to the homeowners association. This was particularly upsetting because Civano's marketing propaganda had promised a collaborative community-building process. The residents determined that, although they could not affect the business negotiations, they would "turn the lights on," making sure any weakening of Civano's standards at the city level occurred publicly.[138]

The threat of lowered environmental standards seemed to have rallied some formerly indifferent residents and turned them into environmental crusaders. What had been just one aspect of the planned community became its focal point when residents perceived it was threatened. In responding to the threat of a takeover by Diamond Ventures, the residents articulated their values in a fight for power with the city authorities. Coming together behind the environmental principles on which Civano had been founded, the residents followed their exhaustive letter-writing campaign with a formal petition demanding that the Tucson city council maintain the Civano energy standards. The council issued a verbal statement in support of the Civano energy standards in late October, and in December of 2000, Diamond withdrew from negotiations to purchase Civano.

Residents believed that it was their active organization and vocal protest that kept Civano's standards intact, but they recognized that the victory was only partial. According to one local observer, the Don Diamond incident showed residents they had the power "not to make the decisions but to be a participant in how the decisions are going to be made and what factors will be considered." The fact that Diamond did not purchase Civano does not mean that another developer will not come along and push a personal agenda sometime in the future, but such a developer will be more likely to open a dialogue with residents as well as managers.

In January 2004, residents were reportedly optimistic because of the sale of neighborhoods two and three to Pulte Homes, a developer that was willing to make a commitment to Civano's environmental principles, outlined in the Civano IMPACT system memorandum of understanding. The neighborhood association met with Pulte regularly throughout the purchasing process and early on lent its support to continuing discussions. The sale made residents feel that they had some ability to guide decisions according to their values—but whether, in the long run, these values would continue to be expressed at Civano remained to be seen. In 2004, in a worrying development, it looked as if Pulte Homes would be shying away from following many of the New Urbanist principles that had attracted so many residents.[139]

The Expression of Values in Grand Bois, Civano, and the United States

The cases of Grand Bois and Civano are, on the surface, different in the extreme. Grand Bois is a community of poor, undereducated, racial minorities, many of whose families have lived in the same spot for a century or more. Civano is made up of upper-middle-class, predominantly white residents who began to move in only in 1999. Most of Civano's residents migrated from outside the Tucson area, and that fact underscores another difference between the two communities: a difference of privilege and political power. Civano's residents enjoy the luxury of choosing their community and location, and they are vocal in their demands to mold the community to their liking. The residents of Grand Bois face much greater constraints about where they live, and when they speak out, it is not to protect their vision for the community but to protect themselves and their families from harm.

By probing the two communities' values we can learn about the choices some Americans make—or are free to make—about their environments. Until a crisis hit, most Grand Bois residents rarely thought about how their values defined their relationship to the environment. In fact, they lived next door to toxic waste for more than a decade, and not until the problem reached a certain threshold were they spurred to action. In Civano, many residents have become acutely aware of their values through the process of choosing a home and a community. They are conversant with the New Urbanist vision and environmentally sensitive technologies, and they have molded their community based upon New Urbanist and environmentalist values.

In both Grand Bois and Civano, residents' commitment to place was profound, but for different reasons. In Grand Bois, the families of those harmed by the toxic waste had lived in the area for a century or more. Before the crisis, their sense of place and appreciation for the natural environment were strong, and most would never have dreamed of leaving their community. After the poisoning, however, many came to realize that they *could not* leave because their homes, thanks to oilfield waste, were now unsalable. The longtime familial attachment to the land was now accompanied by resentment born of an unattainable desire to flee. In Civano, on the other hand, all the residents were newcomers, most from outside the Tucson area. Although a few moved to Civano specifically because of their appreciation for the community's environmental standards, most came for other reasons. Once there, however, many residents experienced an environmental "awakening." Learning about Civano's environmental goals, which Fannie Mae had deliberately downplayed in its marketing strategy, increased the residents' appreciation for the environment and for their new homes. Thus the degree of commitment to place in these two communities changed in the course of our cases, becoming weaker in Grand Bois and stronger in Civano. As former Civano project manager John Laswick has noted, people come to Tucson "because they are attracted to living in the desert. As time goes by, they become desensitized. It's the newcomers who have a higher level of awareness of their impact on the deserts."[140]

Natural resource–use ideologies also changed over time for the residents of both regions. Back in the 1920s, long before the arrival of the oil and gas industry, Louisianans had called for habitat protection. In 1925, for example, an official of Louisiana's Department of Conservation argued that the draining and reclaiming of marshes was a major factor in the decline of the state's native wildlife. "The scenic effects throughout this country [the wetlands]," he wrote, "have served and still serve as inspiration to the poet, philosopher and artist, and the legend and romance of the swamp and marsh country is still being written."[141] But few people ventured into the region's marshes, and as a result, Louisiana's early conservationists perceived the area as vast and its resources as forever renewable. These attitudes lingered for decades, contributing to the initial inaction when the oil and gas industry began to pollute the state. It took a crisis on the level of Grand Bois to begin to change these views.

In the Sonoran Desert, resource-use ideology has long been premised on growth and expansion, and, consequently, it has focused on resource consumption. The desert was vast and empty, and it was up to rugged settlers to people it and improve it. The original vision of Civano declined to challenge the idea that growth was good, instead adjusting the methods of growth. And by letting go of some of the development's original environmental goals, the advocates of modified New Urbanism also contributed to the perpetuation of this pro-growth ideology.

The third category of values at play in the two cases relates to marketing and economics. In both cases, it is hard to disentangle economic arguments from environmental ones. In Grand Bois, Houmas and Cajuns were heavily dependent on the oil industry for their livelihoods. Residents were forced to choose between revolting against the oil companies that supported them and protecting their health, homes, and communities. For many, this was an impossible choice. One community organizer lamented that even after the court fight many of her neighbors had remained tied into the oil industry because that is what brought in the "fat paychecks." Even among those who sought to protect themselves and their families, economics (specifically, the impossibility of selling their homes) often prevented them from doing so.

In Civano, market economics dictated substantial changes in the original vision of the community, as the solar village concept was eclipsed by New Urbanism. The developers figured that New Urbanism would sell, and environmentalism would not—so their marketing strategy downplayed the community's environmental goals they did retain. At the same time, the economic benefits of living in the new community were touted to potential residents. Many people moved into Civano because they were attracted by the idea of lower energy bills—and only after signing on for the economic benefits did they come to know and appreciate the development's environmental goals.

The communities can be distinguished by their differing sense of political efficacy, which had a lot to do with the degree to which each could express values in public policy spheres. Both communities struggled to protect themselves in the face of powerful monied interests. In Grand Bois, residents responded to the advice and support of the church, scientists, and policy makers who stood behind their cause. They took their grievances to court—but in the end, despite policy changes, many still felt that their voices had not been heard. A weak sense of political efficacy has a long history among Louisianans, who according to former state Secretary of Environmental Quality Paul Templet, are "not well-educated or -organized. They tend not to participate in government, and Louisiana has one of the lowest voter turnout rates in the country. . . . Louisiana is not what you would call a democratic state because of the influence of industry and the lack of accountability within [state government] agencies."[142] In Civano, on the other hand, the middle class residents assumed from the start that they had every right to speak out on their own behalf. They formed their own community organization with its own Web site distinct from that of the developer, lobbied officials, and protested attempted buyouts by developers they believed would not be true to their vision. In both cases, residents eventually resorted to the ultimate American solution—litigation. The two communities came away with very different ideas about the effectiveness of such involvement, however—the Grand Bois plaintiffs were disappointed by small settlements, whereas the Civano residents could congratulate themselves on the success of their efforts.

In the Grand Bois case study, we see the winners and losers clearly, and we see the role of race and class in determining who they are. In Grand Bois, because of a history of absorbing refugees from British rule and because of racial mixing, the Houma Indians, Louisiana's largest Indian tribe, were denied federal recognition as a Native American tribe and the relative protection such status offers. For the Houmas ever to attain federal recognition, they will have to prove that they have maintained their society and culture in a particular geographic area for hundreds of years. Thus, even if they had the financial means to relocate, leaving Grand Bois would not only endanger the continuation of their culture and community but also end any hopes for recognition as a tribe.

As the Houma subsistence economy has disappeared, the Houmas have become dependent on the wage labor system and tied to industries that harm their environment. Today the oil industry that pays their wage simultaneously poisons them. In this sense, the Houmas are complicit in their own destruction, yet the federal and Louisiana governments prevent them from influencing in any large measure the way the industry operates in their community. Depositing toxic waste in Grand Bois and other poor minority communities protects more affluent communities from being harmed by byproducts of the industries upon which their standard of living relies.

In stark contrast to Grand Bois, the main actors in the Civano case are a group of white privileged developers, with the largely white middle class residents also playing a role in shaping the community. Situating Civano within the broader context of resource politics in the Sonoran Desert, however, reveals that the dynamics of race and class are also operating in this case. The less powerful (and unrecognized) stakeholders include the Hopi and the Navajo, who have sacrificed their lands to feed urban growth. Both tribes are federally recognized, and, as such, as the U.S. Supreme Court has ruled, they are entitled to reserved water rights to guarantee a viable subsistence economy and federal oversight of resource extraction contracts. Despite these protections, the federal government, state governments, resource extraction industries, and southwestern developers have effectively conspired to place these Indian nations in a position resembling that of third world colonies—and not unlike the situation of the Houma in Grand Bois. The surrounding governments recognize Navajo and Hopi sovereignty yet take their natural resources at a fraction of market value to support relatively affluent areas like Tucson and Civano in a desert environment hundreds of miles away. The Navajo and Hopi tribes have recourse to the federal court system and the Bureau of Indian Affairs, yet these are the very offices of the U.S. government that have created the current system and the tribes are cautious about the amount of support they can expect from them.

At the same time it would be wrong to overstate the power held by Tucson residents in general and Civano community members in particular. Tucson includes the silent inner-city poor that city councilwoman Molly McKasson and homeless advocate Don Chatfield speak for. And despite their socioeconomic advantages over their Grand Bois counterparts, Civano residents still struggle against the power of entrenched business interests in the form of developers like Don Diamond. Again, it was in the course of such struggles that their own values were clarified and articulated, a process that resembles the experience of Grand Bois residents.

Four Insights

Ecosystem degradation, the introduction and spread of alien species, changes to the course of a major river, aquifer depletion, and suburb construction are all forms of human engagement in the natural world. Government policies guide and limit that engagement but not the diversity of meanings that inform it. In the United States, policies typically are instrumental, in the sense that they seek to maximize the use of a valued resource. Maximization of resource consumption often (but not always) involves competing costs and benefits to environments, economies, and people. Also typically, instrumental policies further the sense that humans and their creations are distinct from the natural world—that culture stands apart from nature. These two attributes of American policy partially account for the disjuncture between environmental policy and values. Insofar as policy makers see their efforts as promoting only human concerns, they have some justification for minimizing the importance of environmental effects. Environmental values that are at odds with the instrumental rationality of the state can then be downplayed—as in Vice President Cheney's comment that conservation, as a mere personal virtue, is less important than an energy policy that efficiently exploits natural resources.

Yet in a symbolic maneuver that rejoins nature and culture, we may wish to see the natural in the canals of the Central Arizona Project, and the unnatural in jumbo shrimp off the coast of southern Louisiana; the natural in oil wells and the unnatural in pygmy owl preservation. Perhaps the needed shift in environmental values, and environmental policy, is a major ontological reorganization that shakes loose the cultural presuppositions that maintain the division between humans and the rest of nature, so that we see a culture-nature link where we once saw a culture-nature divide. Problems of nature-culture—what Richard White in his study of the Columbia River calls the "organic machine," or what might also be called the domesticated wild—center on the relationship between humans and the world we inhabit, a relationship for which there is no adequate single term.[143]

Our studies of Louisiana oilfield waste policy and Arizona desert conservation and their impacts on environmental values point directly to the relationship between humans and our world, a relationship partially of our devising and partially outside our ability to devise. The studies suggest at least four insights about the relationship between policy and its impact on people's relationship with the natural world:

1. Policy decisions at multiple levels of government shape the expression of environmental values—in some cases suppressing them altogether. As an example at the national level, the congressional decision not to regulate oilfield waste as hazardous waste under the Resource Conservation and Recovery Act required Grand Bois residents to find other, and ultimately less-efficacious, means to bring their problems to the attention of government officials. Their environmental values were couched in terms of health and community life, but had to be expressed in a regulatory context that placed a priority on American oil supplies and its economic and security benefits and gave favorable treatment to polluting oil companies, thereby allowing the ongoing contamination of their environment. Grand Bois residents finally resorted to legal action and public exposure of the toxic-waste disposal practices through national media. Significantly, however, their legal case was settled out of court and the results are sealed, protecting oilfield waste companies from further public scrutiny.

An example of local policy shaping the expression of environmental values is Tucson's zoning regulations, which required Civano developers to bulldoze the land prior to building. Part of the zoning rationale was directed at flood control. The development needed to be graded to allow rain to flow out of the development. It is impossible, however, to preserve a local desert environment while scraping it bare and rearranging its contours. As an expression of environmental values, desert preservation was no match for flood control. Local policy encompassed a set of environmental values, which the subjects of that policy could accept or try to modify. Recourse for change, however, is unwieldy and in some cases can require litigation, legislative reform or both. To have practical effects, local environmental values must be mediated by political economic relations and large bureaucracies, both of which impose their own constraints on environmental change.

2. In general, local concerns trump regional or national concerns in the expression of environmental values. As a consequence, destructive policies may continue: local people see only a small portion of their effects, and thus may advocate policies that have deleterious consequences elsewhere. In addition, local environmental values, as they are reflected in the activities of people's daily lives, do not appear to encompass larger issues or larger connections. For example, oilfield pollution in Louisiana, and desert sprawl and diminishing water supplies in Arizona, are historically linked because both involve the development and use of cheap energy supplies, but the environmental subjects—the people affected by environmental policies—often remain unaware of this connection. In the case of Civano a link that is rarely a part of the policy discourse is the fact that Tucson's growth, including environmentally sensitive developments like Civano, relies on a water supply that is heavily dependent on the Navajo aquifer.

3. Environmental values become part of public discourse only when they serve a pragmatic goal—preservation of human health in Grand Bois, and sustainable desert life in Tucson. The implication is that each local culture will find different ways to express environmental values. Therefore how a community responds to the effects of economic globalization, for example, is dependent on the cultural meanings it has

developed around these issues as well as the sensitivity of local policies that mediate globalization's effects to local values. Further ethnographic and historical work will continue to uncover local cultural specificity.

4. The cases of Civano and Grand Bois demonstrate that environmental values are embedded in a range of other values—those connected with family, work, and community. For environmental values to change, these other values need to change as well. Therefore it is difficult to identify a distinctive sphere of environmental values; rather values towards the environment are related closely to values towards family, community, health, and livelihood.

In Grand Bois, in particular, where many residents expressed suspicion of the environmental movement, environmental values were constantly invented and invoked, but rarely as values specifically oriented toward the environment. Civano, an overtly environmental project, probably comes as close as one can get to an example of where environmental values are expressed as values towards the environment. But even in the case of Civano, we saw how in the implementation of the project to create a sustainable community, other values—particularly economic and community values—became paramount.

Ultimately the question is whose values will prevail. At stake is the interpretation through policy of human-environment interactions and the means to justify and implement that interpretation. Also at stake is the reproduction of local culture. Grand Bois and Civano show the limits, as well as the possibilities, of local people's power to affect the process of constructing and engaging environmental values that have a policy impact. The question, which this study does not answer, is whether the better incorporation of these values in policy will be sufficient to alter destructive environmental practices, slow the pace of such practices, or simply remain marginal to the larger economic and policy forces that dominate human-environment relations in the United States.

Notes

*This chapter, revised and abridged by David Jenkins, Joanne Bauer, and Scott Bruton, is based on an unpublished report: Diane Austin, Thomas McGuire, Erin Dean, Trenna Valado, Allison Davis, Candice Clifford, Jane Moody, and Colin Seay, "Exploring Environmental Values and Policy in the United States: Case Studies in Arizona and Louisiana" (Bureau of Applied Research in Anthropology [BARA] at the University of Arizona, September 2001). David Jenkins, who worked with the BARA team and was its representative at the meetings in Beijing, Udaipur, and Tarrytown (New York) for the project upon which this book is based, wrote the introduction and the "final insights" sections. Vivian Bertrand, Anna Ray Davies, Lauren Osborne, and Jilan Kamal also assisted in writing this chapter. The original research report is available at www.carnegiecouncil.org/forgingenvironmentalism.

1. Joseph Kahn, "Cheney Promotes Increasing Supply as Energy Policy," *New York Times,* 1 May 2001.

2. As we use it in this chapter, the term *community mapping* refers to a technique by which local residents help identify who lives in every household in their community, how long they or members of their family have lived there, and what the heads of households do for a living.

3. In the Louisiana case, the BARA research team conducted the interviews from the

summer of 1999 through the spring of 2001. For the Sonoran Desert case, a second research team from BARA interviewed residents and potential residents from April 2000 to May 2001 and conducted a resident survey. For survey methods, sampling, and results see www.carnegiecouncil.org/forgingenvironmentalism. All participants in interviews conducted by the BARA teams are identified by a number in brackets rather than name because BARA's research protocol calls for keeping the identities of participants confidential. Vivian Bertrand and Joanne Bauer of the Carnegie Council on Ethics and International Affairs carried out supplementary interviews by phone in 2003 and 2004. For these interviews, interviewees are identified by name. All interviews were semistructured and ranged in length from thirty minutes to ninety minutes.

4. J. Timmons Roberts and Melissa Toffolon-Weiss, *Chronicles of the Environmental Justice Frontline* (New York: Cambridge University Press, 2001), 144.

5. Thomas Petzinger, Jr., and George Getschow, "Oil's Legacy: In Louisiana, Pollution and Cancer Are Rife in the Petroleum Area, Region Is Littered with Pits of the Chemicals Poured in Wells During Drilling," *Wall Street Journal*, 23 October 1984.

6. U.S. Code 42, chap. 82, section 6921, 1980 ed.

7. The Gulf Coast field comprises a 650-mile strip extending from the U.S.-Mexico border on the west to the Mississippi River on the east and extending a hundred miles inland from the waters of the Gulf of Mexico. This field once contained the largest deposit of oil in the United States and has been continuously exploited since the early 1900s.

8. For a list of references see www.carnegiecouncil.org/forgingenvironmentalism.

9. *Report to Congress on the Management of Wastes from the Exploration, Development, and Production of Crude Oil, Natural Gas, and Geothermal Energy, Vol. 1: Oil and Gas* (Washington, D.C.: Environmental Protection Agency, Office of Solid Waste and Emergency Response, 1987).

10. 53 Federal Register 25, 446–25, 457 (1988). More precise estimates are impossible because the constituents of oilfield waste vary enormously depending on a range of factors such as geological features and type of drilling "mud." In addition, and as a direct result of the exemption, the wastes have never been analyzed systematically.

11. In 1989 they rejected an offer to participate in a review by the Interstate Oil Compact Commission of state oil and gas management programs. And given their frustration with and lack of trust in the state review process, few environmental activists were willing to participate in the state review process by the end of the decade.

12. See www.carnegiecouncil.org/forgingenvironmentalism for a list of member groups.

13. Gary Snellgrove, Commercial E&P Waste, Office of Conservation, Louisiana Department of Natural Resources, phone interview 23 May 2003.

14. As indicated in note 3, the numbers in brackets refer to interviewees and are intended to protect their identities.

15. *Times-Picayune*, 16 October 1989, cited in Kevin C. Rung, "Treatment, Storage, and Disposal of Nonhazardous Oilfield Waste in Louisiana," *Tulane Environmental Law Journal* 4, no. 1 (1990): 95–111.

16. Roberts and Toffolon-Weiss, *Chronicles of the Environmental Justice Frontline*, 146.

17. Paul Templet, e-mail communication, 29 April 2004. According to Templet, "These days the DEQ isn't a much better home. It has become captured by its clients in the chemical and manufacturing sectors, in my opinion." Templet, who headed the Louisiana Department of Environmental Quality under Governor Roemer from 1988 to 1992, is now a professor at Louisiana State University.

18. Paul Templet, interview, 23 May 2003.

19. Maureen O'Neill, interoffice memorandum, 15 August 1988.

20. William H. Spell to Those Concerned with Naturally-Occurring Radioactive Material (NORM), Nuclear Energy Division, Louisiana Department of Environmental Quality, memorandum, 30 November 1988.

21. William J. Guste, letter to the deputy secretary of the U.S. Department of Energy re: delaying produced water regulations, 10 September 1990.

22. Cited in Roberts and Toffolon-Weiss, *Chronicles of the Environmental Justice Frontline,* 148.

23. The histories and identities of these peoples are complicated and contested, but they have both been historically excluded from Louisiana's plantation economy.

24. F. B. Kniffen, H. F. Gregory, and G. A. Stokes, *The Historic Indian Tribes of Louisiana: From 1542 to the Present* (Baton Rouge: Louisiana State University Press, 1987), 92.

25. Charles D. Marshall to Bruce Babbitt, secretary of the interior, letter, 27 October 1995. The Bureau of Acknowledgement and Recognition's proposed finding on the tribe's petition was negative and as of 2004 was on appeal.

26. Thomas McGuire and Diane Austin, "Gulf Coast Communities: Land, Water, Work, and Education" (draft report prepared for the Minerals Management Service, Gulf of Mexico Region, 1999), 110–12.

27. In April 1963, a U.S. District Court ruled that the public schools could not discriminate against Indian students (*Margie Willa Naquin et al. v. Terrebonne Board of Education,* U.S. District Court, Eastern District of Louisiana Civil Action 13, 291). As a result, in 1964, Houma students in Lafourche, one of the two parishes that Grand Bois straddles, were offered the choice between attending a church-run settlement school or the public elementary school.

28. Until recently, many residents believed the Louisiana Land and Exploration Company, the corporation that acquired much of the bayou country, was a Louisiana company, when in fact it was based in Maryland.

29. McGuire and Austin, "Gulf Coast Communities," 108–9.

30. When the market for furs dropped precipitously in the 1980s due to nationwide protests against those who made, sold, and wore fur garments, many residents in Southern Louisiana turned to oilfield-related work. A decline in the shrimp industry hastened the transition for others.

31. In response to significant and obvious problems associated with industrial contamination of the environment, in 1980 Congress passed the Comprehensive Environmental Response, Compensation, and Liability Act, also known as Superfund. Sites are designated for attention by being placed on a National Priority List, based on factors such as level of hazard, routes of possible exposure, and magnitude of the affected population.

32. U.S. EPA Archive, NFRAP, Sites, EPA, ID LAD980501522. There is no clear documentation about why the pit was removed from the list. It was most likely dropped as a relatively minor site during a review of sites.

33. A good deal of controversy exists over the exact composition of this waste. Many involved in the incident (including Wilma Subra, according to a phone interview with her on 14 May 2003) believed that the pits did not contain produced water, but rather only solid and semi-solid waste and that the problem was not one of radioactivity, which is an issue with produced water, but one of beneze and heavy metals. In court documents, however, Exxon acknowledged that the March 1994 load contained "produced water, hydrocarbon fluids, sludge and rainwater as well as fluids from process equipment, vessels, and tanks," and that this material had been piped into the cell at the facility (Lafourche County Courthouse, Grand Bois Lawsuit, Book 1 of 40). In addition, the *New Orleans Times-Picayune* reported that "the facility accepted 1.2 million barrels of waste in 1995, more than 50 million gallons. Some of it arrives as produced water, a combination of saltwater and organic chemicals that come to the surface when oil and gas wells are drilled" (Chris Gray, "Pits Cause Stink in Lafourche," *New Orleans Times-Picayune,* 14 July 1997).

34. The Toxic Release Inventory is a compendium of information on toxic substances released by manufacturing facilities. Disclosure of this information is required under the federal Emergency Planning and Community Right to Know Act of 1986.

35. Roberts and Toffolon-Weiss, *Chronicles of the Environmental Justice Frontline,* 140.

36. Quoted in Leslie Zganjar, "Small Town in Louisiana Fighting to Shut Down Waste Pits," Associated Press, 23 January 1988.

37. Roberts and Toffolon-Weiss, *Chronicles of the Environmental Justice Frontline*, 142.

38. The lawsuit was initially filed as *Clarice Freloux, wife of/and Danny Freloux, Sandra Matherne, wife of and Blake Matherne, Pamela Matherne, wife of/and Lonnie Matherne, Stacy Molinere, wife of/and R.J. Molinere, Joyceline Dominique v. Campbell Wells Corporation and Tillman Trehan*. Many of the names were misspelled.

39. The amended suit was *Clarice Friloux et al. v. Campbell Wells Corporation, Daniel Trehan and Exxon Company U.S.A.*

40. Patricia Williams, "Grand Bois Community Health Assessment, Vol. 1" (report prepared for the Occupational Toxicology Outreach Program, Department of Medicine, Louisiana State University Medical Center, Shreveport, 1997).

41. CBS, *On Assignment: Town Under Siege*, 23 December 1997.

42. For a pessimistic assessment, see C. Paul Hillard, "State Reveals Waste Testing Procedure," *American Oil and Gas Reporter* 41, no. 4: 175–77.

43. Mike Dunne and John McMillan, "Grand Bois Deliberations Resume Today," *Baton Rouge Advocate*, 11 June 1998. This story as well as the dialogue in the courtroom is recounted in detail in Roberts and Toffolon-Weiss, *Chronicles of the Environmental Justice Frontline*, 155–57. As the authors explain, Exxon claimed that it had not hidden documents; they had simply been misplaced.

44. Janisse Ray, "Guardian of Grand Bois," *Sierra Magazine* (May/June 2002), available at www.sierraclub.org/sierra/200205/profile.asp, accessed 20 July 2004.

45. Roberts and Toffolon-Weiss, *Chronicles of the Environmental Justice Frontline*, 157; Mike Dunne, "Grand Bois Defendant Settles with Plaintiffs: Exxon Now Stands Alone Against Allegations," *Baton Rouge Advocate*, 8 August 1998.

46. Williams, "Grand Bois Community Health Assessment."

47. Roberts and Toffolon-Weiss, *Chronicles of the Environmental Justice Frontline*, 154.

48. John McMillan and Mike Dunne, "Exxon Cleared of Most Claims," *Baton Rouge Advocate*, 10 August 1998; John McMillan, "Exxon Faces Sanctions in Grand Bois Litigation," *Baton Rouge Advocate*, 30 October 1999, and "Exxon to Pay $325,000 for Documents Sanction," *Baton Rouge Advocate*, 1 January 2000.

49. Ray, "Guardian of Grand Bois."

50. Patrick Courreges, "Oilfield Waste Rules Presented to Panel," *Baton Rouge Advocate*, 28 November 2001.

51. Carroll Wascom and Gary Snellgrove, "Regulatory Changes for Commercial E&P Waste Facilities in Louisiana," State of Louisiana, DNR, Office of Conservation, Baton Rouge, LA, available at www.gwpc.org/meetings/AF02-proceedingsCD/papers/Carroll_Wascom_AF02—1.pdf, accessed May 7, 2003. *E&P waste*—i.e., exploration and production waste—was the government's new term for the wastes previously labeled nonhazardous oilfield wastes. The new term continued to distract attention from the hazardous nature of the wastes, in spite of progress made in regulating them.

52. Society of Petroleum Engineers, "New Louisiana Waste Rules," available at www.spe.org/pdf/ehas_Louisiana-offsite_wasterule.pdf, accessed 29 May 2003.

53. Ray, "Guardian of Grand Bois."

54. Kristin Shrader-Frechette, *Environmental Justice: Creating Equality, Reclaiming Democracy* (New York: Oxford University Press, 2002), 167.

55. Louisiana Catholic Conference, Resolution #87-A-(87–26), 1987.

56. U.S. Catholic Conference, "Seven Key Themes of Catholic Social Teaching," 1999: 6, available at www.usccb.org/sdwp/projects/socialteaching/excerpt.htm, accessed 26 September 2005.

57. The child was born in 1999 and is doing well; the results of medical tests conducted at the time of his birth were not shared with his parents.

58. Unidentified woman, R.J. Molinere, and Anna Matherne, all interviewed on *60 Minutes*, 23 December 1997.

59. "Big Oil in Louisiana and a Community's Bottom Line," *Human Rights Dialogue*, series 2, no. 2, available at www.carnegiecouncil.org/viewMedia.php/prmTemplateID/8/prmID/617.

60. Available at www.ci.tucson.az.us/lv-goa111.html, accessed 16 May 2003.

61. One acre-foot equals 325,851 gallons, or 1,233 cubic meters.

62. Adrian H. Griffin estimates 23 million acre-feet in "An Economic and Institutional Assessment of the Water Problem Facing the Tucson Basin" (Ph.D. dissertation, University of Arizona, 1980).

63. Sean Patrick Reilly, "Gathering Clouds: Arizona's Navajo and Hopi Tribes Have Won a Water-Rights Battle against the Coal Company That Has Sustained Their Fragile Economies. But on the Threshold of Impending Victory, a Sobering Question: Now What?" *Los Angeles Times Magazine*, 6 June 2004, 10.

64. According to journalist Paul Vandevelder, "The entire Hopi tribe lives on less water than that sprayed through whirly-gigs on a single golf course in Phoenix" ("Between a Rock and a Dry Place," *Native Americas: Hemispheric Journal of Indigenous Issues* 17, no. 2 [2000]: 11–25).

65. M. Kelso, W. Martin, and L. Mack, *Water Supplies and Economic Growth in an Arid Environment: An Arizona Case Study* (Tucson: University of Arizona, 1973).

66. Michael Lafleur, "CAP Mix Will Flow in May," *Tucson Citizen*, April 17, 2001.

67. Vicki Hart, "CAP Is Still Crap," *Tucson Weekly*, 23–29 October 1997, 72.

68. There is little incentive for municipalities to pursue safe yield, because there is no penalty for not doing so. See Mitch Tobin, "Lack of Water Might Stunt Tucson's Growth," *Arizona Daily Star*, 1 May 2001.

69. This plan was updated in 2001 to cover transportation, water, open space, air quality, and growth cost; see Tony Davis, "Land Use Plan to Be Linked to Outline for Conservation," *Arizona Daily Star*, 18 April 2001.

70. Tony Davis, "150 Gather to Discuss Land-Preservation Plan," *Arizona Daily Star*, 31 May 2001.

71. The rest of the land has been set aside as tribal lands, state and national parks, and state trust land. State trust land is protected from development, but much of the land is actually not fit for development because it consists of rugged, mountainous terrain.

72. Tony Davis, "Desert Sprawl: Tucson Paves Its Way Across a Fragile Landscape," *High Country News* (Paonia), 18 January 1999.

73. For example, in response to the rumor that the Fish and Wildlife Service would push back by several months its deadline for surveying the area and for receiving the required public comment, the Washington-based group Defenders of Wildlife issued a press release on November 11, 1998, stating: "We are tired of these delaying tactics. For nearly a decade the Fish and Wildlife Service has ignored its legal obligations, acquiescing to the pygmy owl's imminent extirpation from Arizona, all because of rampant development." See www.defenders.org/releases/pr1998/pr111198.html, accessed 30 September 2005.

74. Tony Davis, "State Agency Against U.S. Plan Protecting Pygmy Owl Habitat," *Arizona Daily Star*, 30 March 1999.

75. Tony Davis, "Development Guidelines Approved," *Arizona Daily Star*, 6 June 2001.

76. See Joe Burchell, "Owls May Thwart Plan for Girls Home on Northwest Side," *Arizona Daily Star*, April 7, 2001; and Garry Duffy, "Supes Reject 0.91 Acre Rezoning in Owl Area," *Tucson Citizen*, 19 May 2001.

77. Rob Bailey, "Growing Pains Vex Community," *Arizona Daily Star*, southeast section, 20 March 2001.

78. Douglas Jehl, "Rare Arizona Owl (All 7 Inches of It) Is in Habitat Furor," *New York Times*, 17 March 2003.

79. Tony Davis, "Strict Limits Put on Rezoning of Outlying Desert," *Arizona Daily Star*, 3 March 1999.

80. The plan came under fire in 2001, however, when a bill was introduced in the state legislature that would have required the approval of the governor, the state land commission, the department of water resources, and the Arizona Game and Fish Department to implement new land use plans. See www.carnegiecouncil.org/forgingenvironmentalism for an update.

81. *Renewable Energy Annual* (Washington, DC: U.S. Department of Energy, 1996), available at www.eia.doe.gov/cneaf/solar.renewables/renewable.energy.annual/contents.html, accessed 4 June 2004.

82. Victor Dricks, "Sun Sets on Solar," *Phoenix Gazette*, 22 November 1992.

83. These revenues came from the Oil Overcharge Restitution Fund, which was set up by the federal government in 1986 as a result of a settlement with oil producers stemming from price gouging between 1974 and 1981. Each year, states receive an allocation from this fund for energy-related projects that benefit the public.

84. The Urban Lands Management Act, passed in 1981, gave the state land department new authority to plan, zone, and sell trust lands around the state's urban areas, and required public involvement. Prior to the act, the state sold land at current value, usually grazing value, to a developer who could profit enormously by changing the zoning after purchase. As Moody explained to us, the Tucson Solar Village was the first time that planning for a parcel had occurred before a contract with a developer was signed.

85. Only Tucson Electric Power (TEP) reached its voluntary goal of five megawatts of renewable energy, which were generated at a methane recapture facility located at the Los Reales landfill. Alan D. Fisher, "Renewable-Energy Push," *Arizona Daily Star*, 25 April 2000. In 1996, TEP paid $5 million for a 50 percent interest in Global Solar, a solar panel manufacturer.

86. As part of this initiative, Tucson received about $150,000 for the development of solar technology. Rob Bailey, "Applying a Bit of Energy," *Arizona Daily Star*, Southeast Section, 20 March 2001.

87. David R. Wilcox, Thomas McGuire, and Charles Sternberg, *Snaketown Revisited*, Arizona State Museum Archeological Series 155 (Tucson: University of Arizona, 1981), 212.

88. City of Tucson, available at www.ci.tucson.az.us/specproj.htm, accessed 28 May 2003.

89. By 1995, a sixth goal had been added: to make 20 percent of the houses available to people of low and moderate income, but it appears that this goal has not been met. According to John Laswick, in 2004, the median price for a house in Civano was "a little more than the median price for a house in the city of Tucson."

90. In 1989, Tucson mega-developer Don Diamond's proposal to build two resorts and a planned community on 6,380 acres of the old Rocking K Ranch, east of the Saguaro National Monument, was met with fervent protests by nearby residents. Meanwhile, however, southeastern Tucson continued to grow.

91. Mark Smith, "Integrating Sustainable Design and Programming into Mainstream Real Estate Development," *Environmental Design and Construction*, 24 January 2001, available at www.edcmag.com/CDA/ArticleInformation/features/BNP_Features_Item/0,4120,19210,00.html, accessed 28 May 2003; National Town Meeting for a Sustainable America, Detroit, Michigan Learning Session (LS) Summary, 1999, available at www.sustainableusa.org/proceedings/LS217.cfm, accessed 28 May 2003.

92. Available at www.sustainable.doe.gov/success/civano.shtml, accessed 17 December 2003.

93. This was owing to "provincial political indecision," according to the Web site of the Trust for Sustainable Development, available at www.tsd.ca/bamberton.html, accessed 28 May 2003.

94. Available at www.newurbanism.org/pages/416429/index.htm, accessed 17 December 2003.

95. Dave Devine, "Cloudy Horizon: The City-Subsidized Development Has Lost Its Shine." *Tuscon Weekly*, 7–13 May 1998.

96. In June 2001, the city dropped the permit requirement in an attempt to increase use of gray water systems, raising the hopes of some that future neighborhoods at Civano may be able to incorporate this more environmentally and economically sound alternative to the bulky reclaimed water system. See Mitch Tobin, "Gray Water Users Are No Longer Scofflaws," *Arizona Daily Star*, PM Update, 7 June 2001.

97. Available at www.fanniemae.com/company/index.html, accessed 4 June 2001.

98. City of Tucson, special projects, available at www.ci.tucson.az.us/specproj.htm#civano, accessed 28 May 2003.

99. Available at www.tsd.ca/civano.html, accessed 13 January 2004.

100. Al Gore, letter to Civano community partners, 1999.

101. Joe Burchell, "'Future Community' Is Now," *Arizona Daily Star*, 17 April 1999.

102. Former staff of Case Enterprises and Civano Development formed CDC Partners in January 2000 to manage the project on behalf of Fannie Mae.

103. A 17 June 2002 report by Al Nichols Engineering, an engineering firm owned by a resident of Civano, Al Nichols, who was also involved with outlining environmental standards for Civano, shows that "in total, Civano homes use fifty-six percent of the heating and cooling energy of Tucson at-large homes. . . . Overall, Civano total energy use is sixty-seven percent of Tucson at-large homes, and sixty-eight percent of Tucson 1998–99 homes"—those built the same year as the Civano homes under study.

104. U.S. Department of Energy Smart Communities Network, available at www.sustainable .doe.gov/success/civano.shtml, accessed 28 May 2003.

105. Civano's various solar interest groups are confusing. The first, the Tucson Solar Alliance, was formed as a nonprofit community partnership when President Clinton announced his Million Solar Roofs Initiative in 1997, a plan to install solar energy systems on the roofs of a million buildings in the United States. As part of this initiative, Tucson received more than $150,000 for the development of solar technology. It includes engineers, scholars, community leaders, and activists. Then there is the Tucson Solar Coalition, whose wide membership includes the city of Tucson, John Wesley Miller, Global Solar, and other building and construction companies. The coalition is not incorporated, but rather is controlled by Tucson Electric Power, which, the alternative press has pointed out, signals a potential conflict of interest. See "Sun Stroke," *Tucson Weekly*, 15–21 April 1999.

106. Paul Huddy, quoted in Devine, "Cloudy Horizon: The City-Subsidized Development Has Lost Its Shine."

107. "Civano: Remote but Vital," *Arizona Daily Star*, 21 April 1999.

108. Wayne Moody, phone interview, 22 July 2003.

109. Rhonda Bodfield Sander, "Which Mayoral Vision Do City Voters Want to See?" *Arizona Daily Star*, 10 October 1999; and Burchell, "'Future Community' Is Now."

110. M. Logan, *Fighting Sprawl and City Hall: Resistance to Urban Growth in the Southwest* (Tucson: University of Arizona Press, 1995), 61; C.L. Sonnichsen, *Tucson: The Life and Times of an American City* (Norman: University of Oklahoma Press, 1982), 286.

111. Neil Smith, *The New Urban Frontier: Gentrification and the Revanchist City* (London: Routledge, 1996), 137.

112. Jeannine Relly, "Revitalization Worries Homeless," *Arizona Daily Star*, 27 December 2002.

113. City of Tucson, Special Projects, available at www.ci.tucson.az.us/specproj.htm#civano.

114. Fannie Mae's Arizona public relations firm asserts that, as of 31 December 2002, Civano was sixty-one jobs above its target of one job for every two housing units (Angela Jamison, e-mail to Vivian Bertrand, 28 July 2003). Civano Neighbors representative Simmons Buntin, however, was less certain. In an e-mail message dated 30 December 2003, he wrote, "Many of those who work at Civano as of the end of 2002 likely do not live here. The two largest employers—Global Solar and Civano Nursery—are primarily 'staffed' by non-residents. However, the number of full-time home-based businesses continues to grow . . . and I believe with

the exception of Global Solar and Medallion Real Estate Services, all of the commercial-area businesses are owned/run by Civano residents (such as Al Nichols Engineering, Ballet Rincon, Civano Nursery, and Wolfsong Infomatics)."

115. *Town Crier* (Civano Neighbors Neighborhood Association newsletter), July 2003.

116. "A Bright and Shining Lie," *Tucson Weekly*, 29 April–5 May 1999.

117. Burchell, "'Future Community' Is Now."

118. John Laswick, phone interview, 7 January 2004.

119. Angela Jamison of Gitenstein & Assadi Public Relations, correspondence with Vivian Bertrand, 28 July 2003.

120. Laswick interview.

121. Tom Beal, "Civano: New Urban Life Civano Is Eco-Living," *Arizona Daily Star,* 30 June 2002.

122. Kristen Cook, "Custom/Cozy Early Civano Resident Pleased," *Arizona Daily Star,* 30 January 2000.

123. President's Council on Sustainable Development, "Eco-Industrial Park Workshop, Proceedings," 17–18 October 1996, available at http://clinton4.nara.gov/PCSD/Publications/Eco_Workshop.html, accessed 28 May 2003.

124. "EPA Official Talks at Civano," *Arizona Daily Star*, 21 January 2003.

125. Laswick interview.

126. Civano testimonials, available at www.civano.com/aboutcivano/testimonials.html.

127. For full survey results, see the BARA report, available at www.carnegiecouncil.org/forgingenvironmentalism.

128. This refers to unplanned subdivisions, originally used as a way to circumvent zoning laws, available at www.tucsonweekly.com/tw/2001-02-08/skinny.html, accessed 28 May 2003.

129. Simmons Buntin, "Per Simmons: The Town That Wouldn't Be?" *Town Crier*, September 2003.

130. Available at www.civan01.com, accessed 9 June 2003.

131. It is interesting to note that there was some confusion about this fact among residents who thought the developer had even more control than it does. We heard from residents that the developer might hold as many as three to five votes per empty lot, versus one vote per occupied lot, while the reality is that every lot is worth one vote on the HOA.

132. Anonymous Civano resident, phone interview, 18 July 2003.

133. Tim Ellis, "Putting Principle into Practice," *Arizona Daily Star,* 18 June 2002.

134. "Bylaws Approved; We'll Be 'Official' Soon," *Town Crier*, October 2002, available at www.civanoneighbors.com.

135. Civano Advisory Council, "A White Paper by Civano's First Residents: Safeguarding Civano's Destiny," 9 August 2000, available at www.melblack.com/CivanoWhitePaper1.html, accessed 1 August 2003.

136. The residents were not uniformly against Diamond; some were relieved that an experienced businessman would be stepping in to push the development along and avoid situations like the one with RCG, the builder that defaulted.

137. Field notes from neighborhood meeting, 1 October 2000.

138. Ibid.

139. Laswick interview.

140. Ibid.

141. Percy Viosca, Jr., "Louisiana Wet Lands and the Value of Their Wild Life and Fishery Resources," *Ecology* 9, no. 2 (April 1928): 216–29.

142. Paul Templet, phone interview, 23 May 2003.

143. Richard White, *The Organic Machine: The Remaking of the Columbia River* (New York: Hill and Wang, 1995).

PART II

Understanding Values Cross-Nationally

5

The Value of *Legality* in Environmental Action

Sheila Jasanoff

What is the place of law in a study of environmental values? Complex in itself, the question becomes even more complicated in the context of a comparative study such as this because the meanings multiply when we look across many cultures. How we answer it depends in part on how we conceive of the law itself—whether, more particularly, we see law as embedded in culture and thus as an instrument for the articulation of disparate social values, including environmental ones; or whether we view the law as standing above culture, ideology, and political economy, and hence as a vehicle for overcoming purely local understandings and disseminating values of *legality* that are, in some sense, transcendental. If we adopt the first perspective, we might be inclined to ask how the country studies presented in this book exemplify the workings of the law, how national legal processes reflect or condition values related to nature and the environment, and whether the law has affected the uptake of environmental values into policy in distinctive ways in each of the countries examined here. If we approach the topic from the second perspective, we will instead ask whether environmental values and environmental policy in each country are subordinated to seemingly universal ideas of lawfulness or legality, and whether the power of the law can bring about, through such subordination, convergence among disparate national systems of environmental values.

The evidence gleaned from these extremely rich studies suggests that our approach to analyzing the role of law should take account of both perspectives. Much in the country cases points to the specificity of legal institutions and processes. They grow out of particular histories, subscribe to varied doctrinal traditions,[1] occupy distinctive niches in relation to the other organs of the state, and offer different forms of access and remedy to citizens. Formal law is overlaid in each country on divergent living traditions of informal dispute resolution and community building; *environmental* law, more specifically, regulates and makes explicit only certain aspects of human accommodations with nature. Civil society, too, imagines the role of law quite differently in the four nations: as a reliable companion in projects of social and political self-expression in the United States; as a largely invisible and inaccessible source of policy directives in China; and, depending on circumstances, as both in Japan and India. Law relating to the environment, moreover, is formulated and enforced at different levels of government, from international organizations and national authorities down to regions and municipalities, with the precise blend of formal power and informal custom varying in each national context.

Yet despite these differences, in no country has environmental policy taken shape without the active involvement of legal institutions. This is not altogether surprising. The earliest recorded law codes in history dealt not only with the rights and responsibilities of individuals toward one another but also with their uses and abuses of nature's resources. Nearly four thousand years ago, for instance, the Code of Hammurabi laid out provisions regulating what should happen if a man negligently floods another's field or steals the implements with which water is drawn for irrigation. Today, some functions of the law in relation to nature, such as compensation for damage and standard-setting for management, are so widely acknowledged as to appear almost independent of culture. At a more abstract level, environmental and legal thought are connected in every modern state through interactive, sometimes mutually reinforcing conceptions of naturalness, rightness or appropriateness, ownership, justice and equity, and the importance of knowledge. Thus, what is natural is also frequently taken as right or just, and what is fair or equitable can be seen as natural, in managing environmental resources. In these senses, adherence to the law is itself a value that structures the expression of environmental values everywhere.

This essay, then, looks at the nexus of law and environment both as a site where the particularities of national value systems with regard to nature are expressed and affirmed and as a place where conflicts of knowledge, ownership, and power in relation to the natural world are negotiated or, as often, fought out. To acknowledge these tensions between valuing nature and wishing to appropriate it, as well as to capture broad similarities and differences among extraordinarily disparate legal cultures, we have to move the discussion of law away from formal categories such as "tort law," "contract law," and even "environmental law"—a term that has no fixed definition even within a single national legal system. Instead, we must follow the law as it is invoked by citizens and governmental bodies in their attempts to navigate the contrary currents of environmental protection and resource appropriation. How, we ask, has the law been deployed in making fundamental choices about how people will live with their physical surroundings, including natural resources and other living things? These choices can be grouped under five topical headings that serve to organize the remainder of this chapter: (1) allocation and planning; (2) compensation; (3) standards; (4) knowledge-making; and (5) resistance. We conclude with observations about the cross-national similarities and differences in environmental legal thought that these comparisons bring to light.

Allocation and Planning

Environmentalism is often equated with ecological consciousness, which emphasizes notions of conservation and stewardship, and it is contrasted with the values of production and consumption, which are broadly labeled economic. The conflict between these values is starkly felt in most corners of the world, and the countries considered in this volume are no exception. While the term *sustainable development*[2] tries to balance the two concepts, suggesting a theoretical possibility of harmonizing the goals of production and conservation, in practice all efforts to meet the demands of the present while respecting the needs of the future remain highly contested. One of the law's most central roles in environmental policy is to resolve these tensions; not only justice but *distributive* justice is the goal to be attained, but this effort to allocate costs, benefits, and resources necessarily presses the law into playing politics on a grand scale. The rules of this game, as the studies show, vary considerably from country to country.

At the heart of the legal dilemma of redistribution is how to make allocations that will command respect from stakeholders with radically different economic, social, and political commitments. Setting workable, defensible limits on two seemingly irreconcilable principles—production and protection—is a challenge of no mean proportions, and, not surprisingly, legal institutions have had varied success in silencing environmental controversies. Paradoxically, legal authorities have themselves felt a need for legitimation as they are drawn into the essentially political acts of distribution and redistribution. This need is perhaps least pronounced for a democratically accountable legislature that acts through formal lawmaking, but when decisions are made by less representative bodies—such as courts, agencies, or planning commissions—additional resources such as expert knowledge (as discussed below) and public participation may be needed to confer legitimacy. The mix of strategies used by actors in the reported cases reflects a nation's legal traditions, as well as the particular kinds of allocative decisions that need to be made.

Allocation in the environmental domain is often conceived as a matter of distributing scarce resources so as to avoid adverse outcomes such as the "tragedy of the commons."[3] Examples of governmental action designed to prevent the overuse of resources can be observed in far-flung places around the world: one need only consider the regulation of fishing off the coast of Kerala, in southern India; dam construction to manage water at Lake Biwa and on the Nagara River in Japan; or the establishment of the Sanjiang Nature Reserve in China. What emerges with enormous clarity from these cases, however, is that regulatory interventions often represent not so much a policy for safeguarding a resource as a verdict for or against an entire way of life. Even in a late-modern, capitalist society such as the United States, restrictions on hunting and trapping in the Cajun country affect people's capacity to adjust to fluctuations in the economy and to the rise and fall of fish populations. Similarly, efforts to assure water supply for urban dwellers along the Nagara River or around Lake Biwa influence the livelihood and ways of life of Japan's traditionally poor fishing families. The establishment of a nature reserve in China's Fuyuan County effectively makes distinctions among the economic and even the survival prospects of farmworkers, long-term migrants, and new migrants. In all these cases, only a highly reductionist reading of "the law" would credit it with simply safeguarding environmental values. Rather, law operates as an instrument of social order, determining how much respect should be accorded to different ways of living in the environment.

The Kerala fisheries case and the Delhi pollution case in India most starkly underline the lifestyle-determining role of the law in poor countries. In Kerala, both formal legislation and expert committees (e.g., the Kalawar Committee) sought to accommodate the competing claims of two different fishing cultures: the "artisanal" sector, with its initially less advanced technological capabilities, and the "mechanized" sector, with its more powerful trawlers and greater range and adaptability. Although law and policy in this case were conscious of the need to mediate between lifestyles—and not just to set quotas or make technical determinations of "sustainability"—the legal-institutional response was unprepared for the rapid changes that occurred within the so-called artisanal culture in response to macroeconomic forces. This problem of cultural fluidity is perhaps most pronounced in developing countries meeting the challenges of globalization, but (as even the Louisiana oilfields case suggests) challenges arise for the law in any contexts, rich or poor, where resource allocation decisions must be enforced against a background of shifting social identities and sociotechnical practices.

Compensation

One way to justify environmental allocations that favor some groups or individuals at the expense of others is to compensate those who have been hurt or damaged by these allocations. Issues of compensation in environmental law commonly fall under two broad headings: private law proceedings to remedy damage inflicted by human activities, and public law processes that limit property rights in order to protect a public good, such as valued ecosystems, endangered species, or clean air. Although both kinds of problems have appeared in all four countries, some striking differences can be observed in the implementation of, and social responses to, compensation processes.

In the United States, the private law of "torts"[4] plays a pervasive role in people's lives. Its overall effect is to frame many social ills in terms of wrongs committed by one private party against another and, within that framework, to offer many people a possible remedy that is not available from legislatures. A celebrated example of this privatization of grievances in an environmental context was the lawsuit brought in the 1970s by Vietnam veterans against manufacturers of the defoliant Agent Orange.[5] In this protracted, contentious process concerning what was in essence a compensation claim for environmentally induced disease, the veterans ultimately received through a court-ordered settlement the monetary award they had been unable to gain from the U.S. Congress. In Grand Bois, similarly, vain efforts to move local and state officials to act against the Campbell Wells and Exxon oil facilities inexorably led to lawsuits and numerous out-of-court settlements. Officially sealed to all but the participants, such settlements are routine in American law, where they may play a cathartic role for victims, but only dubiously further the tort law's goals of providing publicly visible punishment and, in this way, effective deterrence.

The struggle for compensation for environmental injuries contributed to the rise of environmental awareness in Japan. By the late 1960s, widespread illnesses attributed to air and water pollution had spurred legal recognition of the "polluter pays principle," along with various judicial and administrative compensation schemes for the victims. In both Kumamoto-Minamata and Niigata, the pollution of drinking water by methyl mercury and the resulting deaths and disabilities gave rise to two different remedial strategies: the informal, personalized "gift money" approach exemplified in Chisso Corporation's payments to disease victims in Minamata; and a more formal, litigated approach resulting in the certification and compensation of claimants in Niigata. Kada et al.'s chapter in this volume equates the latter strategy with modernization and a contractual view of social relations, as contrasted with a communitarian culture of responsibility and blame.

The Japanese victims' ambivalence about seeking compensation through court action highlights a greater resistance in Japan than in the United States to translating personal injuries into monetary terms, as well as a greater sensitivity to the inadequacy of money in compensating for long-term communal impacts of environmental pollution. Fishers at Lake Biwa, for example, belatedly realize that legally mandated "fishing compensation" is a one-time payment, a political compromise that does not properly reflect the lost income flow from a lifetime of fishing. Some Minamata disease victims, like Ogata Masato openly resisted the monetization of their grief and loss. Others, like the Minamata residents who opposed the creation of a museum named for "their" disease, and who to this day fight any association between their locality and the disease, express by these means a strongly felt lack of fit between compensation law's contractual, individualistic orientation and the hurt to communal relationships that inevitably accompanies environmental disasters. It is not that communal values are unappreciated or considered insignificant in other nations,[6] but at least in the United States the social processes of individuation and privatization have proceeded to a point where it is difficult to recognize and respect such collective sensibilities within established legal structures.

A quite different type of compensation claim potentially arises when private property is taken to create a public good. Examples include the creation of nature parks or reserves, limitations on takings of or trade in endangered species, and restrictions on land use for environmental purposes. The different responses to these types of actions in the national case studies reveal not only structural dissimilarities among countries, for instance in socialist versus pluralist planning regimes, but also in the degree to which the very concept of an "environmental public good" has anchored itself in different national contexts. The vocal opposition of the Southern Arizona Home Builders Association to the protection of the pygmy owl in the U.S. case, for example, illustrates a broader American trend toward the reassertion of private property rights at the expense of public environmental values. Several recent decisions of the U.S. Supreme Court have reflected and reaffirmed this trend by forcing state institutions either to compensate property owners for "takings" in the name of environmental protection or to justify land-use restrictions through more stringent technical analysis.[7]

Whereas these U.S. decisions reaffirm the rights of well-to-do property owners, and arguably elevate individual interests in wealth-creation above public interests in environmental conservation, comparable claims by poor laborers and landowners have fared less well under the law in developing countries. The Delhi pollution case can be read from one angle as a success story in that it mobilized the nation's highest court for a "green" cause. But as Baviskar argues, Justice Kuldip Singh's orders and judgments relocating polluting industries outside Delhi's National Capital Region can equally be seen as a victory for urban, middle class health interests over the subsistence rights of workers, many of whom were forcibly relocated or lost their jobs without adequate compensation. The court, for institutional reasons, could not implement or enforce the administrative mechanisms it created to protect the workers. In this respect, the Delhi judgments mark a break with earlier cases of public interest litigation in which the Indian Supreme Court sought to establish minimal environmental standards for poor city-dwellers. The Chinese nature reserve case also appears to exemplify the triumph of middle-class environmentalism—sustained in part through the globalizing influence of international law, money, and activism—over the livelihood concerns of poor farmers and recent migrants. In this case, however, legal compensation did not arise as an issue, and the dispossessed, as we see below, expressed their resistance primarily through actions outside the law.

Standards

The operation of the law depends at every turn on classification. For the law to perform fairly its core functions of permission, prohibition, and punishment, there must be ways of clearly identifying which cases are like each other, which are unlike, and which fall outside the permitted limits of the law. Like cases must be treated alike in the interests of justice, and only those actions that society classifies as unlawful may be prosecuted or penalized. Of course, to classify cases, we must have standards, and a major function of the law is to provide the means of establishing and enforcing them.

In environmental law, the need for standards comes continually into play as authorities try to determine what is pollution, who is a polluter, who is a victim, what is risk or safety, what resources need protection, and how much use of such resources is warranted. Comparison across countries shows that a commitment to standards, and to underlying notions of legality and justice, is shared everywhere, but the emphasis on particular types of standards varies, as do the processes through which standards are determined and applied. These differences in turn point to variations in the values that people assign to the environment, as well as to divergent preferences for how to order the relations between nature and society through law.

The Objects of Standard-Setting

One notable cross-cultural difference centers on the question of what is to be standardized for purposes of the law. Is it features of nature "out there," distinct from society, that are subjected to objective observation, measurement, and classification; do people themselves, as biological entities, need to be standardized for certain purposes, and what is the role of the law in taking such a step? Or, alternatively, do standards apply to the ways in which human beings conduct their relations with nature, including the artifacts they produce and the ways in which they live in the world? How do law and ideas of legality play out under the second, more hybrid framing? Looking across the case studies, we can discern both patterns of standard-setting. For convenience, we may call the former *modern* and the latter *antimodern*.

The modern approach is familiar to any student of contemporary environmental law. It involves several sequential steps designed to produce a technical-rational basis for control: the identification of the object or phenomenon to be regulated through the law (e.g., pollution, risk, wetlands, endangered species, air or water quality); the generation of scientific knowledge about this entity; the establishment of (usually numerical) limits of quality, safety, or sustainability; the creation of legal penalties for failing to meet the standards; and the establishment of implementing agencies to enforce the applicable standards. In this bureaucratic approach to regulating the environment, science and law serve as allies in the regulatory project, and the thing or condition being standardized, whether it is an ecosystem or a pollutant plume or a type of harm, is treated as a detachable, objectively knowable, and independently manageable element of nature. Often, however, these things or concepts associated with them exist only to satisfy the needs of the law: people might die and species might disappear in the course of industrial development, but regulatable phenomena such as "emissions," "acute toxicity," or "endangered species" are *legal* constructs; they have little or no meaning outside the standardizing impulses of the law. Such entities come into being as a result of people's commitment to ordering their relations with nature. The law, in this sense, creates new environmental ontologies in the very process of seeking to protect the environment.

Examples of modernity's legal metaphysics are scattered throughout the case studies: "water quality" in Lake Biwa and "certified victims" in Minamata; "excess cancers" or "detectable [health] impacts" around the Grand Bois oil fields; "monsoon trawl ban" and "optimum mesh size" for fishing nets in Kerala; "migratory fowl" in the Sanjiang wetlands; and many others. Because so many of these categories and entities depend on new and emerging scientific knowledge, their use in environmental policy is clouded by uncertainty and frequently embroiled in controversy, as the lawsuits discussed in the national case studies in this volume amply document. In this respect, environmental standards illustrate, wherever they are deployed, the phenomenon of "reflexive modernization"—a dynamic of post-industrial society in which the attempt to generate certainty about distant futures produces its own destabilizing uncertainties, and which prominent sociologists have identified as a signature characteristic of modernity.[8] Science is relied on as a source of legal and political legitimacy in controlling increasingly complex and speculative problems; yet this increased reliance heightens uncertainty and conflict, weakening or undermining the legitimating potential of science. The case studies demonstrate a similar vulnerability on the part of legally empowered administrative agencies, which are science's constant partners in the rationalizing enterprise of modernity.

Against this pervasive yet troubled use of legally established and enforceable environmental standards, the country stories also illustrate a contrasting approach to standardization—one that does not isolate "natural" phenomena such as risk and pollution from the social conditions in which they arise but focuses instead on collective accommodations to living in the environment. What is standardized in this second framework is more an integrated lifestyle than a detached object or phenomenon; the disciplining associated with standards occurs here too, but it is a discipline that grows from within the community rather than from conjunctions of highly professionalized legal and scientific experts. The values of legality are adhered to, as discussed below, in the sense that quite restrictive norms are established and enforced, but without formal recourse to the law.

In his pioneering work on legality and governance in modern societies,[9] Michel Foucault noted that the exercise of power over multitudes no longer requires extreme force or violent exercises of authority. Instead, control becomes possible through normalization, the process by which people adapt themselves to dominant standards of behavior and action under constant surveillance, whether vertically by the state or horizontally by others within society. Foucault termed this kind of disciplining force *biopower* because it operates on the bodies of living subjects, in effect defining how we see them through traits and markers that help to distinguish the normal from the deviant. The results are lawlike in the efficacy of their control, but they do not necessarily depend on formal legal institutions, operating instead through a wealth of other disciplining agencies, such as hospitals, schools, and armies.

That the Foucauldian notion of discipline can extend to ways of engaging with the environment is strikingly apparent in the Chinese case. Here, the permeability of social discipline and environmental control is reflected in the army's enthusiastic (and to some degree voluntary) embrace of environmental protection. Already schooled in techniques of self-control, the soldiers eagerly become amateur naturalists; willing to be schooled in the systematic observation of nature, they learn to identify birds and plants, build a specimen room, and even enjoy "planting trees and making nests for birds in their leisure time" (p. 71).[10] A similar centrally guided discipline influences morale and behavior among the officers of the Sanjiang Nature Reserve Management Bureau (SNRMB), although discipline for this group is further strengthened by the promise of a bright economic future. As their director observes, "Environmental protection is a sun-rising sector in our country" (p. 69).

While Foucault and others have associated the rationalizing, classifying, and controlling power of standards with modernity and the growth of the centralizing state, we perceive in the case studies some instances in which such discipline seems to have grown instead from a more bottom-up urge to live harmoniously with the environment. Ironically, this less formalized approach to standards can be observed both in poor, marginalized, premodern societies, such as the artisanal fishers of Kerala, and among wealthy, postmodern communities such as the Civano residents in Arizona.[11]

This is why I characterize this approach not as premodern or postmodern, but as *antimodern*—in refusing to externalize and manage nature, but rather deriving cues for sustainable living from it.

In the Kerala case, for example, the fisherman K.M. George reports that he used to be able to see fish—eagle rays and sting rays—from the shore and would run to his fishing boat to catch them only after seeing them. This practice respected the Mother Sea, who rewarded the fishers' respect with adequate supplies of fish. The trawlers, equated by some with foreigners, disrupted this natural, harmonious, and sustainable relationship, presumably by catching the fish before they had a chance to replenish themselves and to make the resulting plenitude visible to fishers on the shore. It is no wonder then that the fisherwoman Sheela complains, "There are no fish in our sea. . . . If they stopped trawling, the fish would lay eggs"(p. 232). For the local fishers, the trawlers represent an alien incursion into the established rhythms of life in the sea and life on land, bound and regulated by the personified sea herself. Technology breaks the rules of sustainability set by nature, and the consequent disorder and loss of livelihood are only to be expected.

Curiously, an environmentally "advanced" American community has developed a similar, quite unmodern mix of trial and error and personal compromise, balancing community values with economic interests, to arrive at acceptable standards. According to John Laswick, the city of Tucson's project manager for Civano, developers decided that Civano had to be more than just an environmental project, even if it meant sacrificing some of the original features of green design:

> New urbanist principles really reinforced the kind of environmental principles that Civano or sustainable developments were trying to promote, which was not just an environmentally better community, but a socially more interesting and dynamic community, which made money and flourished in the marketplace. So you have the three legs of environmental, economic, and social benefits. And what I think new urbanism brings to development is essentially "curb appeal"—not everyone wants to live in a house that is energy efficient but isn't particularly attractive. You need both.

There is no pretense here that houses have to be built in conformity with environmental standards alone; rather, they have to accord well with a total way of life. In Japan, the replacement of a "comprehensive development" plan for Lake Biwa with a more community-based approach to "comprehensive environmental protection" represents a similar turn from a modernist to an antimodernist framing of water issues. A comparable story can be told about the opposition led by the naturalist writer Amano Reiko to dam construction on the Nagara River in order to protect an established way of living with nature.

Standard-Setting Processes

A second area of difference among the case studies has to do with the nature and transparency of standardization. How explicit or formal is the process of standard-setting? Is it seen as expert-based and value-neutral, as fundamentally rational but subject to political contamination, or as intrinsically political and social and therefore needing the participation of affected publics? Are standards established from the top down or the bottom up? Who, more generally, participates in standard-setting and through what procedural channels? What means exist in the law for challenging standards that affected parties deem arbitrary? While detailed answers to these questions should be sought in the case studies themselves, a few general observations are in order here.

Prior comparative studies of environmental policy established that the United States is unique among Western nations in its highly legalistic, formal, open, and often adversarial approach to setting environmental standards.[12] The case studies in this volume further highlight that uniqueness. In Asian countries too, environmental standards are more likely to emerge from interactions between state agencies and their expert advisers than through explicit notice and comment proceedings or hearings (like those required of U.S. regulatory agencies), which make state authorities directly accountable to the public. These procedural distinctions correlate with features of the framing of environmental issues and, in turn, the values that tend to be crystallized and given prominence in policy debates. More specifically, the U.S. focus on legalized proceedings tends to favor the articulation of individual interests more than collective norms about the value of the environment or the obligations of the state; it thus increases the likelihood that individual rather than group values will be expressed through the administrative process. Interestingly, even Christopher Stone's classic 1972 essay on the intrinsic value of "natural objects" (trees in his case) was couched in the individualistic language of rights and "standing."[13]

The form of proceedings necessarily affects who participates and on what grounds. Adjudicatory-style proceedings, whether they occur in the United States, Japan, or India, invite participation only by acknowledged "stakeholders." Since economic stakes are the most widely recognized, legalized processes tend to favor those whose property or business interests are affected by a proposed standard. American environmental laws on the whole allow the broadest range of interested and affected parties, including environmental groups, both to participate in regulatory proceedings and to sue agencies if their regulations are deemed inconsistent with the law. Offsetting this extraordinary breadth in the kinds of people who may participate, however, is a relative narrowness in the grounds on which people may challenge agency actions. Grounds must be found within the framework of existing legislation and hence are limited largely to technical errors committed by administrative agencies in their performance of the law.

By contrast, India's public interest litigation (PIL) process, initiated by "writ petitions" addressed directly to the Supreme Court, has allowed parties to complain of inaction or nonperformance by the other branches of government, even in the absence of specific legal guarantees. Baviskar argues, however, that PIL actions may lead to unenforceable judgments, as well as to actions favoring middle class health and environmental interests over the working class interest in job security.

Finally, it is worth noting that standard-setting processes initiated from below, without recourse to the state's administrative apparatus, may produce constraints on human-environment relations that are no less stringent in practice than those imposed from above by the state. Yet these bottom-up standards may be more easily tolerated by those subjected to them. In Arizona's Civano development, for example, participants were willing to put up with endlessly detailed restrictions on the kinds of materials they could build with, as well as the manner in which they could use water and energy. The fishing customs of the fishworkers in India represent every bit as much a discipline—though, in this case, the self-discipline of tradition—as "modern" standards that regulate the timing, location, or intensity of industrial agriculture. The success of these alternative models of standard-setting is consistent with findings that, even in highly modernized, science-dependent societies such as the United States, standards of responsible environmental behavior, particularly with regard to the use of common pool resources, often come about through agreements on shared norms and a shared sense of place rather than through the formal exercise of legal power.[14]

Knowledge-Making

In all four countries described in this volume, a holistic local knowledge of nature, usually predating the time of law and regulation, contrasts with the turn to science that seems inevitably to accompany the legal protection of nature. From India's artisanal fishers, who are striving to retain a way of life in which they do not disturb Kadalamma ("Mother Sea") to the fishers and hunters who eke out difficult, marginal livings on the fringes of extractive modern industries in China, Japan, and the United States— each country study confronts us with nostalgic memories of a time when people apparently knew how to live well with the environment. Law's allocative, compensatory, and standard-setting functions were not called for in those days; nor was science a prerequisite for environmental sustainability. But this remembered era is everywhere yielding to one in which science is very much on the scene, usually in active partnership with the law.

Although the connection between law and knowledge production is intimate, science plays highly variable roles in environmental policy-making in the four countries, as well as in the case studies within each one. Legal institutions and processes affect not only how much knowledge is produced but also what kinds of issues are considered worth investigating and what forms of knowledge are considered credible. In this way, the law collaborates with science to shore up certain framings of environmental problems and the values associated with them.

Given the pervasiveness of legal processes in the United States, it is perhaps not surprising that this is where law-science interactions have received the most sustained attention, both from scholars and from participants in the policy process. Well-known features of the U.S. administrative culture include a legally sanctioned demand for a reasoned, objective, preferably quantitatively expressed justification of policy decisions and an associated push toward translating value controversies into scientific terms.[15] In the sheer production of environmental research, it would be difficult for any country to compete with the United States, where science is everyone's favorite ally.[16] It can serve as an instrument for advancing the public interest when agencies or citizens generate evidence in support of health and safety claims; equally, it becomes a powerful mechanism for defending private interests when companies or private property owners sponsor studies to debunk claims of risk. The term "tobacco science" gained currency in U.S. political circles in the 1990s as an especially egregious example of such cooptation of scientific discourse by business interests.

But the intense collaboration between law and science in American environmental policy-making also has more subtle and less well-recognized implications. Perhaps most significant in the context of this volume is the weighting of the U.S. policy system toward certain ways of coping with uncertainty and complexity over others, and thus a preference for framing issues in terms of risk, which can be scientifically assessed, rather than precaution, which more openly admits the limits of knowledge; a tendency to locate risk in the inanimate world rather than in human behaviors and lifestyles;[17] and a concomitant preference for investigating nature through methods that detach the observer from the observed. We see instances of all these dynamics in the U.S. cases: for example, petroleum companies in the Grand Bois region fund studies of produced water discharges to contest government findings; Grand Bois residents unite over the rituals of health testing, needing science to confirm their community's perceptions of environmental deterioration; a Louisiana environmental department undertakes emergency action to sample produced water for radioactivity levels; meanwhile, in Arizona, technical controversies develop over the costs and benefits of a plan to protect the pygmy owl.

Science is nowhere else so public or so contested as in these and many similar U.S. episodes, and the visibility of the scientific process correlates interestingly with the formality of the law. For example, in China, where decisions concerning environmental protection are reached for the most part without explicit, formal procedures, no apparent controversies have arisen about the nature or quality of the evidence supporting the state's decisions. This is the case even though many suspect that the corrupt desire to collect and pocket monetary fines drives the development of forest and wetland protection measures more than science does. Nature reserve officials' commitment to the environment, for its part, rests on an array of factors from which science is noticeably absent. "While," as the case study tells us, "reserve officials acknowledged the long-term importance of preserving the Sanjiang wetland, the constellation of values that guides them includes ambitions for modernity and internationalism, career aspirations, socialist values of discipline and dedication to a cause, and kinship values resting on networks of loyalties and mutual favors" (p. 70). One could hardly imagine a greater contrast with the situation across the Pacific in the United States.

In Japan, recourse to science is again closely coupled with recourse to law, as in the lawsuits by Minamata pollution victims. Systematic knowledge-production through science is deemed necessary in these cases, but whereas an American community can find common cause through the rituals of testing for shared afflictions, in the Japanese cases investigation by scientific researchers, like formal legal proceedings, seems almost antithetical to community building. In the Kumamoto-Minamata case, in particular, the dynamics of blaming and victimization, compensation, and restoration all proceed with near-complete disregard for both science and law. Similarly, rural communities around Lake Biwa are reluctant to conceptualize the lake only in terms of its researchable characteristics, such as water quality or the concentrations of particular chemical constituents. Yet, as the Lake Biwa case also shows, when citizens do unite in a communal project of environmental protection, they are prepared to undertake scientific studies of such commonplace phenomena as changes in firefly populations; similarly, Minamata residents wished to create an international mercury pollution research network as part of their efforts at rebuilding community through shared experiences of disaster.

The Indian stories likewise show a strong correlation between recourse to science, with its explicitness, and recourse to the law, with its formality. Ever since the environmental lawyer M.C. Mehta's landmark 1985 lawsuit to get a polluting industry relocated outside the Delhi city limits, efforts to monitor and curb toxic discharges in the capital region have steadily grown. As in the United States, the marriage of science and law has proved a formidable lever with which to promote green objectives. But what the Delhi air pollution case makes clear is that in developing countries, unlike the United States, for instance, the capacity to enlist either the law or science for one's political causes remains most unequally distributed. Despite heroic efforts at data gathering and documentation, the Manch, a federation of trade unions and human rights organizations, cannot get the Indian Supreme Court interested in the statistics it has compiled about the impact of environmentally motivated factory closures on the numbers of jobless and displaced. Accordingly, the contract workers—for whom "environmental sustainability" in a metropolitan setting meant, above all, access to work and a minimal level of economic subsistence—did not fare so well under law as those who could produce evidence of urban decay and pollution-related illness such as asthma.

Resistance

The law has been harnessed to many ends in late modernity, serving multiple, sometimes contradictory purposes, from the safeguarding of production, trade, and markets to the prevention of pollution and the protection of natural resources. The core objective of this preeminent social technology remains, however, the rendering of justice. In concluding our comparative review, we may ask, then, how far the law has been engaged in the service of *environmental* justice. To what extent and under what circumstances do people see the law as an instrument for registering grievances, obtaining redress, or pressing for new allocations in relation of environmental resources and rights? Is the law seen as a solution to the problem of unsustainability, or is it part of the problem?

Strikingly, resistance in all four countries seems to be targeted as much *at* the law—or, more generally, at legally supported regimes of environmental governance—as *through* the law. The clearest cases of resistance are those in which the state is perceived as using the law-making apparatus wholly in its own self-interest or else as acting to further powerful commercial interests at the expense of citizens. Stealing and poaching are rife in the Sanjiang Reserve, for example, and a local reserve officer resignedly offers this comment on his powerlessness to stop them: "The new migrants are desperate. They make money from all kinds of risky things, and we might suffer from their crazy retaliation if we strictly enforced the laws" (p. 80).

In India, from as far back as colonial times, resource allocation decisions made by the state have repeatedly led to protest actions, and even social movements. Where such decisions are coupled with concerted governmental support for some forms of production over others, as in the case of the Kerala fishworkers, protest may be of little use, whether it is conducted with or without the aid of law. In other cases, however, Indian protest movements have succeeded brilliantly in dramatizing the environmental concerns of the poor. The best-known example here is the "Chipko" (hug the tree) movement that originated in a small village the Himalayan foothills but achieved international renown by the late 1980s as an inspiring example of women's activism and local resistance. Like the Chipko demonstrators, the Kerala National Fishworkers' Forum similarly tied environmental and economic issues together through its 1989 campaign, organized around the slogan "Protect Water, Protect Life" (p. 224). Public demonstrations such as these project to the world a holistic conception of the nature-culture relationship that seems inconsistent with the spirit of much formal environmental law.

In Japan, as in India, legal institutions are often rejected or only reluctantly embraced by the environmentally concerned, although the issue here is the law's felt divisiveness rather than its hegemonic regulatory power. Victims of pollution, for example, find legal actions alienating because they are variously too public, too impersonal, too partial, and too threatening to the life of the community. In addition, the framings of the environment that the law permits are deemed inadequate by some of the activists and spokespersons who appear in the Japanese case studies. They place a higher value on the preservation of multiple meanings of the environment, including historical memories of the places that they wish to protect—or, in the case of Minamata, to regenerate. The complexity of environmental experience, Kada et al. suggest in their chapter, cannot easily be captured by legal processes, which promote a more reductionist, objective, analytic vision. To fight this oversimplification, Japanese environmental framers, like their Indian counterparts, have chosen to turn to forms of communal action other than multiparty lawsuits.

No comparable ambivalence about the framing effects of the law can be discerned in the United States, where a fondness for judicial remedies unites even those who firmly oppose each other on issues of environmental allocation and compensation. It is not the law but the concept of legitimacy itself that seems most under attack in the United States. Who, after all, can command real authority in environmental policy-making? Citizens sue corporations for environmental misconduct and blame state agencies for insufficient regulation and enforcement, while firms and landowners, vigorously defending themselves against citizens and the state, sue the government for overregulation and challenge its scientific findings. In the end, no actor unproblematically derives authority from the law. Each act of embracing the institutions of the law paradoxically becomes an act of resistance against claims of lawfulness by others. Environmental conflicts in the United States thus illustrate in perhaps the most extreme form the contradictions of an all-too-pervasive rule of law. Just as reflexive modernization—the phenomenon in which people find new uncertainties in the process of trying to narrow other uncertainties—leads to an undermining of scientific authority by the power of science, so, too, does hyper-legalism in the U.S. mode entail a hollowing out of legal authority through the very operation of the law.

Concluding Reflections

For as long as people have tried to live at peace with one another, the law has existed as the instrument that makes ordered existence possible. With growing populations, resource use, and recognition of the biosphere's limited capacity, no nation or polity can disregard the need for law in its attempts to order human interactions with nature. It is next to impossible to imagine any regime of environmental governance, from the most local to the most global, without the active involvement of legal institutions and legal modes of thought. That said, however, nations differ in the ways they interweave the formal institutions of the law with other sources of communal principles and norms. Cross-national variations in environmental policy arise, in part, through divergent accommodations among folk beliefs, traditional cultural practices, and explicit invocations of the law.

The centrality of the law for environmental policy is amply documented in each of the four country studies. Five domains of legal activity emerge as salient in the production of sustainability: allocation of scarce resources; compensation for environmental harm; standard-setting; knowledge-making; and resistance against perceived threats to established ways of life. To the extent that all nations and all actors within them accept the need for law in pursuing these functions, they can all be said to subscribe to a common value of *legality*. They recognize that ordering nature demands a simultaneous ordering of society—and that such ordering can most easily be accomplished through a disciplined engagement with the law. Thus, their commitment to environmental law can be regarded as a transcendent human value.

Yet the way in which each nation constructs the role and limits of legality for environmental purposes remains persistently culture-bound. The differences among nations can be sketched along five principal dimensions. One is the relationship between public and private law. Environmental disputes between private parties are most common in the United States, resisted to some degree in Japan, and least common in India and China. A second dimension of difference is the openness and formality of legal procedures, with the United States again occupying an exceptional

Table 5.1

Law and Environment in Comparative Perspective

	China	India	Japan	United States
Legal frameworks: public/private	Public regulatory actions. No private litigation.	Public regulatory actions. Public interest litigation (PIL).	Public regulatory actions. Administrative compensation proceedings.	Public regulatory actions. Private liability litigation.
Openness/ formality/ explicitness of process	Extremely low.	Low in public proceedings; moderate/high in PIL.	Moderate to high, but culturally resisted.	Extremely high in all cases; culturally prized.
Public science: investment and demand	Low investment; low demand.	Low investment; low demand.	Moderate investment; moderate-to-low demand.	High investment; high demand.
Nature/society relationship: separatism vs. holism	Official separation of nature and society.	Integration of nature and society in administrative decisions and some protest movements.	Official separation of nature and society. Integration in some citizen initiatives.	Official separation of nature and society. Some integration in private behavior.
Modes of innovation: top-down/ bottom-up/ interactive; legal vs. extralegal	Top-down regulation. Bottom-up resistance.	Top-down regulation. Bottom-up protests and PIL.	Top-down regulation. Bottom-up community building.	Interactive regulation. Bottom-up challenges through lawsuits.

position in its commitment to open, adversarial processes. A third important dimension is the extent to which nations invest in producing public knowledge in support of regulatory judgments and rest their environmental policies on explicit scientific justification. The United States takes the lead, with India, Japan, and China following significantly behind. A fourth and closely related dimension is the degree to which law and science work together to separate natural from social phenomena. Arguably capitalist United States and socialist China have separatist orientations in common, as against the more holistic environmental movements of India and Japan. Finally, there are differences among countries regarding where in society resistance originates and the extent to which the law serves as a source of environmental innovation. While some environmental initiatives have taken shape without recourse to the law in all the country cases, citizens of the four nations compared here differ in their willingness to seek bottom-up solutions and to do so through institutions other than those of the law. (Table 5.1 summarizes these contrasts.)

Environmental law, we conclude, at once actively frames and passively reflects culturally grounded expectations about the ways in which human societies wish to live with one another and with their natural surroundings. With the progress of modernity, a particular model of legality continues to spread throughout the world. This is the model of modernity that separates nature from culture, standardizes both, and defends its prescriptions for good conduct through rational scientific argumentation. It has, however, met with resistance in the environmental context, not only because the resources of rationality are expensive and unequally distributed but because this form of legality runs into two additional, culturally sensitive problems. In many parts of the world, the modernizing thrust of the law seems not to satisfy people's deep-seated commitments to place, community, and forms of life. And even where such feelings no longer predominate, the growing managerial ambitions of law and science produce their own contradictions, which neither institution can satisfactorily resolve. It remains to be seen whether the law in its infinite plasticity will find workable and, dare we say, soul-satisfying alternatives to the contested, though now globally disseminated, prototype of modern environmental regulation.

Notes

1. India and the United States are common law countries, although the reception and development of the common law has proceeded in very different ways in the two jurisdictions. Japan's modern legal system was built on continental civil law models, especially those of Germany and France, but was modified in the American direction after World War II. China's legal system, developed since 1949, builds on a socialist model with some civil law characteristics, but since 1979 it has increasingly incorporated elements of foreign law, especially in the sphere of economic regulation.

2. This term was inserted into global environmental discourse by a United Nations commission in preparation for the 1992 Rio Earth Summit. World Commission on Environment and Development, *Our Common Future* (Oxford: Oxford University Press, 1987), 43.

3. In this scenario, unrestricted use by a collection of individuals leads to depletion of the common resource. Garrett Hardin, "The Tragedy of the Commons," *Science* 16, no. 2 (1968): 1243–48.

4. *Tort*, derived from the French word for wrong, is the legal name for an injury inflicted by one private party on another. Tort law provides the standard vehicle for recovery in most environmental injury cases, such as pollution of groundwater, toxic releases into air or water, oil spills, chemical-induced fish kills, and so forth. Persistent problems in environmental tort cases include the difficulty of establishing a causal connection between particular human activities and damage to health or environment and the difficulty of placing a monetary value on environmental harms.

5. Peter Schuck, *Agent Orange on Trial: Mass Toxic Disasters in the Courts* (Cambridge: Harvard University Press, 1986).

6. See, for example, Kai Erikson, *Everything in Its Path: The Destruction of Community in the Buffalo Creek Flood* (New York: Simon and Schuster, 1976).

7. According to *Palazzolo v. Rhode Island*, 533 U.S. 606 (2001) property owners are not

foreclosed from challenging the application of land-use restrictions imposed before they acquired their properties; *Dolan v. City of Tigard*, 512 U.S. 687 (1994) required a municipality to demonstrate a reasonable relationship between environmental restrictions placed on a proposed development and its likely impact.

8. Ulrich Beck, *Risk Society: Towards a New Modernity* (London: Sage, 1992), 153–256; see also Ulrich Beck, Anthony Giddens, and Scott Lash, *Reflexive Modernization: Politics, Tradition and Aesthetics in the Modern Social Order* (Cambridge: Polity Press, 1994).

9. Michel Foucault, *Power/Knowledge: Selected Interviews and Other Writings 1972–1977* (New York: Pantheon, 1980); *Discipline and Punish: The Birth of the Prison* (New York: Random House, 1979); *The History of Sexuality, Vol. 1* (New York: Pantheon, 1978).

10. Possible correspondences between training citizens and training skilled observers of nature can also be found in Western political thought and practice. See, in particular, Lewis Mumford, *Technics and Civilization* (New York: Harcourt, Brace and World, 1963); also Claire Waterton and Rebecca Ellis, "Environmental Citizenship in the Making: The Participation of Volunteer Naturalists in UK Biological Recording," *Science & Public Policy* 31, no. 2 (2004): 95–105; Claire Waterton and Brian Wynne, "Building the European Union: Science and the Cultural Dimensions of Environmental Policy," *Journal of European Public Policy* 3, no. 3 (1996): 421–40.

11. Originally this project also included studies of the Koiter shifting cultivators in Bastar, India, and the Sonora co-housing in Tucson, two cases that even more profoundly exemplify this point.

12. See Sheila Jasanoff, *Risk Management and Political Culture* (New York: Russell Sage Foundation, 1986); David Vogel, *National Styles of Regulation* (Ithaca: Cornell University Press, 1986); Ronald Brickman, Sheila Jasanoff, and Thomas Ilgen, *Controlling Chemicals: The Politics of Regulation in Europe and the United States* (Ithaca: Cornell University Press, 1985).

13. Christopher Stone, *Should Trees Have Standing: Toward Legal Rights for Natural Objects* (Los Altos, CA: William Kaufmann, 1974).

14. See particularly Elinor Ostrom, ed., *Governing the Commons: The Evolution of Institutions for Collective Action* (Cambridge: Cambridge University Press, 1990). Also see Sheila Jasanoff, "Compelling Knowledge in Public Decisions," in *Saving the Seas: Values, Scientists, and International Governance,* ed. L. Anathea Brooks and Stacy D. VanDeveer (College Park, MD: Maryland Sea Grant, 1996), 229–52.

15. Sheila Jasanoff, *The Fifth Branch: Science Advisers as Policymakers* (Cambridge: Harvard University Press, 1990); and *Risk Management and Political Culture* (New York: Russell Sage Foundation, 1986). For a historical account of these phenomena, see Theodore Porter, *Trust in Numbers: The Pursuit of Objectivity in Science and Public Life* (Princeton: Princeton University Press, 1995).

16. For more on this phenomenon, see Yaron Ezrahi, "Science and Utopia in Late 20th Century Pluralist Democracy—with a Special Reference to the U.S.A.," in *Nineteen Eighty-Four: Science between Utopia and Dystopia, Sociology of the Sciences VIII,* ed. Everett Mendelsohn and Helga Nowotny (Dordrecht, NL: Kluwer, 1984), 273–90.

17. On these points, see particularly Sheila Jasanoff, "Technological Risk and Cultures of Rationality," in *Incorporating Science, Economics, and Sociology in Developing Sanitary and Phytosanitary Standards in International Trade,* National Research Council, Board on Agriculture and Natural Resources (Washington, DC: National Academies Press, 2000), 65–84; and "The Songliness of Risk," *Environmental Values* 8 (1999): 135–52.

6

Environmental Transformations and the Values of Modernity

Arun Agrawal

If modernity is the name of the project that posits a direct relationship between the pursuit of knowledge, reason, and human progress,[1] we are all witting or unwitting participants in that project.[2] Multiple shades of meanings, and translation into multiple programs of action, make modernity appropriable and indeed, desirable to a degree that few rival concepts can match. Poor families wanting a more comfortable livelihood; corporations pursuing ever higher profits and sales; elected and autocratic leaders promising a better tomorrow; idealists imagining a democratic and participatory society; progressive academics invested in greater equity; and well-meaning NGOs attempting a more just world—for them all, modernity is the condition to be desired and inhabited. Modernity is phenomenologically coincident with particular forms of values such as reason, legality, equality, and democracy.[3] One can therefore argue that attempts to question modernity rest on the possibility of reason and logic. Thus, even the questioning of modernity is thoroughly modern.

But modernity is also undoubtedly a spatial condition. Recent books, from Appadurai's *Modernity at Large* to titles that implicitly or explicitly emphasize geography— *African Modernities, Mapping Modernities, Geohistorical Modernities, Melanesian Modernities,* and *Provincial Modernity*—suggest that modernity is neither universal nor uniform. It arrives at its own pace in different locations. Certain characteristics help constitute modern spaces, including but not restricted to science and its products —such as print media, electricity, and industrial production—and social developments such as the de-linking of birth and status, equality before law, and companionate marriage based on love.

Drawing on the case studies in the first part of the book, this chapter explores how modern values shape and are reflected in social-environmental outcomes. Of course, environmental action is often at first strongly influenced by existing social values that are premodern in the sense that they predate the belief that reason and progress are of a piece. But over time environmental crises and movements can generate new, modern values and seed them into national or local contexts. In turn, new environmental values can influence future social mobilization and legislation.

Notably, in each of our case studies, an environmental crisis helped introduce modern values into local contexts, or changed how local people viewed the environment. Thus, the Minamata disaster encouraged a reevaluation of classical Japanese beliefs in tradition, hierarchy, and the place of victims. In China, the disappearance of Benxi from satellite pictures because of air pollution helped launch a wholesale program of environmental rectification. Similarly, the 1998 floods in Heilongjiang Province prompted Chinese officials with jurisdiction over the Sanjiang Plain to take seriously international calls for wetland preservation. In both China cases, the relevant actors came to see full membership in the international community —an important value of modernity—as a desirable end. Environmental crises discussed in the other country chapters—sudden and dramatic drops in fish catch in Kerala, energy and water scarcity in Civano, the red tide in Biwa, the oleum leak in Delhi, and benzene-laden wastes in Louisiana—brought environmental issues dramatically to the social forefront. These crises fostered a renewed appreciation for nature and its fragility (as in Civano, Biwa, and Grand Bois) or a recognition of the need for a healthy environment in order to achieve sustainable livelihoods (as in Kerala) or healthy lives (as in Delhi).

While environmental crises can promote modern thinking, the instruments of modernity can in turn help advance environmental causes. Twentieth century technologies, for instance, allow environmentalists to elevate objects and phenomena associated with the environment into potent symbols—witness the billboards in Delhi announcing pollution levels or the publicity surrounding the discovery that Benxi is invisible in satellite images. These symbols, one of presence and the other of absence, can be deployed to dramatic effect by environmentalists. Before launching into the main part of this chapter, I would like to point out that modernity and its values, especially in the context of environmental action and change, are "essentially contestable";[4] that is, the manner in which they deal with and simultaneously gloss over a diversity of interests encourages multiple interpretations of the events at stake. The plethora of values that modernity commodiously encompasses makes the task of jointly considering the values of modernity and the environment easy in some ways, difficult in others.

This chapter therefore relies on an interested reading of a number of writers on modernity to focus on some key ideas they see as an important part of what it means to be modern. Three overarching values relationships frame the ensuing discussion: (1) the connection between science and progress-defined-as-growth;[5] (2) the role of science in the creation of what counts as the environment in the different cases;[6] and (3) the presumed equality of modern individuals[7]—before the law and in opportunity—in relation to environmental change. These modernity-related themes, highly visible in all the country chapters, give rise to two additional discussions: the emergence of the individual[8]—as, for example, in the Japan cases—and the web of connections that link humans to each other, often internationally or globally[9]—as for example, in the China cases.

Modernity and Growth

The modern value perhaps most relevant to environmental change is the belief in knowledge as a means to progress.[10] Economic growth and development are the critical index most national leaders use to measure progress and improvement. Indeed, growth and development are deeply held values beyond leadership strata, for everyday citizens' desire for secure jobs and greater incomes match national growth and development goals. These goals are called into question for environmental reasons only when their pursuit collides with some version of local limits on development (as in the resource-use cases of Sanjiang, Biwa, Nagara, Kerala, and Civano) or directly conflicts with something even more basic, such as health or bodily integrity (as in the cases of Benxi, Minamata, Delhi, and Louisiana). The relationship between environmental crises and ill-considered and hastily implemented plans for growth is thus the starting point for all the case studies. Indeed, many people first form the idea of the environment as something to be protected and cherished as a direct result of unrestrained economic growth. Environmental devastation wrought by unchecked growth forces people to become aware of and rethink their values with regard to nature.

Variations in national growth strategies, implicitly described in Part 1 of this book, also suggest that poorer countries with some success in growing rapidly seem even more interested in pushing for growth than those that are already highly developed or that have not seen much success in their plans for growth. Postwar Japan, and China and India today, are good examples. But growth is a value so enshrined in most national economic policies that it can be easy to overlook the vulnerability of localities and groups to its chilling consequences.

The connection between aspirations for economic growth and the willingness to ignore or minimize the adverse health effects of industrial development is seen most fully in postwar Japan, where economic growth was so highly valued that even clear evidence of mercury poisoning in the local population did not at first end the dumping of effluent into Minamata Bay. But there are interesting parallels between the faith in industrial development exemplified in Minamata and the way Louisiana and U.S. legislation shielded (and continues to shield) powerful oil and gas companies by permitting indiscriminate toxic waste disposal. For over a decade Grand Bois residents unknowingly lived next to a toxic waste site because Louisiana, like Japan in the 1960s, had no legislation that would have penalized the indiscriminate dumping of toxic oil field waste. The residents of Grand Bois, like the Minamatans, faced government officials sympathetic to large corporate actors and relatively unconcerned about the environmental effects of their actions. Similarly, officials in Benxi, China's steel-producing capital, never did anything about air pollution until the United Nations Environment Program publicized satellite images of Benxi obscured by particulate matter.

Minamata, Grand Bois, and Benxi exemplify the excesses connected with unchecked development. But nearly all the other cases also suggest that environmental problems stem from overreliance on irresponsible development strategies—as in Japan's dam-building program, China's overexploitation of forests and reclamation of wetlands for agricultural development in the Sanjiang region, the capital-intensive interventions to boost the fish catch off India's Kerala coast, and the push to attract new business to Tucson amid a growing regional water crisis. In all these cases, growth involved a Faustian bargain that increased incomes for some and compromised the health, livelihoods, and lives of others.

Though the governments and societies involved in all the cases placed high value on economic growth, the extent to which and ways in which governments value growth differ from one nation to another. Indeed, the value placed on growth even varies among different stakeholders in a given country or locality. The cases suggest that three variables are critical: the country's level of development; how benefits of growth and its costs, including environmental costs, are distributed; and the timeline along which individuals and groups experience the effects of environmental problems.

Low levels of development and per capita income appear to make national governments eager to favor growth over environmental protection. The converse also likely holds. These propositions are evident in the Japan and China cases, and for the fisheries case for India. At the time the Minamata disaster occurred, Japan was still relatively underdeveloped, and the Ministry of Construction enjoyed enormous influence over the country's economic decision-making. It was only in later years, when Japan enjoyed high levels of development, and in no small measure because of the experience of Minamata, that officials and citizens alike have become far more conscious of environmental issues.

Two of the cases stand out against this generalization: Grand Bois and Delhi. In these two cases, political-economic realities trumped values brought to the fore by environmental crises. Environmental costs of growth fall on the poor in Louisiana, and the tight relationship between state officials and corporate actors protected the powerful oil and gas interests from the just consequences of their actions.

The case of industrialization around Delhi is more complex. The middle class consumer-residents of Delhi and the poor workers employed in the factories faced and valued the costs and benefits of industrial pollution quite differently. Although some of the relatively well-off factory owners profited from polluting industries, relatively few middle class and elite Delhi residents depended on these industries economically, and yet they bore the costs of pollution emitted by the industries. They prevailed upon the Supreme Court to take action despite the importance that the Indian state attaches to economic growth, but only because upper status Delhi residents *are,* by and large, the Indian state.

The factory workers, for their part, were willing to put up with pollution because their livelihoods were so intimately tied to the polluting factories. But environmental pollution threatened the health of a more powerful social group, and many members of that group came to define the poor as part of the pollution of which Delhi needed to be rid. Further, in the Indian case the timing of the issue also helped the anti-pollution campaign. The Supreme Court would likely not have rendered a similar decision in the 1960s or 1970s, when even a narrowly elite-based environmental movement was missing from India. Since the 1980s and 1990s, when environmental organizations first came on the Indian scene,[11] awareness of environmental issues has grown, at least among urban elite Indians, often accompanied by a willingness to act when hazardous substances threaten their health. Elite awareness of the West's stricter environmental standards fuels a desire for equally strong standards in India as the elite strive to become part of the modern world.

The varying impacts of values connected with economic growth on the cases in this volume suggest that these values affect outcomes but not necessarily by themselves. Instead, the values act in concert with other political, economic, and societal factors. High levels of development in a country, many economists and some political scientists have argued, are often accompanied by increasing concern for environmental issues,[12] but the cases illustrate that there is little reason to assume that environmental protection will emerge victorious only or always after values connected with economic growth have found expression.

Modern Reason and Environmental Problems

Faith in knowledge as the means to progress, together with the formation of discrete domains of knowledge that underpin this faith, is another important characteristic of modernity. In modernity human activities are divided into separate spheres, and the distinct domains of society—the state, the economy, and culture—are born. These domains of human endeavor become available to reason and science for further investigation and analysis. At the same time, modernity also witnesses the birth of concepts through which different domains of human life can be analyzed and understood: class, gender, power, utility, discourse, and so on.

The emergence of discrete domains of analysis and action is as true in the environmental sphere as it is in other spheres of the social world. In modernity, the environment itself becomes an object of knowledge and analysis as part of the modern valorization of science and the attendant proliferation of intellectual disciplines. To paraphrase the noted cultural studies scholar Stuart Hall it is not that observations about nature were absent before modernity—rather, modernity transformed nature into environment,[13] a "separate and distinct form of reality, which could be analyzed . . . and laid out for rational investigation and explanation."[14] Scientific investigation of the natural world can reveal the precise causes of problems and the mechanisms through which causes and effects are connected, and it can point to solutions to the problems. Further, science can help evaluate alternative solutions so that the best possible policy and legislation can be adopted.

The corollary of this objectification of nature is a shift toward a more abstract and secular conceptualization of the environment, described in the Japan chapter in terms of "disembeddedness." Particular individuals and groups in modernity value nature, but typically as the environment—something to be protected and cared for through scientific investigation and examination. But nature loses its divinity when it comes to be perceived as the "environment" (*kankyo mondai*), a domain fit for scientific investigation and group action. While the divine is fundamentally unknowable, environmental action presumes environment's knowability.[15]

As environmental sociologists Taylor and Buttel suggest, "We know we have global environmental problems because . . . science documents the existing situation and ever tightens its predictions of future changes. [Moreover] science supplies the knowledge needed to stimulate and guide social-political action."[16] Long before Rachel Carson wrote about the effects of pesticides on songbirds, scientists have been postulating cause and effect relationships between human actions such as forest clearing for agricultural expansion or timber harvesting, and their environmental impacts, such as soil erosion and flooding.

The case studies in this volume highlight the extent to which scientific studies are crucial in demonstrating how particular toxic chemicals affected soil, water, food, and health. Scientific evidence led to conclusions about the kinds and extent of environmental damage in the industrial pollution cases of Benxi, Minamata, Louisiana, and Delhi. This evidence included satellite pictures of the earth, medical research on the effects of organic mercury on fish and human health, and EPA reports on wastes generated in the course of oil production, scientific findings-based newspaper reports of the pollution of the Jamuna River, a tributary of the Ganges. Similarly, land-use planning in Sanjiang, analysis of water availability in the Lake Biwa region, impact assessments of trawling in Kerala, and zoning regulations in Tucson all relied upon science. In each of these cases, science counts whether its users seek objective answers to questions of public policy or are cynically deploying scientific evidence to advance narrow self-interest. Science has such power in environmental conflicts that scientific studies favoring one position can only be discounted on the basis of other scientific studies. Thus, when adherents of a particular position dislike the results of a scientific study, they always call for further studies. We encounter such calls for more evidence and analysis in the Grand Bois or Minamata cases as well as today's conflict over global climate change.

But science and reason do more than simply identify environmental problems, help us find their causes, and suggest solutions. They also help us constitute our views about the environment. Certain kinds of human impacts—on soil, water, plants and animals, food supply, air, and through these media on human health—are typically classified as "environmental." Tetsuro Yoshimoto's statement in the Minamata case that the word "environment" is frequently used by government officers and scientists "who are detached from actual contact with land and water" is instructive (p. 135), pointing to how the environment itself is constructed through a process of abstraction. The abstraction and classification of particular effects as environmental (and others as economic, or cultural, or political) is therefore a product of tacit or explicit values. For example, tropical deforestation through much of the 1950s and 1960s was viewed as a perfectly reasonable strategy to achieve higher levels of development. Conversion of forests into cropland was, thus, development. But the abstraction of particular species and assemblages of organisms in forests as biodiversity and greater awareness of the ecosystem services forests provide has transformed deforestation into environmental degradation.

The division of knowledge into different domains also enables specialized investigations that require their own vocabulary, techniques, and rhetoric. The idea of "the environment," for instance, depends on the accumulation of certain facts about the world, techniques to describe and connect these facts, and strategies to present them to different audiences. Once certain kinds of effects are imagined and classified as "environmental" in one context, similar kinds of classification become easier in other situations. Once deforestation in the Amazon is viewed as reducing global biodiversity, deforestation in other tropical nations is easier to classify and accept as being an example of biodiversity loss. As particular facts, symbols, techniques, responses, and policy mechanisms get established as having an environmental content, they can be unhitched from the contexts in which they were produced and deployed in other, new and foreign contexts. Such mobility of concepts and strategies across contexts helps to spread the idea of environment, environmental problems, and environmental protection more rapidly across the globe.

Consider an example from the cases in the book. The international Ramsar Convention lays out the general criteria on the basis of which certain lands can be classified as "Wetlands of International Importance."[17] By creating the category wetlands (and thereby elevating the status of what was previously considered "swampland"), outlining the procedures through which they can be formed and administered, and clarifying the criteria that prospective wetland sites should meet (as well as the availability of international funds for wetlands protection), the convention aided the creation of the Sanjiang Nature Reserve. Those interested in environmental protection in Sanjiang were able to classify many local phenomena such as soil erosion, changes in land cover, alteration of vegetation, disappearance of some species (including megafauna such as the Siberian tiger), agricultural runoff, illegal hunting, and overharvesting as environmental effects. They all needed attention. Chinese urban environmental activists, government agencies, and international actors came to believe that devoting 30 percent of the Sanjiang Plain to wetland reserves would begin to address the above problems. The value placed internationally on environmental protection of wetlands worked powerfully to help in the creation of a "wetland of international importance," as specified in the Ramsar Convention. The portability of abstract environmental principles thus helped to produce concrete local outcomes.

But the constitution of the domain of the environment, as the cases show, occurs in relation to different overarching values of modernity. In both Minamata and Biwa, according to the authors of the Japan chapter, environmental activism is influenced by the wish for a restoration of a stronger connection and a more equal balance between humans and nature. Community activism and local participation are crucial to this restoration of natural connections, even if such actions are sometimes shaped by relations between local groups and international organizations or their aspirations. On the other hand, in places like Benxi and Sanjiang, the relationship of environmental activism to international standards, funds, and activists promotes environmental mobilization. Some of this emphasis on international connections in the China cases can be explained by the fact that such connections can bring new resources and funds into domestic contexts. But quite possibly, the appeal to international standards also confers greater legitimacy on the leaders of the two local government-led campaigns.

Science, Equality, and Environmental Solutions

The equality of all modern individuals—the belief that all humans are equal before the law[18]—plays a crucial role in the way state and social actors respond to the environmental crises described in the case studies. Modern democratic governments and their laws rest, at least in the abstract, on the leveling of hierarchies and barriers to equality. Environmental crises powerfully motivate the proliferation of new regulations and enforcement mechanisms, whether the crises involve land use around Lake Biwa and in Sanjiang, fishing in Kerala, land classification and zoning in Tuscon, or toxic waste in Minamata, Delhi, Benxi, and Louisiana. The value of equality constantly encourages the creation of new rules and regulations to address these problems and others like them.

The cases highlight a particularly complex aspect of environmental problems: that the burden of environmental problems falls unequally upon different social groups. From Louisiana to Kerala to Sanjiang to Minamata, the cases deliver an important lesson about how environmental outcomes affect different social groups differently. As Anil Agarwal and Sunita Narain show, even a seemingly universal environmental issue as global climate change can be, and needs to be, discussed in terms of the contribution by different countries to the problem and the problem's effects on different countries and social groups.[19] Agarwal and Narain's well-known response to the World Resources Institute report on global warming in 1991 undermined the supposition that environmental problems are global: in contrast to the rhetoric of "one world" they showed that the origins and impacts of global warming are highly differentiated. Environmental problems today can scarcely be described credibly in terms of a universal common future.[20] Even the value of community that animates some environmental struggles and seems significantly at play in the creation of Civano, for example, has been called an unsound basis for environmental action because of the multiple axes along which most communities are fractured.[21] Scholars of environmental justice in the United States and political ecologists and environmental feminists internationally have pioneered the analysis of political and distributive environmental conflicts to show how environmental problems do not affect members of a society equally.[22]

Those who advocate environmental equity and call attention to the different environmental interests of different social groups tend to believe that similar processes, characteristic of modernity, are responsible for both environmental and social distributive outcomes.[23] Underlying the modern focus on equality and distributive fairness is the assumption that all human beings have an equal claim to the benefits of development. Since all humans are equal, the unequal impacts of environmental outcomes—from global climate change to biodiversity loss—need to be critiqued.

Further, forms of redress need to be established, with more compensation to those who disproportionately bear the costs of environmental changes.

It is the essential equality of human beings that compels environmental mobilizations against powerful corporate interests, uncaring state bureaucracies, and the anonymous forces of globalization. The discussions in this volume of mercury poisoning (in Minamata and Niigata-Minamata) and inadequate disposal of toxic oilfield waste (in Grand Bois) treat equality quite explicitly. But a similar concern for equality also motivated protests, collective and individual, against judicial orders and labor displacement in Delhi's polluting industrial units, against the way trawlers undermined livelihoods among Kerala's traditional fishermen, and against the corruption of officials who hunt illegally in the Sanjiang Nature Reserve.

Several of the cases, however, show that, when it comes to policy reform, concerns about equity can be compromised by existing social values. In the Delhi case, coauthor Amita Baviskar informs us, the weight of upper- and middle-class worries about pollution overwhelmed poor people's concerns about their jobs. The middle class desire for cleaner air and water is less about unsullied nature for all and more about better health for individual members of the elite and the upper middle classes. Moving the courts proved to be a cost-effective way for environmental entrepreneurs.

Although political and economic factors slowed the recognition and treatment of Minamata's mercury poisoning victims, social values also harmed them. Views about disease being the responsibility of the sick, about a social hierarchy in which the technocrats and Tokyo University graduates of the Chisso managerial class stood at the top and fishers at the bottom, and about the need to heal the social body through forgiveness and reconciliation all worked against equality in this case. In short, traditional social and communitarian values competed with the modern value of equality, slowing the wheels of justice. The belief that those who are superior also know better meant that the stances adopted by the Chisso Corporation, scientific researchers from Tokyo University sent by the national government, and the Japanese state were questioned and overturned only after the dimensions of the disaster turned out to be horrifyingly large. But in other ways, the belief in equality and in knowledge as the means to a better world prevailed even in the Minamata case. As the authors of the Japan chapter point out, the Minamata experience led to a national pollution policy of "protecting people and punishing polluters. Today, victims of pollution are certified based on the Pollution-Related Health Damage Compensation Law, which bases certification criteria on medical science" (p. 121).

If the value of equality ultimately enables greater bureaucratization with the passage of environmental regulations and a machinery to ensure compliance, it also fosters the emergence of the ordinary individual, potentially with the ability to accomplish all that is humanly possible. Modernity, which values equality and knowledge as the basis of progress, makes it possible for the anonymous individual to become a central historical figure. A person's poverty, gender, ethnicity, caste, and physical disabilities are no longer an automatic bar to his or her potential to lead or know. In modernity, leadership, intelligence, knowledge, and other forms of excellence are distributed randomly among the population. The anonymous individual—anonymous in the sense of being unmarked by the vagaries of birth—is capable of being the expression of his or her historical period and social circumstances.

The anonymous individual is an expression of modernity precisely because of his or her role as the figure capable of representing what is essential about a context or a period. It is out of a particular moment and conjuncture, rather than the inherent qualities of the individual that endow the ordinary individual with historical significance.[24] Again and again, the case studies in this volume illustrate these two aspects of modern individuals—the potential of almost anyone to emerge as a leader, and the fact that the significance of the individual person lies in the context she or he inhabits. Environmental leaders described in the Japanese case studies, people such as Hosoya, Kamakura, and Amano, emerged out of a specific instance of environmental crisis, action, mobilization, and legislation. But their actions were motivated by the values that bloom with modernity—the significance accorded to science and knowledge, equality among humans, and the identification of scientific knowledge with progress. Environmental crises described in the other cases also brought to the fore ordinary individuals like Clarice Friloux in Grand Bois and M.C. Mehta in Delhi. It is not their birth or social status that endowed them with special social traits but their actions in a particular context that helped mobilize others.

The openness of the modern political process to interventions by citizens and experts also means that modernity creates a new uncertainty in the evolution and resolution of environmental crises. Depending on the relative balance of pressures resulting from political and economic forces, material interests, and societal values, environmental crises may lead to outcomes in which economically and politically powerful groups get what they want (as in Delhi) or groups who are socially and economically weak influence environmental policy (as in Minamata and Southern Louisiana). Environmental values may force outcomes that environmentalists favor, as in Sanjiang, or they may take the backseat, with developers using environmental idioms to advance claims for greater access to funds and resources, as in Civano.

Conclusion: Modernity's Influence on Environmental Outcomes

Many environmentalists—consider deep ecologists or anarchists—reject modern forms of development and progress. For them, each environmental crisis heralds the need to return to a more natural existence because every technological fix only prepares the ground for the next disaster. What Freud called civilization's "discontents" and Weber saw as the "rationalization" and "disenchantment" of the modern world finds its echo in these activists' advocacy of a simpler, more rooted lifestyle, away from the complication and pollution of urban, industrial living. Whatever one might think of such rejectionism and the traditionalist values it embodies, the questioning and rejection are themselves nonetheless part of modernity. Pessimistic assessments of modernity, grounded as they must be in some form of reason, do not stand above modernity but are rather part and parcel of modern science and reason. More generally, it is only after a place or people have become modern that it becomes possible to raise questions about the values that modernity takes as universally desirable. As Frederic Jameson rightly points out, questions about meta-narratives are themselves founded on some different meta-narrative.[25] The use of conservationist environmental values to raise doubts about other forms of modernity—in particular, development and growth—is thus only another example of the workings of modernity. The anti-modern environmentalist is acting on thoroughly and deeply rooted modern impulses when counterpoising conservation to development.

An interesting instance of rejectionism occurs in the Minamata case study, when Ogata Masato, whose father had suffered a difficult death from the Minamata disease in the 1950s, abandoned his court case because he was unwilling to monetize his grief. Instead, with other activists, he installed stone statues on the land reclaimed from Minamata Bay as a way to commemorate victims of the disease and foster spiritual values. His actions show the power of rejectionist gestures, especially when they are coupled with efforts to transcend the personal.

However, the more common response to the environmental problems in our cases is to mobilize—for ends like environmental health, as in Louisiana, or more-sustainable resource use through better technologies, as in Kerala. Even the founders of Civano were not rejecting technology but designing new forms of settlement that take advantage of modern technologies to reduce the environmental impact of human habitation. This unwillingness of important stakeholders to turn away from core values of modernity, such as those related to the use of science to promote better livelihoods and greater equality, suggests the powerful attraction of modernity in people's daily lives.

The case studies in this book document the ways in which important modern values influence environmental outcomes. The valorization of growth as the most important goal of national policy (except perhaps security) produces the problems to which environmental activism and policies seek solutions. The value placed on scientific knowledge generates the discrete domain of environment as a field to be investigated and analyzed. And the value placed on equality, which is often at odds with the value placed on growth, works in a variety of ways to affect environmental outcomes: it fractures the presumption of universal environmental outcomes, it promotes proliferation of environmental laws and greater bureaucratization so that these laws can be applied, and it encourages the emergence of the ordinary, anonymous individual as an environmental activist or leader.

Notes

1. David Harvey, *The Condition of Postmodernity* (Cambridge, MA: Blackwell, 1989).
2. This is despite the thorough discrediting of the belief that reason and pursuit of knowledge necessarily generate progress. See Alain Touraine, *Critique of Modernity* (Cambridge, MA: Blackwell, 1995). Believers in modernity can require knowledge to be the basis of progress without believing that knowledge will necessarily produce progress.
3. Note that the desire to relate modernity in its temporal sense to different forms of reason leaves sufficient room for the possibility that there are other forms of reason that are neither

modern nor to be dismissed. See Dipesh Chakrabarty, *Provincializing Europe: Postcolonial Thought and Historical Difference* (Princeton: Princeton University Press, 2000).

4. William E. Connolly, *The Terms of Political Discourse* (Princeton: Princeton University Press, 1983).

5. David Harvey, *The Condition of Postmodernity.*

6. Peter J. Taylor and Frederick H. Buttel, "How Do We Know We Have Global Environmental Problems? Science and the Globalization of Environmental Discourse," *Geoforum* 23, no. 3 (1992): 405–16.

7. Stuart Hall, "Introduction," in *Modernity: An Introduction to Modern Societies,* ed. Stuart Hall, David Held, Don Hubert, and Kenneth Thompson (Cambridge, UK: Polity Press, 1995), 3–18.

8. Henri Lefebvre, *Everyday Life in the Modern World* (New Brunswick: Transaction, 1984).

9. Arjun Appadurai, *Modernity at Large* (Minneapolis: University of Minnesota Press, 1996).

10. See also James C. Scott, *Seeing Like a State: How Certain Schemes to Improve the Human Condition Have Failed* (New Haven: Yale University Press, 1998). Scott defines high modernist ideologies as "the rational design of social order commensurate with the scientific understanding of natural laws."

11. Emma Mawdsley, "India's Middle Classes and the Environment," *Development and Change* 35, no. 1 (2004): 79–103.

12. Kenneth J. Arrow, Partha Dasgupta, and Karl G. Maler, "Evaluating Projects and Assessing Sustainable Development in Imperfect Economies," *Environmental and Resource Economics* 26, no. 4 (2003): 647–85; and R. Inglehart and S. Flanagan, "Value Change in Industrial Societies," *American Political Science Review* 81, no. 4 (1987): 1289–319.

13. Arun Agrawal, *Environmentality: Technologies of Government and the Making of Subjects* (Durham: Duke University Press, 2005).

14. Stuart Hall, "Introduction," in *Modernity,* 3–18. Hall is speaking about how the constitution of the social as a distinct domain of analysis is a thoroughly modern phenomenon, but his point applies equally to the environment, as several chapters in this volume attest.

15. Jerry Williams, "Knowledge, Consequences, and Experience: The Social Construction of Environmental Problems," *Sociological Inquiry* 68, no. 4 (1998): 476–97, discusses several models of environmental problem definition. These include a "natural decline model," as described in Anthony Downs, "Up and Down with Ecology: The Issue-Attention Cycle," *Public Interest* 28 (1972): 38–50; a "natural history model," as described in Malcolm Spector and John Kitsuse, *Constructing Social Problems* (New York: Cummings, 1977); and a "public arenas model" as described in Stephen Hilgartner and Charles Bosk, "The Rise and Fall of Social Problems: A Public Arenas Model," *American Journal of Sociology* 94, no. 1 (1988): 53–78. In each of these models, science and reason are crucial to the definition and construction of environmental issues.

16. Peter J. Taylor, and Frederick H. Buttel, "How Do We Know We Have Global Environmental Problems? Science and the Globalization of Environmental Discourse," 405.

17. The transformation of bogs and marshes into wetlands and the positive or negative valence attached to these terms is itself a fascinating theme. See S. Anderson and B. Moss, "How Wetlands Are Perceived by Children: Consequences of Children's Education and Wetland Conservation," *International Journal of Science Education* 15, no. 5 (1993): 473–85.

18. Wendy Brown, *States of Injury: Power and Freedom in Late Modernity* (Princeton: Princeton University Press, 1995).

19. Anil Agarwal and Sunita Narain, *Global Warming in an Unequal World* (New Delhi: Center for Science and Environment, 1991).

20. Titles such as *Our Common Future,* by WCED (World Commission on Environment and Development) (Oxford: Oxford University Press, 1987), and *One Earth, One Future,* by

Silver et al. (Washington, DC: National Academy Press, 1990), express the hope that human beings are equally subject to the changing environment. See Paul R. Ehrlich, *Healing the Planet: Strategies for Resolving the Environmental Crisis* (Reading, MA: Addison-Wesley, 1991).

21. Donald Moore, "A River Runs Through It: Environmental History and the Politics of Community in Zimbabwe's Eastern Highlands," *Journal of Southern African Studies* 24, no. 2 (1998): 377–403.

22. See P. Mohai and B. Bryant, "Environmental Racism: Reviewing the Evidence," in *Race and the Incidence of Environmental Hazards,* ed. B. Bryant and P. Mohai (Boulder, CO: Westview Press, 1992); and Robert Bullard, ed., *Confronting Environmental Racism: Voices from the Grassroots* (London: South End Press, 1993), on environmental justice. Bina Agarwal, "The Gender and Environment Debate: Lessons from India," *Feminist Studies* 18 (1992), 119–58; Ramchandra Guha, *The Unquiet Woods: Ecological Change and Peasant Resistance in the Himalaya* (New Delhi: Oxford University Press, 1989); Vandana Shiva, *Staying Alive: Women, Ecology, and Survival* (London: Zed Books, 1988); Nancy L. Peluso, *Rich Forests, Poor People: Resource Control and Resistance in Java* (Berkeley: University of California Press, 1992), introduce variant claims about environmental justice in the international arena.

23. David Harvey, "What's Green and Makes the Environment Go Around?" in *The Cultures of Globalization*, ed. Frederic Jameson and Masao Miyoshi (Durham: Duke University Press, 1998), 327–56.

24. Michel de Certeau dedicates *The Practice of Everyday Life* (Berkeley: University of California Press, 1984) "to the ordinary man."

25. Frederic Jameson, *Postmodernism, or the Cultural Logic of Late Capitalism* (Durham: Duke University Press, 1991).

7

Evaluating Environmental Justice Claims

Robert Melchior Figueroa

The term *environmental justice* has come into popular use by environmental and social justice activists and scholars. In its most common usage it pertains to distributive justice—the equitable distribution of environmental risks, such as toxic waste and other forms of pollution. As the case studies in this volume demonstrate, environmental justice is also related to the distribution of environmental goods—in other words, how resources are used. Distributive justice is a critical form of environmental justice, but environmental justice also takes a second form, related to who gets to make environmental policy decisions and who does not. Environmental injustice occurs when a policy elite disrespects traditional environmental practices and excludes the least empowered and most economically vulnerable groups from environmental decision-making. These concerns have generated what I have come to call the "environmental justice paradigm," a concept that emphasizes the interrelatedness of distributive justice and political recognition.[1] Besides representation and participation, political recognition also requires that individual and group identity is respected, which entails an appreciation for local experience and knowledge, traditional beliefs, and environmental heritage.

The environmental justice paradigm finds its political expression in the environmental justice movement (EJM): an amalgamation of many grassroots efforts to identify, remedy, or at least ameliorate, injustices by confronting government, social, and corporate power. Fusing civil rights, labor, women's, and indigenous people's movements, the EJM has exposed a global trend of environmental elitism that compounds the disenfranchisement of environmental victims from the policy decisions that most affect them. At the local level, an environmental justice movement is one in which the people who mobilize to tackle an environmental threat identify as a group communally and culturally—not simply as interest-maximizing individuals with common goals, but as people similarly situated in a particular geographical, cultural, and historical experience.

Most of the case studies in this volume involve local environmental justice movements that fight political inequality and social discrimination as reflected in environmental practices. They demonstrate clearly the ways in which these movements are able to transform power relationships both at the institutional level, as reflected in law and policy, and at the cultural level, in terms of a shift of public values and attitudes. They also demonstrate the range of transformative responses available within the environmental justice paradigm: redistributing environmental benefits and burdens, reconfiguring the political arena for greater participation in decision-making, healing communities, obtaining political recognition for previously unrecognized groups, shifting environmental values, and respecting the environmental heritage of minority populations.

In this chapter I examine the case studies according to the dimensions of the environmental justice paradigm. Where there is no apparent environmental justice movement, as in the China cases and Civano, I explore why this is so and the ways in which the cases still fit the environmental justice paradigm. To ensure that we bear in mind the connection between social justice and environmental quality—the earmark of environmental justice as opposed to other forms of environmental analysis—we will need to pay attention to whether the environmental destruction in a given case resulted in the first place from existing forms of social injustice, such as discrimination, marginalization, and disenfranchisement.

Distributive Justice

The distributive justice dimension of environmental justice can be divided into two broad categories: distribution and compensation. In both, environmental justice is concerned with the equitable balance of benefits and burdens. Some social groups benefit from modern industrial development in terms of jobs, education, economic and natural resources, infrastructural improvements, and international respect. Environmental justice provides a critical lens through which to view the enjoyment of such benefits against the suffering of the associated burdens by other social groups.

Distributive Arena

In all our cases an action that harmed a particular community also benefits another group, and sometimes the benefits extend well beyond the locale of the environmental assault. For instance, the Chisso Corporation's Minamata plant, the source of Minamata disease, also contributed to Japan's national economic development. Locally, despite the recognition of the plant's catastrophic practices, the Minamata public still honors Chisso as the city's economic linchpin. Likewise, the Lake Biwa Comprehensive Development Plan (LBCDP), which harmed the lake's ecology, transformed the lake into the "water jug" for a burgeoning urban population in Osaka, the commercial center of Japan. Japanese bureaucrats promoting Japan's dam projects could boast benefits for industrial development even though the costs to the local population were evident. In China, starting with the period of Mao's Great Leap Forward, Benxi, a center of steel production, and a primary source of air pollution, produced vast economic benefits for China while its population suffered from respiratory ailments. The Sanjiang Nature Reserve provides environmental benefits (biodiversity, protection against sandstorms and floods), enhances China's diplomatic and international prestige, and promotes national security (through forest cover that prevents spying from over the Russian border). In the American Southwest, the desert housing development of Civano was envisioned by planners and government supporters as a solution to the scarcity of resources, including water and energy, and an opportunity to test new technologies, creative forms of resident participation, and new forms of community interaction. Grand Bois, a quintessential American environmental justice case, illustrates the all-too-common claim that local residents, while harmed by oilfield waste, also benefited from jobs in the oil industry at a time when traditional occupations and practices were no longer remunerative. Furthermore, the benefits of the oil industry extended across the nation and well beyond its borders. In Kerala, mechanization reaped the benefit of a profitable export industry for India and the mechanized sector of the Indian fishing industry, while threatening traditional fishing practices and communities. The despair of displaced laborers in Delhi contrasts with the benefits of improved environmental quality for city residents.

The environmental justice paradigm forces us to notice costs as well as benefits, particularly in terms of their fair distribution. There are often disturbingly clear inequities in the distribution of the costs of toxic waste dumping, as in the Minamata and Grand Bois cases. At the same time, the environmental justice paradigm also calls attention to the need to evaluate the justice of resource use decisions. In fact, competing demands on limited resources make resource distribution a key issue in environmental justice. Civano provides a very good example. Civano's planners envisioned a housing development that would inspire sustainable community living and offset the environmental and social harms caused by urban sprawl and tract development. However, local social justice advocates denounced the city of Tucson's decision to back this project, charging that, instead of supporting the development, which fundamentally embraces the growth paradigm, the city should have directed its financial resources toward containing sprawl and reversing urban blight. Tucson councilwoman Molly McKasson, for example, criticized the social and environmental incongruities of Civano's goals and impacts—in particular, the environmental impact of commuting from Civano—and the city's failure to channel economic resources to populations with more immediate needs, such as Tucson's Mexican Americans and the burgeoning homeless population. Other distributive injustices apparent in the case, although not voiced by the critics cited there, relate to the complex system of water distribution needed to meet the demands of a growing metropolis and the city's energy system, which exploited the resources of the Navajo and Hopi Indian reservations upstream. These Indian nations alleged that their aquifer was being depleted in order to transport coal that is strip-mined from their lands.

Weighing the benefits accruing from Civano against these environmental burdens may seem unfair, since a single sustainable community cannot be expected to resolve all of a region's environmental contradictions. Yet, while Civano may be touted for attempting creative solutions to resource scarcity in the desert, the environmental justice paradigm moves us to question whether the Civano plan was also environmentally just. It forces us to see that some forms of environmentalism—in particular, "mainstream environmentalism" typically taking the form of conservation movements by elites—often discriminate in their tendency to maintain the social status quo. In the case of Civano, the beneficiaries of the innovations in housing design, creative funding schemes, and further sprawl were primarily the Civano residents, who are overwhelmingly affluent.

Ironically, the benefits of environmental policies and other actions that lead to pollution and resource degradation can sometimes harm the beneficiaries as well as others. Wolfgang Sachs identifies this phenomenon as the "boomerang effect" of environmental injustices.[2] In Kerala, in an effort to curtail the incursion of foreign factory ships, the "fishery capitalists," or local trawler owners, found themselves in the position of needing to join forces with the traditional fishing communities—the historical "losers" in the conflict with these same trawler owners. Yet the factory ships were part of the very mechanization revolution that had reaped inequitable benefits for trawler owners at the expense of traditional fishers as well as the fishery resource. Thus, the initial "winners"—the local trawler owners—saw their own mechanized methods boomerang against them, to the benefit of bigger corporate players. It is the boomerang effect of a harmful practice on its supposed beneficiaries that often leads them to halt the practice. In Grand Bois, for instance, the public benefiting from jobs in the oil and gas industry paid little attention to the risks connected with oilfield waste dumping, despite abundant scientific evidence, until they started getting sick. When more affluent citizens outside Grand Bois began to fear that they might also suffer the consequences of an unregulated oil industry practice, the people of Grand Bois had the opening they needed to argue for just compensation.

The emphasis on *who* is at risk, versus the nature of the harm, is a central feature of the environmental justice movement. Mainstream environmentalism, by contrast, generally receives funding and political support from the more affluent members of the society, who do not directly pay the costs of environmental degradation; thus it tends to be chiefly concerned with impacts of human activities on nature and only indirectly with their impacts on people. Mainstream environmentalism and the environmental justice approach represent two sets of environmental values, with environmental justice dealing with livelihood issues and power relations, and mainstream environmentalism speaking the language of conservation and preservation.[3]

The Delhi pollution case appears to defy this distinction. Here, the environmentalism of the middle class is expressed not in terms of nature preservation but in terms of concerns about human health and the preservation of national heritage sites, such as the famous Taj Mahal.[4] Nonetheless, the Indian middle-class environmentalism exhibited in this case dovetails with the affluent mainstream versions around the world insofar as it dismisses the impact of environmentalist measures upon vulnerable workers and by the its failure to notice that "environmentalist" responses do not protect all people equally. As chapter coauthor Amita Baviskar explains, the "organizing fiction" of "the idea of 'public interest' . . . *conceals the class-specific effects of the air pollution initiative*" (p. 214; italics added). This discriminatory environmentalism—

in which mainstream environmental agendas do not account for the interests of marginalized peoples—contrasts with the environmental justice movement, which insists upon equitable protection against environmental burdens. Of course, the polluting industries—which, by the way, fail to provide safe working conditions and job security for their workers—require closer scrutiny. Yet the environmental justice perspective requires that the social impact of environmental decision-making be accounted for alongside the assessment of environmental burdens.

As in Delhi, Benxi's environmental campaign, which was led by government, was embraced by the white collar class and resented by laid-off workers, who told interviewers that a greater priority should be placed on jobs and social welfare than on greening the city. While the Benxi case clearly involves social justice issues, I would argue that it also needs to be evaluated in terms of *environmental* justice since there are allegedly inequities in the distribution of costs of environmental improvement. For instance, some residents speculated that a greener city could attract more investment and therefore create jobs. To be just, however, such a scheme needs to be backed by evidence that the number of jobs created by the green campaign is greater than that created under an alternative allocation of resources. We also need to investigate whether funds that might have gone towards job creation and to support pension programs were diverted to the city's antipollution effort and who actually benefits from that effort.

Compensatory Arena

Ever since Aristotle's *Nichomachean Ethics,* just compensation—the act of redistributing benefits and burdens to achieve equity among citizens—has been recognized as a key to social justice.[5] When a government, a business, or a private citizen harms a person's livelihood, compensation, usually in the form of money, is commonly accepted as a remedy. However, by no means does compensation fully redress environmental injustices. Our cases indicate four ways in which compensation may actually further exacerbate environmental injustices:

1. compensation typically does not necessitate a redistribution of the burden to advantaged communities or the responsible parties, nor does it require a cessation of burden-producing practices;
2. compensation, whether agreed upon by the parties or ordered by a court, can generate antagonisms within communities;
3. victims of environmental injustices can suffer social stigma as a result of compensation programs;
4. compensation may be used to limit future claims against responsible parties.

In particular, inequity can be perpetuated when for cultural or other reasons society relies upon the "good faith" of the responsible party to compensate the injured parties. In the Minamata disease and Lake Biwa cases, informal and traditional *mimai kin* (sympathy money), was paid to victims. But as the cases show, *mimai kin* and out-of-court settlements can reinforce the marginalization and disempowerment of victims of environmental injustices in two ways that may be entirely acceptable under the law: by allowing the responsible party to continue environmentally destructive practices and by preventing victims from bringing future claims against the polluters.

In Minamata, the initial settlements of *mimai kin* stipulated that disease victims could seek no further compensation from Chisso. In Grand Bois (and throughout the United States), out-of-court settlements apply to the property damages suffered by residents—usually according to the fair market value of the affected property. Yet the compensation amounts were paltry and could not cover the medical costs associated with unusual strains or clusters of cancer. And in both cultural contexts, Grand Bois and Minamata, a cessation of the destructive practices does not accompany the initial compensation schemes—not by current or former polluters, not by Exxon, Campbell Wells, or U.S. Liquids, and not by Chisso or Showa Denko (the offending corporation in the Niigata instance of the disease outbreak).

In Kerala, by contrast, the zoning for traditional vessels and modern trawlers is compensation in the form of policy change. If the best form of compensation from an environmental justice perspective is one that allows people to sustain their forms of livelihood, the zoning policy was on the right track, since it aimed to restrict the harm done to traditional fishers by mechanized fishing practices and offered a chance of increased catches in the traditional fishing zones. Nevertheless, Kerala's zoning policies still permitted the continuation of practices that result in overfishing. In fact, efforts to prevent overfishing have had limited effect because even the rigid policy restricting fishing during the monsoon seasons, when fish spawn, exempted the Neendakara trawler base, the center of mechanized fishing in the state. In other words, even the most proactive compensatory measure may fail to cease the practices that generate environmental injustices. In this case, the unsustainable fishing practices are a concern for environmental justice advocates because the least well-off were hit the hardest.

The second drawback of compensation is that it can dissolve community cohesion. Compensation is sometimes given to only a few members of a community, either through official compensation packages that require the registration and certification of victims or by out-of-court settlements or court-ordered payments in legal cases brought by the victims of the worst property damage or health consequences, or by the more vocal residents of the affected area. The unity among residents who organize against the responsible party in environmental justice cases is often rather precarious, and thus the buying out of individual residents is an effective and common divide-and-conquer strategy for polluters. As I have argued elsewhere, compensatory victories—especially out-of-court settlements for poor communities—are typically Pyrrhic at best. Community members may benefit but at too great a cost to the traditions and cohesion of the community as a whole.[6]

In Grand Bois, this was so even though all 301 residents were granted some compensation and even though residents did continue to pursue legal action against Exxon after reaching out-of-court settlements with Campbell Wells and U.S. Liquids. The disempowering effect of the settlements was still felt in a wide range of experiences: court records were sealed; infighting broke out between community members because of unequal and inadequate compensation; and new feuds resulted from the tensions between community values and self-interest. As a community leader commented in an interview, the legal battle was "costly in both social and psychological costs. . . . It split families to the extent that family members don't talk to each other because of it" (p. 289).

The Delhi air pollution case presents another divisive policy. The Supreme Court ordered the affected industries to compensate only their permanent workers, while the vast number of "informal," or temporary, workers—the city's most vulnerable—received no compensation. The environmental justice paradigm would have required a different approach to enforcing Delhi's pollution policies, one that included offers of alternative employment for discharged workers and compensation for informal workers.

Yet another divisive effect of compensation involves disagreement over who are the *true* victims. In Kerala, the top-down means by which the Indo-Norwegian Project brought mechanization divided the fishing community into haves and have-nots. Because of asymmetries in the distribution of the tools of mechanization and in the distribution of costs, each group maintained different perceptions of who are the actual victims. The artisanal fishers believed themselves to be victims of the inequities posed by trawlers' mechanized overfishing; while, following the adoption of the 1991 New Deep Sea Fishing Policy, the trawlers perceived themselves the victims of invading transnational fishers employing supermechanized methods.

The third way in which compensation can aggravate injustice involves the social stigma recipients suffer when they get marked as traitors to the community or as fakers trying to abuse the system. The Minamata fishers suffered from marginalized social status even before falling victim to the debilitating disease. Resisting the token sympathy money meant stepping far outside the cultural norm and behaving in a way inappropriate for a person of such low social status. Even worse was to request fair compensation and thereby threaten to undermine Chisso, the city's economic powerhouse. There was little public sympathy for the idea that Chisso had a duty to remedy the offense. As the chapter authors explain, "To this day, Minamata victims are referred to in Japanese as 'patients,' reflecting a persistent cultural predilection to avoid attributing the cause to a particular perpetrator" (p. 128). Therefore, perhaps the worst stigma was that attached to certified victims who actually accepted compensation.

Can legislation reduce the social stigma attached to compensation? As the Japan chapter's comparison between the outbreak of Minamata disease in Minamata and the subsequent outbreak in Niigata demonstrates, the passage of the Relief Law, which legislated a right to be compensated by state procedure and aid (as opposed to *mimai kin*) did not by itself ensure protection against the social stigma attached to compensation. This was because of the sociocultural context in which the law was applied. Chisso was (and is) so deeply interwoven into the social fabric of Minamata that filing a suit against the company was considered an unacceptable act against another member of the community. But in Niigata, residents did not consider Showa Denko, which was located upstream from the affected community, as a member of that community. Thus, for Niigata residents, taking up a lawsuit against Showa Denko, no matter the firm's economic importance, did not subject them to further social discrimination in their community.

As these cases demonstrate, the very process of compensation sometimes subjects the least well-off to further discrimination. They are left without a voice in future decision-making over the distribution of environmental burdens; they are denigrated for their attempts to seek compensatory justice, which they deserve by custom and law; and they are alienated from their own self-empowerment because compensation may weaken the spirit of a grassroots resistance movement.

Recognition Justice

Compensation alone, as we have just seen, cannot alter a pattern of injustices; communities must also have a voice in environmental policy. In its political recognition dimension, environmental justice calls for the institutions of mainstream environmentalism to be transformed to include the voices of those most affected by the environmental burdens. Otherwise, harmful environmental practices are likely to continue. Thus, while compensatory justice is an important dimension of environmental justice, political recognition is central to the project of ending environmental injustice.

Any discussion of political recognition, or *recognition justice*, requires us to consider the question of political representation within a given social structure. Are all groups with vital interests in environmental decision-making represented in their own voice? Are local knowledge systems accounted for in the analysis of the problems and the formulation of solutions? Are the environmental identities and environmental heritage of the affected community represented and respected in the process?

The concept of recognition justice developed some thousands of years after distributive justice had been philosophically and politically established. Defenders of recognition justice argue that persistent cultural discrimination cannot be addressed by material redistribution alone. Distributive justice cannot adequately address fundamental questions about who has the power to redistribute. Communities that face environmental discrimination *and* discriminatory environmentalism, as in the Delhi pollution case, need a political voice before they can overcome the prejudices that undermine political equality and environmental equity.

In the Civano case, the Urban Lands Management Act, passed in 1981 by the Arizona legislature, not only allowed the city of Tucson to establish building codes before developers stepped in but also required public involvement in planning and zoning decisions and in decisions to sell trust lands. Such requirements are commonly part of contemporary environmental and zoning regulations across the United States, and are stipulated in many state environmental laws; while they are not always complied with, they have proven to be a formidable tool for grassroots movements in their response to environmental injustices. Perhaps the best-known example of the efficacy of public-input requirements involves a 1991 Kettleman City, California, case where a state judge ruled against the siting of a toxic waste incinerator because the environmental impact assessment, filed in English, violated the right to participate of predominantly monolingual Spanish-speaking residents.[7]

For Civano, public participation was mandated at nearly every step of the approval process. Like the 1981 legislation, the city's 1992 master development plan also mandated public participation, as did the Metropolitan Energy Commission, a key actor pushing the process. On the other hand, once the Civano planners encountered financial difficulties and Fannie Mae became the project's sole owner, initial visions of deliberative and inclusive participation degenerated into conflicts between competing interest groups.[8] Initially heralded for its grand vision of sustainability and public participation, Civano sacrificed its innovative hydrological plans by conforming to the city's problematic standards of water resource management, and its solar energy specifications were watered down.

Eventually the residents moved in and developed their own voice to counter Fannie Mae through the Civano Neighbors Neighborhood Association and other mechanisms. But the values and interests of Tucson's lower income residents, who were affected by the diversion of city resources to the mammoth development from which they stood to gain little (most of Civano's residents were upper middle class), remained unrecognized as stakeholders and left out of decisions surrounding Civano's development. Ultimately, the vision of a sustainable community became limited to those who could afford the cost of buying a Civano home. This outcome raises the environmental justice question of just who is the "public" whose participation is required by so many laws and regulations. The environmental justice paradigm would require the participation of the inner city Mexican immigrants in Tucson as well as the Hopis and Navajos who were affected upstream.[9] The inner city residents, in particular, also contributed to the city tax-base, had a vested interest in the new developments and urban sprawl, and were the most vulnerable of the city's population.

In contrast to the Tucson case, where public participation is mandated by law, the China cases demonstrate the workings of a political order that systematically restricts public participation. As the authors of the China chapter suggest, the Chinese public's political impotency translates easily into dependency on the government, whereby collective problems are seen as the responsibility of the government and "not a matter of individual concern" (p. 90). There is also a reluctance among many Chinese citizens to get involved in politics, a lingering effect of strict government control under the Maoist regime, as Judith Shapiro notes in her foreword to the chapter. A result of government policies in the Sanjiang Plain, Sanjiang farmers and fishers receive no compensation or even recognition for their lost lifestyles and resources, which would likely not have happened (at least without a fight) had there not been severe restrictions on local organizing. Adding insult to injury, common fishing, herding, and logging practices have been outlawed for the sake of environmental preservation.

The need for recognition justice in Grand Bois is equally acute. After the hazards of siting oilfield waste facilities near residential communities became known, and during a brief window of progressive government, state officials made some progress in regulating the oilfield waste disposal. There was also an unprecedented spate of public meetings and opportunities for public participation, but the state and national policy debates over produced water and other oilfield waste bypassed such geographically remote and politically and socially marginalized communities as Grand Bois, and the election of a pro-business governor left the community undefended against Big Oil's dumping practices. Grand Bois is a testimony to the fact that even with the best intentions professional environmental agencies will overlook the interests of marginalized local communities unless those communities have full participation in environmental decision-making.

A major obstacle to participatory parity, and all other aspects of environmental justice, is corruption, which all too often accompanies environmentally irresponsible business practices. Corruption in some form is an element in all our cases. In the Sanjiang Nature Reserve case, the researchers saw evidence of illegal hunting by the very officials charged with enforcing the wildlife protection laws. Yet if the hunters and herders who once depended upon these activities for their livelihoods did the same, they would be arrested. Similarly, officials of the industrial giant Benxi Iron and Steel Company were charged with corruption, which was widely publicized in the local press. The association of the company with the environmental campaign— it had received preferential loans and other benefits from the state to help it meet the demands of the campaign—made the swelling population of economically vulnerable Benxi residents increasingly distrustful of the campaign itself. In Delhi, amid the loss of over a quarter of a million jobs as a result of the Supreme Court–ordered factory closures, credible yet unproved allegations circulated that certain factories that had paid the appropriate bribe stayed off the list of nonconforming industries. Kerala's exemption of Neendarkara from trawling bans could be traced back to Baby John's political and economic power. And finally, as the major taxpayers and provider of jobs, the industrial powers of Chisso (Minamata) and Exxon and Campbell Wells (Grand Bois), were granted many privileges, most notably in the form of relaxed regulations of their harmful activities, and in the case of the early years of Minamata Disease, government cover from accepting responsibility. Corruption in these cases is seen in the ways in which economically and politically privileged groups are able to circumvent the regulations and attendant costs by virtue of their insider status—a form of participation that would be contained if recognition justice were upheld. Again we see that distributive justice alone fails to mandate a role for the otherwise disenfranchised communities in a fair bottom-up process.

Grassroots Mobilization

Essential to participatory parity, in addition to rules and institutions that enable it, is the capacity and political space for grassroots mobilization. The Grand Bois,

Minamata, and Kerala cases offer prime examples of the transformative character of grassroots activism in which local residents organize to address environmental inequities, challenging and ultimately changing the political institutions behind the injustices. In all three places activists mobilized to address not only the question of who receives the benefits, but also importantly who *determines* the benefits and their distribution.

The China cases, by contrast, where there was no grassroots mobilization, challenge the environmental justice paradigm since the top-down environmental campaigns resulted in undisputed environmental improvements despite the absence of environmental justice movements. The national policy of shutting down dirty and inefficient coal mines in Benxi and the People's Liberation Army's enforcement of the government's nature protection policies are environmental actions that mainstream environmentalists around the world can only applaud. The latter in particular is a highly unusual engagement of the military; typically military operations have adverse environmental impacts—in fact they are responsible for some of the worst environmental destruction in the modern world. Cleaner air for all of Benxi's residents and the enjoyment of the wetlands by the human residents and the wildlife of the Sanjiang Plain widens the distribution of environmental benefits, at least in principle. Can we then say that environmental justice has been achieved in the China cases from a distributive point of view? We cannot fully answer that question without also assessing the recognition aspects of the case, since the two dimensions of justice operate hand in hand. Our cases demonstrate that the two dimensions of justice are interdependent, and they merge at the critical juncture of participatory parity.

The top-down, nonparticipatory environmental projects of Benxi and the Sanjiang Nature Reserve are typical of China's historically repressive government. In the government's view, local residents need to be reeducated as environmentally conscious citizens, particularly when it comes to environmental projects that are perceived to have long-term economic benefits. Yet, environmental education cannot be accomplished through officially sanctioned programs such as those in China. What is needed is a shift in consciousness whereby stakeholders envision their lives as a part of their natural surroundings; in Benxi and Sanjiang the government's policies did little to achieve that. Beyond the question of the effectiveness of China's policy approach, environmental justice demands procedural justice where citizens can find their own voice in the campaign. The establishment of mechanisms for public input in Benxi, such as the environmental hotline, while a step in the right direction, has had limited effect. This is so not only because of the inherent limits of this form of participation but also because of historical conditioning that leaves residents feeling an obligation to learn and follow rather than to make their voices heard in environmental decision-making.

Evaluating the environmental justice of government policies and citizen actions is also a complicated matter in the Lake Biwa case. As the authors point out, a shift in the terms of public debate from *kogai* ("public nuisance" issues) to *kankyo mondai* (environmental problems) occurs in all of the Japan cases, and at Lake Biwa these two sets of values drive two very different grassroots movements. Local fishers, who not only saw the degradation of the fishery resource but also lost their fishing rights to certain areas, mounted the earliest challenges to the water resource development plan. Because they had few allies besides "biologists, ecologists, and some residents in the smaller villages where dam construction was planned" (p. 151), their opposition received little publicity and was ultimately dealt with through *mimai kin,* the *kogai* form of compensation.

The later, much more effective challenge to the government's comprehensive water resources development plan emerges from the soap movement engineered by the "environmentalist" (*kankyo mondai*) administration of the prefectural government and then taken up by a grassroots movement comprising new lakeshore residents. Through new tactics, including legal battles, the soap movement successfully agitated for new policies that grew out of *kankyo mondai* values—an appreciation of the lake itself. The old-style Japanese environmentalism, marked by adherence to traditional forms of compensation and respect for the prefectural officials and directed at the livelihood and constitutional rights of fishers, was eclipsed by new-style environmentalism, which pushed the agenda of more urban, younger, and affluent lakeshore residents.

How should we evaluate these grassroots efforts from an environmental justice perspective? Although older residents share an interest in water quality, the soap movement did not incorporate these residents and their broader concerns into their movement. Thus, in the evolution of environmental values from *kogai* to *kankyo mondai*, as described by the authors, we see the discrimination that is so problematic in mainstream environmentalism. But a return to *kogai*, with its compensatory response of *mimai kin*, will not bring environmental justice either. An environmental justice perspective encourages a new phase of environmental transformation that involves "compassion values," which could motivate soap movement activists to include the original fisher opposition.

Respect for Environmental Identity and Environmental Heritage

Recognition justice demands that we fully account for the situational aspects of group mobilization for environmental justice by understanding the individual and community environmental identities and environmental heritages at stake. An environmental identity is the amalgamation of cultural identities, ways of life, and self-perceptions that are connected to a given group's physical environment. In Minamata, for example, we find that fishers were reluctant to accept the fact that the fish were contaminated because it would mean abandoning their traditional way of life and sustenance. Environmental identity is closely related to environmental heritage, where the meanings and symbols of the past frame values, practices, and places we wish to preserve for ourselves *as members of a community.* In other words, our environmental heritage is our environmental identity in relation to the community viewed over time.

The fact that vulnerable groups are so often victims of the unfair distribution of environmental burdens reflects discrimination against the groups' environmental identity. If the maritime identity of the fishers of Minamata, Lake Biwa, the Nagara River, and Kerala, for example, is socially devalued, so too will be the groups' interest in clean water and sustainable practices. More generally, the distribution of environmental burdens is closely related to the ways in which groups' environmental identities and environmental heritages are respected within a society. Yet environmental identity and heritage are the most commonly overlooked aspects of environmental justice. Even if distributive justice and political recognition are achieved as a result of an environmental justice struggle, the affected groups may still experience harm to their environmental heritage as a result of which they are forced to rethink their self-identity.

For the Houma and Cajuns of Grand Bois an environmental heritage of sharing resources among family and community members predates the oil industry and the legacy of dependence it created. This heritage, passed on in stories from one generation to the next, guides them on the path to personal and cultural security. But the Grand Bois people's narratives are threatened by the local presence of the oil industry. The oil-related ecological destruction that forced Grand Bois residents to abandon long-time fishing and shrimping practices, signatures of local identity, will not be easily mitigated as long as the oil industry remains dominant in the region. This kind of impact on environmental identity and heritage means that remedies to the injustice will involve a more conscientious solution: compensation alone is unacceptable to many residents, who see ecological cleanup and the removal of the offending waste site as necessary to restoring health as well as environmental heritage.

The case of Benxi provides an ironic twist on environmental identity. For an industrial, steel-producing city like Benxi, a toxic identity signifies industrial productivity. It is the turn to a market economy and the downsizing of the state-owned steel enterprises that enables the creation of a model environmental city and the turn to a green identity, thereby transforming Benxi into a national symbol for lightening the environmental burdens of a modern industrial society. The many residents who were left jobless and without a social safety net in the new economy regard this new identity with disdain, however, once again raising the question "environmentalism for whom"? The interviews with Benxi residents in the China chapter indicate that green values have yet to trickle down from the middle classes. Furthermore, we need to consider an older environmental identity that was lost with the advent of the steel industry. To judge from the region's mountainous landscape and abundant verdant beauty, the toxic identity no doubt masks a loss of environmental heritage. Whether it can be recovered through the new efforts to promote tourism is doubtful unless the people of Benxi are brought in as full participants to the policy decisions.

Typical remedies to injustice, such as compensation or other forms of redistribution, cannot repair damage to environmental identity and the rupture of a way of life. If we are stripped of our livelihood, marginalized by virtue of environmental hazards, and ultimately face the loss of our own self-respect, what is the remedy? Recognition justice involves not only giving victims a voice in environmental decision-making, but also cultivating an authentic respect for the ways in which local groups experience the policy process, and for their traditional ways of knowing and responding to environmental concerns.

We must find creative remedies to injustices against environmental identity. One possible remedy is *restorative justice,* wherein mediators bring victims and offenders into a dialogue in order to establish the parameters of apology that will be acceptable to the victims. Recognition justice requires more than compensation and redistribution. As Australian environmentalist Val Plumwood points out: "One has to concede injustice in order to effect a sufficient change to provide any guarantee that the same approach will not immediately be repeated somewhere else where it may be equally damaging—that is, evidence of dispositional change. That's why it's so important to be able to say 'Sorry'."[10] To make the offender more responsible and conscientious, and suture the wounds of the affected people, families, and communities, the harm to environmental identity and heritage needs to be addressed. Restorative justice requires that the victims confront the offenders (although in actual cases this rarely happens face to face) so as to discourage repeat offenses. Through restorative justice, in short, apologies and mediation are added to the recognition and distributive remedies of greater participation and compensation. Restorative justice also involves reforming laws and institutions to ensure the victims a voice in the decisions surrounding environmental practices of the wrongdoers and to prevent future victimization, abuse of science, and irresponsible policy-making. Thus, once a polluting operation is shut down, victims need to be assured that the culpable parties do not simply move on and repeat the offense elsewhere. Public apologies keep the spotlight of guilt on the culpable parties, instead of casting doubt on the good faith of the victims, as happened in Minamata, Grand Bois, and Delhi, where the victims were seen as having violated social custom, harmed productivity, hindered green policy advances, or burdened state tax systems.

Restorative justice is not without its flaws, as the leading legal practitioners in New Zealand and Australia have learned.[11] Victims are often placed under great stress when dialoguing with their offenders. And offenders may in fact get too much credit for agreeing to take part in the restorative justice process, while victims are put in a position where they must take responsibility for rehabilitating the offender.

Nevertheless, restorative justice has been shown to produce good results in one of our cases. The recent history of Minamata represents a fairly successful effort at restorative justice. After decades of conflict over toxic waste and its health effects, the people of Minamata remained divided, with victims and offspring of victims still suffering from the disease, from social stigmatization, from the economic hardships of downsizing at the Chisso plant, and from the environmental destruction of the local landscape. Finally, in the 1990s, the prefectural government took action to reunite the community with its Moyainaoshi Campaign. According to the Japan chapter, this reconciliation effort emphasized "activities that bring the residents face-to-face to discuss environmental issues and to cooperate together on resolving community environmental problems" (p. 114). The community-wide process of healing between residents across generations, which included a public apology from the mayor, memorials, concerts, and sculptures, helped give Minamata a new identity. The process of healing the environment, through the city's recycling system and other *moyainaoshi* projects, was developed expressly to redefine the identity of victims and the city itself. Victims became participating citizens, whose voices counted because they had traditional knowledge that could help forge Minamata's new identity—the very knowledge that for decades legal experts, corporate giants, prefectural and national government officials, medical professionals, and other residents had long dismissed.

The project of *moyainaoshi* remains unfinished. As a movement led by the prefectural government, its credibility is circumscribed. It makes top-down mistakes—for example, inviting victims to the memorial's coffee house but preventing them from working there because of their disabilities. And despite the campaign's efforts to create awareness and social sensitivity, some Minamata people continue to look down on the victim and fisher communities. Many victims and activists disagree with the decision to site the campaign's festivities and memorials on a fifty-eight hectare green that is also the site of the reclamation landfill where the mercury dredged from the sea is buried. The victims themselves remain exhausted from decades of illness and social prejudice, and the healing process depends upon their reliving this painful experience.

**Transformations and the Environmental
Justice Movement**

The China chapter authors summarize the attitude of the people of both Benxi and the Sanjiang Plain toward environmental projects in their regions as follows: "What is the point of a nice environment if people have nothing to eat?" (p. 91). The choice of eating or preserving the environment is a false dichotomy imposed upon marginalized people around the world. The environmental justice paradigm calls us to recognize that environmental practices, values, and politics have serious social repercussions; in order to anticipate, understand, and ameliorate these repercussions, environmental consciousness must be transformed so that we promote justice for both ecologies *and* communities instead of framing the two goals as irreconcilable. The promise of the environmental justice movement lies in its potential to achieve this transformation by empowering individuals and groups, reforming political institutions, and changing our approach to environmentalism itself.

As we have seen in the studies in this book, community mobilization can transform marginalized individuals, living day to day with a sense of resignation, into the powers that be: citizens with a voice in decision-making. In Grand Bois, Kerala, and Minamata, citizens and communities took on major corporations and government bureaucracies. Their demands for recognition, including respect for identity, were articulated in a way that over time gave their environmental values entry and some degree of legitimacy in the domain of policy-making. In encouraging the victims of environmental injustice to confront business-as-usual politics, an environmental justice movement can alter the political arena. The Minamata Disease Victims Certification Association and the fishworkers' movement of Kerala were environmental justice movements to be reckoned with at the highest levels of local *and* national politics, while the Grand Bois Citizen's Committee won revisions in state environmental policy, even though some key demands remained unmet.

In the face of the environmental justice paradigm, not only politics but also environmentalism itself, dominated as it is by affluent classes worldwide, must confront the need for transformation. In several of our cases, mainstream environmentalists inside and outside government were complicit in the social injustices suffered by the most disenfranchised groups. Most notably in Delhi, environmental policies supported by the environmentalism of the new and growing middle class cost desperate workers more than a quarter of a million factory jobs. In the Sanjiang Nature Reserve and in Benxi, it is state-sanctioned mainstream environmentalism that residents suffer from (or in the case of Benxi, perceive they suffer from, as a consequence of misplaced priorities and corruption). Clearly, then, environmentalism is a political movement that must be scrutinized for its social consequences. In addition to showing the shortcomings of mainstream environmentalism, our case studies have also shown the ways in which mainstream environmentalism has faced up to its social responsibility to assist communities in their struggle for environmental justice, as in Grand Bois, where alliances with mainstream environmental groups helped the community gain a political platform and find a voice with which to challenge Big Oil.

The most important transformation that needs to take place, in my view, is with respect to the environmentalism of the dominant class. Driven by a consumerist culture, this class shapes the way in which politics, morality, economics, science, and technology are used to generate the injustices. This is the environmental identity that most of us share in and which we are morally obligated to transform everywhere, particularly in this age of economic globalization. Only by deconstructing and reconstituting our environmental identity to respect the environmental rights of all people can the environmental identity of the victims of environmental injustices be affirmed by the victims themselves and respected by those who once perpetuated the injustices.

Notes

The case studies in this book present so many rare and new avenues for environmental justice studies that the task of conforming my analysis to the goals of the text felt, at times, overwhelming. I therefore especially thank Joanne Bauer for the many times she went beyond the normal duties of editor to assist me with direction and feedback. Many insights and contours of this chapter are owing to the long discussions and countless hours that she generously gave to this chapter. For those moments of guidance and virtual coauthorship I must express my gratitude.

1. There is a great deal of debate among justice theorists over the exact nature of and relationship between the two dimensions. Here and elsewhere I follow the distinctions of Nancy Fraser's "redistribution-recognition problem," which argues that these dimensions are identifiable, distinct, and interrelated. See Nancy Fraser, *Justice Interruptus: Critical Reflections on the "Postsocialist Condition* (New York: Routledge, 1997). For a lengthier account of the role of these dimensions in environmental justice, see Robert Melchior Figueroa, *Debating the Paradigms of Justice: The Bivalence of Environmental Justice* (Ann Arbor: University Microfilms International, 1999).

2. Wolfgang Sachs, *Ecology and Equity: From Rio to Johannesburg 2002*, video recording (Hamilton, NY: Colgate University), March 23, 2002.

3. "Mainstream environmentalists" characterize the distinction as "shallow ecology," which deals with pollution and human environmental health, versus "deep ecology," which places ecological interests on par with strictly human interests.

4. Although it is not mentioned in the case study in this volume, the Supreme Court, in addition to shutting down polluting factories in Delhi, also shut down factories and commercial enterprises that were soiling the Taj Mahal in nearby Agra. See the 1999–2000 annual report of the Central Pollution Control Board, available at www.cpcb.delhi.nic.in/annual_report1999-2000-26.htm, accessed 29 September 2004. See also T.K. Rajalakshmi, "Toxins and the Taj," *UNESCO Courier,* July/August 2000, available at www.unesco.org/courier/2000_07/uk/signe.htm, accessed 10 January 2006.

5. Aristotle, *Nichomachean Ethics,* ed. R. McKeon (New York: Random House, 1941), 1132a: 10.

6. Robert Melchior Figueroa, "Teaching for Transformation: Lessons from Environmental Justice," in *The Environmental Justice Reader: Politics, Poetics, and Pedagogy,* ed. J. Adamson, M. Evans, and R. Stein (Tucson: University of Arizona Press, 2002), 311–30.

7. Robert Melchior Figueroa, "Other Faces: Latinos and Environmental Justice," in *Faces of Environmental Racism: Confronting Issues of Global Justice,* 2d ed., ed. L. Westra and B.E. Lawson (Lanham, MD: Rowman and Littlefield, 2001), 167–86.

8. For a more detailed discussion of pluralistic public involvement versus deliberative participatory processes in environmental justice; wherein the former poses stakeholders as self-interested parties pressuring the others into a concession and the latter involves stakeholders as equal partners in a problem solving venture that is not intended to end in the favor of an individual player or regime of players, but as a collective solution by all present players. See Luke W. Cole and Sheila R. Foster, *From the Ground Up: Environmental Racism and the Rise of the Environmental Justice Movement* (New York: New York University Press, 2001), especially chapter 5.

9. The extent to which upstream parties (Native American Nations) and downstream parties (inner-city Mexican Americans) played a role in the process is not entirely clear from the case study.

10. Val Plumwood, *Environmental Culture: The Ecological Crisis of Reason* (New York: Routledge, 2002), 116.

11. Heather Strang, "Restoring Victims: An International View" (lecture delivered at the Restoration for Victims of Crime Conference, Melbourne, Australia, September, 1999).

8

Framing Shared Values

Reason and Trust in Environmental Governance

Clark A. Miller

At first blush, the accounts presented in Part 1 of this volume may appear to be *local* stories about *local* environmental conflict. Nothing could be further from the truth. To be sure, these stories treat particular struggles in particular locales, like Fuyuan County, China, and Tucson, Arizona. They are not local, however, in the sense of being of import or interest only to those who live in or care about a particular region. They are, instead, stories that inform our understanding of what it means to live on earth at the dawn of the twenty-first century. Although it is sometimes obscured by the messiness of local contexts, values, and politics, these studies offer important insights into environmental governance in an increasingly *global* world.

Environmental governance in the late twentieth century was marked by a profound shift toward *globalism*: the framing of issues in explicitly global terms, as problems that can be understood and managed on a scale no smaller than the earth itself.[1] Increasingly, the lives of people and communities are greatly affected by people and events in other, often distant parts of the globe. "Think globally, act locally," once the signature slogan of the environmental movement, has given way to new policy discourses emphasizing the need for worldwide action to protect key elements of the global environment: the ozone layer, the climate system, and biological diversity. The proliferation of earth images—on everything from the evening news and corporate logos to cereal boxes, coffee mugs, and T-shirts—testifies to the widespread appeal of this new global vision.

To date, most studies of environmental globalism have focused on the production of global narratives and discourses and in particular why some communities have articulated their environmental concerns in explicitly global terms.[2] In the studies in this volume, by contrast, we see the flip side of environmental globalism, as people in particular contexts work to reorder their lives in response to the emergence and spread of globalist discourses. In each study, in line with UN Secretary General Kofi Annan's call to world leaders to "put a human face on globalization," the reader encounters a detailed ethnographic account of what it means to encounter, acknowledge, and grapple with the idea of being an inhabitant, and possibly a citizen, of a global, interconnected world. Together, the country chapters make for a fascinating account of *comparative globalism*, of the different ways in which people confront and interpret key elements of the global environmental agenda—the production and consumption of oil, agricultural expansion into natural landscapes, overexploited fisheries, thick industrial pollution—as they seek to forge governance arrangements that can accommodate (and maybe even transcend) widely conflicting notions of nature, work, wealth, community, identity, justice, health, peace, and tranquility.

In Kerala, for example, we see what is happening to a fishing community marginalized by emerging global fish markets, by industrialization of the fishing fleets, and by the impacts of these phenomena on local fisheries and fish harvests. In Grand Bois, Louisiana, we see the dark side of the production and consumption of oil, the world's principal source of energy, for the communities who depend on the oil industry for their livelihoods but who also live in areas directly affected by oil drilling. In Benxi and Sanjiang, we follow communities struggling to cope with ideas about nature and the environment they have received from conference rooms and laboratories halfway around the world, through the auspices of groups like the International Crane Foundation and the World Bank and through the actions of a state bureaucracy that seeks little or no input from local people. In Japan, local communities are also struggling against a seemingly distant and monolithic state, but one whose environmental ideas are framed not so much by the agendas of the transnational environmental movement but by a hegemonic discourse of economic growth in a competitive global marketplace.

My goal in this chapter is to excavate lessons from these stories that will help us think about the challenges of environmental governance under conditions of globalization. I begin with a brief theoretical discussion of environmental values and governance, highlighting the need to rethink their relationship in contexts like those examined in this volume. In this first section, I offer three analytic concepts that might aid us in developing a new understanding of environmental values and governance: framing, styles of reasoning, and trust. Then, in the next three sections of the chapter, I take each of these lenses separately, looking at the case studies through each in turn. I conclude with some suggestions about how the lessons of these studies might be used as a guide not only for people in other localities who are grappling with the complex challenges of globalization, and the rapidly expanding flows of ideas, people, and products that have accompanied it, but also for the planet as a whole, as humans search for new, more workable forms of global environmental governance.

Environmental Values and Governance

What is the relationship between environmental values and governance? One answer can be found in Edwin Haefele's classic treatise *Environmental Management and Representative Government*.[3] Writing in 1973, Haefele argued that environmental problems would require a fairly radical rearrangement of governance institutions. The problem, as he identified it, was that nature did not obey the political jurisdictions people had laid down. Air, water, animals, plants, insects—all passed easily from one jurisdiction to another, tying together communities whose decision-making processes prevented them from making joint management policies. Upstream communities could therefore make choices with little regard for the views of their downstream neighbors. Only by creating legislative institutions whose jurisdictional authority matched the physical boundaries of the environmental system in question and whose membership fairly represented all whose lives intersected that system, Haefele argued, could political institutions appropriately aggregate citizens' preferences. In the intervening three decades, Haefele's suggestion has become gospel. On everything from air and water pollution and ground water management to climate change and ozone depletion, environmental policies have led to the formation of new decision-making institutions that attempt to mirror in politics the boundaries of nature. Locally, these are known as air management districts or watershed councils; globally, they are known as the conferences of parties of each of the major environmental treaties.

For Haefele, writing within the tradition of liberal individualism, environmental values were simply taken as given. Individuals held preferences about the environment. The purpose of representative government was to aggregate those preferences and reach collective decisions through fair processes of bargaining and voting. End of story. More recently, this paradigm, with slight modifications, has been extended to discussions of international governance. Delivering his 2000 presidential address to the American Political Science Association, Robert Keohane examined the need for international organizations to become more democratic if they were to become legitimate institutions of global governance.[4] In contrast to national legislatures, international organizations lack the political authority to compel assent to their bargained outcomes. Keohane therefore asserted the need for international institutions to look for alternative means of reaching collective decisions, highlighting the ideal of persuasion through reasoned, open communication. In contexts involving bargaining, Keohane asserted, reasoned persuasion can "chang[e] people's choices of alternatives independently of their calculations about the strategies of other players" through an "appeal to norms, principles, and values that are shared by participants in a conversation." In short, following work in the epistemic communities tradition, Keohane emphasized shared values as a key resource for environmental governance.[5]

Missing from Haefele and Keohane's suggestions are a number of insights that come from recent scholarship on the cultural roots of environmental values and conflict.[6] First, where Haefele and Keohane treat environmental values as fixed and outside the realm of social analysis, more culturally grounded approaches emphasize the need to examine closely how and why people come to hold particular environmental values and how those values change over time as people grapple with new social and environmental challenges. Many of the studies presented in Part 1 of this volume highlight the transient, malleable character of environmental preferences. In her account of atmospheric pollution in Delhi, for example, Amita Baviskar illustrates numerous methods by which activist members of India's urban middle class came to be persuaded of the value of a strong clean air policy. In her account and others, environmental values come to be understood as dynamic elements of community relationships and dialogues, shaped by the ways people attribute meaning and importance to scientific facts, weave them into broader social narratives, and embed them in the tacit assumptions and day-to-day practices of institutions and the broader social order.

Second, Haefele and Keohane assume that environmental values can be cleanly separated from other aspects of social life: Haefele, in his wish for special legislative institutions that address ecosystem considerations, Keohane in his tacit acceptance of the current organization of international institutions around distinct issue areas, such as climate change, biodiversity loss, and international trade. The Conference of Parties for the UN Framework Convention on Climate Change, for example, is authorized to make global policies to protect the climate, but its sovereignty does not extend to energy policy, urban transportation, or agricultural subsidies, all of which nonetheless factor into climate policy. By contrast, national and state legislatures typically have authority to address issues in their manifold dimensions. This integrative approach seems more consistent with the culturally grounded approaches to environmental values we have been discussing and with the studies in this volume, which pay careful attention to the close ties people forge between the values they attach to nature and the values they attach to historical tradition, communal identity, meaningful work, and other aspects of their lives. Moreover, it also seems to align more closely with the real-world connections among multiple aspects of environmental degradation, broader patterns of economic development, social relationships, and political order.

To build a more robust model of environmental values and governance, consistent with the insights of culturally grounded approaches, I want to introduce and describe three important analytic concepts. The first is *framing*. Understood dynamically, framing is the process by which communities arrive at shared conceptual frameworks, "worldviews or underlying assumptions that guide communal interpretation and definition" of environmental issues. As I have written elsewhere, framing shapes "the definitions of risk, the terms of participation, the range of policy options considered, and the nature of political debate."[7] One approach to the analysis of environmental governance is to consider the ways in which alternative frames of meaning are articulated, contested, defended, brought into dialogue with one another, canonized, and normalized as part of routine decision-making.[8]

In a now famous essay, "A Place for Stories," the environmental historian William Cronon compares the divergent stories historians have told about the dust bowl years of the American Great Plains. For some historians, the dust bowl reflected a classic example of human overexploitation of nature, leading to ecological collapse. For others, however, the dust bowl was a compelling story of the ability of resourceful people to triumph over nature's limitations. How, Cronon asks in the essay, could competent historians, working from essentially similar historical evidence and facts, arrive at such different interpretations? His answer: they brought very different narrative framings to their work, and so told markedly different stories.

Framing, as Cronon and others have depicted it, is largely a matter of shaping narrative composition, but it is clear that divergent framings also tie into deeper, more systematic variations in the *styles of reasoning* cultures adopt for making sense of risk. Styles of reasoning is my second analytic concept. I borrow this term from the philosopher of science Ian Hacking, who argues that research communities develop distinct constellations of modes of argumentation, objects of study, forms of evidence, approaches to theory development, and notions of expertise in their work. Comparative, cross-national studies of risk analysis and management have observed a similar phenomenon in which countries differ in how they frame risk, arriving at widely differing answers to risk-related questions (e.g., whether the risk of cancer should be treated similarly to or differently from other kinds of health risks and whether climate change is a local or a global risk).[9] The studies indicate that these variations in framing are the result of important aspects of political culture that lead countries to apply very different analytic tools and approaches to understanding and managing risk, differing in how they define expertise, set evidentiary standards, organize scientific advisory committees, develop regulatory programs, and communicate risk to the public.[10] In other words, communities develop distinct civic epistemologies—institutions and practices for generating, validating, and putting knowledge to use in the making of public choices—that guide how they interpret, make sense of, and reason about environmental risks.[11] Environmental values are thus caught up in basic social and cultural arrangements for making sense of the way the world works, for relating human actions to the natural resources and systems on which people rely for a variety of ecological goods and services, and for making collective choices about how to adjust human-nature interactions in the face of both social and environmental change.

The final concept I want to introduce is *trust*. In recent years, social scientists have increasingly deployed this concept as a causal variable, often as part of a broader notion of social capital, to explain variations among societies in economic or political success.[12] In some societies people trust each other and governing institutions more than in others, these authors conclude, allowing them to build stronger economic and political relationships. More recent work on the role of science in public affairs has turned this question around, seeking an explanation of how citizens and governments secure one another's trust, with a particular emphasis on the production and validation of credible knowledge.[13] This work has illustrated the mutually supporting and interdependent character of knowledge and order. Deploying objective knowledge has allowed government agents to appear as neutral, unbiased arbiters whose personal biases have been neutralized through the application of externally imposed constraints.[14] At the same time, governments have become deeply involved in setting standards for the production and application of knowledge in policy settings, regulating appropriate forms of evidence and expertise, auditing research facilities, and mandating public exposition of expert reason. In this way, governments have become essential players in helping to ensure that knowledge is produced in such a way that citizens can trust it as a reliable foundation for making collective choices and can therefore trust the policies built upon it.[15]

This work makes clear that trust and mistrust do not necessarily or merely depend on the good or bad faith of social actors, but also depend on competing rationalities in complex social encounters where it is difficult if not impossible to differentiate cleanly between issues of knowledge and politics.[16] In a study of sheep farmers in the north of England, for example, Brian Wynne found extensive mistrust of government scientists and officials, citing a wide range of complaints, from past untruthfulness ("they've lied to us before") and defects in identity and expertise ("they don't know anything about sheep farming") to problems with the experimental process ("they were measuring in the wrong places") and the scientists' stubbornness ("they kept insisting their models were right, even when their old predictions turned out not to be true").[17] In circumstances like these, which characterize many of the case studies in this volume, the challenge for environmental governance becomes not so much to identify effective policy options but to build institutions that can build trust across significant cultural gaps.

The analytic concepts of framing, styles of reasoning, and trust provide useful starting points, in my view, for approaching questions of environmental values and governance in the global, cross-cultural contexts in which environmental conflicts are increasingly fought out. In the next three sections, I use these concepts as a basis for interpreting the case studies from part 1, arguing in the process that we need to rethink how we understand not only local but also global governance to adjust to new ideas of knowledge and its role in policy processes. Finding democratic approaches to global decision-making, I contend, demands that we take seriously how people reason about the environment and how their frames of meaning and styles of reasoning contribute to their judgments of credibility and trust.

Framing

Across the case studies, it is clear that communities around the world increasingly face cross-boundary flows of ideas, people, and commodities that have a significant impact on environmental governance. Consider, for example, some of the apparent similarities among the cases:

- The hopelessness, the confusion, and the contradictions among individual and community reactions to pollution insults in Grand Bois and Minamata, where residents depend for their income and livelihood on industrial enterprises, often with transnational markets, yet are also at risk from the cutthroat demands of global economic competition.
- The simultaneous emergence of air pollution as a major environmental issue in the late 1990s in Delhi and Benxi, as economic growth created a new, more financially secure middle class in each country, seeking to use newfound wealth to improve living conditions at the same time that international agencies such as the World Bank began to require that countries observe international environmental norms, such as those developed at the 1992 Rio Earth Summit, as a condition of multilateral aid.

- The struggles in the Sanjiang Plain and Kerala between agents of international environmental NGOs and other transnational actors who seek to put nature off limits to human exploitation (e.g., through restrictions on land use or the use of turtle excluding devices) and local inhabitants who see nature as their only reliable source of income.
- People's desire in many of these communities to find ways to reassert control over their lives, to restore some semblance of continuity, community, and security that can protect them against the consequences of actions being taken by others who are seemingly a world away.

Even in these cases, however, where individuals and communities in different places face strikingly similar challenges, people respond differently not only to environmental degradation but also to the larger problems of living in a global world. Comparing environmental politics in China and Japan, for example, one sees almost a mirror image in terms of the way that citizens and the government have framed environmental degradation in the context of broader developments in state-society relations. In both Benxi and Fuyuan County, the Chinese state has framed environmental protection as an issue of direct concern and considerable importance to the national government. In this respect, China follows a pattern set in the United States. Much as Congress has historically written environmental law and set environmental policy in the United States, China's environmental laws and standards appear to flow primarily from Beijing, which also has the power to channel foreign funding to environmental protection activities at the county and provincial level and, as we saw in Benxi, sometimes even funds such activities directly. Benxi's local administrators exploit Beijing's environmental values to generate money and institutional support for programs designed to return Benxi to visibility in satellite surveys. In the case of Sanjiang, the State Council assumed authority over the nature reserve in 2000 in order to assure effective wetland protection. Meanwhile local citizens in Sanjiang—and to some degree also in Benxi—are key opponents of innovations designed to enhance environmental quality.

By contrast, in the cases described in the Japan chapter, environmental progress was achieved only over and against the direct and deliberate opposition of the state and, in the resource use cases of Lake Biwa and the Nagara River, after the passage of legislation that decentralized policy-making, giving new, strong voices to individual citizens and local governments. This pattern is consistent with the findings of other recent research on Japanese environmental politics, which shows that the principal support for environmental improvement comes from citizen-activists and local, small-scale nonprofit organizations that seek to mobilize citizens to oppose government policy.[18] Japanese politics are characterized by strong ties between movements for environmental protection and movements for democratic reform. A broad base of citizens increasingly mobilize around efforts to protect nature, defying the framing of environmental degradation as a necessary cost of Japan's efforts to build a strong postwar economy that has characterized centralized, bureaucratic decision-making by the Japanese state. This close relationship between environmental politics and movements for governmental reform parallels one aspect of U.S. environmental politics in the 1960s and 1970s, decades when the environmental movement helped usher in administrative reforms that substantially opened up government processes to public input. In China, by contrast, while increasing numbers of government-approved citizens' groups are cropping up across the country, environmental protection remains for the most part—and certainly in our two cases—under the authority of the central government, and at least in the short term, decentralization seems likely only to weaken support for environmental objectives.

A second, illuminating comparison can be drawn between the United States and India. The environmental conflicts in Kerala and Delhi mirror familiar cases in the United States, including the Grand Bois case presented in this volume. Notably, however, the discourses in which the U.S. and Indian conflicts are interpreted differ dramatically. In the United States, communities tend to frame policy choices regarding natural resources and pollution as a trade-off between environmental protection and economic development. In India, by contrast, particularly in the Delhi air pollution case but also in the discussion of the Kerala fisheries, a second kind of framing shows the conflict in class terms because it pits the poor against people who might elsewhere be termed "nouveau riche" ("the middle class" in Delhi, "successful fish exporters" in Kerala): those people who have made money through entrepreneurial activity, often in the global marketplace. Perhaps the best illustration of the competing frames comes from a comparison of the U.S. environmental justice movement, of which the Grand Bois case serves as an exemplary study, and the case of the movement to address injustice among the urban (formerly rural) poor in Delhi who work in the factories shut down by air pollution regulators. The two movements frame the linkages between justice and environment in opposite directions. The U.S. environmental justice movement has sought to address the injustice of locating polluting factories in poor neighborhoods. Calls for justice by groups like Kalpavriksh, the People's Union for Civil Liberties, and Saajha Manch (the Joint Forum on Urban Issues), by contrast, strive to highlight the injustice of putting poor people out of work in the name of environmental protection. In the United States, justice is framed in environmental terms—who has access to a clean environment. In India, justice is framed in economic terms—whose job is lost in order to protect the environment.

These differences extend into other elements of the framing of American and Indian environmental policy. In American environmental policy, exemplified in the views of a resident of Civano, environmental degradation is increasingly framed in terms of a shrinking planet: "The world is getting too small to [consume excess natural resources] any more" (p. 308). One of the most popular American environmental concepts is the "ecological footprint"—the amount of space people or communities take up in ecological terms as a result of their resource consumption. As another resident of Civano put it, there is a need to "live lightly" on the planet, a goal that is increasingly defined in the United States in terms of "sustainable development," which in turn is almost always defined in terms of consumer choice. The result is most often a search for technologies, from hydrogen fuel cells and hybrid cars to energy- and water-conserving homes, that can reduce environmental impacts while allowing people to improve (or at least maintain) their lifestyles. In short, for most Americans environmental values involve a choice of what to consume, not whether to consume.

As noted above, however, major schools of Indian environmental thought and activism remain staunchly critical of consumerism. In Kerala, fisher activists saw the emergence of a global market for fish, as well as the emergence of a local fishing industry based on trawlers that serve that market, as the fundamental threat to the livelihoods of traditional fishing families. This view is not simply the product of conservatism and unwillingness to change—nor is it a wholesale rejection of market ideas. Traditional fishers use their own new technologies, including outboard motors for their boats, and would like to be able to earn a living selling the catch from their smaller-scale fishing in local markets. But what is at stake is not money so much as maintaining a way of life that increasingly appears to the Kerala fishers as incompatible with the incorporation of their small part of the world into a global consumer society. In Delhi, the activist community likewise sees their problem in terms of the actions of the middle class, newly able to purchase environmental goods, who are creating environmental injustice through the pursuit of clean air policies. Such anticonsumerist sentiments, which compete in India with middle class consumerist ideologies, are all but absent in the United States. They inform key elements of Indian foreign policy vis-à-vis global environmental change, which has argued, for example, that climate change is the result of the profligate spending habits of the world's rich and that climate policies that impose the burden of responding to climate change on the world's poor are highly unjust.[19] For many Indian activists, as for the Indian government, overconsumption and economic inequity are the framing in which environmental degradation and policy should be interpreted, not the other way around.[20]

Connecting Framing to Styles of Reasoning

As we explore the various framings of environmental issues in the studies in this book, we need to recognize that competing framings are as much about how people *know* the environment as about how they *value* it. Writing in the opening pages of her chapter, Amita Baviskar conjures up powerful visual imagery of air pollution in Delhi. This imagery illuminates a larger argument about how societies frame environmental conflicts and how different framings can leave out key elements of broader narratives that link the environment to nonenvironmental aspects of life in diverse communities. Baviskar vividly calls the reader's attention to a city teeming with "rush hour traffic," "trucks and old buses," "unburned hydrocarbons," and "scooters and motorcycles," as well as people with "streaming eyes, coughing bouts, and, later, blinding headaches," "chronic respiratory ailment[s]," "handkerchiefs across their noses and mouths," and "inhalers in their pockets," struggling to live in a "toxic" environment. And the story is told not only in visceral visual images but also in mundane yet equally persuasive health statistics and digital displays of pollution levels strategically located at major intersections, and on the nightly news, where pollution data now "follows the weather forecast."

Caught up in the data and imagery, we struggle to step back and recognize that the Delhi case study is not simply yet another standard account of the health impacts of pollution. The framing of air pollution as an environmental problem has rested in Delhi, as it has in the United States, on visual iconography and quantitative measurement, two tools meant to convey both the immediacy and the extent of the damage air pollution causes to people's health and well-being. As Baviskar relates, however, these tools do not simply provide objective, neutral representations of reality; they are freighted elements of a broader narrative that "conjures up a cause and a constituency, authorizes action" and perhaps most importantly "obscures as much as it reveals." *To choose* these images and statistics is, in effect, *not to choose* others, such as data on hunger or images of malnourishment among children in the families of workers who have lost their factory jobs as a result of Delhi's clean air campaign. Air pollution, according to Baviskar, is a constructed problem—which does not necessarily deny its reality but points to the fact that it is cast in particular way, to a particular end, for the benefit of a particular group of people, and, intentionally or not, to the disadvantage of others.

The framing of environmental values is often treated as a production problem—who has framed the issue, in what way, and for what purpose? Thus described, framing seems like little more than political spin. Here, however, I want to look at the consumption side of framing. In environmental controversies, multiple frames often clutter the political and policy landscape. But only as specific framings of an issue begin to influence individual and collective decisions do they begin to affect social and environmental outcomes. Framings must therefore be credible and persuasive to their audience if they are to be effective. An image of a child with an inhaler in her pocket will have little impact if the viewer of the image fails to associate an inhaler with asthma and asthma with air pollution. Thus, perhaps the most interesting objects in Baviskar's study are the Central Pollution Control Board's digital pollution displays, put up to persuade people who may not already be thinking in terms of air pollution that they, too, are affected by pollutant levels, by "showing" them the health risks they face each time they breathe the air. Thus, novel instruments, methods of knowing, and styles of reasoning about environmental risk enable a new framing of environmental values.

Understood in these terms, the activists' struggle to persuade people of the importance of environmental values is intimately connected to the development of new styles of reasoning. New ways of compiling and presenting data, new instruments, methods, and analytical techniques, and new theories help people connect their own experience of the world to broader narratives and ideas about how the world works. In the process, they acquire not only new approaches to analyzing and managing environmental risks but also new concepts of social identity and organization.[21] Nowhere, perhaps, is this connection clearer than in the case studies from Japan, where the struggle to achieve environmental protection has also been a struggle for more meaningful modes of democratic citizenship. Styles of reasoning are thus properly understood not only as particular ways of thinking about or inquiring into environmental degradation but rather as civic epistemologies, patterns of analysis and reasoning that connect up how communities frame human-nature interactions; how they produce and validate environmental knowledge and apply it to policy problems; and how they organize social and political life.

Institutional Trust

With benefit of the perspective developed in the preceding section, we should not be surprised that the conflict over environmental governance in a globalized world, as it emerges in the case studies in this volume, appears frequently in the guise of conflicting styles of reasoning. It is not simply that communities and cultures frame environmental values differently; those differences are connected to divergent styles of reasoning: sets of practices, networks, and institutions for creating and certifying knowledge and putting it to use in environmental policy and management. One common approach to overcoming competing styles of reasoning is to negotiate or impose uniform standards on all participants. Such standards may take many different forms. Unless styles of reasoning can be harmonized as well, however, such an approach risks conceptual confusion and error, not to mention political conflict, because the same standard may be understood and interpreted differently by communities working from different rationalities.

Precisely because styles of reasoning tend to be well grounded in cultural attitudes and expectations, as well as forms of social and political organization, Sheila Jasanoff has suggested that efforts to learn to *reason together*—that is to bring varying styles of reasoning into productive dialogue with one another—may be a more fruitful approach than standardization.[22] If scientists, public officials, and citizens are to identify and construct shared styles of reasoning and shared frames of meaning when it comes to environmental change, they need, argues Jasanoff, to recognize, acknowledge, compare, contrast, and integrate across multiple styles of reasoning. Moreover, she suggests, governance processes need to excavate and make more transparent the ways in which styles of reasoning are connected to differing notions of citizenship and constitutional constraints on the exercise of power. Particularly in the area of environmental standard-setting, there is a need for participants to be more reflective about and accountable for the tacit assumptions and values embedded in the methods of analysis and reasoning they bring to the process and their relationship to broader notions of democratic legitimacy, accountability, and authority.[23]

The studies in this volume suggest Jasanoff may be right. Failure to account for divergent styles of reasoning and frames of meaning has exacerbated the challenges of environmental governance in several cases. In China, greater willingness on the part of powerful bureaucrats in state agencies to engage with alternative local discourses of nature and local meanings attached to land use and livelihood might have resulted in environmental policies that gave rise to less local resistance (and possibly, therefore, improved environmental protection requiring less coercive means). Baviskar's account of air pollution in India suggests that overreliance on a single framing has likewise been a problem in the Indian courts. State authority in India has become allied with one style of reasoning to the exclusion of others, exacerbating social conflict. In contrast, however, communities in Kerala and in Japan have over time carved out spaces in which citizen perspectives are beginning to be heard and taken seriously as a counterweight to hegemonic market narratives. To be sure, the expression of marginal reasoning styles remains constrained in these cases, precisely because styles of reasoning are so closely connected to political order. In Minamata, for example, victims have faced difficulties both in verifying claims that they suffer from Minamata disease in sufficiently scientific terms to meet the criteria of the 1969 Relief Law and in overcoming community censure when they register for compensation or speak out. Victims' views have received greater acknowledgement more recently, however, especially because the Moyainaoshi Campaign has explicitly sought to bridge differences in cultural attitudes toward mercury poisoning. Further, in 1999, Japan's Environment Agency moved to relax the scientific criteria for proof of Minamata disease and to begin to accept forms of evidence that did not rely on scientific verification.

In the efforts of governments and citizens to create shared styles of reasoning and frames of meaning around nature and the environment through processes of reasoning together, these cases point to the importance of institutional trust. People appear to participate meaningfully only in processes that they perceive will treat their views and perspectives seriously. Such trust can take time to develop, as it did in the instance of the Benxi hotline and the more general growth of the use of hotlines in China as a crucial tool for environmental intelligence gathering. Use of these hotlines has increased significantly over time as citizens apparently become more confident that its use will enable them not only to achieve environmental goods when they report environmental problems and misdeeds but also to avoid the hazards of public exposure by assuring that their privacy will be protected. Likewise, when given the option to register themselves as Minamata disease victims through a process that would require developing scientific proof of their status, many victims expressed their mistrust of the government by opting for another route. Placing their trust in the courts, they believed, gave them a better chance of seeing their own ideas and values given due consideration. Censure of victims by other residents also led to deep cultural rifts and mistrust between segments of the Minamata community that have only begun to be healed through efforts to help community members understand one another's style of reasoning. Indeed, the authors of the Japan case studies note that, despite government efforts to reestablish trust by "re-tying" the bonds of community among segments of the population and also between the government and its citizens, many in the population remain skeptical of the government's motives. Once lost, trust can be extremely difficult to regain.

Trust is clearly connected to notions of identity and identification. In their efforts to rebuild trust in the Minamata case, a major strategy of Japanese officials was to strive to identify with the victims, to acknowledge and legitimize their position and views. Although not yet fully successful, this strategy has had some success in reestablishing a climate of shared identity and trust among victims and nonvictims. Notions of identity were also an important element in the case of the Kerala fisheries. At one point in the conflict, as the fishworkers' movement became more scientifically aware, movement leaders sought to counter the conclusions of government scientists and the international scientific community with alternative scientific perspectives. But before they could do so, they had to build ties of trust with specific scientists. According to observers, many fishers began their relationship with the scientists with the attitude that they, and they alone, truly understood the sea. Only after a long period of interaction did they drop their defensiveness and come to trust the scientists to speak on their behalf.

As the movement began to gather steam, its scientist allies called the movement's attention to cutting-edge scientific questions being addressed by government scientific committees. Armed with the knowledge that these committees' findings would be important in the political process, the movement used its own political leverage to pressure the committees to reconsider their conclusions and to take on board new knowledge provided by the movement and its scientific allies. The process brought multiple scientific research programs into dialogue in a series of committee hearings and reports—enabling the movement to gain a hearing for its views, something it had not accomplished through other means. Ultimately, the process led to recommendations by the panels and committees for a seasonal trawling ban, the approach many fishers viewed (on the basis of their own knowledge of the sea) as the only effective way to manage Kerala's fisheries.

As the Kerala case demonstrates, accountability, as well as identity, is an important element of trust. In this case, the movement was able to use its political leverage to hold accountable government scientific committees. As a result, the movement's members were able to ensure that the committees would grant standing to their ideas and values in institutional deliberations, and so to have a degree of trust that the outcome would not marginalize them. A similar conclusion also follows from the U.S. case studies. In Civano, residents built new institutions, including an independent neighborhood association, to help strengthen community relations and to provide a mechanism for developing consensus community positions when developers appeared unconcerned about their views. They also spoke out frequently about economic decisions, including the sale of the development. While residents had no formal power over either city or developer decisions, they made sure through active mobilization that no decisions were made that did not at least take their views into account. Their success in resisting the developer Don Diamond and encouraging the sale of the development to Pulte Homes gave residents some degree of trust that they could make their voices count. Even so, Pulte's subsequent decisions regarding future development reminded residents why institutions like the neighborhood association that could help them hold others accountable were essential to their ability to maintain the identity of the community over the long term.

Residents of Grand Bois felt much deeper mistrust of local, state, and federal government agencies, as well as the oil industry, than people in Civano felt toward the city and developers. Spaces where Grand Bois residents could have their views heard and given due consideration proved few and far between. Promises to community residents were repeatedly broken, with the result that most of the residents became highly disaffected. Even the law, which has often been the refuge of the otherwise powerless in the United States, largely failed Grand Bois residents; as in Japan, their health claims were tied to an ability to deliver scientific proof, too high a bar for the impoverished residents of the community. A waste facility continues to operate in the town today, and the community itself split into opposing factions during the course of the legal battles. Faced with persistent denial of the value of their stories, many residents have even begun to deny these stories themselves, insisting now that the oil industry has cleaned up its act and that others (e.g., the Army Corps of Engineers) have created worse ecological problems in the region.

Global Environmental Governance

What emerges from these accounts, then, is a model of environmental governance that depends on mutual learning and accommodation among people with highly divergent approaches to defining, analyzing, and managing risk—that is, on learning how to *reason together* about environmental risks. Accomplishing this task demands that institutions recognize the importance of culture as a factor in how communities reason and develop new means to foster cross-cultural dialogue, especially in forums where such dialogue has been limited to date—for example, in technical or scientific institutions. In developing such means, institutions should pay careful attention to governance reforms that (1) give people and communities greater opportunity to express environmental values in their own voice while acknowledging their right to do so and also providing the opportunity and means for relating the values expressed to broader collective narratives, meaning, and myth—in short, enabling their connection to cultural styles of reasoning; (2) foster opportunities to bring competing styles of reasoning into dialogue with another; and (3) increase trust among people with divergent backgrounds, distinct cultural values, and from scattered locations within a country (and even across the planet).

This model has considerable value for those thinking about environmental governance not only in local settings like those described in this volume but also in global environmental conflicts. After the signing of the Kyoto Protocol in 1997, efforts to address global environmental degradation foundered, ending a quarter century of apparent international consensus on environmental values that at times seemed to presage the emergence of a genuine global community. U.S. movement away from the Kyoto Protocol and rising global tensions over the environmental and health implications of trade in genetically modified organisms in the late 1990s and early 2000s stood in stark contrast to the optimism of Montreal in 1987 and Rio in 1992, revealing the extent to which the earth's natural resources and systems had become as much the subject of global conflict as global cooperation. By the end of the 1990s, many of the world's poorest nations saw global efforts to stop climate change and biodiversity loss through regulation as, at best, misguided (because they blamed poverty more than consumption for environmental risk) and, at worst, as deliberate programs to prevent poor nations from achieving standards of living comparable to those of the West. In Seattle, in 1999, anti-globalization rioters dressed as sea turtles used the environment as a rallying point in their efforts to bring down the World Trade Organization and other emerging institutions of global governance. In the early 2000s, violent conflicts in the Middle East, Africa, and Latin America highlighted the exploitation of natural resources—especially drug crops, diamonds, and oil—as a key contributor to the instigation and financing of ethnic genocide, guerilla warfare, weapons of mass destruction, and terrorist networks.

It may seem easy to blame renewed global environmental conflict on the activities of a few extremists in Seattle, Al Qaeda, or the White House. There is little doubt, for example, that the Bush administration's unilateralist, anti-environmental politics dramatically exacerbated tensions over such issues as climate change and genetically modified organisms. But the pullback from global environmental regimes predated the Bush administration, a sign that deeper changes were also at work. In the 1970s, the environment was frequently touted as an issue that could transcend even such deep ideological divides as those between capitalism and communism and between imperial capitals and their former colonial dependencies. Few people are naïve enough to accept that claim today. There is a growing recognition in the rich countries of the North as much as the poor countries of the South that global environmental regimes are places where the future governance of the planet is at stake and that negotiating positions in these forums should reflect broader disputes over the allocation of power in international politics. Growing conflicts over global environmental issues thus have come to mirror deeper, more entrenched value conflicts over the constitutional arrangements of global politics.

In the wake of these developments, efforts to resurrect progress toward global environmental stewardship must go beyond "one world" approaches by acknowledging and dealing with the deep ideological divisions—as well as the fundamental connections between environment, wealth, and power—in global society.[24] The persistence of vast political fissures over international environmental policy and the inability of existing international environmental institutions to close them point to the importance of the project represented in this volume. Since 1972 and the United Nations Conference on the Human Environment in Stockholm, efforts at international environmental cooperation have turned mainly to science, for its presumed ability to provide objective, politically neutral frameworks for identifying, describing, and analyzing environmental problems. In the process, cultural values were relegated to a position of secondary importance, as variables that might explain why, when informed about an environmental risk, countries nonetheless opted not to participate fully in efforts to solve it. Thus, environmental negotiations became settings in which wealthy nations provided "side payments" to these holdouts, forever fixing in people's minds the idea that environmental values were a luxury of the wealthy that the poor could not afford.

The studies in this book offer an alternative approach, grounded mainly in a comparative political analysis, that recognizes that environmental problems are deeply woven into the intimacies of daily life and the broader patterns of cultural styles of reasoning. To put it simply, this book is itself an example of how to reason together. The studies begin from the presumption that knowing something about how these four countries, in particular, value the environment will help us find ways to bridge the differences they bring to the negotiating table. These four countries are not random. Together, the United States, India, China, and Japan encompass nearly one half of the Earth's inhabitants and economic output and a substantial fraction of its military might. Economically, the four span a diversity of approaches to bridging markets and government planning and the three largest economies in the world. They include the widely regarded icon of Western, laissez faire, liberal, free trade economics and the intellectual leader of the non-aligned movement. Politically, they are four of the world's current great powers, including the last remaining communist great power, the world's oldest democracy, and two countries whose current forms of governance have been adapted from legacies of occupation by Western countries with noticeably different notions about how to construct a democratic polity. Their inhabitants include some of the world's richest and poorest peoples, not to mention large, influential populations of many of the world's major religions, including Buddhism, Protestant and Catholic Christianity, Islam, Judaism, Hinduism, and Shintoism. Last, but certainly not least, each possesses a highly regarded, well-funded environmental science community.

To ensure that they can adequately reflect the world described in this book, institutions of global environmental governance must rethink their approach. First, these institutions must find ways to legitimize plurality, especially by acknowledging the link between knowledge and cultural values. Climate change and biodiversity loss, let alone nature and society more generally, simply are not seen or valued the same way in all parts of the world, and global institutions need to find ways to come to grips with that fact. One very interesting experiment is being carried out in the United Nations Millennium Ecosystem Assessment, where "sub-global" units (some geographically defined at levels from towns to subcontinents, some defined in terms that cut across many regions) have carried out ecosystem assessments that link knowledge and values, as well as science and policy, in locally appropriate ways. In turn, the Millennium Assessment has organized a series of meetings for participants in these sub-global assessment units designed to foster cross-group exchange of ideas and methods.

Second, global environmental institutions need to find ways to deepen their engagement with the peoples of the world. They must find ways to relate to people in their daily lives and to engage their attention and secure their trust. It is not enough to negotiate ad hoc agreements among diplomats, scientists, and national leaders. Increasingly, broad publics are expressing their concerns about global policies. Much of the blame for the U.S. failure to ratify Kyoto can be laid at the feet of negotiators who failed to notice just how deeply the American public had come to care about the potential implications of climate policy.

Finally, global institutions need to find ways to promote dialogue among the many communities that make up the world polity, so that they can learn to reason together. Much as many environmentalists would wish it otherwise, this book illustrates that shared environmental values do not exist around the world. Without question, people in all four countries value the environment; but they do so in different ways, in keeping with their cultures and styles of reasoning. Although it would be convenient if it were otherwise, neither a set of universally shared environmental values nor a common style of reasoning about global environmental risks yet exists in global society; instead, a key aspect of global environmental governance in the coming years will be the enormous work required to achieve a common framework for valuing and reasoning about global environmental change among the world's peoples and nations. This is not impossible, but it will require diligence and care. Human institutions have long held the power to establish and shape social norms; the challenge is to do so in a manner that can achieve—on global scales—some semblance of democratic legitimacy and social trust.

Notes

1. See Clark Miller, "Resisting Empire: Globalism, Relocalization, and the Politics of Knowledge," in *Earthly Politics: Local and Global in Environmental Politics,* ed. Marybeth Long-Martello and Sheila Jasanoff (Cambridge, MA: MIT Press, 2004), 81–102.
2. See for example Peter Taylor and Frederick Buttel, "How Do We Know We Have Global Environmental Problems? Science and the Globalization of Environmental Discourse," *Geoforum* 23, no. 3 (1992): 405–16. David Takacs, *The Idea of Biodiversity: Philosophies of Paradise* (Baltimore: Johns Hopkins University Press, 1996); Clark A. Miller, "Climate Science and the Making of Global Political Order," in *States of Knowledge: The Co-Production of Science and Social Order,* ed. Sheila Jasanoff (London: Routledge, 2004).
3. Edwin Haefele, *Representative Government and Environmental Management* (Baltimore: Johns Hopkins University Press, 1973).
4. Robert Keohane, "Governance in a Partially Globalized World" (presidential address delivered at the American Political Science Association annual meeting, Washington, DC, August 31–September 3, 2000).
5. Compare Keohane's speech to Peter Haas, *Saving the Mediterranean: The Politics of International Environmental Cooperation* (New York: Columbia University Press, 1990).
6. See, for example, Thompson and Rayner, "Cultural Discourses," in *Human Choice and Climate Change,* ed. S. Rayner and E. Malone (Columbus, OH: Battelle, 1998), 265–344; and M. Douglas, and A. Wildavsky, *Risk and Culture: An Essay on the Selection of Technological and Environmental Dangers* (Berkeley: University of California Press, 1982).
7. Clark A. Miller, "The Dynamics of Framing Environmental Values and Policy: Four Models of Societal Processes," *Environmental Values* 9 (2000): 211–33.
8. William Cronon, "A Place for Stories: Nature, History and Narrative," *Journal of American History* (March 1992): 1347–76.
9. Sheila Jasanoff, "Product, Process, or Programme: Three Cultures and the Regulation of Biotechnology," in *Resistance to New Technology,* ed. M. Bauer (Cambridge: Cambridge University Press, 1995), 311–31; Sheila Jasanoff, *Risk Management and Political Culture* (New York, NY: Russell Sage Foundation, 1986); Brickman et al., *Controlling Chemicals: The Politics of Regulation in Europe and the United States* (Ithaca: Cornell University Press, 1985).
10. Brian Wynne, "Risk Communication for Chemical Plant Hazards in the European Com-

munity Seveso Directive," in *Corporate Disclosure of Environmental Risks*, ed. Michael S. Baram and Daniel G. Partan (Salem, NH: Butterworth Press, 1990).

11. Clark A. Miller, "New Civic Epistemologies of Quantification: Making Sense of Local and Global Indicators of Sustainability," *Science, Technology and Human Values* 30, no. 3 (2005): 403–32.

12. Frances Fukuyama, *Trust: The Social Virtues and the Creation of Prosperity* (New York: Free Press, 1995); Robert Putnam, "Bowling Alone: America's Declining Social Capital," *Journal of Democracy* 6 (1995): 65–78; Robert Putnam, *Making Democracy Work: Civic Traditions in Modern Italy* (Princeton: Princeton University Press, 1993).

13. Sheila Jasanoff, *The Fifth Branch: Science Advisers as Policymakers* (Cambridge: Harvard University Press, 1990).

14. Yaron Ezrahi, *The Descent of Icarus: Science and the Transformation of Contemporary Democracy* (Cambridge: Harvard University Press, 1990); Theodore Porter, *Trust in Numbers: The Pursuit of Objectivity in Science and Public Life* (Princeton: Princeton University Press, 1995).

15. Sheila Jasanoff, "Science and Norms in Global Environmental Regimes," in *Earthly Goods: Environmental Change and Social Justice*, ed. Fen Osler Hamson and Judith Reppy (Ithaca: Cornell University Press, 1996), 173–97.

16. Sheldon Krimsky and Alonso Plough, *Environmental Hazards: Communicating Risk as a Social Process* (Dover: Auburn House, 1988). For more theoretical discussions, see Steven A. Shapin, *Social History of Truth* (Chicago: University of Chicago Press, 1994), especially chapter 1, and Steven Shapin and Simon Schaffer, *Leviathan and the Air Pump: Hobbes, Boyle, and the Experimental Life* (Princeton: Princeton University Press, 1985).

17. Brian Wynne, "Misunderstood Misunderstandings: Social Identities and the Public Uptake of Science," in *Misunderstanding Science? The Public Reconstruction of Science*, ed. Alan Irwin and Brian Wynne (Cambridge: Cambridge University Press, 1995), 19–46.

18. K. Harada, "Public Access to Environmental Information in Japan: The Case of Sanbanze Wetland" (master's thesis, University of Wisconsin, 2003).

19. Anil Agarwal and Sunita Narain, *Global Warming in an Unequal World* (Delhi: Centre for Science and the Environment, 1991).

20. Sheila Jasanoff, "India at the Crossroads," *Global Environmental Change* (March 1993): 32–51.

21. Jasanoff, *States of Knowledge*.

22. Sheila Jasanoff, "Harmonization—The Politics of Reasoning Together," in *The Politics of Chemical Risk*, ed. Roland Bal and Willem Halfmann (Dordrecht: Kluwer, 1998), 176–93.

23. We have yet to identify appropriate means for accomplishing these goals, but for an example of institutional practices that arguably constitute an approach to learning to reason together, see Clark A. Miller, "Scientific Internationalism in American Foreign Policy: The Case of Meteorology, 1947–1958," in *Changing the Atmosphere: Expert Knowledge and Environmental Governance*, ed. Clark A. Miller and Paul N. Edwards (Cambridge, MA: MIT Press, 2001), 167–218.

24. Marybeth Long-Martello and Sheila Jasanoff, "Introduction: Globalization and Environmental Governance," in *Earthly Politics*, 1–30.

PART III

Reflections on the Study of
Environmental Values

9

How Shall We Study
Environmental Values?

Joanne Bauer and Anna Ray Davies

Values are hard to study because they are changeable, evasive, powerful, and emotive. Values related to the environment in particular defy complete capture by individual disciplines. Environmental professionals contest the meaning and even very existence of environmental values, and publics who have deeply felt connections to the environment are frequently ignored in debates about environmental policy. On the few occasions when publics are asked to comment, they often find the task of articulating their feelings awkward, unfamiliar, and problematic. In part this is because, as noted in the United States country chapter, a study of environmental values involves considering "the relationship between humans and our world, a relationship which is partially of our own devising and partially outside our ability to devise" (p. 317). Yet despite these tricky issues environmental scholars and practitioners increasingly recognize the importance of values to environmental policy-making in a differentiated society filled with uncertainty over environmental risks at multiple scales of policy making. The difficulty we faced in devising the project is encapsulated by British philosopher John Foster, who observes that "the notion of value . . . eludes our definitional grasp with a duplicity characteristic of the really important concepts in human experience."[1]

Having people from different disciplines and cultures conducting research in different places ultimately led to less uniformity than we had originally envisioned for the project. The project's geographical and conceptual breadth posed considerable, but ultimately rewarding, intellectual and practical challenges for all those involved. One issue we revisited and struggled with throughout the project was the question of methodology, or how to elicit, interpret, and convey environmental values for a report by a cross-cultural, transdisciplinary comparative research network. This chapter reflects on some of these negotiations and the strategies they led us to, and explains the assumptions that lie behind the work. It considers the nature of environmental values and how we studied, or reconstructed, them through applied research.

In constructing our research approach, we debated a number of problems related to how we would identify and locate values, particularly across different cultural contexts. How would we identify expressions of environmental value? How do individual values relate to the values of the group (e.g., family, friends, and religious, cultural, and political associations)? What are the different forms of value expression in different societies, and which of those forms is legitimated by the policy process? Could we avoid conferring the researchers' approval on some expressions and not others? How would we acknowledge silences in reporting on the interviews? How would we accurately and responsibly make the connection between the construction and legitimation of environmental values in specific places and the policy changes taking place at the level of nations? How would we take into account the global processes that make cultures increasingly less discrete and avoid essentializing cultures? All these questions involve concerns about translation of vocabularies, the position and responsibility of the researcher vis-à-vis her or his informants and the project, the generalizability of the findings, and the accuracy of comparisons.

Devising a Research Protocol

In planning the project, we determined that answering the central research questions would require fresh empirical material that could be compared cross-nationally. Earlier experiences with multi-country projects suggested that uniform protocols for data collection and analysis often proved too constraining and obscured vast differences among countries.[2] Thus, we sought to devise a research protocol that would address the problems that usually bedevil social science researchers: questions of representation of group views, of translation of value-laden terminology (both between interviewer and respondent and across the four countries), and of comparability, particularly understanding and interpreting causal mechanisms. Survey instruments are one way to tackle these problems, but they have a number of limitations, including a tendency to emphasize short-term preferences; a failure to capture the "density" of feelings attached to a particular place; an oversimplification of the model of a human subject, whereby views on the environment are treated as separate from other social practices in which the subject is engaged,[3] and the problem of categories that do not translate across cultures. On the other hand, interpretivist methods are criticized for a lack of replicability, vague concepts, non-operationalizable measures, and a failure to specify causal relationships, as well as for confounding factual and evaluational propositions and for treating multiple cases in noncomparable ways.

Since we were trying to understand environmental values as social phenomena both in terms of their complexity and the meanings people bring to them, we believed that our methods should involve close, or "intensive," encounters with our informants. In other words we were operating from the perspective that values are discursively constructed and reconstructed through interaction between people during conversations in various social and policy environments, at home, work and at leisure.[4] An important aspect of the intensive approach of open and sustained dialogue with a limited number of informants adopted in this research was the opportunity it provided to probe, cross-check, or clarify interview questions and responses. To probe effectively, an interviewer must listen beyond, such that the researcher achieves a critical awareness of what is being said and is ready to explore issues in greater depth. This is clearly shown in the Japan case, where our researchers ponder what a statement such as "the water is clean" really means to the respondent when the judgment is intuitively felt rather than clearly explained.

This degree of attention to context in making sense of environmental values reflects an appreciation for the fact that values are formulated in particular places and over time. According to two of the participants in the project meetings, "The abstraction of research from its site of production can lead to a loss of vital linkages, [thus] reducing the nuanced understanding of people's experience."[5] We were aware that in order to gain the desired depth of understanding of environmental value [re]construction it was necessary to be selective in choosing interviewees that might leave us open to the criticism that the interviewees are not representative of the wider society. The fundamental point of the research, however, was "to gain access to the cultural categories and assumptions according to which one culture construes the world. . . . In other words, qualitative research does not survey the terrain, it mines it."[6] We were interested as much in what people say as in the actions they take. To some extent values are implicit in people's behavior and policy actions as related in the case narratives—but the interviews allowed us to tease them out further and make them more explicit. Thus, we relied on interviews with a cross section of publics and policy makers, as well as public records and speeches, and used interview material extensively in writing up the research.

To make this project comparative, we tried to steer a course between nomothetic and interpretive approaches by standardizing methodology and encouraging continuous interaction among the research teams. We adopted several strategies as components of our standardized research protocol, all designed to aid comparability. First, the research teams defined four common research questions that would guide every team's field research. In addition, the teams were invited to add questions that they deemed important to their particular case. These questions were selected with an eye toward helping the researchers understand respondents' moral judgments, including their ideas of fairness and distributive justice. The common research questions were first developed in meetings prior to fieldwork and then revised collectively at a meeting in Kusatsu, Japan, in July 1999, after an initial round of fieldwork. The questions, which appear in the project's consolidated guidelines," are the following:

1. How do the interested and affected parties in the case perceive the problem? This question is designed to help researchers gain a better understanding of how scientific and other "authorities," as defined by the local culture, influence local perceptions and values regarding the environment, and in turn how people make sense of the science background of the case. What are the local standards for what constitutes an "environmental problem"? How do the various actors involved invoke science, engineering, and technological knowledge? What does "environment" mean to people? In addition, this question should lead to a clearer understanding of whether there is a distinctive sphere of environmental values, how "environmental values" relate to other values people hold, and the reasons why they take the position on the issues that they do.

2. *How have values changed and how are they changing?* If more-sustainable policies are to be instituted, policy makers and analysts need to know more about the values that can support those policies and the factors that can lead to value change. For example, in China since Deng Xiaoping and in postwar Japan the dominant set of values driving policy was pro-development values. However, policy makers in both countries have come to see the importance of protecting the environment, and are both responding to public and international demands for higher environmental standards while at the same time searching for ways to promote environmental values broadly among their publics in order to achieve new public policy goals. Therefore, in order to encourage this trend it is important to understand how that value change occurs among both elites and non-elites.

3. *How and to what extent do outside ideas, money, and standards impact environmental values?* This question is designed to capture the way in which globalizing forces are effecting value change. It emphasizes the relationship between local and international discourses and the effects of international discourses both on value formation and policy. It acknowledges that those effects can be both positive (e.g., regulatory standards, technology transfer, transfer of best practices by multinational corporations) as well as negative (e.g., the imposition of foreign legal norms and practices that do not take into account local norms and conditions). Furthermore, *outsider* can be defined in terms of community, tribal, regional, or even international boundaries. The researcher's aim should be to discover who is considered an insider, who is considered an outsider, and what impact these designations have on values and value change.

4. *How and why do certain values come to inform the policy process?* This question is designed to shed light on how value conflicts are resolved in the policy process and how that process, which ultimately leads to the inclusion or non-inclusion of certain values in policy, affects values and values change. To answer it requires an understanding of which values enter into debates, policies, and legal decisions, which values are screened out, and which are silenced. It also involves gauging the level of public trust in the government institutions and policies and the science those policies depend upon, which in turn sheds light on values and value formation. Finally, the question is intended to help us understand how different values affect the way in which scientific information is incorporated into decision-making.

Each question demanded that the researcher balance scientific understanding of the environmental problem with perceptions and values. Generally speaking, the first is obtainable through secondary research and verifiable through interviews, while the second and third can be discovered through interviews, document analysis, media analysis, the analysis of public hearings and community meetings, and where appropriate, focus groups and workshops. The collection of data on what we called the "science stream" involved the flows and distribution of scientific and local knowledge in the community—for example, in the form of environmental assessments, media coverage of environmental issues and local folklore. We paid attention to the standards different stakeholders used for defining and recognizing the severity of an environmental problem and how they create expectations for air or water quality. For the "values stream" research teams considered a wide array of factors in relation to the community under study: the repositories of values over time, including artifacts, institutions, individuals, or texts; the different ways in which these values are communicated (for example, through families, schools, media, festivals, literature, arts, scientific information, and policy decisions); the degree to which social actors explicitly invoke history, culture, and values in debates over the environment; the social constructions of nature (for example, as fragile or resilient); and local patterns of interaction with the environment and how they change over time (for example, changing technologies and land uses). Finally, learning about the "policy stream" involved paying attention to the processes of value change, particularly what determines the depth and speed of change (for example, crises, policy failures, and scientific findings); the values that are incorporated into environmental policy (for example, ideas of fairness and conceptions of nature); the effect of styles of governance and conflict resolution on which values dominate the policy process; and how values and patterns of dominance change, as observed (for example, in the relative power of government bureaucracies, courts, and NGOs). In addition to all these research methods, we undertook demographic and socioeconomic analysis, as well as documentary analysis of scientific reports, scholarly texts, legal information, and local newspaper accounts.

All of the research teams studied the following broad categories of institutions in sufficient detail to reveal important differences and similarities: families, schools, industry/business, neighborhood communities, scientists, nongovernmental (voluntary) organizations, religious groups, governmental agencies (local, regional, national), and where appropriate, international organizations. At the same time we tried to account for the wide variation in the ways in which societies organize themselves, and the fact that the terms we used to describe institutional arrangements may be specific to a particular setting or culture. For example, "nongovernmental" organizations may be more or less governmental depending on where they are operating. Similarly, the term stakeholder as used in India seemed not to include those who lack the power to claim a stake in the matter at hand but are directly and sometimes tragically affected. We also had many discussions about the danger of presuming that any one respondent wears a single hat; thus, in their interviews teams explored the informants' own sense of who they are and with what group they identify or represent as well as how they are generally perceived, and how they deal with their multiple allegiances.

Research teams had the latitude to employ the fieldwork tools appropriate to the site and to the fieldwork tradition of their country. The Japan team used historical photographs of the area to stimulate candid discussion of environmental change. They asked questions about life histories and childhood experiences to encourage participants to express their positions in their own words. The U.S. team used a form of community mapping whereby local residents document who lives in their neighborhood. In China because of the limits on press freedoms and widespread public cynicism toward official news accounts, media analysis was not a reliable means of assessing what people know. At the same time, a careful probing of media rhetoric could reveal important insights about value priorities. Propaganda, after all, can indicate which values public officials hope to instill in the public or the existing public values to which their reports aim to appeal. As part of our collaborative process, researchers shared, debated, and evaluated the methods we used in each of the countries, considering the kind of insights they yielded and their transferability to other research contexts.

From early on there were problems of translation of concepts across the disciplines and across cultures, and these were revealing. For example, both the Japan and China teams had problems translating "environmental value" into their respective languages in such a way as to ensure that the meaning of the term went beyond financial worth to a more expansive sense of *value*. In addition, we found that the terms "social welfare," "environment," "governance," and "culture" did not necessarily mean the same thing for all the country team members, especially the non–native English speakers. We also encountered differences between different regimes of knowledge (such as those of government-based scientists versus those of local fishermen) as well as academic or disciplinary dimensions. Thus, we found it necessary in discussions to ensure that all participants had a common understanding of the meanings of key terms and concepts. As difficulties became apparent, we wrote out the terms, discussed them, and added our understanding of them to the project guidelines.

As we noted in the introduction to this volume, we deliberately chose cases that allowed project researchers to make comparisons within national contexts, and therefore to capture a wide range of variability and depth of understanding of value construction and change by including different demographics, climates, and ethnic groups. In addition to selecting one resource use and one industrial pollution study in each country, all research teams adopted the following case selection criteria: (1) Cases should be current, yet offer a longitudinal dimension to demonstrate how the problem developed into a policy issue that has caught the attention of the local community; (2) Cases should involve a range of actors and perspectives, and entail several policy options; (3) Research needs to be feasible through a variety of methods (including document analysis and quantitative and qualitative data collection methods) and not excessively bound by political constraints on the research process. In most cases we also chose sites with which the researchers were familiar, either through past or ongoing work in that area. While it is natural to be drawn to a familiar site, for some researchers, as we describe below, having a high level of engagement with a place was a practical and ethical necessity.

Research Politics and Ethics

We were conscious from the start of the hazards of researcher bias in terms of privileging one set of values over another in our reporting and analysis. Bias can appear during the initial delineation of the case, the interview process, or the write-up of the fieldwork. Bias need not be a liability, however; in fact, it can be an asset if acknowledged and properly managed. As American geographer Erica Schoenberger comments, "Questions of gender, class, race, nationality, politics, history and experience shape our research and our interpretations of the world, however much we are supposed to deny it. The task then is not to do away with these things, but to know them and to learn from them."[7] In this context, anthropologist Grant McCracken recognizes the benefits of commonality between researcher and interviewee but also adds a caveat:

> It is precisely because the qualitative researchers are working in their own culture that they can make the long interview do such powerful work. It is by drawing on their understanding of how they themselves see and experience the world that they can supplement and interpret the data they generate in a long interview. Just as plainly, however, this intimate acquaintance with one's own culture can create as much blindness as insight.[8]

Again, we considered communication among the research teams to be fundamental to our effort to integrate the research from all four teams. In addition to comparing methods and results, another means by which we sought to reduce the potential for cultural blindness was by making our biases explicit through self-reflection, active debates, and the processes of clarification that occurred in the meetings.

Project participants were especially concerned about issues regarding the power to speak for others through the medium of academic research, along with problems of viewing a culture as unitary and unchanging (a practice that scholars refer to as "essentialism") when researching others. As bell hooks has suggested, researchers working on studies, such as this one, that involve close encounters need to think about how they speak "of" and "for" others.[9] In an attempt to deal with this concern the researchers sought to build mutually trusting relationships with their informants. To ensure trust and in recognition of their own accountability to the research site, the U.S. research team, for instance, preserves anonymity for its informants and ensures that their final reports are vetted by those informants. For the Japan research, Kada Yukiko chose her team of researchers on the basis of their long-standing commitment to the relevant issues at the research site. Further, she did not use graduate students to conduct interviews because it would have been considered a sign of disrespect to the informants. The association of the researchers with the places being studied and their resident populations meant that a relationship of trust and legitimacy already existed between the research teams and the research participants.

It is generally assumed that power lies in the hands of the researcher as compared to the research subject, but this is not always the case.[10] When interviewees are members of elites, they often have a great deal of experience being interviewed (and if they are politicians or corporate executives, likely to have been trained to deflect difficult questions). In addition, just as language, particularly academic jargon, can set up barriers between the researcher and researched, professionalized discourses can obscure meaning for a researcher. Power relationships of this sort can be difficult to deal with, particularly when the interviewee is a gatekeeper for a research program. For example, in the Louisiana pollution case there were layers of legality and bureaucracy to engage with, and powerful advocates and corporations were able to control information. The same was true in the Delhi pollution case. Interviews proved especially challenging in China, where local respondents are reluctant to talk openly to interviewers who hail from Beijing and are therefore seen as outsiders. Furthermore, qualitative techniques are in an embryonic stage of development in China, and they operate under political constraints. In several instances cautious public officials have even shut down or censored research projects; a recent case involves the husband-and-wife team of Chen Guidi and Chun Tao, whose book detailing the abuses of the peasantry by a local cadre was banned in March 2004.[11] As a result of such constraints, our China researchers had to exercise caution in both their encounters with those in power and in the analysis of their research findings.

In all three of these examples, the respondents, and not the interviewers, control the research process. Nevertheless we were always aware that the researcher's actions and the research produced could further marginalize the already powerless. We recognized that it is impossible to remove power relations from the research context, but that it is possible to be open about the possible effects of those power relations on the information collected and to be clear about the motivations for research. Responsibility, then, was a key concern for the project as a whole.

Tensions arose among us over how to balance our responsibilities to participants with the requirements of a collaborative research project. The original India research team, for instance, strongly felt the need to maintain their allegiance to the voiceless and underrepresented people in their cases, a feeling they referred to when they said, in their 2001 team report, "We are political in a certain sense. There is a methodological bias to our group. And it comes from the political character of our group and the institute we represent. . . . [We are] committed to looking at the problems of democracy and the democratic imagination." They went on to explain, "Our second bias is that we believe that formal structures of articulation sometimes do not capture voices of marginal groups and sometimes do not capture the rationality of a certain kind of political discourse, or the silences in the system." In one of their final reports they expressed deep concern that the "mere reiteration of a few voices actually devalues voice to the margins," and the only way to prevent this was to rely on the interpretation and analysis of the academic as a "trustee" of the site. The problem, in other words, was that formalizing the study in some sense silenced the grassroots voices: the Indian researchers saw an incommensurability of formal academic studies and the responsibility to the voiceless grass roots that led to the impossibility of translating between the two.

In the end, then, the India researchers chose not to complete their study for this volume. The authors of the India chapter that appears in this volume, Amita Baviskar, Subir Sinha, and Kavita Philip, joined us after the research phase, picking up the case studies selected by the original team and developing the research according to the guidelines that had been established by the project. It is noteworthy that Amita Baviskar, like the Indian research team, had reservations about relying excessively on discourse analysis. Instead, as she notes in the chapter, she based her analysis primarily upon her observations. As a long-term resident of Delhi, she explained that she is "able to draw upon tacit cultural understandings that, while often unarticulated into words, powerfully shape the practices of different social groups. . . . When significant silences mark normalized exclusions, attention to practices other than speech is necessary." She also notes that her "proximity to rights-based activist groups in Delhi allowed her "critical analytical insight into these practices, which would otherwise escape attention." In particular, she aimed "to make explicit the consequences of constitutive exclusions and unstated assumptions that invisibly yet powerfully shape the construction of 'public interest'."

The China researchers, by contrast, expressed the importance of maintaining objectivity in the face of research bias. At one of our meetings, the team was questioned for the emphasis their research placed on the official sector in China, compared to the other country studies. A member of the China team explained that the emphasis is justified because the government, as well as affiliated scientists and researchers, has been central to China's environmental policy and value development. At the same time, however, the research team acknowledged that understanding the values of ordinary citizens is essential to ensuring the success of any policy, even in China. In short, the cross-fertilization of ideas within the meetings prompted the Chinese researchers to place more importance on the environmental identities of people affected by the environmental policies described in their cases.

Concerns about responsibility to recognize all stakeholders extended through the write-up phase. Scott Bruton, who joined the project to help shape the U.S. research reports into a chapter for this volume, felt strongly that the Civano study as it stood had given insufficient attention to the broader regional consequences of the Civano development. In particular, drawing upon his own research in the region, Bruton believed it was a mistake not to consider the competing resource demands of the Tucson region and the Hopi and Navajo Indian reservations, though the places were separated by hundreds of miles. Because similar concerns had surfaced at the later project meetings, we determined that the chapter should include that perspective.

No single method is guaranteed to produce a transparent account of people's values. Our research sought to avoid the problem of methodological overextension and universalization, recognizing that each method creates its own values at a particular moment and in a particular place. We took seriously the commitment to represent the voiceless and to respect the trust of our informants. Despite modifications (such as Baviskar's) to the research protocol the problem of representing the voiceless was resolved via selected historical and narrative choices. While imperfect and leaving many silences and gaps (as in any narrative), the methods used by our research teams embraced rather than denied the dynamic complexity of society. In the process we believe we uncovered some accurate and important insights about environmental values, environmental politics, and comparative research.

Notes

1. John Foster, *Valuing Nature? Ethics, Economics and the Environment* (London: Routledge, 1997), 2–3.

2. We are indebted to Edith Brown Weiss and William Clarke for these insights.

3. Phil Macnaghten and John Urry, *Contested Natures* (London: Sage, 1998), 307.

4. Anna Ray Davies, "What Silence Knows—Planning, Public Participation, and Environmental Values," *Environmental Values* 10 (2001): 77–102.

5. Anna Ray Davies and Steve Rayner, "Examining Environmental Values" (Carnegie Council, 2002).

6. Grant McCracken, *The Long Interview* (Newbury Park, CA: Sage, 1988), 17.

7. Erica Schoenberger, "Self Criticism and Self Awareness in Research: A Reply to Linda McDowell," *Professional Geographer* 44 (1992): 218.

8. Grant McCracken, *The Long Interview* (Newbury Park, CA: Sage, 1988), 11–12.

9. bell hooks, *Yearning: Race, Gender and Cultural Politics* (London: Turnaround, 1991).

10. S.J. Ball, "Political Interviews and the Politics of Interviewing," in *Researching the Powerful in Education,* ed. Geoffrey Walford (London: UCL Press, 1994), 96–115.

11. The book, which goes by many English titles, including "An Investigation of Chinese Peasants," was a huge bestseller in China before it was banned and since then has reportedly been highly sought after on the black market.

Index